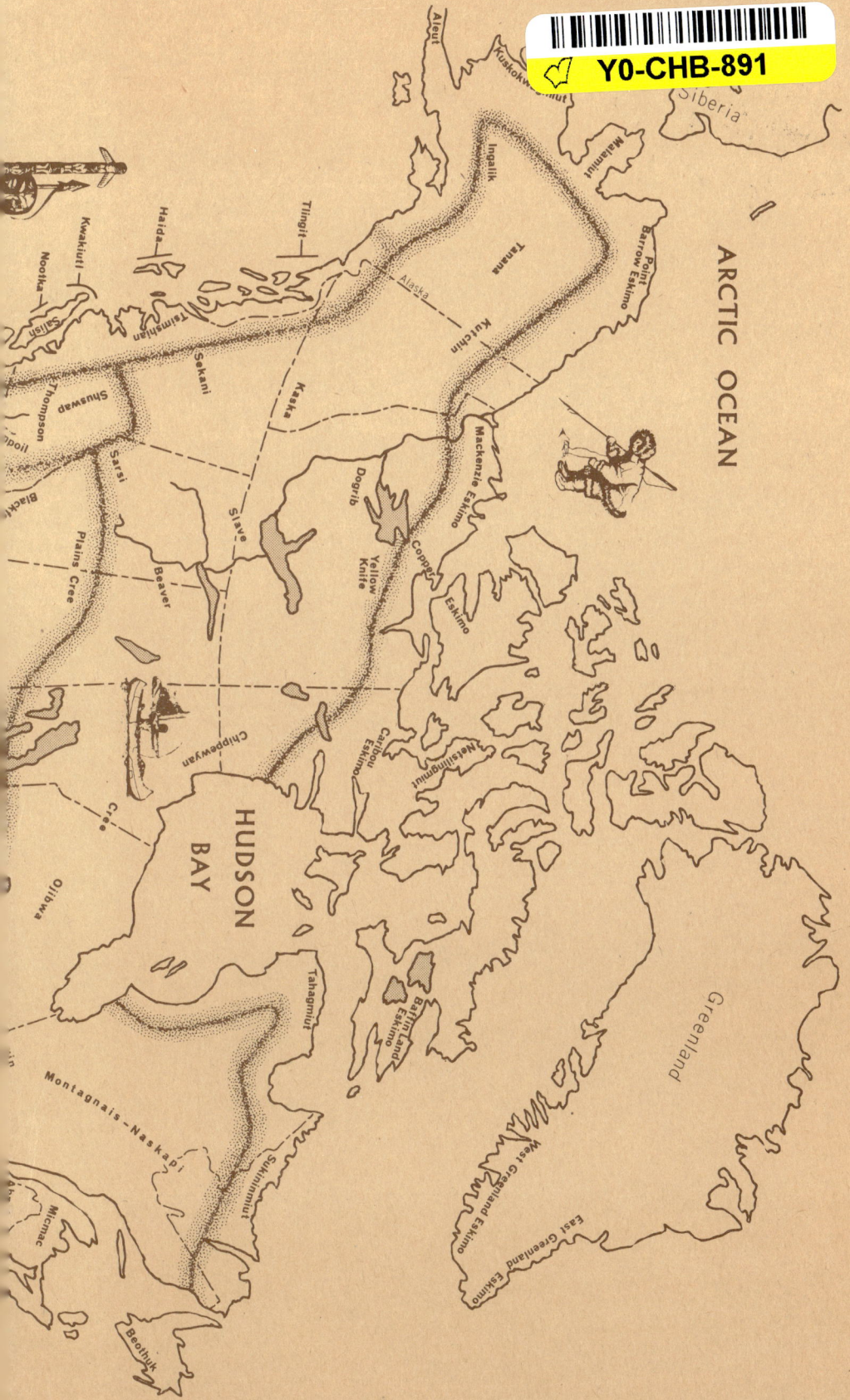

THE NORTH AMERICAN INDIANS
A SOURCEBOOK

Edited, and with Introductions by

ROGER C. OWEN

University of California,
Santa Barbara

JAMES J. F. DEETZ

University of California,
Santa Barbara

ANTHONY D. FISHER

University of Alberta,
Edmonton

THE
NORTH
AMERICAN
INDIANS
A Sourcebook

MACMILLAN PUBLISHING CO., INC.
New York

COLLIER MACMILLAN PUBLISHERS
London

Library of Congress catalog card number: 67-16712

MACMILLAN PUBLISHING CO., INC.
866 Third Avenue, New York, New York 10022

COLLIER-MACMILLAN CANADA, LTD., TORONTO, ONTARIO

Printed in the United States of America

Printing   789101112   Year   34567890

A chief of the Digger Indians, as the Californians call them, talked to me a great deal about the ways of his people in the old days. He was a Christian and a leader among his people in the planting of peaches and apricots on irrigated land, but when he talked of the shamans who had transformed themselves into bears before his eyes in the bear dance, his hands trembled and his voice broke with excitement. It was an incomparable thing, the power his people had had in the old days. He liked best to talk of the desert foods they had eaten. He brought each uprooted plant lovingly and with an unfailing sense of its importance. In those days his people had eaten "the health of the desert," he said, and knew nothing of the insides of tin cans and the things for sale at butcher shops.

One day, without transition, Ramon broke in upon his descriptions of grinding mesquite and preparing acorn soup. "In the beginning," he said, "God gave to every people a cup, a cup of clay, and from this cup they drank their life." I do not know whether the figure occurred in some traditional ritual of his people that I never found, or whether it was his own imagery. At any rate, in the mind of this humble Indian the figure of speech was clear and full of meaning. "They all dipped in the water," he continued, "but their cups were different. Our cup is broken now. It has passed away."

—From *Patterns of Culture,* by Ruth Benedict

PREFACE

This book is intended as a general introduction to the study of the aboriginal populations of North America in college and university courses on the American Indian. We have attempted to include basic, original articles by outstanding authorities so that many interested individuals (students and nonstudents, amateurs and professionals, and elementary school teachers) as well as our colleagues will find the book useful.

The theoretical framework of the volume is implicitly evolutionary, but overtly regional. We have used the time-honored concept of "culture area" as the basis for dividing the book into sections because this format seems to offer the greatest pedagogical value. For those who favor an approach that utilizes either a topical or a structural organization, we have deliberately included articles that will permit such employment after simple rearrangement.

The quantity of literature on the North American Indian is staggering. One need only examine Murdock's *Ethnographic Bibliography of North America* (see p. 700) to grasp this point. Selection of articles and authors has been exceedingly difficult, and it is not easy to explain precisely how our decisions were made. The book has been treated as a whole and, as a result, it has sometimes been necessary to exclude excellent papers and worthy writers because of some other choice. We have attempted to include articles representative of the major theoretical points of view (historical, psychological, configurational, structural, functional, evolutionary), and, as well, the purely descriptive; to cover the major topical areas traditionally of interest to anthropologists (technology, social organization, religion, economics, and so on), as well as to provide examples of writings from various time periods. He who reads through the articles will not only learn a great deal about Indians, but will also note the growth and change in anthropology itself. From the early descriptive papers by Boas and Kroeber, to the theoretically speculative papers by Devereux, Spier, Hoijer, and others, to the more recent syntheses by Newman, Swadesh, Steward, and Ewers, one may observe the gradual development of anthropology.

Unfortunately, editorial considerations make it necessary to eliminate all footnotes except those associated with quotations employed by the various authors. Most articles have been edited; readers wishing to explore an author's original sources should turn to the original article. Great care has, nevertheless, been taken to avoid modification of the intent of any of the abridged papers. All quotations within the articles are cited by a notation within the text such as "(13:426)," which refers to the thirteenth entry in the References Quoted list (see p. 693) and the page number (426) where the material quoted in our selection can be found in the publication where it first appeared.

We have provided an up-to-date list of additional readings, arranged according to subjects of the sections. The books and articles noted there provide a key to the most recent literature in the field. In addition, an annotated directory of 250 educational films on North American Indians may be found following the list of additional readings. We believe this list is inclusive but new films are being made each year, and the interested person is urged to consult the various film catalogues referred to in our lists.

There is no room here to name all those who have contributed to the development of this book. The editors' responsibilities for research and teaching and the geographical mobility common to anthropologists have made its production gradual and much considered. In the last phases of manuscript completion, the burden of final selection and editing of articles fell to the senior editor. The brief introductory paragraphs to be found with each section were also done by him. Of the many students who have participated in phases of the book we would like to mention gratefully Regina and William L. Garrison, George Hunt, Neal Hooker, Penny Hollins, Kathryn Fish, Carole Lockhart, and Frank Lobo, all of whom either patiently typed, Xeroxed, cut, pasted, or searched in the library. The film list was initiated by George Hunt and completed by Frank Lobo. The designs preceding each section and the small maps are by William E. Thompson. The endpaper map was prepared by Richard V. Humphrey, and the index by Sue Lobo.

Without the valuable suggestions and gentle proddings of our editor at The Macmillan Company, John D. Moore, we would not have finished nor even begun. We would like to dedicate the book jointly to our editor and to the Indians, both of whom were prerequisites to the production of the book.

R. C. O.
J. J. F. D.
A. D. F.

CONTENTS

SECTION I

Introduction

Where did American Indians come from? All authorities now agree that the primary and original source of native New World populations was Asia. Earliest access to the New World, perhaps 30,000 years or so ago, was across what is now the Bering Strait. During the terminal Pleistocene, the Bering Strait, now a fifty-six-mile-wide strip of water separating two continents, was a plain a thousand miles or more in width. Since the time when the first hunters and gleaners radiated into the vast continent previously unoccupied by man, other human populations have followed from Asia both by foot and by boat. Until recently, Siberian Eskimos continued to ply easily between the two continents. Furthermore, it is likely that prior to the arrival of Columbus in the Caribbean area, the west coast of the New World had been contacted several times by Southeast Asians, by Polynesians, and possibly by people from the Japanese Islands. As for the east coast, little doubt now remains that Norsemen had landed on the maritime coast of present-day Canada and perhaps had penetrated some distance inland by 1000 A.D. or earlier. Yet, despite these extra-continental contacts, and despite all of the suggestions scholars have made regarding the possible influence of Old World ideas on aboriginal New World cultural developments, the consensus of professional anthropological opinion is that cultural development in the Americas occurred largely without stimulation from Old World centers of civilization. Regarded as even less likely are those fanciful contentions which suggest that the origin of American Indians can be attributed to sunken continents or wandering lost tribes.

The dates of the earliest migration to the New World are still in question. Man was leaving tools and debris in Patagonian caves, near the tip of South America, nearly 10,000 years ago. The gradual population of North, Central, and South America until hunters had reached the extreme tip of the southern continent must have taken additional thousands of years. Few experts now would quarrel with the contention that man has been resident in the New World for 20,000 to 30,000 years, and possibly longer. A few anthropologists suggest that the date of arrival might have been much earlier, as long ago as 40,000 to 60,000 years ago. It should be noted, however, that if this extreme date should ultimately be confirmed, we must expect to discover Neanderthal-like remains in the New World.

Archaeology can clearly demonstrate human presence in the New

World, employing principally the radioactive Carbon₁₄ technique, only to about 15,000 years ago. Numbers of apparently earlier archaeological sites have been studied (Sandia Cave, New Mexico; Lewisville, Texas; Tule Springs, Nevada; Santa Rosa Island, California; and others); but according to general professional opinion, the very ancient dates derived from these excavations are as yet insufficiently documented to be readily accepted. Although the record of ancient New World cultural development is meager, as we move to more recent archaeological times the historical image becomes much clearer. Few major mysteries remain regarding the development of native cultures of the New World for the past 2,000 years; and for some regions, such as the Viru Valley in Peru or the central region of the state of Arizona, the archaeologist is able to present a relatively detailed outline of cultural history and to commence work on specific historical and cultural problems. But over these optimistic comments a note of caution must be raised: much work remains to be done on the prehistory of all New World regions.

In addition to archaeological research, American Indian scholars have studied extensively the physical or morphological attributes of the American Indian, the so-called "Red Man." In fact, the color "red" is frequently added to the simplistic threefold scheme used to describe the "races" of Man: black, yellow, white, and red. Few physical anthropologists regard any of these categories as valid, and many physical anthropologists have come to the conclusion that, in truth, *Homo sapiens* consists of a single race which exhibits considerable variability. In any case, few experts on the American Indian see sufficient physical variation among aboriginal populations in the New World, with the possible exception of the Eskimo, to warrant the suggestion of "racial" variation. It is clear, however, that the American Indian is, physically speaking, more closely related to certain contemporary Asian populations than to any other.

Other clues to the origin and development of the Indian have been sought through the study of his languages. At this time, due to the enormous number of Indian languages that were completely lost in the early stages of European contact, the question of "ultimate" relationships and origins may never be explicitly answered. Highly accurate techniques of linguistic recording and sophisticated tools of language analysis have existed for only the past 30 years or so. Yet, despite great handicaps, linguists have had numerous successes in indicating often unsuspected and exceedingly distant re- lationships. Since the first comprehensive classifications of American Indian languages were made during the last two decades of the nineteenth century, the constant trend has been to reduce the num- ber of seemingly unrelated units and to group specific dialects in ever larger categories of "families," or "macro-families." What may prove to be a near maximal reduction has been achieved by Morris Swadesh in a paper included in this section.

Finally, it should be noted by students of the American Indian that the process which was begun by the earliest migrant to the New World, and continued by subsequent peoples, including more re- cently the Eskimo, the Norse and Columbus, has been and is being perpetuated by the English, Irish, Germans, Italians, Japanese, and the other most recent migrants to the New World continents. It is interesting to speculate how archaeologists of the distant future may view our brief history of only 400 years.

The 1960's brought a reawakening of interest in evolutionary theory throughout American anthropology. More and more, students of primitive societies are interpreting cultural development and change as an orderly process and as a process which has been similar in many ways wherever it has occurred. The reconstruction of the specifics of cultural evolution falls within the province of the archaeologists, and in the article that follows one of the most distinguished of American archaeologists outlines the general trends and specific developments which occurred in the New World prior to the arrival of Columbus.

I Gordon R. Willey

HISTORY AND EVOLUTION OF AMERICAN INDIAN CULTURES*

In attempting to trace the courses and processes of the evolution of New World cultures, we will define, first, the major subsistence and settlement types that are found in prehistoric America. These will then be described and examined within the framework of what are called "basic New World life-patterns." These life-patterns are historical spheres or continuities of great geographic extent and long chronologic persistence. Each is characterized by an underlying natural environmental-subsistence ecology, as well as by particular societal or community types and by cultural institutions. The reconstructions of cultural ecology from natural environmental habitats and tool types, of social units from settlement patterns, and of cultural forms from whatever available clues are, of course, limited by the nature of archaeological data. The quantity and quality of archaeological inference will vary greatly as one moves from the relative security of subsistence and settlement interpretations to those involving the more abstract—and, at the same time, more

* Abridged from "Historical Patterns and Evolution in Native New World Cultures," by G. R. Willey, in *Evolution after Darwin*, Vol. II: *The Evolution of Man*, S. Tax (ed.). Chicago: Univ. Chicago Press, 111–142, 1960.

uniquely and interestingly human—results of men's minds and hands. Inference and its reliability will also vary with the richness or poverty of the record and with the possibilities of injecting into it the reinforcements of ethnohistorical documentation. Nevertheless, any culture history of the native Americas which is to be more than a chronicle account of artifact types must reckon with such inferences.

The extent to which cultural institutions and forms are functionally and causally interrelated with each other and with subsistence and settlement (societal) types is, of course, a major nexus of the problem of human cultural evolution. We cannot pretend to offer many answers in this discussion, but if human beings living in social groups in the natural world are the creators and bearers of culture, it seems likely that such interrelationships exist.

NEW WORLD PATTERNS OF CULTURE

Subsistence Types

There are three principal subsistence types native to the New World: big-game hunting, gathering-collecting, and cultivation.

Big-game hunting refers to the stalking and killing of large mammals as a principal source of food and clothing. It was a mode of subsistence widespread in the Americas in Pleistocene times (antedating 7000 B.C.). In later eras it was also followed on a somewhat more restricted geographic scale. It is, obviously, conditioned strongly by natural environmental circumstances.

Gathering-collecting refers to all those means of procuring food from the natural setting except the hunting of big game or the cultivation and domestication of plants and animals. The nature of the foods may be small animals, fish, shellfish, roots, seeds, nuts, and berries. The occasional taking of large game is not precluded, although this is not a specialization. At one time or another gathering-collecting economies characterized most parts of aboriginal America. Although there are clues to their appearance as early as the Pleistocene, they are more typical of the recent geological era. *Gathering-collecting* may be subtyped into (*a*) *gathering*, where food resources were extremely meager, the techniques for obtaining them simple and unspecialized, and the efforts of the people involved devoted almost wholly to the food quest; (*b*) *collecting*, where there are more ample resources and more effective techniques; and (*c*) *intensive collecting*, which is marked by abundant

resources, specialized techniques, and the accumulation of food surpluses.

Cultivation of food plants is the only major type of food production
in native America. Its origins may begin as early as the close of the
Pleistocene, but the pattern was one of only partial economic significance
until the second millennium B.C., when it became of primary importance
in Nuclear America. Maize was the most important staple crop, and at
the time of the discovery of America by the Europeans it was found
spread over the southern half of North America and the northern two-
thirds of South America. Manioc, another staple, had a more limited
distribution. From the points of view of techniques and productiveness,
native American *cultivation* types may be considered as (*a*) *incipient,*
where either food plants, farming techniques, or both are but partially
developed and the produce has only a minor role in the economy; (*b*)
established, where the primary means of food-getting is farming; and
(*c*) *intensive,* where, as a result of favorable soils, climatic conditions, a
variety of nutritious plants, and the employment of techniques such as
irrigation, terracing, "floating gardens," and fertilizers, a high productivity is assured.

Settlement Patterns

As they reflect the nature of the community, we have classified New
World native settlements into five major types: *camps, semipermanent
villages, permanent villages, towns-and-temples,* and *cities.*

The *camp* site is small in extent and marked by thin and scattered
refuse. There are few or no clues to dwellings or other structures. When
found as the only type of settlement for a society and culture, it is reflective of a small, non-sedentary community unit, probably a wandering
band of less than one hundred individuals. Such bands roamed over territories of varying extent and followed a hunting or a gathering-
collecting subsistence. On the American scene the camp is found in
virtually all parts of both continents and at all time periods.

Semipermanent villages are those which give evidence of substantial
occupation over an appreciable span of time. Traces of perishable dwellings may be found; accumulated refuse is often deep; and cemeteries
may be in or near the site. They were the living places of communities
which appear to have occupied such locations sporadically or to have
shifted their site locus after every few years. Inhabitants must have
numbered several hundred. The semipermanent village marks a shift
from a wandering toward a sedentary life. In some American areas it is

correlated with a change from food-collecting to intensive collecting or to cultivation.

The *permanent village* settlement is the locus of a community which has occupied the same spot steadily over a long period of time. It reflects this sedentism in permanence of architectural features as well as refuse concentration. Its occupants numbered from a few hundred to over a thousand. The social and political organization of these communities may have rested upon kinship, but there are instances from ethnohistory of chiefs and social class distinctions. In the New World the permanent village, in both archaeological and ethnohistoric times, is most often associated with established cultivation. The American data pertain to two subtypes of permanent villages. The first has a unitary or "undifferentiated" settlement plan. In this, the village is a compact unit of dwellings which may contain within itself a special temple or politico-religious structure. The second—a dispersed or "differentiated" subtype—has a nucleus or politico-religious center which is surrounded at varying distances by small hamlet or homestead satellites.

The *town-and-temple* settlement pattern and community type is an enlargement and elaboration of the permanent village pattern. The total community is now likely to be a dispersed and differentiated one. The politico-religious, or "ceremonial," center is the principal focus. It may, or may not, be within the confines of a compact town; but in either case it is usually surrounded by satellite villages and hamlets. The population of the total community probably ran to a few thousand. Their social and political organization was probably hierarchical, with governmental authority supplanting kinship. These towns were the centers of full-time artisans and the residences of rulers, and activities in connection with the temples were directed by an organized priesthood. The town-and-temple settlement is associated with established or intensive cultivation and is best known from Middle America and Peru, although the type is also found in other parts of South and Central America, the West Indies, and in the southeastern and southwestern United States.

The *city*, as distinct from the town-and-temple, cannot be defined upon the basis of settlement features alone, although sheer size and population numbers are among the criteria. The native American city is known only from parts of Middle America and Peru. It was the nerve center of a civilization. It attracted to its precincts the artisans, artists, and specialists. Its temples housed pantheons of deities. It was a focus of trade, of the collection of taxes, and frequently of the military power of the state. It is characterized by monumental architecture, by great arts, and in some places, as in the territory of the lowland Maya, by evidences of true mathematical and astronomic sciences and writing. Its actual settlement pattern may be compact and truly urban, or it may be differentiated into a politico-religious center surrounded at a distance by villages and hamlets. Its traditions may be relatively homogeneous, or it may have a more cosmopolitan cast. Among the native New World cities, some appear to have maintained a rather limited regional scope of power and influence, while others were undoubtedly the capitals of large empires.

HISTORICAL OUTLINES OF BASIC NEW WORLD LIFE-PATTERNS

As noted in the introduction, the "basic New World life-patterns" are conceived of as historical entities of great geographic-chronologic scope, each distinguished by the persistences of certain subsistence and community types and cultural forms. The exact number of such life-patterns in the New World is, of course, debatable and somewhat arbitrary. A few major ones emerge from the welter of archaeological facts, and we shall discuss these and refer also to others with less ample data.

Pleistocene Gatherers (?)

There are suggestions, although the evidence is by no means conclusive, that the earliest inhabitants of the New World were peoples following a very simple gathering type of subsistence. At Tule Springs, Nevada, there is an artifact assemblage of crude chipped scrapers and chopping tools found in association with extinct camel, bison, and horse bones and with a radiocarbon date of about 22000 B.C. The discoveries in Friesenhahn Cave, Texas, of scrapers and choppers date from well back into the Wisconsin glacial stage, if not earlier. Somewhat later, but almost certainly of terminal Pleistocene age, are the rather nondescript scraper-chopper-like stone tools from the lowest levels of Fishbone Cave, Nevada. None of these artifact groups clearly represents a big-game hunting economy. Their extremely unspecialized nature is vaguely suggestive of Old World Lower Paleolithic cultures. Their presence in the Americas may result from man's very early migrations to these continents, of which we have now only the most imperfect record. On the other hand, it is possible that these finds are merely partial or incomplete assemblages of the Pleistocene big-game hunting pattern.

Pleistocene Big-Game Hunters

The earliest life-pattern which can be clearly formulated for the New World is that of the Pleistocene big-game hunters. Its origins are uncertain. In the pursuit of large Ice Age mammals and in the employment of pressure-flaked projectile points it has general Old World Upper Paleolithic parallels, but the forms of the American points and other artifacts differ from those of the Old World. Its age is best defined from the period just antedating and concurrent with the final substage of the Wisconsin glaciation. Radiocarbon dates and geological estimates indicate this to be the span from about 12000 to about 7000 B.C., although there are a few dates which go back earlier. The Sandia and Clovis projectile points and associated flint scrapers and knives, together with mammoth remains and the bones of other extinct fauna, are the best-known earlier representatives of the big-game hunting pattern. The long, fluted, and fishtailed Clovis type point is widely distributed through North America, particularly east of the Rocky Mountains. This fluted point form is peculiarly American; and, although no prototypes have yet been discovered in either the New or the Old World, it is possible to trace its later developments into the Folsom type points. The Folsom complex dates from 9000 to 7000 B.C. and is found in the Colorado and New Mexico High Plains country. The Folsom fluted points display technical improvements over the earlier and somewhat less specialized Clovis forms. The Folsom point is widest just back of the piercing end, and the flutes or channels on each side are longer and occupy a greater surface area of the implement. Such features probably insured a more effective puncturing of the hide of the animal (usually a kind of bison now extinct) and more profuse bleeding. Thus a reasonable argument can be made out for a progressive adaptive efficiency of the Folsom point over the Clovis point.

Early Post-Pleistocene Hunters

In the subsequent post-Pleistocene (*ca.* 7000–5000 B.C.) the trend in the manufacture of points is to drop out the fluting feature altogether. Such types as the Eden, Scottsbluff, Plainview, and Angostura, while retaining something of the lanceolate Clovis-Folsom outline, lack the fluting. This trend may mark a lessening in hunting efficiency, although it is possible that with changes to modern fauna the fluted point became less effective.

The Pleistocene big-game hunting pattern apparently spread from North to Middle and to South America. In these areas, in Pleistocene or early post-Pleistocene contexts, lanceolate, well-chipped, but unfluted points have been found associated with mammoth and other extinct animals.

As noted, the camp type settlement is associated with the Pleistocene big-game hunting pattern. In fact, many of the sites appear to have been little more than "kills" or "butchering stations." All inferences point to small wandering populations. Very little has ever been found other than the equipment used for the hunt and for the preparation of the meat and hides of the animals. Crude paint palettes, stone beads, and little incised bone disks, taken from a Folsom context, are among the few exceptions to this.

Collectors of the North American Desert

The "North American Desert," as the environmental homeland of a food-collecting life-pattern of long persistence, may be defined as the vast arid and semiarid basin, range, and plateau country which in North America lies between the Rocky Mountains and the mountain systems of the Pacific Coast and stretches from southern Canada deep into Mexico. There are indications that it was in this territory that the moist conditions of the Pleistocene first began to give way to those of the warmer, drier Altithermal climatic period. The onset of the Altithermal is placed at about 5000 B.C., but in the North American Desert basin, as might be anticipated, a collecting life-pattern seems to have been established even earlier than this. Its origins may lie, in part, in the possible earlier Pleistocene gathering pattern just discussed; they may be found, also, in a change-over from the big-game hunting pattern to the hunting of lesser animals and seed-collecting that was brought about by the disappearance of the grasslands and the Pleistocene fauna; and the probability also exists of new population movements or diffusions from the north and, more remotely, from the Old World. Levels representative of a Desert collecting pattern in Danger Cave, Utah, are dated as early as 7500 B.C. These contain projectile points of both corner-notched and stemless forms that are reminiscent of other early Desert pattern types. Slab milling stones and twined baskets are also associated with these levels. Among other early dates for what appear to be the beginnings of the Desert collecting pattern are those for the Humboldt phase levels of the Leonard site, in Nevada (*ca.* 9000–5000 B.C.), and for Fort Rock Cave, in Oregon (*ca.* 7000 B.C.). The artifacts at Fort Rock include notched and unstemmed points, scrapers, drills, grinding stones, bone tools, twined basketry, and bark sandals.

Throughout the Desert basin there are numerous locations which show the continuity of these complexes with their varieties of stemmed, notched, and unstemmed projectile points and milling and handstones. The upper levels at Leonard Rockshelter are placed at between 3000 and 2000 B.C. The Danger Cave stratigraphy has a continuation of the Desert collecting pattern, from its early date until 1800 B.C. The Cochise continuum of cultures in southern Arizona and southern New Mexico also demonstrates the long existence of the Desert collecting pattern from before 5000 B.C. up to almost the beginning of the Christian Era. In the Cochise sequence there is a definite trend through time toward more numerous, larger, and more carefully deepened and shaped milling stones and mortars. This trend is almost certainly expressive of an increased "settling-in" and adjustment to the collecting of seed foods. It is correlated with greater stability of living sites at the end of the Cochise sequence, where there is archaeological testimony to semipermanent villages of houses with prepared floors and storage pits. It is undoubtedly of great significance that remains of a very primitive maize have been found in the Cochise sequence, dating back to 2000 B.C., or before. Such maize appears to have been in its initial stages of cultivation and to have served as a supplement to wild plant foods.

Collectors of the North American Woodlands

The collecting life-pattern of the Eastern Woodlands of North America is referred to by archaeologists as the "Archaic" pattern. This mode of existence—the collecting of wild vegetable foods, of shellfish, and the taking of fish and small game—replaced the dependence upon the large Pleistocene fauna that was once present in the East. This replacement was probably a gradual one which kept pace with the disappearance of late pluvial conditions and the big-game animals. Such change is seen in the artifact stratigraphy of Illinois and Missouri caves. The shift-over from big-game hunting to collecting probably began as long ago as 8000 B.C., and by 4000 B.C. it was complete throughout the Eastern Woodlands. The projectile points and tools of the Eastern collecting pattern are large, wide, stemmed, or tanged forms and a variety of mortars, handstones, and pestles.

Between 4000 and 1000 B.C. a number of modifications occur in the Eastern Woodland collecting pattern. These are best seen regionally, and in some cases they appear to be responses to natural settings. It also seems likely that new ideas and migrations of people, of ultimate Asiatic origins, were entering the East at this time. These modifications constitute a definite trend toward adjustment or "living-into" the various niches of the Eastern area. Along seacoasts and river, as in Georgia and Tennessee, shellfishing stations offered opportunities for regular seasonal residence of a semipermanent village kind. With this increased sedentism appear numerous polished stone implements and ornaments, including celts, atlatl weights, vessels, gorgets, and beads. Around the Great Lakes, copper nuggets were fashioned into artifacts by hammering techniques. Finally, toward the close of the period, pottery was made and used. It is with these changes that the collecting pattern of the East becomes, at least in many localities, intensive collecting.

The intensive collecting pattern of the Eastern Woodlands, or a level of "Primary Forest Efficiency," as it has been called, climaxes during the first millennium B.C. in certain regions of the Mississippi and Ohio valleys. This is seen in the Poverty Point and Adena cultures with the construction of great ceremonial earthwork centers. The Poverty Point site, in Louisiana, consists of two huge mounds and a concentric series of earth embankments a half-mile in diameter. The Adena centers of Ohio, West Virginia, and Kentucky are marked by a big earth tumuli constructed over interior burial chambers. The total settlement patterns associated with these monuments are unknown, but it is certain that the societies responsible for such "public works" must have included large numbers of individuals and have necessitated the co-ordination of the efforts of these people, even though their actual living sites may have been of no more than a semipermanent nature. The subsistence basis of these societies is questionable. Some plant cultivation may have been known in the East by this time, but the probable local cultigens seem insufficient as dietary staples, and the presence of maize has not yet been demonstrated. A bit later, between 500 B.C. and A.D. 500, with the advent of the Hopewellian cultures, maize does come into the picture, and it probably was of real subsistence value as a supplement to the intensive collecting pattern. But it is undoubtedly significant that the Hopewellian cultures continue in the earlier tradition of burial-mound earthwork construction and in the traditions of art and ceremonial paraphernalia which draw their symbolism from religious practices and magic associated with hunting.

Other Hunting and Collecting Patterns

The American Plains. Later, big-game hunting patterns on the Plains of North America developed from the older Pleistocene way of life. This transition came about gradually, and, at first, the technological changes were relatively slight. A modern type of buffalo was pursued by these Plains huntsmen, and they combined this activity with some food-collecting. In later prehistoric times horticulture was brought to certain regions of the Plains and became an important subsistence factor, but buffalo hunting continued. In historic times, after the European intro-duction of the horse, the buffalo-hunting pattern enjoyed a renaissance. A similar history can be reconstructed for the Argentine pampas and Patagonia, where the guanaco was the game animal. In both the North and the South American Plains the change-over from Pleistocene to modern climatic conditions appears to have taken place at about 5000 B.C. From this date forward, there are general trends toward smaller projectile points, and these are accompanied by stone food-grinding im-plements, objects of aesthetic, ceremonial, or non-utilitarian usage, and, later, pottery. These trends are associated with sites which could be classed as semipermanent settlement types. Thus it seems probable that these late big-game hunting cultures of the North and South American Plains, although depending primarily upon the chase for their food re-sources, were becoming somewhat more sedentary as the result of other subsistence activities; this increased sedentism is, in turn, related to a development of aspects of culture which are not directly a part of the food quest and the adaptation to the natural environment.

The Arctic. Quite distinct in both natural environmental setting and in history from the later big-game hunting of the Plains is the Arctic hunting pattern. In its earliest phases the Arctic pattern seems to have been oriented toward land hunting. The Denbigh Complex of Alaska is the example. It is possible that there are connections between Denbigh and the early post-Pleistocene big-game hunters farther south. This is suggested by some of the Denbigh parallel-flaked projectile points. But there are other technological traditions in Denbigh flint-work, such as the burins and the micro-core-and-blade forms, which indi-cate diffusions or migrations from northeastern Asia, perhaps as recently as 2000 or 3000 B.C. Following this horizon, the course of Arctic prehis-tory is the story of the development of Eskimo culture. This develop-ment was not an American Arctic phenomenon alone, as subsequent population movements or strong influences may be traced from North America back to Asia; but, viewing the Asiatic-American Arctic sphere as a whole as the home of this evolving Eskimo culture, there is little doubt that the main trends were those of a gradual supplementation of land hunting by sea-mammal hunting and by fishing and by an increas-ing adaptation to an environment of ice and snow. Eskimo sites dating back to the beginning of the Christian Era are fully of semipermanent settlement type. Artifacts of all kinds, in ground stone and ivory, abound; and, from the first millennium A.D. forward, Eskimo culture had achieved that unique and amazing ecological adjustment for which it is famous. It is worthy of note that in such customs and value expressions as the burial of the dead and ivory-carving art there is no steady mounting elaboration. The climactic developments in these come, rather, with the Old Bering Sea and Ipiutak phases, during the first millennium A.D. Subsequent phases show a lessening in the complexity and elaboration of these themes. The supposition is that these refinements of the cult of the dead and of ornamental art had original Asiatic sources outside the severe Arctic zone and that, with the adaptive evolution of Eskimo culture, they were, to some extent, inhibited or sloughed off.

The North Pacific Coast. Along the Pacific Coast of North America it is likely that a food-collecting way of life had its beginnings with migrants from the western interior desert areas who brought to the coast the relatively simple subsistence technology of the Great Basin and Plateau countries. As they settled in the Pacific river valleys and along the coast, their adjustment parallels, in many ways, that of the Eastern Woodland collectors. This adjustment is marked, archaeologically, by the introduction and increasing use of ground and polished stone implements and ceremonial forms and by greater site size and apparent stability of occupation. By 2000 B.C., if not earlier, the Pacific Coastal pattern was of an intensive collecting kind, accompanied by a semipermanent village settlement type. In late prehistoric and early historic times some of the California acorn-gathering or fishing societies were living in what must be considered permanent villages of several thousand inhabitants. Farther north, in Oregon, Washington, and British Columbia, there are comparable sequences showing an increased "settling-in" adaptation to the environment. These societies achieved an intensive collecting pattern well back in prehistoric times, and the salmon-fishing Northwest Coast tribes of the historic period are still in this tradition of abundant subsistence.

Cultivators of Nuclear America

Nuclear American plant cultivation centered in the territories including and extending from central Mexico to southern Peru. Its beginnings were slow and gradual, and in its incipient forms it was grafted upon, or an adjunct to, pre-existing collecting patterns. This is the case in Tamaulipas, Mexico, on the northern border of Nuclear America, where hints of plant domestication go back to 7000 B.C. and where, by 5000 B.C., it is definite. Between that date and 3000 B.C. squash and beans are identified from dry cave deposits, and by 2500 B.C. small cobs of primitive maize have made their appearance. The cultural contexts of these Tamaulipas caves make it evident that these domesticates played but a relatively small part in what may otherwise be considered to be a North American Desert collecting pattern of food-getting. It is noteworthy, however, that in this Tamaulipas sequence of incipient cultivation there is a steady increase in the types and volume of cultigens and also in the varieties and numbers of such seed-grinding implements as mortars, manos, and mullers. With the advent of the final incipient cultivation phase, at about 1600 B.C., improved corn, beans, and Lima beans are all present, and it has been estimated that the cave populations of this period derived about 30 per cent of their sustenance from these crops. In Peru incipient cultivation also appears to be a kind of epiphenomenon superimposed upon the shellfish and wild-plant collecting patterns of the ancient coastal populations. In this setting, squash, beans (*Canavalia*), and miscellaneous roots and tubers were domesticated as early as 2500 B.C., if not long before.

The basic origins and courses of diffusion of the Nuclear American incipient cultivation pattern are difficult to trace. No imperishable and diagnostic tool types can testify indisputably to its presence. Such specialized and definite implements as the maize-grinding metate and mano are more likely to be associated with a fully established agriculture, and the relatively unspecialized seed-grinding implements are as likely to have been used for wild as for domesticated foods. Consequently, unusual conditions of preservation, such as dry caves or completely arid desert sands, are necessary for an accurate determination of cultivation incipience. It may be for this reason that the arid uplands of Middle America and the rainless Peruvian coast now appear as the earliest centers of the Nuclear American incipient cultivation pattern. For it seems probable that experimentation with plant domestication proceeded in many parts of Nuclear America and that its antiquity throughout the zone goes back to 3000 B.C. or earlier. It is unlikely that any one area or region was the *fons et origo* of all the important food plants. Maize (*Zea mays*), which was to become the basic staple of the New World, probably was domesticated first in Guatemala or southern Mexico and spread from there, although the possibilities of more or less separate and independent cultivation of wild pod corn at various localities in the Nuclear zone cannot be discarded.

The societal and cultural context of Nuclear American incipient cultivation ranges from the camp site, with its relatively limited inventory of basketry and ground and chipped stone tools, to semipermanent and permanent villages with much wider assemblages of textile and stone items plus, in some instances, pottery. The coastal locations appear to have been more propitious for settled life. Pottery, of a relatively simple sort, has been found in a coastal shell midden in Panama, dating at 2100 B.C.; and, in Ecuador, coastal shell refuse stations, going back to 2400 B.C., have also yielded pottery. On the Peruvian coast the incipient cultivators lived in stone-and-mud-masonry pit-house villages which probably numbered up to more than one hundred persons, and between 1800 and 1000 B.C. they began to manufacture pottery of a kind probably related to the Panamanian and Ecuadorean varieties.

The line marking the shift from what we have called "incipient cultivation" to established cultivation is drawn at that point where communities derive their major support from farming. In the Middle American area this change is marked by the appearance of the first permanent villages. Some of these villages, like those in the Tamaulipas region which follow the incipient cultivation societies, are quite small. Others, including the early pottery and farming phases of the Valley of Mexico, cover several acres. Still other village units were probably composed of several scattered hamlets which were nucleated around small ceremonial centers marked by temple mounds. In both Ecuador and Peru there was a movement away from the immediate coast back into the valleys at this time, a settlement shift suggestive of the rising importance of cultivation over a fishing and shellfish-collecting subsistence. The Peruvian sites of such early farming phases as the Cupisnique were small hamlets dotted over the river valley floor and along the valley edges, apparently focused upon a ceremonial center.

The beginnings of the established cultivation pattern in Nuclear America are dated at about 1500 B.C. in Middle America and at 1000 B.C. in Peru. The next thousand years or so saw an intensification of this pattern, with increasing population densities and a development and elaboration of technology and art. Public building was on the increase in the form of pyramids constructed of adobe, earth, or stone. These pyramids marked the ceremonial or politico-religious centers and either were surrounded by town type settlements, as in upland Mexico and Guatemala and on the Peruvian coast, or served as nuclei to dispersed hamlets, as in the Maya and Veracruz lowlands. The impressive Middle American art styles and the systems of hieroglyphic writing and calendrics, which were to flower brilliantly only slightly later, had their beginnings in the Formative Period. In Peru, this was also the time of the first great arts, of experimentation in metallurgy, and of the initiation of complex irrigation works.

Intensive cultivation arose from established cultivation in Peru and in certain portions of Middle America. On the Peruvian scene it is clearly defined by the large-scale irrigation and garden-plot networks of the coast and the irrigation and terracing of the highland basins. Such works are dated as early as the beginnings of the Classic period, at about A.D. 1. In Middle America intensive cultivation was more limited in geographic scope, and the evidence for it is more difficult to define archaeologically. In the Valley of Mexico irrigation and chinampa ("floating-garden") farming can be dated with assurance back to the Toltec civilization at around A.D. 900. Before that the case for intensive cultivation is less certain, although it is possible that irrigation was practiced as early as the first phases of the Teotihuacán civilization at the beginning of the Christian Era. In both Peru and Middle America intensive cultivation is associated with towns and temples and, in some instances, with cities.

The history of Nuclear American cultivation belongs not only to the Nuclear zone but to the outlands bordering it to the north and south. The diffusions or migrations carrying the ideas of plant domestication to these areas must have begun on the incipient cultivation level. We have already noted that primitive maize and other plants were being cultivated in the southwestern United States area in the third millennium B.C. by peoples who were essentially Desert collectors. It is also possible that incipient cultivation spread into northern Chile or northwestern Argentina at a relatively early date, although there is no proof of this. Established cultivation patterns, however, are not introduced to, or developed upon, the Nuclear American peripheries until much later. It was not until the last few centuries B.C. that permanent villages based primarily upon farming were established in the North American Southwest, and a comparable date probably is applicable to northern Chile-Argentina. In both the Southwest and in northern Chile-Argentina, elements of intensive cultivation appear sometime after about A.D. 700. The canal systems of the southern Arizona desert Hohokam culture and the agricultural terracing of the southern Andes are examples in point. There seem to be associations between these intensive cultivation patterns and town and temple communities; however, it is also certain that in the southwestern United States such large late prehistoric towns as Pueblo Bonito, in northern New Mexico, came into being without these specialized techniques of complex irrigation or terracing systems.

Other Patterns of Cultivation

There are two other native American cultivation patterns whose histories, if not completely separate from that of the Nuclear American pattern, have sufficient independence to deserve comment. Both are found in lowland wooded areas of adequate or abundant rainfall. Unfortunately, in neither case does the archaeological record give more than a hint of these patterns. They have their respective hearts in the North American Eastern Woodlands and its Mississippian River system and in the South American Tropical Forest of the Amazon and Orinoco Rivers.

The Mississippi Drainage of Eastern North America. It seems likely that the sunflower (*Helianthus*), goosefoot (*Chenopodium*), and pumpkin (*Cucurbita pepo*) were all domesticated here by the beginning of the first millennium B.C. This may have been in response to remote stimulus diffusion from the Nuclear American cultivation pattern, the plants used being the best that the local environment had to offer; or it may have been an entirely independent development. As previously noted, this Eastern Woodland incipient cultivation was a part of a dominantly collecting or intensive collecting life-way of which the Adena and Hopewell cultures represented a climax. It is known that, by 500 B.C., such cultures were in contact with the Nuclear American cultivation pattern for maize. By A.D. 500, established cultivation of a Nuclear American variety, derived from Middle America, dominated the Mississippi Valley. Thus the earlier, non-maize, distinctively Eastern Woodland cultivation never proceeded beyond the level of incipience until it became a part of the expanding Nuclear American pattern.

The South American Tropical Forest. This pattern played a much more important role in native American agriculture. The basic crops were root starches, primarily manioc (*Manihot esculenta*), both bitter and sweet, as well as the sweet potato (*Ipomoea batatas*). Their antiquity as domesticates in Venezuela and Brazil can only be speculated upon, but almost certainly it antedates 1000 B.C.

NEW WORLD CULTURE: HISTORY AND EVOLUTION

Subsistence Efficiency

Nearly all the New World hunting or collecting life-patterns demonstrate, or strongly suggest, a trend through time of increasing adaptive efficiency in the realm of subsistence technology. The North American

Desert pattern, which is known in the full gamut of its development, reveals the growing importance of seed foods in its middle and later stages. This is seen in the increasing numbers and specialization of food-grinding implements. The North American Woodland pattern development parallels this to some extent, but with a strong emphasis upon specialization in weapons and implements used for forest hunting and stream and coastal fishing. On the Pacific Coast of North America there is a similar sequential record of improved adjustment to local environments in which the collecting of vegetable foods or fishing were the specialties. In the South American collecting patterns these same tendencies also exist, and in the far north the Arctic hunting pattern is the example par excellence of the development of a technology to cope with environmental conditions. Only the very earliest patterns—those of the Pleistocene gatherers and the Pleistocene hunters—fail to reveal fully this configuration through time of adaptive subsistence efficiency. For the first, the data are too few to make an appraisal. For the second—the big-game hunters—we see a high degree of specialization to an environment at the outset; and it seems likely that the earlier stages of the pattern, leading up to such complexes as the Sandia or Clovis, are as yet undiscovered. Even with only a part of the chronological range of the pattern revealed, however, there is a hint of the specialization trend in the changes that set the later Folsom complex off from the earlier Clovis. Thereafter, the pattern dissolves with the shrinkage and eventual disappearance of the Pleistocene environments.

The American collecting patterns were not pushed back to marginal positions or terminated by natural environmental change but by the propagation of plant cultivation. The history of this cultivation is a story of several millennia of casual, experimental, or incipient cultivation. During this time plant cultivation did not really constitute an independent subsistence pattern but was an adjunct to food-collecting. Incipient cultivation, although progressing slowly, culminated in the Nuclear American and Tropical Forest established cultivation patterns. Offering a subsistence based largely or wholly upon food production rather than collecting, it spread to all those American areas where it was able to find a receptive natural environment and where it could compete successfully with existing subsistence techniques. In parts of America the more productive and more highly specialized intensive cultivation replaced established cultivation.

Social Integration

Our surveys of New World life-patterns indicate correlations between the increasing efficiency of subsistence adaptations and the increasing size and stability of settlement or community types. Both the North American Desert and the Woodland collectors lived in camp type settlements in their earlier stages. In their later phases the Cochise populations of the Southwest established semipermanent villages, and the tribes of the eastern United States began to "settle in" along rivers and the coast in semipermanent, or possibly permanent, villages. Elsewhere, as on the Pacific Coast of North America or the South American coasts, the intensification of food-collecting also made it possible for larger social aggregates to live together for longer periods of time.

In the Nuclear American and South American Tropical Forest cultivation patterns the stage of agricultural incipience probably marked some increase in community size and stability, although the evidence here is either lacking or difficult to separate from that of the later stages of food-collecting. Undoubtedly, local conditions and available food plants were decisive variables. It was with the established cultivation level, however, that the permanent village came into existence in these patterns. As previously observed, this does not mean that settled village life was impossible without plant cultivation; we have noted its probable existence in certain circumstances of intensive collecting; but it does signify that when the food economy of a society was predominantly agricultural, that society became "anchored" to a relatively small geographical locus. There is considerable range in size and type of site associated with established cultivation. Although the permanent village was the most usual and widespread form in the Nuclear American and Tropical Forest zones as well as in outlying American areas, there are indications that town-and-temple and even city type communities were supported by this kind of farming.

Cultural Forms and Institutions

This brings us to our most difficult step in the attempt to follow out the trends and courses of New World cultural evolution. What configurations of change through time may we generalize about those aspects of culture which are not immediately and intimately related to the subsistence technology-environmental settings or to the sizes and groupings of settlements and societies? And how might these configurations correlate, or fail to correlate, with trends of change in the technological and social orders?

To begin at a low and tangible level, it is observed that manufactures of all kinds increase throughout the histories of our American collecting and cultivation life-patterns. This is most noticeable in the North American Desert and Woodland patterns, where, in the early levels, there is relatively little archaeological residue as compared to later phases. In the later phases not only are there more objects, but many of these have no apparent direct relationship to the food quest. Polished stone items of a ceremonial or ornamental nature are examples. Similar trends are also noted in South American collecting patterns. Within the sequences of the cultivation patterns this same increase in material goods, particularly non-utilitarian goods, is characteristic of the earlier periods; later on, it is less evident. There is, then, in cultural items that might be classed as elaborations of life—ornaments, emblems, religious paraphernalia—an increase that more or less parallels the rise of successful food-collecting and plant cultivation and the appearance of semipermanent and permanent villages. This is not to argue that aesthetic or religious experience was lacking in earlier times or on earlier levels, but the time or desire to give frequent material expression to such emotions must have been lacking before the development of some degree of sedentism.

Architecture, particularly communal or public architecture, is another tangible that seems to describe some significant configurations in its occurrences in the American life-patterns. It is absent from both the Pleistocene hunting and the later hunting traditions. It is given some expression with the intensive levels of the collecting patterns. On the North American Pacific Coast it is known from historic times, and it is probable that communal buildings of impressive size were put up here during prehistoric periods, although these, being of wood, would have left little or no archaeological traces. In the eastern United States the intensive collectors of the Woodlands built large earth monuments for burial and religious purposes. However, it is with the Nuclear American cultures that public building was greatly elaborated.

Art is perhaps the archaeologist's one best clue to the non-material, non-utilitarian heart of things. At least we shall consider it so, for it is the only means at hand so to interpret the preliterate cultures. In the New World life-patterns there is little evidence of it associated with the Pleistocene big-game hunters, although it may have existed in some perishable form. In the North American collecting patterns, art has its beginnings with the small ornamental and ceremonial objects of sculptured stone or bone. The Hopewellian climax of the Woodland collectors represents a florescence of the art of this particular pattern. In Nuclear America there are varying styles of art in small handicraft objects and ceramics in the earlier phases of established cultivation, and relatively early in the Formative Period in both Middle America and Peru monumental art styles, such as the Olmec and Chavín, make their appearance.

The New World as a Whole

Up to now we have considered the question of the evolution of culture in the New World within the confines of the historical units designated as life-patterns. In each of these patterns we have observed certain trends or configurations of occurrence in social and cultural traits. There are similarities in these trends, from pattern to pattern, and there are also distinct differences. These differences, together with the variable chronological and distributional aspects of the life-patterns, suggest that it is possible to conceive of New World prehistoric events as a unitary, if highly complex, history and evolution.

The earliest of the definite American life-patterns—that of the Pleistocene big-game hunters—marks a stage in New World culture history and culture development referred to as the *Lithic,* and *Paleo-Indian,* or the *Paleo-American.* It was a highly specialized way of life, and the pattern was broken with the changing of the natural environment at the end of the Pleistocene. Some of the peoples and societies involved may have perished, but it is likely that others sought new modes of subsistence adaptation. Possibly minor food-getting techniques, of little importance in an economy geared to the mammoth hunt, became the bases of a new orientation. Also, there was probable recourse to borrowing either from peoples newly arrived from Asia or from those descendant in the possible ancient traditions of Pleistocene food-gathering. In some such way the collecting patterns must have come into being.

The food-collecting way of life, although represented in several historically distinct life-patterns, comprises a stage in the development and history of New World subsistence technology. This has been called the *Archaic stage.* The food-collectors were, at first, less well adapted to their environments than the big-game hunters; but, in losing the specialization of their ancestors, relatives, or neighbors, they had been launched upon a course that would eventually lead to a much greater subsistence efficiency and economic security than the chase of the animal herds. After a few thousand years the results of this new specialization, or variety of subsistence specializations, is apparent in the semipermanent villages, the manufacture of "luxury" items, and the beginnings of art and ceremonial constructions.

Carried somewhat like a parasite in the host of the food-collecting patterns was the minor element of plant domestication. Of considerable antiquity, it appears to have remained little more than dormant for millennia. Gradually this incipient cultivation assumed more importance, especially in certain geographical regions where the native wild flora and fauna were not overly abundant. Finally, plant cultivation emerged as the agricultural way of life. This threshold of village communities sustained by farming marks the *New World Formative stage*.

Like the early food-collectors, the first established village agriculturists had a less successful economic adaptation than many contemporary intensive collectors, such as those of the North American Eastern Woodlands or Pacific Coast. But the potentialities were before them, and it was not long before the agriculturally based societies of Nuclear America surpassed the wealthiest of the food-collectors in surpluses and population numbers. With the establishment of the secure cultivation threshold, there were no more major changes in native American subsistence patterns. Intensive cultivation, achieved in some places, was a specialization and a refinement, not a new departure. Thus it is at somewhere near this point that the course of New World culture history and culture evolution can no longer be traced in terms of subsistence efficiency.

Community size, concentration, and complexity of organization do, however, continue to show a configuration of increase after the establishment of cultivation as the primary means of subsistence. Although, to some extent and in some places, this may be attributed to intensive cultivation and to population rise, it is certain that cultural choice entered increasingly into the equation. As towns and cities arose in Nuclear America, during what have been called the *Classic* and *Postclassic stages* of culture development, it is significant that absolute numbers of people did not change so much as did the settlement patterns by which they were organized. The town and the city were not simply the means of containing population masses; they were an organic part of societies organized and integrated over large territories or states.

We have remarked that both monumental art styles and temples occur relatively early in the rise of Middle American and Peruvian civilizations, perhaps less than a thousand years after the first establishment of village life based on cultivation and at the beginnings of what might be considered the town-and-temple community. There followed, then, a series of architectural and artistic developments whose trends cannot be generalized in the sense of "increase," "improvement," or "refinement" but rather as reflective of changes in social and political types and in moral values. Such trends as are suggested are those marking a shift from sacred to secular emphases, from relative peace to times of war, and from the smaller city or regional state to the larger territorial empire. It is from an appraisal of such trends that the distinction between a Classic and a Postclassic stage has been based.

We come, then, to sum up the case for the evolution of culture in the native New World. I would conclude that whatever the contacts with the peoples and cultures of the Old World (and these have been but briefly alluded to in this paper), New World culture did, indeed, evolve in an essentially independent manner. This evolution can be traced in subsistence modes which, within several major historical patterns, describe a configuration of increasing efficiency and environmental adaptation. This same general trend of subsistence efficiency for production can also be projected across these various historical patterns so that it describes an over-all configuration of increase despite the fluctuations which mark the junctures of the patterns. Paralleling subsistence increase is the enlargement of the social unit and its geographic stability. Sedentism and food surpluses are also seen as the conditions necessary for the creation of material wealth and for the memorializing of religious and aesthetic motions in art and architecture. Great skill and sophistication were attained in New World art, including monumental art, well in advance of the rise of the power of the city or the state. The evolution of the city and the state in native America appears to be linked with the growing power of military and secular forces and with attempts to propagate single religious, political, and social views—unified moral orders—to ever widening spheres of influence.

The "culture-area" concept was devised by students of the American Indian because of the necessity of classifying and describing the ways of life of hundreds of culturally and linguistically different Indian groups. Clark Wissler, for many years curator of Anthropology at the American Museum of Natural History, elaborated and popularized essentially the same pattern of culture areas as has been used to organize this book. It should be noted that Wissler himself was well aware that culture areas are, to a large degree, artificial constructs. Boundaries of most areas, for example, are impossible to delineate, as one culture area normally blends into others. Nonetheless, the notion of the "culture area" has served as a very useful tool in the study of American Indians.

2 *Clark Wissler*

NORTH AMERICAN CULTURE AREAS*

CULTURE AREAS

It is customary to divide the continent into culture areas the boundaries to which are provisional and transitional, but which taken in the large enable us to make convenient distinctions. North of Mexico we have nine culture areas: the Southwest, California, the Plateaus, the Plains, the Southeast, the Eastern Woodlands, the Mackenzie, the North Pacific Coast, and the Arctic areas. Each of these is conceived as the home of a distinct type of culture; but when we take a detailed view of the various tribal groups within such an area we find a complex condition not easily adjusted to a generalized type.

Plains Area

In the Plains area we have at least thirty-one tribal groups, of which eleven may be considered as manifesting the typical material culture of the area: the Assiniboine, Arapaho, Blackfoot, Crow, Cheyenne, Comanche, Gros Ventre, Kiowa, Kiowa-Apache, Sarsi, and Teton-Dakota. The chief traits of this culture are the dependence upon the buffalo and the very limited use of roots and berries; absence of fishing; lack of agriculture; the tipi as a movable dwelling; transportation by land only with the dog and the travois (in historic times with the horse); want of

---

* Abridged from "Material Cultures of the North American Indian," by C. Wissler, in *American Anthropologist*, **16**, 447–505, 1914.

basketry and pottery; no true weaving; clothing of buffalo and deer-skins; a special bead technique; high development of work in skins; special rawhide work (parfleche, cylindrical bag, etc.); use of a circular shield; weak development of work in wood, stone, and bone.

In historic times these tribes ranged from north to south in the heart of the area. On the eastern border were some fourteen tribes having most of the positive traits enumerated above and in addition some of the negative ones, as a limited use of pottery and basketry, some spinning and weaving of bags, rather extensive agriculture and alternating the tipi with larger and more permanent houses covered with grass, bark, or earth, some attempts at water transportation. These tribes are: the Arikara, Hidatsa, Iowa, Kansa, Mandan, Missouri, Omaha, Osage, Oto, Pawnee, Ponca, Santee-Dakota, Yankton-Dakota, and the Wichita.

On the western border were other tribes (the Wind River Shoshone, Uinta, and Uncompahgre Ute) lacking pottery, but producing a rather high type of basketry, depending far less on the buffalo but more on deer and small game, making large use of wild grass seeds, or grain, alternating tipis with brush and mat-covered shelters.

Also on the northeastern border are the Plains-Ojibway and Plains-Cree who have many traits of the forest hunting tribes as well as most of those found in the Plains. Possibly a few of the little-known bands of Canadian Assiniboine should be included in this group in distinction from the Assiniboine proper.

These variations from the type are, as we shall see, typical traits of the adjoining areas, the possible exception being the earth-lodges of the Mandan, Pawnee, etc. On the other hand, the tribes of the area as a whole have in common practically all the traits of the typical group. For example, the Mandan made some use of tipis, hunted buffalo, used the travois, worked in skins and rawhide, and armed and clothes them-selves like the typical Plains tribes, but also added other traits, pottery, basketry, agriculture, and earth-lodges. Thus we see that while in this area there are marked culture differences, the traits constituting these differences tend to be typical of other areas and that, hence, we are quite justified in taking the cultures of the central group as the type for the area as a whole.

Plateau Area

The Plateau area joins the Plains on the west. It is far less uniform in its topography, the south being a veritable desert while the north is moist and fertile. To add to the difficulties in systematically characterizing this culture, arising from lack of geographical unity, is the want of definite information for many important tribes. Our readily available sources are Teit's Thompson, Shushwap, and Lillooet; Spinden's Nez Percé; and Lowie's Northern Shoshone; but there is also an excellent summary of the miscellaneous historical information by Lewis. In a general way, these three intense tribal studies give us the cultural nuclei of as many groups, the Interior Salish, the Shahaptian, and the Shoshone. Of these the Salish seem the typical group because both the Nez Percé and the Shoshone show marked Plains traits. It is also the largest, having sixteen or more dialectic divisions and considerable territorial extent. Of these the Thompson, Shushwap, Okanagan (Colville, Nespelim, Sanpoil, Senijixtia), and Lillooet seem to be the most typical. The traits may be summarized as: extensive use of salmon, deer, roots (especially camas), and berries; the use of a handled digging-stick, cooking with hot stones in holes and baskets; the pulverization of dried salmon and roots for storage; winter houses, semi-subterranean, a circular pit with a conical roof and smoke hole entrance; summer houses, movable or transient, mat- or rush-covered tents and the lean-to, double and single; the dog sometimes used as a pack animal; water transportation weakly developed, crude dug-outs and bark canoes being used; pottery not known; basketry highly developed, coil, rectangular shapes, imbricated technique; twine weaving in flexible bags and mats; some simple weaving of bark fiber for clothing; clothing for the entire body usually of deerskins; skin caps for the men, and in some cases basket caps for women; blankets of woven rabbitskin; the sinew-backed bow prevailed; clubs, lances, and knives, and rod and slat armor were used in war, also heavy leather shirts; fish spears, hooks, traps, and bag nets were used; dressing of deerskins highly developed but other skin work weak; upright stretching frames and straight long handled scrapers; while wood work was more advanced than among the Plains tribes it was insignificant as compared to the North Pacific Coast area; stone work was confined to the making of tools and points, battering and flaking, some jadeite tools; work in bone, metal, and feathers very weak.

The Shahaptian group includes tribes of the Waiilatpuan stock. The underground house seems to be wanting here, but the Nez Percé used a form of it for a young men's lodge. However, the permanent house seems to be a form of the double lean-to of the North. In other respects the differences are almost wholly due to the intrusion of traits from the Plains. Skin work is more highly developed and no attempts at the weaving of cloth are made, but there is a high development of basketry and soft bags.

The Northern Shoshonean tribes were even farther removed toward Plains culture, though they used a dome-shaped brush shelter before the tipi became general; thus, they used canoes not at all, carried the Plains shield; deer being scarce in their country they made more use of the buffalo than the Nez Percé, depended more upon small game and especially made extensive use of wild grass seeds, though as everywhere in the area, roots and salmon formed an important food; in addition to the universal sagebrush bark weaving they made rabbitskin blankets; their basketry was coil and twine, but the shapes were round; they had some steatite jars and possibly pottery, but usually cooked in baskets; their clothing was quite Plains-like and work in rawhide was well developed; in historic times they were great horse Indians but seem not to have used the travois either for dogs or horses. The remaining Shoshone of western Utah and Nevada were in a more arid region and so out of both the salmon and the buffalo country, but otherwise their fundamental culture was much the same, though far less modified by Plains traits. The Wind River division, the Uinta or Uncompahgre Ute, it should be noted, belong more to the Plains area than here, and have been so classed. In the extreme western part of Nevada we have the Washo, a small tribe and linguistic stock, who in common with some of the little-known Shoshonean Mono-Paviotso groups seem to have been influenced by California culture. Among other variants, their occasional use of insects as food may be noted. On the north of our area are the Athapascan Chilcotin whose material culture was quite like that of the Salish, and to the northeast the Kutenai with some individualities and some inclinations toward the Plains.

In general, it appears that in choice of foods, textile arts, quantity of clothing, forms of utensils, fishing appliances, methods of cooking and preparing foods, there was great uniformity throughout the entire area, while in houses, transportation, weapons, cut and style of clothing, the groups designated above presented some important differences. As in the Plains area, we find certain border tribes strongly influenced by the cultures of the adjoining areas.

California Area

In California we have a marginal or coast area, which Kroeber divides into four sub-culture areas. However, by far the most extensive is the central group to which belongs the typical culture. Its main characteristics are: acorns, the chief vegetable food, supplemented by wild seeds, roots and berries scarcely used; acorns made into bread by a roundabout process; hunting mostly for small game and fishing where possible; houses of many forms, but all simple shelters of brush or tule, or more substantial conical lean-to structures of poles; the dog was not used for packing and there were no canoes, but used rafts of tule for ferrying; no pottery but high development of basketry, both coil and twine; bags and mats very scanty; cloth or other weaving of twisted elements not known; clothing was simple, and scanty, feet generally bare; the bow, the only weapon, sinew-backed usually; work in skins very weak; work in wood, bone, etc., weak; metals not at all; stone work not advanced. With the single exception of basketry we have here a series of simple traits which tend to great uniformity.

As with the preceding areas, we must again consider intermediate groups. In the south the characteristic linguistic individuality vanishes to make room for large groups of Yuman and Shoshonean tribes; here we find some pottery, sandals, wooden war clubs, and even curved rabbit sticks, all intrusive. The extinct Santa Barbara were at least variants, living upon sea food, having some wood work, making plank canoes, and excellent workers of stone, bone, and shell. In northern California are again the Karok, Yurok, Wishosk, Shasta, and Hupa, and other Athapascan tribes; here sea food on the coast and salmon in the interior rival acorns and other foods; dug-out canoes; rectangular gabled houses of planks with circular doors; basketry almost exclusively twined; elkhorn and wooden trinket boxes; elkhorn spoons; stone work superior to that of central California; the occasional use of rod, slat, and elkskin armor and also basket hats of the northern type. These all suggest the culture farther north.

North Pacific Coast Area

Ranging northward from California to the Alaskan peninsula we have an ethnic coast belt, known as the North Pacific Coast area. This culture is rather complex and presents highly individualized tribal variations, but can be consistently treated under three subdivisions: (a) the northern group, Tlingit, Haida, and Tsimshian; (b) the central group, the Kwakiutl tribes and the Bellacoola; and (c) the southern group, the Coast Salish, the Nootka, the Chinook, Kalapooian, Waiilatpuan, Chimakuan, and some Athapascan tribes. The first of these seem to be the type and are characterized by: the great dependence upon sea food, some hunting upon the mainland, large use of berries; dried fish, clams, and berries are the staple food; cooking with hot stones in boxes and baskets; large rectangular gabled houses of upright cedar planks with carved posts and totem poles; travel chiefly by water in large sea-going dug-out canoes some of which had sails; no pottery or stone vessels, except mortars; baskets in checker, those in twine reaching a high state of excellence among the Tlingit; coil basketry not made; mats of cedar bark and soft bags in abundance; the Chilkat, a Tlingit tribe, specialized in the weaving of a blanket of goat hair; there was no true loom, the warp hanging from a bar and weaving with the fingers, downward; clothing rather scanty, chiefly of skin, a wide basket hat (only one of the kind on the continent and apparently for rain protection); feet usually bare, but skin moccasins and leggings were occasionally made; for weapons the bow, club, and a peculiar dagger, no lances; slat, rod, and skin armor; wooden helmets, no shields; practically no chipped stone tools, but nephrite or green stone used; wood work highly developed, splitting and dressing of planks, peculiar bending for boxes, joining by securing with concealed stitches, high development of carving technique; work in copper may have been aboriginal, but, if so, very weakly developed.

The central group differs in a few minor points; used a hand stone hammer instead of a hafted one, practically no use of skin clothing but twisted and loosely woven bark or wool; no coil or twined basketry, all checker work.

Among the southern group appears a strong tendency to use stone arrowheads in contrast to the north; a peculiar flat club, vaguely similar to the New Zealand type, the occasional use of the Plains war club, greater use of edible roots (camas, etc.) and berries, some use of acorns as in California, the handled digging-stick, roasting in holes (especially camas) and the pounding of dried salmon, a temporary summer house of bark or rushes, twine basketry prevailed, the sewed rush mat, costume like the central group.

Eskimo Area

The chief résumés of Eskimo culture have been made by Boas who divides them into nine or more groups, but his distinctions are based largely upon non-material traits. When we consider the fact that the Eskimo are confined to the coast line and stretch from the Aleutian islands to eastern Greenland, we should expect lack of contact in many parts of this long chain to give rise to many differences. While many differences do exist, the similarities are striking, equal if not superior in uniformity to those of any other culture area. However, our knowledge of these people is far from satisfactory, making even this brief survey quite provisional.

The mere fact that they live by the sea and chiefly upon sea food, will not of itself differentiate them from the tribes of the North Pacific coast; but the habit of camping in winter upon sea ice and living upon seal, and in the summer upon land animals, will serve us. Among other traits the kayak and "woman's boat," the lamp, the harpoon, the float, woman's knife, bowdrill, snow goggles, the trussed-bow, and dog traction, are almost universal and taken in their entirety rather sharply differentiate Eskimo culture from the remainder of the continent. The type of winter shelter varies considerably, but the skin tent is quite universal in summer, and the snow house, as a more or less permanent winter house, prevails east of Point Barrow. Intrusive traits are also present: basketry of coil and twine is common in Alaska; pottery also extended eastward to Cape Parry; the Asiatic pipe occurs in Alaska and the Indian pipe on the west side of Hudson Bay; likewise some costumes beaded in general Indian style have been noted west of Hudson Bay. All Eskimo are rather ingenious workers with tools, in this respect strikingly like the tribes of the North Pacific coast. In Alaska where wood is available the Eskimo carve masks, small boxes, and bowls with great cleverness.

Mackenzie Area

Skirting the Eskimo area from east to west is a great interior belt of semi-Arctic lands, including the greater part of the interior of Canada. Hudson Bay almost cuts it into two parts, the western or larger part occupied by the Déné tribes, the eastern by Algonkins, the Saulteaux, Cree, Montagnais, and Naskapi. The fauna, flora, and climate are quite uniform for corresponding latitudes which is reflected to some extent in material culture so that we should be justified in considering it one great area; this would, however, not be consistent with less material traits according to which the Déné country is considered as a distinct area. For this reason we shall treat the region under two areas.

Our knowledge of the Déné tribes is rather fragmentary, for scarcely a single tribe has been seriously studied. Aside from the work of Father Morice we have only the random observations of explorers and fur traders. It is believed that the Déné tribes fall into three culture groups. The eastern group: the Yellow Knives, Dog Rib, Hares, Slavey, Chipewyan, and Beaver; the southwestern group: the Nahane,

Sekani, Babine, and Carrier; the northwestern group comprising the Kutchin, Loucheux, Ahtena, and Khotana. The Chilcotin are so far removed culturally that we have placed them in the Plateau group and the Tahltan seem to be intermediate to the North Pacific center.

Of these three groups the southwestern is the largest and occupies the most favorable habitat. From the writings of Father Morice a fairly satisfactory statement of their material cultures can be made, as follows: All the tribes are hunters of large and small game, caribou are often driven into enclosures, small game taken in snares and traps; a few of the tribes on the headwaters of the Pacific drainage take salmon, but other kinds of fish are largely used; large use of berries is made, they are mashed and dried by a special process; edible roots and other vegetable foods are used to some extent; utensils are of wood and bark; no pottery; bark vessels for boiling with and without use of stones; travel in summer largely by canoe, in winter by snowshoe; dog sleds used to some extent, but chiefly since trade days, the toboggan form prevailing; clothing of skins; mittens and caps; no weaving except rabbit-skin garments, but fine network in snowshoes, bags, and fish nets, materials of bark fiber, sinew, and babiche; there is also a special form of woven quill work; the typical habitation seems to be the double lean-to, though many intrusive forms occur; fish-hooks and spears; limited use of copper; work in stone weak.

Unfortunately, the data available on the other groups are less definite, so that we cannot decisively classify the tribes. From Hearne, Mackenzie, and others it appears that the following traits prevailed over the entire Déné area: the twisting of bark fiber without spindle and its general use, reminding one of sennit; snares and nets for all kinds of game; the use of spruce and birchbark for vessels and canoes; basketry of split spruce root (*watap*) for cooking with hot stones noted by early observers; the toboggan; in summer the use of the dog to carry tents and other baggage; extensive use of babiche; the short-handled stone adze; iron pyrites instead of the firedrill and fungus for touchwood; the use of the cache; and above all, dependence upon the caribou. These seem to be the most characteristic traits of the Déné as a whole and while neither numerous nor complex are still quite distinctive.

Some writers have commented upon the relative poverty of distinctive traits and the preponderance of borrowed, or intrusive ones. For example, the double lean-to is peculiarly their own, though used slightly in parts of the Plateau area; but among the southwestern

Déné we frequently find houses like those of the Tsimshian among the Babine and northern Carrier, while the Skena and southern Carrier use the underground houses of the Salish, and among the Chipewyan, Beaver, and most of the eastern group, the skin or bark-covered tipi of the Cree is common. Similar differences have been noted in costume and doubtless hold for other traits. Pemmican was made by the eastern group. According to Hearne some of them painted their shields with Plains-like devices. In the northwestern group we find some sleds of Eskimo pattern. Such borrowing of traits from other areas is, however, not peculiar to the Déné, and while it may be more prevalent among them, it should be noted that our best data is from tribes marginal to the area. It is just in the geographical center of this area that data fail us. Therefore, the inference is that there is a distinct type of Déné culture and that their lack of individuality has been over-estimated.

Eastern Woodland Area

We come now to the so-called Eastern Woodland area, the characterization of which is difficult. As just noted, its northern border extends to the Arctic and all the territory between the Eskimo above and Lakes Superior and Huron below and eastward to the St. Lawrence is the home of a culture whose material traits are comparable to those of the Déné. In brief, the traits are the taking of caribou in pens; the snaring of game; the considerable use of small game and fish; the use of berry food; the weaving of rabbitskins; the birch canoe; the toboggan; the conical skin or bark-covered shelter; the absence of basketry and pottery; use of bark and wooden utensils. The tribes most distinctly of this culture are the Ojibway north of the Lakes, including the Saulteaux, the Wood Cree, the Montagnais, and the Naskapi.

Taking the above as the northern group we find the main body falls into three large divisions:

1. The Iroquoian tribes (Huron, Wyandot, Erie, Susquehanna, and the Five Nations) extending from north to south and thus dividing the Algonkin tribes.

2. The Central Algonkin, west of the Iroquois: Some Ojibway, the Ottawa, Menomini, Sauk and Fox, Potawatomi, Peoria, Illinois, Kickapoo, Miami, Piankashaw, Shawnee, also the Siouan Winnebago.

3. The Eastern Algonkin: The Abnaki group, and the Micmac, not to be distinguished from the northern border group save by their feeble cultivation of maize; the New England tribes, and the Delawares.

While the Iroquoian tribes seem to have been predominant, their material culture suggests a southern origin, thus disqualifying them for places in the type group. The Eastern tribes are not well known, many of them being extinct, but they also seem to have been strongly influenced by the Iroquois and by southern culture. We must therefore turn to the Central group for the type. Even here the data are far from adequate, for the Peoria, Illinois, Miami, and Piankashaw have almost faded away. Little is known of the Kickapoo and Ottawa, and no serious studies of the Shawnee are available. The latter, however, seem to belong with the transitional tribes of the eastern group, if not actually to the Southeastern area. Our discussions therefore must be based on the Ojibway, Menomini, Sauk and Fox, and Winnebago.

Maize, squashes, and beans were cultivated (though weakly by the Ojibway), wild rice where available was a great staple, maple sugar was manufactured; deer, bear, and even buffalo were hunted, also wild fowl; fishing was fairly developed, especially sturgeon fishing on the lakes; pottery was weakly developed but formerly used for cooking vessels; vessels of wood and bark were common; some splint basketry; two types of shelter prevailed, a dome-shaped bark or mat-covered lodge for winter, a rectangular bark house for summer, though the Ojibway tended to use the conical type of the northern border group instead of the latter; canoes of bark and dug-out were used where possible; the toboggan was occasionally used, snowshoes were common; dog traction rare; weaving of bark fiber downward with fingers; soft bags; pack lines; and fish nets; clothing of skins, soft-soled moccasins with drooping flaps, leggings, breech-cloth, and sleeved shirts for men, for women a skirt and jacket, though a one-piece dress was known; skin robes, some woven of rabbitskin; no armor, bows of plain wood, no lances, both the ball-ended and gun-shaped wooden club; in trade days the tomahawk; deer were often driven into the water and killed from canoes (the use of the jack-light should be noted); fish taken with hooks, spears, and nets, small game trapped and snared; work in skins confined to clothing; bags usually woven and other receptacles made of birchbark; mats of reed and cedar bark common; work in wood, stone, and bone weakly developed; probably considerable use of copper in prehistoric times; feather-work rare.

When we come to the Eastern group we find agriculture more intensive (except in the extreme north) and pottery more highly developed. Woven feather cloaks seem to have been common, a southern trait. Work in stone also seems a little more complex; a special development of steatite work. More use was made of edible roots.

The Iroquoian tribes were even more intensive agriculturists and potters, they made some use of the blowgun, developed corn-husk weaving, carved elaborate masks from wood, lived in rectangular long houses of peculiar pattern, built fortifications, and were superior in bone work.

Southeastern Area

The Southeastern area is conveniently divided by the Mississippi river, the typical culture occurring in the east. As we have noted, the Powhatan group and perhaps the Shawnee are quite intermediate. These eliminated we have the Muskogean and Iroquoian tribes (Cherokee and Tuscarora) as the chief groups, also the Yuchi, Eastern Siouan, Tunican, and Quapaw. The Chitimacha and Atakapa differ chiefly in the greater use of aquatic foods. The Caddoan tribes had a different type of shelter and were otherwise slightly deflected toward the Plains culture. We have little data for the Tonkawa, Karankawa, and Carrizo, but they seem not to have been agriculturists and some of them seem to have lived in tipis like the Lipan, being almost true buffalo Indians. These thus stand as intermediate and may belong with the Plains or the Southwest area. The Biloxi of the east, the extinct Timuqua, and the Florida Seminole are also variants from the type. They were far less dependent upon agriculture and made considerable use of aquatic food. The Timuqua lived in circular houses and, as did the Seminole, made use of bread made of coonti roots (*Zamia primila*), the method of preparing suggesting West Indian influence. The eating of human flesh is also set down as a trait of several Gulf Coast tribes. Our typical culture then may be found at its best among the Muskogean, Yuchi, and Cherokee.

The following are the most distinctive traits: great use of vegetable food and intensive agriculture; raised maize, cane (a kind of millet), pumpkins, watermelons, tobacco, and after contact with Europeans quickly took up peaches, figs, etc.; large use of wild vegetables also; dogs eaten, the only domestic animal, but chickens, hogs, horses, and even cattle were adopted quickly; deer, bear, and bison in the west were the large game, for deer the stalking and surround methods were used; turkeys and small game were hunted and fish taken when convenient (fish poisons were in use); of manufactured foods bears' oil, hickory-nut oil, persimmon bread, and hominy are noteworthy, to which we may add the famous "black drink"; houses were generally rectangular with curved roofs, covered with thatch or bark, also often provided with plaster walls reinforced with wicker work; towns were well fortified with palisades, dug-out canoes; costume was moderate, chiefly of deerskins, robes of bison, etc., shirt-like garments for men, skirts and toga-like upper garments for women, boot-like moccasins for winter; some woven fabrics of bark fiber, and fine netted feather cloaks, some buffalo-hair weaving in the west; weaving downward with the fingers; fine mats of cane and some corn-husk work; baskets of cane and splints, the double or netted basket and the basket meal sieve are special forms; knives of cane, darts of cane and bone; blowguns in general use; good potters, coil process, paddle decorations; skin dressing by slightly different method from elsewhere (macerated in mortars) and straight scrapers of hafted stone; work in stone of a high order but no true sculpture; little metal work.

Southwestern Area

In the Southwestern area we have a small portion of the United States (New Mexico and Arizona) and an indefinite portion of Mexico. For convenience, we shall ignore all tribes south of the international boundary. Within these limits we have what appear to be two types of culture: the Pueblos and the nomadic tribes, but from our point of view (material culture) this seems not wholly justifiable since the differences are chiefly those of architecture and not unlike those already noted in the Eastern Woodland area. On account of its highly developed state and its prehistoric antecedents, the Pueblo culture appears as the type. The cultures of the different villages are far from uniform, but ignoring minor variations fall into three geographical groups: the Hopi (Walpi, Sichumovi, Hano [Tewa], Shipaulovi, Mishongnovi, Shunopovi, and Oraibi); Zuñi (Zuñi proper, Pescado, Nutria, and Ojo Caliente); and the Rio Grande (Taos, Picuris, San Juan, Santa Clara, San Ildefonso, Tesuque, Pojoaque, Nambe, Jemez, Pecos, Sandia, Isleta, all of Tanoan stock; San Felipe, Cochiti, Santo Domingo, Santa Ana, Sia, Laguna, and Acoma, Keresan stock). The culture of the whole may be characterized first by certain traits not yet found in our survey of the continent; viz., the main dependence upon maize and other cultivated foods (men did the cultivating and weaving of cloth instead of women as above); the use of a grinding stone instead of a mortar; the art of masonry; loom or upward weaving; cultivated cotton as textile material; pottery decorated in color; a unique type of building; and the domestication of the turkey. These certainly serve to sharply differentiate this culture.

While the main dependence was placed on vegetable food there was some hunting; the eastern villages hunted buffalo and deer, especially Taos. The most unique hunting weapon is the flat, curved rabbit stick.

Drives of rabbits and antelope were practiced. The principal wild
vegetable food was the piñon nut. Of manufactured foods piki bread is
the most unique. In former times the villages often traded for meat
with the more nomadic tribes. Taos, Pecos, and a few of the frontier villages used buffalo robes and often dressed in deerskins, but woven robes
were usual. Men wore aprons and a robe when needed. In addition to
cloth robes, some were woven of rabbitskin and some netted with turkey
feathers. Women wore a woven garment reaching from the shoulder to
the knees, fastened over right shoulder only. For the feet hard-soled
moccasins, those for women having long strips of deerskin wound
around the leg. Pottery was highly developed and served other uses
than the practical. Basketry was known, but not so highly developed as
among the non-Pueblo tribes. The dog was kept but not used in transportation and there were no boats. The mechanical arts were not highly
developed; their stone work and work in wood while of an advanced
type does not excel that of some other areas; some work in turquoise but
nothing in metal.

The Pima once lived in adobe houses but not of the Pueblo type, they
developed irrigation but also made extensive use of wild plants (mesquite, saguaro, etc.). They raised cotton and wove cloth, were indifferent potters, but experts in basketry. The kindred Papago were similar,
though less advanced. The Mohave, Yuma, Cocopa, Maricopa, and
Yavapai used a square, flat-roofed house of wood, did not practice irrigation, were not good basket makers (excepting the Yavapai), but
otherwise similar to the Pima. The Walapai and Havasupai were somewhat more nomadic.

The preceding appear to be transitional to the Pueblo type, but when
we come to the Athapascan-speaking tribes of the eastern side of the
area we find some intermediate cultures. Thus, the Jicarilla and Mescalero used the Plains tipi, they raised but little, gathered wild vegetable
foods and hunted buffalo and other animals, no weaving but costumes
of skin in the Plains type, made a little pottery, good coil baskets,
used glass-bead technique of the Plains. The southern Ute were also in
this class. The western Apache differed little from these, but rarely used
tipis and gave a little more attention to agriculture. All used shields of
buffalo hide and roasted certain roots in holes. In general while the
Apache have certain undoubted Pueblo traits they also remind one of
the Plains, the Plateaus, and, in a lean-to like shelter, of the Mackenzie
area.

The Navaho seem to have taken on their most striking traits under

European influence, but their shelter is again the up-ended stick type of the north, while their costume, pottery, and feeble attempts at basketry and formerly at agriculture suggest Pueblo influence.

Thus in the widely diffused traits of agriculture, metate, pottery, and to a less degree the weaving of cloth with loom and spindle, former use of sandals, we have common cultural bonds between all the tribes of the Southwest, uniting them in one culture area. In all these the Pueblos lead. The non-Pueblo tribes skirting the Plains and Plateaus occupy an intermediate position, as doubtless do the tribes to the southwest, from which it appears that after all we have but one distinct type of material culture for this area.

A great many anthropologists have studied specific American Indian cultures or individuals, while a few have studied American Indian culture in totality. Perhaps the foremost scholar in the field of the comparative ethnology of North American tribes was Alfred L. Kroeber, for half a century a leader in American anthropology and "dean" of California ethnologists. Kroeber's interest in item and detail is expressed in the following paper where, utilizing his grasp of the anthropology and history of North America, he attempts to estimate the size of the aboriginal population.

3 *Alfred L. Kroeber*

DEMOGRAPHY OF THE AMERICAN INDIANS*

A posthumous work by James Mooney makes available the first careful and complete tribe-by-tribe series of estimates of the native population of America, north of present-day Mexico, for the period of early

* Abridged from "Native American Population," by A. L. Kroeber, in *American Anthropologist*, **36**, 1–25, 1934.

contact of each group with settling Caucasians. This invaluable study renders possible the examination of population density in terms of cultural or other areas.

The Mooney figures are here used with one consistent modification—a substitution of my total of 133,000 for California in place of C. H. Merriam's 260,000 which Mooney took over; hence with a reduction of the total for the continent north of Mexico from 1,152,950 at 1,025,950, or about 10 percent. I have made this substitution because my total is arrived at through a tribe-by-tribe addition or "dead-reckoning" method, like all Mooney's other figures; whereas Merriam uses a mission to nonmission area multiplication ratio for the state as a whole.

It proved necessary to convert Mooney's data for tribes and bands into terms of the ethnic groups recognized in my own tribal territorial map. This involved some consolidations. In other cases, Mooney gives only combined figures for tribes which I keep separate; thus, Southern Paiute and Paviotso. Accordingly there are overlaps as well as omissions; and an exactly authentic check-up on the conversions from his scheme is difficult. The result is that my rearranged totals fall about 10,000 below his. This discrepancy of 1 percent is negligible since the best of Mooney's estimates can hardly pretend to be nearer than 10 percent to the probable truth, and some may be 50 percent or more from it. It is of still less moment so far as it enters into population densities, because the boundaries of many tribal territories are imperfectly known or in dispute.

Mooney's figures are probably mostly too high rather than too low, so far as they are in error.

All in all, however, Mooney's estimates and computations have clearly been made on the basis of wide reading, conscientiousness, and experienced judgment. Until some new, equally systematic, and detailed survey is made, it seems best to accept his figures *in toto* rather than to patch them here and there. My impression is that Mooney's total of about 1,150,000 reduced to 1,025,000 by the California substitution, will ultimately shrink to around 900,000, but that the respective density ratios of the principal areas will not be very materially affected by such change.

The outstanding fact is the exceptional density on the Pacific coast—both Northwest and California. Next comes the Southwest; but this also extends to the Pacific coast. Even the Columbia-Fraser region, a Pacific coast hinterland, more than holds its own against the fertile East. The

TABLE I

POPULATION DENSITIES OF PRINCIPAL AREAS OF CULTURE

	Culture areas	Population	Territory 100 km²	Density
	Arctic Coast			
1	Eastern Eskimo (W. to incl. Coronation Gulf)	30,900	15,057	2.05
2	Western Eskimo (Mackenzie delta and west)	58,800	7,231	8.13
	Northwest Coast			
1	Northern Maritime (Tlingit, Haida, Tsimshian, Haisla)	28,100	1,666	16.8
2	Central Maritime (all other Wakashans, Bella Coola)	17,300	594	29.1
3	Gulf of Georgia (Salish)	23,700	725	32.6
4	Puget Sound	6,000	357	16.8
5	Lower Columbia	32,300	507	63.7
6	Willamette Valley	3,000	334	8.98
7	Lower Klamath (and S.W. Oregon)	18,000	377	49.8
	Intermediate and Intermountain			
1	Great Basin (incl. Snake r. Shoshoneans)	26,700	10,810	2.47
2	California (excl. N.W. and S. California)	84,000	1,941	43.3
3	Columbia-Fraser (incl. Interior Salish, Sahaptin, etc.)	47,650	6,600	7.15
	Southwest			
1	Pueblo	33,800	446	75.7
2	Circum-Pueblo (Apache and Navaho)	14,500	6,430	2.26
4	Sonoran area (Pima and Papago in U. S.)	10,600	864	12.2
7	NW Arizona (Havasupai, Walapai, Yavapai)	1,600	666	2.4
8	Lower Colorado (River Yumans, Cocopa to Mohave)	13,000	416	31.25
9	Peninsular California in U. S. (Diegueño)	3,000	166	18.1
10	Southern California (Shoshoneans, Chumash)	26,500	683	38.7
	Eastern and Northern			
1	Southeast proper	87,800	5,983	14.7
2	South Florida	4,000	542	7.38
3	South Texas (coastal)	6,400	2,057	3.11
4	Red River (Caddoan group) and Pawnee	25,900	4,563	5.67
5	Plains (high plains, short grass)	50,500	13,978	3.61
6	Prairies (tall grass: C. Siouans, Dakota exc. Teton, etc.)	53,000	11,692	4.53
7	Wisconsin (wild rice area)	18,300	1,461	12.52
8	Ohio Valley (incl. Illinois)	20,000	7,707	2.59
9	Southern Great Lakes (Iroquoian tribes)	42,500	4,421	9.61

Cont.

TABLE 1 *(Cont.)*
POPULATION DENSITIES OF PRINCIPAL AREAS OF CULTURE

	Culture areas	Population	Territory 100 km^2	Density
10	North Atlantic Slope (Micmac, Abnaki)	7,300	3,285	2.22
11	Middle Atlantic Slope (Penacook to Conoy)	46,800	1,828	25.6
12	South Atlantic Slope (excl. Yuchi, Creek)	41,900	2,467	17.—
13	Appalachian Summit (Cherokee)	22,000	1,344	16.3
14	N. Great Lakes (Ottowa, Algonkin, most Ojibwa)	37,300	5,188	7.18
15	E. Sub-Arctic (Algonkins: Montagnais, Cree, Naskapi)	23,000	25,677	1.11
16	W. Sub-Arctic (Athabascans: Chipewyan to Kutchin and Khotana)	33,930	38,944	.87

TABLE 2
POPULATION DENSITIES BY MAJOR AREAS

California	84,000	1,941	43.3
Northwest Coast	129,200	4,560	28.3
Southwest (part within U. S.)	103,000	9,671	10.7
(Intermediate-Intermountain)	158,350	19,411	8.1
Columbia-Fraser	47,650	6,660	7.15
Eastern	426,400	61,328	6.95
Arctic Coast	89,700	22,288	4.02
(Eastern and Northern)	520,630	131,137	3.97
Great Basin	26,700	10,810	2.47
Northern	94,230	69,809	1.35
Total, N. of Mexico	1,000,880	187,067	5.35

Arctic coast, surprisingly enough, has a density more than half as great as that of the East, though this was mostly agricultural; and one approximately equal—on the face of the figures even slightly superior—to the agricultural Eastern and non-agricultural Northern areas combined. This means of course that the latter had much the lowest density of all. The average figure for the continent (north of Mexico) falls somewhat below that for the agricultural East and somewhere above that for the Eskimo.

COAST LAND AND FARM LAND

Two generalizations are obvious: coastal residence did make for heavier population; agriculture per se did not necessarily increase density. The following summary will make these propositions more vivid.

We can first set off the wholly non-agricultural Pacific coast; next, the essentially agricultural areas of the Southwest and East; and then treat the remainder of the continent north of Mexico as a unit.

The Pacific coast may be conveniently taken as extending from the Malemiut Eskimo of Alaska to the Diegueño and Kamia just short of the mouth of the Colorado. The area is that of Pacific coast in the literal sense, not Pacific drainage. The whole Yukon, Fraser, and Columbia river areas are excluded, except for the Eskimo, Coast Salish, and Chinook at the mouths of these streams. California is included as a native culture area, not as a modern political unit; so is the northwestern margin of the Southwest, namely southern California.

TABLE 3
GRAND POPULATION DIVISIONS NORTH OF MEXICO

	Population	Area 100 km²	Density	Percent of total population
Pacific Coast, Bering Strait to mouth of Colorado	295,700	11,745	25.2	29.6
Essentially agricultural areas, E. and S.W.	404,600	39,884	10.1	40.4
Remainder	300,580	135,438	2.1	30.0
	1,000,880	187,067	5.1	100.0

The agricultural region comprises the tribes in whose economy farming plays a significant rather than sporadic part. Excluded are the Walapai, Havasupai, Yavapai, Apache, Navaho, Ojibwa, Abnaki, and the tribes of south Texas and south Florida.

In round numbers, the Pacific coast had 300,000 inhabitants out of a million north of Mexico, or 30 percent of the population in 6 percent of the area, with a density of 25 per 100 km²; the farming regions, 40 percent in 20 percent of the territory with a density of 10; the remainder, 30 percent on nearly 75 percent of the land, with a density barely exceeding 2.

That among non-farming natives a coast or coast-plain habitat was normally far more favorable than interior residence in conducing to an aggregation of population, is not only indicated by the much greater density in the Pacific areas, but by two other facts: first, that the Arctic shore Eskimo are, per area, more numerous than their inland Athabascan and Algonkin neighbors; and second, certain density figures for adjacent Atlantic and Gulf tribal areas. Such are: Massachusetts, coastal, 105, Nipmuc, interior, 14; Montauk 158, Iroquois 7; Powhatan 38, Monacan 9; Chitimacha 32, Natchez 19.

A sharp line of division between coast and interior cannot easily be drawn in the Eastern region, because tidewater in many places runs far inland and because tribal adhesions and territories are so often uncertain. But a review of the itemized tribal data leaves little doubt that on the whole the population density in the farming parts of the Atlantic and Gulf region was perhaps twice as heavy on the coast, including habitats on tidewater or within a day's travel of salt water, as immediately inland thereof.

This means that for the continent as a whole (always unfortunately excluding Mexico), coastal residence, inclusive of that on coastal plains or along the lowest courses of rivers, led to a populational density from five to ten times greater than the interior as a whole, in non-agricultural regions; and probably at least twice as great even in agricultural areas.

This finding may be expectable; but that the non-farming Pacific coast should overtop the farming areas with a two-and-a-half times greater density, is certainly surprising. It means, obviously, that the relation to the land in terms of agricultural utilization by the United States Indian was fundamentally different from our own. He was not a farmer in our sense of the word. Not only did he derive possibly half his subsistence through non-farming; but he utilized for his farming no more than a very small percentage of the land capable of being farmed.

This is particularly true of the East; and the Southwest should be excepted in this connection. The agricultural total in Table 3 breaks up thus: East 347,200 souls, 3,799,762 km², 9.1 density; Southwest, 57,400; 172,200; 33.3. Not only is the gross density nearly four times as great in the Southwest, but the larger part of the territory assigned to the Southwestern agricultural tribes is desert or mountain and unfarmable, or actually unfarmed by ourselves. The native Southwesterners, so far as they farmed, therefore pushed the exploitation of the land to a much higher pitch than the Easterners. This fact implies a different history, and thus further justifies the current sharp segregation of the Southwestern and Eastern native cultures. These essentially different histories, in turn, reinforced by the non-agricultural geographic gap between the areas, indicate separate origins, or at any rate separate branchings from the same southern stem of maize culture.

THE AGRICULTURAL EAST

The basic situation as regards native farming in the Eastern area may be made clearer by a comparison with our agriculture. The average yield of maize per acre today throughout the United States is between 25 and 30 bushels of 56 pounds of shelled corn. Maize notoriously increases its yield per acre but little under improved methods of farming. The improvements which we have made over Indian methods have been mainly in the direction of reducing production costs, especially in labor. The Indian therefore may be assumed to have derived nearly as many bushels from each acre of planting as we. He probably planted somewhat farther apart; but not unduly so, because of the difficulty of clearing and cultivating unnecessary area with his tools. A yield of 15 to say 1000, or a little under 3 pounds a day. This should more than sustain the average person in a community composed of men, women, and children. Beans and pumpkins would vary the diet as partial substitutes for maize without seriously affecting the acreage cultivated. The quantity of farm food consumed was probably less than here computed, because of the supplement of game, fish, mollusks, berries, wild seeds, and roots, which over much of the Eastern region is estimated to have contributed half of the food supply. However, let us keep to our figure of nearly three pounds of maize or equivalent in farm products per head. Since this involves only about one acre cultivated per person, and we reckon 347,200 population in the Eastern agricultural area, the total native plantations in this region aggregated in round numbers only a third of a million acres. Against this, we today plant a hundred million acres of maize alone in the United States—not all, but nearly all, within the native agricultural areas here called Eastern. We add another two hundred million acres in wheat, oats, cotton, and hay—many of these acres perfectly suitable, though not profitable to us, for maize. True, part of our total lies outside the region of systematic Indian farming; but it is a minority part. It does not much matter whether our total is one or two or three hundred million acres and the Indian total one-third or two-thirds of a million: the conclusion remains that the eastern Indian cultivated less than one percent of the area on which he could successfully have grown crops satisfactory to his needs and standards. My own opinion is that the figure was under rather than over one-half of one percent.

Here is another way of conceptualizing the situation. The Eastern agricultural density was 9.1 per 100 km², a little under 9 souls—say 2 families—per township. We allot 144 quarter-sections to 144 families or some 700 persons in a township; and these earn through their crops not only their food but their clothing, tools, vehicles, furniture, taxes, and luxuries—and often support a town in addition. The ratio comes out about the same.

It is clear that two things were fundamentally different in the Eastern Indian and our economics: the land use, or relation to the land; and the place of agriculture in life. "Improvement" of land was confined to minute specks in the landscape. They were comparable in size to oases, although not in the least enforced by nature, being in fact simply selected by convenience or habit from among a hundred times as many sites about equally well utilizable. In other words, there was a hundred-fold surplus of good land over farming population.

Second, while every native household in the area farmed, it becomes doubtful whether many of them did so from real necessity. If the Pacific coast from Bering Strait to the Imperial Valley desert could support 25 souls per areal unit without farming, it is not unreasonable to suppose that the uniformly fertile East might have supported 10 without farming. Agriculture then was not basic to life in the East; it was an auxiliary, in a sense a luxury. It made possible increased accumulation of food against the future, a living in permanent sites and in larger groups, and therefore joint undertakings, whether of council, ritual, war, or building. It thus no doubt contributed somewhat toward the enrichment of cultural life; but there is nothing to show that the culture in its fundamental forms was really resting on agriculture.

Does this mean that agriculture was a recent introduction in the East, not yet fully acculturated and its potentialities still mainly unconceived? Theoretically such might well be the case, but it is not a necessary inference. As long as any other factors kept an originally light population light, the relation to the land, the part-only farm-use of this, might go on indefinitely.

THE SOUTHWEST

The Southwest was different from the East. It had maize as far back as Basket Maker times—less long than Mexico, no doubt, but longer than the East. Population density in the Southwest, also, was intermediate, so far as genuinely agricultural peoples are concerned. The distinctive feature of the Southwest is the presence in it, side by side, of two kinds of population—the fairly densely settled farmers and the very thinly sown non-farmers around and between them. How far back this condition goes historically, is difficult to say, because, as might be expected, the farmers have left abundant and striking archaeological remains, the gatherers few and scattered ones.

The basis of this duality of the Pueblo-Southwestern economic system, whether it is relatively recent or ancient also, lies obviously in the nature of the land. The Southwest is an arid region, steppe and mountain or semi-desert where not desert. Farming, with patience, can be made to yield a fairly reliable subsistence; but only in selected spots. The vast majority of the surface of the Southwest was as useless to the Pueblos, for crops, as it is to us. They could and did farm many spots which we do not farm; but that was because they sought only their food, we a civilized living. Allowing, as before, an acre to a person, the 34,000 Pueblos whom Hodge and Mooney estimate for 1680 would have had under cultivation a total of only some 53 square miles—a township and a half. We may double the allowance of land per head to permit of wider spacing of planting or lower yield in the arid Southwest. We may enlarge the population somewhat to accord with the wider extent of the culture in Pueblo periods 2 and 3. Even this, however, brings the actually farmed land up to a total of only one or two hundred square miles in two or three hundred thousand. This is just about the ratio utilized in the East; but there most of the great unused remainder was farmable, in the Southwest it was not.

The Pueblo, then, resembled the Mexican in using for his crops, if not every inch of productive land, at any rate considerable of the best of it. This makes his subsistence appear more directly of Mexican origin, with but slight transmutations. Where he differed was in that so little of his land was cultivable, and that scattered. He could not become numerous. He therefore did not need states and rulers and a peasantry; the more so as the scattered distribution of his farmable land kept his communities small. On the other hand, once given a concentration in towns, his agriculture became a necessity to him if he was not to starve.

This in turn engendered an attitude, a lack of leisure and lack of sense of freedom and enterprise, which would keep him from plunging into chronic warfare as a social mechanism. His population was kept down not so much by being killed off or expelled and disrupted, as by clinging to a narrow shelf of subsistence mechanism without leeway or recourse.

So far, discussion of the Southwest has been in terms of Pueblos and the non-agricultural tribes immediately enclosing them. But population-ally, this part of the Southwest forms only a smaller half of even that part of the Southwest which lies within the United States, without counting the related parts of Sonora and Chihuahua. It held 48,300 souls out of 103,000 in the American Southwest. Pima-Papago, Lower Colo-rado Yumans, and Southern Californians alone, in the non-Pueblo sphere, with 10,000, 13,000, and 26,500 souls, outnumber the com-bined Pueblo, Apache, and Navaho, even with the Pueblo counted at Mooney's high figure of nearly 34,000. Numerically, then, the pre-ponderant half of the American Southwest was the Gila-Yuman-South-ern California sphere, not the Pueblo one. As regards density, the disproportion is even greater; nearly 20 for the former, against a little over 7 for the Pueblo sphere. It is true that the density of the pure Pueblo territory alone was the highest—around 75. But against this in the other half are figures like 31 for Lower Colorado, and 39 for non-agricultural and semi-desert Southern California. The Pueblo-sphere density as a whole is brought down by the abnormally low density (2.3) of the large included area occupied in historic time by Athabascans. This expresses again the oasis-like distribution of the important population in the Pueblo sphere, and the contrast between town-dwellers and mescal-gatherers, which recalls nicely in many ways the relation of town-farmers and herders in the Sahara, Arabia, and inner Asia. As against this, the Gila-Yuma-California sphere was much more evenly sown with population, irrespective of whether this was agricultural or not. In one sense therefore this area may be considered as having made a healthier adjustment with its arid environment than the Pueblo sphere.

NORTHWEST COAST

The figures for the areas within the Northwest coast also carry a story, though they must be used with a certain reserve because in some of the areas the land itself was so little or secondarily used that length of frontage on shore or river was evidently the decisive factor as regards population. Still the areal densities mean something. They are:

Areas

Lower Columbia (Chinook, etc.)	64
Lower Klamath (Yurok, etc.)	50
Gulf of Georgia (Coast Salish)	33
Central Maritime (Wakashan, etc.)	29
Northern Maritime (Northern-tribes)	17
Puget Sound (Coast Salish)	17
Willamette Valley (inland)	9

Sub-Areas

Central Maritime, South (Nutka, Makah, Quinault)	65
Northern Maritime, Archipelago (Haida, S. Tlingit, Tsimshian)	22
Central Maritime, North (Kwakiutl, Heiltsuk, B. Coola)	17
Northern Maritime, River (Niska, Gitskyan, Haisla)	10
Northern Maritime, Mainland (N. Tlingit)	10

The Willamette area is a wholly inland one. We do not know with certainty whether it should be reckoned as part of the Northwest Coast or the Columbia-Fraser plateau. Puget Sound, although salt water, also extends its inlets far into the interior, and the area is a quasi-inland one. Apart from these two minor areas, the other five range almost in geographical order, with density decreasing from south to north. The sub-areas within the two northern areas again show almost the identical arrangement. Even if Mooney's computations for the Chinook and Gulf of Georgia Salish are taken as somewhat high, the generally greater density of the south as against the north remains fundamentally unimpaired. On this point, too, shoreline density would not invert the situation, the northerly areas having the more irregular, indented shore, whose ratio to the already lighter population would go up faster even than their land areas. The difference seems to lie in this: The northern groups were essentially maritime, mostly lived fronting the beach, and made little use of the land which they owned. The southern groups lived on river and tributary as well as on the shore, perhaps more largely so in fact, and often made genuine use of their landholdings. Their habitat utilization and culture remained more generalized and simpler, those of the northern groups were more specialized and extreme. As in the Southwest, on comparison of Gila-California with

Pueblo sphere, the more generalized method in the long run allowed of a heavier aggregate population.

ESKIMO

For the Eskimo areas, the range of land-area densities is:

Aleut	65
Pacific Coast (excl. Bering sea)	19
Western (Bristol bay to Mackenzie river)	4.9
Central-Eastern	2.3
Caribou	.4
Total Western	8.1
Total Eastern	2.1

Land areas mean particularly little in comparison with shore line in the case of the Eskimo, whose life depends on water and ice far more than on what the land bears. Still, the figures give a crude approximation to shoremile density, even if the Aleut population of 16,000 should prove too high. How far the higher latitude of the three low-density areas may be a factor must also be considered.

Still, the figures on their face show this: Nearly a third of all the Eskimo lived on open Pacific ocean frontage—27,300 Aleut, Kaniagmiut, Chugachigmiut, and Ugalakmiut out of 89,700. From the Malemiut south, that is, roughly, in Alaska from Bering Strait south, were almost 60 percent all members of the stock—53,000 out of 89,700. This is the region of masks and wooden houses and grave monuments and property distribution festivals and war fleet expeditions, traits which we are wont to regard as characteristic of the Northwest Coast. It is also the region where ice-hunting of seals, the sledge and the snow-house, and many other "typical" Eskimo traits are lacking or nearly absent.

In other words, "pure" or characteristic Eskimo culture obtains only among two-fifths of the members of the stock. Three-fifths live in a culture heavily charged with elements usually regarded as Northwest Coast or Asiatic, and lacking much of the inventory of "typical" Eskimo life. It is obvious that our concept of what is Eskimo is due to a first approach from Greenland, and next Labrador, Baffinland, and the Central region. Had our knowledge begun in Alaska, where population centers, and where the comparative density is overwhelming, our most "typical" Eskimo would probably seem merely peripherally reduced and atypical. Just what this means for the origin and history of the culture is hard to say. Most such evidence can be read two ways. The final word must be by specialists on the Eskimo. But the population distribution cannot be left out of account.

〰〰〰

W̶ithin the discipline of anthropology, as in the world at large, there has been a recent ferment about the nature, number, and significance of human races. In the past there have been those who have seen hundreds of human races of all sizes, shapes, and colors, several of whom were thought to be represented in the New World aboriginal population. "Black," "red," "yellow," and ancient "white" men were all believed by some experts to have contributed genes to the American Indians. In recent years, however, a number of leading anthropologists have begun to develop the position that, among all contemporary and recent human populations, the nature and order of differences are not of sufficient degree to warrant use of the concept "race." There are, then, as many races as one cares to see or, on the other hand, only one.

In the following paper, T. Dale Stewart and Marshall T. Newman, two leading authorities on the physical anthropology of the New World, discuss the history of the subject of racial variation in the New World.

4 **T. Dale Stewart &
Marshall T. Newman**

PHYSICAL TYPES OF AMERICAN INDIANS*

VIEWS OF TRAVELLERS IN AMERICA

It was Antonio de Ulloa, the Spanish scientific traveller, who wrote the famous statement. The year was 1772. In its original form it reads

* Abridged from "An Historical Résumé of the Concept of Differences in Indian Types," by T. D. Stewart and M. T. Newman, in *American Anthropologist* **53**, 19–36, 1951.

as follows: *"Visto un Indio de qualquier región se puede decir que se ha visto todos en quanto al color y contextura"* (24:242).* Daniel Wilson, 100 years later, translated it as follows: "If we have seen one American, we may be said to have seen all, their colour and make are so nearly alike" (26:114). Usually, however, it was rendered simply as "He who has seen one tribe of Indians, has seen all." Yet it can be recognized also as the basis for Samuel G. Morton's likewise oft-quoted generalization of 1842: "It is an adage among travellers that he who has seen one tribe of Indians, has seen all, so much do the individuals of this race resemble one another . . ." (19:4).

The influence of Ulloa's words is the more remarkable because they were ridiculed by his contemporaries. For example, Juan Ignacio Molina, the Chilian historian, writing from Italy in 1782, said: "Nothing appears to me to be more ridiculous than the assertion of several authors, that all the Americans resemble each other, and that from seeing one you are able to judge the whole" (18:233).

The effect of Ulloa's words upon subsequent thought, and the degree of their acceptance in spite of such opinion to the contrary, deserve further consideration. We must remember that they were written after the writer's contact with the Indians. Perhaps it is only natural for travellers to recall the homogeneous appearance of strange peoples. Thus in our own country we find Timothy Flint in 1826 reviewing in much the same way his 10 years' experience among the Indians of the Mississippi Valley:

> I have been forcibly struck with a general resemblance in their countenance, make, conformation, manners and habits. I believe that no race of men can show people, who speak different languages, inhabit different climes, and subsists on different food, and who are yet so wonderfully alike. (11:136)

Alexander von Humboldt, in 1811, after his extensive travels in the Americas, recognized the tendency to forget population differences. His reasoning can be characterized briefly in terms of the modern expression, "All Chinese look alike." Humboldt said:

> . . . an European, when he decides on the great resemblance among the copper-coloured races, is subject to a particular illusion. He is struck with a complexion so different from our own, and the uniformity of this complexion

---

* Numbers enclosed in parentheses refer to references and their page numbers listed in the back of this book under References Quoted, p. 693.

conceals for a long time from him the diversity of individual features. (16:140)

On the other hand, some of the early writers who have doubted or taken issue with Ulloa's generalization have not been content to explain it away. They in turn have been very positive about the existence of differences between Indians. Thus Molina said: "A Chilian is as easily distinguishable from a Peruvian as an Italian from a German" (18:233).

And Humboldt: ". . . the American race contains nations whose features differ as essentially from one another, as the numerous varieties of the race of Caucasus, the Circassians, Moors, and Persians, differ from one another" (16:140).

As if this were not enough to confuse the picture, some observers, in addition to stressing tribal differences, have insisted on an overall resemblance between tribes. Thus, Humboldt, in addition to what has been quoted about Indian variability, stated that "The Indians of New Spain bear a general resemblance to those who inhabit Canada, Florida, Peru, and Brazil" (16:140).

Much more recently (1925) Hrdlička combined these ideas in one statement:

. . . we find that the various differences presented by the Indians are often more apparent than real; that actual and important differences are in no case of sufficient weight to permit of any radical dissociation on that basis; and that the more substantial differences which exist between the tribes are everywhere underlaid by fundamental similarities and identities that outweigh them and that speak strongly not only against any plurality of race on the American continent, taking the term *race* in its fullest meaning, but for the general original unity of the Indians. (15:481)

This idea persists even today, as the following quotation from Sir Arthur Keith shows:

I . . . make the bold assumption that the whole Amerind population of America, from Bering Strait to the Strait of Magellan, is the progeny of the original pioneer group or groups. Certainly the American Indians differ in appearance from tribe to tribe and from region to region, but underneath these local differences, there is a fundamental similarity. (17:218)

This disparagement of Indian variability and insistence upon the homogeneity of the Indian type that has been traced from the famous words of Ulloa, is one of the more interesting aspects of the history of the development of anthropology. Daniel Wilson was probably right when he said that "An idea which embraces in a simple form the solution of many difficulties, is sure to meet with ready acceptance" (26:114).

In the foregoing the opinions of travellers in America who were familiar with the appearance of living Indians have been considered. No one can question the extensive contact with Indians of such men as Ulloa, Humboldt, Flint, or Hrdlička. Yet it must be borne in mind that in thinking about the living they were basing their opinions mainly on features that, according to Hooton, display relatively small variation— hair color, eye color, hair form and hair texture, body hair, skin color, and facial form. These superficial features—perhaps to be called Mongoloid features—would seem to be much of the physical structure that Indians possess in common.

VIEWS OF CRANIOLOGISTS

Fortunately, the travellers, besides providing opinions about the Indians, procured their skeletal remains. This brings us to another phase of our subject—the opinions of the craniologists.

The first of these to merit attention is Samuel G. Morton of Philadelphia, who has been called the father of physical anthropology in America. In his famous *Crania Americana* of 1839 he divided the American race into two great families—the Toltecan or civilized tribes and the American or barbarous tribes. The latter he subdivided into four branches. This subdivision appears to have been based on differences in culture rather than on physical differences, for Morton, throughout his anthropological career, stoutly maintained the unity of the American Indian. Indeed, so great was his influence that he was responsible in large measure for the wide acceptance of the generalization embodied in Ulloa's words and for the conversion of Ulloa's words into "an adage."

Doubts as to the correctness of Morton's opinion began to appear about five years after his death. In 1856–57 Daniel Wilson reported that Canadian Indian crania did not conform to Morton's standard type. About this time also Anders Retzius of Sweden divided the Indians into dolichocephalic and brachycephalic groups. Then in 1866, Meigs, after reviewing the Morton collections, together with newer additions, added a third or mesocephalic group.

At the Berlin meeting of the Congress of Americanists in 1888,

Virchow took up the argument, on the basis of his forthcoming *Crania Ethnica Americana,* and declared "the physiognomic characters of American heads show a divergence so manifest that one should definitely renounce the construction of a universal and common type for the American Indian" (25:260).

Virchow's declaration was strongly seconded by Ten Kate at the next meeting of the Americanists. After this for some time there was little expressed opposition to the homogeneity of the Indians. In the meantime we find Hrdlička reaffirming the unity of the Indian at the American Anthropological Association's symposium in 1911. Hrdlička could speak both as a craniologist and as an observer of living Indians. However, at the same time that he was proclaiming this generalization he was busy calling attention to the differences in Indian crania. The rest of his life was devoted to promoting these paradoxical ideas.

The year 1923 marks the beginning of the modern period of opposition to the prevailing view. Dixon in his *Racial History of Man,* published in 1923, said:

. . . in spite of the weight of authority which is ranged on the side of this belief in the unity of the Indian, I believe that it can be shown, by the method of analysis here adopted, that the theory of the homogeneity of the American Indian must be discarded. For not only does it wholly fail to account for certain facts of geographic distribution which have been strangely overlooked, but it breaks down entirely when historical and chronological factors are taken into consideration. (9:394)

Regardless of the defects now recognized to exist in Dixon's methodology, he appears to have been the first to review all the data in their chronological relations. He is also generally credited with first having demonstrated the peripheral distribution of the long-heads in North America. Unfortunately, however, both his terminology and his maps tended to suggest that the American Indians were composed of distinct racial elements, derived ultimately from all the other continents.

The revolt at Harvard, led by Dixon, was soon joined by Hooton. Using the Pecos skeletal remains, the largest collection from one site yet to become available, Hooton undertook another methodological experiment. He subjectively typed all of the crania and applied names to these types that suggested the presence of the same racial elements found by Dixon. In accounting for his findings and extending these ideas to the peopling of America, Hooton has speculated on such things as the white strain in the Iroquois, the Toda-like ancestors of the

Lacandones, and the Negroid admixture in some South American forest tribes. We see the culmination of this trend in Gladwin's use of Hooton's subjective impressions as proof that Negroes and Australians were early migrants to America.

Hooton's students are more conservative. Viewing the racial history of Asia, from which America was peopled, Howells and Birdsell see no possibility of Negroid or Australoid elements in the ancestry of American Indians. To them the American Indians represent a varying mixture of Early White (or Ainuoid) and Mongoloid strains. Also they have not been led astray by Weidenreich's imagination that led him to see—as Hooton has put it—"shocking racial diversity [in] the specimens that lay cheek-by-jowl in the one Upper Cave of Choukoutien" (13:649).

In summarizing the opinions of the craniologists on the unity or plurality of the American Indians, we find Morton at the beginning and Hrdlička recently insisting on unity; otherwise we find many other famous craniologists—among them Retzius, Meigs, Virchow, Ten Kate, Dixon and Hooton—all insisting on racial plurality of varying degrees. There can be no doubt that all of these men had seen lots of Indian crania.

Although Morton and Hrdlička seem thus to be exceptions to the rule, they carried the most weight here in America in their times. For this reason, they reinforced the view on Indian unity expressed by many travellers since the time of Ulloa and made it the majority opinion. As the above cited quotation from Dixon shows, as late as 1923, "the weight of authority [was still] ranged on the side of this belief in the unity of the Indian."

VIEWS OF CLASSIFIERS

The data supplied by travellers in America, by craniologists studying American Indian crania, and by physical anthropologists using other lines of investigation that need not be gone into here, have been utilized in racial classifications. This brings us to the third phase of our subject, and the one farthest removed from that object of reality, the Indian himself. We may now consider the opinions of the classifiers.

Linnaeus (or Linné), the father of taxonomy, from the first (1735) identified four human groups, among which was *Homo americanus rubescens*. Blumenbach emphasized the correspondence of these divisions to the four main land masses and the four colors: white, black, yellow and red, though he added the "tawny-colored" Malay group. Of the important early classifiers, only Cuvier could not bring himself to give the American Indian separate status. However, it was not until early in the 19th century that subdivisions of the American variety began to appear. Desmoulins in 1825 separated a North American group under the name of "Columbians" from a South American group, which he named "Americans." About the same time Bory de Saint Vincent separated the Patagonians from the "Americans" of Desmoulins. This action perhaps reflects the publicity given the Patagonians by exploring expeditions in which Darwin was soon to participate. D'Orbigny in 1839 went further and divided the South American Indians into three races: "Ando-Peruvienne," "Pampéenne," and Brasilio-Guaranienne" (10:247–249).

Although these and other classifiers of the early 19th century mention physical traits, apparently their subdivisions were based mostly upon cultural and geographic considerations. The first to make a classification solely upon physical grounds was Isidore Geoffroy Saint-Hillaire in 1858. His North and South American groups rest upon a difference in nose shape and eye slant—slight and doubtful differences indeed.

Taking this scheme as a model, Topinard in 1878 distinguished the "Peaux-Rouges"—Redskins—of North America from the "Tehuelches," "Guaranis" and "Peruviens" of South America.

Next, in 1889, Deniker, in his famous "attempt at a classification of human races based entirely on physical characters," distinguished the "Peau-Rouge" of North America from the Patagonians and other "Indians of the South" and all these in turn from a Paleo-American group (8:327).

Coming into the 20th century we find Haddon, in 1909, following Deniker closely, but in North America separating the Central Amerinds from the North-Western Amerinds of the Pacific slope on the one hand and from the Northern Amerinds of the Atlantic slope on the other, a classification that still smacks of a geographic bias.

Up to this point classifiers distinguished between the Indians of North and South America. But in 1912 Renato Biasutti, for the first time, cut across this division. His Neo-tropical class includes Sonoran, Central American, Amazonian and East Brazilian groups. His other main classes are: Subarctic, North Atlantic, South Atlantic and Austro-American.

The next significant development is von Eickstedt's 1933 classification of racial types—probably the most ambitious effort so far in this direction. His American types, following Biasutti's lead, cut across continental limits. The eight types that he distinguished have been somewhat modified and renamed by Imbelloni.

Of the classifiers thus far mentioned—Desmoulins, Bory de Saint Vincent, d'Orbigny, Saint-Hillaire, Topinard, Deniker, Haddon, Biasutti, von Eickstedt and Imbelloni—only the last can claim residency in the western hemisphere. As Hooton has perceived:

> . . . the principle of American racial unity, patriotically affirmed by many students of the American Indian who are native to, or naturalized in, the New World, [is] contemptuously dismissed by certain European anthropologists who divide up the American Indian into a variable number of racial types, with the naive irresponsibility of the cloistered savant classifying nebulous savages in remote wildernesses. (12:155–156)

Here in America, in keeping with our well-known scientific conservatism, the differentiation of Indian types has proceeded much more cautiously. Hrdlička, who as we have seen was one of the foremost champions of the principle of American racial unity, began as early as 1908 to identify cranial types. To his Gulf type, described at that time, he subsequently added Algonkin, Siouan, and Shoshonean types. Georg Neumann is currently in the process of describing another set of types. A multiplicity of names for much the same thing—partly linguistic and tribal, and partly geographic—is reducing the subject to chaos.

INTERPRETATION

Thought concerning the physical variability of the American Indian has been largely cast in terms of description and classification. Interpretation has lagged behind. One reason for this lag in the United States was the weight of authority behind the theory of racial unity, which was not successfully challenged until the 1920's. In denying any significant variability among Indians, this theory left little variability to interpret. Another reason for this interpretive lag, which stems from the conservatism of American science, has been a reluctance to make racial classifications or comprehensive interpretations until all the descriptive facts were known. As a result, interpretations by Americanists in this country have been few in number and very general in nature.

In Europe the same lag in interpretation has been present, but the reasons for it are different. In contrast to the Americans, European students have shown no reluctance to classify Indian races on the basis of incomplete data. As late as about 1890, however, these classifications were basically more geographic and cultural than racial, and were therefore unaccompanied by biological interpretations. Yet when the Indian classifications came to be based primarily on physical traits, they were unaccompanied by interpretations, or were uncritically explained in terms of migrations of racially different peoples from the Old World.

It is important to recall that until the 1880's, in the United States and abroad, interpretive efforts in any aspect of the biological sciences were also hampered by the domination of theological concepts. Even when the acceptance of the theory of evolution released the biological sciences from this bondage, students of the American Indian were, however, slow in realizing their new freedom. Then, when they made interpretations of Indian variability, they seemed to have been confused by the welter of opinion on the causes of evolution, and borrowed very little from modern biology. The hesitancy of Americanists to profit from the advances along the frontiers of biological thought constitutes another reason for the lag in interpretive efforts.

In this résumé, the interpretations of the early pre-Darwinian period are of historical interest only, and accordingly are given summary treatment. The interpretations made within the period of essentially modern biology, from roughly 1880 onwards, are the primary concern of this discussion.

Interpretation of the Early Period (1790–1880)

The earliest interpretations of American Indian variability were highly colored by the monogenesis-polygenesis controversy. Monogenesis, the older view, claimed a single creation for man, and used environmental response to explain the development of the Indian from the original creation. Polygenesis, which became popular in the early 19th century, held that the American Indian was a separate creation, and once created was not susceptible to change except through intermixture. Thus the polygenists were the hereditarians, and the monogenists the environmentalists of this period.

Blumenbach, the most notable monogenist to deal with the American Indian, expressed the belief that through climatic and cultural pressures the Indians were developed from North Asiatic Mongolians, who in turn were derived from the originally created Caucasian race. He claimed that the Indians then migrated into the New World ". . . at different times, after considerable intervals, according as various physical, geological or political catastrophes gave occasion to them" (4:274).

Although, as already noted, he made no racial divisions in America, Blumenbach was aware of considerable variation in skin color and face form, and attributed this to climatic factors. Most interesting is his conjecture that because the northern and southern extremities of the New World approximated Siberian climatic conditions, the Eskimos and Fuegians ". . . seem to come nearer, and as it were fall back, to the original Mongolian countenance" (4:274). These views, expressed in 1795, are strikingly modern.

The most influential polygenist in the American Indian field was Samuel Morton. He believed that the Indian was separately created in the New World, and that any physical variability among the aborigines of that area was inconsequential and transient. Morton was inclined to deny ". . . entirely the competency of physical causes to produce the effects alleged [adaptations to environmental stimuli], . . . mainly in consequence of the historical evidence he had accumulated, showing the unalterable permanency of the characteristics of race, within the limits of human records" (20:xlvi–xlvii). Despite Wilson's criticisms, Morton's thesis that the Indian represented one unalterable race was the dominant American view of the mid-19th century. In fact, this view still appeared in the 10th edition (1871) of Nott and Glidden's popular book, and as late as 1887 the elderly Brinton reiterated the dogma of the ". . . really remarkable fixedness of the American type" (7:296). After the turn of the century, Hrdlička devoted a large part of his efforts to the promotion of essentially the same idea.

Interpretations of the Modern Period (1880–1950)

The long-smoldering controversy between the evolutionists and the theologians was revived in 1859 by the publication of Darwin's *Origin of Species*. After a struggle of more than twenty years, a clear-cut vindication of the evolutionary concept resulted, thanks largely to superb marshalling of the supporting evidence. By the 1880's, most biologists had no doubt that evolution had taken place, but they expressed a wide diversity of opinion as to its causes. This diversity was especially great after 1890, when the first strong scientific challenge was leveled against Darwinism, through the first decade or so of the twentieth century. The challenges were aimed largely at natural selection, which was and still is the very heart of Darwinism. Substitute theories were offered. Meanwhile the supporters of Darwinism bolstered natural selection by ridding it of some of its obvious faults, and also developed postulates auxiliary to it.

This diversity of opinion seems to have discouraged Americanists from making biological interpretations of Indian variability. How could they apply biological theories to the Indian, when the biologists themselves were undecided as to which theories were the more valid? One way out taken by some Americanists was to assume that certain of these theories, especially natural selection, did not apply to man. Perhaps because they subscribed to this assumption, the classifiers of Indian types operated with a strongly hereditarian bias, out of keeping with the main stream of biological thought. If explanations were given for their classifications, they were usually to the effect that each Indian "race" represented a separate migration from the Old World. Implicitly, such explanations disavowed the possibility that physical changes could have occurred among New World peoples.

Other Americanists, who eschewed classifications, occasionally interpreted American Indian variability more in terms of their adaptations to differing environments. Their views were more in sympathy with Darwinian biology than were those of the classifiers. But these environmentally oriented explanations were usually so general that they did little more than affirm a belief in the potency of natural selection in the formation of races.

As previously indicated, most of the classifications were made by Europeans, and most of the environmentally oriented interpretations were by Americans. It is the views of these two groups that will now be considered.

Hereditarian Interpretations of the Classifiers. The students of Broca were the first to break away from the mono- vs. polygenesis controversy and to erect racial classifications based largely on physical traits. Neither Topinard nor Deniker, who made the principal contributions along this line, attempted to interpret their classifications. In 1885, however, Topinard toyed cautiously with Darwinian principles, at the same time expressing strongly hereditarian views. He seems to have believed that during the formation of human races, environmental forces had a directing influence upon physical structure, but that when these races were formed, the forces of heredity took over. This is, however, a case of trying to eat one's cake and have it. Yet concepts of this general nature appear basic to the thinking of most serious classifiers.

The first edition (1909) of Haddon's *Races of Man and their Distribution* contains no interpretation of the author's classification of American Indians. Speaking in a very general way in the second edition (1925), he credited environmental factors with a prominent role in race formation, and suggested that these adaptive processes are still going on. He felt that the real issue was essentially Darwin versus Lamarck, with the latter considered in its long-time cumulative sense. Haddon admitted it was hard to tell whether physical deviations away from a supposed average were due to inherent variability, environmental effect, or race mixture. Yet the assumptions underlying at least the New World section of his classification were strictly hereditarian and migrationist, since each of his Indian races was attributed to a separate migration from the Old World.

Hereditarian assumptions underlie the world classifications of Sergi and Biasutti, where racial distributions are explained by migration and mixture. Just as fundamentally hereditarian is Dixon's *Racial History of Man,* which was as much an exercise in method as an exposition of a new classification. Dixon peopled the Americas by a number of "pure race" migrations. Although he believed races were everchanging entities, the only cause he admitted was race mixture, which produced intermediate types.

Another American classifier, of Old World origin, is Griffith Taylor. His *Environment and Race* is, in spite of its title, almost as hereditarian as Dixon's book. Taylor's races were fixed and unchanging entities that migrated over the earth in accordance with climatic stimuli. Although he suggested that stature ". . . reacts very rapidly to changing environment" (23:38), he ascribed the distribution of short-statured peoples on the peripheries of the world-masses to a single and ancient migration. In this way he missed an excellent chance to make an environmental interpretation more in keeping with the title of his book.

Von Eickstedt's sweeping world survey leaned heavily on Sergi and Biasutti for the New World coverage, and included more recent data. Von Eickstedt's assumptions are less insistently hereditarian than those of his predecessors, yet he seems to have ignored genetic, environmental and other factors in erecting his classification. This is particularly the case in his sections on the Americas.

Czekanowski's frequency distribution of types, applied to the New World by Klimek, and the work of the biometricians exhibit a certain hereditarian narrowness. The resulting classifications are not explained except in vague terms of Asiatic relationships.

A rather more moderate hereditarianism was followed by Hooton, in the two editions of *Up from the Ape.* In the first edition he postulated three racially distinct migrations into the New World. Fifteen years later, in the second edition, he saw no reason to change this view. Hooton claimed that these different peoples ". . . intermingled to form the diversified types of the American Indian today. Over all of these types there is a Mongoloid wash of dominant features, especially observable in the cheek bones, the hair form, and the skin color" (13:649). Because of this state of panmixia, Hooton developed the sorting techniques that he used for the Pecos series. As he saw the problem there:

. . . if we discover within the same area, and within one group in that area, individuals who have the same mode of life, the same material culture, and who yet present dissimilar physical types, these differences may be due merely to the perpetuation of family peculiarities, but they may result, on the other hand, from the mixing of racially different strains. The variations can be tested, to some extent, by comparing these individual types in sufficient samples with adequate series of authentic races to which they seem to bear resemblances. (12:168)

Hooton's testing showed varying degrees of crude metric relationship between his samples of individual types and various New and Old World series. These relationships led him to emphasize the racially composite nature of the American Indian, where only an occasional individual would show a combination of traits once pertaining to one of the ancestral types.

Environmentally-oriented Interpretations. Interpretations of this sort were made largely by Americanists who had no classifications to justify, and accordingly were more willing to admit that anthropometric determinations were not always stable in changing environments. As a group, these Americanists did not deny the migrationist postulates of the classifiers, but seemed to believe that hereditarian and environmental explanations could be harmoniously blended in over-all interpretations.

The first Americanist of this persuasion was Putnam, who stated in 1899 that the craniological evidence as correlated with ethnological data

. . . seem to indicate that the American continent has been peopled at different times and from various sources; that in the great lapse of time since the different immigrants reached the continent there has been in many places an admixture of several stocks . . . while the natural environment has had a great influence upon the ethnic development of each group. (21:480)

Putnam, unfortunately, was not a voluminous writer and never expanded these views.

Hrdlička, speaking at the Americanist Congress in 1911, entertained less liberal views. He stated that

. . . Man did not reach America until . . . [he had] undergone advanced and thorough stem and even racial and tribal differentiation; and . . . since the peopling of the American continent was commenced, has developed numerous secondary, sub-racial, localized structural modifications [which] . . cannot yet be regarded as fixed, and in no important features have they obliterated the old type and sub-types of the people. (14:60)

Hrdlička made it clear that these modifications were transient and environmentally produced, invoking natural and linguistic barriers as isolating mechanisms. His dogmatic thesis of a "single American homotype," with its antimigrationist and environmentalist overtones, became the majority opinion in this country, and had much the same hampering effect on American Indian racial studies as did the assertions of Morton almost a century earlier.

In 1912, Boas placed his opinion on record. He felt that the movement of Asiatic peoples into America may have been ". . . a continuous process extending over a long period and bringing different types and languages into our continent" (5:111). He brought in the earliest Indians just prior to the last glaciation which sealed them off from the Old World. Once in the New World

. . . the isolation and small number of individuals in each community gave rise to long-continued inbreeding, and with it, to a sharp individualization of local types. This was emphasized by the subtle influences of natural and social environment. With the slow increase in numbers, these types came into contact; and through mixture and migration a new distribution of typical forms developed. Thus the American race came to represent the picture of a rather irregular distribution of distinct types and the wider distribution of these types, and colors, spread over the whole continent. . . . Notwithstanding the wider distribution of these types, each area presented a fairly homogeneous picture. (6:178)

Boas' views combined an essentially migrationist approach with an appreciation of the factors of population genetics and environmental effect. An elaboration and documentation of these views would have been extraordinarily productive. Instead, Boas devoted most of his energies to other fields, and in this, Indian racial studies were a definite loser.

Perhaps following Boas' lead, Wissler in 1917 plotted out mean statures and cephalic indices on Indian culture area and linguistic maps, observing that ". . . as we pass from one social group to another, there is a gradation of somatic characters and . . . these gradations radiate from centers in much the same way as . . . culture characters" (27:321). He felt that the populations at these centers were physically rather stable, so that an occasional immigrant group coming in would be gradually leveled by intermarriage. The physical characters of the mixed types being "subject to certain very definite laws of inheritance" would be likely to take on various forms (27:340).

The interpretations presented have been made by Americans. Several Englishmen produced environmentally oriented interpretations of a rather different sort. These were considered quite heretical, and consequently were largely ignored. The first was by Thomason who claimed that the nasal index varied directly with climate in the New World. In collaboration with Buxton, he presented this claim as a finished argument in 1923. In 1932 Davies reanalyzed the problem, using more series and better climatic data. For the world, the correlation between nasal index on the living and climate is .60; for 61 American Indian series, .68. Davies concluded that the response of the nasal index to climate was so slow that the index could be used as a racial criterion if specially handled. Yet no special handling of this index is apparent in the work of the classifiers.

A second environmentally oriented contribution was Marett's *Race, Sex and Environment*, published in 1936. His New World treatment is very summary. He begins by deriving the American Indian from Ainu-like and Mongoloid peoples. The postulated Wegenerian shift of the North Pole would have tended to thrust the Ainu-like people to the arid edge of the ice-cap and into the New World. Marett argued that the Ainu-like people would have preceded the Mongoloids, since the former were probably better equipped to stand cold, and less fitted to cope with mineral shortages. With both peoples in America, the retreat of the ice and resultant heavy rains would tend to decalcify the soil. Under such conditions, the Mongoloids would retain their fertility better, and would accomplish the greater part of the peopling of the Americas. This is plainly exuberant, but the soundness of the general approach should have been more widely recognized.

A new and vital opinion on race formation, which bears only indirectly on the American Indian, comes from Coon who believes that many "Mongoloid" characteristics developed as responses to extreme cold. This concept is applicable to American Indians insofar as they possess these "Mongoloid" features.

Following some of the promising guidelines for research outlined in the preceding paper, Newman here departs from the traditional approach to racial classification and attempts an analysis of population variation, employing climatic conditions as the major independent variable. As an attempt to escape from the traditional taxonomic approach to the study of human physical variation, the article which follows has become a classic. The ecological concepts employed by Newman are those being used more and more by American physical anthropologists.

5 Marshall T. Newman

ECOLOGY AND PHYSICAL TYPES OF THE AMERICAN INDIANS*

Correlations between the physical characters of warm-blooded verte-brates and their environments have led zoologists to the formulation of several ecological rules. The generally accepted interpretation of these correlations is that through natural selection, adaptive changes have oc-curred as the result of environmental stresses. In May, 1952, before the American Academy of Arts and Sciences, Coon applied these rules to man on a world-wide basis. Nevertheless the occurrence of adaptive al-terations in recent man has been denied. In large part this denial seems only to reflect an insistence that such human adaptation be demon-strated. It is the purpose of this paper, therefore, to test two of the best validated ecological rules on the aborigines of the New World, namely, Bergmann's and Allen's. Both of these rules deal with the fostering of bodily heat retention or dissipation by respectively reducing or increas-ing the radiating skin surface per unit of body mass.

Bergmann's rule holds that within a single wide-ranging species of warm-blooded animal, the subspecies or races in colder climates attain greater body size than those in warmer climates. Illustrative of this rule is the distribution of body size in the American puma, second only to

* Abridged from "The Application of Ecological Rules to the Racial Anthropology of the Aboriginal New World," by M. T. Newman, in *American Anthropologist*, **55**, 311–327, 1953.

man in the extent of its New World range. The average increase in the puma's body size with higher latitude forms a sustained gradient or cline for each New World continent. The same body size clines are demonstrated by other mammals of more restricted range.

Basic to Bergmann's rule is the principle that ". . . in otherwise similar bodies, the larger one has the smaller skin surface in proportion to mass, since volume and mass increase as the cube of the linear measurements and surface only as the square" (1:462). Greater body size, therefore, increases the body mass/body surface ratio. Chunkier and more compact body builds do the same thing. Increasing this ratio reduces body heat loss by radiation and therefore seems to be a cold climate adaptation. On the other hand, as Schreider (22:823) points out, ". . . the body mass/body surface ratio tends to decrease in climates which, at least during part of the year, put a stress on heat-eliminating mechanisms." In comparable fashion, small body size, or a slender build, increases the skin surface relative to mass, and by fostering body cooling in this way, appears to be a hot-climate adaptation. Although unaware of the Bergmann principle, Coon, Garn and Birdsell developed the same idea and applied it to arctic- and desert-dwelling humans.

Allen's rule holds that warm-blooded animals living in cold climates have their heat radiating body surfaces further reduced by decreases in the size of their extremities and appendages. An example of this rule is seen in the reduction of ear length toward the north among the several North American species of rabbits. Comparable shortening of extremities is seen in a number of other mammals. This sort of reduction also raises the body mass/body surface ratio, and as such seems to be an additional cold-climate adaptation.

While the general validity of Bergmann's and Allen's rules seems to be recognized, in practice their usefulness as interpretative tools in mammalian taxonomy is hampered by certain limitations not present in human studies. For example, in some mammals, especially the Rodentia, the small growth increments throughout life render the determination of adult body size an approximation foreign to students of man. Then, quantitative analyses of body size and proportions demand larger subspecies samples than can usually be amassed, since few taxonomists spend their lives studying one species, as anthropologists do. Moreover, most species, of mammals at least, have rather restricted ranges, which limit the gross climatic variations to which they are exposed. Thus many subspecies differences, if of an adaptive nature, are more likely attributable to local conditions, such as microclimate, than to the gross climatic variations underlying the operation of Bergmann's and Allen's rules.

In contrast, for man we have much larger series of measurements on wholly adult groups distributed over wide areas with tremendous climatic variations. In addition, the considerable body of data on post-Pleistocene human skeletons provides a third dimension usually lacking in taxonomic studies. For these reasons, it is likely that Bergmann's and Allen's rules may be more closely operative in man than in other animals. Man's assets as a test species for ecological rules need not be vitiated by the possession of a culture, since the strongly shielding effect of high culture is only 5–6000 years old anywhere, and in some parts of the world has hardly been felt.

Although testing of Bergmann's and Allen's rules is confined here to New World peoples, I am aware that in certain parts of the Old World they do not seem applicable. Upon superficial examination, the rules do not appear operative in Africa south of the Sahara. Yet, in Europe and the Near and Middle East and in East Asia and Malaysia, there seem to be north-south body size clines conforming to Bergmann's rule. The explanation of these discrepancies in Africa and perhaps elsewhere is not yet apparent.

METHOD

In the course of testing the rules, I have plotted the distribution of a number of mean male bodily and other dimensions and indices on linguistic and tribal maps of the New World. Where only one series is available for a wide-spread group, I have assumed that this series is wholly representative of it.

Clines in Body, Head and Face Size in Indians and Eskimos

The distribution of average male stature shows a conspicuous concentration of short peoples in the lower latitudes. To the north and south there is a progressive irregular increase in stature closely comparable to the body size clines for the puma. In American Indians the sustained nature of these stature clines is the more remarkable in view of the number and scope of well-documented intracontinental movements of people, for example: The Athabaskan push into the Southwest, the late movements into the Plains, the Tupí spread down the Brazilian coast, and the historic invasion of the Pampas by Araucanians. The regularity of the clines is also remarkable in view of the more obvious deficiencies of the basic data—inaccuracies of measurement, small size of some series and the chances of White and other admixture. In northern North America, however, the stature cline is broken by the shorter Eskimo. But the Western Eskimo are not inferior in sitting height to the tallest Indians. Their shorter stature, then, is attributable solely to their short legs. This reduction of extremity length is in accordance with Allen's rule, and probably represents an adaptation fostering body-heat retention. Judging from their equally high relative sitting heights, the Eastern Eskimo also conform to Allen's rule, but are smaller in both stature and sitting height than are the Indians south of them. Possibly the use of heavy tailored clothing in combination with factors of uncertain food supply and periodic undernutrition may cancel out the selective advantage of larger bodies in colder climates, but this cannot be demonstrated. Other than in this way, I cannot account for the Eastern Eskimo's smaller body size, although in Labrador and West Greenland, Stewart suggests there may have been a stature decrease since European contact, due possibly to a less adequate diet occasioned by acculturation. This view is reinforced by the fact that, despite the heavy increments of White genes they have received, these particular Eskimo are still shorter than their Baffin Island and East Greenland neighbors. Other short-statured people in North America, who are surrounded by taller groups, are the Yuki of northern California and the Harrison Lake Lillouet of southern British Columbia.

Clines in Body, Face and Nose Proportions in Indians and Eskimos

So far only body size clines have been considered, all of which appear to follow Bergmann's rule. The trunk-leg proportions of the Eskimo are in accordance with Allen's rule. Confirmatory of the body-build characters of the Eskimo is Rodahl's summary, giving the surface area of different parts of the body in percentage of the total calculated surface area. Forty-two male and 11 female Eskimo from Alaska, and a patently insufficient series of 7 Whites are used. Percentagewise the Eskimo have the larger skin surface of the head, trunk, and hands; the Whites for the arms, thighs, lower legs, and feet.

In facial proportions of the living, the relative elongation of the face with higher latitude. These clines are confirmed by the upper facial index on skulls.

Doubtless related to the progressive elongation of the face is the narrowing of the nose with latitude first pointed out by Thomson. In addition, Davies has offered the unverified explanation that narrow noses represent an adaptation to cold climates where the temperature of the air must be adjusted to a warmth and humidity suitable to the lung tissue, just as a broad nose is of value in providing maximum egress for heated air from the lungs in climates hot enough to render optimum heat dissipation a selective advantage. The distribution of the nasal index on the living is shown where the regular and sustained quality of the clines is remarkable in view of the technical difficulties in the location of nasion. Some, at least, of the five patches of higher indices between California and Central Brazil can probably be attributed to overly low location of nasion in the series reported from there. The clines for nasal indices on the living are paralleled by those on the skull.

The Biological Nature of the Clines in Body Size and Proportions in American Aborigines

The sustained clines in body size and proportions are, in my opinion, due to adaptive changes that took place largely since the New World was first peopled about 15,000 years ago. In their pattern of adaptive change the body size clines seem to follow Bergmann's rule. While the body proportions of the Eskimo probably follow Allen's rule, the clines in facial and nasal proportions are not directly attributable to either rule, although in all likelihood they are due to the same factors of temperature and humidity.

Although gross climatic effect is undoubtedly important in controlling body size and proportions, there are almost certainly other factors. Possibly indications of the presence of such other factors are provided by the exceptions to the sustained nature of the clines: The smaller body size of the Eastern Eskimo, Canoe Indians, Yuki, and Harrison Lake Lillouet. Assuming the samples to be adequate, which is questionable in the last two mentioned, these peoples may be smaller because of inadquacies in food supply and nutrition. Another sort of exception is provided by the Indians living in high altitude cold along the Andes, who are small in body size though relatively large in chest dimensions, and give all indications of a separate problem in adaptation from those considered here.

In the American tropics, and perhaps elsewhere, it seems likely that food supply and nutrition may be as important as temperature and humidity in determining body size. Although we know less about human nutritional requirements in the tropics than in any other broad climatic zone, there are several indications of extra stresses in that area. Mills contends that the thiamine requirements of experimental animals are increased in hot environments, but whether this holds for man is not wholly certain. Again, there are indications that due to higher excretory and other losses, the iron and possibly the calcium requirements of tropic-dwelling man are also heightened. Against these and other possibilities of higher nutritional requirements for man in the tropics, there is Mills' further contention that tropic-raised meats are lower in thiamine content than those raised in temperate climates. If these factors stand up under the scrutiny of controlled assays and other experiments, it is apparent that humans residing in the tropics and subsisting upon locally raised foods are faced with a real dietary dilemma lending selective value to smaller body size.

The extent to which adaptations in body size and proportions are inherited cannot as yet be determined. There are at present only general indications as to the hereditary nature of body build in man. These indications are supported by evidence from other animals. As noted by Rensch, when several subspecies are placed in a common environment, without intermixture, there is no apparent convergence in physical characters over a number of generations. He also cites instances where body-size clines do not correspond to recent climatic zones, but rather to those of the preceding geological period. Finally he notes that there is a higher rate of cell division in the larger-bodied subspecies than in the smaller-bodied ones. Another sort of evidence favoring the inherited nature of body build is provided by production in the laboratory of large-bodied and small-bodied races of mice by pedigree selection for eight generations.

On the other hand, there is convincing evidence that changes in the environment can have a direct non-genic effect on human body build. Lasker summarized the cases where there are definite but limited physical changes that took place in the descendants of immigrants: Europeans, Japanese, Chinese and Mexicans in the United States, Japanese in Hawaii, and North Americans in Panama. Particularly pertinent to the present study are Mills' findings that, age for age, Panama-born North American children are slightly shorter in stature and lighter in weight than those just arrived from the United States. He attributes the retardation of the Panama-born to the growth depression caused by difficulties in dissipation of body heat. If so, the growth depression may be viewed as a non-genic adaptation to a body mass/body surface ratio more favorable to hot-climate living. This point is illustrated by Robinson's determination that in terms of standard physiological criteria, such as pulse rate, small men showed greater physical endurance than large men when both were placed at hard labor under conditions of difficult heat dissipation. Baker's findings that White and Negro soldiers lost body fat under conditions of desert stress, may be interpreted as a rapid somatic adjustment to the problem of body heat loss.

Animal experiments strongly support the evidence for man that the environment can have a direct, non-genic effect on body build. For example, white mice raised at about 65°F have significantly longer and heavier bodies and shorter extremities and appendages than those from the same stock raised at 90°F. The same findings, without the increase in body length, also apply to chicks. Thus the Bergmann and Allen effects are easily duplicated in the laboratory.

From the foregoing, it seems clear that body build is influenced by both hereditary and direct environmental factors. It is likely that the same environmental pressures that provide a selective screen favoring the better adapted body types, also make a somatic impression on the individual during his life span. As Angel has pointed out, through the mechanism of relative growth, both factors—natural selection of hereditary phenotypes and direct non-genic effect of the environment—can produce striking alterations in body size and proportions. The relative potencies of these two factors in man, then, is a problem for future research.

THE SIGNIFICANCE OF THE CLINES IN BODY SIZE AND PROPORTIONS IN NEW WORLD RACIAL STUDIES

Whatever the relative potencies of the factors producing the clines, the clines themselves are based upon most of the standard dimensions usually taken by anthropometrists. Otherwise there would have been insufficient data to plot the clines. Of the remaining standard dimensions, only head form and relative head height show distributional patterns not readily interpreted as adaptive ones. Indeed, the earlier and marginal distribution of long heads and the apparently late arrival of low heads seems best explained by migrations of peoples differing in these regards. But since the diagnostic criteria of most racial classifications of New World aborigines are principally the body size and proportion traits shown here to be adaptive, it is most curious that if explanations of these classifications are attempted at all, they are in terms of a separate migration from Asia to account for each race. Even Neumann used 4 to 6 migrations to account for his 8 North American varieties although he leaned more heavily upon morphological characters in defining his racial varieties than upon the metric features considered here. The extent to which his diagnostic morphological characters are influenced by adaptive changes in head, face, and nose size and proportions remains to be determined.

This extreme hereditarianism of most classifiers makes no allowance for physical change in the Americas except by interbreeding. Without denying that the New World was peopled by successive migrations or infiltrations of physically differing peoples, it is very likely that the American races of the classifiers are at least partly the products of adaptive changes that took place in the New World. This view does not necessarily contest any reality the classifiers' American races may have, since ecological races have definite validity in biology. Rather, it questions the classifiers' insistence that phenotypic traits involving body size and proportions could survive unaltered the vicissitudes of varying environmental pressures for 80 to 600 generations (i.e., 2,000 to 15,000 years) in the New World. It is much more probable that the sharpness of metric resemblance to Asiatic peoples fades with the number of generations in the Americas. Changes in the Asiatic parent- and the American daughter-populations, occasioned by mutation, random genetic drift, adaptation, and intermixture, would certainly blur the original closeness of phenotypic resemblance. On this basis it seems likely that the traditional metric analyses have only short range applicability in space and time to problems of racial affiliations. Effective coverage of the longer ranges may come only from morphological studies using traits whose functional and adaptive natures are understood, and, as Birdsell has suggested, from controlled analyses of the genetically more complicated characters.

Among the linguists who specialize in the study of historical or "genetic" relationships underlying contemporary languages, some are willing to tentatively group together different languages on very slim grounds. These linguists, sometimes called the "lumpers," contrast with another type of scholar, at times referred to as the "splitter," who insists upon maximal evidence prior to the acceptance of historical relationships among particular languages.

At the time of European contact, hundreds, if not thousands, of mutually unintelligible languages and dialects were spoken by the aborigines of the New World. Continuous attempts have been made for the past seventy years or so to bring order out of this complex chaos, to group the abundant languages into related families. The article which follows outlines what one leading linguist, employing rigorous criteria, believed to be the demonstrable relationships in 1946. Although in more recent years the number of accepted linguistic families has been reduced somewhat, many linguists still favor a scheme not radically different from that described here by Hoijer.

6 *Harry Hoijer*

INDIAN LANGUAGES OF NORTH AMERICA*

It is customary to group the American languages into three great geographical classifications: the languages of America north of Mexico, the languages of Mexico and Central America, and the languages of South America and the West Indies. This classification is, however, not a rigid one; there is a good bit of overlapping. Thus, for example, the Piman dialects of northern Mexico, as well as the languages of the Nahuatlan (Aztecan) stock, are clearly related to certain languages north of Mexico; this stock, the Uto-Aztecan, is found in two of our geographical divisions for that reason. It is quite possible that when the remoter relationships between American Indian languages have been established, this geographical classification, a convenient one now, will be abandoned.

Within each geographical area, the languages are classed into genetically related groups or linguistic stocks. There is, however, a considerable difference in the accuracy and completeness with which this can be done in each of the areas. The languages north of Mexico have been studied more thoroughly than those of the other two groups. As a consequence, the genetic classification of the languages north of Mexico,

* Abridged from "Introduction," by H. Hoijer, in *Linguistic Structures of Native America*. New York: Viking Fund Publication in Anthropology, **6**, 9–23, 1946.

while not by any means a solved problem, has a completeness and definiteness lacking in the other two areas, particularly in South America.

THE LANGUAGES NORTH OF MEXICO

The first comprehensive classification of the languages north of Mexico was made by J. W. Powell and his associates, A. S. Gatschet and J. Owen Dorsey, in 1891. Though a number of far-reaching modifications of this classification have been suggested since, the groups set up by Powell still retain their validity. In no case has a stock established by Powell been discredited by later work; the modifications that have been suggested are all concerned with the establishment of larger stocks to include two or more of the Powell groupings. Since most of these modifications have not as yet been indisputably established, we shall list in the following the stocks set up by Powell and indicate where later work has led to larger groupings.

Eskimo-Aleut (Eskimauan)

A large number of dialects extending along the shores of the Arctic from Greenland to the end of the Aleutian chain. There is little knowledge of the interrelationships of the languages included in this stock. On the basis of data presented by Rasmussen, Dall, and Thalbitzer, however, the following major divisions may be set up:

A. Eskimo
1. Central and Greenland Eskimo. Spoken in many mutually intelligible dialects from Greenland to the Yukon River delta in Alaska.
2. Alaskan Eskimo. The dialects south and west of the Yukon.
B. Aleut
1. Eastern Aleut or Unalaskan.
2. Western Aleut or Atkan.

Athapaskan

The Athapaskan languages are generally divided into three geographical groupings: the Northern Athapaskan, the Pacific Coast Athapaskan, and the Southern Athapaskan.

The northern languages, which are spoken in western Canada and Alaska, are divided by Sapir and Osgood into the following substocks:

1. Kutchin.   5. Tahltan-Kaska.
2. Tsetsaut.   6. Sekani-Beaver-Sarsi.
3. Tanaina-Ingalik.   7. Chipewyan-Slave-Yellowknife.
4. Carrier-Chilcotin.   8. Dogrib-Bear Lake-Hare.

The precise interrelations of the above eight groups are far from certain. Each appears, however, to be a group of more or less mutually intelligible dialects. Of uncertain classification are the following: Koyukon, Tanana, Nabesna, Ahtena, Han, Tutchona, Mountain, and Nicola.

The Pacific Coast group apparently forms a single substock, though this conclusion has not as yet been fully established. It includes a number of isolated languages spoken along the Pacific Coast from Washington to northern California. Of these, Hupa, Kato, Wailaki, Chasta Costa, Mattole, and Tolowa are still spoken.

The Southern Athapaskan languages (now called Apachean) are definitely a linguistic as well as a geographical grouping. They may be divided into two main groups: Western Apachean (which includes Navaho, San Carlos Apache and a number of other mutually intelligible dialects, Chiricahua Apache, and Mescalero Apache); and Eastern Apachean (which includes Jicarilla, Lipan, and Kiowa-Apache). All except Lipan and Kiowa-Apache were spoken in New Mexico, Arizona, and the northern portions of Mexico which adjoin these states. Kiowa-Apache was spoken in western Kansas, and Lipan in Texas.

Eyak

A recently discovered language spoken by about 200 people on the Copper River delta in Alaska. Its classification is as yet uncertain, but it may turn out to be a link between Athapaskan and Tlingit.

Tlingit (Koluschan)

A number of loosely related languages spoken on the north Pacific Coast from Alaska to 55 degrees north latitude.

Haida (Skittigetan)

Spoken on the Queen Charlotte Islands off the coast of British Columbia.

Athapaskan, Tlingit, and Haida were grouped together by Sapir in 1915 under the name Na-Dene. Na-Dene is divided into two subgroups: Haida and Continental Na-Dene. Continental Na-Dene, in turn, has two subgroups: Tlingit and Athapaskan.

The complete evidence for this classification is not as yet available. It has however, been attacked by Boas and Goddard, who point out that the similarities listed by Sapir as evidence of genetic relationship may have resulted from borrowing.

Beothukan

An extinct linguistic stock formerly spoken in Newfoundland. Little data is extant on Beothuk. It was suggested by Latham in 1846 that Beothuk was related to Algonquian. Gatschet, however, on the basis of further data, decided that Beothuk was an independent stock. Lately, Beothuk has generally been considered as remotely related to Algonquian though, since the language is extinct, this hypothesis cannot be proven.

Algonquian

A widely distributed stock, extending from Labrador and the north Atlantic Coast to Montana. Bloomfield states as follows (3:85):

The grouping of the Algonquian languages is uncertain, since most of them are scantily or poorly recorded. Following, in the main, Michelson, we may list them as follows:

I. Central-Eastern:
   A. Central Type: Cree-Montagnais-Naskapi, Menomini, Fox-Sauk-Kickapoo, Shawnee, Peoria-Miami, Potawatomi, Ojibwa-Ottawa-Algonquin-Salteaux, Delaware, Powhatan.
   B. New England Type: Natick-Narragansett, Mohegan-Pequot, Penobscot-Abnaki, Passamaquoddy-Malecite, Micmac.
   II. Blackfoot
   III. Cheyenne
   IV. Arapaho-Atsina-Nawathinehena

Kutenai (Kitunahan)

This group of languages is spoken on the Kootenay River in Oregon.

Salishan

A large group of languages spoken in the region about Puget Sound and in-land. A small enclave, the Bella Coola, is found north of this region on the Dean River.

The classification of the Salishan languages is still unclear. Boas and Haeberlin divided them into a coast group and an inland group, and pointed out that this geographical division was in the main accompanied by significant differences phonetically.

Wakashan

This stock is composed of two main subgroups: Nootka, Nitinat, and Makah, spoken on Vancouver Island; and Kwakiutl, Bella Bella, and Kitamat, spoken on the coast of British Columbia north of Vancouver Island.

Chimakuan

A small stock consisting of two languages: Chimakum, spoken about Port Townsend Bay in Puget Sound, and Quileute, which is spoken on the Pacific Coast, south of Cape Flattery.

Yurok (Weitspekan)

Spoken by a small group of tribes occupying the lower Klamath River in northern California.

Wiyot (Wishokan)

Spoken by a small group of tribes in the area just south of the Yurok. A similarity between Wiyot and Yurok has long been noted. Dixon and Kroeber, in 1913, classed the two together under the name Ritwan. Later, Sapir pointed out a number of similarities between Ritwan and the Algonquian languages and set forth the hypothesis that these two were remotely related. This view was attacked by Michelson.

In a later article in the 14th edition of the *Encyclopedia Britannica*, Sapir listed Beothukan, Algonquian, Kutenai, Salishan, Wakashan, Chimakuan, and Ritwan as substocks in a larger linguistic grouping to which he gave the name Algonkin-Wakashan. No evidence was published for this grouping which was admittedly speculative.

Miwok (Moquelumnan)

Spoken in central California, east of the San Francisco Bay area.

Costanoan

Spoken in California on the south coast of San Francisco Bay and along the Pacific Coast to the south of the bay. Gatschet, in 1877, classed Costanoan with Miwok, calling the combined stock Mutsun. Powell, however, rejected this synthesis.

Yokuts (Mariposan)

Spoken in the area east of the Costanoan and south of the Miwok.

Kroeber, in 1904, established the following classification of the Yokuts languages:

1. Valley Division
   a. Northern valley group: Chukchansi, Kechayi, Dumna, and a number of extinct languages.
   b. Main valley group: Yauelmani, Wechikhit, Nutunutu, Tachi, Chunut, Wowolasi, Choinok, and a number of now extinct languages.
   c. Chulamni.
2. Foothill Division
   a. Kings River group: Chukaimina, Michahai, Aiticha, and Choinimni.
   b. Tule-Kaweah Rivers group: Yaudanchi, Wükchamni, and possibly two or three others.
   c. Poso Creek group: Paleuyami, and one or two neighboring dialects.
   d. Buena Vista and Kern Lakes group: Tulamni and one other tribe.

Maidu (Pujunan)

Spoken in California in the area directly north of the Miwok.

Wintun (Copehan)

Spoken in north central California directly west of the Maidu.

In 1913, Dixon and Kroeber combined Miwok, Costanoan, Yokuts, Maidu, and Wintun into a single genetically related group which they called Penutian. The evidence for this classification was published in a larger monograph in 1919. Though this evidence is far from conclusive, it presents an hypothesis which deserves further investigation.

Takelma (Takilman)

Spoken on the Rogue River in Oregon.

Coos (Kusan)

Spoken on the coast of middle Oregon, on the Coos River and Bay.

Siuslaw and Yakonan (Yakonan)

Powell included in this group the Yakona, Alsea, Siuslaw, and Lower Umpqua tribes, all of which lived on the northern portion of the Oregon coast. Wissler, in 1938, lists Siuslaw and Lower Umpqua together and puts Yakona and Alsea in a separate group. He gives no authority for this division of the Powell stock.

Kalapuya (Kalapooian)

Spoken in the valley of the Willamette River in Oregon, well up to the headwaters of the river.

Chinook

Spoken in Washington, at the mouth and along the banks of the Columbia River. There are two major dialect groups: Lower Chinook (now nearly extinct) and Upper Chinook.

In 1918, Frachtenberg published a paper comparing Takelma, Kalapuya, and Chinook and suggested that these languages were sufficiently similar to be classed together. Sapir, in 1921, suggested that these languages, together with certain others, constituted an Oregon Penutian family which was remotely related to Dixon and Kroeber's California Penutian.

Tsimshian (Chimmesyan)

Spoken on the North Pacific Coast directly across from the Queen Charlotte Islands.

Shahaptian

Spoken over a comparatively large area in southern Washington and northern Oregon.

Waiilatpuan

A small group in northeastern Oregon, about in the center of the Shahaptian territory.

Lutuamian

Spoken in south central Oregon, just south of the Shahaptian area.

In 1931, Jacobs suggested that Powell's Shahaptian, Waiilatpuan, and Lutuamian stocks be tentatively combined into a single linguistic stock for which he proposed the name Sahaptin. The complete evidence for this grouping has not as yet been published.

In his *Encyclopedia Britannica* classification, Sapir put into a single linguistic family—also called Penutian—the California Penutian languages, the Oregon Penutian, Chinookan, Tsimshian, the Plateau Penutian (Jacobs' Sahaptin), and a Mexican Penutian group (including Mixe-Zoque and Huave). As in the case of the Algonkin-Wakashan hypothesis, this grouping was tentative and Sapir published no evidence for it.

Karok (Quoratean)

Spoken in northwestern California.

Chimariko

A small stock in northwestern California.

Shasta-Achamawi (Sastean and Palaihnihan)

A large group of languages spoken in the territory east of the Karok in northern California. This connection was first suggested by Gatschet, who did not, however, have the data to prove it. The relationship was demonstrated by Dixon in 1905.

Yanan

A small group of dialects spoken in northern California in the area just south of that occupied by the Shasta-Achomawi languages.

Pomo (Kulanapan)

A group of languages spoken on the coast of California north of San Francisco Bay. Dr. A. M. Halpern, who has recently studied the languages of this group, sends me a tentative statement (as yet unpublished) of their interrelationships, which I have summarized as follows:

1. Southeastern Pomo.
2. Eastern and Russian River Pomo.
   a. Eastern Pomo.
   b. Russian River Pomo. Here are included five languages; Northeastern Pomo, Northern Pomo, Central Pomo, Southwestern Pomo, and Southern Pomo. The relationships within this group cannot now be stated with any assurance.

Washoan

Spoken in the Carson valley, Nevada, just at the Nevada-California state line.

Esselenian

A now extinct group who formerly lived on the coast of California just south of the Costanoan-speaking peoples.

Yuman

A large group of languages spoken in Lower California and in the territory in California and Arizona which centers about the lower Colorado and Gila valleys. The most recent classification has been published by Kroeber, who divides them as follows:

1. Northwest or Upland Arizona: Walapai, Havasupai, the three Yavapai dialects.
2. Colorado River, where this forms the boundary between California and Arizona, and the lower Gila: Mohave, Halchidhoma, Kavelchadom, Maricopa, and Yuma.
3. Colorado Delta, in Mexico: Cocopa, Halyikwamai, Kahwan.
4. Mexican and American California north of 31 degrees: Diegueño, Kamia, Akwa' ala, Kiliwa.

Salinan

Spoken on the coast of southern California south of the Esselenian group.

Chumashan

Spoken on the coast of southern California just south of the Salinan group.

In 1913, Dixon and Kroeber set up a new stock which they called Hokan, subsuming under this head, Karok, Chimariko, Shastan, Pomo, Yana, Esselen, and Yuman. Later, Kroeber linked Seri (in northern Mexico) and Tequistlatecan (in southern Mexico) with the original California Hokan.

Chumash and Salinan were also grouped together by Dixon and Kroeber in 1913, under the name Iskoman. Harrington later suggested a relationship between Chumash and Yuman, thereby linking the Iskoman group with the California Hokan.

In 1917, Sapir published a paper on the Hokan affiliations of Yana, in which he presented evidence relating Shasta-Achomawi, Chimariko, Karok, Yana, Pomo, Esselen, Yuman, Salinan, Chumash, Seri, and Chontal. This hypothesis was accepted by Dixon and Kroeber, who later also added Washo to the Hokan group. It must be remembered, however, that all of these later extensions of the Hokan stock were made on the basis of scanty and, in some cases, poorly recorded materials. Before it can definitely be stated that there is a Hokan stock—even in the limited sense in which it was originally set up by Dixon and Kroeber—a good deal of work remains to be done. The evidences presented so far are far from conclusive and can serve only as a basis for future work.

Tonkawa

Originally spoken in perhaps three or four dialects in the neighborhood of Austin, Texas. Today there are only about ten speakers of Tonkawa alive, who live in the town of Tonkawa, Oklahoma.

Coahuilteco (Coahuiltecan)

A number of tribes, all of which are now extinct, who lived along the Gulf Coast and inland on both sides of the Rio Grande. The little data on these languages was gathered by Gatschet in 1886 or is known from the records of the Reverend Father Bartolome Garcia.

Karankawa

A now extinct tribe formerly found in the neighborhood of Matagorda Bay in Texas. A scanty vocabulary was collected by Gatschet in 1884.

In 1917, Sapir presented data relating Tonkawa, the Coahuiltecan languages, and Karankawa to the newly established Hokan group. Later, in 1925, he added the Subtiaba-Tlappanec languages of Nicaragua to this group to which he gave the name Hokan-Coahuiltecan.

Yuki

Spoken in Round valley, California, north of the San Francisco Bay area.

Keresan

A group of languages spoken by some of the pueblo-dwellers of New Mexico. The Keresan stock may be divided into two groups: Eastern Keresan (spoken at San Felipe, Santa Ana, Sia, Cochiti, and Santo Domingo) and Western Keresan (spoken at Acoma and Laguna).

Tunican (Tonikan)

A group of languages formerly spoken in northern Louisiana on both sides of the Mississippi River. These languages are now practically extinct, only one speaker surviving.

Atakapa (Attacapan)

A group of languages, now extinct, formerly spoken on the Gulf Coast of Texas and Louisiana. The material extant on Atakapa was collected by Sibley and Gatschet. Though this evidence showed a possible relationship of Atakapa to Chitimacha, Powell listed it as a separate stock.

Chitimachan

Formerly spoken in Louisiana, on the Gulf Coast just west of the Mississippi River. Only one speaker now survives.

In 1917, Swanton published a paper in which he compared all the then available material on Tunica, Chitimacha, and Atakapa. On the basis of the similarities so revealed, he concluded that these languages were genetically related and gave the new stock the name Tunican. This hypothesis was accepted by Sapir, who divided Tunican into two subgroups: Tunica-Atakapa and Chitimacha.

Iroquoian

A large group of languages distributed in two discontinuous areas in eastern North America. The largest group (Seneca, Cayuga, Onondaga, Mohawk, Oneida, and Wyandot) is found from the Lake Erie region northeast along the St. Lawrence River to the Gulf of St. Lawrence. Tuscarora was spoken in western Virginia, and Cherokee in North and South Carolina.

Caddoan

A widely distributed group of languages spoken on the southern plains. The Caddoan-speaking peoples ranged from southern Texas and Louisiana north and a bit west to central Nebraska. In addition, a small island of Caddoan speech is found on the boundary between North and South Dakota.

Powell divided these languages into three main groups: Northern Caddoan (the Arikara), Middle Caddoan (the Pawnee), and Southern Caddoan (the Caddo, Wichita, Kichai, and others). Lesser and Weltfish, in a paper published in 1932, give us the latest classification of the Caddoan languages. This may be summarized as follows:

I. Pawnee, Kitsai, and Wichita
    A. Pawnee
        1. Pawnee proper
        2. Skiri Pawnee
        3. Arikara
    B. Kitsai
    C. Wichita
        1. Wichita proper (spoken by six groups)
        2. A dialectically divergent Wichita spoken by two groups
II. Caddo
    A. Caddo proper
    B. Haina
    C. Adai (?)

In his classification of Central and North American Indian languages in the 14th edition of the *Encyclopedia Britannica*, Sapir groups Iroquoian and Caddoan together as one of the substocks of his larger Hokan-Siouan family. As far as we know, no evidence has been published on this relationship.

Siouan

The Siouan languages are found in three distinct areas in mid-western and eastern United States. The largest group is west of the Mississippi River and extends from the southeastern corner of Saskatchewan south and a bit east to eastern Arkansas. A group of Siouan-speaking people also lived in eastern South Carolina, North Carolina, and Virginia, just east of the southern Iroquois. Finally, a small island of Siouan-speaking people (the Biloxi and Ofo) is found on the Mississippi coast of the Gulf of Mexico.

Voegelin divides the Siouan languages as follows:

1. Eastern (Catawba)
2. Ohio Valley (Ofo, Biloxi, Tutelo)
3. Missouri River (Hidatsa, Crow)
4. Mississippi Valley (Iowa-Oto-Missouri, Winnebago, and possibly Dhegiha, Mandan, and Dakota)

A Siouan-Iroquois connection has been suggested by Louis Allen in a paper published in 1931. The author lists a number of lexical and grammatical similarities between the two groups. His conclusions are as follows:

The writer does not flatter himself that he has in these few pages definitely established the genetic connection between Siouan and Iroquoian though he is convinced of such a connection, and believes that it can be satisfactorily established. This comparison makes no pretense of being complete. (2:193)

Yuchi (Uchean)

A small group of languages distributed in two noncontiguous areas in southeastern United States. One island is in northern Alabama, the other on the border between Georgia and South Carolina.

Natchez-Muskogean (Natchesan and Muskogean)

Powell considered these two stocks to be independent of one another. Their connection was first established by Swanton in 1924 and has been confirmed by other investigators since.

Mary Haas provides us with the latest classification of the Muskogean group:

A. Western Division
   Old Choctaw
      New Choctaw subdialects, including Chickasaw
B. Eastern Division
   1. Old Alabama
      a. New Alabama
      b. Koasati
   2. Old Hitchiti
      New Hitchiti, including its subdialect Mikasuki
   3. Old Creek
      New Creek subdialects, including Seminole

Timuquan

An extinct language formerly spoken in northern Florida. Sapir has suggested, in his paper in the *Encyclopedia Britannica*, that Timuquan may be related to the Natchez-Muskogean subgroup of his Hokan-Siouan stock. No evidence for this relationship has been published.

In Sapir's classification of American Indian languages in the *Encyclopedia Britannica,* he sets up the Hokan-Siouan stock in which he brings under one linguistic family all of the groups listed from Karok to Timuquan. His classification, summarized, is as follows:

1. Hokan-Coahuiltecan	5. Iroquois-Caddoan
2. Yuki	6. Eastern group
3. Keres	a. Siouan-Yuchi
4. Tunican	b. Natchez-Muskogean

This hypothesis is, to the best of our knowledge, not supported by any published data. Since many of the substocks of the proposed Hokan-Siouan are still in question, it is clear that much more data must be made available before this hypothesis can be either confirmed or denied.

Uto-Aztecan

This stock, which includes the Powell stocks Piman and Shoshonean, as well as a number of Mexican families, was first clearly defined in Sapir's papers on Southern Paiute and Nahuatl. The exact position of its constituent groups with regard to one another is not yet satisfactorily settled but the validity of the group as a whole has not been seriously challenged.

A classification of the Uto-Aztecan languages is that published by Kroeber in 1934, a summary of which follows:

I. Shoshonean
   A. Hopi (spoken in northeastern Arizona)
   B. Plateau Shoshonean (spoken in eastern Oregon, Idaho, Nevada, Utah, and in western Wyoming and California)
      1. Ute-Chemehuevi
      2. Shoshone-Commanche
      3. Mono-Bannock
   C. Tubatalabal (spoken in Kern County, California)
   D. Southern California Shoshonean
      1. Serrano
      2. Gabrielino
      3. Luiseño-Cahuilla
II. Pima-Tepehuan. Spoken in a narrow belt from the Gila River (in Arizona) to the Santiago River in northern Mexico.

III. Cáhita-Opata-Tarahumar. A number of languages spoken in various portions of northwestern Mexico.

IV. Nahuatl or Mexicano, including Pipil. Spoken mainly in the territory south of Mexico City approximately to the state line of Oaxaca and also along the east coast of Mexico south of Vera Cruz. There is also an isolated group on the west coast of Mexico south of the Gulf of Tehuantepec to the Guatemalan border. Pipil is spoken in Salvador.

V. Grouping uncertain: Cora; with Totorame or Pinome of the coast.

VI. Grouping uncertain: Huichol; with Tecual, Guachichil. This may be more similar to Nahuatl than any of the preceding groups.

VII. Unplaced, for lack of evidence: Jumano and Suma; Lagunero or Irritila; Zacatec; Teul and Cazcan; Coca and Tecuexe; languages of Aguas Calientes, Jalisco, Colima, and western Guerrero west of the Otomi and Tarasco, usually known on maps as Mexicano.

Tanoan

Spoken by many of the pueblo-dwellers of New Mexico. This stock is generally divided into three groups: Tiwa (spoken at the pueblos of Taos, Picuris, Sandia, Isleta, and the extinct Piro); Towa (spoken at Jemez and the extinct pueblo of Pecos); and Tewa (spoken at San Juan, Santa Clara, San Ildefonso, Nambe, Poyoaque, Tesuque, and the Hopi village of Hano).

Kiowa

Spoken in the territory centering about the junction of the Oklahoma, Kansas, and Colorado state lines.

The relationship of Kiowan and Tanoan was first suggested by Harrington but no considerable amount of evidence has been published on this point. The relationship was accepted by Sapir, who, in his *Encyclopedia Britannica* classification, groups them together under the name Tanoan-Kiowa as a subgroup of his Aztec-Tanoan stock.

Sapir's Aztec-Tanoan group linked Uto-Aztecan with Tanoan-Kiowa and Zuni, though the latter inclusion was queried. Recently, Whorf and Trager have published a paper presenting evidences for the relationship between Tanoan and Uto-Aztecan.

The variety of languages to be found in North America, listed in the preceding text by Hoijer, could be the result of dozens of migrations from the Old World by linguistically diverse peoples. Much more probable, however, is the hypothesis that actual migrations were relatively few, and that much of the linguistic differentiation to be seen in aboriginal North America was a result of normal language change and linguistic borrowing which developed during population radiation over the new continent. Language change is a process which occurs continuously, and, in populations which lack the ability to transcribe their speech, it may be extremely rapid. Furthermore, when two societies come into contact with each other, linguistic "meshing" and borrowing normally occurs. Such "hybridization" carried out over thousands of years may utterly obscure genetic-historical relationships between languages. In the text which follows, Morris Swadesh, long prominent in the field of American Indian linguistics, offers what promises to be one of the final syntheses regarding relationships among the aboriginal languages.

7 *Morris Swadesh*

NORTH AMERICAN INDIAN LANGUAGES: A SYNTHESIS*

In the course of recent comparative studies of Amerindian languages, the author found himself not infrequently running across structural features and specific meaningful elements reminiscent of Indo-European and other Old World linguistic groups. This is not an unusual experience for an Americanist, nor was it new for the author. In the past, like many of his colleagues, he has set these similarities down as sheer coincidences, more amusing than significant, and has brought to mind various considerations to explain them in terms of chance. Of course many of the like forms involve divergent meanings which could be the product of differentiation from original identity but might also be attributed to

---

* Abridged from "On Interhemisphere Linguistic Connections," by M. Swadesh, in *Culture in History: Essays in Honor of Paul Radin*, S. Diamond (ed.). New York: Columbia Univ. Press, 894–924, 1960.

the presence of synonyms in every language, which gives the compara-
tivist a choice of elements among which to seek similarities. That is, if a
word of one language does not match one of like meaning in a second
language, one can look around among the synonyms, more or less approximate, and perhaps find one whose form is roughly comparable.
Then again, when we are dealing with a number of languages on each
side of the comparison, we have the combined vocabularies of all of
them in which to seek supposed cognates. However, on this occasion we
were engaged in a broad comparison of Amerindian linguistic stocks and
had found evidence that quite a number of them may go back to a form
that was common perhaps 15,000 years ago. It was striking then, that
similarities with Indo-European were shown by elements and features
that are very widespread in America and which seemed, because of their
spread and their consistent phonology, to go back to the Ancient American proto-language which we are reconstructing. Hence, if our reconstructions are correct, at least in essence, these are not a mere collection
of scattered coincidences from a variety of languages but similarities belonging to a single speech form. And their number seems to be too great
to have resulted from the procedure of picking and choosing among
synonyms. Still, this is only a tentative conclusion which we offer
diffidently because the reconstruction of Ancient American is still in its
beginning stages and comparable work in the Old World still more em-
bryonic. The possible value of presenting it now is that it may stimulate
the study of remote linguistic relations in both hemispheres and may
add something to our orientation in an important problem of prehistory.

In the past there have been many proposals linking New World
languages with certain ones of the Old World, particularly Hebrew, but
also with various others. These ideas have been advanced often without
evidence, sometimes with a few citations of supposedly similar words
which were either too farfetched or too few to carry conviction to the
critical scholar. On the other hand there have been a certain number of
comparisons made by competent persons and supported by impressive
bodies of data. Some of the more serious efforts are: attempts to link
Eskimo-Aleutian with Ural-Altaic by various scholars, beginning with
Rasmus Rask; Sapir's theory of Nadenean connections with Sino-
Tibetan, backed by a large manuscript collection of comparisons though
represented in print mainly by independent materials of Shafer and the
present author; various comparisons of Nahua with Sanskrit and Indo-
European; Rivet's attempts to relate Tsonekan with Australian and
Hokan with Malayo-Polynesian. As will be seen, some of these theories

can be assimilated to the one being offered here, while others would seem to represent later levels of affinity.

The reception of these theories in the scholarly world has ranged from confident acceptance to a flat refusal even to consider them based on the notion that such distant relations can never be scientifically proved. The present author does not share the pessimism of the ultra-skeptical, but on the contrary feels that if we make good use of available techniques of study and proceed systematically, in the main but not exclusively from the easier to the more difficult problems, we are certain to penetrate much farther back in time without loss of accuracy. All the published theories of interhemisphere relations, along with the present one, are not yet adequately supported, but they reaffirm the need for, and perhaps show the feasibility of, this kind of study. In time we will surely see satisfactory proof of these or other theories of interhemisphere linguistic relationships.

There is geologic and archaeologic evidence for various waves of immigration into the New World, beginning perhaps 30,000 years ago by the land bridge which connected America with Siberia when the glaciers were extensive and the sea level low; interrupted by the rising sea but renewed about 15,000 years ago with the new glaciation and the reappearance of the land bridge; again interrupted by the sea, and re-opened some thousands of years later by the development of water travel. Each wave must have brought one or more languages, but not all of them survived. Some may have been swamped out by later arrivals, others lost in the face of languages already present; before disappearing they may or may not have left traces, principally in the form of loan words in other tongues. Those languages which were maintained must have in the course of time split up into dialects, which eventually developed into completely separate languages and groups of languages. All these divergent speech forms may be studied by the comparative method to reveal the number and nature of the earlier languages from which they stem.

Recent research seems to show that the great bulk of American languages form a single genetic phylum going far back in time. They show an inter-graded relationship whose nature and geographic distribution are such as to suggest that the entire phylum developed out of a single speech community in America. The time depth of the complex is too great to be directly estimated by lexico-statistic methods. By noting actual measures of up to about 10,000 years in some of the component parts of the complex, we infer that the age of the group is considerably greater than this figure, and it seems possible that we are dealing with the languages derived from one brought in with the second great migration, about 15,000 years ago. Eskimo-Aleutian and Nadenean seem to stand apart, and may therefore represent later waves of migration; they would then be no more closely related to the remaining American languages than other languages still in the Old World. As for more recent movements, aside from the obvious case of Asian and Alaskan Eskimo, evidently based on a back migration from America within the last several centuries, there is no close interhemisphere linguistic relationship of the type that exists between, say, English and German, nor even one of moderate time depth, like that of English and Hittite. New languages probably came into America in the late millennia just before Columbus, but their speakers must have been absorbed into the earlier speech communities or returned to the Old World without leaving any language that has continued to modern times.

If we are dealing with a linguistic complex going back 15,000 years in America and represented by scores of distinct stocks today, it would be good to find a comparable entity in the Old World with which to compare it. However, remote comparative linguistics in the eastern hemisphere has not yet established any such ancient and far-reaching complex. There are various groups of up to about 6,000 years of time depth and various theories of more remote relationship which have not yet been sifted and coordinated. The various theories taken together may add up to the same thing as Trombetti's monogenetic explanation, whose age must be considerably more than 15,000 years. Just how much older we cannot say, but the total impression one gets from comparing modern linguistic stocks suggests that it probably does not go back to the dawn of human society and may be as recent as about 30,000 years. This would imply that the earlier development of human culture was achieved with a more primitive form of vocal communication, which may have eventually given rise to modern language but was notably different from it. The passage from elemental to true language may have spread from a single subarea within the range of the human species, carrying with it not only its structural innovations but also its specific vocabulary elements.

If proto-Indo-European stems from a dialect identical with or closely related to the one that entered the New World 15,000 years ago, it would be no farther removed from proto-Ancient American than stocks of similar time depth in America, for example Uto-Aztecan or Otian

(Miwok-Costanoan). They would all be about nine or ten thousand years more recent than the common tongue. Yet to establish the connection in the Old World would be harder because in America we can go back step by step, involving each time the next most closely related groups. Some day, when the order of relationships is determined in the Old World, the stepwise comparison can be achieved there in the same way. Under present circumstances, we do not even know which Old World languages are most pertinent to the comparison.

Despite frequent comments by early Christian missionaries to the contrary, all American Indians maintained beliefs in supernatural beings, regular religious ceremonies, and complex cosmological conceptions. Indeed, the importance and prominence of the religious systems of some of the culturally more complex Indians, such as the Arizona and Rio Grande Pueblo peoples, have led some scholars to characterize their cultures as "theocracies." Most North American Indians, however, had not reached the level of sociocultural complexity necessary for the maintenance of complex priesthoods nor of churchlike institutions. With the partial exception of the agricultural Indians of the Southwest and East, most American Indians held beliefs that were highly individualistic and relatively nondogmatic. Ceremonies were most frequently held by small groups, such as families, and were concerned with the more immediate and mundane aspects of human affairs—birth, puberty, marriage, and death. Lack of religious formality, however, does not mean that they lacked a preoccupation with the supernatural. On the contrary, most, if not all, American Indians occupied a world which, from their point of view, was also inhabited by spirits, ghosts, witches, and gods. And in the common American Indian view, man was required to adjust to this perceived reality if he were to survive. Ruth Underhill is widely recognized as an authority on American Indians, especially on their religious life.

8 *Ruth Underhill*

RELIGION AMONG AMERICAN INDIANS*

The American Indian of pre-Columbian days, at least the male, spent much of his time and effort in activity involving the supernatural. With little knowledge of natural science or medicine, with small acquaintance with other peoples outside a few neighboring friends or enemies, a large section of his world was unknown, mysterious, and, possibly, threatening. His techniques for dealing with this unknown, which he conceived as supernatural, I shall speak of as religion.

Few groups had any consistent theology. Their interest was in action which would secure health and prosperity and protect them from danger. Explanations of the spirit world for the average man might be fragmentary and even contradictory, although, as Radin has pointed out, there was usually a group of thinkers who strove toward greater consistency and understanding. Nor had the spirit world much connection with ethics. It is true that in advanced cultures like that of the Pueblos and their pupils, the Navahos, there was an emphasis on peacefulness for those engaged in religious activity. Even there, however, such offenses against society as murder, theft, lying, greed, adultery and so forth were dealt with by the family or council. Only when a group became so large and mixed that these local agencies lost their effectiveness did the priest take over with his threat of supernatural punishment. Such a situation was rare in any group north of Mexico. The spirits did indeed punish, but not for what a modern would call sins against society. What drew their wrath was a breach of taboo, such as failure to perform a ceremony correctly or disobedience to ceremonial rules concerning a mother-in-law or a woman in childbirth. Such emphasis on ceremonial regulations is a familiar stage of religious development, long known in the Old World.

* Abridged from "Religion among American Indians," by R. Underhill, in *Annals of the American Academy of Political and Social Sciences*, **311**, 127–136, 1957.

PRE-COLUMBIAN RELIGIONS

In sketching the religious attitudes of Indians in North America, I shall use the past tense. It is true that many of these attitudes and usages developed from them are still in force. However, many have been given up and many have changed, either in historic times or recently. Therefore, my attempt in the first part of this paper is to outline early religious attitudes.

Mana and Taboo

Most Indian religious attitudes have worldwide counterparts, and some seem so fundamental that they may have been brought by the first paleolithic immigrants. Among these are the concepts of mana and taboo. The Melanesian word *mana* has been standardized by anthropologists to refer to a widespread primitive belief in some invisible force pervading the universe. It can be focused on any object, animate or inanimate, endowing that object, for the time being, with supernatural power. Sacred places, objects used in ceremony, or human beings under certain circumstances can be imbued with this power. The Siouan word *wakan,* the Iroquoian *orenda* and the Algonquian *manitou* all refer to it, and many other tribes have the concept if not the name.

As a corollary, the focus of power was dangerous to one not in a sacred state. This is the familiar concept of taboo which is as worldwide as that of mana. It regards the focus of power as untouchable, not because it is unclean, but because it belongs to the supernatural world with which contact may be dangerous. To meet the situation, an age-old technique has been developed whose remnants are visible even among modern people. Briefly, it requires that anyone who has been in contact with a supernatural power, either voluntarily or involuntarily, must negate the danger by withdrawing both from human society and from bodily activity. As interpreted by various Indian groups, this can mean seclusion; fasting; abstaining from speech, sleep, looking at the sun or at fire, touching the head (the most important part of the body), or touching the lips with water.

The Life Crises

This technique, in whole or in part, was used by many Indian groups at the life crises of birth, puberty, and death. These were occasions when an uncontrollable biological event swooped in to affect human life.

Those under its influence were considered subject to supernatural power, and they practiced the techniques which would keep them safe and also keep others safe from them. Such an attitude was found most often in the food gathering and hunting groups where organization was simple. With agricultural groups, who had a wealth of ceremonies, the seclusion rules, especially those for women, were often obscured or omitted.

Here we must differentiate between girls' and boys' puberty. The acknowledgment of maturity for boys, as we shall see below, is usually accompanied with ordeals and initiations undertaken on the boy's own initiative. A girl's puberty, without any effort on her part, fits her to perform the miracle of childbirth. The menstruant and the parturient are considered under such strong supernatural influence that, unless they withdraw, they would be in danger themselves and would certainly bring danger to men. This attitude is particularly true of the hunting and food-gathering groups. On the Northwest coast, a girl's withdrawal at puberty might last for months and might include the use of a scratching stick and drinking tube to avoid touching hair or lips. With some California groups, as in parts of South America and the Basque region of Europe, the husband was considered so intimately connected with his wife that, after childbirth, he, too, must abstain from action.

There is no theology involved in this behavior. No priest or medicine man needs to participate, for the so-called purification which sometimes follows seclusion does not always take place. Various statements are made as to diseases or misfortunes which may follow if the woman fails to withdraw, but they are not always the same. They seem to belong to an elementary system of magic unconnected with the spirit world. They coexist with various ideas about gods and spirits and are unconnected and unexplained.

With some older Indians, these ideas about women's seclusion are still in force. One reason for their fear of hospitals is the fact that the white nurses are known never to seclude themselves. A male patient cannot tell when they may be spreading supernatural danger. Even converts to Christianity find the taboo hard to forget.

Withdrawal in some degree was practiced by the bereaved after a death, and sometimes by enemy slayers, murderers, even whale killers. Here there is an explanation. There is danger from the soul of the departed which either wishes to take a loved one with it for company or to injure its killer. Here is the beginning of a theory about the supernatural which is different from the pure magic of the restrictions at childbirth. It seems possible to me that, early though such theories are shown to be, the withdrawal at childbirth, unconnected with any spirit, may antedate them.

The Spirits

A belief in spirits and a purposeful attempt to conciliate them is found in every Indian tribe. Spirits of the dead, just mentioned, did not play the all-important part sometimes found in the Old World. True, some far western tribes imagined them as stealing the souls of the living and so causing illness. A few thought of them as acting the part of guardian spirits, and others conceived of them as reincarnated in children. As a rule, it was thought that the average dead person existed in the after-world only until the last person who remembered him on earth was gone. A few might be elevated to powerful spirits or gods.

This afterworld was a shadowy place to which both good and bad went indiscriminately. Days of withdrawal were often observed by mourners or corpse handlers while souls were supposedly on their journey thither, and they were supplied with food for this journey. Some tribes also supplied their dead with goods to keep them contented so they would not return. To this end, too, their dwellings were often destroyed and their names never mentioned. This belief and practices cause difficulty for Indians in going to hospitals, for many have died there, but the building stands replete with supernatural danger. They also make it difficult for white men taking census because names of the dead must not be mentioned.

Other spirits were those of animals, plants, and natural phenomena. To most Indians, there was no sharp dividing line between these and human beings. The Sioux spoke of all living things as the two-leggeds, the four-leggeds, and the wingeds. All these had life and must be treated as fellow beings. So must even the plants and Mother Earth who bore them. A Comanche on being urged to plow and reap objected: "Shall I stab my Mother's breast and cut my Mother's hair!" True, agricultural tribes did dig the earth, but usually they had a tradition of a supernatural visitant, perhaps the corn plant, which had bidden them do so. Every act connected with planting was a religious ceremony. Every wild thing, too, was treated with consideration. The Papago woman asked permission of the plants which she plucked for basketry. The Zuni apologized to the deer he killed.

Although it is hard to reconcile this attitude with the life of the hunter who killed for a living, there was a saving explanation. The plant or animal eaten was only an outward form assumed by an immortal spirit. When that was consumed, the spirit returned to its home. If it had been well treated, by way of ceremony and proper disposal of the remains, it would return in a new dress to serve man again. To this end, seal bladders and salmon bones were thrown into the sea, so that they might return to the seal and salmon villages. Deer horns and buffalo heads were kept in a sacred place. The various "first fruits" ceremonies for plant and animal foods were an example of respect shown to what must be used.

Sometimes mana was thought to be concentrated in a particular representative of a genus; the Algonquians believed in an Owner for each sort of animal. On parts of the Northwest coast, the belief was that the animals, which were so much better able to get food than primitive man, had once owned the earth. They had their present characters but could take human form when they wished. In fact, they can do so still, and thus they appeared to fortunate visionaries. A number of tribes believed that an animal was either the ancestor of a human group, married an ancestor, or magically assisted him. Such totemism might result in clan names, clan functions, sometimes a prohibition against eating the animal as with the Yuchi of South Carolina, or a ceremony involving it as with the Hopi Snake clan. However, there were also kin groups without totemic connections. Nor was it always true that a group with one animal patron must not intermarry. An animal might be the creator of a whole tribe, as the coyote was with the Miwok of California. It might be a culture hero or a trickster-transformer, like the hare with the Winnebago or the raven with the Tlingit. In fact, the word "totem" cannot be used in America without a careful definition of the concept as used in the group concerned.

Animal spirits appeared in some form in almost every Indian group. In addition, the more organized peoples imported or devised anthropomorphic concepts like the War Gods and Kachinas of the Southwest or the False Faces of the Iroquois. A few horrifying beings appeared, like the Cannibal Spirit or the Windigo of the North Woods. (Has the gloom of the forest anything to do with this sort of imagination?) As a rule, there was no sharp division between good and bad forces as is found in monotheistic religions. To use the well-known simile of the electric current, power was thought to harm or benefit according to the channel through which it passed. Thus, the same shaman, according to his attitude, could dispel a disease or use it to kill. A Guardian Spirit helped as long as proper behavior was observed toward it. If not, it might injure or kill its protégé. Occasionally, there is mention of a bad or deceptive spirit, but this concept was a vague one. Nor is there any proof of a High God, keeping the spirit world in order. Certain beautiful expressions occur, such as the Algonquian Great Spirit and the Creek Master of Breath. These generally turn out to have been very limited concepts, either of a distant creator who later ceased to function or merely of a spirit higher than the others.

The spirits were approached in two very different ways and were closely connected with the economics of a tribe and its degree of organization. The two ways are vision and ceremony.

The Vision

Across the northern part of North America stretched an area of hunting peoples. They lived for most of the year in seminomadic small bands with little organization and little chance for large assemblies. Much of the time, the hunter faced his dangerous task alone. His need was for health, courage, and luck for himself, but the fate of others hardly concerned him. In this area the individual male sought a vision which would assure him of the luck phrased as spirit power.

The vision took numberless forms among the different tribes and was sought under varying circumstances. With the Woodland Algonquians of the East, the Salish of the Northwest and some Plains tribes, it was sought at puberty. Here, every boy (and a few girls) hoped for supernatural help to guide his career and ensure success. To that end he practiced seclusion and fasting, sometimes repeatedly, but *before* the supernatural experience, not after as with women. Sometimes he added ordeals to gain the spirits' pity and show his courage. In fact, this was a religious ritual based on a definite theology, not a blind observance of taboo. It served as a substitute for boys' initiation ceremonies, rare in North America.

The puberty vision followed a standard form for which the boy was well prepared. An animal appeared in its human guise and took him to its village in the forest or under the sea or perhaps delivered instruction on the spot. This consisted of a song to be used when power was needed and usually a fetish which was given or which he must find or make. With the fetish went a rudimentary ritual which must be followed on pain of losing power or being injured by it. Even an unimaginative youth was likely to achieve such a vision after repeated trials. Often he

had some supervision from an older man or a whole group of them. If
his hallucination was not of acceptable form he was likely to be told:
"That was a false spirit. Try again."

After the puberty vision, the boy went into an apprenticeship to
realize the promised power. He did this with an absolute conviction of
success and an image of himself as one favored by the spirits. This was a
potent incentive to success. It was just possible that in such an arduous
occupation as whaling, he might fail in spite of this psychological help.
In that case, there was no distrust of the spirits. He decided or was told
that the vision coming to him had been an evil spirit in disguise. We can
hardly overestimate the value of this vision experience at a time when a
boy's character was being formed. The lack of it in boarding schools
seems to me to have been one cause of Indian demoralization. To an
Indian with culture history so different from the white culture, the
Hebrew-Christian teaching rarely provided a substitute.

With the Woodland Algonquian the voluntary, strenuous vision
quest ceased after puberty, but on the Plains it was carried on much
later. In the Sun Dance of the Dakota and Mandan, mature men were
tortured in a group in expectation of a vision to come. Individuals, at
other times, practiced seclusion and torture for added power. In other
Plains tribes, men, at least, prayed and fasted when special help was
needed.

This idea of supernatural help through revelation has much in common with Christian concepts. Some Christian teachers have, indeed,
built on it, only suggesting that the direction of power be changed from
success in war or hunting, now inessential, to success in righteous living.
Most have insisted, however, often without much study, that all the old
practices be swept away. As a response the Indians, particularly in the
Plains area where the vision was prominent, have worked out their own
combination of vision and ethics.

Going west and south from the Plains and the Plateau Salish, the
vision experience becomes less strenuous. It might even arrive unsought. In a large area including the Great Basin and much of California, even some of the Southwest, it came as a dream in sleep. A Mohave
of southern California found himself on the sacred mountain at the
beginning of the world and learned a power like scalping or the right to
sing a clan song from the lips of the creator, himself. Luiseño boys in
California had visions in a group, under the influence of a drug, *datura*.
Along the Pacific coast, beginning in northern California, spirit power
may come unsought (although not always) and even unwanted. One

is reminded of mediums of eastern Asia and the Pacific by the way in which the recipient of power is temporarily affected with either illness or madness. Here the power is less often an animal than the wealth spirit, or the war spirit. With the Kwakiutl of Vancouver Island, the whole power concept is reduced to a dramatic show and a means to prestige. A highborn boy pretends to be kidnapped by the Cannibal Spirit and returns, pretending madness. Lowborn people were not expected to have visions.

The Shaman

The medicine man, or shaman, was the arch visionary. I define such a person as one whose powers came from direct contact with the supernatural, rather than from inheritance or memorized ritual. True, it is impossible to make a clearcut distinction for often the son or relative of a shaman was thought to have a better chance of inspiration than others. Also, his predecessor might teach him some of the sleight of hand which sometimes accompanied exhibitions of spirit power. According to the area, power was obtained, just as it was for the average man, either through quest and ordeal, or often unsought through dreams in sleep. The difference was that the shaman's experience was more prolonged and often more strenuous. Sometimes he had several spirits, providing different powers.

The chief function of the shaman was curing. Here he used a method so ancient and widespread that it may well have been brought over by some of the earliest immigrants. This method rests on the belief that illness is caused by an intrusive object, such as a worm or a stick, shot into the body by some malign influence. The shaman sucked out the object, sometimes varying his process by rubbing, smoking, and blowing. Then he exhibited the object to spectators. Shamans were frequently accused of sleight of hand in this process. Still, I can testify that many actually believed in their power and felt that a few tricks were necessary drama for the ignorant. Granted what we now know of psychosomatic medicine, the faith generated in the patient by the shaman's procedure may have had real therapeutic value.

A less widespread belief about disease and its removal was that of spirit possession. Here the shaman actually exorcised an evil spirit and sent it away. Another belief, found chiefly around the Pacific coast, was that illness was caused by the loss of the patient's soul which had strayed or had been spirited away to the land of the dead. Special practitioners, sometimes in a public ceremony, made a trip to the other world to retrieve the soul. Among the Eskimo, as on the east coast of Asia, shamans dramatized a flight to the moon or to another spirit world.

The shaman's function proliferated, especially in the West, where there were war shamans, weather shamans, bear shamans, and snake shamans. Some were merely diviners, foretelling the future or selecting curing practitioners. This last function was necessary where a number of different curing methods had accumulated in one area. In some form or other, the shaman existed in almost every North American tribe. With the agricultural Hopi, who had ceremonial means of curing, he was reduced almost to disgrace. With the Zuni, he was given the aegis of a society. His curing function had such appeal for the average man that the shaman may often be found in a tribe which has given up most other native practices.

The Communal Ceremony

Standardized ceremonies, at regular dates, required certain conditions. The simplest was that it must be possible for a large group of people to gather and be fed. This was impossible for hunters and food gatherers at most times of the year, since such a gathering would frighten the game animals and use up the wild plants. Second, the people must all have a common interest, so that they all sought from the supernaturals one and the same boon. This, too, did not apply to hunters, except when there was a herd of animals to be surrounded. That was the case when the Southern Paiute held their yearly antelope drive or a Plains group its great buffalo hunt. On each of these occasions, there was a standardized ceremony, although much of the Sioux Sun Dance, it is interesting to see, consisted of a vision quest pursued by several men in company.

The groups whose chief contact with the supernaturals was through standardized ceremony were the agriculturists. True, they retained many elements of the visionary and shamanistic belief, since they had, at some time, lived the hunting life. However, their needs were now different. Much of their work in the fields was co-operative, and the individualistic attitude was not useful. Moreover, the rain or sunshine which they needed must come to all alike. For them, a communal appeal to the spirits was the natural thing. The spirits, too, were new ones, having to do with weather and agriculture. It seems possible that they and their accompanying ceremonies were imported along with the magic-working plants they fostered.

Wherever the ceremonies were worked out, they had a good deal of resemblance to the ritual imposed by a spirit on its individual protégé. In its simplest form this meant a song and the honoring of a sacred object. However, as the place of ceremony remained the same, sacred objects could be elaborated into masks, costumes, images, and even theatrical properties like the Hopi snake at Palülükonti. The song could be expanded into a whole suite of songs and dances. The same officiants could be used from year to year. These tended to standardize the ceremony, learn it by heart, and transmit it to successors.

The Priest

Such a ceremonial officiant I shall call a priest. True, his ritual had a supernatural source, but often it was thought to have been dictated by the spirits long ago, and his present duty was merely to follow it without error. However, he handled sacred paraphernalia and therefore must practice some form of withdrawal, at least seclusion and fasting. The Pueblos, at least, brought in ethical considerations by demanding that he should have only peaceful thoughts. The priest and the shaman were two separate functionaries, often practicing in the same society. However, the line between them might be blurred, the shaman developing a little ritual, the priest supplementing his ritual by vision.

The Ritual Form

The most usual rituals were often for the sake of weather and crop growth. For the latter, there might be two or three rituals, corresponding to the life crises of birth (planting); maturity (green corn) and death (harvest). Others were special pleas for rain, rituals to help or to celebrate war raids, and pilgrimages to obtain blessing—the Papago salt journey or the Pawnee Hako and great ceremonies "to keep the world in order." Ceremonial officials can also cure, but in quite other circumstances than those that call for the shaman. They treat afflictions arising supernaturally from breach of taboo generally connected with a ceremony. The cure consists in performing the ceremony, or the injured part of it, correctly; thus erasing the error. The famous Navaho chant, which is a curing ceremony for an individual, comes partly under this head. It is performed with memorized ritual, on a Pueblo pattern, by a priest for a patient who is thought to be "out of harmony" with the world. However, the myth behind it involves visits to supernatural animals in their villages, in the northern hunter's style.

Each tribe had its own series of ceremonies and its own fostering spirits, often those of the plants themselves. There is not enough space here to name all the ritual acts worked out, but they fall with a large common framework. This included purification of the participants, which might mean all those present or only officiants. It might be by a sweat-bath, as with the Sioux; vomiting, as with the Navaho and Creek; or confession, as with the Iroquois. There were offerings to the spirits: to-bacco, food or, in the Southwest, the feathered wands called prayer-sticks. There was little blood sacrifice. Individual Plains Indians sometimes cut off a finger to gain the spirits' pity. A dog was ritually killed and eaten by some tribes, and the Pawnee killed a human captive to help the crops. The concept of vicarious sacrifice in Christian belief seems, therefore, strange to many Indians.

Other concepts not usual in the communal ceremonies are those of humility and worship. The ordeals of the individual vision seeker, as I mentioned, are sometimes phrased as appeals for pity. In the communal ceremonies, the atmosphere is more often that of a bargain between re-spected allies. The priest, having performed his ceremony and made his offerings without error, expresses his confidence that the spirits will give man the rain and crops he needs. In spite of these differences, thousands of Indians are now members of Christian churches. It is interesting to see which sects have proved congenial to the different tribes—Catholics to the Pueblos, Presbyterians to the Pimas, and Quakers to the Iroquois. Granted that historic opportunity had a good deal to do with the case, still, the Pueblos were already given to pageantry, the Pimas to a town-meeting style of discussion, and the Iroquois to a dream dictation very much like that of the "inner light."

POST-COLUMBIAN RELIGIONS

The coming of the whites brought successively a period of frustration and insecurity to various Indian groups. As has happened all over the world, this usually meant a religious revival and the leadership of some seer or prophet who preached a solution to their problems. In the early days, this solution was simply a return to the old ways with abstinence from all food and equipment which came from the white man. Special ceremonies on an Indian plan might be added.

The promised result was the disappearance of the white man and the return of the old life, either through magic or through successful war. Such movements I may call reversion religions.

Reversion Religions

Some of the most important of these looked forward to successful war. Among them can be named that of Popé, leading to the Pueblo revolt of 1680; that of the Delaware prophet and Pontiac's conspiracy, 1672; that of the Shawnee prophet, brother of Tecumseh, and the Ohio revolt, 1805. All of these wars came to grief.

As time showed the hopelessness of war, the visionaries began to promise a magical solution involving the disappearance of the whites or the finding by the Indians of some new and peaceful land. Such leaders were Kanakuk of the Kickapoo, 1827; Tavibo of the Paiute, 1870; Smohalla of the Sokulk, on the Columbia River, 1889–90. In response to a vision claimed by Wowoka, a Paiute, many tribes, especially from the Plains where disruption was extreme, accepted Wowoka's gospel. This meant the Ghost Dance, with special costume, songs, and dances dictated by the prophet on a Paiute pattern. The contention of the devotees was that they intended no attack on the whites, but expected their magical disappearance. These gatherings among the Sioux were misunderstood by the whites and resulted in the massacre of Wounded Knee. Since its prophecies were not fulfilled, this type of reversion religion died out like the other.

Amalgamation Religions

After Christian teachings had become somewhat familiar, there was a series of what I may call amalgamation religions. These did not contemplate the conquest or disappearance of the whites. Instead, they aimed at peaceful living for the Indians under the new conditions. Though they often kept old Indian customs and eschewed Christian theology, they included definite ethical teachings. The need for such teaching was obvious since Indian groups were breaking up, and the old clan and family influence was not sufficient to control behavior. Above all, liquor was making its inroads, and the new preachers demanded total abstinence as well as peaceful and upright living.

Among such preachers was Handsome Lake of the Iroquois, 1799–1815, who was profoundly influenced by Quaker missionaries. In the Southern Puget Sound country, in 1881, John Slocum founded the Shaker religion, a compound of Christian elements and Indian style vision. Both of these cults are still functioning. The most widespread of all was the Peyote religion, many of whose adherents were brought together in 1918 as the Native American Church.

The Peyote religion teaches an ethical doctrine much like those of the monotheistic religions. However, it eschews specific Christian theology, its exponents often stating that while Christ came to the whites, peyote came to the Indians. This is an obvious reaction to the subordinate place so often given to the Indian converts in a church organization. Indians resent being treated as inferiors in religion as elsewhere.

Their meetings, which have been attended by a number of anthropologists including myself, are like some Protestant prayer meetings, where the program includes singing, prayer, and testimonials. They are held in a tepee strewn with white sage in the Plains manner and with a half-moon shaped earthen altar as in some Kiowa ceremonies. During the evening, a drum and rattle are passed around clockwise, one man singing a song, supposedly of his own composition, while a man on one side of him drums and on the other rattles. Meanwhile heads of the cactus, usually dried, are passed around, each person expecting to eat eight during the evening. After midnight, when the round has been made once, there are testimonials from individuals who have been helped to follow "the straight road," giving up liquor and other faults. At dawn comes a token meal of old Indian foods, then prayers asking God's help for Indians, whites, and all the world.

Statements have been made that Peyote meetings are wild orgies like those due to marijuana. Obviously, these opinions are expressed by persons who have never attended a meeting. The effect of peyote is color visions accompanied by extreme lassitude and unwillingness to move at all. Its principal ingredient, mescaline, is now being investigated by several scientific groups; the conclusion so far is that it is not habit forming. To produce any bad effects such as shortened respiration, at least 350 mgs. of mescaline are needed; white experimenters have taken as many as 700 without harm. The standard buttons (eight) taken at meetings contain only some 107 mgs.

Membership in the Native American Church is growing and for obvious reasons. The Indian is at a point where he really desires to share the advantages of the white man, yet he still feels something of a maladjusted outsider. A religion which provides him with purpose and with self-esteem would seem desirable help, unless we get scientific proof that it is injurious. The areas where it is spreading most are those under present stress, like the Navaho reservation. On the contrary in Oklahoma, the place of its origin, I was told that some of the younger, more fully acculturated men object to the Indian elements in the religion and are joining the white man's church.

E thnomusicology is a discipline with enormous potential for historical and other types of sociocultural analysis. Nettl argues in the following paper that the music of the American Indians is among the best known of any primitive people and yet it is hardly known at all. Furthermore, musical themes, rhythms, and even instruments move from one culture to another rapidly and easily, often without very prolonged or intensive contact among groups; this process could distort or even completely hide historical relationships. The rigorous training necessary to become an ethnomusicologist (training as both an anthropologist and as a musicologist) is sufficiently prolonged and difficult to keep the number of practicing ethnomusicologists very small.

9 *Bruno Nettl*

AMERICAN INDIAN MUSIC

We shall analyze the music of this region by dividing it into "music areas": geographic units whose inhabitants share a relatively homogeneous style that contrasts in important ways with the styles of surrounding areas. Music areas are patterned after the culture area concept. The first serious attempt to devise music areas for North America was a short paper published by Herzog in 1928, in which he uses vocal technique and, to a lesser extent, melodic movement as the main criteria for area differentiation. Herzog does not give complete distributions of the traits he examines in this paper, but he does indicate a main line of demarcation between the northern and southern portions of the continent. In 1936, Helen Roberts published a more detailed study, *Musical Areas in Aboriginal North America.* Her monograph emphasizes the distribution of musical instruments rather than stylistic traits of vocal music, which after all comprises the bulk of primitive musical material. Much more information has been uncovered since her work was published. The conclusions drawn in this chapter agree in part with those of Roberts; but more material is included here, and the distribution of strictly musical phenomena is emphasized more than are culture areas as units of musical homogeneity.

* Abridged and revised from *Music in Primitive Culture*, by B. Nettl. Cambridge, Mass.: Harvard Univ. Press, 106–119, 1956.

In order to be designated a music area, a territory must include musical styles that hold in common one or more important traits, such as identical form types, scale types, or melodic ranges. As is true of division by culture areas, the marginal groups possess elements of both bordering regions. It is sometimes difficult to decide on the exact degree of homogeneity requisite to characterize a music area: areas of various sizes and levels may be designated—continents contrast with other continents, individual tribes with other individual tribes, etc. There are certain aspects of music common to the entire region north of Mexico that are not found on other continents, such as the virtual lack of polyphony, the predominance of pentatonic scales, and heterometric construction. But we shall present here six music areas within this continent, indicating how they differ from each other in significant ways. The areas are fairly large and agree in size with the generally accepted culture areas of North America. The chief criterion used here in determining areas is the frequency of the various traits. Almost every trait occurs in every culture to some degree, because of the long-term intimate contact among the American primitive groups; therefore an area is defined by the traits prevalent in the majority of its songs, even though the same traits crop up sporadically and sparsely in other areas.

THE ESKIMO–NORTHWEST COAST MUSIC AREA

The first area to be discussed contains some of the simplest and some of the most complicated music in North America. It comprises three subareas that are distinguishable primarily because of their varying degrees of complexity. The music of the Eskimos is the simplest. The most complex sub-area is the Northwest Coast culture area, particularly the most culturally advanced tribes—the Kwakiutl, Nootka, Tsimshian, Makah, and Quileute. Occupying an intermediate position in regard to musical complexity are the Salish tribes directly east of the coast and extending to Oregon: the Thompson River Indians, the Bella Coola, the Sliamon, and others directly east of the Northwest Coast tribes.

The significant traits of Eskimo music are intensified in the music of the Salish tribes and even more so in the music of the Northwest Coast sub-area. Among these traits are recitative-like singing and the attendant complex rhythmic organization; relatively small melodic range, averaging about a sixth; and melodic prominence of major thirds and minor seconds, in contrast to the minor thirds and major seconds conspicuous in other areas. Among the Eskimos, melodic movement is undulating;

among the Salish and Northwest Coast Indians it is pendulum-type, leaping in broad intervals from one limit of the range to the other. Eskimo music is not well-known, and as more information becomes available it becomes increasingly evident that there is a good deal of variety. There is some Eskimo music which resembles that of the Plains; and there is also a good deal of material which fits into the Eskimo-Northwest Coast style only by virtue of the relatively complex drumming.

The Northwest Coast music is among the most complicated on the continent, especially in regard to rhythmic structure. Percussive accompaniments to songs have rhythmic designs of their own, intricately related to the melody, and rigid percussion instruments are commonly used. In this sub-area, rudimentary polyphony has been discovered, although to my knowledge it has never been recorded. It consists either of a drone or of parallelism at various intervals. Antiphonal and responsorial forms are also used. Pulsation and vocal tension characterize the style of singing, although these are typical of several other music areas too. The extreme tension in the vocal chords produces dynamic contrast, ornamentation, and rhythmic pulsation: sudden accents without special articulation may occur several times during one sustained note. This may be responsible for the sharp contrasts between very long and very short tones.

THE GREAT BASIN MUSIC AREA

Most of the desert tribes of Utah and Nevada are part of the Great Basin music area, as are some tribes in southern Oregon. The most familiar tribal names here are the Paiute, Ute, and Shoshoni of the Basin, the Modoc and Klamath of Oregon, and some tribes in Northern California such as the Yana and Yahi. This area is sparsely settled, with a population slightly over 10 per cent of that of the Eskimo-Northwest Coast music area. Its music is not nearly so well known. The style is extremely simple; it has small melodic ranges averaging barely over a perfect fifth, many tetronic scales, and very short forms. Most songs are iterative, with each phrase repeated once, although songs with multiple repetitions are found occasionally. The Modoc and Klamath Indians have many songs that consist of only one repeated phrase, and many of their scales are ditonic and tritonic.

In the late nineteenth century, the Great Basin style was carried to many tribes of the Great Plains and surrounding areas by the Ghost

Dance religion. This cult, which originated among the Paiute, arose in reaction against the white supremacy that was forcing the aboriginal cultures to dwindle. It taught that if a particular dance were performed, all whites would die and all dead Indians return to life. The ceremony spread from the Great Basin and with it went the style of the songs, which is characterized by paired-phrase patterns very strongly and by a relaxed, nonpulsating vocal technique. Thus the Plains Ghost Dance songs were originally part of the tradition of the Great Basin music area.

Herzog describes another group of songs that are related to the Great Basin area, albeit somewhat less closely. The group consists of many of the lullabies, songs from tales, and gambling songs that are sung all over the continent, and is characterized by its great simplicity. It is this quality that relates it to the Great Basin, together with other more concrete features. Some scholars believe that these songs are survivals from a really archaic layer of music; and it may well be that the entire Great Basin style is also a remnant of ancient days, protected from acculturation by its relatively isolated cultural position.

The Basin tribes have also been greatly influenced by the Plains styles; accordingly, repertories such as those of the Ute contain a good many songs in the Plains patterns, and during the twentieth century, these seem to have become predominant.

THE CALIFORNIAN–YUMAN MUSIC AREA

The California-Yuman music area consists of most of California and part of Arizona, and includes such tribes as the Pomo and Miwok of central California, the Luiseño, Catalineño, and Gabrieliño of southern California, and the Yuman tribes—the Mohave, Yuman, Havasupai, Maricopa, and others. This area is characterized chiefly by one striking trait: the presence of the rise in almost all of its songs. The vocal technique of the area is relaxed and nonpulsating, resembling some of the techniques of Western cultivated music. Other significant traits are the use of a fairly large amount of isometric material, some isorhythmic tendencies, simple rhythmic organization, pentatonic scales without half tones and with an average range of an octave, sequences, and syncopated figures like the following:

The use of the rise by these tribes exemplifies particularly well how the frequent occurrence of one trait can determine the boundaries of a music area. The forms of the rise are not necessarily identical throughout the area. Usually the rise contains new melodic material and is related to the non-rise parts of the song by virtue of the rhythmic structure. In some instances, the tones used in the rise are no higher in pitch than the highest tones of the non-rise portion; but the rise is nonetheless distinct because it includes a much greater number of the high-pitched tones. The relationship between the rise and the non-rise portions of a song form varies considerably from tribe to tribe. In central California the non-rise portion is usually a single reiterated phrase, a litany-type form, with the rise consisting of the same melodic material transposed up an octave. Among the Yuman tribes, the non-rise portion consists of longer repeated units, each comprising several phrases, while the rise usually consists of a single unit of three to five phrases that is rendered only once. In southern California the forms tend to be progressive, although the two just described are also found.

THE PLAINS–PUEBLO MUSIC AREA

The Plains-Pueblo area is the largest geographically and the third largest in population. It occupies the central portion of the United States, roughly coinciding with the Louisiana Purchase but extending farther to the southwest. At one time its musical style was supposed to be racially inherent in the Indians and shared by all of them. This premise was assumed because most of the Indian material available early in the twentieth century came from the Plains-Pueblo area. Even today this area is by far the best documented, and the sampling of tribes presented here is more extensive than for the other areas.

The chief musical traits of the entire area are extreme vocal tension and pulsation, with resulting ornamentation; tile-type melodic contour; relatively complex rhythm, including the use of several durational values per song; and a type of form that we call the "incomplete repetition type." This form consists of two large sections, the second being an incomplete rendition of the first; the first phrase of the first section is also frequently repeated. Typical schemes are ABC, BC and AABC, ABC. Each large section has tile-type contour. The form is governed by the textual structure; the first half of the text is composed of meaningless syllables, and the second half, sung with the incomplete musical repetition, is meaningful.

A number of songs from other music areas are found in the Plains-Pueblo repertories. This is true of all music areas but especially noticeable here because of the central location of the Plains-Pueblo area, which is contiguous to all the others. We find, for example, Great Basin songs—lullabies, songs from tales, gambling and Ghost Dance songs—and Peyote songs that originated among the southern Athabascans.

This area is so large and well documented that it is possible to identify five sub-areas, units with relatively homogeneous styles that contrast with each other but have in common the characteristics mentioned above. The easternmost sub-area is around Lake Superior and Lake Michigan, and includes the Ojibwa, Menomini, and Winnebago Indians. The musical style is differentiated from the others by particularly large melodic ranges (averaging over a twelfth) and by the use of isorhythmic material in at least one-third of all songs, a larger proportion than elsewhere. Some songs are entirely isorhythmic, others have isorhythmic segments or slightly modified isorhythmic patterns.

Directly south of these tribes, in Missouri, Kansas, and Nebraska, the tribes of the Southern Prairies culture area constitute another sub-area. These tribes, primarily the Pawnee, Osage, and Omaha, are related somewhat more closely to the tribes of the southeastern United States in musical style than are the other Plains-Pueblo tribes. Their forms are more complex, often consisting of several short sections interwoven in iterative and reverting relationships. The average range is smaller than in the music area as a whole, and the scales are likely to have more tones—tetratonic scales are rare, hexatonic relatively common.

The most typical sub-area, and in some ways the simplest in style, comprises the central Plains tribes. It is evidently under less influence from other music areas than are the other sub-areas. The main tribes are the Blackfoot, Crow, Dakota, Cheyenne, Arapaho, Kiowa, and Comanche, stretching in one line just east of the Rocky Mountains from Canada into Texas. The material here is characterized by extreme pulsation and vocal tension, a preference for perfect fourths in the melody, rhythmic complexity, and a relative proponderance of tetratonic scales. These traits are intensified in the center of the area, among the Arapaho and Cheyenne. The range of the songs averages about a tenth. In the northern part, particularly among the Blackfoot, the material is simpler, the ranges smaller, and the scales have fewer tones, while in the southern part the influence of tribes in the southeastern and southwestern United States is evident, causing greater complexity and variety. In the Plains, too, the relationship between percussive accompaniment and the melody is not constant; drum beats coincide only approximately with the important durational values of the melody, resulting in an apparently discordant relationship. The typical Plains style seems to have been developed most vigorously in the central Plains, by the Dakota, Arapaho, and Cheyenne. The tribes at the edges of the area do not have it in such a pronounced manner. For example, the Blackfoot repertory contains also many songs sung in a less tense and pulsating style, songs which have a smaller range and which have more complex forms consisting of various relationships among several short phrases. On the other hand, the typical Plains style is found in many songs of the Eastern Pueblos.

The sub-area most complex in musical style is that of the Pueblo of New Mexico and Arizona, including the Hopi, Zuni, Taos, San Ildefonso, Santo Domingo, and many others. The style here is one of the most complex on the continent and differs most markedly from the rest of the Plains-Pueblo styles. The songs tend to be much longer and to have more variety in form and melodic contour. The types of percussive accompaniment are more varied and they occasionally have rhythmic designs related to those of the melody. The ranges are between an octave and a twelfth, and the rhythmic complexity is about equal to that of the Plains sub-area. The scales tend to have more tones than they do elsewhere on the continent—hexatonic and heptatonic scales are common. The most complex songs are the Katchina dance songs, sung by masked dancers impersonating clan ancestors. The most complex varieties of the Pueblo style are found in the western part of the sub-area, in Hopi and Zuni material, while the eastern Pueblos, including the Tanoans and Keresans, partake of a simpler style intermediate in complexity between those of the Plains and the western Pueblos.

The Pima and Papago tribes, located in southern Arizona, are marginal in style, having traits of both the Plains-Pueblo and the California-Yuman music areas. Their melodic movement and vocal technique are similar to that of the Yumans, although they do not have the rise, while their forms and rhythmic materials are related to those of the Pueblos. A detailed comparison of Pima and Pueblo styles has been made by Herzog.

THE ATHABASCAN MUSIC AREA

The Athabascan-speaking tribes of the Southwest, the Navaho and Apache, have a distinct musical style, although the repertories of the Apache have been considerably influenced by those of the Plains and

Pueblos, while the Navaho have evidently learned much from the Pueblos and perhaps the Yuman tribes. There is some evidence that their styles are related to those of the Northern Athabascans in Western Canada, but the music of the latter is not sufficiently known to make definite conclusions possible.

The southern Athabascan style is characterized chiefly by the limited number of durational values, usually no more than two to a song. The rhythmic organization is also simple in other respects. The typical melodic contour is arc-type. The melodic range is wide, especially among the Navaho, and the melodic intervals tend to be large: major and minor thirds and perfect fourths and fifths predominate, while leaps of an octave are not rare. Broad acrobatic maneuvers in the melody are characteristic. As a result, the scales usually have few tones; tritonic and tetratonic scales are very common, usually occurring in triad-like formation. The typical southern Athabascan song form is strophic. The vocal technique is characterized by the use of falsetto, pulsations, and a nasal sound that is especially distinctive.

The Peyote songs found primarily in the Plains-Pueblo area are evidently related to the Athabascan area also, both stylistically and historically. The Peyote religion was spread among the Plains-Pueblo tribes by the Apaches, either directly or deviously. Some Apache musical traits carried over into the Plains-Pueblo adaptations of the Peyote songs. The songs are now composites of both styles: they have the two durational values and the predominant thirds and fifths of the Apaches, plus the tile-type melodic contour, incomplete repetitions, and isorhythmic tendencies characteristic of Plains-Pueblo music. The Peyote vocal technique is closer to the Athabascan than to the Plains-Pueblo one, and the Peyote cadential formula may be another Athabascan feature.

THE EASTERN MUSIC AREA

The section of the continent between the Mississippi River and the Atlantic makes up the Eastern music area. The music of the entire area is not well known; only the southeastern part and the Atlantic Coast are musically well documented. The tribes of the Southeast, and the Iroquois, who are related linguistically to some of them, have the most complex style; they include the Creek, Yuchi, Cherokee, and Choctaw. The Algonquian-speaking tribes, such as the Delaware and Penobscot, have simpler music. The Shawnee, although Algonquian, have lived so close to the southeastern tribes that their style is relatively complex.

The main musical characteristics of the Eastern area are short phrases in iterative and reverting relationships; the use of shouts before, during, and after songs; pentatonic scales without half tones; simple rhythmic and metric organization; and, probably most important, a great deal of antiphonal and responsorial technique with the accompanying rudimentary imitative polyphony. The melodic movement is usually unspecialized and tends to be gradually descending. A moderate amount of pulsation and vocal tension is present. The characteristics given here are not found in a majority of the songs of the Eastern area, but to the extent that they are found they distinguish the area. It should be noted, however, that the Eastern area is more varied than the others, and that its western portions have close ties to the styles of the Plains.

The music areas of North America partially coincide with the culture areas of the continent. The Eskimo-Northwest Coast music area contains the two culture areas from which it takes its name, the Great Basin music area covers the same territory as the Great Basin culture area (or sub-area, according to Kroeber's scheme). The boundaries do not usually match so closely; some music areas contain parts of several culture areas. The California-Yuman music area, although compact in itself, contains parts of the Southwest culture area as well as California. Conversely, the Southwest culture area contains parts of the California-Yuman, the Athabascan, and the Plains-Pueblo music areas. This type of arrangement is the rule throughout the continent. In both music and culture areas, the diversity of traits is greater in the western part of the continent than in the eastern. The western half is also divided into more areas than the eastern.

The correlation of music areas with linguistic families or linguistic structural types is less pronounced than with cultural units. The only close correlation is found in the Athabascan music area, where almost all tribes speak only the Athabascan languages. An area as homogeneous in musical style as the Plains-Pueblo includes tribes speaking the Athabascan, Algonquian, Siouan, Uto-Aztecan, and Kiowa languages.

Certain traits of Indian music, especially some rather specialized ones, have a distribution that is interesting. These traits are also relevant to the reconstruction of the history of Indian music. Among them are incomplete-repetition form, polyphony, tense vocal technique, and the rise, which we shall use as an example here. The rise is characteristic of the California-Yuman area, where it occurs in the majority of the songs, but it is also found elsewhere in other varieties and with less frequency. The specific form of the rise tends to agree with the fundamental princi-

ples of each area where it occurs; for example, on the Northwest Coast
the rise is used with variation and iteration, which are characteristic of
the area as a whole. In the southeastern United States, forms using the
rise tend to include the reverting relationships that are common there.
The rise is found in about 20 per cent of the music of the Northwest
Coast sub-area of the Eskimo-Northwest Coast music area. It is present
in about 15 per cent of the songs in the southeastern United States and
in a few songs farther north in the Eastern area. The proportion differs
in every tribe, and the sampling on which these estimates are based may
not be accurate, but it is probable that these percentages indicate at least
the relative frequencies within the tribes.

CHRONOLOGICAL DEVELOPMENT OF AMERICAN
INDIAN MUSIC

Of the North American styles known at the present time, the oldest is
probably that of the Great Basin area. Its age is attested to by its relative simplicity and by the fact that its style is represented throughout
the continent in lullabies, gambling songs, and songs from tales. Similar
styles are found throughout the Old World in widely scattered musical
cultures of great simplicity. The period during which this style was
common to all of North America antedates the development of advanced cultures in Mexico, Middle America, and Peru. On this style
were superimposed others, and it has remained dominant only in the
isolated and culturally simple Great Basin.

With the development of the advanced cultures in Mexico came a
style characterized by relaxed vocal technique and probably by the rise.
Whether this style still exists in Mexico or whether it was replaced
there before the advent of the white man cannot be ascertained now, because we know so little of Mexico Indian music, especially that of the
advanced cultures. At any rate, this style spread northward, particularly
along the coasts. It is the basis for the styles of the California-Yuman
and the Eastern areas. Besides the rise, these areas have in common relative rhythmic simplicity, isometric material, pentatonic scales without
half tones (to a greater extent than elsewhere), and forms consisting of
short sections. The differences between their styles are probably due to
later contacts with other music areas. Whether the Mexican style spread
into the central part of the continent, including Texas and environs, we
cannot conjecture. If it did, it was later replaced by the Plains-Pueblo
style.

At about the same time, three separate waves of musical style reached

North America from Asia. They had a number of traits in common, notably tense and pulsating vocal technique. All three came across the Bering Strait, and their influence is evident today in the styles of some of the Paleo-Siberian tribes, like the Chuckchee, Yukaghir, Koryak, and others in the extreme east of Siberia. The three styles are represented in the Plains-Pueblo, Athabascan, the Eskimo–Northwest Coast areas, and may have come to America in that order. They spread south on the continent and eventually came in contact with the movements initiated in Mexico. It is at the southernmost points of all three areas that the most complex material is found: on the Northwest Coast, in the Pueblos, and among the Navaho. Contact between the Northwest Coast and Mexico seems implausible because of the great geographic distance and the intervening Great Basin style, yet the presence of concrete musical phenomena like bird-shaped whistles in both areas is evidence that it did take place. Since the Navaho were undoubtedly the last of these peoples to reach the South (they did so probably no more than eight hundred years ago), they probably had no direct contact with the Mexican movements but were influenced indirectly by way of the Pueblos.

The Plains-Pueblo area extended throughout the central part of the continent, influencing the surrounding areas and imparting much of its tense vocal technique to the Eastern area. This process continues today: tribes of all areas are learning Plains songs whenever contact exists, but the Plains Indians rarely learn songs from tribes whose musical styles are unrelated to theirs.

Thus, the three centers of musical complexity—the Pueblos, the Northwest Coast, and the southeastern United States—although they all represent mixtures of northern and Mexican elements, consist of different combinations. The Pueblos have the culmination of the northern elements; the Gulf of Mexico, with its cultural similarity to ancient Mexico and its use of polyphony, shows the Mexican influence predominantly. The Northwest Coast probably represents a mixture of Mexican and northern elements, with polyphony being the chief Mexican contribution.

Finally, it should be emphasized again that not only the historical recapitulation presented above but also the classifications of the tribes in music areas are highly tentative and subject to revision. Very little is yet known about North American Indian music, although relatively more than is know about primitive music on other continents, and very few tribes are known intimately. Many of the tribes have disintegrated, and there is no hope now of ever discovering their musical traits.

SECTION II

The Eskimo

The Eskimo is the most recent aboriginal arrival to the New World, having begun moving from Asia some 3,000 years or so ago. Rudimentary Eskimo culture—houses, weapons, lamps and cooking devices, cutting implements, type of social organization, shamanistic emphasis, and many more specific features—is clearly related to known cultural complexes of northwestern Siberia. These general Siberian patterns appear, in turn, to have their roots in the Mesolithic patterns of North China and perhaps, ultimately, in the Upper Paleolithic cultural patterns of Northern Europe. Swadesh has noted that there are possible relationships between the Eskimo-Aleut language family and a widespread Old World stock, Ural-Altaic, which includes such languages as Finnish, Estonian, Turkish, Tartar and, perhaps, Mongol.

Despite the general agreement among scholars that Asians early passed to the New World through what is now Alaska, no archaeological finds of truly ancient age have yet been made in the Arctic. Pre-Eskimo material has been found, dated at perhaps 10,000 years, but most archaeological materials from the Arctic are much more recent in time—5,000 years old or less. Definite roots of recent Eskimo culture were to be seen in the Bering Sea region hundreds of years before the beginning of the Christian era. Beginnings of divergence also appeared at that time, seen more recently between the Eskimo proper and the Aleuts (inhabitants of the Aleutian Islands). Regional differentiation continued from that time onward, especially in southern Alaska; but everywhere—with the exception of a few inland groups in Alaska and in the vicinity of James and Hudson's Bay—the Eskimo had a maritime-oriented, land-mammal-using, technologically specialized, band-type society. The particular character of the Eskimo culture, and perhaps its very viability, was due to the Eskimo's ability to utilize sea mammals, especially the many varieties of seals, as well as sea lions and whales.

Between 1100 and 1200 A.D. there was a rapid expansion of a culture type called "Thule" from the Point Barrow region of the Alaskan coast eastward to Greenland. The Thule people were intensively maritime in orientation, and lived in permanent, semi-subterranean houses made of driftwood, whale bones, turf, and stones. At the time of European contact, the Eskimos of Greenland and of the Point Barrow region had cultural patterns which were remarkably alike; considering the vast distance separating the two areas, even more incredible is the fact that they spoke very similar dialects. This attests not only to their cultural stability, but also to the Eskimos' enthusiasm for travel, as well as to the low population densities throughout the region which forced Eskimos into marriages with distantly located females. However, in the James Bay area of Canada, and in the central region of the Arctic in general, perhaps due to fluctuations in sea mammal populations, the Eskimos lost their classic Thule adaptive patterns and became much more strongly devoted to land life and to caribou hunting.

A still unfolding chapter of Eskimo prehistory is that which deals with the contacts between Norsemen and the aboriginal inhabitants of Greenland and Labrador, beginning perhaps a thousand or more years ago. These Norsemen, who may also have established settlements on the maritime coast of what is now Canada, introduced forged iron and other metal tools to the Eskimo as long ago as 1000 A.D.

In the opening article of this section, W. S. Laughlin discusses the historical relationships between the native of the Aleutian Islands and the Eskimo proper. The article is a rare example of anthropological versatility, drawing as it does on linguistic, morphological, archaeological, and sociocultural evidence.

10 *William S. Laughlin*

THE ALEUT-ESKIMO COMMUNITY*

Along the coast of northern North America, Greenland and a small area in Siberia, there exists a genetically, linguistically and culturally related population which provides one of the most outstanding examples in human history of the linear distribution of a population. By virtue of its unusual contiguous linear extension this stock offers a number of basic problems concerning the process of racial, linguistic and cultural change. It is first necessary to appreciate the ways in which these peoples are related, to assess their ecological relationships and their relative time depth, before the processes by which they have become differentiated into geographical variants can be profitably studied. It is now apparent that there is sufficient evidence for considering these peoples as one unified stock, physically, linguistically and culturally. Researches of the last five years which have included dialectical studies, dental and morphological researches, blood typing, ethnological and archaeological studies, have brought to light much information which demonstrates the nature of the relationships of the contemporary people and, especially with the finding of core and blade industries, the relatively great time depth of the proto-Aleut-Eskimos. At the same time these researches have indicated the great fertility, the creativity and innovative genius of these pragmatically oriented people.

To the extent that both the variability and the structure of Aleut-Eskimo culture have been ignored, the racial polymorphy unappreciated, the ecological framework disregarded and the time depth minimized, there has been an accompanying lack of attention to process. As a consequence, there has been a frequent resort to migration of unrelated peoples from the most improbable places to explain various traits which were felt to be aberrant.

In the study of Eskimo culture, as well as in the racial background, the

* Abridged from "The Aleut-Eskimo Community," by W. S. Laughlin, in *Anthropological Papers of the University of Alaska*, **1**, 25–43, 1952.

underlying assumption that change or evolution took place "somewhere else" is frequently manifested. Thus, an amazing medley of peoples ranging from the Ainu, Tungus and Kamchadals on the one hand to various American Indians such as Athabascans on the other hand have been cited as the authors or bearers of Aleut-Eskimo traits. Consideration of genetic processes in race, language and culture, plus the fact that there has been ample time for substantial changes to have taken place, when added to the known examples of change and development *in situ,* obviate the excessive dependency upon external sources to explain the elaboration of culture or race among these highly adaptable people. It is the intent of this paper to examine certain aspects in the nature of the Aleut-Eskimo relationship, to call attention to the variability, to cite various examples of internal change and to point out the need for the study of the actual processes of change.

IS THERE AN ALEUT-ESKIMO RACIAL UNITY?

Much of the answer to this question concerning the unity of the Aleut-Eskimo stock hinges purely upon which of two major approaches to the recognition of a race is used: the typological approach or the population approach. The deficiencies of the older typological approach have been exposed sufficiently elsewhere to exclude that method from serious consideration. When we turn to the question of whether or not these people constitute one over-all breeding population we are in a position to deal with the problem scientifically. Present evidence indicates that Eskimos have habitually interbred with Eskimos, Aleuts with Aleuts, within their several breeding isolates, and that Aleuts mated with Eskimos. The frequencies of intermarriage between the different dialectical and language groups have surely varied considerably. In the case of the greatest linguistic barrier, that between Aleuts and Eskimos, there are ample references in the traditional accounts of the people to demonstrate beyond any question that the Aleuts frequently raided the Koniags for wives and slaves and that the Koniags did likewise. The Koniag Eskimos are the only people with whom the Aleuts have been in immediate contact. Keeping in mind that it is the breeding population which is the race, and not a type abstracted from the population, it is immediately apparent that the Aleut-Eskimo peoples constitute one breeding population and therefore constitute a sub-race or race depending on the taxonomic value to be assigned their degree of distinctiveness from other breeding populations.

Once it is recognized that these people do intermarry, at different rates between the many breeding isolates, and that there is gene flow throughout their geographical range, we are in a position to assess the differences between the breeding isolates within this population. This view simply recognizes the polymorphy of these people and the large number of geographical variants in contrast to the inaccurate typological system of assuming a type and considering all differing isolates to be deviations from that type.

The question of Indian intermixture has been dealt with previously. The essential points are: (1) little or no mixture with Indians has taken place, and (2) there are not enough Indians in the contiguous areas to notably affect the larger populations of Eskimos or Aleuts. The possible exception of certain peripheral groups of Eskimos such as those about Hudson Bay can be admitted but, since they constitute a numerically insignificant part of the Eskimo population, random mixing between Indians and them, if demonstrated, would make little difference in the overall genetic constitution of the Aleut-Eskimo population.

The physical characteristics shared by most isolates of the Aleut-Eskimo sub-race are varying amounts of blood type, with more A and O, a generally Mongoloid physiognomy, small hands and feet, large relative sitting height, small nose, mandibular torus, shovel-shaped incisors, and a number of other dental characters. In some of these characters, such as blood type B, the adjacent Indians appear to be totally lacking in the necessary gene; in the other characters the frequencies of the traits distinguish the Aleut-Eskimo peoples from the Indians. It is interesting to note that selected similarities between Eskimos and Indians in Canada have been used as evidence of inland origin for the Eskimos whereas selected similarities between Indians and Eskimos in southwestern Alaska have been used as evidence of admixture. That the Indians should be considered contemporary representatives of ancestors in one case and adulterating agents in the other case is an unscientific coercion of the data in an attempt to justify a particular theory of the origin of the Eskimos. The Aleut-Eskimo population is also characterized by variability in head form. However, the majority of Eskimos and Aleuts are brachycephalic or high in mesocephaly. Brachycephaly reaches a climax among the later representatives of the populations in the area of the eastern Aleutians and Kodiak Island, and declines again in the western Aleutians.

The four factors responsible for changes in a population are selection, mutation, genetic drift, and migration or mixture. Past theorists have placed primary reliance upon mixture to explain the variants in the population. This has been accompanied by the attempt to analyze race on the basis of a single skull. It can only be reiterated that a race is a population and that one individual is an inadequate sample of any contemporary population. Owing to the variability in all Mongoloid populations, as in other populations, there is much overlap in most of the northern peoples, Neo-Asiatics and Paleo-Asiatics, including the Aleut-Eskimos. On the basis of morphological classification it is often possible to place a particular individual in any one of several populations.

An example of internal change appears to exist in southwestern Alaska where an earlier population, designated in the Aleutians as Paleo-Aleut, has been largely superseded by a later population, Neo-Aleut. This same succession is known to have occurred in the prehistory of the Kuskokwim Eskimos and the Koniag Eskimos. The fact that the Neo-Aleuts have their heaviest concentration in the eastern Aleutians, and that this population succession took place in adjacent areas to the east, is sufficient in itself to exclude the importation of "Tungids," from Asia. On the basis of their higher blood type N frequency alone, the "Tungids," the Ainu, and other Asiatics may be exempted from a rather ambitious voyage from Asia to southwestern Alaska. Additionally, the relative population size must always be kept in mind when mixture is suggested for the origin of a particular trait or type. Hybridization of the population of southwestern Alaska would have been no mean task for a considerable number of extremely fertile "Tungids." One has only to note the minor genetic effect of the Russian occupation on the Aleuts to roughly estimate the required numbers.

Only patient examination of large numbers of stratigraphically derived skeletal collections will provide the details of the origin of the many geographical variants among the Aleut-Eskimo stock. Undoubtedly different processes have been more important at one time than another. Additional increments of Mongoloid populations may have come across Bering Strait from time to time. The distribution of the people into small breeding isolates and these into small village communities provides an ideal situation for the process of genetic drift.

LINGUISTIC UNITY OF THE ALEUT–ESKIMO STOCK

Perhaps the most adequately documented example of the common background of the Aleut-Eskimo stock lies in language. As a result of the studies of both European and New World scholars there is at least a

little information on most of the divisions and in many cases much information. Though Rasmus Rask had recorded a list of words spoken by
two Aleut brothers in St. Petersburg in 1819 and correctly linked Aleut
with Eskimo, neither he nor later researchers had sufficient first-hand
material nor had fundamental structural comparisons been made until
the recent studies of G. H. Marsh and Knut Bergsland which have been
conducted in a number of Aleut villages and in all the dialects. The theoretical importance of the Aleut linguistic studies to the problem of the
relationship and origins of the Aleut-Eskimo peoples may be indicated
by an earlier quotation from Sapir:

> Had the historical significance of linguistic differentiation been more gen-
> erally appreciated, I doubt if the theory, for example, of the distribution of
> Eskimo tribes from the west coast of Hudson Bay as a centre would have
> received quite such ready acceptance. I do not wish expressly to oppose this
> theory, but merely to point out that it does not well agree with the linguistic
> evidence. The Eskimo linguistic stock is sharply divided into two dialectic
> groups, Eskimo proper and Aleut. Inasmuch as Aleut is confined to Alaska
> and as a considerable number of distinct Eskimo dialects are spoken in Alaska
> besides, it seems very probable to me that the earliest at present ascertainable
> centre of dispersion of the tribes of Eskimo stock lies in Alaska. (4:82)

Those divisions to which Sapir referred as dialectic groups are now
recognized as languages.

Recognizing the fact that the fundamental structure and some of the
basic vocabulary correspond in the two languages, it is possible to
estimate the time of divergence from a common proto-Aleut-Eskimo
language by a method based on the percentage of basic vocabulary correspondence. Such an estimate suggests a period of 4,000 years of separate
development. This is, happily, compatible with the archaeological
record of a relatively great time depth in southwestern Alaska, a record
based on carbon-14 dating. A shorter period of time, some 1,500 years,
is estimated for the time of separation between Yupik and Inupik.

Past attempts to find similarities indicative of relationship with other
peoples, such as the Ainu or the Kamchadals, has been unsuccessful.
This is quite understandable when the probability of Alaska as the
homeland of the proto-Aleut-Eskimo of some five thousand or more
years is recognized. No non-Aleut words have been found in the Aleut
dialects, excepting, of course, the recent accretions of Russian and English. There can be extremely little basis for an assertion of any basic similarity of immediate interrelation between Aleut on the one hand and

the Chukchi-Koryak-Kamchadal family of languages on the other. The phonologic system in the two groups of languages is more or less dissimilar. The morphologic pattern is likewise rather remote, and the lexicon shows tenuous connections if any at all. Furthermore, as a side point, if one is going to compare the Chukchi-Koryak-Kamchadal (or Lucravedlan) family with Aleut, Kamchadal is the least probable member of that family from which to demonstrate. Of the three, Kamchadal shows the most aberrant form and is also the most clearly permeated with the rather striking Uralic or Altaic (most likely Altaic in the case of Kamchadal) phonologic features which all three of these languages manifest. There is the vague possibility of some remote comparisons between Chukchi-Koryak-Kamchadal and the Aleut-Eskimo stock in general, but the comparisons that might be made will have to be on the proto level, with the assumption that an ancient substratum of proto-Aleut-Eskimo overlain by a dominant Uralic-speaking element might have produced languages such as we see in the East Siberian group. In view of the fact that the Aleuts have been separated from contact with Indians by the intervening populations of Eskimos, and from Asia by a minimum distance of 180 miles to the uninhabited Kommandorski Islands, non-Aleut words would have to be accepted before their movement out onto the chain. This would mean a time span of at least 4,000 years and it is unlikely that they would be identifiable at this date.

The over-all importance of the linguistic unity of the Aleut-Eskimo people is manifested in at least three ways. First, the linguistic community serves as an isolating mechanism to define the breeding population. Second, the fact that there is an underlying unity means that the differences are due to divergence which demonstrates the nature of change which has taken place and removes the process of borrowing from any important place in understanding the differentiation. Third, the linguistic relationships indicate the major divisions with sharp lines of demarcation having been created within the community. In the absence of contact this can only indicate that there have been periods of separation of various divisions and that there has been considerable time for the operations of linguistic differentiation.

The sharp breaks in language, at Norton Sound between the two Eskimo languages, and on the Alaska Peninsula between Aleut and Eskimo, provide a powerful demonstration of the extent to which change has taken place without the intervention of alien cultures. The existence of intrusive peoples at either of these places, past or present, would alter considerably the picture of cultural elaboration over a linear distribution of contiguous peoples.

The theoretical model provided by the differentiation within the stock is valuable for both the racial and cultural analogies. Since all contemporary forms go back to a proto-Aleut-Eskimo, no one is more Eskimo than another anymore than dissimilar siblings of the same parents where some of the children bear more physical resemblance to the phenotype of the parents are any more or less valid children. It is not possible to have a contemporary ancestor; though it is possible that some of the divisions have changed less than other divisions, it is evident that all have changed to some extent from the original form or forms.

This linguistic model also demonstrates the necessity for distinguishing between origins of the Aleut-Eskimo stock and the areas of characterization. It appears to be a patent certainty that the ultimate source of the Aleut-Eskimo stock is Asiatic and that its progenitors entered the New World across the Bering Strait. However, it appears that the languages, as well as other portions of the culture, assumed their definitive aspects in southwestern Alaska.

TIME DEPTH AND VARIABILITY IN MATERIAL CULTURE

Without considerable time depth it would not be possible to understand the linguistic differentiation and physical differentiation which has taken place inside the Aleut-Eskimo stock. Archaeological studies reveal a time depth well in excess of 3,000 years and a correspondingly great variability in the material culture. It is this degree of variability which has, in fact, made difficult the recognition of "Eskimo" traits in the absence of skeletal remains. In some cases archaeological assemblages have been accepted as Eskimo even though skeletons were not present and there was no indication of the language spoken. This is possible in many cases though there are certainly many subliminal claimants to the designation of Eskimo on the North Pacific Coast and in southern Canada and northeastern United States. When one considers the trait differences in excess of certain basic traits in Dorset, Thule, Koniag, Aleut, Ipiutak and St. Lawrence Island it is necessary to admit a high degree of local variation. Considered solely in time depth the problem of the point at which Eskimo begins and its predecessors end is equally a problem which will require the presence of skeletons or, at least, of traits which are well associated with skeletons at some other point in time, linked by an unbroken sequence. Such a problem is raised by the important discoveries of the Denbigh Flint Complex and associated industries using lamelles to a great extent. Asiatic connections are as clearly evidenced in this industry as they are in the Ipiutak culture some 5,000 years later. It is significant that a core and blade industry is found in the Aleutian Islands and that tools made from these blades are found in the lower levels of the oldest known site on Umnak Island. The skeletal materials from this portion of the site are those of the Paleo-Aleuts, who are morphologically similar to many other western Alaskan Eskimos. On the basis of visual inspection they appear similar to the Ipiutak population, especially in the presence of the occipital "bun."

The nature of the archaeological sequence in the Aleutians was obscured by the chance selection of sites dug by W. Jochelson. He excavated sites which belonged wholly or predominantly to the later portions of the known sequence. This has been demonstrated by our excavations in which we went to some of the same sites he used and compared the artifacts with those of the long Chaluka sequence at Nikolski, Umnak Island. Since no great time sequence was suspected the minor amount of change he demonstrated was accepted with little question. The excavations of A. Hrdlicka did not add a great deal to the picture in terms of change, for he kept little or nothing in the way of archaeological records and mixed the artifacts by collecting them in boxes which were convenient but not chronological.

A study of Aleut archaeology reveals no traits which do not have a good basis in the elaboration of the original artifact inventory carried into the Aleutians from the Alaska mainland or which have subsequently been introduced from the east. The sequence does reveal considerable innovation of styles and is in harmony with a minimum date of entry of some 4,000 years ago.

UNIFORMITY, VARIABILITY AND STRUCTURE IN THE ALEUT-ESKIMO CULTURE

An ecological preface is necessary to an over-all view of the cultural uniformities of these peoples. The important aspect of their distribution is not that it is Arctic, a common misapprehension, but first, that it is primarily littoral and second, that it is a linear distribution of contiguous groups (usually remaining in contact with each other to the relative exclusion of Indians) running from the sub-Arctic into the Arctic. In accordance with their littoral distribution their main subsistence is derived from the hunting of sea mammals and fish, and the major portion of their culture is dedicated to this end. Other subsistence factors associated with the sea are the presence of driftwood and the presence of ice. Access to land animals is another major factor and especially one which has permitted deviation due to local opportunity. Deviation is here used to mean less frequency and not to imply less validity. Access to land animals must also be considered with reference to the extent to which these could be pursued inland. Thus, on the Alaska Peninsula and the southern coasts land animals were added to a rich inventory of sea mammals: caribou, bear, mountain goats, mountain sheep, weasel, marten, fox, ground squirrels, beaver and wolves. However, the presence of mountains close to the sea, such as the interior mountains of Kodiak Island, or the mountains of the Alaska Range, the Aleutian Range, etc., did not permit these people to go inland and still maintain their familiarity with sea hunting techniques. One conclusion which may be drawn from this is that the early southwestern Alaskan populations had familiarity with the hunting of land animals, in addition to their intimate knowledge of sea hunting, and migrating groups were able to draw upon this cultural background for more specialization where the local area presented the opportunity. Where land hunting is practiced the bow and arrow becomes of greater importance. Thus, those Aleuts living on Unimak Island and the Peninsula, where caribou were present, used the bow far more than the Aleuts to the west of Unimak Island. The Aleuts west of Unimak used the throwing board and retrieving harpoon almost exclusively, since they were much more adaptable to use from skin boats, and reserved the bow for warfare, a form of land animal hunting. Similarly, ice hunting techniques are used where ice is present, and if people must spend long periods of time on the ice the snowhouse is used also. The sled has not been used at either end of the Aleut-Eskimo range, southern Alaska or southern Greenland. At the same places ice hunting cannot be practiced. There has been a consequent elaboration of kayak hunting, at least in southern Greenland; it was probably antecedent in southern Alaska.

Kroeber has listed twenty-five regional variants of Eskimo economic culture and the list could well be extended. In spite of the adaptation to each local region a number of traits are rather uniformly present:

1. A great group of similar utensils, tools, and weapons: the ulu, whittling knives, men's meat-cutting knives, side-bladed knives, toggle and other harpoons, comparable spear types, leisters, pronged bird spears, flat throwing boards, semilunar pots, sewing implements, fish-hooks, grapling hooks, nets, weirs, similar bows and the same type of arrow-head mounting, bolas, bag-nets, lamps, drums, etc. For ornamentation the dot-and-circle, animal figures and human heads all used on tools.

2. Two types of boats: the community boat, the bydar, and the individual boat, the bydarky.

3. Communal houses (houses for one family alone seem to be found only in North Greenland and in the present-day Aleut after long contact with whites).

4. A distinction between summer and winter houses, the winter (in a few places the summer) house being a communal dwelling and relatively permanent either in structure or location, the summer being temporary and for only one family per shelter on the whole—the main distinction, again, being between communal and individual, as with boats.

5. The use of stone and whale-bones in house construction even where wood is available (our few oldest Aleut house remains show the stone element, and whalebone is obvious everywhere).

6. The dichotomy between land and sea mammals not only in methods of hunting but also in methods of eating.

7. A similar type of social organization with emphasis on maintaining a co-operating group in spite of personal frictions and antagonisms. The keeping of personal antagonisms in restraint unless continued and cumulative irritation aggravated the relation to the point of explosion leading to murder and consequent blood-feuds. Specific mechanisms for maintaining group cohesiveness, of which the most widespread is the arbitrary name-sake relation (anaaqisax), whereby people who acquire the same name in some arbitrary fashion must form a mutual-relationship pair (in some Eskimo areas this consists in intentionally naming a child after an older person; among the Aleut besides intentional naming accidental naming also occurs).

8. Proper age for starting the instruction of children is 10–12. Before that they learn by watching, imitating, playing, and so forth, but after that the older people definitely undertake to teach the skills and behavior belonging to adult life. Among other things the instruction of children includes training in survival techniques (even in the Aleutians,

which are outside the Arctic proper and have a relatively mild climate): inurement to cold, training in observation, bodily health and strength, survival foods.

9. Control of the population through indirect socially sanctioned restraints on promiscuity. Though the general exercise of sexual promiscuity or restraint is an individual matter, there are various organized tabus and injunctions on both men and women: e.g. boys can't walk out at night, and can't attend dances before 20; hunters refrain from intercourse with their wives before hunt and with other women during hunting period; girls are confined at menarche and tabued regularly during menstruation; women mustn't be unfaithful to husbands who are out hunting; there are boogy-men to keep the women in at night; widows and widowers are confined after death of the spouse and a "mourning period" before they remarry is recommended, and such like. On the other hand there seems to be population control in the other direction through socially sanctioned promiscuity especially to encourage breeding with outsiders and strangers (there are some hints of this among the Aleuts).

10. The use of labrets and tattooing. Tattooing is mainly for women, where in the Aleut and Kanyag area women and transvestites could be distinguished at times only by their tattooing and ear ornaments.

11. Tailored garments, involving the elaborate piecing together of materials both for structure and for ornament. This feature sets the whole Aleut-Eskimo stock off from any of their Indian neighbors.

12. Tending of the lamp, working with grass and the gathering and handling of vegetable products, are specifically women's jobs.

13. No secret societies. (This is not certain for the Aleuts simply through lack of information on the subject, but if they had existed they probably would have been important enough to have made their way into the literature.)

14. Flexed burial. Not only flexed burial but the attempt to cover up the corpse seems to be a general Aleut-Eskimo custom (exposure is found in only a restricted area). Grave goods are also sufficiently prevalent to be common to the stock.

15. Differential burial for important and unimportant people with the attempt to preserve the bodies of the important people to retain their spirits. (There may not be sufficiently large distribution of this trait among the various Eskimos to maintain it as a trait characteristic of the stock as such.)

16. Mourning customs involving dietary tabus.

17. A number of beliefs about the supernatural seem to belong to the whole stock:

    a. The spirits of the dead participate in the affairs of the living (hence Aleut mummies).

    b. A method exists for destroying the power of the soul of an annihilated person (the method is not everywhere the same, but the existence of a method is widespread—Aleut, disjointing; Bering Strait, cutting off fingers and toes; farther east, eating part of the heart of the killed person).

    c. Spirits, notably ones that whistle, inhabit places, especially bodies of water.

    d. The moon is an important being, is everywhere a man, and is probably throughout the stock connected with the fertility of women.

18. A Headman who functions as coordinator of activities simply providing ideas and suggestions and then organizing a group to carry them out.

19. The cooperative gathering and communal sharing of food with fixed formulas for the division of the highly prized animals (whether whales, bearded seals, sea otter, or other, depending on the area).

Unfortunately the time depth of all these traits cannot be uniformly documented. A list of traits common to most Aleut-Eskimos of 2,000 years ago might differ somewhat. Such a trait as the labret, which appears before the 3,000 year level at Chaluka, Umnak Island, must have been shared by the proto-Aleut-Eskimo and has probably been discarded by the Eskimos who went into the Arctic.

Another cause of variation which operates in addition to local ecological adaptation is that of style preference. Where the choice is presented in the method of removing salmon from a trap, as in the Aleutians, the people may prefer to use a gaff hook instead of a net simply because it is "more fun." More important, whales can be successfully hunted using essentially the same equipment as that for seals or for humans and without the addition of heavier tackle. Thus, some eastern Aleuts used a light spear with a stone point set in a whalebone socket and after spearing the whale waited for him to die, at which time they secured a line in his lower lip and towed him to shore. The Aleuts possessed togglehead harpoons and could have used techniques similar to those further north. It is of interest to note that as part of their complex whaling techniques the Aleuts used "poison," composed of such things as a kind of isopod and bumble bee legs, which was placed in the slot beneath the stone point.

Consideration of the variability in single material traits alone forces one to place more emphasis on the processes of innovation. The ground slate semi-lunar knife, common among the recent Aleuts and Eskimos, is confined to the later strata in the Aleutians. It was, however, preceded by a chipped semi-lunar knife which was, in turn, only one of several kinds of knives. If the single category of knives were considered for all past and present Aleut-Eskimo cultures, it would be apparent immediately that there has been considerable innovation. The number of such traits is so far in excess of the number uniformly found among all the peoples that neither diffusion from neighboring peoples nor migration of more distant peoples can be very useful in explaining their presence. One is perforce led to consider the processes of innovation. In view of the fact that innovation is known to have been specifically encouraged, this area of the culture must receive more thorough consideration before the "sources" of Aleut-Eskimo culture can be exposed.

Variability not due solely to ecological adaptation has provided the basis for dividing Eskimo groups into the heterogeneous and the homogeneous, or the pure and the impure. Thus, Kroeber has used the term "purer" to apply to the eastern Eskimo as contrasted with the western Eskimo. By this is meant those things in the race, language and culture which are "more characteristically or undilutedly" Eskimo. However, this greater variability of the western Eskimos and Aleuts should not be taken to mean that they are any less "Eskimo." In this case greater variability is a characterizing trait in itself, just as great variability is a characteristic of the gibbons and does not suggest that they are any less valid anthropoid apes for this characteristic.

Obviously, western Alaska has been exposed to influences coming from Asia across Bering Strait. The larger populations of western Alaska with greater food supplies and opportunity for incorporation of new traits, in the absence of the restricting limitations of near survival subsistence of the Arctic, have been able to maintain a greater inventory of traits. Moreover, they have at the same time been able to innovate more traits and to elaborate them into multitudinous variants. Whereas various eastern Eskimos have one kind of kayak, the Aleuts have three, depending on the number of hatches. The three-hatch skin boat may be excepted in view of the fact that it was an innovation apparently stimulated by the Russians. In hunting techniques the degree of elaboration is comparatively great. In hunting the seal several methods were used, a

decoy behind which the hunter lay, nets, clubs, and a variety of retrieving harpoons with or without attached bladder. In disposal of the dead
another variety of methods is seen, which depended on the fact that
there was not a fear of the dead in the same way characteristic of the
Arctic or eastern Eskimos; bodies were kept about the house for varying
periods of time, mummified and placed in caves or in special log tombs,
buried in the habitation area, buried in special little homes, or, in the
case of slain enemies, dissected for study purposes or dismembered and
thrown in the ocean.

Almost any trait that is found among the eastern Eskimos and western Eskimos will have many more variant forms or embellishments in
the west, within a comparable dialectic group. When the total variants
of the different groups are placed together the variability of west as opposed to east is shown in equally clear relief. The situation is then quite
comparable to that of the linguistic differentiation or the physical differentiation. At the same time it is more difficult to abstract particular traits
and assign their origin to non-Aleut-Eskimo peoples.

The variability of western Eskimo culture, both material and non-
material culture, is closely related to the population size. The size of the
population in turn is related to ecological background. In the Aleutians
and in southern Alaska south of the Kuskokwim River the size and
number of archaeological sites substantiate the population estimates
which indicate that one third of the Eskimo speakers (including Aleut)
lived on the Pacific Ocean frontage and that roughly three-fifths of all
Eskimo, indicated also by sites to the north of the Kuskokwim, lived
south of Bering Strait. Relative to the Indians and eastern Eskimos
comparatively large populations were made possible in the southwestern
area by the presence of annual salmon runs and many kinds of marine
fish, in addition to a large inventory of sea mammals, including walrus,
whale, sea lion, seal and sea otter. The fur seal were especially important and were conveniently available owing to the necessity of passing
through the Aleutian Islands on their annual trip to the Pribilof breeding grounds. Large numbers of octopus, shell fish and edible sea weeds,
as well as land plants, enabled many communities to survive the lean
spring period when storms prevented hunting at sea and the winter
stores had been depleted. The presence of land animals comparatively
close to the shore line villages provided an additional source of food for
the peoples of the mainland and adjacent Unimak and Kodiak Islands.

The population size contributed to the elaboration of the culture in at
least two major ways; first, there were simply more people available for

the production of new traits and these people were provided with a wealth of plastic materials, ivory, wood, stone and bone. Second, more indirectly but none-the-less influential, the comparative ecological wealth of southwestern Alaska explains in part the early occupation of this area insofar as the proto-Aleut-Eskimo peoples are concerned, thereby providing more time, clearly in excess of 4,000 years, for the characterization and elaboration of the Aleut-Eskimo culture to take place.

In summary, two points may be emphasized. First, "marginal cultures" in general are characterized by heterogeneity resulting from local invention. This point has been made by Lowie who, in an article which includes a reference to the invention of the vaulted snowhouse by the Eskimo, concludes, "The ecological adaptations of marginal peoples reveal an astonishing inventiveness. The religious, magical and social aspects of their cultures exhibit imagination and logical power. *A fortiori*, the occurrence of items belonging to these categories need not arouse our amazement . . ." (3:7). Second, the Aleut-Eskimo culture in particular is characterized by an especially high degree of heterogeneity within a common structured framework. This variability is the result not only of local adaptation but of an explicit pattern for innovation. Finally, this culturally sanctioned emphasis on innovation in both the individual and the village community has been one of the major factors enabling the Aleut-Eskimo stock to enter into inhospitable areas with success and still retain its over-all unity.

STRUCTURAL REGULARITIES

The simple tabulation of trait inventories of the Aleuts and Eskimos has some limitations in analyzing variants within the over-all culture and in contrasting it with that of the Indians. Cultural traits cannot be easily coerced into comparative tables for such reasons as: (1) some traits have changed greatly and recently while others have changed little, slowly, or long ago; (2) environmental limitations preclude certain traits; (3) cultural interests select or delete others, deletions due to style preferences not always being distinguishable from deletions due to environmental selections; (4) the same traits may be differently patterned in different areas. Aside from the brute similarities of external form which can be easily appreciated in material traits and their uses, it is necessary to know the meaning and the function of the traits to be compared. Thus, on the level of material ethnography, the Aleuts, like all members of the Aleut-Eskimo stock, possess the throwing board. However, the form not only has certain regular distinguishing features such as the uniform breadth of the handle and blade, but the ivory pin is conceived to be a ziphisternum and is thus named; the upper end is conceived as a forehead and bears the name for forehead, the back is painted black and represents fur, while the belly is painted red and represents blood. While the primary function of the throwing board remains everywhere the same, the meanings connected with it probably do not.

The use of anatomical names for the various parts of the throwing board and for other material traits of the Aleuts assumes more significance when it is realized that anatomical concepts and interests form a major orientation in several aspects of Aleut culture. This anatomical orientation, plus other orientations, is as distinctive of Aleuts as is their language. Neither intelligible comparisons nor studies of the process of change can be managed until the form, the meaning and the functions of the traits are known. And, until these are studied, the structural regularities, the themes and patterns of the culture must be neglected or inaccurately conceived.

It is precisely in the field of these major orientations that some of the most significant uniformities of the Aleut-Eskimo culture are to be found. These major orientations, like the linguistic and genetic similarities, testify to the historical unity of this stock and easily distinguish them from the Indians.

The briefest characterization of the Aleut-Eskimo culture is given by Kroeber where he states, "The Eskimo, again, are very sensory, immediate, concrete and discrete in their ethos" (1:606). In contrasting Eskimos with Indians he states, ". . . but their primary and dominant orientation is realistic," and "The cause for this orientation can perhaps be sought in the extraordinary trying circumstances of survival in the Arctic. The Eskimo must be mechanically-minded, able-bodied, manually skillful, and practical" (1:603). In contrasting the use of magic between Eskimos and Melanesians he says of the Eskimo, "They are far more practical, competent with tools, and self reliant" (1:308). The point here is that these same characterizations apply equally well to all the Aleuts, as evidenced in the following quotation, "In common with other members of the Eskimo stock mechanical innovations have played a major part in the remarkably successful adaptation of the Aleuts to their environment. In their case this has often been the result of deliberate comparative experiments. Their culture is directed toward the development of self-sufficient individuals within the framework of a highly cooperative group" (2:84). It is possible to recognize a considerable body of evidence from many different workers which illustrates this uniformity of a pragmatic orientation to the environment, a concentration on technical details of practical importance, and the development of self-sufficiency or self-reliance. Upon these common structural regularities the Aleut division appears to have advanced with reference to the use of deliberate comparative experiments. An appeal is frequently made to superior functional performance as the explanation for a particular practice by the Aleuts. In their traditions they describe such things as a boat race between two villages west of Umnak which was held to decide which method of preparing food, steaming or boiling, was preferable for the development of great wind and endurance. Again, two children were raised in two different fashions to determine what method of child raising would give most satisfactory results. In the development of their extensive anatomical knowledge the resort to empirical investigation is seen in many ways. Persons who died were dissected in an effort to determine the cause of death. Sea otter were dissected as late as 1910–13 for the purposes of true comparative anatomy. The Aleut explanation for the use of the sea otter is that it is most similar to humans and, in fact, it does possess the most morphological similarities of any available sea mammal, as evidenced in the humerus, femur and flat grinding molars. The use of the dead for dissection and the use of their supernatural powers provided by mummification may not be as distinctive as they first appear when more is known about the Eskimos to the east. The Koniags are known to have made use of mummies and may also have built up a body of anatomical knowledge.

Another example of the necessity of knowing the meaning of a trait, and thus being enabled to understand its place in a pattern and of the place of the resulting patterns in a theme or major orientation, is shown in the belief in a supernatural power which resides in the body. In brief, the separate elements may be found among other Eskimo groups, but in the eastern Aleutians they have a particular relationship which may not be duplicated elsewhere. Thus, the discrete practices of joint binding of pubescent girls, the dismemberment of slain enemies, mummification of the honored, joint binding of the widow and the dismemberment of the hawk and owl are all brought together by the belief that the power in the body can be regulated or removed completely. These various practices were employed to either protect the living individuals or enable them to use the power of a person who had suffered corporeal death or for both purposes. It is apparent that the eastern Aleuts do not believe that a person who had power gave it up simply by the act of dying.

In summary there are sufficient uniformities in both the material and the non-material culture to demonstrate the historical unity of Aleut-Eskimo culture. Variations are seen not only in the mechanical innovations but in the structure of the culture as well. The patterning in the culture, the relations of the traits to each other, cannot be known without a thorough knowledge of the form, meaning, function and use of each trait. Aleut-Eskimo culture has placed a premium upon innovation and this in itself constitutes a major characteristic of the culture as well as a major source of Aleut-Eskimo traits.

SUMMARY

The primary purpose of this paper has not been merely to consider new data concerning the problem of Aleut-Eskimo relationships but to consider this problem by means of a more comprehensive method of evaluation. Specifically, this involves a study of those elements which set these people apart as a distinct population, a study of those elements common to all the divisions of the people and, following this, a consideration of the factors of internal change which are primarily responsible for the variations within the stock. Viewed in time depth these changes are manifested racially in the development of a brachycephalic population from an originally mesocephalic population, linguistically by the differentiation into languages and dialects, and in the material culture by the abandonment of the core and blade industry and the innovation of many mechanical adaptations. At the same time it is necessary to appreciate the geographical variants represented by dialect groups, breeding isolates with distinctive morphology and local variants in the overall culture. To those documented examples of change must be added those in the structure of the culture. A catalog of traits, no matter how large and complete, does not take into account the patterning of the traits. Just as the terms Aleut and Eskimo are useful abstractions imposed upon the people and their culture, so it is useful to compare the abstractions of pattern and ethos, as given, for example, by Kroeber. To the extent that these are empirically derived they can be valid and useful. Without the inclusion of these patterns the genius of Aleut-Eskimo culture must receive inadequate attention.

The practical effect of this point of view, the recognition of variability and change within a common framework, is to focus more attention on the processes of change within the people of the Aleut-Eskimo stock and, therefore, to place less reliance upon speculative and unproven suppositions of extraneous migrations from distant peoples or upon premature and factually exiguous suggestions of culture contacts with Asiatic peoples across the Pacific Ocean rather than across Bering Strait. The speculative migrations presuppose the existence of traits, physical and cultural, which have not developed within the culture nor been accepted from their immediate neighbors. Historical evidence indicates that traits have been declared atypical or alien when only a portion of the stock has been selected as a type model, or when only a portion of a complex was known, and that this arbitrary selection has given a false appearance of homogeneity. Traits have been wrenched from their context in part because the context has been so poorly known. Only after the time depth has been more thoroughly explored and the limits of variability of the over-all culture better known can there be profitable comparisons with alien cultures on a sound basis.

Eskimo religion is principally concerned with the "here" and the "now," and only secondarily with the obscure fate of the dead, or with distant nature, or with such questions as the origin of the universe. In essence, Eskimo religion is a set of beliefs and practices, developed, modified, and elaborated over a period of thousands of years, which grew from the world in which the Eskimo lived. If not always so overtly or obviously so, these beliefs were as important to Eskimo survival as were the ulu, *the* umiak, *and the* igloo. *The Eskimo and their relatives, the Aleut, well exemplify the adage that "fantasy is one of the most human of human attributes."*

II Gordon H. Marsh

ESKIMO-ALEUT RELIGION*

This is to be a study of the basic beliefs and their systematization; a study of the religion rather than its techniques.

* Abridged from "A Comparative Survey of Eskimo-Aleut Religion," by G. H. Marsh, in *Anthropological Papers of the University of Alaska*, **3**, 21–36, 1954.

The religion of the Eskimos and Aleuts is essentially a pure animism, i.e., all the powers of the universe are conceived as animistic beings essentially anthropomorphic. Its only non-animistic features are the powers connected with certain amulets, magic spells and chants, and the practice of sorcery.

Eskimo-Aleut religion comprises a set of beliefs about the supernatural plus a body of public rituals and a body of private rituals for dealing therewith. It provides its practitioner with an essentially pragmatic system for treating with the forces of nature so as to control the weather and the food supply, to ensure protection against harm and disease, to provide a means of curing sickness and disorders, and to prognosticate coming events. It arises from an acute introspective analysis of human life and projects a psychic structure into the universe. Its basic assumptions are that the psychic structure of the universe is naturally harmonious and is neutrally or even well-disposed toward men unless irritated and angered by thoughtless negligence or willful disobedience on the part of humans. Thus, men through their own sins are responsible for bringing upon themselves their discomforts, either hunger, harm, or unhappiness. The powers of the universe, in the words of an Iglulik Eskimo quoted by Rasmussen, are seen to keep a right balance between mankind and the rest of the world.

The basic beliefs, structure and mechanisms are the same from the western tip of the Aleutians clear to the eastern shores of Greenland. However, there are two elements found throughout the whole of Alaska but lacking in the Central and Eastern areas, viz., personal guardian spirits and the "persons" of animals, and two elements found in the Central and Eastern Arctic that are largely absent in Alaska, viz., the predominance of female divinities and *tupilait*. One other feature that distinguishes Alaska from the regions to the east is the public ceremonials.

The basic structure of Eskimo-Aleut religion comprises five categories of powers, which are: (1) charms, amulets, talismans and magic formulas; (2) the immortal and perpetually reincarnated souls of men and animals; (3) the "persons" of creatures; (4) the demonic spirits of the earth and air; and (5) the "persons" or spirit-powers directing the universe and forces of nature. All these five categories of powers interact on each other and their system of interaction is the *modus operandi* of the universe or the means whereby humans may exert control over the operation of the universe.

First, to discuss these categories separately.

CHARMS

In most of the Eskimo-Aleut groups the power of charms, talismans, magic formulas and songs seems to be conceived as simply inherent in these objects themselves without the operation of an associated spirit-being. Thus in a technical sense they belong rather to a system of mana and magic than to the animism of the rest of the religious structure. These may represent survivals of an earlier stage of development, since especially the magic spells are thought by the Eskimos to descend from the ancient ancestors who inhabited the world in its primeval epochs when men and animals were all the same and words alone had power. Nevertheless, in western Alaska at least, the charm system has become integrated into the animistic portion of the religion since charm powers are regarded as derived from the "persons" of objects, places or creatures. Likewise with magic songs and to a certain extent also with magic spells. The tendency in Eskimo-Aleut religion to align the magic portions of the system with the animistic is doubtless the logical conclusion of what may be a long prior development.

Charms, consisting of talismans and amulets, magic formulas and songs, are used to provide hunting luck and other desired boons, and to ensure protection from all harms and ills. Practically every Eskimo and Aleut from earliest infancy to his demise possesses a collection of charms, which he has obtained through gift, legacy or personal acquisition. The details of their material content need not concern us here. The practice of sorcery likewise involves almost entirely magic, chiefly incantation or spell-casting, the most potent spells being those that have been passed on through several generations of sorcerers. Sorcery does not seem to have been extensive except in certain areas, and the details do not shed much light on our present discussion. More consideration of *tupilait*, on the other hand, will appear below.

SOULS

Souls belong only to men and animals and are immortal and imperishble. Humans and dogs possess two kinds of souls, a breath-soul and a name-soul. All other animals have only the breath-soul. The various terms designating the breath-soul contain the notion of either breath, life, image, shadow or appearance. This soul is what gives life and what makes a man a man, a bear a bear, and so on. And yet, though souls determine the species to which the body belongs, in subsequent reincarnations they are at will or through the action of other powers interchangeable between animals and people. These souls are variously envisaged by the different Eskimo-Aleut peoples as either a small image of the creature, residing in a certain organ or area of the body, or simply as a life-sized image or a general principle suffusing the whole body. They are invisible except to certain shamans, and have the power to come and go from the body while the latter is still alive. This occurs during sleep, trance, or coma, though usually the prolonged absence of the soul occasions sickness or death. Departed or unincarnated souls of both men and animals have the power to influence other souls, specifically those currently incorporated in live bodies, and hence they can affect the game supply and also the health of humans. They can likewise to a limited extent influence the weather and nature. Souls can also turn into demonic spirits.

For our present discussion we are leaving out the eschatological beliefs.

The personal names of people and dogs constitute for the Eskimos and Aleuts another class of spiritual essences. The name carries with it bodily and mental characteristics—strength, skill, endurance, intelligence, and magic power. All these characteristics are transferred through a name from all previous forebears to the current holder. As a Netsilik Eskimo shaman explained it to Rasmussen, there is behind each person a long line of namesakes guarding him as long as he observes the rules of life. Hence a man often has as many names as possible to protect him, and a woman possesses several names to protect her future sons. Throughout the Eskimo-Aleut region the name is of prime importance in providing a child with the strength to survive the rigors of infancy. In Central and Eastern Arctic it also provides a person with a guardian during his whole life. However, in Alaska, generally the name is only important in adult life for the set of living associates that it provides to an individual through certain fixed types of mutual relationships which accompany names. It is doubtless significant that the words for name are cognate throughout the entire Eskimo and Aleut regions even in Aleut which shares only about a third of its lexicon with the Eskimo languages.

The name-soul actually belongs to a different order from the breath-soul. It seems to function through the breath-soul, primarily for protective purposes. Theoretically it is not immortal, as the disuse of a name would cause the disappearance of that name-soul, and it does not go after death to any special abode of souls nor does it become a demonic spirit. In fundamental nature and function it belongs to the "person" category of spirit-beings that we are about to examine.

"PERSONS"

The class of spirit-beings referred to in the Eskimo tongues as "persons" (*inua, yua, sua, tayaruu*—a word often translated as "its owner") is particularly significant for comparisons between Alaska on the one hand and the Central and Eastern Arctic on the other. The basic class of "persons" of objects and places is a fundamental element in all Eskimo-Aleut areas. All objects, things, or places have, at least in theory, their respective "persons." In practice it is only such objects as obtrude themselves on people's notice for some reason, whose "persons" actually become functional. The "person" of an object is nothing more, from our point of view, than a psychic projection of the object's existence. When the object disappears or is destroyed, its "person" ceases to exist. Thus, the "person" of a fire vanishes when the fire goes out. Or, since in the Eskimo view the "person" of any object is a being, if the "person" can be destroyed, the object itself will thus be eliminated. This portion of their system of belief has applications, in certain regions, in medical practices and sorcery, since every organ or member of the body has its "person" (a concept often misinterpreted by Western commentators as a "soul"), which may depart, thereby causing the associated member to ail or atrophy. "Persons" are not in their nature immortal beings, but it is obvious that the "person" of a cliff, lake, or island, will have from a practical standpoint a permanent existence. Likewise the "person" of something such as grass is not in reality the "person" of a given patch of grass or of a given year's growth of grass, but is in fact what we could describe as the "person" of the idea of grass, and this likewise from a practical standpoint has a perpetual existence.

"Persons" are thus a distinct order of spirit-beings from the immortal souls of men and animals and also from the corps of immortal demonic spirits that we shall discuss presently. This category of spirit-beings represents in the Eskimo-Aleut religious system an animistic and not a manaistic explanation of the operation of the universe in that (a) they are designated by the word meaning "human being," (b) they are envisaged as looking and behaving like humans, and (c) although they act directly upon the material universe, they can also act upon the rest of the spirit-structure of the universe in the same manner as souls and daimons. Their function in the system is largely explicatory, i.e., accidental deaths, disappearances and the like are thereby given a cause. Nevertheless we shall see that especially in Alaska they have a further function.

The significance of this portion of Eskimo-Aleut cosmology lies in the presence of an additional feature of it in Alaska which is absent to the east. In the beliefs of the entire Eskimo-Aleut region of Alaska there are, besides the "persons" of places and objects, also the "persons" of animals and all other non-human creatures. These "persons" of animals are spirit-beings distinct and apart from the souls of animals. The "persons" of animals are envisaged (and also depicted) as humans, while the souls take the form of their respective species. And whereas the souls of animals are the spiritual counterparts of individual creatures, the "persons" of animals are as a matter of fact the spiritual projection of the idea of each type. Thus they are the "persons" of groups or species. The "person" of the walrus, for example, is not the "person" of one specific walrus, but the "person" of the type walrus; in fact, of the ideal walrus. Hence the "persons" of animals have a perpetual existence. Furthermore, since the "person" of any given species of animal is in actuality the "person" of the ideal animal of that species, this animal "person" stands in relation to all the individuals of that species or band as a headman of a human household or community to his fellow members. Therefore this animal "person" is thought to control the activities of all the members of his band or species.

Intimately allied with the Alaskan belief in the "persons" of animals are two other aspects of the religion also lacking in the Central and Eastern Eskimo regions. These are (1) the concept of personal guardian spirits belonging to each and every member of the community, with the rituals and customs attendant on this concept; and (2) public communal ceremonies aimed at establishing cordial relations between the people and the "persons" of animals, and also between the "persons" of animals, the hunting paraphernalia, and the souls of animals. The great bulk, if not the totality of personal guardian spirits, are drawn from the category of "person"-spirits, chiefly from the "persons" of animals (mammals, birds, fish, and invertebrates), with a rare one from the "persons" of plants or of inanimate objects like qayaqs. Personal guardian spirits, not to be confused with shamans' tutelary spirits, provide their owners with hunting luck, protection against harm and danger, and power in combat. The methods of securing guardian spirits are varied and often multiple, involving both individual acquisition and legacy. The public religious ceremonials centered around the "persons" of animals (and including the "persons" of the universe as well) are the bladder-festivals of western Alaska, similar festivals of the Aleutians and south coast, the sitting-ceremony of Point Hope, and certain portions of the memorial feasts for the dead.

From the mouth of the Mackenzie east to Greenland we find nothing of the "persons" of animals in the religious system. Instead we find that individual guardian powers—those that supply each human prowess and luck in obtaining game and protection from evil—are centered in charms and the name-soul. The mechanism of charms exists throughout Eskimo-Aleut society and is simply put into more extensive practice in the Central and Eastern areas. Because life in these regions is so much more precarious than in Alaska, these Eskimos have had to utilize to the extreme certain means of protection and assurance and methods of manipulating the universe which are supplied by their religious traditions. Hence the traditional prescriptions and injunctions are more strictly observed, and the number and variety of amulets and charms is more extensive. These Eskimos thus have greater recourse to the magical portions of their religion for the individual's protective powers. The Alaskan Eskimos and Aleuts on the other hand have derived the bulk of their guardian powers from the animistic portions of their religion. Even the charms and amulets have been largely integrated into the "person" category in much of Alaska. The majority of the talismans in Nunivak Island, for example, are simply effigies of the tutelary animal "persons" with which each individual is in relation, and power songs are likewise acquired from and obtain their effectiveness from the "person" guardian spirits.

The name-soul, which is of such importance among the Central and Eastern Eskimos, must from a functional point of view be regarded as more closely allied to the "person" category than to the categories of immortal spirit-beings. The name is really the "person" of humans (and dogs). Like the "persons" of animals it is not the "person" of an individual creature but that of a band or species. In the case of humans (and also dogs) this band is actually an arbitrary lineage established through the transmission of the name, a sort of "nominal" rather than a genealogical clan.

There are two other features from the Central and Eastern Eskimos that it seems to me we must juxtapose with the Alaskan concept of the "persons" of animals. The first of these is the *tupilak*. A *tupilak* is always a grotesque animal figure fabricated out of parts of several creatures by a sorcerer for the purpose of working harm on someone at a distance. By magic incantations the sorcerer induces life into his *tupilak* and then subsequently nourishes it to make it grow, usually putting it into the sea where it can feed itself and whence it returns to prey upon its intended victim. If this were all, one would ask wherein lies the relation to the Alaskan concept of the "persons" of animals. But it happens that the Central and Eastern Eskimo word *tupilak* is directly cognate with the word used for the personal guardian spirit in the Inyupik-speaking regions of Alaska about Bering Strait. This word is *tupitkaq*. There must therefore by an historical connection between the *tupilak* mechanism of the east and the guardian-spirit complex of the west. I am prepared to suggest that this historical connection lies in the loss of the guardian-spirit complex among the Eskimos that peopled the Central and Eastern Arctic with the consequent remodeling or assimilation of the concept of "persons" of animals into the *tupilak* mechanism. The *tupilak* mechanism is doubtless also ancient in the prehistory of the Eskimo-Aleut stock as it is shared by several Eskimo, northwest coast Indian and Paleo-Siberian groups, but it belongs to the magical stratum of their religious history along with the charm system and the tabu system. At Point Hope, for instance, the making of grotesque effigies for sorcery is practised, where the guardian-spirit complex also exists. Such an effigy is called *kikituk*. What I am suggesting here is that the guardian-spirit system, or something basic to it, is likewise old in Eskimo-Aleut prehistory, though this belongs to the animistic stratum of the religion. The eastern *tupilak* is an animal effigy associated with specific power. The western *tupitkaq* is also an effigy of the guardian spirit or a mask or costume which the owner dons to transform himself into his guardian to acquire its powers. The common element is the fabricated representation of an animal spirit-power. In Siberia the grotesque animals sent by a sorcerer to wreak vengeance do not require the concoction of an effigy since the magic incantations will of themselves bring the monster into being.

The personal guardian-spirit complex is of course well exemplified among the northwest coast Indian groups, in a system very comparable to that of the Alaskan Eskimos and Aleuts. Among Paleo-Siberian peoples, the feature most closely resembling the personal guardian spirit derived from the "persons" of animals is the *pejul* of the Yukaghir. Although the Yukaghir *pejul* is actually the spirit-protector of a band or species of animals and not a human being, it is by an intimate association with a given *pejul* that a given Yukaghir hunter obtains his hunting luck and his proper relation to his animal food supply. The other Paleo-Siberian peoples—Chukchi, Koryak, and Kamchadal—possess a system similar to that of the Central and Eastern Eskimos, in which each individual's personal fortune and protection come largely from his ancestors and from powers derived from fetishes, talismans, and incantations. It is therefore extremely noteworthy, in comparisons with the Paleo-Siberians, that the Alaskan system has its closest parallels among the Yukaghir, whereas the Central and Eastern Eskimo system seems most allied to that of the Luorawedlan-speaking group.

The second item of comparison between the Eastern and the Alaskan Eskimos is contained in an incidental bit of information from the Polar Eskimos of northwest Greenland, which points toward another remnant of the guardian-spirit system in an area where this latter seems to be lacking. We read in Kroeber's account that each Eskimo possesses, in addition to a breath-soul and a name-soul, another which is described as an "evil soul," the *angiyang*. The "evil soul" is envisaged as a bird and is said to cause sickness by pecking its host. Also the "evil soul" dies when the person dies. Thus the *angiyang* appears to be a negative guardian spirit, or at least one more likely to work harm than good. This may give us a clue to the disappearance of the guardian-spirit complex in the Central and Eastern areas. With the extreme rigor of life in the Central Arctic, the harmful effects of nature are more vivid than the beneficial. This is apparent in the attitude of the Central Eskimos toward the universe, whose powers are easily angered so that human life becomes a constant vigil against antagonizing and toward appeasing such readily irritable beings. Under such an attitude, the guardian spirit could easily have become the obverse of what it originally was, now becoming a being needing constantly to be humored and propitiated like the other spirit-beings of the universe, and more liable to turn upon its host for failure to behave properly than to assist him when he does follow the straight and narrow path. Another factor in the religion of the Central and Eastern Eskimos which must also have operated toward the displacement of the guardian-spirit complex is the emphasis on dealing with the sources of food and the forces of nature through the controlling deities of the universe, rather than the guardian-spirit mechanism of treating directly with the game animals. This shift in emphasis accompanied the rise of the shaman in the Central and Eastern culture to the position of chief specialized manipulator of the powers of the world. The rest of the members of the community were thus relegated to the use solely of the magical mechanisms of their religious system. We also see the replacement of almost all public ceremonials in which the whole community actively participates in favor of the shaman seance at which the public become largely passive participants. There may originally even have been active proselytizing by shamans against the guardian-spirit complex.

DEMONIC SPIRITS

The fourth set of spirit-powers in the Eskimo-Aleut cosmology are the demonic spirits or daimons. These inhabit all parts of the world away from human habitations, and, although entirely non-corporeal, are mobile and live in bands like humans, hunting, marrying and reproducing. They are conceived as monstrous and grotesque people and animals. Their closest link in the rest of the cosmological system is with the souls of men and animals. Many of them, if not all, are actually thought to have arisen from human and animal souls mistreated by people, and they tend to be inimically inclined toward humans. Though of a nebulous substance they can make themselves visible to men, most commonly to shamans. From their ranks are derived the shamans' tutelaries. Most of them come in colonies of all one kind with specific habitats. In a number of the Eskimo areas their association with the forces of nature and their ubiquity have produced their designation as a category as "persons of the weather or world," *silap inui*, although they work primarily on people and animals. A number of types have widespread extension throughout Eskimo-Aleut regions. Dwarfs and giants seem to be universal, though the latter are relatively unimportant. The former are often described with pointed heads, great strength and agility, and remarkable hunting powers. Half-people and -animals are common, and cannibal women are not rare. Beings with pinchers on their heads constitute a motif reported from both Alaska and Greenland. Nonetheless their forms are legion, limited only by the shamans' powers of imagination.

The Eskimo name for demonic spirit from Greenland clear to the mouth of the Kuskokwim is some variation of the word *tunraq*. From Nunivak Island and the Chugach of the south coast of Alaska we find the terms *kalla* and *kalhaaq/kalhagaq*, a word perhaps to be compared to Chukchi *kele* and Koryak *kala*. The Kanyagh word is *iggaq* and the Aleut is *qugar*. The term for shaman in southern and southwestern Alaska, including the Aleutians, means, "the one who has a daimon." The more widespread Eskimo term, that ranges from the Kuskokwim

River to Greenland, is *angatlkuq/angatkuq/angakkuq.* The daimon-complex within the Eskimo-Aleut religious structure is, like the concepts concerning the immortal souls of men and animals, one of the components of the system that shows the least variability from one end of the range to the other.

"PERSONS" OF THE UNIVERSE

The last category in the Eskimo-Aleut hierarchy of powers are the spirit-powers controlling the forces of nature. There is quite some diversity in this part of their religious structure. One common basic element seems to be the conception of the chief powers of the sky and upper atmosphere as masculine and those of the land and sea as feminine, also the tendency for each primary power to have a secondary associate or consort of the opposite sex. There is in this portion of the religion, as in the portion comprising the lesser "person" powers, a difference between the Alaskan area on the one hand and the Central and Eastern on the other. The essence of this difference is the fact that in Alaska the principal world power is masculine, whereas in the Central area it is feminine, while in Labrador and Greenland we again encounter a chief male power or a division of jurisdiction between a male and a female power.

Throughout the Alaskan area male divinities are paramount. The "person of the world, sky or atmosphere," *lham sua,* and the Moon-man are the prime powers in this category. In the various areas it is not possible to determine from the information whether these are two separate divinities or two aspects of the same divinity. On Nunivak, for instance, *lham sua,* "the person of the world," seems to control the forces of nature, the game supply and the souls of men and animals, while *lham inga* "the eye of the world" (? a name for the Moon-man), watches over the observance of the traditional prescriptions and injunctions. Among the Chugach Eskimos the "person of the sky," *lham cua,* is associated with the sun, though the conception of him is vague and connected chiefly with control of the weather. In the Aleutians the paramount divinity was called *agudar* or *agurur,* a name meaning "creator" (now used for the Christian God), and he also appears to have been related to the sun. His functions, as indicated in the fragmentary evidence still available, were concerned with hunting luck, protection from harm, and the reincarnation of souls. At Point Hope the first and chief sacred image hung up at the sitting-ceremony was the "daylight," and the Moon was prayed to for new life and hunting luck, but the concepts of a primary divinity are otherwise extremely vague in the modern evidence. In Alaska it is clear that, except as a regulator of the general forces of nature and of the reincarnation of souls and as a vague source of sanction for the traditional rules of life, the functions of a central deity were relatively unimportant. This is because of the fact that the people dealt more immediately and directly with the powers controlling their food supply through the personal guardian spirits, through the system of private rituals (i.e., the traditional prescriptions and injunctions), through the performance of public ceremonies, and to a lesser extent through the operations of shamans and the use of charms. And of course for the Alaskan Eskimos and Aleuts, as for all other Eskimos, the divinities had no special relation to the mechanisms for treating maladies and injuries, nor for divination.

From widely separated areas in Alaska we encounter the concept of certain female powers of the world in addition to the male ones. Among the Chugach the "person of the sea," *imam sua*, and the "person of the land," *nunam sua*, are both women. The latter influences the land animals, the former those of the sea and also gales. These two powers are, however, in their scope and function more like the "persons" of animals and objects, and individuals can acquire their services as personal guardian spirits. The Aleuts also have a "person of the sea," *alarum tayaruu* or *alarum isuu*, whose sex, however, is not indicated. This being does not seem to be important in their cosmology and is, rather, a grotesque creature with long hair, which if seen by people portends danger at sea. From Point Hope on the other hand, we possess the account of a ceremony connected with the spring whale hunt, in which a shaman goes down through the shore crack in the ice to the undersea whale-hunting camp of a tribe of spirit beings termed *itiviyai*. At this camp is a man with long ears who hears everything said in Tigara village. There is also a man (it is not specified whether he is the same as the other man) with a tail like a dog, who lives with his wife. This man is said to go up into the air to the source of the weather to change the wind to the north. His wife, whose name is *nirivik* "the food-place or -dish" (the same name used in Greenland for the Old Woman of the Sea), goes out to make the sea calm. It is obvious that here these two beings, the man and his wife, are only subsidiary powers in the cosmology of the Tikirarmiut. Nevertheless their association with the male power of the atmosphere and the female power of the sea so important in the Central and Eastern cosmology should not be overlooked.

The Eskimos of the Central Arctic, from the mouth of the Mackenzie

River to Baffin Island, are unique among all Eskimo-Aleut peoples in conceiving one dominant power of the universe which is feminine. For the coastal groups this is the Old Woman of the Sea, variously designated as Nuliayuk "little wife" by the Mackenzie and Netsilik Eskimos, as "That terrible one or woman down there below" by the Copper and Iglulik Eskimos, as Siitna by the Baffin Islanders, and with one or two other names also known from these regions. She is the mother of the sea-mammals (though whales are seldom included) in that they originated from her cut-off finger joints. She therefore controls all the sea animals, and to a certain extent also the land animals. She likewise dominates the male powers of the universe who exist along with her, namely the Moon-man and the Weather (*Sila* or *Naarsuk*). Furthermore she is the enforcer, if not the originator, of the traditional prescriptions and injunctions—those traditional private rituals described by the Eskimos as "the rules of life." Actually the rules with which she is concerned are those pertaining to unclean women, those associated with game and the various products of sea and land, and those connected with ritual cleanliness, dietary restrictions and the like. It seems that the rituals for the dead, on the other hand, are not part of the province of the Old Woman of the Sea. She is thus paramount over that portion of the religious system that is directed toward ensurance of the food supply and protection against danger while obtaining food. It is in this capacity that she also directs the weather by getting the "person of the weather," *Sila* or *Silap inua,* to do her bidding.

Among several of the Central Eskimo groups there is in addition to the Old Woman of the Sea a "mother of the caribou," who is, interestingly enough, also associated with the walrus. Except for the account of her fashioning the caribou she is a very indistinct personage in the traditions as actually preserved and has pretty well been assimiliated to the Old Woman of the Sea. Notwithstanding the vague characterization of the "mother of the caribou," what appears to me most noteworthy is that there exists the tradition of a separate female spirit-power of the land obviously originally distinct from the female power of the sea. Among the Caribou Eskimos the setup is even more unique than that of the other Central Eskimo peoples. They being practically entirely an inland-dwelling population, we find, needless to say, that the chief female divinity is the "mother of the caribou," called *Pinga* or *Pivzuma*. Actually Pinga is not conceived as the mother of the caribou as such, nor is there any legend of the origin of animals. She is simply the guardian of all life both man and animal. She has in fact taken over the position of *Hila* "the atmosphere" and is thus associated with the upper regions as well as the earth. She reincarnates the souls of men and animals into new bodies, and is the executor of the sanctions on the rules of life in the same manner as the Old Woman of the Sea for the coastal Eskimos. However, unlike her coastal counterpart she never interferes with the animals. Although *Pinga* has largely usurped the realm of *Hila* "the atmosphere," and is often confused with him, the latter male deity retains a few of his ancient characteristics. He is still in some way chief of the demonic spirits, since it is to his pity that the shamans exhibit themselves through exposure when seeking their tutelary spirits, though even in this function he has been supplanted by *Pinga* in the conception of some of the Caribou Eskimos. The Moon-man occupies also a small place in Caribou Eskimo cosmology as a servant of *Pinga*. He it is who during the dark of the moon brings human souls down to *Pinga* to be reincarnated either as men or animals. Thus we see that although the Caribou Eskimos are unique among the Central Eskimos in the importance of their female deity, they do not diverge significantly from the basic cosmology of that area. They have simply carried to a greater extreme the development characteristic of the Central Arctic in relegating practically all powers to a single chief female divinity.

When we turn to the Eastern Eskimo areas—Labrador and Greenland—we encounter again important male powers of the universe. For most of Labrador we learn of a female deity, *Superguksoak,* who rules the land animals, and a male deity, her husband, *Turngarsoak,* "the chief daimon," who rules the sea animals and also the spirit world. In the northern and northwestern parts of the Labrador Peninsula *Turngarsoak* (or *Tungarsuk*) likewise controls the caribou and lives in the mountains or in caves as a huge white bear. Around Cape Chidley the Old Woman of the Sea reappears in the cosmology, but as a subsidiary power who rules the sea beasts and receives offerings thrown into the water. Thus everywhere throughout Labrador, as far as our somewhat scanty information goes, the paramount power of the world is a male divinity, with a subsidiary female divinity in control of only one province, either the land or the sea.

In Greenland the Old Woman of the Sea recurs under the name *Nirivik* or *Nirrivik* meaning "the food-place or food-dish," a name we also encountered at Point Hope which may thus be the old Thule Culture designation of this female deity. She occupies in Greenland the same position in the cosmology as in the Central Arctic, i.e., she governs the food supply and all the traditional rules of life connected with its ensurance. She shares control of the spirit-powers of the universe with *Turngarsuk* who rules the realm of the demonic spirits and with the Moon who plays a minor role as chief of the skyland in a vague way associated with the souls of men and with hunting luck. Greenland thus falls closer than Labrador to the cosmological pattern of the Central Eskimos.

We may conclude these observations on the Eskimo-Aleut spirit powers of the universe by hazarding a reconstruction of the basic pattern from which the features of the various areas seem to have diverged. The following elements are common to all the areas and may thus be taken to be aboriginal: (1) The controlling powers of the universe are divided into male powers for the atmosphere and sky and female powers for the sea and land. In this concept the ancestors of the Eskimos and Aleuts resembled the Chinese, not to mention many other peoples. (2) Perhaps originally each of these spirit-powers also had a consort or counterpart of the opposite sex, though these are seldom represented in Alaskan mythology. In the Central and Eastern Eskimo areas these counterparts perform a merely complementary or counterbalancing function. The Moon has his sister the Sun, and also his wife or female relative the Disemboweler. The Atmosphere (*Sila* or *Naarsuk*) has a vague associate in the female "person of the blizzard or sharp ice." *Turngarsoak* in Labrador has his wife *Superquksoak*. The Old Woman of the Sea has her husband the Dog and her father the Punisher. The Caribou Eskimo *Pinga* shares certain of her functions with the male power of the weather *Hila*. This concept of an element of the opposite sex accompanying the dominant powers of the universe is paralleled in China, not to mention India also. (3) The spirit-powers of the universe are "persons" controlling specific realms of the cosmos. The functional elements of the system appear to be these: (a) The Moon was the ruler of the skyland and of the souls of men and animals, in which capacity he could influence abundance of game and fertility in women; (b) the Person of the Atmosphere/World controlled the meteoric elements and was chief of the demonic spirits, who are often lumped together as *silap inui*, "the persons of the atmosphere/world"; (c) the Person of the Sea, was a female who had dominion over the sea and its creatures both in their bodily and spirit forms; (d) the Person of the Land, was a female whose sway comprehended the elements and creatures of the Land. From this point of view the most archaic situation is preserved among the Chugach Eskimos of Alaska's south coast. We need not assume *à priori*, however, that the Moon and the Atmosphere were separate distinct powers in the era of the common ancestors of the Eskimos and Aleuts. Nor need we assume that the "persons" of both sea and land were aboriginally distinguished. This division on the basis of specialty may have taken place subsequent to the separation of some of the Eskimo and Aleut groups, which would account for the diversity. It is just as possible that one male power of the upper regions originally controlled the sky, the atmosphere, souls, and daimons, while one female power of the earth ruled the land, the sea, and the underworld. The greatest degree of specialization actually occurs in the Central Arctic where the above four basic functions are relegated to four more or less separate spirit beings. In Alaska the distinction between the Moon and the Atmosphere is never very clear. In the Central Arctic the distinction between the Persons of Sea and Land is vague. Among the Caribou Eskimos, in Labrador and in Greenland the people distinguish in essence only two world powers, whereas in the Aleutians these all appear to have been reduced to one.

Whether the aboriginal ancestors of the Eskimo-Aleut stock started with four world powers or with two (or even with three like the Yukaghir), we see two divergent strains of realignment. In Alaska with the emphasis on the personal guardian-spirit complex whereby the people dealt with their sources of food and protection directly with the more immediate spirit-powers that controlled these, the universal spirit-powers play a secondary role. In the Central and Eastern Arctic, on the other hand, where the shaman-seance complex was emphasized, the governing powers of the world occupy the chief position, and the shamans become the sole specialist operators who may treat with these. These two divergent developments, with their associated features, constitute the essential difference in the religious systems of the Alaskan Eskimo-Aleuts on the one hand and the Central and Eastern Eskimos on the other.

RULES OF LIFE

A word about the private rituals, the so-called rules of life, in relation to the spirit-powers of the world. These prescriptions and injunctions in reality receive their fundamental sanction through being traditional. They are stated to be the rules discovered to be effective by the ancestors and hence they are followed. Yet this sanction from tradition has been reinforced by a sanction from the cosmological structure as well. This is particularly notable in the Central and Eastern Arctic, where these injunctions are more strict, where they derive their rationale from the preferences of the chief female deity, and where their enforcement, not to say elaboration, depends on the supervision of the shamans. Since the greatest onus of these observances falls upon the women, we may admire the psychological tour de force of these Eskimos in specifying the obligation as coming from a female divine power. It is probable that the Moon as the guardian of souls of men and animals was more anciently the supervisor of these rules since their infringement affects first and foremost these souls, and is in fact the main cause for the latter's becoming demonic spirits. This function the Moon (or sometimes the Person of the Atmosphere) still performs, both in Alaska and in the Central Arctic. However, the Moon is now not the source of sanction but simply an admonisher in the latter region. In Alaska the sanction usually comes from the tradition which has established not only the prescriptions themselves but also the harm to both the individual and to the community that will result from infraction of each custom. Where the sanctions for the traditional rules of life have been incorporated into the cosmological system, we are justified in surmising, I believe, that this is an element of the complex that goes with the development of the shaman into the specialized religious practitioner for the community, a complex that I would venture to suggest may have entered Alaska from Siberia long subsequent to the arrival of the first proto-Eskimo-Aleut immigrants, probably at the period just prior to the eastward spread of the ancestors of the Thule culture.

<hr/>

All human societies provide controls to enforce desired behavior. These "sanctions," as they are sometimes called, may be positive or negative, formal or informal, sacred or secular. Law, as we know it, is a set of written directives and prescriptions regulating sanctions behind which stands the force of the entire society. It is an attribute of more complex societies. Simple societies of the band or tribal type tend to have few if any formal sanctions, but usually have an extensive system of informal and sacred ones. In such societies each individual, in conjunction with relatives sympathetic to his cause, is responsible for pressing his own case; any individual, then, may serve as prosecutor, judge, or executioner during his lifetime.

The following selection by Spencer shows a simple society dealing with its common situations: wife-stealing, witchcraft, adultery, the "bully," and so on.

12   *Robert F. Spencer*

ESKIMO CUSTOMARY LAW*

A yardstick by which to measure social behavior, social controls, and individual responsibility is best provided by an analysis of actions which deviate from the social norm. Even though, like many other primitive groups, the Eskimo of northern Alaska lacked an elaborated system of legal procedures, there was, nonetheless, a strong sense of customary sanctions, resulting in patterned ways of dealing with the deviant. It is clear that the primary mechanism of social control lay in the family, the solidarity of the family being defined and enhanced by the strong sense of collective responsibility. Properly speaking, no crimes could be said to exist; offenses of any kind related to interfamily disputes. These relate almost exclusively to murder. Sorcery, likewise, might be regarded as significant in interfamily quarrels, but this was de facto murder.

The causes for murder were several. Any offense, real or imaginary, by one individual against another might result in bloodshed and so, by the regulation of collective responsibility, involve the families of the two disputants. In the main, however, offenses relating to property would not result in killing. If a man were cheated, if some of his property were stolen, if a piece of property were wantonly destroyed, the injured party had only to air his complaints to the community at large and to allow public opinion to pass on the merits of his claim. His satisfaction thus lay in obtaining a balance of public opinion in his own favor; only in the rarest instances would he seek further retribution.

This can best be illustrated by example: When, at Barrow, there was the general breakup of the reindeer herds and the collapse of the industry, one of the men who had received government training as a

---

* Excerpt from "The North Alaskan Eskimo: a Study in Ecology and Society," by R. F. Spencer, in *Smithsonian Institution, Bureau of American Ethnology, Bulletin 171*, 97–121, 1959.

herdsman became involved in a dispute with a family which had lost a good many head of deer. Failing to understand the herding system and the governmental policies relating to it, the family, not surprisingly, attached blame to the herdsman. When he proved unable to give them satisfaction, the woman of the family destroyed a umiak belonging to him, cutting the skins with her ulu, and breaking the frame. He might have gone, at this period, to the United States Marshal and demanded retribution. Instead, however, he told anyone in the community who would listen what the woman had done, at the same time pointing up his own virtuous patience in the matter and saying that, although he had been wrongfully treated, he would take no action. Since the reindeer herding was a sore spot at this time, it is doubtful that the herdsman got the community support which he wished. Behavior of this kind may be noted for the earlier culture as well. It was unusual for an offended party, whether the injury were real or fancied, to do more than to destroy property. Nor does the litigation seem to have gone further than to call for a judgment of public opinion. Offenses arising between partners often followed a similar pattern and resulted in the end of the partnership.

The misanthropic person, and it is clear that there were such, who made a practice of taking petty vengeance on others by damaging or destroying their property, was marked for death. In this case, a family involvement was inevitable. Here again is encountered the "bully," the nonconformist personality. How far such an individual could go in violating public opinion was variable and depended on the amount of backing he could get from family, or from such associations as his crew or with the supernatural. A long-suffering community would put up with such an individual over a long period of time, each person being anxious to avoid "trouble" and submitting patiently to his irascible antisocial behavior. At last, however, when his backing became less strong or when his unpleasantness reached a peak, he might be murdered. And here again, public opinion would decide the legitimacy of a claim of vengeance. Not that the community could prevent a feud, but members of families other than the two involved might take occasion to point up to the dead man's kin that the situation was now better for all concerned. It frequently happened that the murderer would present himself unarmed before the family of his victim and invite their vengeance. If they demurred, not killing the murderer on the spot, it would be unusual for them to claim later vengeance. Nor would public opinion support them if they did.

The blood feud was thus not necessarily a perennial thing. When it arose within a community, it could usually be quickly settled and forgotten. More frequently, it would continue between communities, the relatives of a murdered man in other groups or settlements being less concerned with the justification for homicide and more eager to keep the idea of vengeance to the fore. This serves to explain the attitude toward the stranger; he was treated with hostility because of the possibility of his involvement in a remote murder-feud situation. But within the group, the justification of a homicide was important. Even if crime as such could be said not to exist, the recidivist murderer was regarded as a criminal menace. He was put out of the way, not, it must be mentioned, by group action, but rather by being killed by an individual. The fact that the recidivist murderer could occur in the society is explainable only because no one, at the first murder, was willing to take action.

But killings arose less because of antisocial behavior relating to food and personal property than because of sexual involvements. Sexual rights were de facto property rights and it was this area which provided a strong motivation for action. The stolen wife, the disrupted betrothal, the love triangle—all might lead to ultimate homicide. In addition, strife and discord could arise in rape, in the mistreatment of a a wife by a husband, or again, in the sexual appetites of the "bully." Adultery, too, was a cause for dispute, particularly if an affair were protracted. Again, however, adultery is less easy to define; a husband might beat an unfaithful wife but it is apparent that he inclined to take no action against her lover unless emotional problems arose to create additional difficulties. The majority of cases collected point to legalistic involvements over sex. Indeed, the Eskimo say of themselves: "It's always the woman who causes the trouble."

The nature of collective responsibility, the solidarity of the family system, and the relations of dispute to the group or community at large are best illustrated by the actual cases. Older informants recall the details of these quite vividly, giving names and specific particulars of events which may have taken place a century and more ago. While a selection such as the following cannot cover all aspects of customary law, sufficient is given to throw the nature of family and community solidarity and interpersonal relations into somewhat sharper perspective. It is apparent that some of these instances have become classic and are recalled for their dramatic appeal, others are more recent.

CASE A

There was a man named Masagaroak who lived to the north of Brower's station. He had the reputation of a drunkard, having learned to distill flour and molasses. One day, he came down from the whaling station and was quite drunk. He made for one of the houses in Utkeaaɣvik, looking for a woman he knew. The woman was Kavenaceaq, wife of a man named Pukuk. The couple had an adopted daughter and shared a house with Pukuk's brother, Uweeguraq, and his family. When Masagaroak entered the house shared by these two families, he asked for a drink. Everyone in the house was frightened and the women ran outside. A relative of Pukuk, a man named Ilʸuusiɣiroak, came in to see what the row was about. Masagaroak grabbed him by the hair and banged his head against the posts of the house. As soon as he let go, all ran out of the house, leaving Masagaroak alone. When all were outside, they discovered that the baby, the adopted child of Pukuk, had been left with Masagaroak alone. They feared that he would harm the child but they were all afraid to go into the house while he was there. Actually, he lay down on the floor and fell asleep.

But meanwhile, Pukuk and Ilʸuusiɣiroak debated what to do. Since incidents like this had happened before, it was decided that it would be best to kill Masagaroak. They agreed that Pukuk would get Masagaroak out of the house and that Ilʸuusiɣiroak would kill him when he came outside. Pukuk went back inside his own house, awakening Masagaroak, who by now docilely agreed to leave. As he stumbled back toward his own house, Pukuk followed him at a distance. By the time Masagaroak reached the ravine, his head had cleared somewhat and he walked without staggering. At the ravine, he met Ilʸuusiɣiroak. The latter said: "Are you Masagaroak?" Knowing what was intended, Masagaroak began to run. Ilʸuusiɣiroak waited a moment and then raised his rifle and shot Masagaroak in the back.

This Ilʸuusiɣiroak was a shaman of great power. Masagaroak had four brothers living in Utkeaaɣvik. They swore revenge but were fearful of the power of Ilʸuusiɣiroak. They did go about saying that they would get their revenge. Some time later, the four were camped with their families at one of the fishing stations. It happened that Ilʸuusiɣiroak passed by that place. When he saw them, he came over to them and said: "I hèar that you wish to kill me; if you want to do so, kill me now," and he handed them his rifle. They stood looking at him and made no reply. He then picked up his gun and went away. The matter was not mentioned by them after this and the trouble between them was over.

When one of the sisters of Masagaroak heard what her brothers had done, of their failure to take advantage of the opportunity for vengeance, she was furious. She went about saying that she would kill Ilᵞuusiɣiroak. But she, too, was afraid of his power and made no attempt against him.

Everyone at Utkeaaɣvik thought that Masagaroak had been justly treated and had got no more than his actions deserved. Opinion was strong against carrying the feud further.

CASE B

Payyaq was a man of the Nuunamiut. He was "crazy" and killed many people. He had committed several murders among the inland people. At one time, during a food shortage, he had murdered a whole family and taken their food. Since the family was camped out alone, he was not suspected. On a later occasion, however, he murdered another family, and his activities became known.

A man named Tuvli, despite public opinion, had married two women, a mother and daughter. In the family of Tuvli was also an adolescent girl who had been adopted by the older wife. This girl had been promised as a wife to Qiwaq, from whom this narration was obtained. Tuvli had lived at Utkeaaɣvik with his family and Qiwaq had visited them there. He had had sexual relations with the girl but had not yet settled down with her. Tuvli also had had sexual relations with his wife's adopted daughter and was somewhat opposed to her marriage with Qiwaq. It was for this reason that he took his two wives and his wife's adopted daughter inland, hoping that Qiwaq would marry someone else.

As Tuvli and his family were camped, Payyaq arrived. Tuvli himself was out hunting at the time and the three women were in the camp alone. The younger wife was pregnant and was, in fact, just getting ready to enter the birth hut for her confinement when Payyaq arrived on the scene. He first went into the tent and murdered the older woman. Then he came out to the birth hut and called the younger wife out. When she came out, he killed her. The adolescent girl, meanwhile, ran away and escaped the killer.

When Payyaq had killed the two women, as well as two younger children who were with the group, he sat down to await Tuvli. As soon as the latter arrived, Payyaq persuaded him to go to the birth hut, perhaps by saying that the younger wife was having her child. As Tuvli turned, evidently to investigate, Payyaq drove an arrow through his back and killed him.

Then Payyaq became aware of the girl's tracks leading away from the encampment. He followed them and succeeded in tracking her down. He did not kill her but kept her with him thereafter, marrying her in effect, in that he demanded work from her and had sexual relations with her. The couple now moved away from the camp where the murders took place and settled down among some others. Payyaq kept close guard on his wife to see that she talked to no one.

But it became evident to the others in the encampment that Payyaq was not using the heads of the animals he killed. People commented on the fact that caribou heads were piled up near his tent. They then remembered that he had a personal taboo on using the heads of animals for some time after he had killed a person. This was, in fact, a not unusual personal prohibition. Hence, although they recognized that he had taken a human life, they did not know who his victim was. As people began to wonder about it, Payyaq became aware of their gossip and left, taking his wife down to Utkeaaɣvik.

At Utkeaaɣvik there lived Iilʸaveraq, brother of Tuvli. He had for some time been expecting his brother and his sisters-in-law. He was beginning to be rather concerned at their failure to appear. When Payyaq came, bringing with him the adopted daughter of Tuvli's wife, Iilʸ-averaq guessed what had happened. Awaiting his opportunity, he finally got the girl alone and learned from her of Payyaq's murders. He then attempted to get help against Payyaq. He enlisted his own kinsmen but also asked help of others, largely to determine on what kind of community support he could count. He approached Qiwaq, for example, to enlist his aid in killing Payyaq. Qiwaq, although he had lost the girl whom he had desired as his wife, refused to help. The problem arose because Payyaq was on the alert. He was a man of tremendous strength and reputedly had considerable supernatural power. He bullied and blustered his way about the community, intimidating everyone, and threatening to kill Iilʸaveraq. The latter, to whom everyone looked to avenge his brother Tuvli, was extremely hesitant to take action. But community sentiment began to build up in favor of Iilʸaveraq. As Payyaq became more and more troublesome with his bullying, it was feared that he would do other violence. Although he and his wife spent the winter at Utkeaaүvik, it was not until spring that anything definite could be done.

After the spring whaling, nalukataq was held and with it the football game. Payyaq played in the game. The men who played with him, led by Iilᵞaveraq, knocked him down and trussed him up. Then they picked him up and began to carry him over to the karigi called Serelᵞuara-amiut. As they were carrying him, he began in a loud voice to call to his mother. At this, several of the men in the procession became frightened and ran away, it being known that Payyaq's mother was dead. Iilᵞave-raq, however, was too far committed to abandon his purpose. He continued to drag Payyaq up to the karigi. When they got there, Payyaq was laid before the karigi door and Iilᵞaveraq cut his throat.

When he had killed Payyaq, he went into the karigi and brought out the oil which had drained from the lamp there. This he poured on the dead man's head to allay the supernatural powers of his victim. Then he cut off the little fingers of the corpse and thrust them into its mouth. The other men came to drag the body away.

Even though Payyaq had some supporters in the community, no one came to his defense and the matter ended there. The facts about the murder of Tuvli became known. This, together with his unpleasantness in the community, was sufficient to prevent any further retaliatory action. Qiwaq thought then of taking over the dead Payyaq's wife. He decided against it, however, and the girl married another man.

CASE C

There was a man at Utkeaaүvik named Kayaakpuq who was married to an attractive woman named Kallikcuk. Another man, Tiguaceak by name, desired this woman even though he had a wife of his own. She responded to his suit and would meet him from time to time. She would pretend that she was menstruating and would leave the community. Some distance away she would join her lover. After a time, Kayaakpuq, discovering the affair, got his bow and attempted to kill his rival. Tiguaceak, however, was warned by his relatives and carried his own bow. The two men exchanged a volley of arrows but each missed the other. When this duel occurred, Kallikcuk left her husband and went to live in the house of Tiguaceak as his second wife. From time to time, she would go back to her former husband and have sexual relations with him. People in the community said: "This isn't right; this doesn't seem right."

The man Tiguaceak then decided that he had best kill his rival, Kayaakpuq, before the latter killed him. He informed his kinsmen about his decision. When his second wife, Kallikcuk, heard about this, she told her former husband of Tiguaceak's intentions. Kayaakpuq said, on hearing of the plan to kill him: "Let me go and stand where he can see me. He can shoot me there, let him kill me." After that, however, the kinsmen of Kayaakpuq watched him closely, giving Tiguaceak no chance to get at him. They even guarded him while he slept. Kayaakpuq would get up in the morning and go to an open place and stand there, waiting for his enemy to come and kill him.

It so happened that the family of Kallikcuk sided with the former husband. One of her brothers came each day to stand guard over Kayaakpuq. One day, Tiguaceak came, an arrow fitted to his bow. Kallikcuk's brother walked toward him. Each man had a reserve of about 20 arrows. These they discharged from a distance. At length, Tiguaceak succeeded in hitting his opponent in the upper arm. The wounded man came back to where Kayaakpuq was standing. Kallikcuk's father was present and came forward to assist his wounded son. He drew the arrow from the wound, remarking to Kayaakpuq: "Unless you go after him now, you'll always be afraid of him." Kayaakpuq did not reply but took his former brother-in-law's bow and remaining arrows and went out, walking slowly through the houses toward Tiguaceak. The latter came out again and exchanged arrows with him. At last, an arrow shot by Kayaakpuq struck Tiguaceak in the ear and he fell dead. It was a long and lucky shot. As he fell, his first wife came out of the house and ran to him. She was a shaman and attempted, by her powers, to get the arrow out. Had she succeeded, she could have sung over him and perhaps restored him to life. But she was menstruating at the time and her powers were hence nullified. Kayaakpuq then walked back and forth among the houses in the community, crying in a loud voice: "If any is against me, let him come forward now." But no one took up his challenge and the matter was thus ended. Everyone in the community felt that Kayaakpuq had acted "honestly," and his former wife, Kallikcuk, now came back to his household.

CASE D

The following case occurred in the 1870's. An uncle of the informant was indirectly involved in that he accompanied one of his kinsmen when the latter discovered the abduction of his wife.

A kinsman of the informant's father had married several women in succession. His last wife was much younger than he. Although they had lived together for some time, he had no children by her. In the community, Utkeaaɣvik, was a man who had recently arrived. He was single and looking for a wife. He awaited his chance, having selected the wife of the informant's relative. One day the woman came out of the house on her way to an ice cellar for water. The man seized her, threw her to the ground, and raped her. He then dragged her back into the house in which he was living. So far as public opinion was concerned, she now had become his wife. The man whose wife she had been debated as to his own course of action and called in his relatives to discuss the matter. Since the abductor had kinsmen in the community, his own relatives were reluctant to begin a feud and urged caution.

The ultimate decision was to do nothing. Sometime later, the deprived husband was walking through the community with the uncle of the informant. They came on the abductor of his wife sleeping in the summer sun in a sheltered place. His team was staked nearby. The former husband took the lead dog and tied it to his sleeping rival's leg. When the man awoke, he knew at once that the man he had offended had passed by and done this to him. He knew that the man had had the opportunity to kill him and had let it pass.

He then called his own kinsmen and told them of the incident. They passed the story around and all in the community were much impressed with the "honesty" of the husband who had been deprived of his wife. While the abductor kept the woman he had taken, he and the former husband became close friends. They called each other "aɲutawkun," that is, men who have had intercourse with the same woman. Everyone in the community felt obliged to comment on the "honorable" way in which the man had let his wife go.

CASE E

This incident took place at Wainwright. There was here a man who had recently married. He and his wife had built a house and were living together. Another man in the community went after the woman, making frequent attempts to talk with the woman and to persuade her to have an affair with him. The husband forbade his wife to have anything to do (i.e., sexually) with that man. One day the woman went a little way off from the village in order to dump some trash. Her pursuer waylaid her, threw her on the ground, and attempted to rape her. She was wearing caribou skin trousers. Her attacker ripped them up one leg and was trying to get them off. The woman began to scream. Her husband, hearing her, came running up and threw the attacker off his wife. The two began to wrestle, the husband attempting to strangle the other man. The latter managed to throw him off and struck him in the ribs with his knee. The husband, winded, sat down, and the attacker ran away.

Other men had come to see what was happening. One of them, the brother of the attacker, came over and asked the husband: "What are you going to do?" "I'm going to kill him," was the answer. "Ah, don't do that; he has a wife already; there won't be any more trouble," said the attacker's brother. And he urged the husband to go home and forget the whole thing.

But the offended husband went over to his relatives and talked the matter over with them. He finally reached the decision to do the same thing to the wife of his wife's assailant. His kinsmen urged him to forget the whole thing and watched to see that he had no opportunity to be alone with the other woman. They constantly urged peace between the two men.

But one day the husband whose wife had been attacked was making a sled. He was working outside on a cleared place. The wife of his enemy passed by. He chased after her, knocked her down, and attempted to rape her. He tried to get her belt off and broke it in pulling it. Then he saw that she wore another pair of trousers underneath the first, fastened with another belt. He broke this too, got his hand inside her trousers and touched her vulva. He stopped there and let her get up. Weeping, she went back home.

Her own husband was now enraged. He demanded revenge and started off after the other man. Then the relatives of both sides came together and stopped them both. They talked the matter over with both men and the two finally agreed to let the matter rest. After that, the bad feelings between the two came to an end.

---

*T*he nature of the world and the origin and place of man in the universe are topics examined in American society by a number of agencies: schools, churches, philosophers, and others. The story of Adam and Eve, the parable of the book of Genesis, and the growing myth of

Lincoln are examples of legendary accounts which provide symbolic
understanding of the world to those who are interested. In preliterate
societies, such as the Eskimo or any other aboriginal North American
group, oral literature provides an educational medium of enormous im-
portance. Even in our own sophisticated society, religious themes are
frequently presented through myths, especially to children. The Sedna
myth, outlining the origin of the Central Eskimo's "sea goddess," con-
veys the grim aspect of many Eskimo legends.

13 Franz Boas

TALES FROM THE CENTRAL ESKIMO*

SEDNA AND THE FULMAR

Once upon a time there lived on a solitary shore an Inung with his
daughter Sedna. His wife had been dead for some time and the two led
a quiet life. Sedna grew up to be a handsome girl and the youths came
from all around to sue for her hand, but none of them could touch her
proud heart. Finally, at the breaking up of the ice in the spring a fulmar
flew from over the ice and wooed Sedna with enticing song. "Come to
me," it said; "come into the land of the birds, where there is never
hunger, where my tent is made of the most beautiful skins. You shall
rest on soft bearskins. My fellows, the fulmars, shall bring you all your
heart may desire; their feathers shall clothe you; your lamp shall always be filled with oil, your pot with meat." Sedna could not long resist
such wooing and they went together over the vast sea. When at last
they reached the country of the fulmar, after a long and hard journey,
Sedna discovered that her spouse had shamefully deceived her. Her
new home was not built of beautiful pelts, but was covered with

* Excerpt from *The Central Eskimo*, by F. Boas. Lincoln: Univ. Nebraska Press,
175–177, 190–192, 1964. (Originally published as part of the 6th Annual Report of
the Smithsonian Institution, Bureau of Ethnology, 1888.)

wretched fishskins, full of holes, that gave free entrance to wind and snow. Instead of soft reindeer skins her bed was made of hard walrus hides and she had to live on miserable fish, which the birds brought her. Too soon she discovered that the had thrown away her opportunities when in her foolish pride she had rejected the Inuit youth. In her woe she sang: "Aja. O father, if you knew how wretched I am you would come to me and we would hurry away in your boat over the waters. The birds look unkindly upon me the stranger; cold winds roar about my bed; they give me but miserable food. O come and take me back home. Aja."

When a year had passed and the sea was again stirred by warmer winds, the father left his country to visit Sedna. His daughter greeted him joyfully and besought him to take her back home. The father hearing of the outrages wrought upon his daughter determined upon revenge. He killed the fulmar, took Sedna into his boat, and they quickly left the country which had brought so much sorrow to Sedna. When the other fulmars came home and found their companion dead and his wife gone, they all flew away in search of the fugitives. They were very sad over the death of their poor murdered comrade and continue to mourn and cry until this day.

Having flown a short distance they discerned the boat and stirred up a heavy storm. The sea rose in immense waves that threatened the pair with destruction. In this mortal peril the father determined to offer Sedna to the birds and flung her overboard. She clung to the edge of the boat with a death grip. The cruel father then took a knife and cut off the first joints of her fingers. Falling into the sea they were transformed into whales, the nails turning into whalebone. Sedna holding on to the boat more tightly, the second finger joints fell under the sharp knife and swam away as seals (*Pagomys fœtidus*); when the father cut off the stumps of the fingers they became ground seals (*Phoca barbata*). Meantime the storm subsided, for the fulmars thought Sedna was drowned. The father then allowed her to come into the boat again. But from that time she cherished a deadly hatred against him and swore bitter revenge. After they got ashore, she called her dogs and let them gnaw off the feet and hands of her father while he was asleep. Upon this he cursed himself, his daughter, and the dogs which had maimed him; whereupon the earth opened and swallowed the hut, the father, the daughter, and the dogs. They have since lived in the land of Adlivun, of which Sedna is the mistress.

THE FLIGHT TO THE MOON

A mighty angakoq, who had a bear for his tornaq, resolved to pay a visit to the moon. He sat down in the rear of his hut, turning his back toward the lamps, which had been extinguished. He had his hands tied up and a thong fastened around his knees and neck. Then he summoned his tornaq, which carried him rapidly through the air and brought him to the moon. He observed that the moon was a house, nicely covered with white deerskins, which the man in the moon used to dry near it. On each side of the entrance was the upper portion of the body of an enormous walrus, which threatened to tear in pieces the bold intruder. Though it was dangerous to pass by the fierce animals, the angakoq, by help of his tornaq, succeeded in entering the house.

In the passage he saw the only dog of the man of the moon, which is called Tirie'tiang and is dappled white and red. On entering the main room he perceived, to the left, a small additional building, in which a beautiful woman, the sun, sat before her lamp. As soon as she saw the angakoq entering she blew her fire, behind the blaze of which she hid herself. The man in the moon came to meet him kindly, stepping from the seat on the ledge and bidding the stranger welcome. Behind the lamps great heaps of venison and seal meat were piled up, but the man of the moon did not yet offer him anything. He said: "My wife, Ululiernang, will soon enter and we will perform a dance. Mind that you do not laugh, else she will slit open your belly with her knife, take out your intestines, and give them to my ermine which lives in yon little house outside."

Before long a woman entered carrying an oblong vessel in which her ulo lay. She put it on the floor and stooped forward, turning the vessel like a whirligig. Then she commenced dancing, and when she turned her back toward the angakoq it was made manifest that she was hollow. She had no back, backbone, or entrails, but only lungs and heart.

The man joined her dance and their attitudes and grimaces looked so funny that the angakoq could scarcely keep from laughing. But just at the right moment he called to mind the warnings of the man in the moon and rushed out of the house. The man cried after him, "Uq-sureliktaleqdjuin" ("Provide yourself with your large white bear tornaq"). Thus he escaped unhurt.

Upon another visit he succeeded in mastering his inclination to laugh and was hospitably received by the man after the performance was finished. He showed him all around the house and let him look into a small additional building near the entrance. There he saw large herds of deer apparently roaming over vast plains, and the man of the moon allowed him to choose one animal, which fell immediately through a hole upon the earth. In another building he saw a profusion of seals swimming in an ocean and was allowed to pick out one of these also. At last the man in the moon sent him away, when his tornaq carried him back to his hut as quickly as he had left it.

During his visit to the moon his body had lain motionless and soulless, but now it revived. The thongs with which his hands had been fastened had fallen down, though they had been tied in firm knots. The angakoq felt almost exhausted, and when the lamps were relighted he related to the eagerly listening men his adventures during his flight to the moon.

It is related in the course of this tradition that the man in the moon has a qaumat, some kind of light or fire, but I could not reach a satisfactory understanding of the meaning of this word. It is derived from qauq (daylight) and is used in Greenland for the moon herself. Among the Eskimo of Baffin Land it is only employed in the angakoq language, in which the moon is called qaumavun, the sun qaumativun. Another name of the moon is aninga (her brother), in reference to the first legend. The natives also believe that the man in the moon makes the snow. He is generally considered a protector of orphans and of the poor, and sometimes descends from his house on a sledge drawn by his god, Tirie'tiang, in order to help them.

KADLU THE THUNDERER

It is said that three sisters make the lightning, the thunder, and the rain. The names of two of them are Ingnirtung (the one who strikes the fire) and Udluqtung (the one who rubs the skins), whose second name is Kadlu (thunder), while that of the third I could not ascertain. They live in a large house the walls of which are supported by whale ribs. It stands in the far west, at a great distance from the sea, as Kadlu and her sisters do not like to go near it. If an Eskimo should happen to enter the house he must hasten away or Ingnirtung will immediately kill him with her lightning. Even the stones are afraid of her and jump down the hills whenever they see the lightning and hear the thunder. The faces of the sisters are entirely black and they wear no clothes at all. (?) Ingnirtung makes the lightning by striking two red stones together (flint). Kadlu makes the thunder by rubbing sealskins and singing. The third sister makes the rain by urinating. They procure food by striking reindeer with the lightning, which singes their skins and roasts their flesh. The Akudnirmiut say that beyond Iglulik, on the continent of America, a large tribe of Eskimo live whom they call Kakiʾjoq. The women of the tribe are said to have rings tattooed round their eyes. These natives offer the dried skins of a species of small seals to Kadlu, who uses them for making the thunder.

What a man is to do when his economically productive prime is past is a problem which must be dealt with by all humans. In simpler societies, attrition is such that large numbers of aged persons are rarely present. Complicated childbirth, accidents, feuds, warfare, disease, and malnutrition are all factors which work in conjunction with a high infant mortality rate to keep populations in check. Yet, in all societies some people survive to grow old and, finally, senile. Among the present Indians of Baja California, an aged or injured man must fend for himself; among the Seri of the Sonoran coast a very feeble old person may have sand poured into his mouth. In more developed societies, homes, institutions, even whole communities may be set apart for those who have either lost or distributed their ability to contribute to the society economically.

"Placing grandmother on the ice" has long been regarded as a mark of the barbarity of Eskimo culture. Yet, for those who have seen the lonely faces and unkempt persons of the aged in the country homes of more "advanced" societies, the simple dignity of the passing of Naterk may appear to be an attractive alternative.

Peter Freuchen

THE PROBLEM OF THE AGED
IN ESKIMO SOCIETY*

Mala had killed a reindeer.

He had cut off the choicest pieces, placed them in the skins and tied them up so that he could drag the load on a strap. The hair on the skins made them slide easily over the surface of the snow. He hardly noticed that he was pulling a heavy burden. It was lucky, too, that the wind came from behind, and so he walked on and on. But he was not sure whether he was striking out in the right direction or whether the wind had shifted. Still he hurried not only because he was afraid that his boys might be cold and he had a house to build for them, but also because of all the good things he had brought for his family. The reindeer stomachs were full of bitter-sweet herbs, and the entrails of the animals were well filled, too. If pressed out, they would furnish the finest broth. Yes, there would be great joy when he got back to the camp.

It was growing darker and soon the light failed altogether. The wind blew stronger than before. It was impossible now to find the trail. As Mala did not know where to look for the sledge, he stopped and built himself a little hut, just big enough to shelter him and his burden of reindeer meat. Then he lay down to sleep, thinking of his boys and of the ships he was soon to visit. He thought of the white men he would see again and their marvelous language which he would hear once more.

Next day, he started out early and at last he found his way back to his home.

"My, oh my, big men must be living here. Big men who build a big house! I am so afraid to enter!"

Mala was always full of fun when he came home from the hunt. He invariably returned in the best of humor and today, especially, he was in

* Excerpt from *Eskimo*, by P. Freuchen. (Trans. by A. P. Maerker-Branden and E. Branden.) New York: Liveright, 10–20, 1931.

good spirits. Was he not bringing reindeer meat, and marrow bones, and tallow and other delicious things?

"Reindeer, reindeer, big reindeer," shouted the boys.

"Leave it to Mala," said Old Naterk.

Iva only smiled at the husband.

Mala liked to see his folk gay and so he grew still more jovial.

"Oh, I only got a couple of pitifully lean animals," he remarked with mock modesty. "Really nothing much to speak of. Merely two of a big herd. Now, if I could only learn to hunt reindeer! It's a shame, you poor people hardly ever get reindeer meat to eat. You see, I have all but forgotten how to hunt them. I really do not know any more how to stalk them."

The women laughed and shook their heads over big, strong, funny Mala who never went hunting in vain.

"I am certainly a poor hunter. I am afraid I don't even know how to skin reindeer," Mala ranted on in a good-humored way. "Oh, why don't you take pity on me? And why don't you tell me who built this snow house here?"

"Just an attempt of a simple woman to put some blocks together," Iva replied. "Do you think, Mala, that women can't build houses at all?"

"How marvelous! Isn't it splendid that my wife can do what I left undone because I'm a lazy good-for-nothing."

The festive meal was soon ready. They ate and ate of the marrow bones and tallow and frozen meat and boiled meat and broth made from the half-digested contents of the reindeer's paunch. This certainly was a happy home, and nobody was upset at all that Orsokidok had not come back yet. He had not returned to Mala after following a wounded reindeer. But he would find his way back to the sledge all right. After all, it was only the orphan who was missing, a boy without any family. He was just a little assistant who happened to be be around.

Orsokidok arrived the next day at noon. He was hungry and tired. He had not killed an animal, and for two days he had gone hungry. He was in poor humor when he returned but when the others laughed— why shouldn't he join in? Wasn't it funny that there were people who just lay around eating lots of meat while others stayed away simply because they did not want to return? It was the old story that he who tries to get more, in the end gets nothing at all. Finally Orsokidok was given a whole pot of meat which he ate with relish.

They did not continue their journey that day, sleeping instead. Old

Naterk was grateful for the rest, for her old legs often hurt her now, and when she breathed there was a rattling noise in her windpipe.

For a little while she walked beside the sledge, half leaning against it for support. Soon, however, she could not keep up with the dogs at all. They had to stop and wait for her. When she finally caught up with them, her face was as red as if she had run a race on a hot summer's day.

"Sit on the sledge and rest," Mala said.

"As if the sledge were not hard enough for the dogs to pull and for you to steer. It is always best for a human being to walk."

Again she stumbled on ahead of the team as was her wont. Mala now saw to it that the dogs did not run too fast. Each time there was a stop he would make it his business to examine the runners very thoroughly and smooth the ice that covered them. He always took so long that Old Naterk, for the greater part of the day, succeeded in keeping well ahead of the sledge. However, she was too weak to find any satisfaction in this feat. The exertion was altogether too great for her. Mala stopped early that day, out of consideration for his brave, old mother.

During the evening, Old Naterk had no appetite; she just lay around, panting heavily like a walrus rising to the surface of the sea.

Puala took a marrow bone which Mala had broken open for him, picked out the marrow, which was not unlike a long, fat worm. Holding the delicacy in front of his grandmother's mouth, he smeared her lips with the choice morsel.

"Eat," he encouraged her. "I shall go out and kill a big reindeer for you."

Old Naterk was touched and told him he was a great hunter who brought his grandmother wonderful things.

"No, I am not," objected Puala, "but I want you to eat when everybody else is eating. If one does not eat, one can't be happy."

"Good, then your old grandmother will eat some of your prey."

Old Naterk could find no rest while the others slept soundly. Her head was hot, there was that rattling noise whenever she took a breath, and she had aches and pains all over her body. She put a few pieces of snow on her forehead and concentrated on some formulas of powerful magic which had helped her frequently before. But the magic words brought no relief. Perhaps she shouldn't have mumbled them while the others were around. She was afraid that she would wake them if she got up now and left the snow hut. So she stayed where she was but somehow could not sleep. She remembered all the amusing nonsense that

men had told her when she was young and they were making love to
her. Simply everything crowded into her head. She was glad when
morning came and the others awoke.

Old Naterk needed a good long time to dress Upik in his clothes, his
shoes and mittens. It was even harder for her to get into her own furs
and crawl out into the fresh air. How her back ached, when she tried to
raise herself! Slowly she walked up a little knoll, sat down and looked
around. Then, loosening her belt, she tied the strap around her left
foot. There Old Naterk sat, with nobody near her, summoning the
spirits to ascertain her fate. She tried to invoke the spirit that had
guided her feet and had always solved her problems before. Today,
however, the spirit would not respond. One must be strong minded and
convinced of one's power to commune with these spirits, otherwise they
simply will not come.

She returned just as Mala was preparing the sledge for an early departure.

"I have something to say to you and it is important too," Naterk said.

Mala understood that his mother had something on her mind that
was more than the usual woman's talk. Her eyes had an expression that
made him feel once more like a little boy. He bowed his head and listened.

"I am tired and I am old. You must build me a snow house because I
shall go on a very long journey all alone."

"Please do not speak like that, mother. We all wish to see your face
among us always. I shall certainly not build a snow house for you. Let
us hurry down to the white men and the ships, where we can get tea and
tobacco."

"Oh, Mala my son, but I am tired and must have rest."

"Remember the children, mother. How badly they will miss you.
They are sure to cry. Iva always needs your help and good advice. And
I—have I not always had you with me? I could not do without you,
mother."

Old Naterk did not answer. She mumbled a few words and stared at
the horizon. In the far distance, she perceived the bare mountains where
the Great Spirit inhaled reindeer through his nostrils whenever he
breathed. Here she had lived as long as she could remember.

"Give me my stick," she ordered. "I shall go ahead."

Mala rushed over to the pot, sucked his mouth full of water from it,
and squirted it against the runners of the sledge for a new ice coating.
Nobody must see how his mother's words affected him. He was dirty

with soot because each time he took a mouthful of water the lampblack smudged his face.

Old Naterk stumbled on as well as she could and it took the others quite long before they finally caught up with her. There were so many obstacles to surmount that day!

In the middle of the day, Naterk tired once more. Mala, being the leader of the party, demanded that she ride on the sledge. There she sat and shivered while the others pulled her along and Iva alone broke the path for the dogs.

During the night, Naterk complained that her old back bothered her and that she had severe pains in her whole body. She did not stir when Iva lighted the lamp. Perspiration ran down her wrinkled face; she had strange thoughts and mumbled strange words which nobody understood.

Iva dressed, sat down next to Naterk and spoke to her. But Naterk would not answer. Iva finally pulled a strand of hair from Naterk's head. She threw it into the fire so that the smell of the burning hair might chase away the evil spirits and the root of the disease might be destroyed in the flames. This magic really helped. Old Naterk's thoughts were orderly once more. She took a couple of pieces of dried reindeer meat left over from last year. The pieces were all mouldy but she cleaned them with her finger nails and handed them to the children.

Next morning the sun shone brightly and the journey was continued. But in the course of the day, Naterk put up her fur hood and waited for Mala to come abreast of her.

"My son," she addressed him. "I have firm words to say to you and you must not make any objection. I have lived many years and my legs are tired. Build me a snow hut. When I asked this favor of you before you would not listen to me. Don't wait until it will be necessary for me to command my son to do what his mother bids him."

She busied herself with the load and brushed some snow off Upik who had fallen while playing.

Mala did not answer this time. He took his stick, probed the snow and started to build a house.

"Are we resting for the day already?" the children asked.

"Yes," answered Iva. "That is what father has decided to do."

Thus Mala built a house.

As usual the two women unloaded the sledge, filled in the cracks between the blocks and covered the whole structure with loose snow. The boys took a seal's skin, tied a strap to it and used it for a sledge. As

Puala, being a big boy already, wanted to help his father with the building, Upik was left alone. He wanted to play and called to his grandmother.

"Come, grandmother, and pull me. I want to go asledging."

The old woman came.

"You must run quickly."

But her old legs were too weak. Suddenly, her lips quivering, she stopped and tears streamed down her cheeks.

"Grandmother is crying. It's no fun to play with her when she is crying." Upik decided he would rather play alone after all.

When they came in later on, Old Naterk started to get busy on a pair of mittens for the little one. Upik lost so many of them.

Mala went outside and built another igloo. Nobody helped him and he did not ask for any assistance either. Orsokidok had gone with bow and arrows to look for some likely prey. When Mala had finished the house he came in and brushed the snow off his clothes.

"Has anything happened?" Iva asked.

"Nothing at all. I've built a house, that's all." He turned away quickly and walked over to a little mound to look around for Orsokidok.

The old woman collected her belongings. She took one skin after the other, scrutinized it and put it aside. Finally she picked an old, almost hairless skin, rolled it up and was ready to leave the hut. Then she stopped and looked around. Emotion almost overcame her. She stepped over to the sleeping children, but her mouth to their noses and sucked. There was a squirting noise and Puala awoke. What was that for? He was no little boy any more. He could blow his nose himself! But grandmother was so strange today and so rough. She pulled off the boys' hoods, exposing their left shoulders. Right there she dug her teeth in, because the bite of an old woman is a lucky omen for children. Although it did not hurt much, as grandmother's teeth were dull from chewing skins for years and years, the two boys were thoroughly aroused by now and they cried without restraint.

Grandmother was certainly acting strangely today. And there were new mittens and new pants at her place. But she did not speak about it.

"The time to leave has arrived," she said simply, and took her old skin and departed.

"Are you going outside?" asked Iva but she kept on sewing.

The boys lay down and quickly fell asleep again. Life inside the snow hut was just as it had been before.

Outside, the old woman first looked around. The world was beautiful, but her back was so tired and, oh, how she longed to rest her weary bones. Then she crawled into the house built for her and quietly stretched herself out on the old skin.

Soon Mala came. He had seen her enter the hut. He now took his knife, cut a block of snow and walled up the entrance with it. There was not one word spoken when Mala closed up Old Naterk's last house.

There, then, the old woman reposed, waiting for death. She seemingly never tired of thinking. She listened to the children come out of the other house and ask questions about her snow hut. She heard the father tell the children that they must not go into grandmother's hut. She heard Orsokidok come home. He had killed a reindeer, a young calf, a mere yearling. Naterk always used to get a piece of tongue. Tongue of a yearling was soft and easy to chew for old teeth. But why should she think of that now? And then again she heard the boys playing with the sledge they had fashioned from skins. Once the children came so near the hut that she could hear the snow crunching under their little feet. Upik fell down and hurt himself; he set up a great wail.

"I'm hurt, I'm bleeding, oh, mother, grandmother!"

How hard it was to play dead. But Old Naterk was no longer to be reckoned among the living. To the others she had passed on; she was gone. Iva came out and called: "Come in for your food. I have nice boiled meat for you."

"Where is grandmother?" Puala inquired. "Isn't grandmother coming to eat with us?"

Tears welled in Naterk's eyes and her mouth watered. Now she was lying here prostrate. Life, surely, was much more wearisome than death. But the most wearisome thing of all was this slow transition from life to death.

She was still tossing sleeplessly on her hairless skin when dawn came. She listened intently when she heard Mala getting the sledge ready. In her thoughts, Old Naterk followed their every movement: Now the dogs would rush into the deserted hut to fight for the bones left there. Now the load was strapped on the sledge; now the children inquired whether grandmother would walk ahead as usual. Then the travelers departed and everything became quiet.

Alas, they had started and left her all alone. Perhaps, after all, Mala should not have permitted her to remain behind. He, who was always so good a son—had he really deserted her now? Naterk arose and tried to leave the house but her old limbs were too weak to carry her. She wanted to follow the others and she wanted to stay behind.

Darkness came, spreading its sheltering wings over her. Old Naterk, once born into this world, had lived her full life. Now she was no more.

In the evening it was very quiet in Mala's snow house; gaiety had fled. Little Upik wanted to know why they were building a house before grandmother had caught up with them. Iva told him to keep still, and nobody said one word more that night than was absolutely necessary. Upik finally cried himself to sleep. Next day they rested and this day and the succeeding days, Mala went hunting but he did not go far; he stayed right in the proximity of the house. The boys became impatient and wanted to know whether they would not soon get down to the ships.

At last Mala went back to the spot where his old mother had gone into her last house. Drifting snow had covered the igloo. No animal had approached it; all around was the silence of death. Mala took his knife and cut a hole in the roof of the house so that Old Naterk's soul could depart.

Returning to Iva, he did not bring any prey that night. He told her that he had come from a visit that grieved him terribly.

"I opened the roof," was all he said and he sat down silently without taking a bite of food.

The children were not permitted to play; they were not even allowed to talk. Iva herself cut snow for drinking water and it was she, too, who cut the meat for the pot—just as if she were a man. Mala did not stir. His hood put up, he sat inside the house all night long, fully dressed. The children, too, were not undressed. Everything seemed so strange.

"The lice are eating me, the lice are eating me," the boys whimpered during the night and scratched themselves furiously. But they were not permitted to take off their furs.

After five days had passed, the children were left alone. The others went back to Naterk's snow house. Mala went ahead and the others followed in his tracks. He cut a hole through the rear of the hut, and they entered Old Naterk's last abode. There she lay in a huddled heap, her pelt hood over her face, her knees pulled up. Mala suddenly remembered when his mother was a young woman and he a little boy. She had always so much to tell him about the men who were ready to fight for her but had never won her. What a splendid mother she had been, what a brave mother—and now—

They dragged the body out of the house to a nearby spot. Where loose stones were scattered over a mighty rock they prepared Old Naterk's grave. She, who had lived, was now dead, and her name must nevermore be mentioned by any living soul. Only those who still breathe are human, and only in their company may one abide. Because they had touched the corpse, they took off their mittens and stuffed them between the stones.

On the way home, they were careful to step into the tracks they had made before. They held their hands close to their bodies so they would not freeze. Now and then Mala would turn back, effacing their tracks with his knife, so that Death should not follow them.

It was evening when they returned. Iva at once took two bags with new clothes and they put on new garments. As Orsokidok had no suit to spare, he just turned his fur coat inside out. All the old clothes were packed up in a bundle and next morning Mala returned to the grave with it. He stayed away a long time and when he retraced his steps, he took care to obliterate his tracks.

At last they journeyed on. Every day they painstakingly wiped out their tracks. Eventually they forgot about it in their eagerness to make quick progress. Ships and the white men beckoned to them and spring was almost upon them. Eider ducks winged their way inland, sea swallows arrived, and big flocks of wild geese, screeching madly overhead, made for the north.

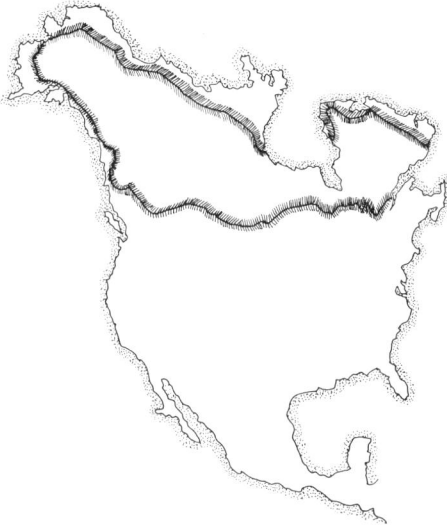

SECTION III
The Northern Hunters

In the study of the American Indian, it is easy to lose sight of the fact that most of the continent of North America was inhabited by simple hunters and gatherers, not by agriculturalists. Virtually all of the terrain north of the present Canadian border was inhabited by such simple societies. These Indians subsisted principally through the hunting of large land mammals (caribou, moose, deer, bear, and buffalo), supplemented by fishing and the gathering of nuts, berries, and other plant products. After European contact, some of these people adopted various trappings of more complex societies. The added complexity was usually based on either the introduction of the horse and/or gun, the economic stimulus provided by the fur trade and the associated trading posts, or, as no doubt occurred in some cases, by simple population amalgamation following general demographic disruption.

The Algonkian-speaking tribes are to be found in the northeastern portion of the continent, including the present maritime portion of eastern Canada, as well as the vast area north and east of the Great Lakes. The Athabascan-speakers, more recently arrived on the continent, are located in the northwestern portion of the continent including interior Alaska and interior British Columbia. These Indian hunters, both Athabascan and Algonkian, everywhere to the north crowd upon the Eskimo, while to the south they gradually blend into the semi-agricultural and agricultural Prairie and Woodlands Indians.

The archaeology of this enormous region is not well known. Long winters with deep snow and a sparse modern population have inhibited archaeological research throughout most of the woodland region of Canada. Furthermore, the very small aboriginal population in this region during the early horizons of human occupation will always make it difficult to locate the very early sites. There is little doubt, however, that the northern forests harbor the remains of the earliest migrants from Asia into the New World, who must have been sub-arctic hunters themselves before venturing into North America.

Despite the relatively recent movement of the Athabaskan-speaking Indians from Asia and, in contrast, the apparently great antiquity of the Algonkian-speaking Indians in the New World, local groups of the two widely dispersed linguistic families are similar in many cultural respects. Regional differences among the numerous Indian bands appear to be more dependent upon local ecological circumstances and proximity to other culture areas than upon ethnic history and linguistic origin.

15 *Diamond Jenness*

HUNTING BANDS OF EASTERN AND WESTERN CANADA*

EASTERN CANADA

Beothuk

The word Beothuk meant probably "man" or "human being," but early European visitors to Newfoundland considered it the tribal name of the aborigines who were inhabiting the island. They gave them also another name, "Red Indians," because they smeared their bodies and clothing with red ochre, partly for religious reasons, apparently, partly as a protection against insects. They may have been lighter in colour than the Indians of the Maritime Provinces, from whom they differed in several ways. Thus, they had no dogs, and did not make pottery, but cooked their food in vessels of birch bark. For sleeping places within their bark wigwams they dug trenches which they lined with branches of fir or pine. Their canoes, though made of birch bark like those of other eastern tribes, were very peculiar in shape, each gunwale presenting the outline of a pair of crescent moons; and they speared seals with harpoons modelled on an archaic Eskimo type. Many of their graves contain bone ornaments of curious shapes and etched with strange designs. We know nothing concerning their political organization except that they were divided into small bands of closely related families, each with its nominal leader. Some meagre vocabularies of their language suggest that they spoke two or three dialects of a common tongue, although the entire tribe could hardly have numbered much more than five hundred individuals when Cabot discovered Newfoundland in 1497. The European fishermen who settled around the shores of the is-

* Excerpt from "The Indians of Canada," by D. Jenness, in *Bulletin of the National Museum of Canada* **65**, *Anthropological Series* **15**, 265–286, 377–404, 1955.

land in the sixteenth, seventeenth, and eighteenth centuries resented their petty pilfering, and shot them down at every opportunity, the French even placing a bounty on their heads; and the Micmac who crossed over from Nova Scotia in the eighteenth century hunted them relentlessly far into the interior. The Beothuk attempted to retaliate, but, armed only with bows and arrows, they could not withstand the combined attacks of white and Micmac, and the last known survivor died in captivity at St. Johns in 1829.

Micmac

The Micmac ("Allies"), who united with the French and English settlers to exterminate the unhappy Beothuk Indians of Newfoundland, occupied at the time of their discovery not only the whole province of Nova Scotia, including Cape Breton Island, but the northern portion of New Brunswick and the neighbouring Prince Edward Island. They were a typical migratory people who lived in the woods during the winter months hunting moose, caribou, and porcupine, then moved down to the seashore in spring to gather shell-fish, to fish at the mouths of the rivers, and to hunt the seals near the coast. Like most Algonkian tribes they lived in conical wigwams covered with birch bark, and they made canoes and household utensils from the same material; but they manufactured also large wooden troughs for boiling their food, and even cooking pots from clay—unless indeed the numerous fragments of pottery found in Nova Scotia shell-heaps were the work of some earlier tribe. Their canoes resembled the peculiar Beothuk type more than the usual Algonkian, and their dialect was so different from those of the tribes around them, and from the Algonkian dialects spoken about the Great Lakes, that it suggests they may have been late intruders into the Maritimes, coming perhaps from the northwest.

The tribe was divided into several exogamous clans, each having its own symbols which its members tattooed on their persons, painted or worked in porcupine quills on their clothing, carved into ornaments to wear on their chests, and painted on their canoes, snowshoes, and other possessions. One clan used a cross as its symbol, to the great astonishment of the early missionaries, who immediately reinterpreted it for the promotion of Christianity. The chiefs of the various bands had comparatively little authority; one of their main duties, apparently, was to assign hunting territories to the different families. The war leaders were often not the actual chiefs, but men who had distinguished themselves in intertribal fighting; for in spite of their rather isolated position the

Micmac fought with Algonkian tribes in the south, Iroquoian tribes in the west, and Eskimo and Montagnais on the north shore of the gulf of St. Lawrence. Their weapons were stone tomahawks, bows and arrows, spears with two-edged blades of moose-bone, and bone or stone knives for scalping their foes. From mimic fights beforehand they augured the issue of their war-parties, and they celebrated their victories with savage feasts and dances at which they generally tortured to death their male prisoners, but spared the women and children for absorption into the tribe.

Micmac mothers strapped their babies to wooden cradles ornamented with painted designs, wampum and porcupine-quill embroidery. Marriage was a solemn ceremony preceded by a year or more of betrothal, when the youth resided with the parents of his future bride and gave them the products of his hunting. Equally solemn were the funeral rites, when the Indians wrapped their dead in birch-bark rolls, deposited them, seated as in life, within round, shallow graves, and burnt, or buried with them, all their implements and utensils to serve their needs in the after life. Elaborate ceremonies, too, attended the installation of chiefs, at least in historical times. It is, therefore, very surprising that the writers of the seventeenth century, to whom we owe most of our information concerning the Maritime Indians, record no ceremony or ritual for the period of adolescence, which Indian tribes elsewhere regarded as the greatest crisis in a man's or woman's lifetime. Yet it is highly probable that every youth fasted to obtain a guardian spirit, since the medicine-men who pretended to cure diseases by incantations, by breathing and blowing on their patients, and by various juggling tricks, made the usual claim that it was through fasting and prayer they had gained the favour of the supernatural world. No youth, in any event, could participate in the councils of the tribe until he had proved his manhood by killing either a moose or a bear.

These old customs of the Micmac have long since disappeared and are now practically forgotten; for the tribe quickly took up agriculture, submitted to the teachings of the Jesuit missionaries, and intermarried freely with the French colonists who settled in their midst. Like their neighbours, the Malecite, they were faithful allies of the French throughout the wars of the seventeenth and eighteenth centuries. It is doubtful whether any pure-blood representatives of the tribe still exist, but their mixed descendants, to the number of nearly 4,000, which about equals the original population, occupy several small reserves in the Maritime Provinces and in Quebec, and a few families survive in

Newfoundland. Of their old handicrafts only basketry persists to any great extent, and even this has been modified to meet the requirements of the market. In their mode of living to-day the majority of the Micmac are hardly distinguishable from poor whites.

Algonkin

Adjoining the Montagnais in the east, and merging in the west with the Ojibwa of the Great Lakes region, were a number of scattered bands commonly classed together as Algonkin, from the name applied by Champlain and his contemporaries to the bands below Ottawa, who made common cause with the Montagnais against the inroads of the Iroquois. As in their geographical position, so also in their customs and beliefs, they held an intermediate place between the peoples that flanked them on either side; they had the wooden cradle-board, the double-headed drum, and, in the western bands at least, the annual festival to the dead and the totemic clan system of the Ojibwa, but they lacked, like the Montagnais, the rice and maple-syrup industries and the secret medicine-society of the western tribe. A few bands along the Ottawa, through their proximity to the Hurons, learned to grow a little maize, and a few squashes and beans; but their methods were so primitive, and their dread of Iroquois raids so constant, that agriculture added but little to their food supply. In the seventeenth century the Iroquois drove them to the north and east away from the lower Ottawa and St. Lawrence rivers, but when the power of the Iroquois declined they gradually drifted back to their old territories. Few in numbers, and scattered in small bands over a large, densely wooded area where the best hunting and trapping districts lay in the hills away from the main routes of travel and settlement, they exercised hardly any influence and received very little attention throughout historical times. Many of their women married white trappers, lumbermen, and pioneer farmers, and their descendants have merged imperceptibly into the civilized communities that now occupy their territory. The remainder, numbering a little over 2,000 (the majority, perhaps, of mixed blood), are restricted to a few reserves in eastern Ontario and western Quebec. There, some raise a little garden produce, and serve as licensed guides to the sportsmen who visit their districts to fish and hunt. Others, notably the Tête-de-Boule band on the upper waters of the St. Maurice River, still support themselves in their old nomadic fashion by hunting and trapping, but purchase with their furs, at the trading-posts, most of the necessities of life except food.

Ojibwa

Numerically the Ojibwa or Chippewa (both are forms of the same word, which signifies "people whose moccasins have puckered seams") were the strongest nation in Canada, totalling even today around 20,000. They controlled all the northern shores of Lakes Huron and Superior from Georgian Bay to the edge of the prairies, and at the height of land north of Lake Superior where the rivers begin to flow towards Hudson Bay they united with their near kinsmen, the Cree. So numerous were they, and so large a territory did they cover, that we may separate them into four distinct groups or tribes, viz., the Ojibwa of the Lake Superior region, the Missisauga ("people of the large river-mouth") of Manitoulin Island and of the mainland around the Missis-sagi River, the Ottawa ("Traders") of the Georgian Bay region, and the Potawatomi ("people of the place of fire") on the west side of Lake Huron within the state of Michigan, some of whom moved across into Ontario in the eighteenth and nineteenth centuries. Three of these four tribes, the Lake Superior Ojibwa, the Ottawa, and the Potawatomi, formed a loose confederacy that became known in the eighteenth century as the Council of the Three Fires.

Each tribe, as among other Algonkians, was subdivided into numerous bands that possessed their own hunting territories and were politically independent of one another, though closely connected by intermarriage. The majority of the bands were small, numbering probably not more than 300 to 400 individuals; and each contained an indefinite number of exogamous totemic clans in which the children inherited the totems of their fathers. These clans had no political functions and very little religious significance, but being distributed among all the bands they gave the nation a certain unity, since fellow clansmen regarded one another as close kinsmen even when they belonged to different tribes. The real political unit was the band. Each had its own leader, who normally handed on his rank to his son; but the power and prestige attached to the position varied with the individual. There was no chief for a whole tribe, still less a leader who could unify the entire nation.

The chief of a band was generally, but not always, its war captain. If he planned a raid against the Sioux or the Iroquois, the principal enemies of the Ojibwa, he first consulted his own followers, then sent either his personal lieutenant or a selected envoy with a pipe and tobacco to invite the participation of neighbouring bands. The envoy delivered his message to the assembled hunters, lit the pipe and handed it around the company. Those who were unwilling to join the war party passed it on without smoking; for no man who put it to his lips could refuse, without deep disgrace, to take part in the enterprise. The Ojibwa were braver warriors than most of the eastern Algonkians, and preserved much stricter discipline on the march. They used the same types of arms as their enemies—the bow and arrow, knobbed wooden club, knife, and a round shield covered with moosehide; and while the fighting lasted they spared neither man, woman, nor child. Whoever slew an enemy carried home the scalp for the victory dance, and thereafter enjoyed the privilege of wearing an eagle feather in his hair. Unlike the Micmac, however, the Ojibwa never tortured their prisoners, and regarded the Iroquois with special loathing because of their inhuman conduct toward enemies who fell into their hands.

All the Ojibwa tribes subsisted to a considerable extent on vegetable foods. They gathered and stored away, in the late summer, vast quantities of the wild rice that grew in the shallow water around the edges of the lakes. In spring they collected the syrup from the maple trees, and in summer large stores of berries, which they preserved for the lean months of early winter. So, although they did not practice agriculture (except some of the Ottawa bands adjacent to the Hurons), they were not so completely dependent on fish and game as other Canadian tribes that did not cultivate maize. Nevertheless, they were as keen hunters, and as keen fishermen, as other Indians. Every winter the families scattered into the woods to pursue the moose; in spring and summer they killed beaver and smaller game, and caught suckers, pickerel, and pike; and in autumn, at the close of the rice harvest, they speared the larger fish—trout, whitefish, and sturgeon—that spawned at that season close to shore. These varied resources caused their lives to be no less migratory than those of their kindred to the east, whom they closely resembled in their extensive use of birch bark for canoes and wigwams. The more southern Ojibwa, in early historical times at least, made clay pots, but too few to supersede the birch-bark utensils which, after all, were more satisfactory for a people constantly in motion.

Partly because the living conditions were a little easier, perhaps, and partly because they were in contact with more advanced tribes in southeastern Ontario, in Michigan, Wisconsin, and Minnesota, the Ojibwa enjoyed a richer social life than the other Algonkian tribes of eastern Canada. The clans held annual feasts, and in the autumn of each year the people celebrated an All Souls' Day or Festival of the Dead, when they burnt a little food for the shades of the departed and feasted and danced until morning. A pleasing ceremony accompanied the naming of each child; when the relatives and friends had gathered for the feast, the grandfather (or another elderly kinsman) took the child in his arms and called on all the great powers in the spiritual world to impart their blessing to its name. Neighbours joined in a feast over every bear laid low by a hunter's club, and they partook of the first game a boy killed, even if it were no larger than a rabbit. There was much jollity, too, in the sugar-making camps of early spring, and at the rice harvesting later in the summer. Food was generally plentiful at those seasons, giving leisure for dances and other pastimes. The men played lacrosse or gambled with bone dice, while the women either watched them or played a special ball game of their own.

The most notable event of the year, however, was the holding of the Midewiwin, or celebration of the Grand Medicine Society, a secret religious organization, open to both sexes, that exercised great influence among the Ojibwa, but existed nowhere else in Canada except among some of the neighbouring Cree. The full organization recognized four grades of membership; even the lowest required a long period of preliminary instruction and the payment of heavy fees, and as the fees increased with each grade, only a few individuals ever attained the highest. The members, *mede*, were the principal doctors or medicine-men of the communities, and, like our own doctors, generally derived much profit and prestige from the practice of their profession. In treating the sick they employed mainly herbal remedies, some of them undoubtedly beneficial, such as the application of balsam gum to wounds, the majority utterly useless. Yet they effected many cures, most often, it would seem, from psychological causes, because the Ojibwa ascribed a soul and power to every tree and stone, and believed that their medicine-men, through the favour of the supernatural world, could attach this power to human beings. But they also believed that many supernatural spirits were unfriendly, and that by enlisting the aid of these hostile powers, or sometimes by purely sympathetic magic, the medicine-men could harm and even slay their fellowmen. So, a dread of witchcraft constantly infected their minds, converting into the grossest superstition what might have been a really beautiful religion.

In early historical times the Ojibwa recognized both a supreme good spirit, a sky-god who ruled the universe through a host of subordinate spirits, and a supreme evil spirit, sometimes regarded as a monstrous supernatural serpent. This dualism arose, probably, through Christian teaching, although the belief in a great sky-god may belong to aboriginal times. Men often prayed to the good spirit and offered him smoke from their pipes, or on special occasions a burnt offering of white dogs. But, regarding him as too remote to concern himself often with human affairs, they generally trusted to the subordinate spirits, and made each adolescent boy fast and dream in solitude to obtain one as his guardian. Every hunter of note carried a "medicine-bag" containing herbs, roots, feathers, wooden images, and other objects revealed to him in his visions or taught him (for a price) by some medicine-man; usually, too, a drum to accompany his medicine-songs. In addition to the *mede*, or members of the Grand Medicine Society, there was an unorganized class of seers or conjurors who delivered their oracles from within cylindrical shrines exactly after the manner of the Montagnais.

The Ojibwa buried their dead in the ground and deposited with them food and tobacco for the four days' journey to the land of souls, whose ruler, according to the esoteric doctrines of the *mede*, was Nanibush, the great trickster and culture hero of the tribe and the secret patron of the Grand Medicine Lodge. There, the souls dwelt in happiness, hunting and feasting and dancing as on earth. Hence relatives, while throwing away their own property to display their grief, dressed a dead man in his best apparel and deposited in the grave all his tools and equipment so that he might use their souls in his new abode. If a chief had won great renown in war his kinsmen sometimes placed his body on a high scaffold, and suspended beside it the scalps he had taken, and other tokens of his valour. Thus they ensured that the prestige, and honour he had gained during his earthly career would attend him without fail in the hereafter.

Despite their numbers and the large extent of territory they occupied, the Ojibwa did not play a very prominent part in the history of the Dominion. They fought with the Sioux southwest of Lake Superior, participated in the wars against the Iroquois, and supported the French in their struggle against the English. The Ottawa were close friends of the Hurons, from whom they learned to cultivate maize; and their proximity to the Ottawa River gave them control of the main route to the lower St. Lawrence and the trading-posts of the early colonists, for the upper St. Lawrence was blocked by the hostile Iroquois. After destroying the Hurons, therefore, the Iroquois turned their arms against the Ottawa and drove them from Georgian Bay. Some fled west towards Lake Superior; others took refuge with their Potawatomi kinsmen in the United States. Half a century later many of these refugees returned to Manitoulin Island and the north shore of Lake Huron, where their descendants still survive.

Cree

The Cree (Cree: contraction of Kristineaux, the French form of a name of unknown meaning, that a portion of the tribe applied to itself) were closely related and almost equal in number to the Ojibwa, whom they flanked on the north and west. Like the Ojibwa, too, they occupied an immense area of country. On the north they were bounded by the coast-line from Eastmain River nearly to Churchill; on the east by lakes Mistassini and Nichikun. Their western limits are uncertain, but in the early sixteenth century they appear to have wandered over part of the country west of Lake Winnipeg, perhaps between the Red River and the Saskatchewan. As soon as they obtained firearms from Hudson Bay, however, they expanded westward and northward, so that by the middle of the eighteenth century they controlled northern Manitoba and Saskatchewan as far as Churchill River, all northern Alberta, the valley of Slave River, and the southeastern part of Great Slave Lake. Some of them had even raided up the Peace River into the Rocky Mountains, and others down the Mackenzie to its delta almost within view of the Arctic Sea, preceding in both directions the explorations of Sir Alexander Mackenzie. The acquisition of firearms by surrounding tribes, and a terrible epidemic of smallpox that devastated them in 1784, checked their further expansion. The Cree then became demoralized through spirituous liquors, underwent constant attack from the Blackfoot confederacy, and were decimated by a second epidemic of smallpox about 1838. From these disasters they never recovered, but remained scattered in whatever districts they found themselves, earning a meagre livelihood by hunting and trapping. Like some of the Athapaskan peoples, they took on the color of the tribes with whom they had most contact, so that today we can divide them into two large groups:

(1) Plains' Cree, living on the prairies.
(2) Woodland Cree, usually called Swampy Cree or Muskegon. They include not only the bands around the southern part of Hudson Bay, but those living on Peace, Athabaska, and Slave rivers and on Athabaska and Great Slave lakes.

Like the Naskapi—but to an even greater extent—the Cree embellished themselves with tattoo marks, a practice not common among Algonkian tribes. Their women had a widespread reputation for beauty; in fact, so experienced a traveller as Mackenzie considered that they were better proportioned, and possessed more regular features, than any other Indians within the boundaries of Canada. In the more southern parts of the area the Woodland Cree dwelt in birch-bark wigwams, either dome-shaped like the Ojibwa wigwam, or conical like the dwellings elsewhere in the east; farther north, where the birch trees were small and stunted, they substituted coverings of pine bark or the hide of the caribou. The bands living around James Bay often used soapstone pots for cooking their food instead of the usual birch-bark vessels, a practice they learned probably from the Eskimo. For scraping their skins, too, they employed a curved knife that resembled the everyday knife of Eskimo women, although bands west of Moose Factory used a chisel-shaped tool after the manner of the Plains' tribes. Since the winter was rather more severe in the territory of the Woodland Cree than farther south, many of them eschewed the tanned hides of the Ojibwa and Algonkians, and wore in their stead coats and blankets made of woven hare skin, or of soft, warm caribou fur, similar to the coats of the Naskapi and some of the Montagnais. Other features differentiating them from their southern neighbours were the absence of mats, and of baskets made from roots or split twigs, together with the relative unimportance of fishing, which the Cree scorned in early days as unworthy of a hunter, and resorted to only from necessity.

The game in most repute were the woodland caribou, moose, beaver, and bear, but owing to the relative scarcity of these animals many bands subsisted in winter principally on hares, which they caught in snares made from the bark of the willow. Hares, like several other northern mammals, undergo periodic increase and decrease; they disappear almost completely every ninth winter and remain scarce for a year or two afterwards. During these seasons shortage of food caused many natives to die of starvation and sometimes led to cannibalism, which inspired no less horror among the Indians than among us. It must have occurred fairly frequently, however, for the early fur traders and explorers mention several instances and it occupies a prominent place in the legends of the tribe, which abound in stories of *windigos*—human beings transformed into supernatural man-eating giants through the eating of human flesh. In spring and autumn the Cree secured many ducks and geese, and in the winter many grouse and ptarmigan; but naturally these minor foods could only supplement, not replace, the meat of the larger mammals.

As among most Algonkian tribes, the only real social units were the bands and the families. Some bands from the Albany River westward developed totemic clans on the analogy of the Ojibwa, but these never gained a firm foothold and are now practically forgotten. Adolescents passed a period in seclusion fasting for visions, and men served their wives' parents for a term, although there was no formal marriage ceremony. Widows and orphans received the kindly treatment usually afforded them by Algonkian Indians, who differed in this respect from the Eskimo and from most of the Athapaskan-speaking tribes. Old people who could no longer keep up on the march were abandoned to starve, or killed at their own request. The dead were buried in the ground amid much lamentation and self-torture, and every year the Cree held a feast in their honour.

All these customs the Cree shared with the Ojibwa, like whom they had a ceaseless fear of witchcraft. Conjurors, indeed, wielded more influence than the so-called chiefs. In many districts there was a secret religious organization copied from the Grand Medicine Society of the Ojibwa, but its celebrations were concealed from the sight of the laity and its power was comparatively slight. More deeply embedded in the lives of these Indians were the innumerable taboos and hunting customs intended to propitiate the spirits of the game. Every hunter carried a medicine-bag to help him in the chase, and in many bands every hide was ceremonially decorated with stripes and dots of red paint.

Even in Sir John Franklin's day the Cree had degenerated and were no longer the adventurous hunters and warriors who had traversed half the Dominion. The white man's liquor and the white man's diseases had left their mark, and recurring epidemics of diseases only intensified the effect. Tuberculosis became almost endemic in many districts, as it has among the tribes of the Mackenzie valley; and the Cree suffered heavily from epidemics of influenza in 1908 and 1909, and again in 1917. Their number (including the Plains' Cree) seems to have fallen away but little, for they registered about 20,000 in 1924; but many of the present day Cree carry a perceptible strain of European blood.

WESTERN CANADA

If we omit from consideration the tribes dwelling along the coast, and a small group of Eskimo who occupied the northeast corner of the continent, all the inhabitants of North America beyond about the 56th parallel spoke dialects of that Athapaskan tongue which Sapir suggests may be remotely connected with the Tibeto-Chinese-Siamese group of languages in eastern Asia. They were essentially woodland peoples like the Algonkians of eastern Canada; the treeless seacoast of the Arctic repelled them, and the "barren lands" with their herds of caribou and musk-oxen drew from most tribes only brief and hurried incursions. Winter was long and severe in their territory, and game, though generally plentiful, subject to wide seasonal variations both in numbers and in movements. Perhaps for these reasons, perhaps for others not so readily discernible, the Athapaskans appear to have been always pressing southward in the centuries preceding the coming of Europeans. To the southeast the Algonkian Cree blocked all passage; in that direction the northerners could make no headway. One tribe, the Sarcee, familiar perhaps with the hunting of buffalo in the Peace River area, drifted out into the open prairies and linked its fortunes with the Blackfoot; but none of its fellow-tribes ventured to follow in its footsteps. Some, keeping to the woodlands, crossed the Rocky Mountains into British Columbia, or starting from the basin of the upper Yukon River, followed down the western flank of the mountains and established a line of "colonies" from Alaska to southern California. The majority, however, lingered in the northland, where they continue to occupy almost the entire basins of the Mackenzie and Yukon rivers.

Sekani

The Sekani ("People of the Rocks," i.e., Rocky Mountains) controlled the basins of the Parsnip and Finlay rivers, and the Valley of the Peace as far down as the modern town of Peace River.

The Sekani were, first and foremost, hunters, living on moose, caribou, bear, porcupine, beaver, and smaller game. They employed the same weapons in hunting as in war, the bow and arrow, a club fashioned from the jawbone of a moose, and a spear which for beaver-hunting was fitted with a toggle head; but their weapons procured them less game than their snares of babiche, which they used for every animal from the marmot to the moose. Unlike the neighbouring Carrier, they hunted in winter and summer alike, and resorted to fishing only when driven by sheer necessity. Then they used nets of willow bark or nettle-fibres, fish-hooks of bone set in a wooden shank, and tridents wielded from a canoe by the light of jackpine torches, or through the ice when the lakes were frozen over. Although the fish-baskets of more western tribes were unknown to them, they sometimes constructed weirs of brush near beaver-dams, broke the dams, and collected the stranded fish as the water drained away.

Like most Athapaskan tribes, the Sekani made far less use of stone than of wood, bone, horn, and antler. Indeed, their only stone implements seem to have been spear- and arrow-points, adze blades, and sometimes knives; in the last they often used beaver teeth. Their cooking vessels were made of spruce bark or woven spruce roots, their dishes of wood or bark, their spoons of goat horn or wood, and their bags of hide or babiche netting. Canoes and dwellings both had coverings of spruce bark. Living as they did by the chase, the Sekani had no permanent villages, but erected rough, conical lodges of poles covered with spruce-bark, or still cruder lean-tos overlaid with bark, skins, or brush. Food that they were unable to carry along with them they cached in trees (later, when they obtained steel axes, on specially built platforms) and carefully peeled the bark from the trunks to prevent the ascent of the crafty wolverine. All their clothing, like that of most Canadian tribes, was of skin. Men wore a sleeveless shirt, at times laced together between the legs in lieu of a breech-cloth (which they adopted only after contact with the Cree); leggings that reached to the thighs, and moccasins with in-soles of groundhog or rabbit fur. Women wore a similar costume, except that they either lengthened the shirt or added a short apron, and their leggings reached only to the knees. A robe, a rounded cap, and mittens, provided additional protection in winter. Shirt and moccasins were commonly embroidered with porcupine-quill work. Hunters wore necklets of grizzly-bear claws, and both men and women had bracelets of horn or bone; but only a few natives possessed ear pendants of dentalia shells, and none of them wore anklets. Rather exceptionally, too, the Sekani seem not to have practiced tattooing, although they used paint freely enough on their persons and clothing.

The political organization and social life were exceedingly simple. The tribe was divided into several independent bands, each under the guidance of a leader who possessed little or no real authority. Common customs, a common language, and frequent intermarriage gave the bands a feeling of unity, but families of different bands frequently quarrelled and started blood feuds. There was no name for the entire tribe; the term Sekani applied to one band only, the band that controlled McLeod Lake and the headwaters of the Parsnip River.

The Sekani regulated marriage solely by the degree of consanguinity. They permitted polygamy, favouring especially marriage with two sisters; but they disclaim the wrestling for wives that occurred so frequently among the Beaver and Mackenzie River tribes, and assert that there were few instances of polyandry. The bridegroom had to hunt for his parents-in-law until the birth of his first child, or else for a period of from twelve to eighteen months, but he and his bride maintained the dignity of their new status by always building a separate lodge for themselves. Babies, who were carried in bags of groundhog or rabbit fur, received names associated with the dream guardians of their fathers or relatives, "Moose-antler," for example, if the dream guardian happened to be the moose. Girls underwent the usual period of seclusion to protect the community from harm, and boys of corresponding age fasted and dreamed for guardian spirits. Every boy obtained a guardian spirit, always from an animal or a bird, but he could count on its aid only in great emergencies. If he were fortunate, he might obtain through dreams in later life other guardian spirits, either from the animal world or from such forces as wind and thunder; and on their aid he could rely at all times. He then became one of the recognized medicine-men of the community, able to cause and cure diseases, and to deliver the people in times of famine. Real deities seem to have been lacking in the old Sekani religion; and if there were local spirits, supernatural beings that haunted special localities, the present generation of Indians has forgotten them. Yet they still believe that man and the animal world are linked together in some mysterious way, and that the animals possess special powers which they may grant the Indian if he seeks them in the proper manner.

Chipewyan

The Chipewyan ("Pointed Skins," a Cree term referring to the form in which the Chipewyan dried their beaver skins) was the most numerous Athapaskan tribe in northern Canada in the first half of the eighteenth century, and controlled the largest area. Although its exact boundaries are uncertain, and probably fluctuated at different periods, it seems to have claimed possession of the vast triangle enclosed by a line from Churchill to the height of land separating the headwaters of the Thelon and Black rivers, another running south past the eastern ends of Great Slave and Athabaska lakes to the Churchill River, and a third east to the coast a little south of Churchill. After the Hudson's Bay Company established its post at Churchill in 1717 the Chipewyan, well supplied with firearms, drove the coast Eskimo northward, and oppressed the two Athapaskan tribes in the northwest, the Yellowknife and the Dogrib, by denying them access to the trading post, forcing them to exchange their furs for a tithe of their value in European goods, and even robbing them outright of their possessions and women. With the Cree on their southern border they kept an uneasy peace after the Hudson's Bay Company established a truce between them in 1715, but with the section of the Cree that drove the Beaver and Slave Indians from the Athabaska and Slave rivers they fought intermittently until about 1760, when the two tribes concluded an armistice. In 1781 smallpox destroyed the majority of the Chipewyan (nine-tenths of them, according to Hearne), and when Fort Chipewyan was established on Lake Athabaska in 1788 most of the remainder preferred to carry their furs to the new trading post rather than undertake the long and arduous journey to Churchill.

The Chipewyan were an edge-of-the-woods people. They followed the movements of the caribou, spearing them in the lakes and rivers of the barren grounds during the summer, and snaring them in pounds or shooting them down with bows and arrows during the winter when they took shelter in the timber. Buffalo, musk-oxen, moose, and smaller game tided them over periods when caribou were lacking. They snared, too, numerous water-fowl, and caught many fish with spears, bone hooks, and nets of babiche. Some bands kept almost entirely to the timber, moving from one grove to another. Others spent the greater part of the summer on the barren grounds, carrying their tent-poles (which they converted into snow-shoes in the autumn), and pounding their dried meat into pemmican, or eating raw meat and raw fish like the Eskimo.

Life under these conditions was hard and uncertain. Moving about the country were many independent bands, some large, some small, whose leaders had no authority or power to keep their followers under control. Strong men plundered the weaklings, and forcibly carried off their women. The latter ranked lower than in any other tribe; separated from all boy companions at the age of eight or nine, married at adolescence, often to middle-aged men, and always subject to many restrictions, they were the first to perish in seasons of scarcity. In winter they were mere traction animals; unaided, they dragged the heavy toboggans. In summer they were pack animals, carrying all the household goods, food, and hides on their backs. The aged and infirm of both sexes were abandoned by their companions and starved to death on the trail. A superstitious horror of bloodshed checked murder within the tribe, and though the Chipewyan massacred enemies from other tribes without respect to age or sex, they imposed on themselves afterwards many severe penalties and taboos. They seldom covered their dead, but left them to be devoured by birds and animals. Families destroyed their property on the death of kinsmen, widows cut off their hair and went into mourning for a year, but widowers suffered no restrictions.

It required from eight to eleven caribou skins to make a complete costume for one man (robe, shirt, leggings, moccasins, breech-cloth, cap, and mittens), and as many more to furnish him with a tent, lines, nooses, and nets for fish and beaver. A skilful hunter enjoyed great prestige and could maintain several wives; he needed them indeed to pack all his hides. Men depended for success in the chase on dreams and visions in which they conceived, like other Indians, that they were communicating with a supernatural world. Medicine-men claimed a similar derivation for their supposed powers; they could both cure and cause disease with the aid of familiar spirits, according to the judgment of their tribesmen, who employed no herbal remedies and ascribed all illness and death to witchcraft. For the Chipewyan seem to have recognized no deities, offered up no public prayers, and possessed no real religion except this belief in guardian spirits. The souls of the dead, they thought, entered a stone boat and travelled along a river to a beautiful island abounding in game. Only the good reached the island in safety; when the evil came within sight of it the stone boat sank and they struggled in the water forever. A few souls, after remaining on the island for a time, might be born again, but the prospect of possible reincarnation left the Indians coldly indifferent.

Although the best known of all the northern Athapaskan tribes, the Chipewyan seem to have possessed the weakest culture, with the exception of their near relatives, the Yellowknife. Some of their traits, indeed, they borrowed from their neighbours. They tattooed their faces in the same way as the Yellowknife and Dogrib, with three or four parallel bars across each cheek. From the Yellowknife, probably, they learned to use copper for hatchets, ice-chisels, awls, knives, and arrow- and spear-heads; from the Cree, perhaps, they acquired birch-bark vessels for boiling their food, since other tribes in the Mackenzie River basin used vessels of spruce bark or of woven spruce roots. They had no feasts or ceremonies of their own except the performances of medicine-men, but they imitated the feasts and dances of the Cree. Women did not use cradle-boards or bags, but carried their babies on their backs after the manner of Eskimo women; and some of the men used the Eskimo double-bladed paddle. Art was confined to some very crude painting on wood, and a little work in porcupine-quill and moosehair that was much inferior to the work of tribes along the Mackenzie River.

Kutchin

The Kutchin or Loucheux group of tribes inhabited the basin of the Peel River from its source to its junction with the Mackenzie and the

entire basin of the Yukon from the mouth of the Pelly River downward, except for a small strip of country around its delta at Bering Sea.
There were several distinct tribes within this area, some of them devided
into bands; but the lists given by different authors by no means agree,
band names being often confused with tribal names. The dress and customs of the Kutchin in what is now Canadian territory varied but little,
and the traveller would have encountered no marked change in the dialect until he reached Fort Yukon within the boundaries of Alaska. The
Hare Indians of the lower Mackenzie could understand the speech of
the Peel River Kutchin, but it was only partly intelligible to the more
distant Chipewyan.

To the north of the Kutchin were the Eskimo, with whom they alternately fought and traded; to the south the highly organized Tlinkit Indians of the gulf of Alaska, who were accessible by passes through the
mountains. Both these neighbours influenced the culture of the Kutchin,
although at basis it followed much the same pattern as the culture of the
tribes in the basin of the Mackenzie.

The Canadian Kutchin devoted most of the summer to fishing, and
the winter to hunting caribou, moose, hare, and other game. They used
snares just as extensively as other tribes in northern Canada, and constructed the same kind of caribou-pound. Their fishing-gear included a
rather peculiar hook, a spear (double-gaff) modelled on an Eskimo
weapon, and a long dip-net and a fish basket of willow that they probably copied from Pacific Coast types. Seines of willow bark were made
by some of the Alaskan Kutchin, but not by the Canadian, apparently,
except by those who frequented the lower Mackenzie. The bow was
almost identical with the Eskimo bow, being made of three pieces of
wood jointed together and backed with a strong lashing of twisted
sinew. One tribe, the Han, that lived where the towns of Dawson and
Eagle now stand, attached a wooden hand-guard to the "grip" of the
bow, but none of the others seems to have favoured this contrivance, although it was used by Indians frequenting Great Bear Lake. All the
Kutchin adopted the Eskimo sled instead of the usual Indian toboggan,
and built their birch-bark canoes with flat bottoms and almost straight
sides like the Eskimo umiak. They made wooden food-trays of Eskimo
type, with bottoms inset as in a cask, although they also used birch-bark
trays; and they cooked their food in woven baskets of spruce or tama-
rack roots, as did other Indians of northern Canada.

The dress of the Kutchin, too, reflected Eskimo influence. The
caribou-skin shirt was short waisted and had long tails before and behind
like the shirt of the Eskimo. The women sometimes enlarged it behind

so that they could carry their babies against their naked backs after the manner of Eskimo women; but more often they used a peculiar birch-bark cradle shaped something like a Mexican saddle. The leggings, of one piece with the moccasins, were so full that they hardly differed from Eskimo trousers, and they carried embroidery of beads or porcupine-quills along the sides where Eskimo trousers had bands of coloured skin. Common to both peoples were the long mittens necessitated by short shirt sleeves, and the hood replacing a cap that was worn by Eskimo of all ages, but among the Kutchin mainly by children. The Kutchin shirt was peculiar in one respect; it had long fringes decorated with seeds or with beads of dentalia shells, and bead or porcupine-quill embroidery on breast, shoulders, and back. Men wore head-bands, necklaces, and nose-pendants of the same shells (which constituted, indeed, a regular cur-rency), painted their faces with red ochre and black lead, and planted bright feathers in their hair, after plastering it with grease and red ochre. Their proud bearing and colourful dress called to mind the Indi-ans of the plains rather than the sombre and depressed natives of the Mackenzie River Valley who were more nearly akin. Women tattooed radiating lines from the lower lip to the chin similar to the lines on Eskimo women, but they never pretended to rival the men in the adornment of their persons.

The dwellings of the Kutchin showed a certain originality. They en-larged the domed sweat-house that was almost universal throughout the upper half of North America, left an opening in the roof for a smoke-hole, banked snow around the outside wall, and strewed the floor with fir boughs. With a small fire burning within, this novel home was fairly comfortable even in the coldest weather. Most of the tribes used the same type of tent in summer also, but some bands of the Vunta tribe that frequented the lower Mackenzie at that season erected oblong huts of poles, brush, and bark to serve both for dwellings and for smoke-drying their fish.

The social organization was rather unusual, although it was obviously connected with the systems current along the Pacific Coast. The Kutchin were divided into three exogamous phratries that counted descent in the female line; yet they recognized no distinctions of rank, knew nothing of crests or totems, and held no potlatches except those in honour of the dead. Chiefs were chosen for courage or wisdom alone, and possessed little more authority than the chiefs or leaders in the tribes along the Mackenzie. Men without relatives or friends found security only by at-taching themselves to leading families, a very mild form of servitude compared with the slavery of the Pacific Coast. The Kutchin never purchased slaves, and never acquired any in their petty wars; for they massacred men, women, and children without mercy, sparing only some of the younger women to carry away for wives. Their own women received no gentle treatment; they performed nearly all the hard work in camp, transported all the family possessions, ate only after the men had eaten, and had no voice in family or tribal affairs except the one prerogative of selecting husbands for their daughters. Mothers often killed their girl babies to spare them the hardships they themselves had undergone; and old or infirm men and women who could no longer support themselves were strangled, sometimes at their own request. Yet life was not all hardships, even for the women. The Kutchin were passionately fond of games, and of singing and dancing; and young and old, women as well as men, took part in these diversions.

We know very little about the religion of the Kutchin. Their hunters often prayed to a moon-deity before starting out on their expeditions, and burned fat in the fire to obtain success in the chase. They had the same belief as other Indians in supernatural beings that haunted special localities, and they tried to propitiate them with offerings of beads. Every misfortune was attributed to witchcraft, and the Kutchin paid great deference to the medicine-men who claimed to acquire special powers from the unseen world through the usual fasting and dreaming. The dead were either burned immediately and their ashes suspended in bags from the tops of painted poles, or, if persons of note, deposited in trees within wooden coffins and burned several months later when the flesh had decayed; for the Kutchin dreaded burial in the ground. Relatives destroyed their property, lacerated their bodies, and made the same display of grief as the Mackenzie River Indians, but they also adopted from the Tlinkit the custom of holding a memorial feast or pot-latch within a special enclosure, when the guests sang mournful songs, danced, and indulged in various games, and departed with gifts for which they subsequently made a partial return.

There are perhaps 700 Kutchin living within the borders of Canada today. A census made by the Hudson's Bay Company in 1858 gave a population of 1,179. Seeing that even then the tribes had declined greatly through infanticide, wars, and European diseases, Mooney estimates a pre-European population of 3,000.

Those who would classify anthropology as the dismal science which examines only the relationships of broken rocks to shattered bones are often surprised to discover the writings of Paul Radin, Ruth Benedict, Margaret Mead, Irving Hallowell, or others concerned with "psychological" anthropology. Far from attempting to piece together a skull, or the past, these scholars have attempted to discover the systems of perception and cognition employed by members of other cultures; they have attempted to explain how the Indian sees the world, or how he classifies experience, or how he objectifies the unverifiable. This subdiscipline, sometimes called the study of "culture and personality," attempts to characterize the psychological or philosophical processes of individuals in other cultures, just as philosophers or psychoanalysts would clarify our own culture.

Irving Hallowell is widely known for his theoretical contributions to modern anthropology and for his outstanding studies of the Indians of the northern portion of the continent.

16 *A. Irving Hallowell*

OJIBWA WORLD VIEW *

It has become increasingly apparent in recent years that the potential significance of the data collected by cultural anthropologists far transcends in interest the level of simple, objective, ethnographic description of the peoples they have studied. New perspectives have arisen; fresh interpretations of old data have been offered; investigation and analysis have been pointed in novel directions. The study of culture and personality, national character and the special attention now being paid to values are illustrations that come to mind. Robert Redfield's concept of world view, "that outlook upon the universe that is characteristic of a people," which emphasizes a perspective that is not equivalent to the study of religion in the conventional sense, is a further example.

* Abridged from "Ojibwa Ontology, Behavior, and World View," by A. I. Hallowell, in *Culture in History: Essays in Honor of Paul Radin*, S. Diamond (ed.). New York: Columbia Univ. Press, 19–52, 1960.

"World view" [he says] differs from culture, ethos, mode of thought, and national character. It is the picture the members of a society have of the properties and characters upon their stage of action. While "national character" refers to the way these people look to the outsider looking in on them, "world view" refers to the way the world looks to that people looking out. Of all that is connoted by "culture," "world view" attends especially to the way a man, in a particular society, sees himself in relation to all else. It is the properties of existence as distinguished from and related to the self. It is, in short, a man's idea of the universe. It is that organization of ideas which answers to a man the questions: Where am I? Among what do I move? What are my relations to these things? . . . Self is the axis of "world view." (8:30)

In an essay entitled "The Self and Its Behavioral Environment," I have pointed out that self-identification and culturally constituted notions of the nature of the self are essential to the operation of all human societies and that a functional corollary is the cognitive orientation of the self to a world of objects other than self. Since the nature of these objects is likewise culturally constituted, a unified phenomenal field of thought, values, and action which is integral with the kind of world view that characterizes a society is provided for its members. The behavioral environment of the self thus becomes structured in terms of a diversified world of objects other than self, "discriminated, classified, and conceptualized with respect to attributes which are culturally constituted and symbolically mediated through language. Object orientation likewise provides the ground for an intelligible interpretation of events in the behavioral environment on the basis of traditional assumptions regarding the nature and attributes of the objects involved and implicit or explicit dogmas regarding the 'causes' of events" (5:91). Human beings in whatever culture are provided with cognitive orientation in a cosmos; there is "order" and "reason" rather than chaos. There are basic premises and principles implied, even if these do not happen to be consciously formulated and articulated by the people themselves. We are confronted with the philosophical implications of their thought, the nature of the world of being as they conceive it. If we pursue the problem deeply enough we soon come face to face with a relatively unexplored territory—ethno-metaphysics. Can we penetrate this realm in other cultures? What kind of evidence is at our disposal? The forms of speech as Benjamin Whorf and the neo-Humboldtians have thought? The manifest content of myth? Observed behavior and attitudes? And what order of reliability can our inferences have? The problem is a complex and difficult one, but this should not preclude its exploration.

In this paper I have assembled evidence, chiefly from my own field work on a branch of the Northern Ojibwa, which supports the inference that in the metaphysics of being found among these Indians, the action of persons provides the major key to their world view.

While in all cultures "persons" comprise one of the major classes of objects to which the self must become oriented, this category of being is by no means limited to *human* beings. In Western culture, as in others, "supernatural" beings are recognized as "persons," although belonging, at the same time, to an other than human category. But in the social sciences and psychology, "persons" and human beings are categorically identified. This identification is inherent in the concept of "society" and "social relations." In Warren's *Dictionary of Psychology* "person" is defined as "a human organism regarded as having distinctive characteristics and social relations." The same identification is implicit in the conceptualization and investigation of social organization by anthropologists. Yet this obviously involves a radical abstraction if, from the standpoint of the people being studied, the concept of "person" is not, in fact, synonymous with human being but transcends it. The significance of the abstraction only becomes apparent when we stop to consider the perspective adopted. The study of social organization, defined as human relations of a certain kind, is perfectly intelligible as an objective approach to the study of this subject in any culture. But if, in the world view of a people, "persons" as a class include entities other than human beings, then our objective approach is not adequate for presenting an accurate description of "the way a man, in a particular society, sees himself in relation to all else." A different perspective is required for this purpose. It may be argued, in fact, that a thoroughgoing "objective" approach to the study of cultures cannot be achieved solely by projecting upon those cultures categorical abstractions derived from Western thought. For, in a broad sense, the latter are a reflection of *our* cultural subjectivity. A higher order of objectivity may be sought by adopting a perspective which includes an analysis of the outlook of the people themselves as a complementary procedure. It is in a world view perspective, too, that we can likewise obtain the best insight into how cultures function as wholes.

The significance of these differences in perspective may be illustrated in the case of the Ojibwa by the manner in which the kinship term "grandfather" is used. It is not only applied to human persons but to spiritual beings who are persons of a category other than human. In fact, when the collective plural "our grandfathers" is used, the reference is primarily to persons of this latter class. Thus if we study Ojibwa social organization in the usual manner, we take account of only one set of "grandfathers." When we study their religion we discover other "grandfathers." But if we adopt a world view perspective no dichotomization appears. In this perspective "grandfather" is a term applicable to certain "person objects," without any distinction between human persons and those of an other-than-human class. Furthermore, both sets of grandfathers can be said to be functionally as well as terminologically equivalent in certain respects. The other-than-human grandfathers are sources of power to human beings through the "blessings" they bestow, i.e., a sharing of their power which enhances the "power" of human beings. A child is always given a name by an old man, i.e., a terminological grandfather. It is a matter of indifference whether he is a blood relative or not. This name carries with it a special blessing because it has reference to a dream of the human grandfather in which he obtained power from one or more of the other-than-human grandfathers. In other words, the relation between a human child and a human grandfather is functionally patterned in the same way as the relation between human beings and grandfathers of another-than-human class. And, just as the latter type of grandfather may impose personal taboos as a condition of a blessing, in the same way a human grandfather may impose a taboo on a "grandchild" he has named.

Another direct linguistic clue to the inclusiveness of the "person" category in Ojibwa thinking is the term *wíndīgo*. Baraga defines it in his *Dictionary* as "fabulous giant that lives on human flesh; a man that eats human flesh, cannibal." From the Ojibwa standpoint all *wíndīgowak* are conceptually unified as terrifying, anthropomorphic beings who, since they threaten one's very existence, must be killed. The central theme of a rich body of anecdotal material shows how this threat was met in particular instances. It ranges from cases in which it was necessary to kill the closest of kin because it was thought an individual was becoming a *wíndīgo*, through accounts of heroic fights between human beings and these fabulous giant monsters, to a first-hand report of a personal encounter with one of them.

The more deeply we penetrate the world view of the Ojibwa the more apparent it is that "social relations" between human beings (*änícinábek*) and other-than-human "persons" are of cardinal significance. These relations are correlative with their more comprehensive categori-

zation of "persons." Recognition must be given to the culturally constituted meaning of "social" and "social relations" if we are to understand
the nature of the Ojibwa world and the living entities in it.

LINGUISTIC CATEGORIES AND COGNITIVE ORIENTATION

Any discussion of "persons" in the world view of the Ojibwa must
take cognizance of the well known fact that the grammatical structure of
the language of these people, like all their Algonkian relatives, formally expresses a distinction between "animate" and "inanimate"
nouns. These particular labels, of course, were imposed upon Algonkian
languages by Europeans, it appeared to outsiders that the Algonkian
differentiation of objects approximated the animate-inanimate dichotomy of Western thought. Superficially this seems to be the case. Yet a
closer examination indicates that, as in the gender categories of other
languages, the distinction in some cases appears to be arbitrary, if not
extremely puzzling, from the standpoint of common sense or in a naturalistic frame of reference. Thus substantives for some, but not all—
trees, sun-moon, thunder, stones, and objects of material culture like
kettle and pipe—are classified as "animate."

If we wish to understand the cognitive orientation of the Ojibwa,
there is an ethno-linguistic problem to be considered: What is the meaning of animate in Ojibwa thinking? Are such generic properties of
objects as responsiveness to outer stimulation—sentience, mobility, self-
movement, or even reproduction—primary characteristics attributed to
all objects of the animate class irrespective of their categories as physical
objects in our thinking? Is there evidence to substantiate such properties
of objects independent of their formal linguistic classification? It must
not be forgotten that no Ojibwa is consciously aware of, or can abstractly
articulate the animate-inanimate category of his language, despite the
fact that this dichotomy is implicit in his speech. Consequently, the
grammatical distinction as such does not emerge as a subject for reflective thought or bear the kind of relation to individual thinking that
would be present if there were some formulated dogma about the
generic properties of these two classes of objects.

Commenting on the analogous grammatical categories of the Central
Algonkian languages with reference to linguistic and nonlinguistic orders of meaning, Greenberg writes: "Since all persons and animals are
in Class I (animate), we have at least one ethnoseme, but most of the

other meanings can be defined only by a linguiseme." In Greenberg's opinion, "unless the actual behavior of Algonquian speakers shows some mode of conduct common to all these instances such that, given this information, we could predict the membership of Class I, we must report to purely linguistic characterization" (3:15–16).

In the case of the Ojibwa, I believe that when evidence from beliefs, attitudes, conduct, and linguistic characterization are all considered together the psychological basis for their unified cognitive outlook can be appreciated, even when there is a radical departure from the framework of our thinking. In certain instances, behavioral predictions can be made. Behavior, however, is a function of a complex set of factors—including actual experience. More important than the linguistic classification of objects is the kind of vital functions attributed to them in the belief system and the conditions under which these functions are observed or tested in experience. This accounts, I think, for the fact that what we view as material, inanimate objects—such as shells and stones—are placed in an "animate" category along with "persons" which have no physical existence in our world view. The shells, for example, called *mígis* on account of the manner in which they function in the Midewiwin, could not be linguistically categorized as "inanimate." "Thunder," as we shall see, is not only reified as an "animate" entity, but has the attributes of a "person" and may be referred to as such. An "inanimate" categorization would be unthinkable from the Ojibwa point of view. When Greenberg refers to "persons" as clearly members of the animate grammatical category he is, by implication, identifying person and human being. Since in the Ojibwa universe there are many kinds of reified person-objects which are other than human but have the same ontological status, these, of course, fall into the same ethnoseme as human beings and into the "animate" linguistic class.

Since stones are grammatically animate, I once asked an old man: Are *all* the stones we see about us here alive? He reflected a long while and then replied, "No! But *some* are." This qualified answer made a lasting impression on me. And it is thoroughly consistent with other data that indicate that the Ojibwa are not animists in the sense that they dogmatically attribute living souls to inanimate objects such as stones. The hypothesis which suggests itself to me is that the allocation of stones to an animate grammatical category is part of a culturally constituted cognitive "set." It does not involve a consciously formulated theory about the nature of stones. It leaves a door open that our orientation on dogmatic grounds keeps shut tight. Whereas we should never expect a stone to manifest animate properties of any kind under any circumstances, the Ojibwa recognize, *a priori,* potentialities for animation in certain classes of objects under certain circumstances. The Ojibwa do not perceive stones, in general, as animate, any more than we do. The crucial test is experience. Is there any personal testimony available? In answer to this question we can say that it is asserted by informants that stones have been seen to move, that some stones manifest other animate properties, and, as we shall see, Flint is represented as a living personage in their mythology.

The old man to whom I addressed the general question about the animate character of stones was the same informant who told me that during a Midewiwin ceremony, when his father was the leader of it, he had seen a "big round stone move." He said his father got up and walked around the path once or twice. Coming back to his place he began to sing. The stone began to move "following the trail of the old man around the tent, rolling over and over, I saw it happen several times and others saw it also." The animate behavior of a stone under these circumstances was considered to be a demonstration of magic power on the part of the Midé. It was not a voluntary act initiated by the stone considered as a living entity. Associated with the Midewiwin in the past there were other types of large boulders with animate properties. My friend Chief Berens had one of these, but it no longer possessed these attributes. It had contours that suggested eyes and mouth. When Yellow Legs, Chief Berens's great-grandfather, was a leader of the Midewiwin he used to tap this stone with a new knife. It would then open its mouth, Yellow Legs would insert his fingers and take out a small leather sack with medicine in it. Mixing some of this medicine with water, he would pass the decoction around. A small sip was taken by those present.

If, then, stones are not only grammatically animate, but, in particular cases, have been observed to manifest animate properties, such as movement in space and opening of a mouth, why should they not on occasion be conceived as possessing animate properties of a "higher" order? The actualization of this possibility is illustrated by the following anecdote:

A white trader, digging in his potato patch, unearthed a large stone similar to the one just referred to. He sent for John Duck, an Indian who was the leader of the *wábano,* a contemporary ceremony that is held in a structure something like that used for the Midewiwin. The trader called his attention to the stone, saying that it must belong to his pavilion. John Duck did not seem pleased at this. He bent down and spoke to the boulder in a low voice, inquiring whether it had ever been in his pavilion. According to John the stone replied in the negative.

It is obvious that John Duck spontaneously structured the situation in terms that are intelligible within the context of Ojibwa language and culture. Speaking to a stone dramatizes the depth of the categorical difference in cognitive orientation between the Ojibwa and ourselves. In the anecdote describing John Duck's behavior, his use of speech as a mode of communication raises the animate status of the boulder to the level of social interaction common to human beings. Simply as a matter of observation we can say that the stone was treated *as if* it were a "person," not a "thing," without inferring that objects of this class are, for the Ojibwa, necessarily conceptualized as persons.

Further exploration might be made of the relations between Ojibwa thinking, observation, and behavior and their grammatical classification of objects but enough has been said, I hope, to indicate that not only animate properties but even "person" attributes may be projected upon objects which to us clearly belong to a physical inanimate category.

THE "PERSONS" OF OJIBWA MYTHOLOGY

The Ojibwa distinguish two general types of traditional oral narrative: (1) "News or tidings" (*täbätcamowin*), i.e., anecdotes, or stories, referring to events in the lives of human beings (*änícinábek*). In content, narratives of this class range from everyday occurrences, through more exceptional experiences, to those which verge on the legendary. (The anecdotes already referred to, although informal, may be said to belong to this general class.) (2) Myths (*ätísoʻkanak*), i.e., sacred stories, which are not only traditional and formalized; their narration is seasonally restricted and is somewhat ritualized. The significant thing about these stories is that the characters in them are regarded as living entities who have existed from time immemorial. While there is genesis through birth and temporary or permanent form-shifting through transformation, there is no outright creation. Whether human or animal in form or name, the major characters in the myths behave like people, though many of their activities are depicted in a spatiotemporal framework of cosmic, rather than mundane, dimensions. There is "social interaction" among them and between them and *änícinábek*.

A striking fact furnishes a direct linguistic clue to the attitude of the

Ojibwa towards these personages. When they use the term *ätíso'kanak*, they are not referring to what I have called a "body of narratives." The term refers to what we would call the characters in these stories; to the Ojibwa they are living "persons" of an other-than-human class. A synonym for this class of persons is "our grandfathers."

The *ätíso'kanak*, or "our grandfathers," are never "talked about" casually by the Ojibwa. But when the myths are narrated on long winter nights, the occasion is a kind of invocation: "Our grandfathers" like it and often come to listen to what is being said. In ancient times one of these entities (*Wísekedjak*) is reputed to have said to the others: "We'll try to make everything to suit the *änícinábek* as long as any of them exist, so that they will never forget us and will always talk about us."

It is clear, therefore, that to the Ojibwa, their "talk" about these entities, although expressed in formal narrative, is not about fictitious characters. On the contrary, what we call myth is accepted by them as a true account of events in the past lives of living "persons." It is for this reason that narratives of this class are significant for an understanding of the manner in which their phenomenal field is culturally structured and cognitively apprehended. As David Bidney has pointed out:

The concept of "myth" is relative to one's accepted beliefs and convictions, so that what is gospel truth for the believer is sheer "myth" and "fiction" for the non-believer or skeptic. . . . Myths and magical tales and practices are accepted precisely because pre-scientific folk do not consider them as merely "myths" or "magic," since once the distinction between myth and science is consciously accepted, the acquired critical insight precludes the belief in and acceptance of magic and myth. (1:166)

When taken at their face value, myths provide a reliable source of prime value for making inferences about Ojibwa world outlook. They offer basic data about unarticulated, unformalized, and unanalyzed concepts regarding which informants cannot be expected to generalize. From this point of view, myths are broadly analogous to the concrete material of the texts on which the linguist depends for his derivation, by analysis and abstraction, of the grammatical categories and principles of a language.

In formal definitions of myth (e.g., *Concise Oxford Dictionary* and Warren's *Dictionary of Psychology*) the subject matter of such narrative often has been said to involve not only fictitious characters but "supernatural persons." This latter appellation, if applied to the Ojibwa characters, is completely misleading, if for no other reason than the fact that the concept of "supernatural" presupposes a concept of the "natural." The latter is not present in Ojibwa thought. It is unfortunate that the natural-supernatural dichotomy has been so persistently invoked by many anthropologists in describing the outlook of peoples in cultures other than our own. Linguists learned long ago that it was impossible to write grammars of the languages of nonliterate peoples by using as a framework Indo-European speech forms. Lovejoy has pointed out that "The sacred word 'nature' is probably the most equivocal in the vocabulary of the European peoples . . ." (6:12) and the natural-supernatural antithesis has had its own complex history in Western thought.

To the Ojibwa, for example, *gízis* (day luminary, the sun) is not a natural object in our sense at all. Not only does their conception differ; the sun is a "person" of the other-than-human class. But more important still is the absence of the notion of the ordered regularity in movement that is inherent in our scientific outlook. The Ojibwa entertain no reasonable certainty that, in accordance with natural law, the sun will "rise" day after day. In fact, *Tcakábec*, a mythical personage, once set a snare in the trail of the sun and caught it. Darkness continued until a mouse was sent by human beings to release the sun and provide daylight again. And in another story (not a myth) it is recounted how two old men at dawn vied with each other in influencing the sun's movements.

The first old man said to his companion: "It is about sunrise now and there is a clear sky. You tell the sun to rise at once." So the other old man said to the sun: "My grandfather, come up quickly." As soon as he had said this the sun came up into the sky like a shot. "Now you try something," he said to his companion. "See if you can send it down." So the other man said to the sun: "My grandfather, put your face down again." When he said this the sun went down again. "I have more power than you," he said to the other old man, "The sun never goes down once it comes up."

We may infer that, to the Ojibwa, any regularity in the movements of the sun is of the same order as the habitual activities of human beings. There are certain expectations, of course, but on occasion, there may be temporary deviations in behavior "caused" by other persons. Above all, any concept of *impersonal* "natural" forces is totally foreign to Ojibwa thought.

Since their cognitive orientation is culturally constituted and thus given a psychological "set," we cannot assume that objects, like the sun, are perceived as natural objects in our sense. If this were so, the anecdote about the old men could not be accepted as an actual event involving a case of "social interaction" between human beings and an other-than-human person. Consequently, it would be an error to say that the Ojibwa "personify" natural objects. This would imply that, at some point, the sun was first perceived as an inanimate, material thing. There is, of course, no evidence for this. The same conclusion applies over the whole area of their cognitive orientation towards the objects of their world.

The Four Winds and Flint, for instance, are quintuplets. They were born of a mother (unnamed) who, while given human characteristics, lived in the very distant past. As will be more apparent later, this character, like others in the myths, may have anthropomorphic characteristics without being conceived as a human being. In the context she, like the others, is an *ätíso'kan*. The Winds were born first, then Flint "jumped out," tearing her to pieces. This, of course, is a direct allusion to his inanimate, stony properties. Later he was penalized for his hurried exit. He fought with *Misábos* (Great Hare) and pieces were chipped off his body and his size reduced. "Those pieces broken from your body may be of some use to human beings some day," *Misábos* said to him. "But you will not be any larger so long as the earth shall last. You'll never harm anyone again."

Against the background of this "historic" event, it would be strange indeed if flint were allocated to an inanimate grammatical category. There is a special term for each of the four winds that are differentiated, but no plural for "winds." They are all animate beings, whose "homes" define the four directions.

The conceptual reification of Flint, the Winds and the Sun as other-than-human persons exemplifies a world view in which a natural-supernatural dichotomy has no place. And the representation of these beings as characters in "true" stories reinforces their reality by means of a cultural device which at the same time depicts their vital roles in interaction with other persons as integral forces in the functioning of a unified cosmos.

ANTHROPOMORPHIC TRAITS AND OTHER-THAN-HUMAN PERSONS

In action and motivations the characters in the myths are indistinguishable from human persons. In this respect, human and other-than-human persons may be set off, in life as well as in myth, from animate beings such as ordinary animals (*awésiak*, pl.) and objects belonging to the inanimate grammatical category. But, at the same time, it must be noted that "persons" of the other-than-human class do not always present a human appearance in the myths. Consequently, we may ask: What constant attributes do unify the concept of "person?" What is the essential meaningful core of the concept of "person" in Ojibwa thinking? It can be stated at once that anthropomorphic traits in outward appearance are not the crucial attributes.

It is true that some extremely prominent characters in the myths are given explicit human form. *Wísekedjak* and *Tcakábec* are examples. Besides this they have distinctive characteristics of their own. The former has an exceptionally long penis and the latter is very small in size, yet extremely powerful. There are no equivalent female figures. By comparison, Flint and the Winds have human attributes by implication; they were born of a "woman" as human beings are born; they speak, and so on. On the other hand, the High God of the Ojibwa, a very remote figure who does not appear in the mythology at all, but is spoken of as a "person," is not even given sexual characteristics. This is possible because there is no sex gender in Ojibwa speech. Consequently an animate being of the person category may function in their thinking without having explicitly sexual or other anthropomorphic characteristics. Entities "seen" in dreams (*pawáganak*) are "persons"; whether they have anthropomorphic attributes or not is incidental. Other entities of the person category, whose anthropomorphic character is undefined or ambiguous, are what have been called the "masters" or "owners" of animals or plant species. Besides these, certain curing procedures and conjuring are said to have other-than-human personal entities as patrons.

If we now examine the cognitive orientation of the Ojibwa towards the Thunder Birds it will become apparent why anthropomorphism is not a constant feature of the Ojibwa concept of "person." These beings likewise demonstrate the autonomous nature of Ojibwa reification. For we find here a creative synthesis of objective "naturalistic" observation integrated with the subjectivity of dream experiences and traditional mythical narrative which, assuming the character of a living image, is neither the personification of a natural phenomenon nor an altogether animal-like or human-like being. Yet it is impossible to deny that, in the universe of the Ojibwa, Thunder Birds are "persons."

My Ojibwa friends, I discovered, were as puzzled by the white man's conception of thunder and lightning as natural phenomena as they were by the idea that the earth is round and not flat. I was pressed on more than one occasion to explain thunder and lightning, but I doubt whether my somewhat feeble efforts made much sense to them. Of one thing I am sure: My explanations left their own beliefs completely unshaken. This is not strange when we consider that, even in our naturalistic frame of reference, thunder and lightning as perceived do not exhibit the lifeless properties of inanimate objects. On the contrary, it has been said that thunder and lightning are among the natural phenomena which exhibit some of the properties of "person objects." Underlying the Ojibwa view there may be a level of naïve perceptual experience that should be taken into account. But their actual construct departs from this level in a most explicit direction: Why is an avian image central in their conception of a being whose manifestations are thunder and lightning? Among the Ojibwa with whom I worked, the linguistic stem for bird is the same as that for Thunder Bird (*pinési;* pl. *pinésíwak*). Besides this, the avian characteristics of Thunder Birds are still more explicit. Conceptually they are grouped with the hawks, of which there are several natural species in their habitat.

What is particularly interesting is that the avian nature of the Thunder Birds does not rest solely on an arbitrary image. Phenomenally, thunder does exhibit "behavioral" characteristics that are analogous to avian phenomena in this region. According to meteorological observations, the average number of days with thunder begins with one in April, increases to a total of five in midsummer (July) and then declines to one in October. And if a bird calendar is consulted, the facts show that species wintering in the south begin to appear in April and disappear for the most part not later than October, being, of course, a familiar sight during the summer months. The avian character of the Thunder Birds can be rationalized to some degree with reference to natural facts and their observation.

But the evidence for the existence of Thunder Birds does not rest only on the association of the occurrence of thunder with the migration of the summer birds projected into an avian image. When I visited the Ojibwa an Indian was living who, when a boy of twelve or so, saw *pinési* with his own eyes. During a severe thunderstorm he ran out of his tent and there on the rocks lay a strange bird. He ran back to call his parents, but when they arrived the bird had disappeared. He was sure it was a Thunder Bird, but his elders were skeptical because it is almost unheard of to see *pinési* in such a fashion. But the matter was clinched and the boy's account accepted when a man who had *dreamed* of *pinési* verified the boy's description. It will be apparent later why a dream experience was decisive. It should be added at this point, however, that many Indians say they have seen the nests of the Thunder Birds; these are usually described as collections of large stones in the form of shallow bowls located in high and inaccessible parts of the country.

If we now turn to the myths, we find that one of them deals in considerable detail with Thunder Birds. Ten unmarried brothers live together. The oldest is called *Mätcíkíwis*. A mysterious housekeeper cuts wood and builds a fire for them which they find burning when they return from a long day's hunt, but she never appears in person. One day the younger brother discovers and marries her. *Mätcíkíwis* is jealous and kills her. She would have revived if her husband had not broken a taboo she imposed. It turns out, however, that she is not actually a human being but a Thunder Bird and, thus, one of the *ätíso'kanak* and immortal. She flies away to the land above this earth inhabited by the Thunder Birds. Her husband, after many difficulties, follows her there. He finds himself brother-in-law to beings who are the "masters" of the duck hawks, sparrow hawks, and other species of this category of birds he has known on earth. He cannot relish the food eaten, since what the Thunder Birds call "beaver" are to him like the frogs and snakes on this earth (a genuinely naturalistic touch since the sparrow hawk, for example, feeds on batrachians and reptiles). He goes hunting gigantic snakes with his male Thunder Bird relatives. Snakes of this class also exist on this earth, and the Thunder Birds are their inveterate enemies. (When there is lightning and thunder this is the prey the Thunder Birds are after.) One day the great Thunder Bird says to his son-in-law, "I know you are getting lonely; you must want to see your people. I'll let you go back to earth now. You have nine brothers at home and I have nine girls left. You can take them with you as wives for your brothers. I'll be related to the people on earth now and I'll be merciful towards them. I'll not hurt any of them if I can possibly help it." So he tells his daughters to get ready. There is a big dance that night and the next morning the whole party starts off. When they come to the edge of Thunder Bird land the lad's wife said to him, "Sit on my back. Hang on tight to my neck and keep your eyes shut." Then the thunder crashes and the young man knows that they are off through the air. Having reached this earth they make their way to the brothers' camp. The Thunder Bird women, who have become transformed into human form, are enthusiastically received. There is another celebration and the nine brothers marry the nine sisters of their youngest brother's wife.

This is the end of the myth but a few comments are necessary. It is obvious that the Thunder Birds are conceived to act like human beings. They hunt and talk and dance. But the analogy can be pressed further. Their social organization and kinship terminology are precisely the same as the Ojibwa. The marriage of a series of female siblings (classificatory or otherwise) to a series of male siblings often occurs among the Ojibwa themselves. This is, in fact, considered a kind of ideal pattern. In one case that I know of six blood brothers were married to a sorority of six sisters. There is a conceptual continuity, therefore, between the social life of human beings and that of the Thunder Birds which is independent of the avian form given to the latter. But we must infer from the myth that this avian form is not constant. Appearance cannot then be taken as a permanent and distinguishable trait of the Thunder Birds. They are capable of metamorphosis, hence, the human attributes with which they are endowed transcend a human outward form. Their conceptualization as "persons" is not associated with a permanent human form any more than it is associated with a birdlike form. And the fact that they belong to the category of *ätinso'kanak* is no barrier to their descending to earth and mating with human beings. I was told of a woman who claimed that North Wind was the father of one of her children. My informant said he did not believe this; nevertheless, he thought it would have been accepted as a possibility in the past. We can only infer that in the universe of the Ojibwa the conception of "person" as a living, functioning social being is not only one which transcends the notion of person in the naturalistic sense; it likewise transcends a human appearance as a constant attribute of this category of being.

The relevance of such a concept to actual behavior may be illustrated by one simple anecdote. An informant told me that many years before he was sitting in a tent one summer afternoon during a storm, together with an old man and his wife. There was one clap of thunder after another. Suddenly the old man turned to his wife and asked, "Did you hear what was said?" "No," she replied, "I didn't catch it." My informant, an acculturated Indian, told me he did not at first know what the old man and his wife referred to. It was, of course, the thunder. The old man thought that one of the Thunder Birds had said something to him. He was reacting to this sound in the same way as he would respond to a human being, whose words he did not understand. The casualness of the remark and even the trivial character of the anecdote demonstrate the psychological depth of the "social relations" with other-than-human beings that becomes explicit in the behavior of the Ojibwa as a consequence of the cognitive "set" induced by their culture.

METAMORPHOSIS AS AN ATTRIBUTE OF PERSONS

The conceptualization in myth and belief of Thunder Birds as animate beings who, while maintaining their identity, may change their outward appearance and exhibit either an avian or a human form exemplifies an attribute of "persons" which, although unarticulated abstractly, is basic in the cognitive orientation of the Ojibwa.

Metamorphosis occurs with considerable frequency in the myths where other-than-human persons change their form. *Wisekedjak*, whose primary characteristics are anthropomorphic, becomes transformed and flies with the geese in one story, assumes the form of a snake in another, and once turns himself into a stump. Men marry "animal" wives who are not "really" animals. And *Mikīnäk*, the Great Turtle, marries a human being.

The senselessness and ambiguities which may puzzle the outsider when reading these myths are resolved when it is understood that, to the Ojibwa, "persons" of this class are capable of metamorphosis by their very nature. Outward appearance is only an incidental attribute of being. And the names by which some of these entities are commonly known, even if they identify the character as an "animal," do not imply unchangeableness in form.

Stith Thompson has pointed out that the possibility of transformation is a "commonplace assumption in folk tales everywhere. Many of such motifs are frankly fictitious, but a large number represent persistent beliefs and living tradition" (9:258). The case of the Ojibwa is in the latter category. The world of myth is not categorically distinct from the world as experienced by human beings in everyday life. In the latter, as well as the former, no sharp lines can be drawn dividing living beings of the animate class because metamorphosis is possible. In outward manifestation neither animal nor human characteristics define categorical differences in the core of being. And, even aside from metamorphosis, we find that in everyday life interaction with nonhuman entities of the animate class are only intelligible on the assumption that they possess some of the attributes of "persons."

So far as animals are concerned, when bears were sought out in their dens in the spring they were addressed, asked to come out so that they could be killed, and an apology was offered to them. The following encounter with a bear, related to me by a pagan Ojibwa named Birchstick, shows what happened in this case when an animal was treated as a person:

One spring when I was out hunting I went up a little creek where I knew suckers were spawning. Before I came to the rapids I saw fresh bear tracks. I walked along the edge of the creek and when I reached the rapids I saw a bear coming towards me, along the same trail I was following. I stepped behind a tree and when the animal was about thirty yards from me I fired. I missed and before I could reload the bear made straight for me. He seemed mad, so I never moved. I just waited there by the tree. As soon as he came close to me and rose up on his hind feet, I put the butt end of my gun against his heart and held him there. I remembered what my father used to tell me when I was a boy. He said that a bear always understands what you tell him. The bear began to bite the stock of the gun. He even put his paws upon it something like a man would do if he were going to shoot. Still holding him off as well as I could I said to the bear, "If you want to live, go away," and he let go the gun and walked off. I didn't bother the bear anymore. (4:397)

These instances suffice to demonstrate that, at the level of individual behavior, the interaction of the Ojibwa with certain kinds of plants and animals in everyday life is so structured culturally that individuals act as if they were dealing with "persons" who both understand what is being said to them and have volitional capacities as well. From the standpoint of perceptual experience if we only take account of autochthonous factors in Birchstick's encounter with the bear his behavior appears idiosyncratic and is not fully explained. On the other hand, if we invoke Ojibwa concepts of the nature of animate beings, his behavior becomes intelligible to us. We can understand the determining factors in his definition of the situation, and the functional relations between perception and conduct are meaningful. The Indian was not confronted with an animal with "objective" ursine properties, but rather with an animate being, who had ursine attributes and *also* "person attributes." These, we may infer, were perceived as an integral whole. I am sure, however, that in narrating this episode to another Indian, he would not have referred to what his father had told him about bears. That was for my benefit!

Since bears, then, are assumed to possess "person attributes," it is not surprising to find that there is a very old, widespread, and persistent belief that sorcerers may become transformed into bears in order better to pursue their nefarious work.

An old-fashioned informant of mine told me how he had once fallen sick, and, although he took various kinds of medicine these did him no good. Because of this, and for other reasons, he believed he had been bewitched by a certain man. Then he noticed that a bear kept coming to his camp almost every night after dark. This is most unusual because wild animals do not ordinarily come anywhere near a human habitation. Once the bear would have entered his wigwam if he had not been warned in a dream. His anxiety increased because he knew, of course, that sorcerers often transformed themselves into bears. So when the bear appeared one night he got up, went outdoors, and shouted to the animal that he knew what it was trying to do. He threatened retaliation in kind if the bear ever returned. The animal ran off and never came back.

In this case there are psychological parallels to Birchstick's encounter with a bear: In both cases the bear is directly addressed as a person might be, and it is only through a knowledge of the cultural background that it is possible fully to understand the behavior of the individuals involved. In the present case, however, we can definitely say that the "animal" was perceived as a human being in the form of a bear; the Indian was threatening a human person with retaliation, not an animal.

A question that I have discussed in *Culture and Experience* in connection with another "bearwalk" anecdote, also arises in this case. Briefly, the Ojibwa believe that a human being consists of a vital part, or *soul*, which, under certain circumstances may become detached from the body, so that it is not necessary to assume that the body part, in all cases, literally undergoes transformation into an animal form. The body of the sorcerer may remain in his wigwam while his soul journeys elsewhere and appears to another person in the form of an animal.

This interpretation is supported by an account which an informant gave me of a visit his deceased grandchild had paid him. One day he was traveling in a canoe across a lake. He had put up an improvised mast and used a blanket for a sail. A little bird alighted on the mast. This was a most unusual thing for a bird to do. He was convinced that it was not a bird but his dead grandchild. The child, of course, had left her body behind in a grave, nevertheless she visited him in animal form.

Thus, both living and dead human beings may assume the form of animals. So far as appearance is concerned, there is no hard and fast line that can be drawn between an animal form and a human form because metamorphosis is possible. In perceptual experience what looks like a bear may sometimes *be* an animal and, on other occasions, a human being. What persists and gives continuity to being is the vital part, or soul. Dorson goes to the heart of the matter when he stresses the fact that the whole socialization process in Ojibwa culture "impresses the young with the concepts of transformation and of 'power', malign or benevolent, human or demonic. These concepts underlie the entire Indian mythology, and make sensible the otherwise childish stories of culture heroes, animal husbands, friendly thunders, and malicious serpents. The bearwalk idea fits at once this dream world—literally a dream world, for Ojibwa go to school in dreams" (2:31).

We must conclude, I believe, that the capacity for metamorphosis is one of the features which links human beings with the other-than-human persons in their behavioral environment. It is one of the generic properties manifested by beings of the person class. But is it a ubiquitous capacity of all members of this class eqaully? I do not think so. Metamorphosis to the Ojibwa mind is an earmark of "power." Within the category of persons there is a graduation of power. Other-than-human persons occupy the top rank in the power hierarchy of animate being. Human beings do not differ from them in kind, but in power. Hence, it is taken for granted that all the *ätíso'kanak* can assume a variety of forms. In the case of human beings, while the potentiality for metamorphosis exists and may even be experienced, any outward manifestation is inextricably associated with unusual power, for good or evil. And power of this degree can only be acquired by human beings through the help of other-than-human persons. Sorcerers can transform themselves only because they have acquired a high order of power from this source.

Powerful men, in the Ojibwa sense, are also those who can make inanimate objects behave as if they were animate. The *Midé* who made a stone roll over and over has been mentioned earlier. Other examples, such as the animation of a string of wooden beads, or animal skins, could be cited. Such individuals also have been observed to transform one object into another, such as charcoal into bullets and ashes into gunpowder, or a handful of goose feathers into birds or insects. In these manifestations, too, they are elevated to the same level of power as that displayed by other-than-human persons. We can, in fact, find comparable episodes in the myths.

The notion of animate being itself does not presume a capacity for manifesting the highest level of power any more than it implies person-attributes in every case. Power manifestations vary within the animate class of being as does the possession of person-attributes. A human being may possess little, if any, more power than a mole. No one would have been more surprised than Birchstick if the bear he faced had suddenly become human in form. On the other hand, the spiritual "masters" of the various species of animals are inherently powerful and, quite generally, they possess the power of metamorphosis. These entities, like the *ätíso'kanak*, are among the sources from which human beings may seek to enhance their own power. My Ojibwa friends often cautioned me against judging by appearances. A poor forlorn Indian dressed in rags might have great power; a smiling, amiable woman, or a pleasant old man, might be a sorcerer. You never can tell until a situation arises in which their power for good or ill becomes manifest. I have since concluded that the advice given me in a common sense fashion provides one of the major clues to a generalized attitude towards the objects of their behavioral environment—particularly people. It makes them cautious and suspicious in interpersonal relations of all kinds. The possibility of metamorphosis must be one of the determining factors in this attitude; it is a concrete manifestation of the deceptiveness of appearances. What looks like an animal, without great power, may be a transformed person with evil intent. Even in dream experiences, where a human being comes into direct contact with other-than-human persons, it is possible to be deceived. Caution is necessary in "social" relations with all classes of persons.

DREAMS, METAMORPHOSIS, AND THE SELF

The Ojibwa are a dream-conscious people. For an understanding of their cognitive orientation it is as necessary to appreciate their attitude towards dreams as it is to understand their attitude towards the characters in the myths. For them, there is an inner connection which is as integral to their outlook as it is foreign to ours.

The basic assumption which links the *ätíso'kanak*, with dreams is this: Self-related experience of the most personal and vital kind includes what is seen, heard, and felt in dreams. Although there is no lack of discrimination between the experiences of the self when awake and when dreaming, both sets of experiences are equally self-related. Dream experiences function integrally with other recalled memory images in so far as these, too, enter the field of self-awareness. When we think autobiographically we only include events that happened to us when awake; the Ojibwa include remembered events that have occurred in dreams. And, far from being of subordinate importance, such experiences are for them often of more vital importance than the events of daily waking life. Why is this so? Because it is in dreams that the individual comes into direct communication with the *ätíso'kanak*, the powerful "persons" of the other-than-human class.

In the long winter evenings, as I have said, the *ätíso'kanak* are talked about; the past events in their lives are recalled again and again by *änícinábek*. When a conjuring performance occurs, the voices of some of the same beings are heard issuing from within the conjuring lodge. Here is actual perceptual experience of the "grandfathers" during a waking state. In dreams, the same other-than-human persons are both "seen" and "heard." They address human beings as "grandchild." These "dream visitors" (i.e., *pawáganak*) interact with the dreamer much as human persons do. But, on account of the nature of these beings there are differences, too. It is in the context of this face-to-face personal interaction of the self with the "grandfathers" (i.e., synonymously *ätíso'kanak*, *pawáganak*) that human beings receive important revelations that are the source of assistance to them in the daily round of life, and, besides this, of "blessings" that enable them to exercise exceptional powers of various kinds.

But dream experiences are not ordinarily recounted save under special circumstances. There is a taboo against this, just as there is a taboo against myth narration except in the proper seasonal context. The consequence is that we know relatively little about the manifest content of dreams. All our data come from acculturated Ojibwa. We do know enough to say, however, that the Ojibwa recognize quite as much as we do that dream experiences are often qualitatively different from our waking experiences. This fact, moreover, is turned to positive account. Since their dream visitors are other-than-human "persons" possessing great power, it is to be expected that the experiences of the self in interaction with them will differ from those with human beings in daily life. Besides this, another assumption must be taken into account: When a human being is asleep and dreaming his *òtcatcákwin* (vital part, soul), which is the core of the self, may become detached from the body (*mïyó*). Viewed by another human being, a person's body may be

easily located and observed in space. But his vital part may be somewhere else. Thus, the self has greater mobility in space and even in time
while sleeping. This is another illustration of the deceptiveness of appearances. The body of a sorcerer may be within sight in a wigwam,
while "he" may be bearwalking. Yet the space in which the self is
mobile is continuous with the earthly and cosmic space of waking life. A
dream of one of my informants documents this specifically. After having
a dream in which he met some (mythical) anthropomorphic beings
(*mémengwécīwak*) who live in rocky escarpments and are famous for
their medicine, he told me that he had later identified precisely the
rocky place he had visited and entered in his dream. Thus the behavioral environment of the self is all of a piece. This is why experiences undergone when awake or asleep can be interpreted as experiences
of self. Memory images, as recalled, become integrated with a sense of
self-continuity in time and space.

Metamorphosis may be *experienced* by the self in dreams. One example will suffice to illustrate this. The dreamer in this case had been
paddled out to an island by his father to undergo his puberty fast. For
several nights he dreamed of an anthropomorphic figure. Finally, this
being said, "Grandchild, I think you are strong enough now to go with
me." Then the *pawágan* began dancing and as he danced he turned into
what looked like a golden eagle. (This being must be understood as the
"master" of this species.) Glancing down at his own body as he sat there
on a rock, the boy noticed it was covered with feathers. The "eagle"
spread its wings and flew off to the south. The boy then spread his
wings and followed.

Here we find the instability of outward form in both human and
other-than-human persons succinctly dramatized. Individuals of both
categories undergo metamorphosis. In later life the boy will recall how
he first saw the "master" of the golden eagles in his anthropomorphic
guise, followed by his transformation into avian form; at the same time
he will recall his own metamorphosis into a bird. But this experience,
considered in context, does not imply that subsequently the boy can
transform himself into a golden eagle at will. He might or might not be
sufficiently "blessed." The dream itself does not inform us about this.

This example, besides showing how dream experiences may reinforce
the belief in metamorphosis, illustrates an additional point: the
pawáganak, whenever "seen," are always experienced as appearing in
a specific form. They have a "bodily" aspect, whether human-like, animal-like, or ambiguous. But this is not their most persistent, enduring

and vital attribute any more than in the case of human beings. We must conclude that all animate beings of the person class are unified conceptually in Ojibwa thinking because they have a similar structure—an inner vital part that is enduring and an outward form which can change. Vital personal attributes such as sentience, volition, memory, speech are not dependent upon outward appearance but upon the inner vital essence of being. If this be true, human beings and other-than-human persons are alike in another way. The human self does not die; it continues its existence in another place, after the body is buried in the grave. In this way *änícinábek* are as immortal as *ätíso'kanak*. This may be why we find human beings associated with the latter in the myths where it is sometimes difficult for an outsider to distinguish between them.

Thus the world of personal relations in which the Ojibwa live is a world in which vital social relations transcend those which are maintained with human beings. Their culturally constituted cognitive orientation prepares the individual for life in this world and for a life after death. The self-image that he acquires makes intelligible the nature of other selves. Speaking as an Ojibwa, one might say: all other "persons" —human or other than human—are structured the same as I am. There is a vital part which is enduring and an outward appearance that may be transformed under certain conditions. All other "persons," too, have such attributes as self-awareness and understanding. I can talk with them. Like myself, they have personal identity, autonomy, and volition. I cannot always predict exactly how they will act, although most of the time their behavior meets my expectations. In relation to myself, other "persons" vary in power. Many of them have more power than I have, but some have less. They may be friendly and help me when I need them but, at the same time, I have to be prepared for hostile acts, too. I must be cautious in my relations with other "persons" because appearances may be deceptive.

THE PSYCHOLOGICAL UNITY OF THE OJIBWA WORLD

Although not formally abstracted and articulated philosophically, the nature of "persons" is the focal point of Ojibwa ontology and the key to the psychological unity and dynamics of their world outlook. This aspect of their metaphysics of being permeates the content of their cognitive processes: perceiving, remembering, imagining, conceiving, judging, and reasoning. Nor can the motivation of much of their conduct be thoroughly understood without taking into account the relation of their central values and goals to the awareness they have of the existence of other-than-human, as well as human, persons in their world. "Persons," in fact, are so inextricably associated with notions of causality that, in order to understand their appraisal of events and the kind of behavior demanded in situations as they define them, we are confronted over and over again with the roles of "persons" as *loci* of causality in the dynamics of their universe. For the Ojibwa make no cardinal use of any concept of impersonal forces as major determinants of events. In the context of my exposition the meaning of the term *manitu*, which has become so generally known, may be considered as a synonym for a person of the other-than-human class ("grandfather," *ätíso'kanak, pawá-gan*).

In an essay on the "Religion of the North American Indians" published over forty years ago, Radin asserted "that from an examination of the data customarily relied upon as proof and from individual data obtained, there is nothing to justify the postulation of a belief in a universal force in North America. Magical power as an 'essence' existing apart and separate from a definite spirit, is, we believe, an unjustified assumption, an abstraction created by investigators" (7:350). This opinion, at the time, was advanced in opposition to the one expressed by those who, stimulated by the writings of R. R. Marett in particular, interpreted the term *manitu* among the Algonkians, *orenda* among the Iroquois and *wakanda* among the Siouan peoples as having reference to a belief in a magical force of some kind. But Radin pointed out that in his own field work among both the Winnebago and the Ojibwa the terms in question "always referred to definite spirits, not necessarily definite in shape. If at a vapor-bath the steam is regarded as *wakanda* or *manitu*, it is because it is a spirit transformed into steam for the time being; if an arrow is possessed of specific virtues, it is because a spirit has either transformed himself into the arrow or because he is temporarily dwelling in it; and finally, if tobacco is offered to a peculiarly-shaped object it is because either this object belongs to a spirit, or a spirit is residing in it." *Manitu*, he said, in addition to its substantive usage may have such connotations as "sacred," "strange," "remarkable" or "powerful" without "having the slightest suggestion of 'inherent power', but having the ordinary sense of these adjectives" (7:349–50).

With respect to the Ojibwa conception of causality, all my own observations suggest that a culturally constituted psychological set operates which inevitably directs the reasoning of individuals towards an explanation of events in personalistic terms. *Who* did it, *who* is responsible, is always the crucial question to be answered. Personalistic explanation of past events is found in the myths. It was *Wīsekedjak* who, through the exercise of his personal power, expanded the tiny bit of mud retrieved by Muskrat from the depths of the inundating waters of the great deluge into the inhabitable island-earth of Ojibwa cosmography. Personalistic explanation is central in theories of disease causation. Illness may be due to sorcery; the victim, in turn, may be "responsible" because he has offended the sorcerer—even unwittingly. Besides this, I may be responsible for my own illness, even without the intervention of a sorcerer. I may have committed some wrongful act in the past, which is the "cause" of my sickness. My child's illness, too, may be the consequence of my past transgressions or those of my wife. The personalistic theory of causation even emerges today among acculturated Ojibwa. In 1940, when a severe forest fire broke out at the mouth of the Berens River, no Indian would believe that lightning or any impersonal or accidental determinants were involved. *Somebody* must have been responsible. The German spy theory soon became popular. "Evidence" began to accumulate; strangers had been seen in the bush, and so on. The personalistic type of explanation satisfies the Ojibwa because it is rooted in a basic metaphysical assumption; its terms are ultimate and incapable of further analysis within the framework of their cognitive orientation and experience.

Since the dynamics of events in the Ojibwa universe find their most ready explanation in a personalistic theory of causation, the qualitative aspects of interpersonal relations become affectively charged with a characteristic sensitivity. The psychological importance of the range and depth of this sensitive area may be overlooked if the inclusiveness of the concept of "person" and "social relations" that is inherent in their outlook is not borne in mind. The reason for this becomes apparent when we consider the pragmatic relations between behavior, values, and the role of "persons" in their world view.

The central goal of life for the Ojibwa is expressed by the term *pīmä-däzīwin*, life in the fullest sense, life in the sense of longevity, health and freedom from misfortune. This goal cannot be achieved without the effective help and cooperation of *both* human and other-than-human "persons," as well as by one's own personal efforts. The help of other-than-human "grandfathers" is particularly important for men. This is why all Ojibwa boys, in aboriginal days, were motivated to undergo the so-called "puberty fast" or "dreaming" experience. This was the means by which it was possible to enter into direct "social interaction" with "persons" of the other-than-human class for the first time. It was the opportunity of a lifetime. Every special aptitude, all a man's subsequent successes and the explanation of many of his failures, hinged upon the help of the "guardian spirits" he obtained at this time, rather than upon his own native endowments or the help of his fellow *anícinábek*. If a boy received "blessings" during his puberty fast and, as a man, could call upon the help of other-than-human persons when he needed them he was well prepared for meeting the vicissitudes of life. Among other things, he could defend himself against the hostile actions of human persons which might threaten him and thus interfere with the achievement of *pīmădăzīwin*. The grandfather of one of my informants said to him: "you will have a long and good life if you dream well." The help of human beings, however, was also vital, especially the services of those who had acquired the kind of power which permitted them to exercise effective curative functions in cases of illness. At the same time there were moral responsibilities which had to be assumed by an individual if he strove for *pīmădăzīwin*. It was as essential to maintain approved standards of personal and social conduct as it was to obtain power from the "grandfathers" because, in the nature of things, one's own conduct, as well as that of other "persons," was always a potential threat to the achievement of *pīmădăzīwin*. Thus we find that the same values are implied throughout the entire range of "social interaction" that characterizes the Ojibwa world; the same standards which apply to mutual obligations between human beings are likewise implied in the reciprocal relations between human and other-than-human "persons." In his relations with "the grandfathers" the individual does not expect to receive a "blessing" for nothing. It is not a free gift; on his part there are obligations to be met. There is a principle of reciprocity implied. There is a general taboo imposed upon the human being which forbids him to recount his dream experiences in full detail, except under certain circumstances. Specific taboos may likewise be imposed upon the suppliant. If these taboos are violated he will lose his power; he can no longer count on the help of his "grandfathers."

The same principle of mutual obligations applies in other spheres of life. The Ojibwa are hunters and food gatherers. Since the various species of animals on which they depend for a living are believed to be under the control of "masters" or "owners" who belong to the category of other-than-human persons, the hunter must always be careful to treat the animals he kills for food or fur in the proper manner. It may be necessary, for example, to throw their bones in the water or to perform a ritual in the case of bears. Otherwise, he will offend the "masters" and be threatened with starvation because no animals will be made available to him. Cruelty to animals is likewise an offense that will provoke the same kind of retaliation. And, according to one anecdote, a man suffered illness because he tortured a fabulous *windigo* after killing him. A moral distinction is drawn between the kind of conduct demanded by the primary necessities of securing a livelihood, or defending oneself against aggression, and unnecessary acts of cruelty. The moral values implied document the consistency of the principle of mutual obligations which is inherent in all interactions with "persons" throughout the Ojibwa world.

One of the prime values of Ojibwa culture is exemplified by the great stress laid upon sharing what one has with others. A balance, a sense of proportion must be maintained in all interpersonal relations and activities. Hoarding, or any manifestation of greed, is discountenanced. The central importance of this moral value in their world outlook is illustrated by the fact that other-than-human persons share their power with human beings. This is only a particular instance of the obligations which human beings feel towards one another. A man's catch of fish or meat is distributed among his kin. Human grandfathers share the power acquired in their dreams from other-than-human persons with their classificatory grandchildren. An informant whose wife had borrowed his pipe for the morning asked to borrow one of mine while we worked together. When my friend Chief Berens once fell ill he could not explain it. Then he recalled that he had overlooked one man when he had passed around a bottle of whiskey. He believed this man was offended and had bewitched him. Since there was no objective evidence of this, it illustrates the extreme sensitivity of an individual to the principle of sharing, operating through feelings of guilt. I was once told about the puberty fast of a boy who was not satisfied with his initial "blessing." He demanded that he dream of all the leaves of all the trees in the world so that absolutely nothing would be hidden from him. This was considered greedy and, while the *pawágan* who appeared in his dream granted his desire, the boy was told that "as soon as the leaves start to fall you'll get sick and when all the leaves drop to the ground that is the end of your life." And this is what happened. "Overfasting" is as greedy as hoarding. It violates a basic moral value and is subject to a punitive sanction. The unity of the Ojibwa outlook is likewise apparent here.

The entire psychological field in which they live and act is not only unified through their conception of the nature and role of "persons" in their universe, but by the sanctioned moral values which guide the relations of "persons." It is within this web of "social relations" that the individual strives for *pīmådäzīwin.*

SECTION IV
The Basin-Plateau

Inland from the Pacific Ocean, between the Cascades and the Sierras on the west and the Rockies on the east, lies a vast stretch of of intermontane country which is called the "Great Basin" (to the south) and the "Plateau" (to the north). This region, intermediate between the Pacific littoral and the continental divide, is a zone of cultural blending.

The Basin (mainly California, Nevada, Utah, and western Colorado desert) was inhabited by hunting and gathering Indians, usually referred to by the generic term "Shoshone." This term includes Indian groups such as the Ute, Paiute, Goshute, Bannock, Snake, Paviotso, Panamint, and Chemehuevi. Faced with a generally inhospitable environment and possessing only crude technology, these Indians were as culturally deprived as any people studied by anthropologists.

That the cultural poverty of these people was a result of historical rather than racial or biological inadequacy is amply demonstrated by the Northern Shoshone who, when they obtained the horse in the early nineteenth century, became buffalo-hunting warriors similar to the better known Plains Indians.

The Plateau, which comprises the interiors of the present states of Oregon and Washington, northern Idaho, western Montana, and portions of interior British Columbia, was occupied by a different variety of Indian culture. In contrast to the linguistic homogeneity of the Basin, where nearly all bands spoke closely related dialects, the Plateau region contained languages from four major families. In addition to its linguistic diversity, the Plateau is also a region of much greater geographical diversity than is the essentially arid Basin. The Plateau is drained by the salmon-bearing Columbia and Fraser Rivers, and because of heavier rainfall than occurs to the south, it is generally more heavily wooded. Furthermore, the Plateau people were strongly influenced by Plains cultures to the east, and by Northwest Coast cultures to the west.

Relatively complex social stratification, which included slavery, developed among a few tribes of the Plateau, and in some tribes a strong orientation toward warfare became prominent.

Despite the apparent cultural and linguistic divergence of the aboriginal populations of the Plateau in contrast to the Basin, the two regions were remarkably similar in many respects. Indeed, from Baja California to interior Alaska stretched a cultural province which displayed many apparently ancient and simple features associated with human adaptation to relatively inhospitable environments. If we could filter out all that has entered into the native cultures since European contact, in the following papers by Steward and by Ray we would be reading a close account of the life led for thousands of years by many of the inhabitants of the New World.

The length of man's residence in the Basin-Plateau zone is still undetermined, but there are indications of possible antiquity greatly exceeding 10,000 years. A famous archaeological site, Tule Springs, Nevada, was once thought to contain cultural material in excess of 23,000 years of age; considerable doubt, however, surrounds this early date. By 8000 B.C., an ancient culture type called the "Desert" culture was widespread over western North America, characterized by a heavy reliance upon plant foods. The Desert culture type survived throughout much of the Basin-Plateau area until the arrival of Europeans; it has been said that some of the Shoshone practiced essentially a Desert-type culture into the late eighteenth century. Though undoubtedly small changes did occur in traditional life, the endurance of the Desert culture pattern over such an extensive period testified to the effective adaptation and to the general cultural isolation of the Indian groups of the region.

In the first article of this section, Julian Steward presents his important and well-known outline of the social organization and ecology of the Basin Indians.

17 Julian H. Steward

THE GREAT BASIN
SHOSHONEAN INDIANS*

The Shoshonean-speaking Indians—the Ute, Western Shoshoni, and Northern Paiute of western Colorado, Utah, Nevada, and eastern Oregon and California—acquired most of their hunting and gathering techniques from other peoples, but their general adaptation to the intermontane steppes and deserts was so distinctive that they constitute a special culture area usually called the Great Basin or Basin-Plateau area. In a quantitative sense, this culture was extremely simple. An "element list," which breaks the culture down into details such as basket weaves and shapes, religious beliefs, social practices, and other details, includes a total of about 3,000 items. By comparison, the U. S. forces landing at Casa Blanca during World War II unloaded 500,000 items of material equipment alone. The total "elements" of modern American culture would probably run to several million.

Shoshonean culture, however, is of interest for the nature of its organization as much as for its quantitative simplicity. Virtually all cultural activities were carried out by the family in comparative isolation from other families. A contrast with modern America helps clarify this point. In the United States today, people are highly specialized workers in an economic system geared to national and international patterns; education is increasingly standardized and the community or state takes over this function from the family when the child is six years old or younger; health practices are dictated largely by research carried out on an international scale and in part administered by the state and community; recreation more and more involves the consumption of products made by national organizations; religious worship is carried on in national or

* Abridged from "The Great Basin Shoshonean Indians: an Example of a Family Level of Sociocultural Integration," in *Theory of Culture Change: The Methodology of Multilinear Evolution,* by J. H. Steward. Urbana: Univ. Illinois Press, 101–121, 1955.

international churches. These growing functions of the community, state, and nation increasingly relieve the family of functions it performed in earlier historical periods. It is perhaps difficult to imagine that a family, alone and unaided, could obtain virtually all the food it consumed; manufacture all its clothing, household goods, and other articles; rear and train its children without assistance; take care of its sick except in time of crisis; be self-sufficient in its religious activities; and, except on special occasions, manage its own recreation. Why this was so in the case of the Shoshoneans is explainable largely in terms of their cultural ecological adaptations.

Owing to the nature of the natural environment of the Great Basin area and to the simple hunting and gathering techniques for exploiting it, it was inevitable that the individual family or at the most two or three related families should live in isolation during most of the year. "Family" in this case signifies the nuclear, biological or bilateral family, consisting of mother, father, and children. Unlike many primitive peoples, the Shoshoneans were not organized in extended family or lineage groups and, although, as we shall see subsequently, the immediate family was frequently enlarged through plural spouses and different families were closely allied by marriage, the functioning unit was the nuclear family, augmented only by a grandparent, aunt, or uncle who otherwise would be homeless.

ENVIRONMENT AND RESOURCES

The natural resources which were exploitable by Shoshonean culture were so limited that the population was extremely sparse. In the more fertile portions of this area there was perhaps one person to five square miles, while in the vast stretches of nearly waterless terrain the ratio was one to fifty or even one hundred square miles. The mean for the whole area was between one person to twenty or thirty square miles.

The territory once inhabited by the Shoshonean Indians is extremely arid, but technically most of it is classified as "steppe" rather than true "desert" although there are large areas devoid of vegetation. The country consists of large arid valleys lying between mountain ranges which run north and south. These valleys are from five to twenty miles wide and twenty to eighty miles long. The greater portion of the Shoshonean habitat lies within the Great Basin, a vast area of interior drainage between the Wasatch Mountains of Utah and the Sierra Nevada Range of California and Oregon, but it also includes portions of the Columbia

River Plateau of Idaho and eastern Oregon and the Colorado River Plateau of eastern Utah and western Colorado.

The flora and fauna of all these areas are very similar. There are several biotic zones, which set the basic conditions for a society equipped only with very simple hunting and gathering techniques. In the valleys, which lie between 4,000 and 6,000 feet elevation, the low rainfall—five to twenty inches a year—together with high evaporation supports a predominantly xerophytic vegetation, that is, such drought-resisting plants as sagebrush and greasewood. This vegetation has very limited value to human beings or animals. Plants bearing edible seeds and roots occur in some abundance immediately along the stream banks, but, except in favored areas, such as the piedmont of the Wasatch Mountains and the Sierra Nevada Mountains, the streams are small and widely-spaced. In the Great Basin, the streams end in saline marshes or lakes. In the vast sandy areas between the streams, the quantity of edible plants depends directly upon rainfall, which varies from year to year and from place to place. These plants only afforded small quantities of food for the Indians, and they could not support game in herds comparable to the bison of the Great Plains or the caribou of the far north. The two species of greatest importance to the Indians were antelope and rabbits. These not only supplied meat and skins, but the communal hunts in which they were sometimes taken were among the few collective cultural activities. The numbers of both species, however, were limited, and the hunts were infrequent.

It is impossible to estimate the quantitative importance of different animal foods in the valley zone, but the Shoshoneans probably ate more rats, mice, gophers, locusts, ants, ant eggs, larvae of flies which breed in the salt lakes, snakes and lizards than large game. In the rivers, such as the Owyhee, John Day, Crooked, Snake, Truckee, Carson, Walker, and Humboldt rivers, fish were an important supplement to other foods but the runs were seasonal, the quantity did not compare with that of fish in coastal rivers, and the fish were evidently not suited for preservation and storage.

The zone of piñon and juniper trees lies between about 6,000 and 8,000 or 9,000 feet. This zone is largely restricted to the flanks of the mountain ranges since most valleys lie below this altitude. The juniper had little value to the Indians except for its wood, but the piñon (*Pinus monophylla* in the north, *Pinus edulis* in the south), which occurred throughout the Shoshonean area to a little north of the Humboldt River in Nevada, yielded pine nuts which were the most important of all food species. North of the piñon area, the seeds of certain other species of pines were eaten, but they were a relatively minor item in the diet. Since there was greater rainfall in the piñon-juniper belt than in the valleys, this zone afforded more seeds, roots, and grasses, and it had more game, especially deer. But it constitutes only a small portion of the total area, and the growing season is short. A few mountain ranges rise above 8,000 or 9,000 feet into the zone of the ponderosa pine, where vegetation is lush and where mountain sheep as well as deer were hunted.

The Shoshonean tribes were of necessity gatherers of vegetable foods and lower forms of animal life rather than hunters. They utilized nearly a hundred species of wild plants. The more important of these yielded small, hard-shelled seeds, which were collected in conical basketry containers, roasted with live coals in shallow baskets, ground on flat stones or metates, and eaten from basketry bowls. In the higher altitudes and latitudes where rainfall is greater, roots were relatively more important as food. When seeds and roots could not be had, especially in early spring, leafy vegetables or greens from many plants were eaten.

SOCIALLY FRAGMENTING EFFECT OF THE CULTURAL ECOLOGY

All of the plant and animal foods had in common the extremely important characteristic that the place and quantity of their occurrence from year to year were unpredictable, owing largely to variations in rainfall. A locality might be very fertile one year and attract large numbers of families, but offer little food for several years thereafter. Few localities had foods in sufficient quantity and reliability to permit permanent settlements. Throughout most of the area, the families were concerned predominantly with warding off potential starvation by moving from place to place. These movements were determined by reports from friends or relatives about the probable quantities of food to be had. Families from different localities would assemble at places where food was temporarily plentiful, but, owing to the impossibility of storing large quantities of food for the future, they soon dispersed to seek elsewhere.

The typical Shoshoni family living in the piñon area of Nevada traveled alone or with one or two related families during the spring and summer, seeking seeds, roots, various small mammals, rodents, insects, larvae, and other edible items. In the late summer when a family heard reports that the pine nuts seemed very promising in a certain portion of a mountain range, it arranged its travels so as to arrive in that locality in late October or early November, when the first frosts would have opened the cones and made the nuts ready to harvest. Other families who had also been foraging for food within a radius of perhaps twenty to thirty miles of that locality came there for the same reason.

In gathering the pine nuts, each family restricted itself by common understanding to a limited area, because there were so many pine nuts in the locality as a whole that no one could gather them all before they dropped and because each family could harvest more if it worked alone. The different families remained from several hundred yards to a mile or more apart. Each gathered pine nuts as rapidly as it could and stored them in earth caches. If the harvest was good, it might support the family throughout most of the winter.

The winter encampment consisted of perhaps twenty or thirty families within easy visiting distance of one another. Early spring generally found the people suffering more or less acutely from hunger. The families then had to go their separate ways to forage for greens, game, and any other foods they could find. Throughout spring and summer, the migrations of a particular family, although limited in general to the terrain it knew well, were determined almost week to week by its knowledge of available foods. It might learn that sand grass seeds were promising in one place, rabbits numerous elsewhere, fly larvae abundant in a certain lake, and antelope ready for a communal hunt under a shaman or medicine man over in the next valley.

Although the pine nut was perhaps the most important factor in determining the whereabouts of the winter encampment and which families would be associated in it, most other foods had a very similar effect in causing seasonal variations in interfamilial contacts. Owing to yearly and local variations in rainfall, the whereabouts of other wild seed and root crops and animal resources was unpredictable. Rabbits might be so numerous in a portion of a valley in a given year that people would assemble from considerable distances to hold a communal hunt. Several years might then follow before it was worth while to hold another such hunt in the same place, whereas rabbits were ready for a hunt in an adjoining valley the next year. The same was true of antelope. A cooperative hunt would so reduce the antelope that it required eight or ten years for their number to be restored. Even such foods as grasshoppers and locusts, or "Mormon crickets," were unpredictable. In certain years locusts occurred in such numbers as to be a major source of food to the Indians—and a plague to the modern farmers—and then during several years they were of no importance.

A limitation of the value of animal products was the absence of preservation and storing techniques. Rabbits, antelope, and fish might afford more meat than the people who assembled to take them could eat, but after a few days or weeks, they spoiled. Fish, unlike other animal species, occurred with some annual regularity in fixed places. During runs, a considerable number of families came from far and wide to fish for a few weeks, after which they had to disperse in search of other foods. Had the Shoshoneans been able to dry and smoke fish, like the Northwest Coast Indians, it is possible that fairly large permanent populations might have developed along certain of the better fishing streams and lakes. In the absence of this possibility, the winter inhabitants of these areas were limited to the few families who used fish as a supplement to other foods. Consequently, the effect of fishing resources on social groups was like that of other foods; it permitted large aggregates of people to assemble for short periods and it helped tide a small number of local families over the winter.

Shoshonean society was affected not only by the erratic and unpredictable occurrence of practically all principal foods and by the limited technical skills for harvesting and storing most of them, but it was also shaped by the predominant importance of wild vegetable products, which put a premium upon family separatism rather than upon cooperation. Anyone who has gathered wild berries in a party knows that he can pick far more if he finds a patch of his own. Unlike certain forms of hunting—for example, collective rabbit drives or antelope hunts—participation of many persons in seed and root gathering not only failed to increase the per capita harvest, but it generally decreased it so greatly that individual families preferred to forage alone so as not to compete with other families.

The competitive aspect of seed and root gathering together with the erratic annual occurrence of practically all principal foods and the inability of the people to store foods in any locality in sufficient amount to permit considerable numbers of families to remain there for a major portion of the year, all contributed to the fragmentation of Shoshonean society into nuclear family units, which moved about the country seasonally and annually in a unpredictable itinerary.

PROPERTY

The concept of property rights among the Shoshoneans was directly related to their mode of life. These Indians assumed that rights to exclusive use of anything resulted from work expended by particular individuals or groups and from habitual use. This is a rather obvious, simple, and practical concept, and it seems to have entailed a minimum of conflict.

In most parts of the area, natural resources were available to anyone. The seeds gathered by a woman, however, belonged to her because she had done the work of converting a natural resource into something that could be directly consumed. If a man made a bow or built a house, these were his, although prior to making objects of them, the trees he utilized belonged to no one. Any family might fish in a certain river or stream, but if a group of families built a fish weir, it alone had the right to use that weir.

When a number of families came into potential conflict in the utilization of natural resources, the same principal held. In seed gathering, it was "first come, first served." The families which entered a seed plot or piñon grove selected the best portion and, by virtue of having started to work on it, had prior rights. Other families gathered pine nuts elsewhere, which was reasonable and necessary because if they gathered in competition with the first family, all would have harvested less. In rabbit drives, the person who clubbed or shot a rabbit or who owned the net which caught it had first claim. In deer or mountain sheep hunting, the man whose arrow first entered the game was entitled to the skin and the choice portions of the meat.

This principle of property rights was essential to survival in the Shoshonean area. Owing to the erratic annual and local occurrence of foods, the arbitrary exclusion of territorially delimited groups of families from utilization of other territories would have caused starvation and death. With few exceptions, the habitat of most families always provided such uncertain subsistence that the territorial interpenetration of families living in different localities was necessary to the survival of all. The absence of property claims of local groups to delimitable areas of natural resources upon which work had not been expended was the corollary of a fragmented nature of Shoshonean society.

In a few portions of the Great Basin, such as Owens Valley in eastern California, which was occupied by Northern Paiute, the many streams flowing from the high Sierra Nevada Range afforded food resources which were comparatively so abundant and reliable that each family could be reasonably certain of finding enough to eat within one or two days' travel from a permanent village. Instead of wandering an unpredictable course determined by the vicissitudes of nature, these families were able to make forays from permanent headquarters. Habitual use of resources within readily accessible portions of the terrain led to the concept that each local village or group of villages had exclusive rights to resources within bounded areas. This economic stability and permanent residence of a particular group of families provided a basis for association, leadership, and organization in band groups.

CO-OPERATION AND LEADERSHIP AS INTEGRATING FACTORS

The typical Shoshonean family was independent and self-sufficient during the greater part of the year, perhaps during 80 or 90 percent of the time. It subsisted and fulfilled most cultural functions with little assistance from other familes. It probably could have survived in complete isolation.

But human history provides no instances in which nuclear families had progeny and perpetuated their culture without associating with and intermarrying with other families. Moreover, nuclear families have always co-operated with other families in various ways. Since this is so, the Shoshoneans, like other fragmented family groups, represent a family level of sociocultural integration only in a relative sense. It is relative in that most societies having a higher level of integration possess patterns of co-operation and leadership among a permanent membership. I classify the Shoshoneans as an exemplification of a family level of sociocultural integration because in the few forms of collective activity the same group of families did not co-operate with one another or accept the same leader on successive occasions. By another definition, however, it might be entirely permissible to view this ever-changing membership and leadership as a special form of suprafamilial integration. While the Shoshoneans represent a family level of sociocultural integration in a relative sense, their suprafamilial patterns of integration involved no permanent social groups of fixed membership despite several kinds of interfamilial co-operation.

Collective Hunting

The most important co-operation consisted of collective hunts. In these hunts, rabbits, antelope, deer, and mud hens were the principal species taken. Communal hunts could be held, however, only when there was sufficient game, when a considerable number of families could assemble, and when an appropriate leader was available. Under these circumstances, co-operation yielded many times the quantity of game that individuals, expending the same effort, could take alone.

The principal collective hunt was the rabbit drive. It could be held fairly often, and it yielded not only meat which could be consumed during a short period but furs which, cut into long strips and twisted, were woven into robes and blankets. The only distinctive technical feature of these drives was a net of about the height and mesh of a modern tennis net but often several hundred feet long. A number of these nets were placed end to end to form a huge semicircle. Men, women, children, and dogs beat the brush over a wide area, gradually closing in so that rabbits which were not clubbed or shot by the drivers became entangled in the nets, where they were killed.

Custom determined the several crucial aspects of the drive and the division of game. Experienced men—in recent years called rather appropriately "rabbit bosses"—were given supreme authority to co-ordinate all activities in this fairly complex operation. They chose the locality of the drive, directed disposition of nets, regulated the drivers, and divided the game according to customary understandings. Anyone who killed a rabbit with a bow or throwing stick in the course of the drive could claim it. Since, however, only a few families owned rabbit nets, net owners received a somewhat greater portion of the rabbits caught in the nets.

In spite of the rather rigid direction of these drives, there were several reasons why they did not bring about permanent integration or cohesion of territorial or social groups or fixed membership. First, drives were held only when rabbits were sufficiently numerous in a particular locality. Second, participants in the drive consisted of families who, because of the rather fortuitous annual occurrence of seeds and other foods in one place or another, happened to be in the locality where the drive was worth holding. Third, the drive was held only if an experienced leader and families owning nets happened to be present. Since the occurrence of these factors was rather haphazard, since the place, the participants, and the leaders were never quite the same in successive years, the drives provided only temporary bonds between independent families. A given family was under no obligation whatever to participate in a drive with a fixed group of families under a permanent leader. And, since, the "rabbit boss" held authority only during the drive, the family paid little heed to him in other times, places, and contexts.

The communal antelope hunt had a social function like that of the rabbit drive. It was held in any given locality at intervals of several years and the participants consisted of those families which happened to be in the vicinity. It was held less frequently than the rabbit drive because it took much longer for the antelope herds to recover their number. A major difference in form rather than function between the rabbit drive and the antelope hunt is that whereas the former were led by men of experience and prestige—qualifications which anyone might develop —the latter were led by "antelope shamans." According to Shoshonean belief, these men were qualified less by their practical ability—though no doubt they were far from incompetent—than by their possession of supernatural power which enabled them to charm the antelope into a state of helplessness.

The practical procedures in the antelope drives were as appropriate to the situation as those in the rabbit hunts. The people built a brush corral from which wings, consisting of piles of brush or stones, extended outward a half mile or so. Drivers spread out several miles from the corral, formed a line across the valley, and slowly closed in, urging the antelope between the wings and into the corral. Antelope differ from rabbits in that they not only flee from something threatening but they are drawn by curiosity toward strange objects. The antelope shaman evidently became one of the chief functionaries in native Shoshonean culture because his role combined this peculiarity of antelope with a basic belief about sickness. It was thought by many primitive peoples, including the Shoshoneans, that sickness might be caused by loss of one's soul. While the antelope shaman was not a curer of human ills, he was thought to possess the power to capture the souls of antelope before the hunt began and thus irresistibly to draw them into the corral, where he stood during the drive.

The shaman's authority was very great during these drives, but he had no voice in other activities. Moreover, even this socioreligious leadership like the lay authority found in rabbit drives failed to integrate social groups of fixed membership.

The other hunting activities involved much less co-operation than rabbit and antelope drives. Mud hen hunts were held only by small groups in the lake areas, while deer drives, held in the mountains, were infrequent and involved few persons.

Dancing, Gambling, and Visiting

The interfamilial associations of the Shoshonean Indians had to be adapted, as previously shown, to the exigencies of obtaining food by means of the techniques known to them. Although these families foraged throughout most of the year in isolation, their contacts with other families over many generations had contributed certain social patterns which strengthened bonds between them.

Whenever groups of Shoshonean families were together, they carried out certain recreational activities, such as dancing and gambling. Dancing, although popular, was originally limited to the circle dance, a performance in which men and women formed a circle and side-stepped to the accompaniment of singing. Gambling games were extremely numerous and included several forms of dice, the hand-game, sports such as racing and hockey, and games of skill such as the hoop-and-pole game and archery. Both dancing and games, however, could be held only when local abundance of food, such as rabbits, locusts, antelope, or pine nuts, made large gatherings possible. After a rabbit or antelope drive, for instance, people might dance and gamble for several days until the meat supply was exhausted, when each family had to go its separate way in the unending food quest.

Interfamilial contacts were not limited to such formalized activities as hunting, dancing, and gambling. Visiting was an important integrating fact since people were always eager to associate with one another whether or not they danced and gambled. They preferred to visit with relatives, but when food was plentiful, a large number of unrelated families could assemble.

Hostilities and Warfare

In aboriginal times most of the Shoshonean people had no national or tribal warfare. There were no territorial rights to be defended, no military honors to be gained, and no means of organizing groups of individuals for concerted action. When war parties of neighboring people invaded their country, the Shoshoneans ran away more often than they fought.

Hostilities generally consisted of feuds, not organized military action, and they resulted largely from the suspicion of witchcraft and from woman-stealing. They were therefore as often intratribal as intertribal. Death was generally ascribed to supernatural causes, especially to shamans, whose normally beneficent power had turned bad, perhaps even without the shaman's knowledge, and it was avenged by slaying the suspect. Usually, the malignant shaman was identified either as the person who had treated the deceased or as a member of a somewhat distant group. Accusations of witchcraft were rarely directed against relatives because kinship relations were too important to be endangered. It was, in fact, one of the most important kinship obligations to avenge the death of a relative. Once revenge had been taken, a series of reprisals and counter-reprisals might follow. These were purely personal and could not involve definable suprafamilial groups, for such groups did not exist.

The Rise of Predatory Bands

After the Shoshonean tribes acquired horses and the territory was occupied by white settlers, warfare of a collective nature developed. Under aboriginal conditions, horses had little value because they consumed the very plants upon which the Indians depended while contributing little to the hunting of rabbits, antelope, or deer. The few horses acquired in early times were eaten. When immigrant trains crossed the area and when white settlers introduced irrigation, crops, and livestock into the country, horses enabled the previously dispersed families to amalgamate and remain fairly constantly together in *predatory bands*, which lived somewhat parasitically by raiding the whites. Warfare involved in raiding and in defense against white reprisals was the principal if not sole function of these bands, and the chiefs had authority over little other than raiding activities. It was only among the Northern Shoshoni of Wind River, Wyoming, and of eastern Idaho and the Bannock, who probably acquired horses by 1800, that bison hunting and native warfare of the Plains type were also functions of the native bands. The Ute received horses sometime after 1820, and their bands were essentially predatory, first in raiding people outside their territory and later in raiding the Mormons and other white settlers inside it. The Western Shoshoni and Northern Paiute continued to be dispersed in family units until about 1845, after which mounted bands rapidly developed. Mounted bands were dissolved among the Shoshonean peoples by 1870 or soon thereafter when the United States Army defeated them.

In understanding the quite specialized nature of these predatory bands and the restricted authority of the chiefs, it is important to note that the bands probably never involved all the people of any region. During the early phases of band operations, there were many families which had no horses and continued to live according to the older pattern of family separatism while some of their friends and relatives engaged in raiding. Later, when the United States Army opposed the raiders, the Indians had to decide whether to continue to fight or whether to accept peace, relinquish certain territory, and live on reservations. At this stage, there were two kinds of chiefs. The first were leaders of predatory bands which were now on the defensive. The second were spokesmen for those who advocated peace and the signing of treaties.

After the Indians were defeated, the division between peaceful and warring factions soon faded and the functions of war leaders were eliminated. Thenceforth, the principal need for leaders was to deal with the white men, especially with the officials of the United States government.

Religion

Religion integrated families with one another only to a minor degree. Shoshonean culture lacked collective social and economic activities and common interests, except the communal hunts, dancing, and gaming previously mentioned. There was no functional need for ceremonialism dedicated to group purposes and led by priests holding a definite office. The communal antelope hunt was directed by a special shaman, but this leader did not serve any permanent group.

The relationship between human beings and supernatural powers was conceived largely as a matter of individual concern. Every person hoped to acquire a supernatural power or guardian spirit. This power, manifest in the form of animals, plants, clouds, mountains, and other natural phenomena, came to him in dreams and gave him special abilities, such as gambling luck, hunting skill, endurance, and others of benefit to himself alone. Shamans' powers differed from those of ordinary persons mainly in the ability to cure sickness in other people. The shaman did not lead group ceremonies. His curing performances might attract large numbers of families which happened to be in the vicinity because they liked not only to watch his singing, dancing, trance, laying-on-of-hands, and other rites but to visit other families. Shamans were influential because their curing abilities gave them prestige while their presumed capacity for practicing black magic made them feared, but they carried no specific authority.

A minor collective religious activity designed for the common good was the circle dance, which, according to the belief of some of the Western Shoshoni, promoted general fertility and benefited everyone. Harris reported that the Tosavits or White Knife Shoshoni of northern Nevada held group ceremonies for general welfare. It is more likely, however, that the principal feature of such ceremonies was the circle dance, which was held by whatever families came together at various stages of their food quest, and that the religious aspect was secondary and incidental to the recreational purpose. The "dance boss" was certainly not a religious leader. Similarly, the bear dance of the Ute was primarily recreational and only secondarily religious in heralding the spring season and providing protection against bears. Its leader, like that of the circle dance, was a layman.

Winter Encampments

The only prolonged accessibility of families to one another occurred in the winter encampments. These winter quarters have sometimes been called villages, but they were not tightly nucleated settlements which constituted organized communities. Instead, family houses were widely scattered within productive portions of the piñon zone. The location of each household was determined primarily by its pine nut caches and secondarily by accessibility to wood and water. The scattered families were able to visit one another to dance, gamble, and exchange gossip, and the men occasionally co-operated in a deer or mountain sheep hunt. Although dances and collective hunts required co-ordination, the leaders had no authority outside the particular activity.

Other interfamilial and interpersonal relationships were determined by customary usage. Disputes and hostilities arising from such matters as murder, theft, wife-stealing, and other violations of custom were settled between families. None of these was a "crime" against the community, for the community did not exist in any corporate or legal sense. Violations of custom threatened families, not larger socially integrated units. Thus, the very concept of crime presupposes some kind of suprafamily level of integration, some collectivity, which has a common purpose that must be protected against antisocial behavior by its members.

In addition to the leaders of special activities, each village or local area of scattered winter houses usually had a man of some importance whom modern Shoshonean informants frequently call the "village chief." So far as "chief" implies permanent authority over an identifiable group, this term is a complete misnomer, for this man had no authority and he served only one function. This function, however, was extremely important. It was to act as a clearing-house of information about where foods could be found. Since the Shoshoneans were constantly on the verge of starvation, especially at the end of winter, knowledge of where greens, seeds, rabbits, insects, and other foods were to be had made the repository of such information the most importan‛ person in the village.

The winter village cannot be considered a genuine suprafamilial form of social integration because it lacked permanent membership and even permanent location. Each year, families came from a general area to a locality of abundant pine nuts. Leaders were accepted by common consent to control such collective activities as required coordination. It was only in the few regions of uncommonly abundant and reliable food that a group of fixed membership occupied one or more permanent villages throughout most of the year and had a true village chief and permanent leaders of other activities.

Food-Named Groups

Considerable confusion concerning the nature of groups named according to special foods is found in the literature starting with the early accounts of the Shoshoneans and perpetuated in modern ethnographic studies. It was the native custom throughout practically all of the area to name the people occupying different localities by some important or striking food found in them. Thus, several different and widely-separated groups were called Rabbit Eaters and Fish Eaters. Other names were Pine Nut Eaters, Ground Hog Eaters, Grass Seed Eaters, and the like. These names, however, did not designate definable groups but were merely applied to whoever happened to be in the locality. Since there were no bands and no territorial limitations on movements in search of food, families frequently traveled from one food area to another and were known by the local name in each. Just as a Washingtonian today becomes a New Yorker upon living in New York, so a Ground Hog Eater of western Idaho became a Salmon Eater if he moved to the Snake River.

Most of the early accounts of the Shoshoneans were written after wars with the whites began and predatory bands developed. Sometimes these bands were named after their leaders and sometimes after the food area from which the leader and many of his followers came. Writers therefore assumed that the inhabitants of these food-named localities constituted aboriginal, territorial bands under over-all chieftainship. Data previously cited show clearly that this could not have been the case. The food-named areas were far too large for a foot people to associate in collective activities, even had the nature of Shoshonean subsistence not precluded integration in bands. After the whites entered the country, the "chief" of predatory bands not only failed to enlist the support of the peace faction in their own place of origin but their followers included persons from many other food-named areas.

Throughout the greater part of the area, therefore, food-names were a designation of people in a certain large region and nothing more. They implied no economic, recreational, religious, social, or political co-operation that would require collective action and lead to suprafamilial forms of integration.

KINSHIP RELATIONS

The economic and social relations of Shoshonean families previously described may be likened to a net in that each family had occasional associations with families on all sides of it and these latter with families farther away and these with still others so that there were no social, economic or political frontiers. The entire area consisted of interlocking associations of family with family. So far as subsistence, recreational, and religious activities are concerned, however, the analogy of a net is not entirely apt because no family was necessarily and consistently associated with certain other families. The net lacked knots; each family was at liberty to associate with whom it pleased. Kinship relations, however, supplied the knots and made a fabric of what otherwise would have been a skein of loose threads, each of which shifted about somewhat randomly. This is not to say that Shonshonean society was based on extended ties of kinship which gave cohesion to any definable group. The activities of a given family month by month were dictated primarily by the food quest, which took precedence over every other consideration. But marriage bonds were fairly enduring, and they created a strong fabric of close relationships, which extended from one locality to the next. They also made interfamilial economic and recreational associations somewhat less random, for kin preferred to co-operate with one another when possible. Moreover, the very absence of socioeconomic unity among inhabitants of local areas made the kinship ties seem relatively more important.

The irreducible minimum of Shoshonean society was the nuclear or biological family. Isolated individuals could not well survive in this cultural-environmental or ecological situation, and unmarried or widowed persons generally attached themselves to a nuclear family. This family was able to carry out most activities necessary to existence, for husband and wife complemented each other in food-getting and together they procreated, reared, and socialized their children. Women gathered vegetable foods, made the baskets needed for this purpose, and prepared all food. Men devoted most of their time to hunting, which, though not very rewarding, was extremely important and time consuming. It was important not only because meat was a desired dietary item, but because hides and furs were needed for clothing. The scarcity of game and the difficulty of hunting is evidenced by the fact that few men were able to kill enough deer or antelope to clothe their families in skin garments or even to make moccasins. Many persons were naked and barefoot during the summer, and in the winter had only a rabbit skin blanket which served both as a robe and as bedding.

In the household, women maintained the home and took care of the children. Men also played an important part in child-rearing. In the absence of toys and games designed expressly for children, boys played with small bows and arrows and other objects used by men, while girls imitated their mothers. In this way, children quickly learned the rudiments of adult functions and absorbed the attitudes, values, and beliefs of their parents. This learning was accomplished largely within the context of the family, for association with other families was limited.

In the course of the very uncertain wanderings and activities of Shoshonean life, the most frequent associates of the members of a nuclear family were members of families with which they had intermarried. These families were companions on seed and root gathering trips, when there was enough food for several families to travel together, and they co-operated in hunting. Relatives were the favored visitors, and often a few families would camp together and spend evenings gossiping and telling legends. Relatives were to be counted on for support if suspicion of witchcraft led to a feud. And they, more than others, were willing to share food in times of shortage.

These close interfamilial bonds were expressed in the marriage system. Marriage was more a contract between families than between individuals. The preferred arrangement was several marriages between the children of two families. When a young man married, it was desired that his wife's brother marry his sister. Several brothers and sisters might marry several sisters and brothers. Shoshonean culture permitted plural spouses, wherein the same principle prevailed. If a man took several wives, custom prescribed that they be sisters, and penalties were imposed for failure to follow this custom. If a man's wife died, he was obligated to take her sister as his next wife. In a parallel way, a certain amount of polyandry, or plural husbands, was permitted. A woman might take a younger brother of her husband as a temporary spouse until he found a wife. If the husband died, his family was obligated to furnish a brother of the first husband if possible.

It was, of course, biologically impossible that the number and sex of siblings in two intermarrying families should be such that this cultural ideal could be met. Moreover, marriages of the parental and grand-parental generation extended marital ties to many families. While marital ties often linked the younger generation of two families to one another somewhat more closely than either was linked to other families, the general pattern was one of innumerable interfamilial linkages extending over a wide area. It meant that a family in a given locality could probably find consanguinal or marital kin of one kind or another among a large proportion of the families which ranged its own territory and among many families farther afield.

These interfamilial marital and kinship bonds were not unbreakable, for, despite the contractual nature of marriage, separations or divorces were common. Individual temperament, incompatibility, and other factors were not to be discounted. Nonetheless, the cultural ideal ascribed these arrangements considerable importance. And this importance derived largely from the fact that these kinships bonds were the principal integrating factors in a cultural-environmental situation where the subsistence pattern prevented the development of bands, villages, or other social units consisting of permanent members having prescribed relationships to one another.

These marital and kinship ties were the knots of the social fabric of the various peoples in the Shoshonean area, but they did not constitute sociocultural frontiers. Marriage was contracted most often between families in contact with one another, but it was not governed by territorial or political units. While it united strands in the netlike fabric of Shoshonean society, it could not consolidate or integrate local groups in a political, social, or economic sense. To the contrary, it cut across local boundaries, making interfamilial ties diffuse and thus actually militating against band or community development.

THE THEORETICAL SIGNIFICANCE OF THE SHOSHONEANS

In a classification of cultures based on the concept of area, the Shoshoneans should probably be included in the Greater Southwest; for more of their culture elements, especially their material culture or technology, seem to have been derived from the Southwest than from any other area. Their economic, political, social, religious, and hostility patterns—general configurations which are not reducible to culture elements—were, however, wholly unlike those of the Southwest. Owing to the cultural ecological processes—to the exploitation of their particular environment by means of the techniques available to them— families functioned independently in most cultural activities, and the few collective interfamilial pursuits did not serve to give permanent co- hesion to extended families, bands, communities, or other higher levels of sociocultural integration as in the Southwest.

*O*ne of the most characteristic features of all American Indian cul- tures was the "shaman," usually a self-trained and self-appointed reli- gious leader. Popularly referred to as a "medicine man" or "witch doctor," the shaman was entrusted with the curing of illness and the exorcising of evil spirits. But he was usually much more than this. As a man of intellectual ability, as a specialist in a world of nonspecialists, as an authority on matters of birth and death, sickness and health, the shaman frequently came to wield sociopolitical power as well. The com- mon tendency to view such practitioners as charlatans and frauds is clearly incorrect. It is probable that most shamans believed in their powers, as did their peers and patients. Even from the vantage point of mid-twentieth century scientific medicine, confidence in the doctor and in his medicines are known to have profound influence on the practi- tioner's effectiveness.

18 *Willard Z. Park*

PAVIOTSO SHAMANISM*

The spirit beings which are everywhere in the Paviotso world are the sources of supernatural power. Spirits of the fauna, spirits from certain mountains and of rocks, as well as the elements, bestow on individuals the power (puhá) through which sickness is controlled and cured. In addition to securing power from these spirits, shamans also derive

* Abridged from "Shamanism in Western North America," by W. Z. Park, in *North- western University Studies in the Social Sciences*, **II**, 15–29, 1938.

supernatural aid from ghosts of the dead (sa'abᵊ) and from the dwarf-like creatures called water-babies that live in certain water-holes, lakes, and water-serpents thought to inhabit the lakes.

Indians were put here on this earth with trees, plants, animals, and water, and the shaman gets his power from them. One shaman might get his power from the hawk that lives in the mountains. Another may get his power from the eagle, the otter, or the bear. A long time ago, all the animals were Indians (they could talk). I think that is why the animals help the people to be shamans. Some strong shamans get their powers from the sun. (Joe Green)

Anyone can get to be a shaman by dreaming. In the dreams, spirits such as those from the eagle, bear, owl, snake, antelope, deer, mountain sheep, mole, or falling star appear. The spirit that comes in the dreams is the shaman's power. It helps him to doctor sick people.

Several informants described the water-babies that are also believed to be a source of supernatural power:

Some shamans get their power from the water-babies. They are the only people who can talk to them. They tell the rest of the people not to make fun of water-babies. These shamans can take the water-babies out of the lake.

The water-babies came to life by their own power. They formed themselves. Some water-babies live in water-holes, and these holes never dry up. People call these water-babies the "breath of the water-holes." There is a cool breeze all the time in the mountains where they live. They have the power to cause wind to blow, even a very strong wind. The wind is their breath.

There are also women in the lakes where the water-babies live. These women are like the water-babies. They have the same power. Big serpents live in the lake, too. Like the water-babies, these serpents have strong power. They give power to some shamans. (Rosie Plummer)

It appears that the spirit of the coyote was never a source of power, although Coyote is the most prominent character in Paviotso tales.

Shamans never got power from Coyote. According to the old stories the Indians tell, Coyote always spoils everything. Coyote is bad. Sometimes he tries to get the soul of someone. He says, "I am going to get you and when you die, I will eat you." The coyote cannot be heard to say this, but when he has said it, it makes the victim sick. (Joe Green)

Shamans do not get power from Coyote. Coyote causes sickness. Dogs are almost like Coyote. When a shaman doctors, dogs are kept away, otherwise he would not be successful in curing the sickness. (Rosie Plummer)

Fear of the wrath of water-babies and water-serpents noted in accounts above is not held for other spirits, save those of the elements, particularly the thunder. There seems to be no danger in ridiculing or showing lack of respect for the spirits of the animals and birds.

The Indian doctors know the wind, clouds, and rain. A shaman talks to them. They are just like people, and they come. Anyone who makes fun of the thunder will be killed. One time a man at Schurz heard the thunder, and said, "That is nothing, I am going to fight that thunder." He went outside the house, and the thunder was heard overhead. He was hit by lightning and killed. (Tom Mitchell)

Another aspect of the supernatural spirits which are the source of shamanistic power is their invisibility to all but the shamans. Only the shaman can see the spirit or spirits from which he derives his power. Even when he invokes his supernatural aids at a doctoring, they are visible to him alone. Their presence is known to the others only through the shaman's account of his conversation with them. Supernatural spirits never appear to, nor are they ever head by, anyone but those upon whom they bestow power.

ACQUIRING SHAMANISTIC POWER

Both men and women acquire and exercise shamanistic power. A shaman of either sex is a puhágəm. The power possessed by either a man or a woman is likewise known by a single term, puhá. The ratio of male to female shamans, as well as the proportion of practitioners to the total population, no doubt varied considerably from generation to generation.

In theory, female shamans may become as powerful as the male doctors. In practice, however, it appears that all the outstanding practitioners are, and have been, men. On the other hand, female shamans are highly respected and are on an equal footing with their male colleagues; some may even have stronger powers than the less prominent male shamans. Moreover, according to several informants, women can acquire powers which are used, as with men, for purposes other than curing.

Apparently berdaches never became shamans. The several transvestites who are remembered by people living today were certainly not shamans. Lowie recorded only one case of sex-reversal among the Pyramid Lake Paviotso. This occurred some twenty years before his visit, and apparently shamanistic powers were not ascribed to the individual. Sarah Winnemucca mentions the case of one cowardly warrior who was forced to don women's clothing and perform tasks allotted to that sex, but there is no reference to the possession of power. This as well as the evidence in my own notes suggests that berdaches were of relatively infrequent occurrence and of slight importance. Certainly they became shamans rarely, if ever, and clearly never as the result of their condition.

Acquiring shamanistic power, and later the exercise of power, is an individual affair. This is true both for the power derived from unsolicited dreams and from the voluntary quest. Power is never acquired by people in groups or at public performances, but is the result of private personal experiences.

The acquisition of power involves more than the development of a personal relationship with a particular spirit. When shamanistic power is conferred, the candidate not only secures a spirit helper but also acquires those special abilities or capacities necessary for coping with sickness; these in turn impose responsibilities and potential danger. Consequently, the possession of supernatural power signifies to the Paviotso more than is suggested by the term "guardian spirit."

The central idea in the acquisition of supernatural power is dream experience. Often these dreams come unsolicited to a prospective shaman. In addition to these involuntary experiences, dreams may be deliberately sought in a number of places in the mountains. Supernatural power may also be inherited, but it is in dreams that the power is actually bestowed on the heir. It is, then, through the experiences in dreams, which may either be sought or may be spontaneous, that a shaman characteristically acquires his power. One shaman may say that power came to him unasked, another may claim to have inherited his power, and a third relates that he acquired power in a certain cave in the mountains. Still, each gained a supernatural spirit as a familiar and as a powerful ally in certain undertakings, also an exacting and cruel taskmaster, through the same medium. In short, all shamans gain power from a fundamentally similar experience, differing only in the way in which it is initiated.

Supernatural power is usually acquired after maturity. Children were known to have had shamanistic power, however, and even to have doctored the sick.

Life crises, such as puberty or the period of mourning for husband, wife or child, are not recognized as times when shamanistic power is to be acquired or lost. Those who seek dream-experiences in caves are always adults. Statements of informants indicate that power may come at any time during life at the volition of the spirits or powers.

Power that comes unsolicited makes itself known through repeated dreams. The spirit which is the source of power appears repeatedly in these dreams to instruct the dreamer.

A man dreams that a spirit of deer, eagle, or bear comes to him. The spirit tells him that he is to be a doctor. When a man first dreams this way he does not believe it. Then the dream comes again. He dreams this way for a long time. The spirit tells him to collect eagle feathers, wild tobacco, a stone pipe, a rattle, and other things. When he gets these things he becomes a doctor. He learns his songs when the spirit comes and sings to him. (Nick Downington)

The dreams, both in form and in content, conform to no rigidly fixed pattern. One person may see an animal or a ghost in his dreams; another may only hear the voice of the spirit which gives him his power. There seems, however, to be an emphasis on auditory experiences in dreams. Usually in the first dream, the prospective shaman only hears the spirit singing and talking. In later dreams the spirit is seen. This is not always the case, for some shamans had visual evidence of the presence of supernatural powers in their first, as well as in later, dream-experiences.

An account of the dreams by which power was given to one shaman will serve to illustrate the characteristic features of this sort of experience.

I was getting to be a doctor. My father was a doctor, and I got to be one just the same as he. In my dream, I heard a song. It was coming from the north. It was coming just a few feet above the ground. I heard that song. I heard it just one night. The song came all night. That was all I heard the first night.

In dreams after that I saw a horse coming from the east. When I first heard him, he was on the other side of the mountain. Then I saw him come over the ridge. He came toward me and when he got close, he made a big circle around me. Then he went back. That horse had nothing to do with my power.

My father used to doctor. He had power from the otter. I had the same power. After I dreamed about the horse, the otter came to me in my dreams. He told me to get his skin and to cut it into a strip about four inches wide down the length of the back from the head to the top of the tail and including the eyes and ears. Then he told me to get two eagle tail-feathers and put them in two holes in the skin at the neck and to tie them inside with buckskin. The feathers lay flat on the fur side of the skin. The otter told me to keep the skin and the eagle-feathers. He told me to use the skin and feathers when sickness is bad and hard to cure. He said, "When there is very bad sickness and no doctor can cure it, take the skin out of your sack and put it in front of you. Then you are going to try to cure." I was ready to doctor then. When I doctored, the otter gave me my songs.

This account then goes on to relate how a mistake was made in the care of the paraphernalia and, as a result, the informant lost his power. This illustrates the belief that if the exact details of the instructions given by the supernatural spirit are not followed, the offending shaman will suffer illness and loss of power.

Very often dream-experience, if not understood, will result in sickness. In this event it may be necessary to have a shaman interpret dreams and restore the dreamer to health.

A man has the same dream a number of times. Then he knows the power to be a shaman is in him. Sometimes it makes him very sick. He must do what the power tells him. One man, who is still living here [Reno], was sick about a year. He almost died. When he was sick he went into trances and his body was stiff as a board. He dreamed that he went to the land of the dead. He dreamed that way all the time when he was sick. He said that ghosts of dead people came and tried to steal his soul. His father was a shaman. The man almost died, but his father finally cured him. (Harry Sampson)

In addition to those who receive shamanistic power from involuntary dreams, there are individuals whose desire for power is sufficiently strong to cause them to undertake a voluntary quest. There are certain places, such as caves in the mountains, where power can be acquired. Eight or ten such places are known today, and perhaps formerly there were still others which are now forgotten.

The success of the power-quest is dependent upon the seeker's undeviating adherence to the traditionally recognized form of procedure. If he does not go to the right place or if he refuses to stay in the cave the entire night, failure will attend his efforts. Also, as in unsolicited dreams, the instructions of the spirits must be carefully followed. Consequently, only those who do not abide by these conditions fail in the quest for power. Several informants related anecdotes of men who were unable to acquire power owing to their failure to follow the correct procedure in the quest.

Happy Dave heard about the cave where power is acquired. He went there, but he did not want to go inside the cave. He tied his horse above the cave and made his bed outside. A lizard came to Dave. It ran up one arm and down the other and then up one leg and down the other. Then it went back on the rock. After the lizard went away the wind came up. It blew very hard. Happy Dave heard the owl down by the river. He could hear the owl in spite of the wind. Later the owl came up from the river and talked to Happy Dave. The owl told him that he had not done the right thing and that he was wasting his time. He told Happy Dave that he should go home. He was to go down to the river and bathe and put iˑbi [white paint] on the horse. This was to purify both the man and the horse [to prevent the sickness that would result from his improper conduct in relation with supernatural spirits]. Happy Dave told me about his experiences. It happened a long time ago. He is now dead. He never got to be a doctor. (Dick Mahwee)

With some, shamanistic power is inherited from parents or other relatives. This is not to be regarded, however, as inheritance of property in the usual sense of the term. The shaman's outfit, like other personal property at the death of the owner, is invariably destroyed. Commonly the Paviotso manifest a very strong fear of the evil consequences that would surely overtake anyone who retained personal property of the dead. The heir of shamanistic power must have that power bestowed on him in dream-experiences precisely as would any other shaman. Inheritance here is simply a strong tendency on the part of one of the children, or other relatives, of a shaman to acquire power from the same source some time after the shaman's death.

CAUSE OF DISEASE

The Paviotso attribute disease to supernatural agencies. Minor ailments, however, are recognized and cured by "home remedies." The knowledge of these treatments is even today widespread and is by no means restricted to the professional equipment of the shaman. Therefore, only illness which results from supernatural causes and which requires the exercise of the shaman's power to bring about recovery will be considered here. Many informants made a strong contrast between sickness today and formerly. It is said that before the whites came, the diseases of the present time were not known; that the Indians suffered only from aches and pains which were caused by sorcery, by dreams, or other supernatural causes.

Two concepts of the cause of disease widespread in the primitive world are current among the Paviotso. It is believed that sickness results from the intrusion of a pathogenic tangible object, or again, an individual may die as a result of the loss of his soul. Shamans may also suffer from the breach of tabu, that is, as the result of breaking any of the restrictions which are placed upon them by their powers. Yet these three categories of the causes of disease are somewhat artificial, as the Paviotso do not clearly distinguish among them. According to their notions, sickness results from a dream, and in such cases a shaman may at one time suck out an intrusive object to bring about a cure, whereas on another occasion it may be necessary to return the lost soul of the patient. Again from the point of view of the Paviotso, sorcerers can cause sickness; but here too, both soul loss and intrusive objects are involved. Therefore, it would seem from the point of view of native belief that a more realistic classification of the causes of disease would take into consideration sickness caused by such agents as sorcery, dreams, ghosts, and animals, as well as the illness of shamans resulting from mistakes or disobedience either of the practitioner or of others.

Dreams (nɔsi) are commonly the cause of sickness. That is, the dream itself is directly responsible, not prophetic of, illness. The experiences in such dreams usually are connected with ghosts of the dead or visions of sickness and death. Often the dreamer will not suffer the ill effects of his dream, but a relative or a member of the household is the victim of the illness so caused. These disease-causing dreams seem to be entirely involuntary; one dreams—with no conscious desire to cause harm—that another is, or will be, ill; and shortly thereafter that individual becomes sick. Thus, illness among children is commonly believed to result from the dreams of parents. A father will dream that his child is ill; a few days later the child is stricken and a shaman must be called in. If the shaman is not called very soon after the first manifestation of the sickness, the child will die. Visitors, as well as the parents, may bring about the illness of children as the result of dreams.

Ghosts are greatly feared as a source of evil, especially as they cause illness. These dreaded spirits are the souls of dead people. Even among the living, the soul wanders in dreams from its place in the body. The seat of the soul is placed by some in the head and by others in the chest.

The soul or spirit is designated by either the term sɔ́yəp, or num-əmugu"[a]. Frequently these terms are rendered in English by interpreters as "the mind." Also in speaking of the loss of the soul, such expressions as "he lost his mind" or "his mind was gone" are employed. It is believed that when breathing stops, the soul leaves the body. Instead of departing at once for the land of the dead, the souls of the dead may turn into ghosts (sa'abə) and plague the living. The ghost's intentions, however, may not be malicious. It is thought that one may linger near the camp in order to take along the soul of some member of the family of the dead person for company on the journey to the land of the dead. It is said that other ghosts, especially, "those of people who were mean during life," may be intentionally malignant. These ghosts often assume the form of animals, especially coyotes, and in such forms appear to the living and cause illness. It is therefore evident that ghosts seen either when awake or in dreams are causes of illness.

Sickness caused by ghosts may, in part, be related to the loss of the soul, for, as has been stated, some ghosts attempt to steal souls from the living in order to have the company of loved ones on the journey to the land of the dead. However, all cases of illness resulting from the visits of ghosts are not of this order. Many suffering from such experiences are cured, not by the return of the soul, but by following the instructions which the shaman receives from his powers when he goes into a trance to diagnose the case. Moreover, soul loss is not entirely due to the kidnaping by ghosts of souls of the living. Several people are reported to have had their souls restored by shamans when they were thought to have died. In these cases, it is claimed that the soul has strayed, in which case it must be found by the shaman and returned. Another explanation frequently given is that souls start for the land of the dead and that they either loiter along the way or are refused admission at the entrance to the afterworld, where they are told that they are not yet ready to join the dead. In either event, the shaman has the opportunity to find the soul and attempt to induce it to return.

It is thought that the soul often leaves the body during sleep. When this happens, serious harm will result if the sleeper is suddenly awakened. Shamans are especially subject to this danger. Accordingly, a sleeping shaman is not disturbed.

It is believed that animals as well as ghosts can bring sickness to man. Apparently, such sickness may result from a deliberate malicious effort as in the case of the coyote; with other animals it may be involuntary or the means of punishment.

Once a man dreamed that three coyotes came to him. They said, "Tell us who is a good man. We will get him and eat him. If you do not tell us, we will come and eat you." The man believed them, so he told them about a woman. A few days after the man had this dream, the woman was sick. They got a shaman to doctor her. He sang for two nights before he knew what made her sick. Then he saw three coyotes in a cloud. Only the heads could be seen. He saw that they were coming to get the woman. He told the woman's family what the coyote had done. They were coming then. When they came close and saw the shaman, they were afraid. They went away and never bothered the woman again. The shaman told her to put red paint on all her joints. She was to paint red and white bands around her joints. [Treatment in this fashion is customary in curing illness caused by dreams.] Coyote could see that paint when he was a long way off. He did not like it so he never came again. (Joe Green)

Other game animals, especially large game, such as antelope and mountain sheep, can also cause illness. The owl appears, prophetically perhaps, in dreams to bring sickness. Gophers, too are thought to be a sign of sickness and death, but it is doubtful that they cause either. When gophers are caught, they are skinned and the skin is spread over the belly of the carcass. Both are then hung up on the south side of a bush, tree, or house. Gophers may also be burned until only ashes remain. In the course of either operation, a prayer in some such words as these is recited: "You tried to give me bad luck. Now you will be destroyed."

Sorcery is an extremely potent source of illness. The sorcerer secures his power from the same sources and in the same way as the shaman who practices for the general good. In fact, to the Paviotso a sorcerer is a shaman who utilizes his power not in the socially accepted way but in a dangerous and anti-social fashion; he has corrupted potentially beneficial power in such a way as to cause harm. The sorcerer is frequently designated by the term for shaman, puhágəm. There is, however, another word for the sorcerer, numətukə́dꭓ (eater of people), but the former seems to be more commonly used.

The sorcerer recites no incantations, nor does he work spells, to overcome his victims. Cast-off clothing, nail-parings, hair-combings, and the images of intended victims, are not used by the sorcerer in causing sickness and death. In fact, none of the techniques usually associated with the practice of either sympathetic or contagious magic is to be found among the Paviotso. Frequently the sorcerer achieves his end simply by concentrating his thoughts on the desired end, the wish for the destruction of the victim by sickness. A sorcerer may also cause illness by touch-ing a person, by handing him food, or giving him a pipe to smoke. The sorcerer does not allow even his victim to become aware of the effort being made to harm him. Discovery of the sorcerer's practices comes only when a shaman is successful in diagnosing the malady of the vic-tim. It is said that sorcerers can cause people either to die suddenly or to suffer a lingering illness.

Often, when sickness results from sorcery, a tangible substance enters the victim's body. That is, in the current categories of such concepts, the sorcerer brings about "disease-object intrusion." These objects are vari-ously described as a small stone, a little black lizard, a worm, insects, a sliver of obsidian, and miniature figures of men, animals, or birds. None of these is thought to have been "shot" into the victim; nor are such objects used in any way to bring about sickness. In the words of one in-formant, "The sorcerer thinks about a lizard and that is what causes sick-ness." The sorcerer then simply concentrates on something, and with the assistance of his power it, or its miniature, is injected by some super-natural process into the victim and sickness results. The disease-object must be sucked out in order to bring about the victim's recovery.

Sorcerers appear never to practice their art for material gain or at the request of another. Securing the services of a sorcerer by means of per-suasion or bribery to wreak vengeance on an enemy is totally foreign to Paviotso thinking. The sorcerer works in secret entirely for his own ends. At least this is true when he first uses his power for evil purposes. Later, after he has caused the illness and death of a number of people, he is powerless to withstand the impulse to kill. Then his activities be-come completely involuntary and he is unable to restrain his lust for murder.

If he has sufficient power, a shaman who has been the victim of a sorcerer may extract the cause of disease and without the aid of another practitioner cast off the ill effects of his enemy's magic.

As sorcerers are believed to cause so much of the illness afflicting the Paviotso, they are greatly feared. Anyone suspected of sorcery is treated with every respect and consideration in order not to arouse his wrath and ill-will. It is said that any request or demand made by a known sor-cerer is never refused out of fear of the revenge that might be taken through witchcraft. Those who fear a particular shaman will, if possible, avoid accepting anything from him or touching his person.

In aboriginal times, sorcerers were put to death when detected in fre-quent killings. Their guilt was established then as now, by shamans who determined not only the nature of sickness but also the person responsible. An accusation of this sort by a shaman of standing was probably tantamount to conviction. When a sorcerer claimed several victims, the entire group became concerned and demanded the death of the guilty person. The execution was carried out by several men appointed for the task, or a large number of people fell upon the sorcerer and killed him. The usual practice was to burn the house over the murdered sorcerer; otherwise the body was buried in the usual manner.

If a sorcerer had not become notorious, members of a victim's family might take it upon themselves to avenge the death of a relative. The sorcerer, known to them from the shaman's diagnosis, was stabbed, clubbed, or shot. As in the communal execution, the house was burned with the corpse inside. As far as can be learned, the sorcerer's family rarely attempted retaliation for these murders. In so far as pre-Caucasian conditions can be determined from the memories of living people, it can safely be said that the fear of sorcery was easily the chief source of intra-tribal strife and violence; that the charge of witchcraft more frequently than anything else led to the killing of one Paviotso by another. Suspicion of sorcery is in itself sufficient to endanger social relations and even life. . . .

The Plateau Sanpoil are regarded by many as one of the more typical cultural groups of the Plateau region. They were only lightly influenced by the post–fur trade developments of the Northwest Coast, and they did not use the horse, unlike, for example, the Plateau Nez Perce. It is important to note that the important social group among the Sanpoil was the village or band, as was true among the Shoshone to the south. Social groups larger than the single village developed only upon the encroachment of Europeans and American governmental agents. V. F. Ray, an outstanding expert on the Plateau region, focuses in the following paper upon "pacifism" and "equality" as two outstanding and important attributes of the Sanpoil in particular, and of most Plateau social groups in general.

19 Verne F. Ray

THE LIFE CYCLE OF THE PLATEAU SANPOIL*

The term Sanpoil is a French corruption of the native name (snpui.' lux") of the people who lived at the confluence of the Sanpoil and Columbia rivers. Other early renderings were Sans Poil, San Poil and Sanpuell. Nespelem, likewise, was derived from a native name (snspi.' ləm), that of the people at the mouth of the Nespelem river. Sanpoil has been interpreted as a descriptive name, indicating either that the people were relatively hairless or that they were poor and had no furs to sell to the traders. Any such assumption is definitely in error.

Thus originally the names Sanpoil and Nespelem were applicable only to two definite settlements among the many autonomous groups occupying that portion of the Columbia river. But through subsequent usage by government agents and white traders the names of these two major groups came to be applied to the surrounding peoples as well. The terms, however, were not used consistently or in mutually exclusive senses. Sometimes Sanpoil was meant to include the Nespelem; at other times it was not. The natives themselves have never adopted these designations. A man's nativity is still indicated by the old village group name, consisting of the village name plus a personifying prefix and suffix.

There is, however, a certain justification for grouping together certain villages under a common name for the sake of description. Although politically autonomous, all of the villages from the Nespelem river to Hunters were culturally and dialectically identical. Moreover they formed a definite social unit. They felt far closer ties between one another than between themselves and the people below (sinəqaie'th ") or the ones above (Colville). Also, the sinəqaie'th " groups affiliated closely with each other to the exclusion of the up-river villages, and the Col-

* Abridged from "The Sanpoil and Nespelem: Salishan Peoples of Northwestern Washington," by V. F. Ray, in *University of Washington Publications in Anthropology*, **5**, 9, 25–30, 1932.

ville probably had true tribal organization—at least they had a group name (sxoie'ʇp ").

Certain dominant trends in Sanpoil culture vitally affected the life of every individual born into that culture. They colored the whole outlook upon the world and determined the attitudes taken toward it. Conservatism and radicalism, faith and skepticism were defined in terms of these concepts. They were: pacifism and the equality of men.

Pacifism was carried to such a degree that heinous offenses by raiding parties were left unrevenged. After one such raid the offenders were pursued for a short distance but the chief soon dissuaded the injured ones from attempting retaliation. "Our children are dead and our property is destroyed. We are sad. But can we bring our children to life or restore our property by killing other people? It is better not to fight. It can do no good." The Sanpoil returned home. Such action was not unusual. The most eloquent speeches of Sanpoil chiefs were delivered in the interest of maintaining peaceful relations with all peoples. These efforts were successful. Theory was put into practice. No warface, either offensive or defensive, could be recalled by the father of any living man. Nor was the principle of pacifism applied only to foreign relations. On the contrary, this ideal was even more important in fashioning the daily lives of men. From earliest infancy the child was drilled in the tenets of peaceful existence with his fellows. The pugnacious man was a public enemy with whom respectable people associated as little as possible. It was clearly one of the principal duties of the chief to see that the peaceful life of the community was not disturbed. This he accomplished by counselling his people, arbitrating petty differences and presenting a good example by his own conduct.

The success of the principle was especially evident within the household. Groups of ten or twenty persons lived together over periods of many years without the development of a single serious altercation. A safety valve was provided. It was a person's privilege to leave at any time and he could always find a home elsewhere. But one was not privileged to remain and demand his "rights" when he developed a grievance. As a result family trouble was unheard of.

Insignificant matters and major problems alike were decided with reference to what action would make for the greatest harmony. Even in the mythology this basic attitude was reflected. For example, the man who decided not to take revenge upon his brother who had stolen his wife, was commended for his decision.

Sanpoil insistence upon the equality of men was of an impressive order. Class distinctions were unthinkable. Slavery was an unaccountable custom of foreigners. When a new chief had to be selected any man was eligible. The selection was made by popular vote on the basis of moral character alone. He remained one of the people. He was as approachable as any man in the group. His powers were preponderantly advisory rather than dictatorial. Every adult citizen was a member of the general assembly of his village. Nor did wealth carry with it an advance in status. Indeed, wealth was rare. Only shamans could properly be counted rich men and whatever prestige they possessed was the result of their unusual supernatural powers, not their riches. The scarcity of wealth was again an outcome of the belief in the equality of mankind. Why should one man have more than another? Yet nature was bountiful—was not every man deserving of a living? The solution of these questions was a modified communistic organization. The huge catches of salmon made each summer at the great fish traps were divided entirely equally between all present, foreigners included. A man need have taken no part in the fishing activities to be entitled to a share in the daily distributions. Likewise the meat obtained on a hunting expedition was divided evenly among all those who had taken part regardless of what members actually killed the game. But room was left for individual initiative. Salmon taken with a spear was the property of the individual spearman (but every man was given his turn on the fishing platform). And game taken by the individual hunter was his personal property (except that the first deer killed by a boy had to be divided among the townspeople to the exclusion of himself). Women always retained the products of their individual labors at berry picking or root gathering. Yet it was never necessary for a person to go hungry if there was food in the village. A single meal or a whole winter's lodging and meals were never denied a man.

Thus almost the whole economic life of the Sanpoil was built around the principle that one man was equal to another. Other quite foreign aspects of life were affected as well. Social control was simplified. Stealing was practically unknown. Why should one steal? The usual executive, judicial and police organization for dealing with criminals was minimized with the absence of one of the commonest of criminals, the thief. The deeply instilled dislike of conflict worked to reduce still more the number of torts committed.

In the quest of supernatural power we see equality again playing a part. This sponsorship was open equally to every man and every woman, not to only a privileged few as in some other parts of North

America. There were very few Sanpoil men who did not succeed in the quest to the extent of gaining at least one guardian spirit.

It is not argued here that all individuality was levelled down by these dominating cultural tendencies or that other cultural drives of consequence were not present. Not all conformed alike to the ideals of peacefulness and equality. As great a range of individual variation was evidenced as in any comparable culture and greater than in many. There were nonconformists and skeptics. There were those who liked conflict, those who deemed themselves superior to their fellows and those who liked to accumulate private property. But these types were in the minority. They were the undesirables, the radicals. They were the individuals who made social problems.

It is interesting to note that here in the center of the Plateau, an area hitherto considered a cultural mixture of Northwest Coast and Plains traits, we find one of the outstanding cultural trends in direct contrast to the Coast, the other to the Plains. At opposite poles were the Sanpoil principles of equality and the rigid Coast system of classes and preferences. And the Sanpoil ideal of pacifism was utterly foreign to the central theme of Plains life, the exhibition of bravery in warfare.

Life began anew for the Sanpoil with the coming of each spring. After the enforced extreme inactivity of the winter months the first signs of spring were occasion for rejoicing. Moreover, fresh food would soon again be available to replace the winter diet of dried products broken only by an occasional meal of venison. The underground houses were deserted at the first opportunity. Temporary camps were established nearby for the sake of a change in surroundings and fresher air. This transfer of residence was usually made during the month called skənćumən, "time that the buttercups bloom," which corresponds roughly to March. The new quarters were occupied for two or three weeks during which time the men gathered shell fish and hunted fowl and rabbits. At the same time the women were digging the few early edible roots which had appeared on the warm sandy hillsides near the river, and were gathering prickly pears, which were eagerly eaten after the spines had been burned off and they had been roasted. At this time those who had spent the winter away from home returned one by one to their own villages.

During the early part of the following month, kəpatcɫta'n, "time that the leaves come out," there was a general removal from the Columbia to the root digging grounds on the plains south of the river. Before leaving, the winter mat houses were dismantled and all goods which were not to be transported were cached in trees or on elevated racks and platforms. Village groups did not move in a body across the river but bands formed of four or five families each and journeyed to their favorite spots. Each band before leaving notified the chief of its intended destination. The largest group usually went with the chief.

The root digging activities opened with the celebration of the first roots ceremony at which the first products of the ground were ceremonially eaten. For the women the ensuing period was one of industrious labor. A whole year's supply of roots had to be gathered and dried. It was necessary to move camp often in order to be near fresh fields. This was a considerable task in itself even though the mats for the conical shelters were fairly light and the hut designed to be erected quickly. The men did not assist in this work. Indeed, the man's life at this time was as leisurely as his wife's was arduous. He occasionally hunted rabbits and antelope but spent much of the time lolling about camp gossiping or gambling with other men. His time of intense activity, the summer fishing season, was yet to come.

The old and ill and crippled remained during this time at the winter camps on the river along with a few able bodied persons to care for them. The extensive travelling during root digging made it impractical to take the incapacitated along. When the travellers returned home with their products they were shared with those who had had to remain.

The summer fishing season began about the first of May, when sturgeon and small fish were available. Trout and salmon appeared soon afterwards. Most of the members of each winter village built summer mat shelters at the fishing grounds nearest that village but some preferred to go elsewhere. The largest traps were located at the mouth of the Sanpoil river, the mouth of the Spokane river and at Kettle Falls. These places always drew persons from far and near. Like the root digging, the salmon season was initiated with a ceremony, the first salmon rite. This observance was the most elaborate ceremony outside of the winter season. During a five day period of feasting and celebration the salmon was handled and eaten in a rigidly prescribed fashion. Social as well as economic life was intense from the opening rite to the end of the season at the end of August. Each day was punctuated with the distributions of the salmon at which time everyone gathered together. Visitors were constantly coming and going and gambling was rampant. The greatest amount of travel occurred toward the end of the season when the fish became scarce. There was always the hope that some distant site might prove more productive. The women were far from idle while the men were fishing and gambling. Theirs were the tasks of cooking and drying the salmon and of gathering berries in any spare time.

About the first of September the dried salmon were temporarily stored on the flat tops of the summer shelters and a general disbanding of the group took place. Some went into the mountains to gather the fall roots and to hunt. Others went directly to the fall fishing grounds where they speared the silver and dog salmons from canoes or caught them with seines. The shelter used at this time was the same type as that in the spring, a conical mat hut. A closed structure was necessary for the fall salmon had to be dried indoors by the heat of the campfire. The heat from the sun was no longer great enough.

Winter villages were reoccupied about the middle of October. All dried foods were placed in their permanent storage places, the underground houses were cleaned and repaired, the long winter mat houses were rebuilt and general preparations were made for a winter of seclusion. Most of the work at this time fell to the lot of the men. The winter houses were made exclusively by the men except for the mats which were woven and sewed by the women. Men also cut or gathered the supply of wood but the women carried it in. They, too, gathered rye grass to cover the floors.

The three midwinter months were descriptively named: kumi′kutǝn, "time that it snows"; kt'a't'sa'ttδ′n, "time that it gets cold"; and spa′kǝt', "time that it is white." It was necessary to spend most of the time indoors because of the severity of the weather. Women made baskets and mats, fashioned and mended clothing and prepared the meals. Men went on occasional hunting trips but were left with much unoccupied time which they spent playing games, telling stories or sleeping. There was one welcome break in the monotony of the season. The great ceremonial period of the year came at midwinter. Dances were held in continuous succession for as long as two months. Families travelled from one dance to another for the duration of that period. Guardian spirit songs were sung and shamanistic performances executed. Emotion was built up and released. At the end of the series of dances all were more content to await the coming of spring.

The summer day often began before sunrise in the Sanpoil household. With the aid of dry pine needles or sagebrush bark an old woman, always the first to arise, brought to life the fires which had been banked the night before with hardwood and knots. This accomplished, she wakened the children, prodding them on the soles of the feet with the fire tongs if they were slow. Immediately upon leaving their beds the boys and girls ran to their respective bathing places on the river. They plunged into the water two or three times, the bolder ones diving, then hurried back to dry themselves around the fires. While they stood there they were tutored by the old woman in the knowledge and ideals of their people. Men were allowed to rise at their leisure but the old woman called and chided the younger women if they were not soon out of their beds. Babies were permitted to sleep as long as they would.

The younger women departed immediately to pick berries or discharge other duties while the morning was yet cool. The children soon left to play in the sands of the river bank. The old women swept the floors, rolled up the unoccupied bedding and kept the fires burning. When the men arose they went to their sweat lodges or to the fishing platforms to spear salmon. Old men bathed and returned to sit around the house. As soon as the babies awakened they were bathed in baskets of warm water and placed in their cradles.

About ten o'clock those who had been away returned. The women turned to preparing the morning meal. Water was brought from the river in which to cook the salmon. The fish were cut up and put in the cooking basket with hot rocks with which the water was boiled. After the water had been kept boiling for about twenty minutes the food was ready. The salmon were removed from the basket with a sharp stick to be placed on the eating mat which had been unrolled on the floor. Fresh berries were served in a basket. If camas had been cooked with the salmon the cooking basket itself was placed on the mat along with a large horn spoon. The men and children were called and all seated themselves around the mat. The men sat with their legs beneath them, or outstretched; women sat on one foot or folded their legs together under them. Children ate with their elders only if no strangers were present. Invalids were fed later.

After the meal was finished the mat was laid out in the sun and the baskets were washed and hung on pegs in the lodge. Men devoted the remainder of the morning to dressing. Women did not take as long; when they were through they combed their husbands' hair. The early afternoon was given over to social activities, particularly gambling and visiting.

The evening meal was served at dusk. It differed little from the morning meal. Afterwards the children gathered around the reclining old people and begged for stories. The young men went out to smoke and discuss affairs of the day with their comrades. The young women attended to small duties about the house. Bedtime came soon for the children; they were not allowed to remain up after dark. The men retired soon after dark and after them the women; this order was observed because the women would have been ashamed to be seen in bed by men who were still up.

The daily routine during the winter was much less diversified except for the ceremonial season when life was fullest. The time of arising, as in the summer, was before dawn, but the actual hour was later. Children bathed in the icy waters of the river; adults washed in baskets of unwarmed water or went to the sweat lodges. The morning meal was dispensed with during the winter. One meal a day was considered sufficient during this time of inactivity and shortage of food.

Morning tasks included cleaning away freshly fallen snow from about the house and the paths to water and fuel. This was done with a paddle-like shovel of wood and brooms of sagebrush.

Men departed early in the morning if a hunting expedition had been planned. Otherwise they spent the day mainly indoors, smoking and chatting. Children played outside in the snow. Women attended to the household tasks and made baskets.

The daily meal was served late in the afternoon (some families preferred to have it in the morning). Dried foods were boiled. Often salmon alone constituted the meal.

Smoking and story telling occupied the evening. All went to bed soon after dark.

People of many cultures believe in mischievous "trickster" gods or spirits. The djinns of the Near East, the leprechauns of Ireland, and the gremlin of the United States are all conceptions of this type. Among North American Indians, "Raven," "Crow," "Mink" and other animals are elevated to the trickster status, but principally it is "Coyote" who occupies the pre-eminent position in Indian mythology. Coyote aids man and hinders him, is alternately wise and foolish, appears to explain but also confuses. The coyote of Indian mythology, in short, behaves much like man. Through the telling of the tales, however, Coyote makes human frailty and duplicity obvious to children and adults. Such stories provide a valuable socialization device which, as James Teit's article indicates, are remarkably resistant to destructive forces. Teit was himself a "squaw-man," resident with the Salish.

20 James A. Teit

SHUSWAP COYOTE STORIES*

An old Indian named Siҳwi'lexken told me as follows:

When I first remember, about sixty years ago, the people of my tribe had very many stories, far more than they have now. In each house they told them almost every night throughout the winter. The fullest versions of some stories were only known by certain individuals. When a fresh story was told, at first the young people flocked to hear it, and afterwards it went the rounds of all the houses. The half-breeds of the Hudson Bay Company sometimes camped with or lived for a time among the Indians. They were very fond of listening to and of telling stories. I think they probably introduced some stories into the tribe. Also, when Indians had been away for a time, among people who lived at a distance—such as Kamloops, Spences Bridge, Chilcotin River, or The Fountain—they sometimes heard and learned fresh stories, which they related upon their return. Some of these new stories took root for a while, but eventually died out or were forgotten. I remember having heard stories a few times, and never again afterwards. It is possible, however, that some of the stories introduced this way became permanent. Many of the stories which were commonest when I was a boy are now seldom told, or have been forgotten altogether. Thus the number of stories has decreased, and no new stories have taken their place, excepting (of late years) some Bible stories introduced by the priests. These are looked upon, however, as forming a different class, and are not considered the same as myths of the speta'kuɫ. Tales of every kind are not told as often as formerly among the people. When I was a boy, very many stories were told about the Old-One or Chief, who travelled over the country teaching people, and putting things to rights. Many wonderful tales were related of him; but the men who told these stories are now all dead, and most of the "Old One" tales have been forgotten. The majority of the Coyote tales have survived, however, and are often told yet; for they are funny, and children like to hear them. Formerly Coyote stories were

* Excerpt from "The Shuswap," by J. A. Teit, in *Memoirs of the American Museum of Natural History*, **IV**, F. Boas (ed.), 447–758, 1909.

probably commonest of all. Long before the arrival of the first white miners, a Hudson Bay half-breed told the Shuswap that after a time strange men would come among them, wearing black robes (the priests). He advised them not to listen to these men, for although they were possessed of much magic, and did some good, still they did more evil. They were descendants of the Coyote, and like him, although very powerful, they were also very foolish, and told many lies. They were simply the Coyote returning to the earth in another form. If the Indians paid attention to and followed the directions of these "black-robes," they would become poor, foolish, and helpless; and disease of all kinds would cut them off. If they avoided them, they would remain contented, happy, and numerous. Some Indians believed what was told them, and for this reason called the first priest whom they saw "Coyote." At the present time some Indians wonder whether, if they had taken the half-breed's advice, it would have turned out as he said, and whether it is really the priests and their religion that are the cause of the people dying so much, and not being so well off as they might be.

COYOTE AND GRISLY MAKE THE SEASONS, AND NIGHT AND DAY

Grisly Bear met Coyote and said, "I am greatest in magic of all the people. When I wish a thing to be, it has to be so. Now I am displeased with the short time that it is dark. I think it will be better if it is dark all the time. I intend to make it so." Coyote answered, "No. That would inconvenience the people too much." Grisly said, "Well, I will have it my way." And Coyote answered, "No, you can't." So the former danced and sang, saying, "Darkness, darkness, darkness! Let it be always dark." And Coyote also danced and sang, saying, "Light, light, light, light! May it be light!"

Thus they danced and sang a very long time; and sometimes the Bear got the ascendancy, and darkness would prevail; and, again, Coyote got the ascendancy, and light would prevail. They struggled for a long time, and neither beat the other.

At last the Bear got tired, and said, "Let there be half darkness, and half light." Coyote agreed to this, and said, "Henceforth it shall be light from the time the sun prepares to rise until he sets: the rest of the time shall be night. Thus every day the sun shall travel; and when he leaves, the night will follow him until next day he rises again."

Then Grisly Bear said, "I am displeased with the length of the year and the duration of winter. It is far too short. Let it be the same number of moons that there are feathers in the tail of a blue grouse." Coyote counted them, and found twenty-two. Thus Grisly Bear wanted each winter to last twenty-two moons. Coyote said, "No. The people cannot endure such a long winter. They will all die. Let it be half that number." Grisly Bear objected: so Coyote said, "Let there be the same number of moons in a year as there are feathers in the tail of the red-winged flicker." Grisly Bear thought there were many feathers in the flicker's tail, so he assented. Then Coyote continued, "Half of these feathers shall represent the number of moons it may snow; and the other half, the number of moons it may not snow or be cold." Grisly Bear assented, as he thought the winter would thus be almost as long as he desired. He got a flicker's tail, and was surprised, when he counted the feathers, to find only twelve; but it was then too late to make any change. Coyote said, "Henceforth the year shall consist of six moons of warm weather, and six moons in which it may snow or be cold." Thus Coyote saved the people from having to live in darkness and cold; and he determined the seasons and days as they are now.

COYOTE MAKES WOMEN MENSTRUATE

Formerly the men menstruated, and not the women. When Coyote was working in the world, putting things to rights, he considered this matter, and said to himself, "It is not right that men should menstruate. It is very inconvenient, for they do all the hunting and most of the travelling. Women stay more at home, and therefore it will be better if they menstruate, and not the men." Whereupon he took some of the menstrual fluid from men, and threw it upon the women, saying, "Henceforth women shall menstruate, and not men."

COYOTE AND THE HUNTING-CANNIBAL

Coyote, while travelling about, met a Cannibal who was hunting. The latter said to him, "Come help me hunt deer! There is a band of deer just coming around the shoulder of the hill yonder." Coyote looked where the Cannibal had pointed, and saw many people travelling along the hillside. He said, "These are not deer, they are people." The Cannibal answered, "No, they are deer, and good food. Let us go and drive them." Coyote said, "I tell you, they are not deer. They are people going to visit another village."

When the Cannibal and Coyote had thus spoken to each other four times, Coyote said, "I will show you deer." He stepped up to a tree, took some of the roots, and transformed them into a buck-deer with large antlers. Then, after showing the animal to the Cannibal, he took some of the meat and cooked it. Coyote ate some of the meat first and invited the Cannibal to do likewise; but at first he refused, for he was afraid it might poison him. At last he ate some, and acknowledged it to be good. Coyote said, "This meat is food, flesh of people is not food. Now we will go together, and I will show you how to hunt and kill deer."

After hunting for some time, they found a band of deer; and Coyote shot one with an arrow, cut it up, and cooked some of the meat. After they had eaten their fill, Coyote took the Cannibal's sack, which contained human flesh, emptied out the contents, and replenished it with venison. Then Coyote said, "I ordain that henceforth no one shall eat human flesh. There shall be no more cannibals in the world. All people shall eat deer-meat." Some say that, on leaving, he transformed the Cannibal into an owl.

COYOTE AND HOLXOLI'P

Holxoli'p was in the habit of amusing himself with his eyes by throwing them up in the air and letting them fall back again into their orbit. When doing this, he called out "Turn around, stick fast!" (X̱a'lxalē'k, x̱êqxê'qa!) Coyote came along, and, seeing him do this, he thought he would do the same. Taking out his eyes and throwing them up, he called out the same words; but his eyes would not fall back into their orbits properly. He tried many times; but, even when they did happen to fall back into their proper places, they would fall out again. Meanwhile Raven came along, and, seeing Coyote throwing up his eyes, he seized them and made off with them. Coyote was now completely blind, and said to himself, "What a fool I was to attempt doing a thing I knew nothing about! If I could only get some bearberries, I could make very good eyes of them." He crawled about on the ground, feeling for bearberries, but he could find none. Finally he found some rose-bushes, and, taking two rose-berries, he put them in his orbits, and was able to see; but his eyes were now large and red, and he could not see as well as formerly.

COYOTE AND FOX

Coyote, while travelling about, came to an underground house which was inhabited by very small, short people. They were the rock-rabbits.

He said to himself, "They are too short for people. I will kill them all and eat them." After slaughtering them, he tied all their bodies on a string, and carried them over his shoulder. It was very hot, clear weather, so he sought the shade of a large yellow pine-tree, where he heated stones, and, digging an earth oven, put all the rock-rabbits in to bake. Then he lay down in the shade to sleep until they should be cooked. Meanwhile Fox came along, and, seeing Coyote asleep, he dug up and took out the contents of the oven, and began to eat. He had eaten about half the rock-rabbits when Coyote awoke, but, feeling too lazy and overcome by the heat to get up, he said to Fox, "Spare me ten." The latter never heeded, but kept on eating. When Coyote saw there were only ten left, and Fox still continued to eat, he said, "Spare me nine." But Fox paid no attention; and, although Coyote continued to ask him to spare the rest, Fox continued to eat until there was only one rock-rabbit left. Coyote was still too lazy to rise, so he said, "Spare me half a one." But Fox ate the last one up, and then crawled away, having eaten so much that he could hardly walk.

At last Coyote became energetic enough to rise. Saying to himself, "I will kill that fellow!" he set out to follow Fox's tracks. Soon he came upon Fox sleeping in the shade of a very thick fir-tree. Coyote, by his magic, made the tree fall on Fox; then he laughed loudly, saying, "I told the tree to fall on him, and now he is dead." The tree was so branchy, however, that it had fallen over Fox without the trunk touching him, for the many branches had hindered the trunk from reaching the ground. Soon Fox crawled out from underneath the tree and walked away.

Reaching a place where the wild red-top or rye-grass was very thick and tall, he went into the middle of it and lay down to sleep again. Coyote followed him, and set fire to the grass all around; but Fox, waking up, set counter-fires around himself, and thus made Coyote's fire harmless.

When the fires had died out, Fox went on, and entered a piece of country overgrown with reeds, where hares were very numerous. Coyote, following, set fire to the reeds, saying, "They will burst, and then Fox's eyes will burst also." When the fire spread, the hares ran out in large numbers; and Coyote was so intent clubbing them, that Fox escaped, and was some distance away before Coyote noticed him. The latter then said, "Fox, you may go."

Then Coyote travelled on, and came to a place where magpies were very numerous. Here he set snares, and, catching many of these birds, he made a robe of their skins. He put his robe on and admired it very much,

saying, "What a beautiful robe I have! and how the feathers shine!"
Soon afterwards he met Fox, who was wearing a robe thickly covered
with tail-feathers of the golden eagle. Coyote said to himself, "His robe
looks better than mine, and is much more valuable." So he offered to
exchange robes; but Fox said, "How can you expect me to exchange a
valuable robe like mine for yours, which is made of only magpie-
skins?" Just as they were about to separate, Coyote seized Fox, and,
tearing his robe off, went away with it.

Fox sat down and watched Coyote until he was out of sight. The latter, arriving at a lake, took off his magpie robe, and, tearing it to pieces,
threw it into the water. Then, donning the robe of eagle-feathers, he
strutted around, admiring himself, and saying, "If a wind would only
come, so that I could see and admire these feathers as they flutter!"
Just then Fox caused a great wind to come, which blew the robe off
Coyote's back, and carried it back to himself. Then Coyote went back to
the lake to see if he could find his old magpie robe; but the wind had
scattered all the pieces and the feathers, so that only here and there on
the surface of the lake could one be seen. Coyote was now worse off than
at first, and had to travel along naked.

COYOTE AND SALMON

Some time after Coyote had introduced the salmon, he said, "I have
never given a feast yet. Why should I not feast the people?" He
caught and dried great numbers of sockeye and king salmon, and also
made much salmon-oil, and buried much salmon-roe. Then he sent out
messengers to invite all the people. He said to himself, "I will sing a
great song, and perform a dance, when the people assemble. They will
think me a great man."

Then he practised his dance, and sang, going out and in between the
poles where the salmon were drying. While doing so, his hair was
caught in the gills of one of the salmon, and he could not free himself.
He got angry, pulled the whole fish down, and threw it into the river.
Immediately all the salmon came to life, and, jumping off the poles,
ran to the river. The Coyote tried to stop them, but in vain. As he was
endeavoring to catch the last one, he noticed that the oil had also come
to life, and was running to the river. He ran to stop it, but too late. The
salmon-roe he had buried also came out and jumped into the river.
When the people arrived, they found nothing to eat, and were very
angry, for they thought Coyote had played a trick on them.

COYOTE AND WOLF

Coyote lived with Wolf. They hunted together, and killed many deer and elks. Wolf said, "When we kill animals, we should take their skins off before eating them. The skins are not good for us to eat. We might leave the skins wherever we kill the animal, and the people might find them and be glad to have them. They might dress the skins and make clothes and moccasins of them." Coyote answered, "No, that would not do. It would take too long to skin each animal. We will eat the skin with the flesh."

This is the reason that at the present day wolves and coyotes, when they kill or find an animal, always eat the skin with the flesh, leaving nothing but the bones. If Coyote had been more considerate, and not so selfish, but allowed Wolf to have his wish, the people would have been better off.

COYOTE AND THE SWANS

Coyote, while travelling with his son Kałê'llst, passed a lake, on the grassy shores of which they saw four swans. Coyote sang and danced, and thus brought it about that the swans lost their power of flight, and fell a prey to his son, who clubbed them, and tied them together. Coyote said to his son, "We will cook and eat them. You must watch them while I gather firewood. I will cut off the dry top of that tree yonder." Coyote climbed the tree, and was standing on a branch, busily engaged cutting the tree-top, when his son cried to him, "Come quickly, father! The swans have come to life, and I cannot hold them." Coyote got excited, and cried, "Catch them! Hold them!" As he hurriedly descended the tree, the sharp point of a broken limb penetrated his scrotum, and he yelled with pain. Meanwhile the swans all got loose and flew away, and, although Coyote danced and sang, they kept on their way, and alighted far out on the lake.

COYOTE AND THE BLACK BEARS

As Coyote was travelling along, he saw three black bears in a tree—a mother and two cubs. He said to himself, "I will kill· all three, and make their skins into a robe. The two cubs' skins sewed together will make one half of the robe, and the large bear the other half." He took off the robe he was wearing, tore it all to pieces, and, taking up a branch that was to serve as a club, he hid at the foot of the tree.

One of the bears came down, and he struck it with the club, but it ran away unharmed. The other bears also came down; and, although Coyote hit each of them on the head, they ran off unharmed, and disappeared in the timber. Thus Coyote was left without a robe. He picked up the pieces of the robe he had torn, but saw that it would be too much work to sew them together again, for the bits were very small. He travelled on, wearing only his leggings. He was foolish.

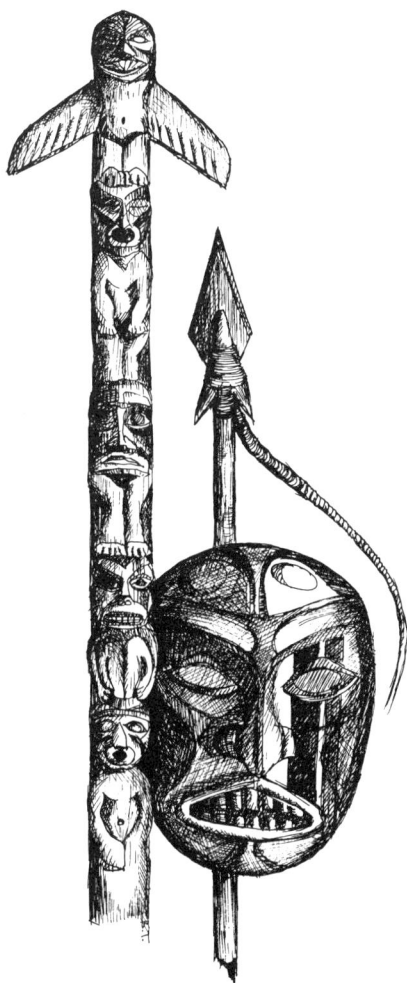

SECTION V
The Northwest Coast

Development of cultural "richness" and complexity is nearly everywhere in the world associated with the cultivation of plants or, at least (as in the case of some of the horse and camel nomads of Asia and North Africa), is found in cultures directly associated with agriculturalists. One outstanding exception to this generalization is to be seen among the societies which developed along the Pacific Coast of North America, from northern California to southern Alaska. Here, a number of societies developed complex social units, elaborate systems of ranked statuses, complicated patterns of inheritance, legal codes, intricate ceremonial rounds, and other appurtenances of life customarily associated with agricultural systems capable of producing social security through the maintenance of a reliable surplus of food.

Northwest Coast Indians, however, instead of basing their subsistence upon the cultivation of plants, made extensive use of the particular richness of the sea, as well as utilizing the abundant resources of the land. Fish (characteristically varieties of salmon, but numerous other species also), sea mammals (seals largely, but also sea lions, otters, and whales), shelled organisms of all types, and even seaweed, provided storable food for the larder. If this were not enough, the land also was filled with animal life, both large and small (from moose, bear, deer, and mountain sheep to turtles and small rodents). Based on this superabundance of food, the Indians of the region developed an elaborate way of life that has intrigued social scientists for the past seventy or more years. It should be noted, however, that like Indians of the Plains area (to be discussed later in this book), what has come to be called an "aboriginal" way of life is, in reality, a pattern of life recorded and studied after serious interference in aboriginal patterns had taken place.

Russians in the 18th century were apparently the first Europeans to contact the Northwest Coast; the Spaniards reached it in 1774. Captain James Cook spent some time in Nootka Sound in 1778. From this time forth, trade in sea otter and other pelts, together with the introduction of firearms and metal tools, provided enormous enrichment to the aboriginal system and brought about drastic change.

As elsewhere in North America, the region under discussion has probably been inhabited for millennia. Just over the coastal mountains in Oregon, Carbon $_{14}$ dates of over 9,000 years have been obtained. Archaeological investigation of the coastal region is still only beginning, but the work that has been done suggests a sequence of several occupations.

Philip Drucker, the author of the first article in this section, is widely known for his syntheses of Northwest Coast culture, as well as for his more descriptive, detailed works.

21 Philip Drucker

INDIANS OF THE NORTHWEST COAST*

THE ENVIRONMENT

Along the shores of northwestern North America from Yakutat Bay in southeast Alaska to Trinidad Bay on the coast of present northern California, lived a number of Indian groups who participated jointly in a unique and rich culture. It is an anthropological truism that development of complex, or "high," culture among primitive peoples is linked with, or, better, results from the notable increase in economic productivity that accompanies the invention or acquisition of agricultural techniques, and within limits, the domestication of animals. This can be documented by archaeological evidence from various early centers of high civilization—the Middle East, the Indus Valley, Middle America. The expansion of the economic base effected by agriculture raises the general standard of living, permits increased settled populations, provides more leisure time to cultivate the arts, to elaborate on religious, social, and political concepts, and to perfect the material aspects of culture: tools, dwellings, utensils, textiles, ornaments, and the rest. The culture of the Northwest Coast, therefore, seems to be an anomaly for it was a civilization of the so-called "hunting-and-gathering" type, without agriculture (except for a few instances of tobacco growing), and possessing no domesticated animals other than the dog. In other words, the natives of the Northwest Coast, like the rude Paiute of Nevada, the Australian aborigines, and others of the simpler cultures the world over, were entirely and directly dependent on natural products for their livelihood. That they were able to attain their high level of civilization is due largely to the amazing wealth of the natural resources of their area. From the sea and rivers, fish—five species of

* Excerpt from "Indians of the Northwest Coast," by P. Drucker, in *American Museum of Natural History Anthropological Handbook* **10**, 1–13, 1955.

Pacific salmon, halibut, cod, herring, smelt, and the famous olachen or "candlefish" (this last so rich in oil that a dried one with a wick threaded through it burns like a candle), and other species too numerous to mention—could be taken in abundance. Some of these fish appeared only seasonally, but were easy to preserve. The sea also provided a tremendous quantity of edible mollusks; "when the tide goes out the table is set," as the saying goes. More spectacular was the marine game: hair seal, sea lion, sea otter, porpoise, and even whale. On shore, land game too abounded. Vegetable foods were less plentiful, although many species of wild berries were abundant in their season. In other words, the bounty of nature provided that which in most other parts of the world man must supply for himself through agriculture and stock raising: a surplus of foodstuffs so great that even a dense population had an abundance of leisure to devote to the improvement and elaboration of its cultural heritage.

The Northwest Coast is a unit, not only in its aboriginal culture patterns, but geographically as well. The Japanese Current offshore moderates the climate so that extreme and prolonged cold does not occur even in the higher latitudes. The same ocean stream releases vast amounts of water vapor that is blown onshore by the prevailing winds, condenses on rising over the coastal mountains and hills, and produces the characteristic heavy rainfall of the area. Consequently, innumerable streams and small rivers with their sources in the Coast Range flow to the sea, as do the major drainage systems like the Columbia, the Fraser, and the Skeena, with sources east of the mountains. Likewise, the heavy precipitation produces a dense specialized vegetation, consisting mainly of thick stands of conifers—Douglas fir, various spruces, red cedar, yellow cedar, yew, and, at the southern tip of the area, coast redwood. Deciduous trees are smaller and more scattered but include several hardwoods, such as maple and oak, and the soft but even-grained alder.

The terrain is of two major types, which grade into each other in the Gulf of Georgia–Puget Sound region. In the north, the Coast Range is composed of towering mountains of raw, naked rock. Deep cañons, gouged out by glacial flow and turbulent streams, cut into them. A general subsidence in ancient geological times has "drowned" many of these valleys and cañons, producing long narrow fiords flanked by sheer cliffs rising hundreds of feet. The scenery is spectacular; travel, except by water and over a few rare passes, is painful and slow. As one goes southward the terrain changes until, around upper Puget Sound and the Oregon and northwestern Californian coasts, one sees steep but rounded coast hills, not mountains; estuaries resulting from the building up of sand bars form at river mouths, indicating the gentler gradients of the lower portions of the stream beds.

The areal fauna, like everything else, is highly specialized. Varieties and abundance of marine forms have been mentioned. The principal large game animals were deer, elk, and, on the mainland from the Gulf of Georgia northward, mountain goats. Where long northern fiords cut entirely or partially through the Coast Range, hunters had access to subarctic faunal assemblages, including caribou and moose. Coastal carnivores included chiefly wolf, black and grizzly bear, and brown bear in the north, mountain lion, and a variety of small fur bearers: beaver, mink, marten, and land otter, among others. A number of intriguing problems related to the distributions of land species, especially in the is-land areas along the Inland Passage, though they have little connection with areal culture patterns, are of passing interest. For example, on the Queen Charlotte Islands there were black bear and a type of small cari-bou, but no grizzly bear or deer. (The modern deer population has de-scended from a few pairs imported by white settlers some forty or fifty years ago. On Vancouver Island deer, elk, wolf, mountain lion, and black bear, among the larger forms, occurred, but neither mountain goat nor grizzly. A small "black bear" with an all-white coat known as Kermode's bear, was found in the vicinity of Princess Royal Island, and apparently nowhere else. Up the coast, nearly every major island from Admiralty Island north seems to have its own distinctive subspecies of Alaskan brown bear. It is possible that the deer population of north-western California tended to show much greater color variation than in other areas. To return from oddities of distributions to the general faunal picture, the Pacific flyway follows the coast for a great part of its length, and enormous flights of waterfowl of many species flew along it on their annual migrational round.

Few modern students of human society will subscribe to a theory of environmental determinism of culture. Yet, while the geographical background of aboriginal Northwest Coast civilization can by no means be said to have defined the culture patterns of the area, it can be shown to have had a certain influence, by permitting, and even inducing, de-velopment along some lines, and inhibiting that along others. Some of the environmentally affected cultural elaborations are included among the patterns that make the areal culture as a whole distinctive, as com-pared with other native civilizations of North America. It is true enough that in other equally important area-wide patterns no environmental factors can be detected, but those in which the physical setting played a part are worth discussing.

Marine resources may be considered first. We have seen that they were tremendously rich, and in addition, partly seasonal (that is, the "runs" of certain important species of fish, such as salmon, herring, smelt, and olachen, occur for a limited period each year). The abundance of these resources made a relatively dense population possible, once techniques had been devised to exploit them properly. Even more basically, it favored the orientation of the areal culture toward the water—the river and sea—with a consequent interest in development of water transport, that is, development of vessel construction and navigation. In fact, in the northern, more rugged half of the area it seems probable that a certain minimum proficiency in canoemanship must have been essential to the earliest human occupancy; it is difficult to see how people could have survived without it. At the same time, it is possible to interpret the richness of the fisheries resource as a limiting factor also: concentrated, as the "runs" of salmon and the other fish were, at the upper ends of bays and channels, or along the beaches, they may have restricted interest in water transport to the foreshore. It is certain that the Indians of the Northwest Coast were not deep-sea navigators in the same sense as the Vikings or the Polynesians. They sailed along the coast, from point to point, and hated to get out of sight of land.

Another feature of the natural environment that affected culture growth was the seasonal aspect of the principal "harvests" of fish. This made for periods of intense activity, put a premium on the development of techniques for the preservation of foodstuffs, and, once such techniques had been developed, permitted lengthy periods of leisure. In fact, once adequate preservation techniques had been developed, not only was there opportunity for leisure, but there was a certain force for seasonal immobility; even a large family group is unlikely to favor a nomadic way of life if they have half a ton of dried salmon to lug around with them. This leisure and temporary immobility was utilized by the Indians of our area for the development of art and ceremonialism. Here of course is where the strictly environmental interpretations of culture break down. The particular fields of interest that were seized on were determined by historical and social factors of human culture, and not by environment at all. All the environment did was to make possible the development of economic techniques that permitted considerable leisure. How that leisure was utilized was not defined by the natural setting—as far as environmental forces were concerned it might as well have been spent at studies of mathematics or crossword puzzles. The important thing is that the natural resources were such that they permitted the expansion of some luxury aspects of culture.

Another environmentally favored development was that of wood-working. As will be brought out, there were undoubtedly historical factors involved in the original interest in this activity, but the fact that the forests of the Northwest Coast were amply supplied with an abundance of readily worked woods made elaboration of this craft possible, and even might be said to have offered a certain inducement to such elaboration. Wood was beyond all question the most abundant type of material available. Moreover, other materials suitable for technological developments were scarce.

Some inhibiting factors of the environment may be pointed out. In the northern half of the area, unquestionably because of the roughness of the terrain, land hunting was a luxury activity, not a major field of economic endeavor. Another example: the mountainous northern coasts were formed of massive blocks of tough igneous rocks; work in stone was of minor importance throughout the area as a consequence, since stone that lent itself to working was relatively rare. There are exceptions. A very tractable form of slate occurs at a few localities in the Queen Charlotte Islands, but given the general absence of a stoneworking pattern, little or no use was made of it until historic times brought new cultural stimuli. Again, the northern half of the area has little land suitable for agriculture. Agriculture is a very minor form of economy today. Even if, in aboriginal times, contacts with agricultural areas had made possible the introduction of the art (as far as we know, there were no such direct contacts), it could never have had much effect on native culture, at least in the north. Even though there was a much-disputed plant—a tobacco or one resembling tobacco—supposed to have been cultivated in the Queen Charlotte Islands, and a true native tobacco was planted and harvested along the lower Klamath River in modern California, agriculture could never have reached a point where it would have modified the prevailing fishing and sea-hunting economy of the coast.

We may summarize our survey of the natural setting as follows: There were certain permissive factors in the environment that allowed cultural developments in certain aspects of native culture. Some of these—dependence on exploitation of marine resources, elaboration of canoe navigation, emphasis on woodworking—came to be distinctive of the areal culture. Some negative characteristics of the area, such as minor importance of land hunting, very rudimentary development of stoneworking, and the like, are due to inhibiting factors of the natural scene which did not provide adequate materials. However, many other features of coastal culture that served to mark it off as different from most other Indian civilizations of North America can be traced only to historical factors, or to the selection of certain solutions to problems posed by functional relationships of strictly cultural, not environmental, phenomena.

THE PEOPLE

Along this rugged but bountiful coast lived a number of Indian nations who differed among themselves somewhat in physical characteristics, differed considerably in language, but shared a number of fundamental cultural patterns that, in combination, comprised Northwest Coast civilization. It must be noted that here, as elsewhere throughout this book, the term "nation" is used with certain reservations, for as will be explained below, there were no nations in the modern political sense. There *were* groups, however, who spoke the same language or dialect of that language, who resembled each other more closely in details of culture than they did their neighbors of alien speech, and who consisted of independent local groups, tribes, or even confederacies, but who were without any sort of over-all "national" political authority or even sense of political unity.

Beginning our enumeration of Northwest Coast peoples in the north, the Tlingit, consisting of fourteen tribal divisions, occupied the coast from Yakutat Bay to Cape Fox. They spoke a language believed by most linguists to be related to the Athapascan stock of the interior. Shortly before the opening of the historic period they were pressing westward. Some of their divisions, probably the Yakutat, had driven the Chugachmiut Eskimo off Kayak Island, and the same or some related tribe established an outpost among the linguistically related Eyak of the mouth of the Copper River. A small Tlingit-speaking group, the Tagish, on Tagish and Marsh lakes (inland from the Chilkat Tlingit, possessed a culture of completely interior, not coastal, pattern, and were apparently an Athapascan people who were in the process of becoming Tlingit-ized through aboriginal trade contacts. According to tradition, the ancestors of some of the Tlingit clans once lived to the south, around the mouth of the Skeena, and subsequently moved northward. Other ancestral divisions migrated from the interior, following the

Stikine River to the sea. If the traditions are to be believed, they reached salt water only after a perilous journey under a glacier that bridged a section of the river.

The Haida, who also spoke a language believed to be related to Athapascan, although differing from Tlingit, inhabited the Queen Charlotte Islands, and the southern part of Prince of Wales Island in Alaska. It is said that the Alaskan Haida, known as the Kaigani, drove out some Southern Tlingit tribe or tribes a little more than two centuries ago. There are two principal dialectic divisions among the Haida. These are called "Masset" and "Skidegate" after two important centers where the speakers of each assembled during historic times, following the sharp decline of the population. Most if not all the Kaigani came from the northern or Masset-speaking villages. Haida traditions relate that some of their ancestors—those belonging to the Eagle phratry (of which more later)—came from the mainland, but claim that the other Haida, whom the newcomers found living on the islands, had been there since the creation of the world.

The Tsimshian nation lived on the mainland and the adjacent islands. Each of the three major subdivisions spoke a slightly divergent dialect, and differed somewhat culturally. The first were the Niska, or Nass River tribes. The second, the Coast Tsimshian, consisted of fourteen tribes who held salmon-fishing villages on the lower Skeena River, and olachen-fishing grounds on the lower Nass. Nine of these tribes had separate winter villages along Metlakatla Pass, just off the modern city of Prince Rupert, and three had winter villages, one off the mouth of the Skeena, the other two to the south. Two Coast Tsimshian tribes, the Kitselas and Kitsamxelam, wintered in their villages just below the cañon of the Skeena. The third major division, the Gitksan, inhabited eight villages above the cañon.

Some linguists classify the Tsimshian language with a proposed linguistic stock, as yet not certainly defined, for which they suggest the name "Penutian." The nearest fellow speakers of this stock were to be found far to the south, within the limits of modern Washington, Oregon, and California. According to Tsimshian tradition, most of their divisions came originally from a legendary place called Temlaxam ("Tum-la-ham"), "Prairie Town," located somewhere far up the Skeena.

South of the Tsimshian were the Kwakiutl, with three major dialectic divisions: that spoken by the Haisla of Gardner and Douglas channels in the north, a second dialect called Heiltsuk, and Southern Kwakiutl.

The Heiltsuk-speakers consisted of the Xaihais, the Bella Bella of Milbanke Sound, a historic confederation of several formerly independent tribes and local groups, and the Wikeno of Rivers Inlet. The traditional origin tales of all these people claim Rivers Inlet and lower Burke and Dean channels as their original homeland. The Haisla, for example, maintain that their ancestors came overland from Rivers Inlet. After settling at the old site of Kitamat, they incorporated a wandering Tsimshian clan. It is interesting to note that the names of their principal villages, "Kitamat" and "Kitlope," are Tsimshian, not Heiltsuk words; a possible interpretation is that their ancestors infiltrated a Tsimshian area and engulfed the former occupants (contradicting the traditional claim that the Haisla were there first). The Xaihais consisted of a number of independent local groups who, as a result of their lack of political unity, were being ground to bits between the warlike Coast Tsimshian and their own equally warlike Bella Bella relatives. The Bella Bella tribes seem to have held their own against all comers. Their drastic historic decline in population was effected by disease, rather than enemy successes.

The Bella Coola villages were located in the upper reaches of Dean and Burke channels and the lower parts of the Bella Coola River valley. These people spoke a Salishan language, fairly closely allied to the speech of the Coast Salish to the south, from whom they were separated by a considerable distance. Bella Coola traditions assert that this nation was created at the beginning of the world in the same locality where Alexander Mackenzie found them in 1793. However, in view of their linguistic affiliations, it seems more probable that their ancestors split off from the main body of Salish and migrated to their northern location. Various aspects of Bella Coola culture suggest either that they have been exposed to Heiltsuk influences a relatively short time or, more likely, that they were remarkably conservative in certain culture traits. Their material culture, their ceremonials, and their mythology check almost point for point with those of their Heiltsuk neighbors. In the field of social organization, however, particularly with respect to rank and social status, they have apparently retained to a great extent the amorphous, loosely organized Salish patterns rather than the precisely and rigidly defined ones of their neighbors.

The Southern Kwakiutl consisted of a large number of independent local groups and tribes occupying the bays and inlets around Queen Charlotte Sound and the entire northern end of Vancouver Island, as far south as Cape Cook. Like the Bella Coola, they insist that their ancestors were created in the region they now occupy; the possibilities are that they have occupied it for a considerable length of time. There is little evidence of any major population shifts among them, other than the expansion of the southernmost tribe, the Lekwiltok, into the Cape Mudge area at the expense of the Salishan Comox, and the separation of the Matilpe from the Fort Rupert confederacy. The Lekwiltok deserve special mention as one of the most warlike groups of the entire coast. Their original territory dominated Yucluta Rapids and Seymour Narrows, passes between Vancouver Island and the mainland. They exacted tribute or attacked anyone who traveled these roads, whether the party was a peaceful one going on a trading expedition or to a potlatch, or whether it was a Haida war party bent on slave raiding in Puget Sound. They were, of course, frequently attacked in retaliation, but always gave a good account of themselves.

On the southwest coast of Vancouver Island, or as it is locally known, the "West Coast," and on Cape Flattery, the extreme tip of the present state of Washington, live the Nootka. The Nootka language is distantly related to Kwakiutl; in fact, linguists consider that the two represent a single stock termed the Wakashan. It has been suggested that this stock, together with Salish and some other languages of the interior, may ultimately be related to Algonkian, a relationship that has not yet been demonstrated. There were two, or possibly three, dialectic divisions of Nootka—Nootka proper, spoken by the people from Cape Cook down to Barkley Sound—and Nitinat-Makah. It has not been established as yet whether Nitinat and Makah were minor variants of a single dialect, or whether they warrant separation into two distinct dialects. The Nootka possessed a specialized form of Northwest Coast culture—one extremely well adapted to the region. Only they (aside from a few neighbors of the Makah who learned the art from that last-named division) hunted the largest game on the coast—whales. Their basic canoe pattern was widely copied, and Nootka-made canoes were bought with eagerness by most of their neighbors because of their excellent lines and seaworthiness. The only territorial changes known to us from historical records or traditions are internal ones in which one Nootka local group or tribe exterminated or dispossessed another in order to acquire the victims' territories.

The land of the Coast Salish, aside from that of the Bella Coola, included the circumference of the Gulf of Georgia, Puget Sound, a good portion of the Olympic Peninsula, and most of western Washington, down to Chinook territory at the mouth of the Columbia River. One

Salishan group, the Tillamook, resided south of the Columbia on the Oregon coast. As the name indicates, these Salish-speaking people were part of a larger linguistic entity, the bulk of whom lived in the interior to the east of the Cascades. This coast versus inland division appears to have been correlated with a major dialectic break, as well as with a differentiation between cultures of coast and inland genre. Great diversities of minor dialectic variants are recognized among the Coast Salish —the inhabitants of almost every drainage system, or at most, two or three contiguous valleys, had their own subdialects. There was a certain amount of intercourse between these coast people and their interior relatives. It is generally assumed that the coast divisions were relatively late entrants into the area, pushing down the Fraser River and spilling over the Cascades into western Washington. Such scant archaeological evidence as is available corroborates this theory, although the length of time the Salish have lived along the coast is not yet known.

A number of small enclaves of linguistically diverse groups occupied western Washington. On either side of the Nootkan Makah on the tip of Cape Flattery lived small divisions—the Chemakum on the Straits, and the Quileute on the Pacific Coast. Both of these spoke closely related languages, or dialects of the same tongue, but one not closely related to any other native North American language, although some authorities suggest a distant affiliation to a proposed group that includes Salishan, Wakashan, and Algonkian. The Chemakum became extinct too early for us to salvage any significant amount of linguistic or cultural data. We know that the Quileute borrowed heavily on the cultural side from their Makah neighbors, so that in historic times they varied from the Makah only slightly. A now extinct group, the Klatskanie, is reported to have held a sizable tract of territory in the midst of the Salish Chehalis. We know virtually nothing of this group, except that they spoke an Athapascan tongue. Presumably, they were culturally fairly similar to their Salish and Chinook neighbors. They were reputed to have been very warlike. Some time during the early historic period, they are reported to have moved from their territory on the Chehalis River across the Columbia to take up residence on the Clatskanie River in present Oregon. Another small Athapascan-speaking enclave, the Kwalhiokwa, about whom even less is known, held a tract along the Willapa River. One wonders if they may not have been a subdivision of the Klatskanie.

Along the lower Columbia, from The Dalles down to the sea, lived the various divisions of the Chinook. The exact relationship of their language to any other is unknown, although affiliation with the proposed widespread Penutian stock has been suggested. The great fame of the Chinook nation stems from the fact that they were middlemen in aboriginal trade north and south along the coast and between the coast and the interior. They traded slaves from the Californian hinterland up the coast for Nootka canoes and the prized dentalium shells, and exchanged many other products as well. It was through their hands that the strings of dentalia from the west coast of Vancouver Island eventually reached the Plains tribes east of the Rockies.

The central coast of Oregon, south of Tillamook territory, was occupied by several small groups now virtually extinct—the Alsea, the Siuslaw, the Coos, and the Umpqua. Very little information is available on these tiny divisions. Such as there is has been collected from informants who lived their lives in the cultural hodgepodge of Siletz and Grande Ronde reservations, on which all the Indians of western Oregon were assembled and thrown into intimate contact in the 1850s. Culturally these small tribes seem to have stood midway between the Salish-Chinook patterns and those of northwestern California; if anything, they inclined slightly more toward the former.

Another segment of the Athapascan linguistic family lived in south western Oregon. Villages of these people, who were sometimes referred to as the Tolowa-Tututni, after two of the better-known divisions, were situated along every stream course from the upper Umpqua to Smith River in northern California. These groups were culturally marginal to—that is to say, in many respects pallid imitations of—the civilization of the lower Klamath River. In this last-named region, representatives of three linguistic stocks—the Yurok of proven Algonkian affiliation, the Hupa of the Athapascan family, and the Karok of uncertain relationship—shared a set of cultural patterns modified from the basic motifs of the Northwest Coast and elaborated in a number of unique ways. Their civilization, simple and poor as it may seem in comparison with that of the northern tribes, was complex indeed as compared with that of their Oregon coastal neighbors and most of the native groups of California.

These, then, were the Indian nations participating in the unique patterns of the civilization of the Northwest Coast. Each group's manifestations of the fundamental motifs of areal culture differed a bit. All were not of the same intensity. Some groups were obviously borrowers, not elaborators, of ideas. Some may even have been "Johnny-come-latelies" to the coastal scene. Yet all shared and utilized a series of concepts that, like the weft strands in weaving, connect the various elements—in this context the local cultural variants—into a unit distinctive and unique among native American cultures.

〜〜〜〜〜

*C*oast Salish" refers to one of the more southerly groups in the Northwest Coast area. They differ from their northerly compatriots, such as the Tlingit, in showing closer affinities to Great Basin cultural patterns than they do to those of the Eskimo. A conclusion which may be drawn in light of present evidence is that the ancestors of the Coast Salish moved down from the Great Basin, perhaps through the Fraser River Valley, and then on to the coast where they came into contact with an already resident, maritime-oriented population.*

22 Homer G. Barnett

THE COAST SALISH OF CANADA*

With the exception of the Bella Coola, the adjective Canadian defines rather precisely that aspect of Coast Salish culture which provides the basis for this summary. The Puget Sound tribes, though Salish and immediately adjoining, are not included in it because of a lack of original information about them and because it is intended that this should be a digest of field data rather than a synthesis of existing material. The limitation is therefore an arbitrary one and not founded upon a cultural discontinuity; in fact there can be no doubt that the transition at the present international boundary was a more gradual one in prehistoric times than that between the Comox and Nanaimo, for example. Specifically the area under consideration lies on both sides of the Strait of Georgia, between Vancouver and Bute Inlet on the mainland, and from Victoria to Salmon River on Vancouver Island.

* Abridged from "The Coast Salish of Canada," by H. G. Barnett, in *American Anthropologist*, **40**, 118–141, 1938.

This is a region of extremes in environment and cultural specialization. In part, the latter has been stimulated by the Kwakiutl immediately to the north, themselves in a very similar habitat. For the rest, the Salish have made their own adjustments to a remarkable land and water configuration. The strait nowhere exceeds a breadth of twenty-five miles, and its waters are not subject to the violent storms which occur on the outer coast. A number of large and small islands are scattered just off shore and add to the irregularity of the land pattern. These features create a maximum of sea shore and become a significant factor in the culture-environment relationship. An extensive hunting ground emerges at low tide: mollusks and waterfowl abound on the mud flats. A pronounced tidal differential—a variation of well over ten feet is not uncommon—brings this feature into still greater prominence. The islands, natural refuges for man and animal, once harbored numerous birds and even deer. Porpoises were abundant; halibut banks were known on the southern part of Vancouver Island; and every river and creek once literally seethed with salmon in the spawning season.

These and other characteristic natural conditions are pertinent to a proper understanding of the cultural accents of this area. Among the Salish, as farther to the north, they have fostered a predominately fishing and sea hunting population. The rich assemblage of aquatic life was exploited to the full, while an almost equally exuberant land fauna played a secondary role in the bill of fare. Protected harbors and inlets ramifying inland further favored the utilization of waterways. On the mainland especially, mountains descend abruptly into the water and are covered as elsewhere with a dense undergrowth topped by heavy stands of conifers. A variety of roots, berries, fibers, and workable timber was derived from these resources, but gainful penetration was difficult and foreign to the genius of the culture. Canoes were therefore indispensable; travel on foot was distinctly the exceptional mode. Habitation sites were almost exclusively on rocky beaches at the water's edge.

All of the area was ranged over and claimed in one fashion or another. This does not mean that the burden of population was critical: to judge by native accounts there was no want on the subsistence level, nor have I any record of contest over territorial claims. On the mainland at least boundary lines were rather well defined.

Occupational sites were of two kinds: permanent villages and temporary summer encampments. At the mouth of every river of any size there was a cluster of plank dwellings. These were the foci, the winter retreats, of semisedentary groups who counted and preserved their distinctness by reason of this habit of seasonal convergence. With the coming of spring the inhabitants of each center radiated over its acknowledged territory, setting up shelters at favored spots for clamming, egg gathering, and fishing. These groups are to be regarded as cultural units, homogeneous within themselves and differing to some degree from the others. Strictly speaking they should not be called tribes. Each was composed of from one to five named house clusters, often within shouting distance of one another, to which the term village is here applied. There were, for example, twelve named villages on the Cowichan River from Duncan to the mouth of the bay. Aboriginally the whole group, as at Cowichan Bay, had no inclusive name for itself, no head chief, and no coordinated political structure. Such unity as it achieved was founded upon a community of interests arising from near or remote degrees of kinship between its members, and a common traditional background.

Eleven of these ethnic groups have been investigated. There is nothing to suggest an internal source for their names; in almost every case the names seem to have come from an outsider and are not the names of villages. Minor differences between any two groups are recognizable, but there are certain cultural cleavages which make it impossible to treat the area as a homogeneous one. A division into three sub-areas is indicated by the data.

The most aberrant group, from the Salish point of view, is that of the Comox proper (Vancouver Island). They show a decided bias toward the Kwakiutl, a fact which was long ago noted by Boas and is voluntarily remarked on by present day informants. With them go the Pentlatch. Their nearest linguistic congeners, the Homalco, Klahuse, and Slaiämun, form another, but less certainly defined, sub-area, having been only moderately (and lately ?) influenced from the north and exhibiting now and again features suggesting interior contacts. Related to them, though not so intimately as they are to one another, are the Sechelt. Across the Strait, the Nanaimo, Cowichan, and Sanetch are in pronounced cultural agreement, except for a few traits which have filtered around the tip of Vancouver Island from the Nootka. In the same category perhaps should be placed the Point Grey group (Muskwium) and the Squamish. I am uncertain about their classification in terms of the outline given here, for while their social structure fits in well enough with the classification suggested here, their technologies reveal an up-river adaptation.

Linguistically the area is divided as follows: To the Comox dialect belong the Pentlatch, Homalco, Klahuse, and Sechelt. The Cowichan and Nanaimo speak another dialect differing only slightly from that of their nearest relatives on the Fraser River as far up as Yale. The Sanetch are most closely connected with the Sooke and Songish around Victoria and the Klallam in Washington. The Squamish are set apart as distinct from the other Salish dialects around them, their nearest affinity being the Nootsack of Washington.

SUMMARY OF THE CULTURES

Salmon, the staple food, were commonly taken by means of weirs, nets, gaffs, and harpoons. Straight shanked hooks and cylindrical basketry traps were not used extensively. The various types of dams and enclosures were constructed of cedar laths and were in use whenever the depth and current of the streams permitted. Harpoons were of the two pronged variety known widely on the Pacific Coast; the detachable head consisting of a simple piercing point bound fast between two wings. They, like the long handled bag net, were operated from platforms standing alone or in connection with dams.

Fish netting was commonly made of nettle fiber. Gill nets were known on the southern part of Vancouver Island, but never attained the popularity of a distinctive variety of seine. Called a reef net, it was operated between two canoes near the mouths of favorable rivers.

Halibut and cod were caught on plain U-shaped hooks of bent hardwood. They were suspended in pairs and held almost everywhere by hand. Cod were also speared, lured upward by a spinning shuttle-cock device. Rock enclosures, and some of stakes, were so situated that at low tide they would effect the stranding of fish. Remains of these structures are still visible on many of the beaches.

A herring rake—"comb" gives a better idea of the construction of this implement—was swept through waters teeming with these fish to impale them on its sharp teeth. During the spawning season roe was collected on submerged branches. Clams were everywhere a never failing source of food, except at the mouth of the Fraser and to some extent that of the Squamish, and while the epithet "clam-digger" had somewhat the same connotations as our own "peasant," the food itself was a part of the daily fare of every class. They were dug by means of a plain pointed stick identical with the one used for roots.

The hunting of sea mammals was a precarious and exacting pursuit. The common man did not engage in it since it involved certain traditional prerogatives, considerable training, and, at least theoretically, some supernatural sanction by way of a dream. Seals and porpoises were generally approached by canoes manned by two hunters. The man in the bow wielded a large scale replica of the salmon harpoon to which was attached a line and several inflated bladders.

The flesh of these animals was a prized delicacy. Their fat was rendered in wooden dishes by means of hot stones and stored, among the Comox, in distended kelp bulbs; over the rest of the area the animal's bladder was used for this purpose. The oil was a relish for dipping dried roe, berries, and roots before eating. Sea lions were also hunted sporadically and similarly utilized; their gut in particular served as cordage.

On the Fraser and Squamish Rivers sturgeon took the place of seals. A long shafted harpoon was used to probe the murky water, or a large pocket net was pulled through it between two canoes. Sockeye, scarce elsewhere, were plentiful on the Fraser, olachen (candle fish) ran on the Squamish, but neither of these places afforded opportunity for cod, halibut, or sea mammals. In fact, the people living on these rivers drew a distinction between themselves and the "salt water people," by which they meant mainly those on Vancouver Island.

Considerable traffic at one time took place between some of the groups, though there is some reason for doubting the antiquity of such free intercourse. All accounts agree that the West Sanetch had well established fishing privileges on Boundary Bay, inside of Point Robert, and regularly resorted there in summer; so did the Lummi. The Cowichan and Nanaimo frequently came to a camp on Lulu Island, either to fish for sturgeon and sockeye themselves or to bargain for them with dried clams. The Squamish in summer came out of Howe Sound, in part, it is said, to escape the mosquitoes. Some camped about Point Robert, others, so another report goes, congregated with the Sechelt and Cowichan at the head of Jervis Inlet. There may have been some contact with the Lillooet in this direction, as there seem to have been inland connections between the Squamish and Sechelt.

In all probability the activities associated with land hunting were more developed in these inland going cultures than among those across the Strait. Certainly it was only on the upper reaches of the inlets that hunting expeditions set out, and these preponderantly in search of mountain goats. For the rest, large animals were plentiful and getting them was a matter of setting traps or of occasional excursions along the water's edge. The familiar pits, dead-falls, and slip-loop snares were universal for capturing elk, deer, and bear. Hunters generally set out alone, but there were some occasions for group drives.

Nets were a favorite device for entangling all kinds of animals. Depending upon the requirements of mesh and purpose, they were made of cedar withes, bark, or sinew. Deer were driven into strong webs set across their runways; circular ones, operated by a release, surrounded rocks frequented by seals. A characteristic Salish net was strung on high poles near marshes to enmesh frightened waterfowl at dusk.

Night hunting developed a number of tricks with flares and blinds. Deer, coming down to drink, were shot when fascinated by a torch. Cod were attracted by the phosphorescence of stirred up water and by lights in canoes. Frequently a fire was built in front of a blind in the fore part of a canoe carrying two men. One of them quietly maneuvered the vessel among flocks of settled ducks while the other drew them in with a multi-pronged spear.

Dogs were valuable and were treated accordingly. Some of them— there are indications that they were of a different breed from those reared for their wool—were put through a course of training involving magical applications along with a more realistic regimen. They were taught to drive deer and elk into deep water and to raise mountain goats. They were well cared for in winter and put on small islands during the summer season.

A number of magical practises clustered about the taking of seal, goat, and to some extent bear, deer, and salmon. Some men were believed to be especially favored by a supernatural helper in acquiring the first two, in return for which, continence and ceremonial purification were requisite. The hunter must not comb his hair, nor could his wife engage in any activity while he was away. For success in sealing, especially, she was cautioned to remain inactive or to move gently. The bones of most animals, including the salmon, were carefully disposed of and never given to dogs. Special restrictions hedged about the treatment of goat heads and organs. An attenuated bear ceremonialism existed among the Homalco, Klahuse, and Slaiämun in the form of speeches to the bear before or after death and ritual disposal of the head; with this was the common belief that it licks its paws during hibernation.

A young man never ate of the first animal he killed. It was always given to the old people, and he was ceremonially painted and sprinkled with down. The first salmon ceremony, a familiar feature on the Pacific Coast, was not performed by the Sechelt, Slaiämun, Klahuse, or Hoalco. Within our restricted area this rite coincides rather closely with the distribution of sockeye, for which it was specifically reserved except at Squamish and Nanaimo.

Food was prepared in one of three ways: by roasting on a spit, by baking in an earth oven, or by stone boiling in wooden vessels. Salt seems not to have been in demand, for only the Comox and some of the northeastern groups made use of seaweed cakes. The mortar was unknown, as were other stone vessels. Cooking and serving utensils were of maple or alder with some abalone inlay decoration and conventionalized modeling to represent animals. The animal crest feasting dishes so dear to the Kwakiutl had spread only as far south as the Pentlatch and Slaiämun. Sheep horn ladles did not get beyond Comox, although the smaller black ones of goat horn were in use everywhere, the raw material being supplied by the mainland tribes. Water pails, chests, and other containers were made of cedar boards, steamed, bent, and sewed.

The importance of wood working helps to explain in some measure the secondary position of basketry. Information on this subject is confusing and difficult to get because of the specialized nature of the craft and its virtual non-existence today, but at least this much can be made out, that the forms, techniques, and uses of baskets were relatively few. The carrying basket for roots, berries, and clams was known universally in rectangular shape with the bottom smaller than the top. In the finer specimens the opening was constricted, giving a "parenthetical" aspect to the four corners. The technique was wrapped twine, the only one employed in rigid basketry except for two isolated reports of split warp and crossed warp variations of plain twining. Soft rush bags in plain twine and/or checker prevailed on Vancouver Island, while most groups were familiar with the same sort of container using cedar bark and the checker-work technique.

Rectangular sewed baskets, imbricated and of the style referred to as Klikitat, were common all along the mainland. Individual specimens undoubtedly got across the Strait, but to judge from the earliest collections and from two explicit denials by informants, it seems safe to infer that they were not made there. A variety of sewing, using rings instead of spiral coils, should also be noted.

Other fabrics were made of wool, cedar bark, and rushes. The twilled wool blanket came from the well known Salish roller loom. To the basic dog wool was added that of goats, if it was to be had, or some other fibrous substance such as cattail pappus or duck down. Associated with the loom was a large spindle, spun in the two hands with a tossing motion.

Another weaving complex, presumably derived from the Kwakiutl, included the suspended warp, twining, and a small spindle rolled on the shank. It had spread as far south as Pentlatch on the one side and Slaiämun on the other. If the somewhat ragged information can be trusted, checker-work cedar mats had the same distribution, as did a twined fabric of the same material. Over all the area, wall and floor mats were of rushes threaded together with a long needle.

The accent upon cedar, and vegetable fibers generally, carries over into articles of everyday dress. It was not uncommon for men, the older ones especially, to go naked, but when this was not the case they wore as an under garment a bark clout or fringe. Women wore a shredded bark or rush knee length skirt, usually of one piece. As a protection against the weather both sexes provided themselves with fur robes or woven blankets caught up over the left shoulder. Those who could afford it used wool. Basketry hats, of cedar root and of southern Kwakiutl design, had not reached lower Vancouver Island nor beyond Sechelt. Even there they were rather reserved for formal occasions.

Some departure from the above dress pattern is discernible on the mainland. Buckskin is more in evidence. Three descriptions of knee length trousers and one of a fitted shirt come from this side, but they may be late borrowings. Leggings and mittens formed a part of the hunter's outfit, as did two piece moccasins. Snowshoes with trailer and upturned toe must be set down as another trait not ordinarily associated with the coast Indian.

Body ornamentation involved a minor amount of tattooing, head deformation, and a piercing of the ear and nose. The mainland tribes avoided the first of these; the others occasionally striped the cheeks or chin of their women and assertedly drew more elaborate figures on the chests and thighs of the men. Both sexes of the well-to-do were given to wearing heavy abalone pendants from the ears and nose. A minimum of copper and some bone work adorned their necks, wrists, and ankles. Olivella shells were strung as beads in the southern part of the area, but, curiously, no group but the Sanetch knew the dentalium.

Canoe building, like sealing, was a specialized pursuit. The hereditary element entered, but was not an indispensable prerequisite. Of more importance psychologically were certain sympathetic songs or incantations bestowed, in the first instance at least, in token of a personal contact with some supernatural assistant. Very often this was a woodpecker. The critical operations such as splitting or steaming were undertaken in privacy, at which time the personal ritual was used and several taboos observed by the man and his wife.

The preliminary shaping was accomplished with the aid of fire, wedges, and celt chisels. A spool-shaped hand maul served as a hammer, and practically the only one. The hull was usually burned out, finally to be smoothed down, inside and out, by adz work. The "D" adz was universal, but the Comox and northeastern groups made an elbow type as well. The surface texture resembling hammered bronze resulting from these tools was valued in other woodwork, but the outer surface of canoes was further rubbed down with an abrasive such as dogfish skin for greater efficiency in the water.

There is no adequate treatment of canoe types for this region, nor can the matter be gone into here. Suffice it to say that there existed two well substantiated types and that these were mutually exclusive in their distributions. One was definitely mainland, the other belonged to Vancouver Island. One and all recognize the so-called "West Coast" (Nootka) form as intrusive, as they do for a Kwakiutl model or two which had found its way to some of the northern groups. Indigenous types were hewn from half logs, which put a considerable limitation on their size and made them relatively low at bow and stern. Improvised canoes of folded bark were regularly made for lake travel by the northern mainlanders, and the Homalco made a river canoe of cottonwood. The latter was called a "shovel nose" but any genetic connection with the typical shovel nose of Puget Sound is doubtful in view of its specific nonoccurrence elsewhere.

Paddles were of maple, yellow cedar, and yew. Those of men and women differed in shape and coloration, and despite a variety of forms a distinctive Salish pattern for each sex can be made out. Bailers were of bark. Sails were improvised of boughs or house boards, but matting and thin boards (in the north) were commonly put to this use.

There is some justification for the generally accepted notion that the Coast Salish we are considering lived in very long plank houses with single sloped roofs, the high side facing the water. This association dates from the observations of Fraser, Kane, and other early travelers to their country; and, indeed, it is true that the tribes living on the lower course of the Fraser, and the Squamish as well, knew no other kind. Furthermore, it was the prevailing type around Victoria and Cowichan Bay and rivaled the gable roofed structure at Pender Harbor (Sechelt). Elsewhere it was regarded as indicating inferior means or ambitions, though the rich sometimes set them up at summer locations. Their distribution was therefore coincident with the Salish, but their importance faded away to the north and northeast in favor of another very nearly universal type. Consequently, it would appear that in this respect two histori-

cally diverse impulses have permeated and fused in Salish territory, one
spreading from the outlet of the Fraser, the other seeping down from
the Kwakiutl in a characteristic pattern relative to Vancouver Island and
the mainland coast.

A second impression which has gained currency from the same report
is that these dwellings, in places said to exceed five hundred and more
feet over all, were unsegmented units with a broad unobstructed avenue
running the entire length. Actually, each was composed of a series of
individually constructed units—houses in fact—formed by as many
cross-wise plank partitions. Each house then averaged a twenty-foot
frontage and a fifty-foot depth with family quarters around its four
walls, a "long house" in itself with roof sloping from front to back. The
partition served as a common wall for two houses and indicates at once
the economy which dictated the successive additions and ultimate great
length. The character of the terrain was undoubtedly a factor as well,
for in most places the division was complete and the units became separate structures with an increased frontage. A unique resolution of difficulties was achieved by the largest village at Point Grey. It was circular
in ground plan and comprised seventy-six segments or houses.

In all plank dwellings, gabled and shed alike, the pitch of the roof
was never great. The roof planks were bracket-shape in cross section and
overlapped like tiles. They lay in place by their own weight and could
be shifted aside for light or ventilation. The structure which supported
them was not relied upon for the support of the walls so much as were
secondary uprights between which the horizontal wall boards were
clamped. Around all four walls there was a low bed platform, and
above it at the height of a few feet a mat, or in the north, a plank
canopy. Varying stretches of it were reserved for the individual families
and the divisions were marked by mat or board screens. Smoking and
drying racks were suspended over the several fires, although separate
outside structures were sometimes built for this purpose. The custom
prevailed of naming individual houses after some aspect of their locations, as "across the creek."

Several features relative to houses belong only to the Comox, Pentlatch, and the three northeastern groups, Homalco, Klahuse, and
Slaiämun. Among them are completely enclosed family compartments,
floor excavation—sometimes to more than one level, with a resultant increase in seating capacity for festive occasions—and a greater and lesser
development—or borrowing—of the crest motif. In this last respect
mainland informants clearly recognize their indebtedness to the north,

and in fact date it from the time when the white man put a stop to their inter-tribal wars. The Comox, on the other hand, were thoroughly saturated and at home with it. All of these groups had some zoomorphic dishes (Kwakiutl "house dishes"), made doors to represent animal mouths, and carved their interior house posts into human figures. Some crude painting was done on the house fronts. Projecting beam ends were carved into heads, and the impressive fact is that these and the dishes, even among the Comox, so consistently portrayed only the seal and the sea lion. A few memorial shafts with a small human figure at top and bottom were erected by the Klahuse. It is an evidence of the degenerated nature of these "crests" that Kwakiutl carvers were hired to do them by anybody who wanted to and could afford it, without any pretensions to a traditional right to the particular figure.

The custom of carving anthropomorphic roof supports and also beam ends carried on to the Sechelt and Squamish. Even the Muskwium observed the first of these and added yet another characteristic figure to grave box ornamentation. Here it is entirely possible that we have to do with a second set of influences of up river origin. They barely touched the Sanetch, and the Cowichan and Nanaimo not at all, for the carvings which exist at these places at the present day are repudiated by the better informed natives as alien to their culture.

A few other structures deserve brief mention. The summer shelters were of the sort constructed by the Puget Sound tribes: a lean-to or a four post frame covered over with mats, bark, or sometimes planks. "Pup tent" structures, for the accommodation of one person at a time, were dug out, covered with bark and earth, and used for steam sweating by the tribes on the mainland. For the same purpose the Vancouver Island groups improvised an individual wickiup of branches and mats, or simply steamed themselves under a blanket covering. Of distinct interest from a wider point of view is the presence of semi-subterranean retreats west of the Coast Range. They were known from Howe Sound to Bute Inlet and were used as refuges in time of war. Furthermore, the Muskwium on Point Grey built underground dwellings of exactly the same type as those farther up the valley. They existed side by side with the plank shed roofed habitations already described, and were a luxury for those who could afford them.

Plank houses were built by the cooperative efforts of the occupants. Specific data from which to draw generalizations cannot be obtained beyond the grandparental generation of the oldest informants, but to judge from these, the house building and owning nucleus comprised a man and his sons, or several brothers. Paternal cousins and at times sons-in-law were included. Each retained such equity for himself and his descendants as was accorded him on the basis of labor and materials contributed. An instance is recorded of a quarrel between two brothers at Comox which resulted in the removal of one who stripped his half of the house bare of its walls and roof to set up an independent household with his son-in-law. This was the recourse of a man of means; others could not afford to be so sensitive and preferred for many reasons to maintain their brotherly affiliations. Nevertheless, this process of segmentation of the extended family within a village must be looked upon as the ordinary mechanism of its growth. Not infrequently brothers or cousins owned adjacent houses, and in all probability the principle of kinship through males governed the formation of villages and even the aggregates of villages as at Cowichan Bay.

Residence, with few exceptions, was patrilocal, which brought it about that a man and his brothers, with their extended families in the male line, lived under one roof. Slaves, widows, orphans, and other dependants made up the remainder. One of the men, usually the eldest in the direct line of the founder, was looked to for guidance and protection by the rest of the house mates. He was granted their respect and allegiance on the score of his prestige and influence. By virtue of his aristocratic birth he owned or exercised a controlling interest in certain property rights and ceremonial privileges. His brothers and house mates were not entirely excluded from them and in order to validate his birth right he was expected to improve upon it by industry, generosity, and dignified behavior. Through an intelligent exercise of these qualities he was able to maintain an appreciable control over his retainers. It was power of an informal sort, implicit in the kinship bond which linked him in some way with almost every member of his extended household.

To sum up, we may say that the house governor's authority was founded upon and defined by his rights as an influential relative and property owner. In return for his patronage he expected and received the support and cooperation of his adherents. He could not afford to abuse their dependence, nor could they risk his disfavor. There are stories of tyrants and bullies, but they are rare and recited with disapproval. If the situation became unbearable a man could always move into the house of another powerful relative, especially one on the maternal side. Some men, to avoid embarrassment in difficult domestic situations, preferred to set up a nearby shack of their own rather than insist upon a remote claim within the big house. On the whole the arrangement was beneficial to all concerned: service and deference were traded for economic security and vicarious glory. Outside his house group the governor had no real authority and was able to achieve only as much precedence among his peers as his prestige and influence warranted. Political power was coincident with social status.

These head men are commonly called chiefs by observers on the Northwest Coast. It is important to note, however, that the Coast Salish disavow the implications of the term as they have come to know them through government administration. They say that they had no chiefs, and rightly too, if by that we mean the incumbent of an office. The notion of an office, in the sense of a functionally defined position, was almost nonexistent by comparison with that concept among the Nootka and Kwakiutl. There was no feeling that a house implied a chieftainship as we feel that a state implies a ruler; depending upon their personal attributes, several men—two, three, or four—in the same house might be entitled to the honorific *hegus* or *siem*. For convenience we may translate this as chief; the natives make shift with such equivalents as "gentlemen," "hightone men," "smart men," and "real men."

Property, the outward symbol of rank and status, was recognized in material goods and ritual privileges. Incorporeal property rights will be discussed more fully under rituals, but the same rules of ownership and transmission applied to them as to other valuable possessions. Apart from houses and their furnishings, corporeal property consisted mainly of hunting and fishing lands and appliances. Nets of all sorts were owned, as were pitfalls, deadfalls, fishing and sealing sites. On the mainland goat hunting lands were divided up among a comparatively few families. All of these possessions were expensive and restricted. They were in the hands of the chiefs who shared their produce with their henchmen and retainers. Clamming places were free to all, but root plots were held in severalty by families. Weapons, canoes, and wool blankets were individually owned and highly prized for their potlatching value. Only the Comox traded upon the fictitious values of copper plates derived from the north.

Descent and inheritance were reckoned bilaterally with a decided preference for the patrilineal. There is no reason for believing that a feeling of nearer kinship with the father's people is responsible for this bias, as the bilateral transmission of names and the kinship nomenclature will testify. As a part of the dowry or bride price return, the son-in-law was sometimes given custody of a certain masked dance to be held in trust for his son. The Salish share this mode of transmission with the

Kwakiutl, but for the former at least the evidence seems to favor an interpretation in terms of a bilateral acknowledgment of kin coupled with a development of return giving, rather than as an infiltration of northern matrilineal principles into a purely patrilineal complex.

Primogeniture was the rule, but was not insisted upon as an inflexible principle. Daughters, for example, could inherit important property only exceptionally, and personal aptitudes were a noteworthy consideration in passing along hunting, technical, and ritual property. Sons received from fathers in preference to brothers unless other factors of age and fitness entered. Very much depended upon the circumstances. In the ordinary course of events the most desirable acquisitions clustered about and descended in the lineal strain of eldest sons. From this nucleus there was a more or less gradual shading off into the trivial, and the more so the greater the number of generations, so that the youngest son of a youngest son received precious little of the original patrimony. It must have been extremely difficult for him to improve upon this situation in aboriginal times within the closed system of a well regulated economy. A possible way out was by a fortunate marriage, of which there are traditions and some historic accounts.

From the above it should be clear why the word caste conveys a misunderstanding of class differentiation as it existed among the Coast Salish. Between the highest and the lowest there was a wide gap, but they were intimately connected by a blended scale of free men. In a sense there were noble families (those of first sons), but own cousins of these might be commoners. Hence, the ever reiterated attitude of nobles to commoners was one of tolerance and encouragement. The only class of despised men—and this was a personal matter—were those referred to as "lazy men," those without ambition as it was conceived by the Salish. A Comox man who could once "hold the people" (potlatch) became a real man, though not so "real" as one who had accomplished it several times or more grandly. Commoners who could not achieve this distinction in their own right hunted and worked for their aristocratic kinsmen and were compensated by public acknowledgment of their contribution, by repayment in other goods, or by good will feasts and entertainments.

Slaves were a class apart, totally subservient, but not tortured or physically abused. They were taken on war raids and to own two or three was a distinction given only to men who were in a position either to buy or to capture them. Usually they were taken as children, then reared as menials in the houses of their masters. The dishonor attaching to their station was hereditary; therefore intermarriage with them, except by the lowest of freemen, was unthinkable. There are some indications that the stigma, in the exceptional case, could be lifted by a formal distribution of property but a slave ancestor was always a vulnerable point for the malicious thrusts of an enemy.

As would be expected, the majority of marriages were contracted between social equals. Varying degrees of pomp and ceremony, depending upon the standing of the two families, signalized the union. To add quality to the occasion a fiction of non-acceptance was acted out which recalls the war-like formalities of the Kwakiutl. The groom's party approached the girl's house by canoe even within the same village. The door was barred to them and they had to pay influential sympathizers to "break it down." This consisted of speeches by resident relatives or by the several chiefs accompanying the boy, his father, and his mother as formal representatives. Once admitted, the boy sat humbly near the door for days, saying nothing and eating little of the food which his people were allowed to prepare for themselves. Sometimes they left him alone and stayed with relatives in another house. Each day his father's speakers harangued the girl's people upon the desirability of the match. At length they relented and the two families ate together. Finally, the whole village was called in to witness the union and the exchange of goods.

This ceremony was costly, for every step in the procedure called for a payment. Each speaker was honored with a blanket or two for his "good words." The groom's party always brought a great amount of food, which was divided equally among all those present on the last day; when they left they were given food to be similarly distributed when they got home. The bride price in blankets was turned over to the girl's father who apportioned it immediately among his nearest responsible relatives. It was incumbent upon them to return it with ceremony at some future date, usually at a visit the following winter. In the southern part of the area the return was in equivalence; in the north, on both sides of the Strait, it was more often double.

The exchange of sisters in marriage was common, as was child betrothal. Sometimes an industrious youth without means was taken into the household of a wealthy man as the husband of a younger daughter, but in this, as in every other case, some payment had to be made to legitimatize the union. This was true even of the sororate and levirate, which, by the way, were entirely optional and not more frequent than other forms of remarriage. They were possibilities only; a fact probably to be correlated with institutionalized bride price return.

The Comox aristocrats performed a travesty of marriage without a bride for the sole purpose of acquiring privileges in the exchange. This was their chief concern and consequently marriages were unstable. Over the rest of the area the most important consideration was the consolidation of one's social position through connections with important kin groups in other houses or villages.

There were no preferred mates within the kinship nexus. First and second cousins were not acceptable, third cousins on either side were. This meant that marriages between house mates as well as village members was permissible, though for reasons given above inter-village alliances were sought after.

The kinship system reveals several points of interest. Separate terms were used for father, mother, sister (Comox dialect), husband and wife, but apart from these no distinction was made between male and female relatives. Furthermore, relatives in the same degree of relationship, whether through males or females, were called by the same term. With few exceptions the sex of the speaker made no difference. This brings it about that each of the following sets of relatives was designated by one term: siblings; youngest sibling; oldest sibling(?); older sibling and parent's older sibling's child; younger sibling and parent's younger sibling's child; parent's siblings; sibling's child; child; grandchild and sibling's grandchild; grandparent and grandparent's siblings; stepparent; step-grandparent; husband's brother, brother's wife (♂ speaking), wife's sister, and sister's husband (♀ speaking); husband's sister and brother's wife (♀ speaking; wife's brother and parent-in-law; sister's husband (♂ speaking) and child's spouse.

A reciprocal term also existed for relations through spouses (parent-in-law to parent-in-law and extending to the whole group). After the death of a spouse another term replaced throughout the one which had been used by the relatives through marriage. No avoidance patterns of any sort were practiced. Terms for parent generations back to the sixth were known to the Sanetch, who used the last one to designate an hereditary privilege.

The critical periods in the individual life cycle were heavily laden with ritual forms, the most striking feature of which was the regularity of their reappearance on several diverse occasions. Within the limits of a summary it is not feasible to go into all their details, so that only a few of the more important can therefore be touched upon.

The most elaborate and important rituals were associated with the death of a spouse (of either sex), with girls' puberty, and with the dancer initiation. At the death of a parent less care had to be taken, and still less for the death of a child. The information is not consistent from one group to another, but it seems fairly clear that upon the birth of a first child the parents, in one way or another, had to refrain from their ordinary habits for four days. The birth of twins greatly altered their behavior, for they were required to live apart in the woods for a year or more. Friends and relatives aided them in getting food, while they carefully sought some supernatural favor prompted by a touch of the sacred as it surrounded them at this time. The twins themselves had a certain amount of supernatural power, and were good fishers, since they were related to the salmon.

Girls at puberty and women at childbirth were secluded behind mat partitions in the living house and at times in huts outside. The dancer initiate was also kept behind a screen. The drinking tube and scratcher are prominent features on most of these occasions, one or both even being prescribed for the initiate and the boy pubescent. Few other formal observances applied to the latter but the significant fact is that there was any recognition at all beyond the usual informal Spartan training for manhood. Some other restrictions had an obvious social significance, being designed to induce a decorous and becoming behavior in later life. More of them had a religious import.

With some local exceptions, a consistent pattern which appears at first childbirth (for the father), puberty, initiation, and at the spouse's death is a ceremonial feeding at the end of four or eight days, and for the man a re-introduction into the fundamental daily occupations. Specific trait associations which occur again and again are those which have to do with the importance of wool, bark, down, daylight, the east, hair combing, bathing, fasting, red paint, etc. Most of the life crises were regarded as dangerous situations during which the individual was at once empowered and contaminated by the supernatural. From these influences he had to be relieved by a ceremonial purification after a regular period. Above Nanaimo and Squamish this could be done by the individual himself, coached by an older person, but for the others an hereditary functionary was employed for the service. In fact, there flourished in this southern section a variety of privileged performances which had no other function than to "wash" the dancer novice, the pubescent, and the corpse awaiting burial. They were expensive demonstrations, dances, tricks—shows in effect—which had nothing intrinsically to do with cleansing, but capitalized upon this aspect of crisis rites for their elaboration. The real purificationist (siwın) operated less spectacularly with more esoteric lore.

All of these events, as well as any other which marked a new relationship between the individual and his group, were celebrated by a distribution of property. That was the recognized mechanism by which any public announcement could be made and it was the only one, so that the person without property had no means of asserting status in his society. An institution existed whereby an individual in anticipation of such a distribution was "helped" or loaned blankets by others, while he at the same time called in those which he had previously loaned out. The return among the Comox, Homalco, Klahuse, and Slaiämun was double (100 percent interest) so that it was wholly to a man's advantage to put himself in the position of a universal creditor in advance of his proposed distribution. It might take place any time during the year, but the grand inter-tribal affairs were held in the spring. One man, perhaps two or three, took the responsibility for the calling, but anyone could take advantage of the congregation to give a "cry song" for his dead, name his child, etc.

Crisis periods were auspicious occasions for the seeking of supernatural helpers. The susceptibility of parents at the birth of twins has already been noted. A bereaved spouse was sent into the woods daily and often received a visitation in his or her exhausted half hysterical condition. Puberty was the time par excellence for seeking, though for girls the procedure was milder and offered less reward than for their brothers. The boy stayed in lonely places, fasted, took emetics, and scrubbed himself with boughs. An essential part of his quest involved swimming and diving, often to the point of exhaustion or unconsciousness, in which state he received a vision, a song, a spirit cry, and promise of help according to the nature of his wishes. Otherwise his experience came in a dream. Frequently some startling real occurrence induced the dream; on the mainland the dreamer had a foreboding of a real encounter which knocked him unconscious and replaced the underwater ordeal. Dreams had to recur to be valid. Everyone sought them, since they gave luck in hunting, in acquiring wealth, in fighting, in doctoring. Powers were not inherited and their acquisition was kept strictly secret; hence no image or representation was made to proclaim them. They were almost exclusively from birds, animals, and fabulous spirits or monsters. There were no restrictions on killing such an animal. On the contrary, that very favor was bestowed on the hunting man.

The shaman's quest was exactly like that of any other person but was more intense, was psychologically conditioned for that end, and ceased only with the acquisition of several powers instead of one. Some spirits deemed ineffectual for curing purposes, and others, such as the e-headed serpent, were tremendously powerful and dangerous. The most potent spirits caused a man to bleed from all the apertures of his body at the time their power struck and entered it. There they resided henceforth, to be summoned into activity by singing to do the work of curing. Ordinary individuals also were known to appeal to their spirit helpers in time of stress. There was no initiation or induction ceremony for the shaman, and no societies.

Sickness was caused by soul loss, intrusion of a foreign object or a spirit, contamination, and by magic. There were two souls; one in the head, the other in the heart. They could wander off in sleep, be abducted by shamans and ghosts, or be displaced by a sudden fright. It was the duty of the shaman as defined above to send his powers in search of the soul, or, according to some, to send his own soul. A material object such as hair or a piece of bone was removed by sucking, and an intruded spirit by manual manipulations. Destruction of either of these was harmful or fatal to the sender.

At a curing the shaman sang with the aid of his wife and others. He had no drum, rattle, nor any appurtenance other than a bowl of water which reflected the universe, and some down or bark on which to catch the soul. On the mainland he shook or "danced" in a semi-possessed state; elsewhere he sat with an arm over his eyes.

Two other professional dealers in the supernatural require mention. The first (siŭwŭ) was but a specialized shaman who had received his power from the dead and who functioned as a clairvoyant and treated those afflicted by ghosts. The second class had no connection with dream experiences or spirits but had come by their secret knowledge through instruction. They were called siwɩn from the private word formulæ which they possessed and jealously guarded. Some were well disposed and acted as purifiers and in a ritual capacity, as at the first salmon rite. Others were workers of contagious magic. The siwɩn was not known to the Sechelt, Slaiămun, Klahuse, or Homalco.

The winter ceremonies of the Coast Salish reveal more clearly than anything else a tri-partite division of the area along the lines suggested in the introduction. It would be futile to dwell upon the complexity of the subject, but there is some point in calling attention to the modification and mutation of pattern within this narrow, restricted territory. It affords another good example of the rather abrupt shifts and re-associations which mark the diffusion of ceremonial complexes on the Northwest Coast. Nothing more than an outline can be attempted in this place, and for the reason given, the characterizations will gain in clarity by sub-areal descriptions.

Sanetch, Cowichan, Nanaimo, Squamish, Muskwium. Participation in the winter dances of this group was conditioned by the individual acquisition of a dreamed power, that is, a guardian spirit of the order described above. Lesser animal spirits of all sorts counted for this requirement, along with the powerful ones for hunting and fighting, and a very few nature spirits. They were not inherited, but the important point is that the dancing group was a closed organization requiring a formal initiation. Anyone could join regardless of whether his parents belonged, and regardless of whether he had received a vision. In fact, it was the function of the initiation to instill a power into the novice; if he already had one, it might come through the ordeal or be smothered and replaced by a wholly artificially induced one. This was no less true for a shaman than any other person who danced in the winter ceremony.

The induction was accomplished by a surprise attack upon the boy or girl at the instigation of some relative who was to pay for the four day ritual of initiation. The novice was beaten, smothered, and choked until he was unconscious—"dead," they say—by his attackers, who were of course already members and his constant attendants for the remainder of the season. Immediately he was placed behind a screen in a corner of the big house and an established morning and evening public ritual inaugurated over his exhausted body. Attendants hovered over him using every means to "bring out" the song of his power. At length it welled up, or one was framed for him and drummed into him. On the fourth day he made a circuit of the village, singing and dancing. Throughout this period and for the remainder of the winter season the attributes and accessories of the novice strongly recall the hamatsa and other dancers to the north.

Members danced singly, assisted by the singing and drumming of all the others. Their song revealed the nature of their power, and they wore head dresses of bark and down, but no wooden masks. They were often in an uncontrollable ecstatic state. The only mask known to this group of tribes was the so-called swaixwe, not of northern origin but probably coming from the Fraser River. It was not used for the winter dancing. It was one of the privileged exhibitions already spoken of in connection with crisis rites; an interesting accent which applies with complete regularity to the other inherited privileges, most of which can be recognized by their association with an hereditary song and a rattle.

Comox, Pentlatch. The dancing complex just described was also known to these two tribes, but it was almost entirely submerged under a more highly regarded formal winter ceremonial taken over bodily from the Kwakiutl. Dream singing and possessed dancers were viewed rather condescendingly, as were most things Cowichan. Non-members provoked them into an ecstasy (as they did also to the south) while the members of the masked dancing society looked stolidly on. In reality the latter were actors given to playing out a hollow caricature of this same spirit possession of which they disapproved.

The completely formal overlay had not suppressed spirit seeking for the requisite supernatural aid in hunting, curing, etc., but it had given an overweening importance to transferable spirits as they were represented in masked dances. It is not necessary to describe them, nor the initiation by abduction and seclusion, for the facts do not differ appreciably from those published for the Kwakiutl. The same masks, and the same dancers appear with northern names: hamatsa, hawinɔL, tohwŭt, etc.

Homalco, Klahuse, Slaiämun, Sechelt. With these groups it is difficult to be certain of some of the major patterns in terms of those known to their neighbors. Part of this difficulty lies, I feel sure, in their own misconceptions and confusions over their borrowed traits. The feature which appears to have been basic, and in all probability represents an original winter dance pattern of all the Coast Salish, was an individual performance imitating some animal. Very likely it was connected with a guardian spirit but it seems to have involved more mimicry than similar dances on Vancouver Island. Some dances may have been without a song; most of them certainly were not. The actors did not form a society, and there was no initiation. A person began to dance when he felt secure in his power and after he had taught the professional song leader his song—and when he had accumulated enough for a few presents. These dancers contributed the bulk of the exhibition and were called by a term which signified "shaman." Furthermore, true curing shamans also danced in that capacity, showing off their powers with demonstrations of death and resurrection, decapitation, fire walking, etc. Doctors, as such, did not perform in the winter dances of the other two areas. Their feats were usually shocking and fearful, and the people did not like them.

Along with these unorganized dances, a distinct group was created by a formal initiation requiring a four day secret retirement in the woods.

Returning clad in branches, the novice (hausaulk) danced publicly, and without further ceremony was relieved of his covering. The ritual care so prominent elsewhere was reduced to a minimum, and little prestige seems to have been derived from the perfunctory "initiation." At Sechelt it was so restricted in scope as to be associated with only one of the dozens of dance spirits. The same distinction of an initiated group within a larger unorganized body of dancers characterized the Squamish.

Still a third winter dance pattern gave expression to a stronger interest in hereditary privileges. Its elements were indicative of professional specialization, and theoretically were the property of families with an enviable reputation for hunting or fighting. They were entertaining, and generally took the form of brief dramatic scenes with realistic costumes and effects. It is not unlikely that they had crystallized out of spirit impersonations, but, like the Comox masked performances, they could be used in the profane season as well, any distribution of property justifying their display. To the same category belongs the only mask of certain occurrence north of Squamish. The Sechelt lacked it, but the three other tribes were familiar with the right to display, by inheritance or outright purchase, a modified DZONOQWA mask, whose northern provenience and equivalent they recognized. Two others, of uncertain identity, may have been used by these same groups.

The "potlatch" of the Northwest Coast Indians, together with the "kula ring" of the Trobriand Islands, is one of anthropology's most famous examples of complicated socioeconomic behavior in relatively simple societies. Ruth Benedict popularized the term "potlatch" in her classic book, Patterns of Culture, *in which she discussed one form of it to support her famous thesis regarding the "Dionysian" character of Northwest Coast culture. Benedict's contention that the entire fabric of Northwest Coast society was oriented toward and obsessed with wealth accumulation and competition, was at that time enthusiastically accepted by a number of social scientists. Many experts, however, have repeatedly pointed out that the image drawn by Benedict was perhaps, at best, an exaggeration and at worst, a serious distortion. It is now a widely accepted tenet of social anthropology that cooperative interaction is the basic relationship of human beings in society, not individualistic competition.*

23 Helen Codere

THE POTLATCH IN KWAKIUTL LIFE*

Field work among the Kwakiutl in 1951 produced evidence of a kind of potlatching, play potlatching or potlatching for fun, that has never been described but is of the greatest importance for an understanding of Kwakiutl life. The existence of playfulness in relation to potlatching requires reinterpretation of the character both of this institution and of the people participating in it. The 1951 field data include much new material on home life, child rearing, and humor that supports Boas' claim that the private life of the Kwakiutl possessed many amiable features, but it is the aim of this presentation to show that even in the public life of the ceremonials and potlatches there was mirth and friendliness.

A summary of the relevant interpretations of Kwakiutl life will be given, followed by an examination of Boas' first-hand account of the winter dances and potlatches of 1895–96 in which there are incidents of funmaking. The new material on play potlatching will be submitted and, in conclusion, the evidence will be discussed in relation to necessary reinterpretations of Kwakiutl life and general theoretical implications.

BOAS' "ATROCIOUS BUT AMIABLE" KWAKIUTL AND BENEDICT'S "PARANOID AND MEGALOMANIAC" KWAKIUTL

Ruth Benedict's presentation of Kwakiutl character and culture has received the widest publicity and general acceptance. The picture she drew is so well known and so consistent and free of the complications of

---

* Abridged from "The Amiable Side of Kwakiutl Life: the Potlatch and the Play Potlatch," by H. Codere, in *American Anthropologist*, **58**, 334–351, 1956.

qualification that it is unnecessary to review it in detail; a few of her characterizing phrases will serve as sufficient reminders:

The object of a Kwakiutl enterprise was to show oneself superior to one's rivals. This will to superiority they exhibited in the most uninhibited fashion. It found expression in uncensored self-glorification and ridicule of all comers. Judged by the standards of other cultures the speeches of their chiefs at their potlatches are unabashed megalomania. (1:190)

These hymns of self-glorification were sung by the chief's retainers upon all great occasions, and they are the most characteristic expressions of their culture. All the motivations they recognized centered around the will to superiority. Their social organization, their economic institutions, their religion, birth and death, were all channels for its expression. (1:191)

They recognized only one gamut of emotion, that which swings between victory and shame. . . . Knowing but the one gamut they used it for every occasion, even the most unlikely. (1:215)

The megalomanic paranoid trend . . . [they made] the essential attribute of ideal man . . . (1:222)

Franz Boas' response to this character portrait of the Kwakiutl is comparatively little known, but, in spite of its brevity and incompleteness, it sets problems of great interest and utility for students of culture:

Evidently, the wider the scope of the leading motive of culture the more it will appear as characteristic of the whole culture, but we must not be deceived into believing that it will give us an exhaustive picture of all the sides of that culture.

As an example I may refer again to the Indians of the Northwest Coast of America. The leading motive of their lives is the limitless pursuit of gaining social prestige and of holding on to what has been gained, and the intense feeling of inferiority and shame if even the slightest part of prestige has been lost. This is manifest not only in the attempts to attain a coveted high position, but equally in the endeavor to be considered the most atrocious member of the tribe. Rank and wealth are valued most highly, but there are also cases of criminals (in the sense of the culture we are discussing) who vie with each other in committing atrocities. A loss of prestige in either sense is a source of shame which must be made good by some action reestablishing the lost respect. If it is not possible it leads to suicide. Art consists in the glorification of the family crest or of family histories. A pretense of excessive conservatism, often contradicted by obvious changes of behavior, is closely allied with the jealous watch over all privileges.

These tendencies are so striking that the amiable qualities that appear in intimate family life are easily overlooked. These are not by any means absent.

In contrast to the jealousy with which prerogatives are guarded, everyone within the family circle belittles his position. Husband and wife address each other as "You whose slave I am," or "You whose dog I am." Parents and grandparents designate themselves in the same way when talking to their children, who in turn use nicknames when addressing their parents and grandparents. (3:267)

Boas' criticism of Benedict centers on a denial of her thesis that a culture, or, at least, some cultures, can be described in terms of a dominant character or leading motif. In relation to Benedict's interpretation of Kwakiutl character, Boas' criticism states points of significant difference but is actually very mild, brief, and even self-contradictory. He is in agreement with the substantial part of Benedict's characterization when he states that "the leading motive" of the Kwakiutl is "the limitless pursuit of gaining social prestige." If anything, he outdoes Benedict in his use of the characterizing word "atrocious," for its connotations, or the connotations of some of the possible translation choices like "vicious" or "evil," seem to go further than some of Benedict's stronger words, such as "paranoid." On the sharp point of difference—the simultaneous presence of other and contradictory qualities in Kwakiutl life— the evidence he cites as revealing "amiable" qualities is slight, unclear, and unimpressive. Nevertheless, it is clear that there is a basic conflict of opinion about Kwakiutl life and the Kwakiutl people.

"AMIABLE" FEATURES PRESENT IN THE 1895–96 POTLATCHES OF THE KWAKIUTL AS DESCRIBED BY BOAS

It is precisely in respect to potlatching that such interpretative judgments of the character of Kwakiutl life as "atrocious," "paranoid," "rivalrous," and "grossly competitive" have been made. Qualifications of this sharp delineation have largely taken the form of noting that a certain amount of co-operation on the level of the family or numaym was required in order to sustain and enhance the rivalry of the potlatch and social system. Additional and fundamental qualifications are required, either if the accounts are looked at freshly and in a way undetermined by previous interpretations or if those data in the accounts that do not fit such interpretations are not glossed over as being unimportant and overwhelmed by other data. Boas' 1895–96 description has been selected for examination because it is the most detailed, play-by-play eyewitness account of Kwakiutl potlatching and winter ceremonial.

Some of the skits and incidents that formed part of the ten days of winter ceremonials and potlatches were plain funmaking, and there is nothing in the account to indicate that the funmaking was not a true part of the proceedings, for all instances of it were right in sequence with other dramatizations and potlatches. They occurred after as well as before the distribution of eagle down that signals such sacred tone as there was in the winter dances, and they were particular to no one group such as a "clown" group or one of the three participating Kwakiutl tribes or any of their subdivisions. There are five extremely clear instances of funmaking.

To anyone who would regard Kwakiutl as impelled by an unqualified straining for self-maximization and glorification and triumphing over rivals the following skit would seem peculiar indeed.

A man rose who acted as though he was a Haida. He delivered a speech, during which he made violent gestures, imitating the sound of the Haida language. An interpreter who stood next to him translated the pretended meaning of his speech, which was supposed to be of the nature of thanks to the host for the soap berries, because they were one of the principal food articles of the Haida, and because the speaker was pleased to eat the kind of food to which he was accustomed in his own country. He continued, saying that he carried a box filled with food which he was going to give to the person who would pronounce his name. Then the host's daughter was called upon, and was asked to say his name. He began, G.a′ tsō, which she repeated; Sē′ as, which she also repeated; then followed, spoken very rapidly, Qoagā′ñ Gustatē′ñ Gusgitatē′ñ Gusoa′t Qoag·ê′ns Quqā′xsla. Then she said: "I cannot say this; I must go to school in order to learn it." The Haida asked her to go to school with him for four nights; then she would know it. The girl's father interrupted them, saying that he wanted to wash his daughter before she went to school with him. (2:546)

Boas notes that this "joke has been known for about eight years and is often repeated." The joke is no more broad or subtle than the meaning of the entire incident in humanizing the character of the Kwakiutl and their institutions. Kwakiutl hosts were, above all, the individuals allowed to make grandiloquent speeches and to strike heroically stuffy postures, and their behavior and speeches have been pointed to again and again as central proof of such main themes in Kwakiutl life as a "will to self-glorification," "bombastic," "triumphing over rivals," and so on down the "paranoid" list. Here is a Kwakiutl host who takes a full part in the presentation of a skit in which the type of food he has just given his guests is joked about and in which his daughter, and himself by reflection, is allowed to look foolish and all too human. No one in this skit would seem to care about the kind of false stuff-shirt dignity that must be vigilantly protected in order to be maintained.

Two other skits are of particular interest because they are potlatches, but potlatches given in a humorous frame of reference. This would seem impossible in an unqualified view of Kwakiutl society as obsessed with social prestige that had to be maintained and validated by potlatching. Such view makes potlatching a deadly serious business.

After this was done [after a potlatch distribution in connection with a winter dance presentation was made], a messenger entered the house and said: "Some strangers are on the beach." The speaker of the Nā′q' oaqtôq sent a man out, who took a torch and went down to the beach. Soon he returned and informed the speaker that some white men had landed and asked to be permitted to enter. The speaker sent for them, and the messengers came back leading a young Indian girl, who was dressed up in European costume, with a gaudy hat, a velvet skirt, and a silk blouse. Then they asked Nō′Lq'auLEla what he thought of her; if he thought she was wealthy. They asked him to send her back if she should be poor. He looked at her and said: "I can easily distinguish rich and poor and I see she is wealthy. Let her stay here." Then the speaker looked at her and said: "Oh, that is Mrs. Nū′le." They led her to the rear of the house and asked if she carried anything in her pocket. She produced a roll of silver quarter dollars which the speaker took and distributed among the people. (2:559–60)

Now the door opened, and four men dressed as policemen entered. . . .

The last of these acted the judge and carried a book. He sent the policemen around asking if everybody was present, and KuLE′m asked, "Are all here?" The people replied. "Yes." Then the two other policemen went around, looked at everybody, and stated that one person was missing. They went out, and soon returned leading the old woman Gudo′yo, whose hands were fastened with handcuffs. Then they pretended to hold court over her on account of her absence. The judge pretended to read the law on the case, and fined her $70. She replied that she was poor; that she was able to pay in blankets but had no ready money. KuLE′m, who acted the interpreter, pretended to translate what she said into English, and the payment of 70 blankets was accepted. Then the friends of Gudo′yo turned against the judge and said: "That is always your way, policemen. As soon as you see anyone who has money, you arrest him and fine him." She was unchained, and the policemen went back to the door. [Boas notes here that "this performance was first introduced in 1865, and has been kept up since that time."]

They called K·ēx· and his friends, the killer whales, and told them to fetch the 70 blankets. The cousin of the old woman, who was the speaker of the Maa'mtag·ila, told them where to go, and soon they returned. Gudo'yō's sister, Lē'mElxa'lag·ilîs followed them, dancing. All the people were singing a ha'mshamtsEs song for her. The blankets were distributed in her name. The mā'maq'a of the Nā'q'oatôq received his share first: then the other members of his tribe, and afterwards the Koskimo beginning with the hā'-mats'a. While this was going on, button blankets and bracelets tied to sticks were being carried into the house. A G·ē'xsEm, whose daughter had married Lē'Lelälak", a G·ī' g.îlqam of the Kuē'xa was going to repay the purchase money of his daughter . . . (2:562–63)

Let us consider some arguments against the claim that these two incidents display a rather lighthearted approach to potlatching. The two incidents are in the full context of apparently very serious winter dance presentations and potlatch distributions. Can they be accounted for as comic relief necessary to sustain a seriousness so heavy that it would otherwise be unbearable? Skipping the fact that such an argument would mean a shift of ground from a conception of potlatching as an institution in which there was no levity at all, it seems impossible to discover in what way they form any different kind of potlatching except in their connection with a skit that does anything but make a point of inflating the honor and glory of the donor. The humor of these skits is not uncomplicated. In both incidents the European is lampooned or derided, but in both cases the giver of the potlatch is identified with the European. Careful study of both the pattern and the content of the various types of event occurring in these ten days of festivities (feasts, dances, speeches, potlatches, funmaking) does not reveal these and other instances of funmaking as "comic relief" occurring at any discernibly special or meaningful time. The first follows a winter dance ceremonial ending with a potlatch and is followed by another winter dance. The second follows a winter dance, speech, and potlatch and is, as the quotation above indicates, followed by a potlatch. This is, however, the standard pattern of the entire ten days, and there is nothing that singles out the events of funmaking. They do not seem to occur just before or after moments of particular tension or moments of easing of tension. They were not initiated by members of either the most or the least exalted Kwakiutl group. The same individuals seem to have been involved in both the skit potlatches and the apparently serious potlatches. The amount of property distributed in the skit potlatches is not at all out of line with the amount distributed in other potlatches, except for the fact that there is one serious potlatch during these ten days that overshadows all the rest, serious and skit potlatches alike.

Of the two remaining instances of funmaking in this 1895–96 account both form a part of the winter dance ceremonials. Although Kwakiutl winter dancing should be considered separately at some time in relation to the interpretations of Kwakiutl character based upon it, it can be considered here as the context of potlatching, and it can be noted that as the context it was relieved by funmaking. One episode is so briefly described that its nature as fun must depend upon the fact that Boas labeled it as such. Boas tells of the opening of the winter dance ceremonials, how all three tribes gathered, feasted, sang their songs in turn, teased a Fool Dancer, and how, while the people were eating their second feast course, the different societies uttered their cries:

> "The hens are pecking!"
> "The great seals keep chewing."
> "The food of the great killer-whale is sweet."
> "The food of the foolish boys is sweet."
> "The great rock cods are trying to get food."
> "The great sea lions throw their heads downwards."
> "The great Mosmos said: "It will be awful." (2:545–46)

It is admittedly more than a little difficult to see this as a jolly episode; especially is there the question of whether these society cries might have anything to do with the well-known Cannibal Dance songs of the people. Boas says, however, that, "When uttering these cries the members of the societies lifted their spoons and seemed to enjoy the fun" (2:546), and we know that it was shortly following that the pretend Haida skit was put on. Boas said there was fun and there seems no good reason to doubt his judgment of the incident; neither would it do for any member of our culture to be overskeptical about the amount of fun present in relatively noisy and simple-minded group pursuits.

The second case is far more detailed and involves ceremonial and supernatural power. The violent and atrocious character of Kwakiutl supernaturals and of the dance ceremonials that recreate them has been much emphasized, yet here is a case in which the character of the supernatural has some beneficent aspects and in which the portrayal creates laughter and joy. The progress of the t'ō′X'uît ceremonial is described. The peak of the ceremony was reached when the t'ō′X'uît, followed by the people of her tribe, went to the four houses in the village where visitors of other tribes were staying:

In each house the t'ō'X'uît caught the supernatural power and threw it upon the people, as described heretofore. Every time she threw it the uproar increased. The people shook their blankets to indicate that the power had entered them. They laughed and cried, and kissed each other's wives, for during this time there is no jealousy and no quarreling. (2:583–85)

The series of episodes concerned with the t'o'X'uît has complex meanings: there is the suggestion that a proper winter ceremonial cannot be put on without this performance, that the supernaturally induced laughter is mixed with tears, that it can do harm as well as good, that it is irresistible, and that it sanctions behavioral license in the name of an ideal smoothness in human relations. However, while it is impossible to consider this material as a simple demonstration of the presence of warmth and lightheartedness in Kwakiutl winter ceremonial, it would be equally impossible to derive exclusively dark interpretations of Kwakiutl winter dancing and relation to the supernatural from any body of materials of which these formed a part.

A question might arise as to whether, granting the funmaking and fun-enjoying nature of the episodes described and discussed, they have a sufficiently important place in these potlatches and ceremonials to deserve consideration. They are but five incidents in a great march of events. Going through the report and counting incidents (feasts, potlatches, speeches, and so on) the total comes to over two hundred. The percentage is certainly unimpressive. The first answer to the question is that it might be meaningless. We know neither how to measure the intensity of any incident of fun or pleasure nor how to assess its significance in relation to the other incidents of a day or an occasion; it just seems generally to count. The second answer is to suggest that the contrast between the few incidents of funmaking and the many incidents of the ten days may not be as sharp as it appears. It would have been humanly impossible for Boas to record the entire content of ten days, and he makes no claim of having done so; in fact, in the final two days there is visible evidence of fatigue on his part, for he merely summarizes episodes and begins to note the hour of the night in a way that elicits the anthropological reader's sympathy: "12:30 A.M., 2 o'clock, 3:15, 4 o'clock." Taking all these factors into account, it would seem impossible to ignore or minimize these incidents of fun or lightness.

Incidents of funmaking are by no means the sole type of incident displaying "amiable" features that is to be found in the record Boas made. Limitations of space prevent full examination and discussion of this record here, but the reader is urged to consider, for example, the numerous and impressive instances of the occurrence of courtesy and civility in connection with Kwakiutl speechmaking, a part of Kwakiutl life that has been considered to show unqualified arrogance and braggadocio. It is impossible, for example, to ignore the continual "Friends!" as the form of address and reference to those who are receiving property at a potlatch and as the form used in reply to the self-glorifying speeches of those giving the potlatch. This usage is of the most frequent occurrence in all recorded potlatch speeches. There is certainly a strong possibility that the usage is at times ironic or even sarcastic, but it is equally certain that "Friends!" might mean just what it says or that, at the very least, it indicates an awareness on the part of the potlatch donors that even at the moment of triumph there would be no triumph unless their friendly opponents were co-operating and an awareness on the part of the recipients that the situation would be reversed when it comes their turn to potlatch.

THE KWAKIUTL PLAY POTLATCH

Play potlatching made use of the heavy themes of potlatching to create fun, nonsense, and congeniality. Perhaps it would be better to say that a human capacity for insight and laughter did not miss the stuffy rigidities of potlatching, for a Bergsonian theory of laughter as social criticism seems operationally relevant here until, at any rate, we get a theory of society that includes laughter.

Play potlatching for all the men, women, and children of a village was apparently very widespread, can be recalled by many living informants, and was taking place as recently as 1948. It was not such a recent development, however, that it was not being carried on at the same time as the "serious" potlatching. Older informants are saddened by the passing both of the play potlatch and of the real potlatch.

Boas certainly knew about play potlatching, although he did not publish anything about it. It was one of the many things he had still to communicate about the Kwakiutl. An elderly Kwakiutl woman recalls with evident amusement:

At Fort Rupert when Boas was up there once they had a play potlatch. They gave away handkerchiefs and soap and things like that. Small stuff.

And the women gave away and received too. He gave some too. Funny names go with it. Everyone had a play potlatch name and he was given one at that time, ME'mlaelatse, "Where-the-southeast-wind-comes-from." The southeast wind comes from a rock near Fort Rupert; when water is sprinkled on this rock it brings the southeast wind.

The play potlatch name is funny only if the literary allusion is detailed. MElā'lanukwē, the-owner-of-the-southeast-wind, causes the always bad-smelling southeast wind to blow by breaking wind constantly. The name, therefore, is not overly dainty, but the scatological elements in this, as in other connections with play potlatching, are fairly fastidious and amusing. When, for instance, a clam buyer did not show up, a man caught with a surplus of clams gave a play potlatch in which everyone was presented with a sack of clams and a roll of toilet paper.

Earthiness, ribaldry, spoofing, and plain and simple fun seem to have been the sense of the play potlatch meeting. They were also apparently quite spontaneous occasions, although the accounts indicate that they occurred less often according to the pattern of the clam digger who was stuck with his clams than according to a feeling that the village was in the mood for some entertainment and tomfoolery. What mostly seems to have happened is that men and women put things by with the possibility of such an occasion in mind, somewhat in the spirit of a mother who keeps some children's presents tucked in a drawer.

One informant said, "Even the big chiefs are in the play potlatches and they have more fun than anybody. There are speeches and play potlatch names for everyone and everyone has a good time." From every point of view the play potlatch seemed to have the aspect of a free-for-all. The lowly or the high-ranking might begin it; before it was done everyone was likely to have been involved. The goods distributed ranged from quite useful articles to mere favors or things like the pigs and the chickens that were not properly the donors to give so that the gift was a fraud and a joke. The war between the sexes seems to have been a frequent theme for both the speeches and what little organization of events the gathering had, a feature that does little to set off the Kwakiutl as utterly distinctive in the world! The entertainment was a combination of Halloween and Kwakiutl theatrical art but seemed always to be arranged so that young and old alike might find it amusing. Maybe the salacious songs one informant claimed were occasionally sung were above the heads of the young or they were unable to savor the lampoons of potlatch speeches at the fullest, but they were there and most of the entertainment seems to have been at the level of fairly simple and exuberant play. Most anyone could enjoy the "you are not supposed to laugh" games and pantomimes and the noisy pots-and-pans trap and the pretending to "talk Chinese"—at least for a time. It seems to the writer that, although there is warmth and laughter in Kwakiutl life today, there is nothing ready to replace this healthy and equalitarian community fun, if it were to die out as many thought it would.

The main question would seem to be how to interpret the meaning of Kwakiutl play potlatching and how to determine its place in Kwakiutl life. Play potlatching seems to be a feature of village life, as distinct from the great public life in which several villages gathered and the large and famous potlatches were given; that this means that play potlatching was done in a homely community context is, however, insupportable. Play potlatching was not done in the context of home life or family or private life. The more rivalrous and serious competitions did exist between individuals of roughly similar social rank in different villages but any one village contained several ranked lineage groups numayms, and each of these numayms contained ranked individual standing places that had to be maintained by the individuals within the numayms in relation to one another. It is useful in clarifying Kwakiutl social organization to know that individuals usually refer to themselves as "one-half" from such and such a village and "one-half" from another village and "one-half" from one numaym and "one-half" from another This is by no means a new usage or one that does not fit all existing descriptions of Kwakiutl social organization, and it clarifies the system nicely. Marriages were usually between individuals of different villages Children's ranked positions could come from either parent or, in some cases, both parents. Loyalties to one village and identifications with one village were by no means uncomplicated or undivided. The results are clear: rank order permeated family, numaym, the single village, and the entire series of villages alike, and there could be no private, at home, escape from it. Therefore, there is no question but that play potlatching was engaged in by the same individuals who did serious potlatching with and against each other. The residual question is rather whether the ranking and the maintaining of rank was as unqualifiedly cutthroat, serious, and competitive as has been made out, and the answer to this question would be in the negative.

CONCLUSIONS: REINTERPRETATIONS OF KWAKIUTL CHARACTER AS SEEN IN KWAKIUTL POTLATCHING

Kwakiutl potlatching has been considered the central expression of Kwakiutl character. The details of potlatching have been used repeatedly to document claims that the people, like their premier institution, were characterized by megalomania, paranoia, and, more particularly, by rivalrousness of deadly seriousness and violent intensity. Reservations about incorporating this portrait into general and scientific thinking and usage have been few in number, brief in statement, and relatively narrow in scope of distribution. There are many areas and aspects of Kwakiutl life that force a reconsideration of the nature of the people and their institutions, but, because potlatching is such a critical center of interpretation, it has been the attempt of this study to confront this issue first of all.

Re-examination of the published first-hand descriptions of Kwakiutl potlatching shows them to contain materials that will not permit the construction of unqualified interpretations of the people and their institutions. The existence of incidents of funmaking and horseplay in connection with potlatching necessitates qualification of such characterizations as "paranoid" or "limitless pursuit of . . . social prestige," "uncensored self-glorification," "violence and rivalry that were the heart of the culture." All such generalizing would have to assume that the facts that did not support the generalization were too few, too inconsequential, or too irrelevant to merit consideration. The facts on funmaking in the published material on potlatching are few but they are certainly not irrelevant, and it seems that, little as we know about the place of fun and laughter in society, they are not inconsequential. The new evidence on play potlatching alone would necessitate a more humanized view of the Kwakiutl. It would be useful at this point to have some full cross-cultural study of the degree to which people make fun of their most sacred and important institutions, but, lacking opportunities for immediate comparison, it seems sound to state at least that if the Kwakiutl could laugh at themselves and their potlatch they were not wholly serious about it, they were not obsessed with it and with the rivalry and competitive ranking it involved, but rather they were capable of sufficient objectivity and insight to merit characterization in terms other than those strictly appropriate to human pathology and neurosis.

From the carefully conceived and excellently executed projectile points and knives of the very ancient Americans, through the Mimbres pottery of the prehistoric southwest, to the striking symmetry achieved by the basket weavers of California, the North American Indian was everywhere interested in embellishments on reality that, at their best, stand as art of the first order.

Common elements in American Indian culture included handsome work in stone (chipped and ground), bone (incised, sculpted, polished, and even etched), pottery (none wheel-thrown or glazed, yet of an order of perfection difficult to achieve even with modern techniques), fiber (woven into twined, coiled, or plaited masterpieces), and other materials.

"Primitive" is not a term which may be used blanketly to describe artistic expression of native North Americans, a point that is cogently demonstrated in the discussion of the stylistic complexities of Northwest Coast arts.

24 Philip Drucker

ART OF THE NORTHWEST COAST INDIANS*

Art, particularly carving in relief or in the round, was highly developed on the Northwest Coast. This applies to the region from the lower Columbia northward; the northwestern Californians and their neighbors did not participate in this artistic tradition, although they did decorate some of their small utensils with neat, if simple, geometric patterns. It was among the more northerly nations that the famous sculptural art, one of the finest in aboriginal America, came into full bloom.

There were two major stylistic divisions of this art, as well as several minor derived ones. The two principal strains, which were probably originally related, differed primarily in that one stressed applied design and formalization of representation, while the other was more fully sculptural and three-dimensional, combining realism with an impression-

* Excerpt from "Indians of the Northwest Coast," by P. Drucker, in *American Museum of Natural History Anthropological Handbook* **10**, 161–185, 1955.

istic suppression of non-essential detail. In the north, the Haida, Tsimshian (including all the Tsimshian subdivisions: Coast, Gitksan, and Niska), and, to a slightly lesser degree, the Tlingit, developed a highly standardized style in which conventionalized forms were used to decorate innumerable objects. Symmetry and rhythmic repetition were accentuated. The Wakashan-speaking groups just to the south developed a simpler but more truly sculptural and vigorous style which stressed mass and movement rather than conventionalization (it must be noted that the northern carvers, when they wished, could produce restrained, highly realistic works of great merit, as, for example, portrait masks and helmets).

The Coast Salish imitated the older Kwakiutl and Nootka carving. Much of their work was a simplification of an already boldly simplified style, so that it seems crude in comparison with its prototype. There were several minor local patterns among the Salish and Chinook that appear to reflect minor differences in sources of inspiration—that is, whether the group in question had closer cultural contacts with the Southern Kwakiutl or with the Nootka, and also, the distance from these sources. As far south as the Columbia River, traces of Wakashan stylistic influence may be seen, although the original three-dimensional treatment was crudely reduced to two dimensions, and a few purely local touches were added, perhaps because of influences from the interior.

The origins of the styles are unknown. Most authorities, however, agree that their perfection and standardization indicate a lengthy developmental history. The first European explorers in the area, Cook and Dixon, saw and collected objects at Nootka Sound and on the Queen Charlotte Islands stylistically identical with those made a century and more later. There is no evidence of any important modification of stylistic patterns during the historic period other than their gradual deterioration through disuse toward the end of the last century and the early decades of the present one. This decline resulted from loss of interest due to the rapidly accelerated acculturation of the Indians and to their nearly complete missionization, which was accompanied by pressure brought to bear by missionaires in favor of the abandonment of all pagan customs. The impairment of the art style was also affected to some extent by the legal prohibition of certain customs, like the potlatch, with which much of the art was associated. At the present time this great art is virtually extinct.

Such earlier developments as can be reasonably well documented during the nineteenth century point to its strength and vigor prior to the historical deteriorations just mentioned. For example, some time quite early in the nineteenth century, or perhaps in the closing years of the eighteenth, the Haida began to mine a soft black slate that occurs in one locality in the Queen Charlottes, and to carve it into pipes and pipestems for sale to whites. A number of reasons lead us to believe that this work began under white stimulus. First, the earliest explorers and fur traders who visited the Haida do not mention any articles of slate. Second, pipes were not known to the Haida or their neighbors of the north until smoking was introduced by whites. Finally, the pipes seem to have been made purely for sale or barter, not for native use. By the time the United States Exploring Expedition, under Lieutenant Wilkes, U.S.N., visited the Oregon Territory in 1841, where they were given quantities of specimens from the Queen Charlotte Islands by the Hudson's Bay Company personnel at Fort Vancouver, the Haida were turning out considerable numbers of elaborate and ornate—and most certainly unsmokable—slate pipes, most of them obviously poor imitations of white seafarers' scrimshaw work. Some of these objects show considerable technical skill, but artistically are pretty sad. During the next two or three decades, however, the aboriginal art style, latent in the consciousness of the carvers, began to come to the fore, submerging the clumsy copying of alien patterns. Some of the "pipes" were still made, but came to be decorated with native motifs (even during the "scrimshaw" period, carvers occasionally utilized aboriginal themes, though in a stiff awkward manner). The Haida artists began to carve models of "totem poles," decorated boxes, and feast dishes, in slate, and by the 1880's the ancient style dominated the slate carving to the point where the specimens of purely classic type and of considerable artistic merit were being produced. In other words, the basic tenets of the style were strong enough to dominate the introduced complex, in which a new material was first used to copy new forms (pipes and scrimshaw work) for a new purpose (for sale as curios), suggesting that the native art was firmly rooted in, and thoroughly harmonious with, the native culture.

This whole art, both among the three northernmost nations and the Kwakiutl and Nootka (and the Bella Coola), was aimed at the depiction of the supernatural beings, in animal, monster, or human form, who according to lineage or clan traditions had appeared to some ancestor, or, in some instances, had transformed itself to human form and become an ancestor. In either case the descendants of that ancestor, in the proper line, inherited the right to display symbols of the supernatural being to demonstrate their noble descent. Whether painted or carved, the motifs are often referred to as "crests," and were much like the heraldic emblazonments of European nobility. Similarly the masks and other appurtenances of the dancing societies were hereditary lineage property (although they, and the rituals they represented could be formally bestowed outside the family line under certain conditions, or captured in war). Thus the art style itself, through the objects made according to its dictates, was intimately linked with the social organization, rank, and status, as well as the ceremonial patterns, of the northern groups.

The special features of the northern art style are:

1. Whether two-dimensional (painting or low, flat relief) or three-dimensional (carving in high relief or full round), it was essentially an *applied* art. Thus its forms were typically adapted primarily to the shape of the object decorated. This was true even of the figures carved in high relief, like those on "totem poles" and spoon handles of mountain-goat horn, in which they appear to be contained within the mass of the material. Masks, because of their specialized function, formed the only important exception to this rule.

2. Conventionalization of form was carried to an extreme degree. However, this did not take place in a random manner, in one way in one specimen and differently in another, but according to certain principles. The first of these resulted from adaptation to the object decorated, as just mentioned. The second was based on what amounted to a passion for symmetry and balanced design. This may be observed most clearly in two-dimensional design, where, for balance, the figure was treated as though it had been split lengthwise and spread out flat, as it were, on the level surfaces, or wrapped around the sides of the whole object. There were many ways of accomplishing this. One was by "splitting" the figure into two separate halves, each half then being shown in profile, head to head, tail to tail, or back to back. Another slightly more complex mode of representation was to "split" the subject from the neck back, showing the head and face in front view, with the two halves of the body spread out on either side. Third, the artists emphasized certain areas in which they were interested, such as the head and face, and sometimes the paws or tail, and minimized or suppressed other parts. This trend was related to the fourth factor in conventionalization: the exaggeration and standardization of certain details for identification of

the being represented. As already remarked, the objective of the art was to depict definite symbols, the property of the clans and lineages. To render these symbols recognizable, certain distinctive features were selected, and consistently used. The following list enumerates a few of these typical keys to identification:

> Bear: Short snout, large teeth, protruding tongue, large paws and claws
> Wolf: Long snout, large teeth
> Beaver: Prominent incisors, holding stick in forepaws (forepaws sometimes raised to this position without stick), wide, flat, scaly (crosshatched) tail
> Killer whale: Large mouth with prominent teeth, long "dorsal fin," whale flukes
> Raven: Wings (usually), long straight beak
> Eagle: Wings (usually), heavy down-curved beak
> Sculpin: Two short dorsal fins, spines around mouth

It should be added that occasionally, when realism was required, the artists discarded their conventionalizations and produced portrait masks and helmets of amazing fidelity.

3. There was a strong tendency to fill all vacant areas, showing a sort of horror of blank spaces. For this reason, for one thing, when a series of figures are carved, as on a "totem pole" or a spoon handle, they are interlocked, with no intervening spaces. The "eye element," a rectangle with rounded corners, containing a lenticular form surrounding a circular one (the iris of the eye), was often used simultaneously as filler and to indicate arm and leg joints. Another common technique for avoiding blank space, especially in two-dimensional design, consisted in filling in the body area of the figure with a sort of schematic anatomical view. Occasionally this had a purpose, as in cases in which the being had eaten someone or something in the legendary episode in which he appeared. Even where such "X-ray" views or anatomical sections had no bearing on the myth, however, the device was frequently used.

4. Movement in the artistic sense—that assists in carrying the viewer's eye from one part of the composition to another—was achieved in several ways. The interlocking of a series of figures, mentioned above, contributed to that effect, particularly when the large principal figures were alternated with smaller ones in a rhythmic sequence. This device

was used frequently, though not exclusively, by Tsimshian totem-pole carvers. Painted lines typically vary in width, being thicker at the centers and tapering toward the ends. (In self-enclosing elements, like the "eye" design unit, the upper and lower margins usually taper toward the sides.) Movement as well as accentuation was frequently given to carvings by flowing painted lines.

Two-dimensional design—either painting in red and black, other than that used for accent and embellishment of high relief carving, or incised or very low relief carving—was applied to a great variety of objects: storage boxes, "settees" or chiefs' backrests, cradles, globular wooden rattles, canoe hulls and paddle blades, house fronts, the highly valued shield-like "coppers," "oil cups" of wood or mountain-sheep horn, shamans' charms and "soul catchers" of bone, horn, or ivory, and as well to buckskin, elkskin, or caribou-skin robes. In the field of textiles twined-woven spruce-root hats were painted with crest decorations, and a few plain woven Chilkat blankets have been collected that have designs painted on them. It is not known whether this was an older practice than weaving designs in panels; it may have been, and persisted into historic times. An early historic reference to robes "with designs in blue, yellow, black, and white" can refer only to the usual type of Chilkat blankets that we know from historic times. Incidentally, the typical Chilkat blanket and "dance shirts" with patterns woven in, and the older dance aprons and leggings, are the only objects we know that were regularly made by women in the classic northern art style. It is not that there was a specific taboo involved, but the motifs did not ordinarily lend themselves to the geometricity of basketry decoration. Hence, women did not learn the working principles of the art as did the men interested in painting and carving. (It should be noted that only certain men—not all—learned the principles of the art style and applied them to painting and carving.) There are a very few—and they are few indeed—Tlingit and Haida baskets that bear woven crest designs rather than the usual geometric patterns. As a matter of fact, in the manufacture of Chilkat blankets, male artists made pattern boards that the women weavers, technicians but not artists, carefully and methodically followed. The only other woven representative designs made by women in the area were the whaling scenes, schematic but with a certain verve, imbricated on the spruce-root hats of the Nootka. These, like the male-made Nootkan art products, vary from the northern pattern in their angularity, detail-less motifs, and extensive open areas.

Carving was done in high relief or the full round, in the classic tradition, in diverse materials and applied to a variety of objects. Most authorities are agreed, however, that this type of work was originally developed around a complex of woodworking, and then secondarily extended to horn, bone, ivory (traded from some Eskimo source), and even an occasional piece of stone. The handles of mountain-goat horn spoons, many feast dishes in their entirety, sealing and halibut clubs, figures mounted on canoe prows, "totem poles," the shanks of halibut hooks, speakers' staffs, and a host of other artifacts, were executed in high relief.

The Wakashan version of this art, as was remarked before, differed in a number of ways from that of the northernmost nations. Basically, it was more frankly sculptural, and less an applied art. Whereas even in full-round carving the work of the northerners gives the impression of being contained within the original volume of the log, horn, or bone on which the carving was done, Kwakiutl and Nootka artists did away with the confines of their material, cutting it away into new planes, and expanding beyond it by adding appendages—for example, the outstretched wings of a Thunderbird, or the prominent "dorsal fin" of the killer whale (occasionally northern artists added pieces to carvings, especially long beaks of certain birds carved on "totem poles," but this was not characteristic of their work). The Wakashan carving was less often applied to objects of utilitarian use, and hence was freer of the restraints of an applied art. The themes depicted were much less rigidly conventionalized; instead, there was a stress on realism of significant areas. At the same time large open areas were tolerated, and minor details were suppressed, so that the sweeping lines lead directly to the key areas and the eye is not distracted by secondary space-filling motifs. All these features of the Wakashan style combine to give great strength and force. Its impressionistic simplicity gives it a certain "primitive" cast, but also boldness and vigor. It is interesting to note that where Tlingit art differed from that of the neighboring Haida and Tsimshian, it was in the same direction, toward a simplified realism. Some Tlingit work is very similar to Wakashan art in treatment and forcefulness. It may be that such carving is closer to the original style from which Haida and Tsimshian (and some Tlingit) art was evolved.

Archaeological materials, chiefly from the lower Fraser, reveal an old art style that contrasts markedly with the classic northern pattern. Yet these ancient objects fit the artistic traditions which the historic Coast Salish derived from their Kwakiutl and Nootka neighbors. This archaeological material thus fits the hypothesis just suggested: that the Wakashan style, and its Salish derivatives, may have been the old form. Gradually the ancestors of the historic Tlingit, Haida, and Tsimshian modified that basic pattern into the subtle, more symmetrical, and also more static and more rigidly standardized style that was in use at the time of early historic contacts and was continued with no essential change till the closing decades of the nineteenth century.

No discussion of classic Northwest Coast art can be complete without a mention of the famous "totem poles." The term is quoted because it is something of a misnomer. Strictly speaking, a totem among primitive peoples the world over is a creature or object associated with one's ancestral traditions, *toward which one is taught to feel respect and reverence*—true totemism involves a basic attitude of religious awe. The Australian aborigines, like many other totemic peoples, do not kill their totem animals for food, even in times of hardship. Other groups have rituals to propitiate their totemic species. Not so the Northwest Coast Indians. There a person with an Eagle, Raven, Bear, or other crest had no particular regard for creatures of that species. It was not the biologic species in general that was of importance in his clan or lineage tradition, but a single specific supernatural being who had used the form of an eagle, raven, or bear. The Indian had no compunctions whatsoever about killing contemporary representatives of these species. In discussing pride in one's ancestry, we have already drawn the comparison between the crests and European heraldic quarterings. From the point of view of use, the crests can be compared to a cattle brand that the modern Western cowman burns not only on his animals to establish legal ownership, but on the gatepost of the corral, on the wings of his chaps, on the doorjamb of his house, and all sorts of places, because it is his brand and he likes it. Similarly, the northern nations along the coast took pride in their crests and sought to display them as often and in as many ways as possible.

Several varieties of totem poles (we may dispense with the quotes now and use the popular term) with varying functions were set up. The first was the memorial pole, erected by a deceased chief's heir as part of the process of assuming his predecessor's title and prerogatives. Such poles were erected along the beach in front of the village. Among the Southern Tlingit and the various Tsimshian divisions this was the principal kind in use in historic times. Another type, the mortuary pole, was set up alongside the grave of the deceased chief. Sometimes it actually constituted the grave, since the box containing the remains might be placed in a niche in the back of the pole, or was supported on top of it. The house-portal poles were a third type. They were built onto the front of the house and rose high above it, with a large opening, forming the doorway, at or near the base. Carved structural members of the houses, posts, and sometimes the beams, form another category. Finally, some poles symbolized some special privilege. Among the Southern Kwakiutl and Nootka, the tall slender poles surmounted by a bird-like figure marked the house of the Beach-Owner—the chief who had inherited the prerogative of being the first to invite important visitors to the village to a feast. Some authorities have disagreed as to which of these types are and which are not to be considered totem poles. The only reasonable solution is that *all* are, since they all consist of symbols which belonged to a particular lineage or family and referred to events in the lineage tradition giving the right to display such a symbol, and which could be displayed by the head of that lineage. Of course the crests used on either a memorial or mortuary pole were part of the lineage property, which both the deceased chief and his successor (who had the pole carved and set up) were entitled to use. The only variation to this consistent lineage-right pattern was a specialized type of Haida pole associated with house building that sometimes included crests of both husband's and wife's lineages.

It was stated above that the crests displayed on totem poles and elsewhere represented encounters by clan or lineage ancestors with supernatural beings. In its broadest terms, the phrasing should have been that the crests represented important events in the family history, for the Indians believed the legendary encounters with spirits and monsters to have been actual historical events. By accepting the native viewpoint, we can account for two specialized types of carvings, used chiefly by Southern Tlingit and Kaigani Haida. In one of these, figures of white men and European sailing vessels were carved. On one famous pole in the Alaskan Haida village of Old Kasaan, several personages who obviously represent nineteenth-century Russian priests are to be seen. The significance of these figures is that Chief Skowl, for whom the pole was carved and set up, was inordinately proud of the fact that he had successfully resisted the attempts of the Russian priests to convert him and his people to their faith. This he regarded as an important phase of his life, and so the figures of the priests were carved to symbolize it. In addition, according to the Indian concept, by thus publicly referring to the "defeat" of the foreign priests by the chief, they were ridiculed.

This brings out another use of the totem pole: to refer to success over a rival, and in this way to humiliate him. When, after an altercation, a chief managed to humilitate another publicly, that event was important enough to be recorded either contemporaneously or on the victor's memorial pole. Under these circumstances the successful chief and his lineage had to be certain enough of their own strength to have no fear of desperate attempts at revenge by the chief and lineage whose disgrace was thus advertised.

The few old poles still standing in their original positions give an impression of great age, with their surfaces weathered to a silvery gray, and bits of moss growing here and there in cracks and crevices. It therefore comes as a surprise to many people to discover that few of the individual poles are even a hundred years old. After all, the wet climate must destroy even the durable red cedar, or at least the base of a pole set in soggy ground, in less than a century. In reaction to this really not very surprising discovery, a few persons have interpreted this to mean that the custom of carving and setting up totem poles was of recent origin, a conclusion completely incompatible with the facts. First of all, the earliest European explorers to visit the permanent (winter) villages saw various kinds of poles. Meares (1788) and Boit (1799) describe elaborately carved portal poles at the Nootka village of Clayoquot. Among other early voyagers, Marchand (1791) describes both portal and mortuary poles at the Haida village of Kiusta. In 1793 the Malaspina Expedition observed a tremendous Bear mortuary post set up at a chief's grave at Lituya Bay in Huna Tlingit territory. The second point of importance is that the most common functions of the totem pole—aside from such specialized variants as the Haida combinations of husband's and wife's crests (not well understood by ethnologists) and the Southern Kwakiutl–Nootka Beach–Owner posts—are related to mortuary rites and/or memorials to the dead. It has been demonstrated that the northern Northwest Coast is only part of a larger area of distribution in which some kind of pole or post, painted, plain, or with attached ornaments, was erected at or near a grave in memory of and in honor of the dead. This practice prevailed over a wide area in northeastern Siberia, among the Western Eskimo in Alaska, and southward through the interior of northwest North America at least as far south as the Columbia Basin, where we have archaeological records of cedar posts set up at the head of prehistoric graves. On the coast this widespread ancient custom was elaborated until, long before first European contacts, the totem-pole complex was evolved.

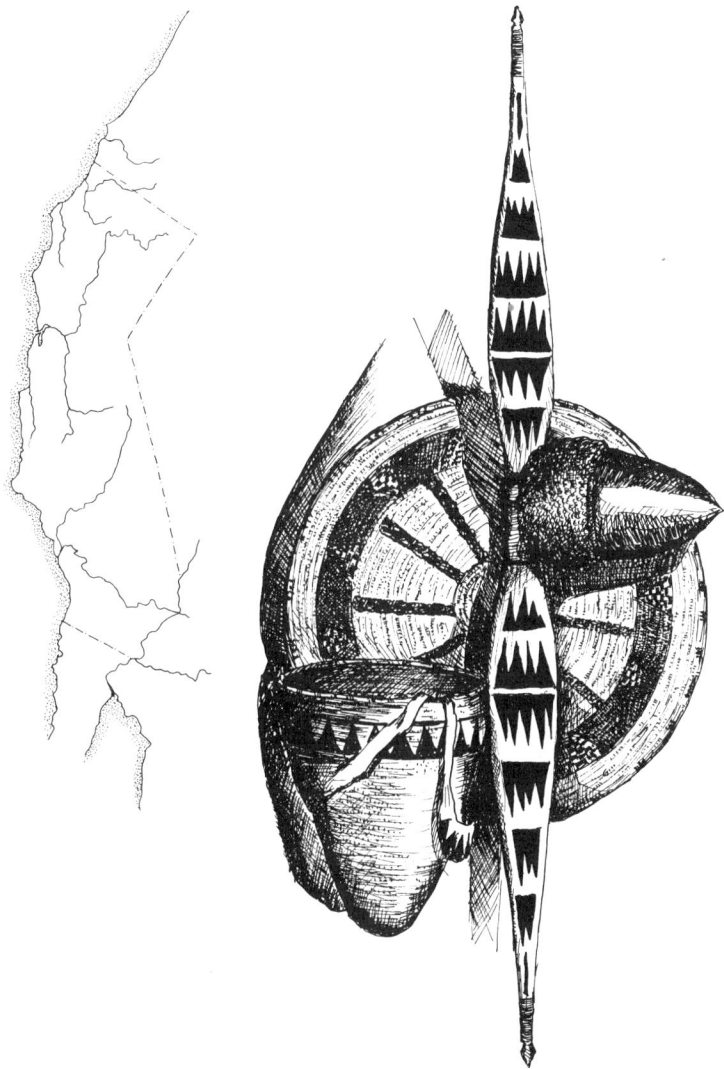

SECTION VI
California

The boundaries of the aboriginal California culture area approximated those of the present state. The zone harbored considerable cultural variation as well as great linguistic diversity. Over 500 miles in length, the region contained many differing climatological and topographical types, a variety which encouraged a great deal of cultural specializations. The northern portion of the culture area was well watered and well wooded, with temperatures ranging from cold to temperate; but through most of the desert interior and along the central and southern coast the climate was relatively warm (to very hot), and relatively dry, so that vegetation tended to be sparse. The regions of higher elevation in California might have frost any month of the year, and heavy snows blocked most of the high Sierra passes for periods of six to ten months at a time. The parched desert denizens of the present Owens Valley might look perpetually upon the snow-capped peaks of the Sierra Nevada and, of course, they might utilize the ecological variety so provided.

Despite the specific regional differences, a common series of traits and complexes were to be found in most of the cultures of California: simple band or rudimentary tribal social organization, simple technology, subsistence based heavily upon wild plants (especially the oak, and the piñon pine), and shamanistic religion.

Agriculture developed only along the Colorado River and, with a few possible exceptions, pottery had the same distribution. Along the coast and streams of the rainy and cold north, salmon and seafood provided a richer base upon which to build; in the region of Santa Barbara an unusual coastal island configuration made available especially large quantities of sea mammal flesh. The Cocopa, Yuma, Mohave, and others who had developed corn horticulture were undergoing population growth and territorial expansion when Europeans arrived; these, however, were the exceptions. The inhabitants of the central valleys, the deserts, and the less abundantly endowed coastal strips were among the simpler of native North American populations.

Although a considerable amount of detailed work has been done on the archaeological and cultural history of California, many problems remain. The absence of pottery throughout most of the state robs the archaeologist of perhaps his most valuable informant; and certainly a paucity of formal architectural remains further complicates an already difficult task. Moreover, the ethnologist, chiefly a twentieth-century figure, has found himself forced to work in California with simple Indian cultures that underwent major social and cultural modifications 300 years ago. Population depletion, group amalgamations, and sociocultural disintegration must have occurred everywhere, further obscuring California cultural and linguistic relationships. It is known, for example, that in areas such as the peninsula of Baja California, perhaps as many as half of the people died prior to personal contact with Europeans because of the indirect introduction of an epidemic disease, such as smallpox.

California's coast and deserts have been occupied for a long time. Carbon$_{14}$ dates place Man on the coast 9,000 or more years ago, and simple desert hunters may have made camp 15,000 years ago around presently dry lake beds in Los Angeles County; some specialists believe that California's desert regions and coastal islands as well as other parts may have been occupied for 30,000 or more years. This contention is supported by the exciting finds in the Mohave Desert of a number of stone tools that are indeed reminiscent of Middle and Upper Paleolithic tools from Europe. Further support for the theory of great antiquity for human occupation on the West Coast is drawn from a number of apparently "barbecued" dwarf mammoth skeletons unearthed on Santa Rosa Island, one of the Santa Barbara Channel islands. However, clear and unequivocable association of hunters with the mammoth "kills" remains, sadly enough, problematic.

If it must be noted that the California region was filled with simple sociocultural groups, mention should also be made of a number of minor cultural triumphs that occurred in the area. Nowhere in the world were fiber baskets superior to those widely designed and woven in California. Most notably, the Pomo, but also the Chumash and the Chemehuevi, made baskets which are now valued art objects in museums or in private collections. The manufacture of enormous numbers of polished stone artifacts and of shell beads was particularly well developed along the southern coast. Also, perhaps the most artistically exciting series of cave paintings in North America were done by the Santa Barbara Chumash and their ancestors. The Mohave, fierce in war and morbidly concerned with death, were renowned widely as dreamers and singers; many now unintelligible songs still sung by Indians in California and in the Southwest are reputed to be Mohave in origin.

In the opening article, A. L. Kroeber, the outstanding expert on California Indian life, presents a classic summary of the variety to be found in California Indian culture.

25 *Alfred L. Kroeber*

THE INDIANS OF CALIFORNIA*

SOCIETY

Political Organization

Tribes did not exist in California in the sense in which the word is properly applicable to the greater part of the North American continent.
When the term is used it must therefore be understood as synonymous
with "ethnic group" rather than as denoting political unity.

The marginal Mohave and the Yuma are the only Californian groups
comparable to what are generally understood as "tribes" in the central
and eastern United States: namely, a fairly coherent body of from five
hundred to five thousand souls—usually averaging not far from two
thousand; speaking in almost all cases a distinctive dialect or at least sub-
dialect; with a political organization of the loosest, perhaps; but nevertheless possessed of a considerable sentiment of solidarity as against all
other bodies, sufficient ordinarily to lead them to act as a unit. The
uniquely enterprising military spirit displayed by the Yuma and Mohave is undoubtedly connected with this sense of cohesion.

The extreme of political anarchy is found in the northwest, where
there was scarcely a tendency to group villages into higher units, and
where even a village was not conceived as an essential unit. In practice a
northwestern village was likely to act as a body, but it did so either because its inhabitants were kinsmen, or because it contained a man of
sufficient wealth to have established personal relations of obligation between himself and individual fellow-townsmen not related to him in
blood. The Yurok, Karok, and Hupa, and probably several of the adjacent groups, simply did not recognize any organization which tran-
scended individuals and kin groups.

* Abridged from "Elements of Culture in Native California," by A. L. Kroeber, in
University of California Publications in American Archaeology and Ethnology, **13,** 259–
328, 1922.

In north central California the rudiments of a tribal organization are discernible among the Pomo, Yuki, and Maidu and may be assumed to have prevailed among most other groups. A tribe in this region was a small body, evidently including on the average not much more than a hundred souls. It did not possess distinctive speech, a number of such tribes being normally included in the range of a single dialect. Each was obviously in substance a "village community," although the term "village" in this connection must be understood as implying a tract of land rather than a settlement as such. In most cases the population of the little tribe was divided between several settlements, each presumably consisting of a few households more or less intimately connected by blood; but there was also a site which was regarded as the principal one inhabited. Subsidiary settlements were frequently abandoned, reoccupied, or newly founded. The principal village was maintained more permanently. The limits of the territory of the group were well defined, comprising in most cases a natural drainage area. A chief was recognized for the tribe. There is some indication that his elevation may often have been subject to popular consent, although hereditary tendencies are likely to have been rather more influential in most cases. The minor settlements or groups of kinsmen had each their lesser chief or head-man. There was no proper name for the tribe. It was designated either by the name of its principal settlement or by that of its chief. Among foreigners these little groups sometimes bore names which were used much like true tribal names; but on an analysis these almost invariably prove to mean only "people of such and such a place or district." This type of organization is likely to have prevailed as far south as the Miwok in the interior and the Costanoans or Salinans on the coast, and northward to the Achomawi and possibly the Modoc.

The Yokuts, and apparently they alone, attained a nearer approach to a full tribal system. Their tribes were larger, ranging from a hundred and fifty to four hundred or five hundred members; possessed names which usually did not refer to localities; and spoke distinctive dialects, although these were often only slightly divergent from the neighboring tongues. The territory of each tribe was larger than in the Maidu-Pomo region, and a principal permanent village looms with prominence only in some cases.

The Shoshoneans of Nevada, and with them those of the eastern desert fringe of California, possessed an organization which appears to be somewhat akin to that of the Yokuts. They were divided into groups of about the same size as the Yokuts, each without a definite metropolis, rather shifting within its range, and headed by a chief possessing considerable influence. The groups were almost throughout named after a characteristic diet, thus "fish eaters" or "mountain-sheep eaters." It is not known how far each of these tribes possessed a unique dialect: if they did, their speech distinctness was in most cases minimal. Owing to the open and poorly productive nature of the country, the territory of each of these groups of the Shoshonean Great Basin was considerably more extensive than in the Yokuts habitat.

Political conditions in southern California are very obscure, but are likely to have been generally similar to those of north central California. Among the Chumash, towns of some size were inhabited century after century, and these undoubtedly were the centers if not the bases of political groups.

The Mohave and other Yuman tribes of the Colorado valley waged war as tribal units. Their settlements were small, shifting, apparently determined in the main by the location of their fields, and enter little into their own descriptions of their life. It is clear that the Mohave's sense of attachment was primarily to his people as a body, and secondarily to his country as a whole. The Californian Indian, with the partial exception of the Yokuts, always gives the impression of being attached first of all to a spot, or at most a few miles of stream or valley, and to his blood kindred or a small group of lifelong associates and intimates.

The Chief

Chieftainship is still wrapped in much the same obscurity and vagueness as political bodies. There were no doubt hereditary chiefs in many parts of California. But it is difficult to determine how far inheritance was the formally instituted avenue to office, or was only actually operative in the majority of instances. In general it seems that chieftainship was more definitely hereditary in the southern half or two-thirds of the state than in the north central area. Wealth was a factor of some consequence in relation to chieftainship everywhere, but its influence seems also to have varied according to locality. The northwestern tribes had hereditarily rich men of great influence, but no chiefs. Being without political organization, they could not well have had the latter.

The degree of authority of the chief is very difficult to estimate. This is a matter which can not be judged accurately from the accounts of relations between native groups and intruders belonging to a more highly civilized alien race. To understand the situation between the chief and his followers in the routine of daily life, it is necessary to have at command a more intimate knowledge of this life before its disturbance by Caucasian culture than is available for most Californian groups. It does seem that the authority of the chief was considerable everywhere as far north as the Miwok, and by no means negligible beyond; while in the northwest the social effect of wealth was so great as to obtain for the rich a distinctly commanding position. Among certain of the Shoshoneans of southern California the chief, the assistant or religious chief, and their wives or children, were all known by titles; which fact argues that a fairly great deference was accorded them. Their authority probably did not lag much behind. Both the Juaneño and the Chumash are said to have gone to war to avenge slights put upon their chiefs. The director of rituals as an assistant to the head chief is a southern California institution. Somewhat similar is the central Yokuts practice of having two chiefs for each tribe, one to represent each exogamous moiety. The chief had speakers, messengers, or similar henchmen with named offices, among the Coast Miwok, the interior Miwok, the Yokuts, the Juaneño, and no doubt among other groups.

The chief was everywhere distinctly a civil official. If he commanded also in battle, it seems to have been only through the accident of being a distinguished warrior as well. The usual war leader was merely that individual in the group who was able to inspire confidence through having displayed courage, skill, and enterprise in combat. It is only natural that his voice should have carried weight even in time of peace; but he seems not to have been regarded as holding an office. This distinction between the chief and the military leader appears to apply even to the Yuma and Mohave, among whom bravery was the supreme virtue.

There were no hereditary priests in California. A religious function often passed from father to son or brother's son, but the successor took his place because his kinship had caused him to acquire the necessary knowledge, not in virtue of his descent as such. At that there was hardly a recognized class of priests. The old man who knew most held the direction of ceremonies; and in the Kuksu region a man became clown, or *moki*, or *kuksu*, or some other specific impersonator, rather than a priest as such.

The shaman of course was never an official in the true sense of the word, inasmuch as his power was necessarily of individual acquisition and varied directly according to his supernatural potency, or, as we should call it, his gifts of personality.

Social Stratification

Social classes of different level are hardly likely to develop markedly in so primitive a society as that of California. It is therefore highly distinctive of the northwestern area that the social stratification which forms so important an element in the culture of the North Pacific coast, appears among these people with undiminished vigor. The heraldic and symbolic devices of the more advanced tribes a thousand miles to the north are lacking among the Yurok: the consciousness of the different value of a rich and a poor man is as keen among them as with the Kwakiutl or the Haida.

The northwest is also the only part of California that knew slavery. This institution rested upon the economic basis of debt.

Wealth was by no means a negligible factor in the remainder of California, but it clearly did not possess the same influence as in the northwest. There seems to have been an effort to regulate matters so that the chief, through the possession of several wives, or through contributions, was in a position to conduct himself with liberality, especially toward strangers and in time of need. On the whole he was wealthy because he was chief rather than the reverse. Among the Colorado River tribes a thoroughly democratic spirit prevailed as regards property, and there was a good deal of the Plains sentiment that it behooved a true man to be contemptuous of material possessions.

Marriage

Marriage is by purchase almost everywhere in California, the groups east of the Sierra and those on the Colorado River providing the only exceptions. Among the latter there is scarcely a formality observed. A man and a woman go to live together and the marriage is recognized as long as the union endures. While some form of bride-purchase is in vogue over the remainder of the state, its import is very different according to locality. The northwestern tribes make of it a definite, commercial, negotiated transaction, the absence of which prior to living together constitutes a serious injury to the family of the girl, whereas a liberal payment enhances the status of both bride and groom and their children. In the southern half of the state, and among the mountaineers of the north, payment has little more significance than a customary observance. It might be described as an affair of manners rather than morals. Formal negotiations are not always carried on, and in some instances the young man shows his intentions and is accepted merely on the strength of some presents of game or the rendering of an ill-defined period of service before or after the union. Even within comparatively restricted regions there is considerable difference in this respect between wealthy valley dwellers and poor highlanders: the northern Maidu furnish an interesting case in point.

So far as known the levirate or marriage of the widow by her dead husband's brother was the custom of all Californians except those on the Colorado. The same may be said of the "sororate" or "glorate," the widower's marriage to his dead wife's sister, or in cases of polygamy to two sisters or to mother and daughter. On account of this almost universal occurrence, these customs may be looked upon as basic and ancient institutions. The uniformity of their prevalence in contrast to the many intergrading forms assumed by the marriage act, and in contrast also to the differences as regards exogamy, renders it highly probable that if an attempt be made to bring the levirate and sororate into relation with these other institutions, the levirate and sororate must be regarded as antecedent—as established practices to which marriage, exogamy, and descent conformed.

Various Social Habits

A rigid custom prescribes that the widow crop or singe off her hair and cover the stubble as well as her face with pitch, throughout a great part of central California. This defacement is left on until the next mourning anniversary or for a year or sometimes longer. The groups that are known to follow this practice are the Achomawi, Shasta, Maidu, Wintun, Kato, Pomo, and Miwok; also the Chukchansi, that is, the northern hill Yokuts. Among the Southern Yokuts the widow merely does not wash her face during the period in which she abstains from eating meat. Beyond the Yokuts, there is no reference to the custom; nor is it known from any northwestern people.

A mourning necklace is northern. The northwestern tribes braid a necklace which is worn for a year or longer after the death of a near relative or spouse. The Achomawi and Northeastern Maidu, perhaps other groups also, have their widows put on a necklace of lumps of pitch.

A belt made of the hair cut from her head was worn by the widow among the Shastan tribes, that is the Shasta, Achomawi, and Atsugewi. In southern California, belts and hair ties and other ornaments of human hair reappear, but do not have so definite a reference to mourning.

The couvade was practiced by nearly all Californians, but not in its "classic" form of the father alone observing restrictions and pretending to lie in. The usual custom was for both parents to be affected equally and for the same period. They observed food restraints and worked and traveled as little as possible in order to benefit their child; they did not ward illness from the infant by shamming it themselves. The custom might well be described as a semi-couvade. It has been reported among the Achomawi, Maidu, Yuki, Pomo, Yokuts, Juaneño, and Diegueño. Only the Yurok, Hupa, Shasta, and with them presumably the Karok and a few other northwestern tribes, are known not to have followed the practice. Here too there are certain restrictions on both parents; but those of the father are much the lighter and briefer.

Fear toward twins is known to have been felt by the Yurok, Achomawi, and Northwestern Maidu of the hills. It is likely to have prevailed more widely, but these instances suggest that the most acute development of the sentiment may have been localized in northern California.

The child's umbilical cord was saved, carefully disposed of, or specially treated. The Diegueño, Luiseño, Juaneño, and Chukchansi Yokuts buried it. The Tachi Yokuts tied it on the child's abdomen. The Hupa and Yurok kept it for a year or two, then deposited it in a split tree.

Kinship Taboos

The taboo which forbids parents-in-law and children-in-law to look each other in the face or speak or communicate, was a central Californian custom. It is recorded for the Kato, Pomo, Maidu, Miwok, Yokuts, and Western Mono; with whom at least the southerly Wintun must probably be included. The Yuki, perhaps the Yana, the Eastern Mono, the Tübatulabal, and the Kawaiisu seem not to have adhered to the practice, whose distribution is therefore recognizable as holding over a continuous and rather regular area whose core is the Sacramento-San Joaquin valley. There is no mention of the habit in regard to any northwestern or southern tribe. Actually, the mother-in-law is alone specified in some instances, but these may be cases of loose or incomplete record. Accuracy also necessitates the statement that among the Kato and Pomo the custom has not been reported directly, but it is known that they address a parent-in-law in the plural—a device which the Miwok and Western Mono make use of as an allowable circumvention of the taboo when there is the requisite occasion. The Kato and Pomo were shy toward their parents-in-law, but much less scrupulous about rigidly avoiding all communication with them than the Northwestern Maidu.

As in other parts of America, no reason for the custom can be obtained from the natives. It is a way they have, they answer; or they would be ashamed to do otherwise. That they feel positive disgrace at speaking brusquely to a parent-in-law is certain; but this sentiment can no more be accounted the direct cause of the origin of the custom than a sense of shame can by itself have produced the manifold varieties of dress current among mankind. It need not be doubted that a sense of delicacy with reference to sexual relations lies at the root of the habit. But to imagine that a native might really be able to explain the ultimate source of any of his institutions or manners, is of course unreasonable.

Disposal of the Dead

The manner of disposing of the dead varied greatly according to region in California. The areas in which cremation was practiced seem to aggregate somewhat larger than those in which burial was the custom, but the balance is nearly even, and the distribution quite irregular. Roughly, five areas can be distinguished.

The southern Californian area burned its dead.

Interment was the rule over a tract which seems to extend from the Great Basin across the southern Sierras to the Chumash and Santa Barbara islands. This includes the Chemehuevi, the Eastern Mono, the Tübatulabal, the Southern Yokuts, the Chumash, and perhaps a few of the adjacent minor Shoshonean groups.

A second region of cremation follows. This consists of the entire central Sierra Nevada, the San Joaquin valley except at its head, the lower Sacramento valley, and the coast region for about the same distance. Roughly, the range is from the Salinans and Central Yokuts to the Pomo and Southern Maidu.

A second area of burial takes in all of the tribes under the influence of the northwestern culture, and in addition to them the Yuki, at least the majority of the Wintun, and most of the northern Maidu.

The Modoc in the northeastern corner of the state again cremated. For the adjoining Achomawi the evidence conflicts. It is possible that this northern region was connected with the central area of cremation through the Yahi and Northwestern Maidu of the foothills.

It seems impossible to establish any correlation between custom and environment in this matter. Treeless and timbered regions both cremated and in other cases interred.

It does appear that the southern and central culture areas can be described as regions of prevailing cremation, the northwestern culture and the desert as areas of burial. The practice of each of the two interring regions has to some extent penetrated the adjacent parts of the central area. Interment however extends farther beyond the outer limits of the northwestern culture than almost all other institutions or elements which are definitely characteristic of the northwest, basketry and dentalia, for instance. Furthermore, there is the curious assemblage of burying peoples from the Eastern Mono to the Santa Barbara islands, which can scarcely correspond to any primary cultural stratum.

War

Warfare throughout California was carried on only for revenge, never for plunder or from a desire of distinction. The Mohave and Yuma must indeed be excepted from this statement, but their attitude is entirely unique. Probably the cause that most commonly originated feuds was the belief that a death had been caused by witchcraft. No doubt theft and disputes of various sorts also contributed. Once ill feeling was established, it was likely to continue for long periods. Even a reconciliation and formal peace must generally have left lurking suspicions which the natives' theory of disease was likely at any moment to fan into fresh accusation and a renewal of hostilities.

Torture has been reported as having been practiced by several tribes, such as the Maidu and the Gabrielino. It appears to have been considered merely a preliminary to the execution of captives, which was the victors' main purpose. As a rule, men who could be seized in warfare were killed and decapitated on the spot. Women and children were also slaughtered more frequently than enslaved. There is no record of any attempt to hold men as prisoners.

Scalps were taken in the greater part of California, brought home in triumph, and celebrated over, usually by a dance around a pole. Women as well as men generally participated. Some tribes made the dance indoors, others outside. There was no great formality about this scalp dance of victory. It may often have been celebrated with great abandon, but its ritual was loose and simple. The Mohave and Yuma alone show some organization of the ceremony, coupled with a considerable manifestation of dread of the scalps themselves—a Southwestern trait.

It is rather difficult to decide how far the scalp taken was literally such and how far it was the entire head. A fallen foe that could be operated upon in safety and leisure was almost always decapitated, and his head brought home. Sometimes it is said that this head was danced with. In other localities it was skinned at the first opportunity and the scalp alone used in the dance. The scalp, however, was always a larger object than we are accustomed to think with the habits of eastern tribes in mind. The skin taken extended to the eyes and nose and included the ears. There is no evidence of an endeavor to preserve scalps as permanent trophies to the credit of individuals; nor of a feeling that anything was lost by a failure to secure scalps, other than that an occasion for a pleasant celebration might be missed thereby.

The battle weapon of California was the bow. Spears have been mentioned as in use by a number of tribes, but all indications are that they were employed only sporadically in hand to hand fighting, and not for hurling from the ranks. It is probable that they were serviceable in an ambush or early morning rush upon the unsuspecting sleepers in a village. In a set fight the spear could not be used against a row of bowmen.

Southern California used the Pueblo type of war club, a rather short, stout stick expanded into a longitudinal mallet head. This seems to have been meant for thrusting into an opponent's face rather than for downright clubbing. The Mohave at any rate knew a second form of club, a somewhat longer, straight, and heavy stick, which served the specific purpose of breaking skulls. In central California mentions of clubs are exceedingly scarce. If they were used they were probably nothing but suitable sticks. When it came to hand to hand fighting the central Californian was likely to have recourse to the nearest stone. Stones were also favored by the northwestern tribes, but in addition there are some examples of a shaped war club of stone in this region. This club was a little over a foot long and rudely edged, somewhat in the shape of a narrow and thick paddle blade. This type has affiliations with the more elaborate stone and bone clubs used farther north on the Pacific coast.

Slings seem to have been known to practically all the Californians as toys, and in some parts were used effectively for hunting water fowl. The only definite reports of the use of slings in warfare are from the Wintun of Trinity river and the Western Mono; both mountaineers.

The shield, which is so important to the Plains Indian and to the Southwestern warrior, was known in California only to the Mohave, the Yuma, and the Diegueño, that is to say, the local representatives of the Yuman family. It was a round piece of unornamented hide. There is no reference to symbolism, and it appears to have been carried only occasionally. Not a single original specimen has been preserved. Much as tribes like the Mohave speak of war, they very rarely mention the shield, and its occurrence among them and their kinsmen is of interest chiefly as an evidence that the distribution of this object reached the Pacific coast.

Armor enters the state at the other end, also as an extension from a great extra-Californian culture. It is either of elk hide, or of rods twined with string in waistcoat shape. The rod type is reported from the north-western tribes, the Achomawi, and the northern mountain Maidu. Elk skin armor has been found among the same groups, as well as the Modoc, Shasta, northern valley Maidu, and Wailaki. These closely coincident distributions indicate that the two armor types are associated, not alternative; and that, confined to the northernmost portion of the state, they are to be understood as the marginal outpost of the extension of an idea that probably originated in the eastern hemisphere and for America centers in the culture of the North Pacific coast.

The greater part of central California appears to have been armorless and shieldless.

RELIGION AND KNOWLEDGE

Shamanism

The shamanistic practices of California are fairly uniform, and similar to those obtaining among the North American Indians generally. The primary function of the California shaman is the curing of disease. The illness is almost always considered due to the presence in the body of some foreign or hostile object. Only among the Colorado River tribes is there definite record of belief in an abstraction or injury of the soul. The shaman's usual business, therefore, is the removal of the disease object, and this in the great majority of cases is carried out by sucking. Singing, dancing, and smoking tobacco, with or without the accompaniment of trance conditions, are the usual diagnostic means. Manipulation of the body, brushing it, and blowing of tobacco smoke, breath, or saliva—the last especially among the Colorado River tribes—are sometimes resorted to in the extraction of the disease object.

Cult Religions

The cults or definitely formulated religions of California are too intricate to be described here, so that the following discussion is confined to their interrelations and certain questions of broader aspect.

The religions of north central and southern California, or Kuksu and "toloache" cults, on the other hand, seem to have overlapped in the region of the northern Yokuts and Salinans. It is unlikely that the two cults existed side by side with undiminished vigor among the same peoples; one was probably much abbreviated and reduced to subsidiary rank while the other maintained itself in flourishing or at least substantially full status.

This seems on the whole to be what has happened in southern California, where the jimsonweed or "toloache" religion emanating from the Gabrielino and the system of song-myth cycles issuing from the Colorado River tribes existed side by side to only a limited extent among the Diegueño and perhaps some of the Cahuila and Serrano. Even in these cases of partial mixture it is possible that the condition is not ancient. A recent wave of propaganda for the jimsonweed cult radiated southward and perhaps eastward from the Gabrielino during mission times—may in fact have succeeded in then gaining for the first time a foothold, particularly when Christian civilization had sapped the strength of the older cults in regions where these had previously been of sufficient vitality to keep out this toloache religion.

In any event there are certain ceremonies of wide distribution in California which must be considered as belonging to a more generalized and presumably older stratum of native civilization than any of the four cults here referred to. Most prominent among these simpler rituals is the adolescence ceremony for girls. The dance of war or victory occupies second place. To this must be added in northwestern and north central California the shamans' dance for instruction of the novice, and in north and south central California various exhibitions by classes or bodies of shamans. Generally speaking, all these rites are dwarfed among each people in proportion as it adheres to one of the four organized cults; but they rarely disappear wholly. They are usually somewhat but rather lightly colored by ritualistic ideas developed in the greater cults. Thus the adolescence rites of the Hupa, the Maidu, and the Luiseño are by no means uniform. And yet, with the partial exception of the latter, they have not been very profoundly shaped by the cults with which they are in contact, and can certainly not be described as having been incorporated in these cults. In short, these old or presumably ancient rites—which are all animated by essentially individual motives as opposed to communal or world purposes—evince a surprising vitality which has enabled them to retain certain salient traits during periods when it may be supposed that the more highly florescent great religions grew or were replaced by others.

The mourning anniversary belongs to neither class and is best considered separately.

The Kuksu and toloache systems shared the idea of initiation into a society. This organization was always communal. The aim normally was to include all adult males, and even where some attempt at discrimination was made, as perhaps among the Wintun, the proportion of those left out of membership seems to have been small. Nowhere was there the institution of distinct but parallel or equivalent fraternal religious bodies. The organization of the society was of very simple character, particularly in the south. In the Kuksu society two grades of initiates were recognized, besides the old men of special knowledge who acted as directors.

The Kuksu cult was the only one in California which directly impersonated spirits and had developed a fair wealth of distinctive paraphernalia and disguises for several mythic characters. This is a feature which probably grew up on the spot. It cannot well have reached central California from either the Southwestern or the North Pacific coast areas, since the intervening nations for long distances do not organize themselves into societies; not to mention that the quite diverse northwestern and toloache religions are present as evidences of growths that would have served to block the transmission of such influences as disguises.

To compensate for the simplicity of organization in the Kuksu and toloache religions, initiation looms up largely, according to some reports almost as if it were the chief function of the bodies. Novices were often given a formal and prolonged education. Witness the *woknam*, the "lie-dance" or "school," of the Yuki; the orations of the Maidu and Wintun; the long moral lectures to Luiseño boys and girls. That these pedagogical inclinations are an inherent part of the idea of the religious society, is shown by the fact that the Yurok and Mohave, who lack societies, do not manifest these inclinations, at least not in any formal way. In the Southwest, education is much less important than in California, relatively to the whole scheme of the religious institution; and for the Plains the difference is still greater. It appears that these two aspects, initiation and organization, tend to stand in inverse ratio of importance in North American cult societies.

Perhaps the most distinctive single trait of the two Californian cult societies is their freedom from any tendency to break up into, or to be accompanied by, smaller and equivalent but diverse societies as in the Plains, Southwest, and North Pacific coast regions.

The cults of the Colorado River tribes are bare of any inclination toward the formation of associations or bodies of members. They rest on dreams, or on imitations of other practitioners which are fused with inward experiences and construed as dreams. These dreams invariably have a mythological cast. Ritually the cults consist essentially of long series of songs; but most singers know a corresponding narrative. Dancing is minimal, and essentially an adjunct for pleasure. Concretely expressed symbolism is scarcely known: disguises, ground paintings, altars, religious edifices, drums or paraphernalia, and costumes are all dispensed with.

The northwestern cults adhere minutely to certain traditional forms, but these forms per se have no meaning. There is no trace of any cult organizations. The esoteric basis of every ceremony is the recitation of a formula, which is a myth in dialogue. The formulas are jealously guarded as private property. Major rites always serve a generic communal or even world-renewing purpose, and may well be described as new year rites. Dance costumes and equipments are splendid but wholly unsymbolic. All performances are very rigorously attached to precise localities and spots.

It appears that as these four cults are followed from northwestern California southeastward to the lower Colorado there is a successive weakening of the dance and all other external forms, of physical apparatus, of association with particular place or edifice; and an increase of personal psychic participation, of symbolism and mysticism, of speculation or emotion about human life and death, and of intrinsic interweaving of ritualistic expression with myth. The development of these respective qualities has nothing to do with the development of principles of organization, initiation, and impersonation or enactment; since the latter principles are adhered to in the middle of our area and unknown at the extremities.

The Mourning Anniversary

The anniversary or annual ceremony in memory of the dead bulks so large in the life of many California tribes as to produce a first impression of being one of the most typical elements of Californian culture. As a matter of fact, the institution was in force over only about half of the state: southern California and the Sierra Nevada region. There can be little doubt that its origin is southern. The distribution itself so suggests. The greatest development of mourning practices is found among the Gabrielino, Luiseño, and Diegueño. It is not that their anniversary is much more elaborate than that of other groups—the use of images representing the dead is common to the great majority of tribes—but these southerners have a greater number of mourning rites. Thus the Luiseño first wash the clothes of the dead, then burn them, and finally make the image ceremony. Of this they know two distinct forms, and in addition there are special mourning rites for religious initiates, and the Eagle dance which is also a funerary ceremony. Another circumstance that points to southern origin is the fact that the anniversary is held by nearly all tribes in a circular brush enclosure, such as is not used by the Miwok and Maidu for other purposes, whereas in southern California it is the only and universal religious structure. Finally, there are no known connections between the anniversary and the Kuksu cult of the Miwok and Maidu, whereas the toloache religion of southern California presents a number of contacts with the mourning ceremony.

It is a fair inference that the anniversary received its principal development among the same people that chiefly shaped the toloache cult, namely, the Gabrielino or some of their immediate neighbors. It is even possible that the two sets of rites flowed northward in conjunction, and that the anniversary outreached its mate because the absence or rarity of the jimsonweed plant north of the Yokuts checked the invasion of the rites based specifically upon it.

The Mohave and Yuma follow an aberrant form of mourning which is characteristic of their isolated cultural position. Their ceremony is held in honor of distinguished individual warriors, not for the memory of all the dead of the year. The mourners and singers sit under a shade, in front of which young men engage in mimic battle and war exploits. There are no images among the Mohave and no brush enclosure. The shade is burned at the conclusion, but there is no considerable destruction of property such as is so important an element of the rite elsewhere in California.

An undoubted influence of the anniversary is to be recognized in a practice shared by a number of tribes just outside its sphere of distribution: the Southern Wintun, Pomo, Yuki, Lassik, and perhaps others. These groups burn a large amount of property for the dead at the time of the funeral.

Some faint traces, not of the mourning anniversary itself indeed, but rather of the point of view which it expresses, are found even among the typical northwestern tribes. Among the Yurok and Hupa custom has established a certain time and place in every major dance as the occasion for an outburst of weeping. The old people in particular remember the presence of their departed kinsmen at former presentations of this part of the ceremony, and seem to express their grief almost spontaneously.

On the question of the time of the commemoration, more information is needed. It appears rather more often not to fall on the actual anniversary. Among some of the southern tribes it may be deferred some years; with the Mohave it seems to be held within a few weeks or months after death; the Sierra tribes mostly limit it to a fixed season—early autumn.

Girls' Adolescence Ceremony

Probably every people in California observed some rite for girls at the verge of womanhood: the vast majority celebrated it with a dance of some duration. It appears that in spite of a general basic similarity of the rite, and the comparatively narrow scope imposed on its main outlines by the physiological event to which it has reference, there are very few features that are universal. These few, among which the use of a head scratcher and the abstention from flesh are prominent, are of a specifically magical nature. The wealth of particular features restricted to single nations, and therefore evidently developed by them, is rather remarkable, and argues that the native Californians were not so much deficient in imagination and originality as in the ability to develop these qualities with emotional intensity to the point of impressiveness. There is every reason to believe that this inference applies with equal force to most phases of Californian civilization. It merely happens that an unusually full series of details is available for comparison on the rite for girls.

Poor and rude tribes make much more of the adolescence ceremony than those possessed of considerable substance and of institutions of some specialization. In this connection it is only necessary to cite the Yurok as contrasted with the Sinkyone, the Pomo as against the Yuki, the valley Maidu against those of the mountains, the Yokuts against the Washo, the Mohave against the Diegueño. Precedence in general elaboration of culture must in every instance be given to the former people of each pair: and yet it is the second that makes, and the first that does not make, a public adolescence dance. This condition warrants the inference that the puberty rite belongs to the generic or basic stratum of native culture, and that it has decayed among those nations that succeeded in definitely evolving or establishing ceremonials whose associations are less intimately personal and of a more broadly dignified import.

In the northern half of the state the idea is deeprooted that the potential influence for evil of a girl at the acme of her adolescence is very great. Even her sight blasts, and she is therefore covered or concealed as much as possible. Everything malignant in what is specifically female in physiology is thought to be thoroughly intensified at its first appearance.

So far as known, all the languages of this portion of California possess one word for a woman in her periodic illness; and an entirely distinct term for a girl who is at the precise incipiency of womanhood.

A second concept is also magical: that the girl's behavior at this period of intensification is extremely critical for her nature and conduct forever after. Hence the innumerable prescriptions for gathering firewood, industry, modest deportment, and the like.

This concept pervades also the reasoning of the tribes in the southern end of the state, but is rather overshadowed there by a more special conviction that direct physiological treatment is necessary to ensure future health. Warmth appears to be considered the first requisite in the south. Cold water must not be drunk under any circumstances, bathing must be in heated water; and in the sphere of Gabrielino-Luiseño influence, the girl is cooked or roasted, as it were, in a pit, which is clearly modeled on the earth oven. The idea of her essential malignancy is by comparison weak.

The southern concepts have penetrated in diluted form into the San Joaquin valley region, along with so many other elements of culture. On the other hand the Mohave, and with them presumably the Yuma, practice a type of ceremony that at most points differs from that of the other southern Californians, and provides an excellent exemplification of the considerable aloofness of the civilization of these agricultural tribes of the Colorado River.

The deer-hoof rattle is consciously associated with the girls' ceremony over all northern California. Since there is a deep-seated antithesis of taboo between everything sexual on the one hand, and everything referring to the hunt, the deer as the distinctive game animal, and flesh on the other, use of this particular rattle can hardly be a meaningless accident. But the basis of the inverting association has not become clear, and no native explanations seem to have been recorded.

Boys' Initiations

The description which has sometimes been made of Californian religion as characterized by initiation and mourning rites is not wholly accurate. Mourning customs, so far as they are crystallized into formal and important ceremonies, are confined to a single wave of southern origin and definitely limited distribution—the mourning anniversary. The girls' adolescence rite on the other hand is universal, and clearly one of the ancient constituents of the religion of all California as well as considerable tracts outside.

Boys were initiated into the two great organized religions of the state, the Kuksu and the toloache cult. Important as the initiation ceremonies were in these cults, it would however be misleading to regard them as primary: the cult has logical precedence, the initiation is a part of it. When therefore we subtract these two religions, there is left almost nothing in the nature of initiation for boys parallel to the girls' adolescence ceremony.

The only clear instance is in the northeastern corner of the state among the Achomawi and Shasta, primarily the former. These people practice an adolescence rite for boys comparable to the more widespread one for girls. Among each of them a characteristic feature is the whipping of the boy with a bow string. The Achomawi also pierce the boy's ears and make him fast, besides which he performs practices very similar to the deliberate seeking after supernatural power indulged in by the tribes of the Plains. The entire affair is very clearly an adolescence rather than an initiation rite, an induction into a status of life, and not into an organized group. It may be looked upon as a local extension to boys of concepts that are universal in regard to girls.

In southern California there is sometimes a partial assimilation of the boys' toloache initiation and of the girls' adolescence ceremony. Thus the Luiseño construct ground paintings for both, deliver analogous orations of advice to both, and put both sexes under similar restrictions. The Kawaiisu are said to give toloache to both boys and girls.

But these local and incomplete developments are very far from equating the initiations for the two sexes; and neither balances with mourning ceremonies. The girls' adolescence, the boys' initiation into a society, and the mourning anniversary clearly have distinct origins so far as California is concerned, and represent cultural planes.

Offerings

Offerings of feather wands are reported from the Chumash, the Costanoans, and the Maidu, and may therefore be assumed to have had a considerably wider distribution. The idea is that of the feather stick or prayer plume of the Southwest, and there is probably a historical connection between the practices of the two regions; although this connection may be psychological, that is indirectly cultural, rather than due to outright transmission. This inference is supported by the fact that there is no reference to anything like the offering of feather wands in southern California proper. In fact the practice of setting out offerings of any kind is so sparsely mentioned for southern California that it must be concluded to have been but slightly developed. The Californian feather wand was of somewhat different shape from the Southwestern feather stick. It appears usually to have been a stick of some length from which single feathers or at most small groups of feathers were hung at one or two places. The northwestern tribes are free from the practice.

Another ultimate connection with the Southwest is found in offerings or sprinklings of meal. These have been recorded for the Pomo, the Maidu, the Costanoans, and the Serrano. In some instances it is not clear whether whole seeds or flour ground from them was used, and it is even possible that the meal was sometimes replaced by entire acorns. The southern California tribes should perhaps be included, since the use of meal or seeds in the ground painting might be construed as an offering. The custom seems, however, to have been more or less hesitating wherever it has been reported. It certainly lacks the full symbolic implications and the ritualistic vigor which mark it in the Southwest. Among the Yokuts and probably their mountain neighbors, offerings of eagle down appear to have been more characteristic than those of seeds or meal. The northwestern tribes can be set down as not participating in the custom of male offerings. They blew tobacco, or dropped incense on the fire.

MATERIAL CULTURE

Dress

The standard clothing of California, irrespective of cultural provinces, was a short skirt or petticoat for women, and either nothing at all for men or a skin folded about the hips. The breechclout is frequently mentioned, but does not seem to have been aboriginal. Sense of modesty among men was slightly developed. In many parts all men went wholly naked except when the weather enforced protection, and among all groups old men appear to have gone bare of clothing without feeling of impropriety. The women's skirt was everywhere in two pieces. A rather narrow apron was worn in front. A larger back piece extended around at least to the hips and frequently reached to meet the front apron. Its variable materials were of two kinds, buckskin and plant fibers. Local supply was the chief factor in determining choice. If the garment was of skin, its lower half was slit into fringes. This allowed much greater freedom of movement, but the decorative effect was also felt and used. Of vegetable fibers the most frequently used was the inner bark of trees shredded and gathered on a cord. Grass, tule, ordinary cordage, and wrapped thongs are also reported.

As protection against rain and wind, both sexes donned a skin blanket. This was either thrown over the shoulders like a cape, or wrapped around the body, or passed over one arm and under the other and tied or secured in front. Sea otter furs made the most prized cloak of this type where they could be obtained. Land otter, wild cat, deer, and almost every other kind of fur was not disdained. The woven blanket of strips of rabbit fur or bird skin sometimes rendered service in this connection, although also an article of bedding.

The moccasin which prevailed over central and northwestern California was an unsoled, single-piece, soft shoe, with one seam up the front and another up the heel. This is the Yurok, Hupa, and Miwok type. The Californian moccasin is rather higher than that of the Plains tribes, and appears not to have been worn with its ankle portion turned down. Journeys, war, wood gathering, are the occasions mentioned for the donning of moccasins; as well as cold weather, when they were sometimes lined with grass. They were not worn about the village or on ordinary excursions.

In southern California, the sandal of the Southwest begins to appear. In its most characteristic form it consists of yucca fiber, apparently folded around a looped frame or string. The Colorado river tribes have abandoned the use of this form of sandal if ever they possessed it. In recent years they have worn simple rawhide sandals; but their very slender opportunities to hunt render it doubtful whether this is a type that antedates the introduction of horses and cattle among them. The Chemehuevi are said to have worn true moccasins. There is no clear report of any sandal north of Tehachapi.

The woman's basketry cap, a brimless cone or frustum, is generally considered a device intended to protect against the chafe of the pack strap. That this interpretation is correct is shown by the fact that in the south the cap is worn chiefly when a load is to be carried; whereas in the north, where custom demands the wearing of the cap at all ordinary times, it is occasionally donned also by men when it becomes of service to them in the handling of a dip net which is steadied with the head. The women's cap, however, is not a generic Californian institution. In the greater part of the central area it is unknown. Its northern and southern forms are quite distinct. Their distribution shows them to be direct adjuncts of certain basketry techniques. The northern cap coincides with the *Xerophyllum tenax* technique and is therefore always made in overlaid twining. The range of the southern cap appears to be identical with that of baskets made on a foundation of *Epicampes rigens* grass and is thus a coiled product. There can be no question that tribes following other basketry techniques possessed the ability to make caps; but they did not do so. It is curious that an object of evident utilitarian origin, more or less influenced by fashion, should have its distribution limited according to the prevalence of basketry techniques and materials.

Inasmuch as woven caps and hats are worn all along the Pacific coast to Alaska and through a great part of the Plateau and Great Basin area, the two Californian types are but occurrences in a larger continuous area, and can therefore scarcely be interpreted as having originated quite independently. Rather is central California to be looked upon as a tract that once had and then lost the cap, or possibly always resisted its invasion.

Houses

The houses of native California are difficult to classify except in summary fashion. The extreme forms are well differentiated, but are all connected by transitions. The frame house of the Yurok and Hupa is a definite type whose affinity with the larger plank house of the North Pacific coast is sufficiently evident. Southward and eastward from the Yurok this house becomes smaller and more rudely made. Bark begins to replace the split or hewn planks, and before long a conical form made wholly of bark slabs is attained. This in turn, if provided with a center post, need only be covered with earth to serve as the simple prototype of the large semi-subterranean house of the Sacramento Valley. Again, the bark is often partly replaced by poles and sticks. If these are covered with thatch, we have a simple form of the conical brush house. This in turn also attains the rectangular form characteristic of the perfect form of plank house, but in other cases is made oval or round and domed, as among the Chumash. In this event it differs from the semi-subterranean house only in the lack of earth covering and its consequent lighter construction. A further transition is afforded by the fact that the earth house almost invariably has foliage of some kind as its topmost covering immediately below the earth surfacing. The brush house is often dug out a short distance. The Chumash threw the earth from the excavation up against the walls for a few feet. The earth covered house proper is only a little deeper and has the covering extending all the way over.

From the Chumash to the southern valley Yokuts, communal houses were in use. Yet the larger specimens of the earth lodges of the Sacramento Valley district must also have sheltered more people than we reckon to a family; and the same is true of the thatched houses of the Pomo.

The separate hut for the woman in her periodical illness seems to be a northern Californian institution. Information is irregular, but the groups who affirm that they formerly erected such structures are the Yurok, Karok, Hupa; probably the other northwestern tribes; the Shasta and Modoc; the northern Maidu; and apparently the Pomo. The Yuki and Sinkyone deny the practice, but their geographical situation renders unconfirmed negative statements somewhat doubtful. South of the Golden Gate, there is no clear reference to separate huts for women except among the Luiseño, and the Yokuts specifically state that they did not build them.

The Sweat-House

The sweat-house is a typical Californian institution if there is any; yet it was not in universal use. The Colorado River tribes lacked it or any substitute; and a want of reference to the structure among a series of Shoshonean desert tribes, such as the Chemehuevi and the eastern Mono, indicates that these must perhaps be joined to the agricultural Yumans in this respect; although an earth sweat-house is reported from the Panamint. The non-use of the sweat-house among the Yuma and Mohave appears to be of rather weighty historical significance, since on their eastern side the edifice was made by the nomadic tribes of the Southwest, and a related type—the kiva or estufa—is important among the Pueblos.

The Californian sweat-house is an institution of daily, not occasional, service. It serves a habit, not a medicinal treatment; it enters into ceremony indirectly rather than specifically as a means of purification. It is the assembly of the men, and often their sleeping quarters. It thus comes to fulfill many of the functions of a club; but is not to be construed as such, since ownership or kinship or friendship, not membership, determines admission; and there is no act of initiation.

In line with these characteristics, the California sweat-house was a structure, not a few boughs over which a blanket was thrown before entry. It was earth-covered; except in the northwest, where an abundance of planks roofed a deep pit. In either case a substantial construction was requisite. A center post was often set up: logs and poles at any rate had to be employed.

Warmth was produced directly by fire, never by steam generated by heated stones. While the smoke was densest, the inmates lay close to the floor. Women were never admitted, except here and there on special ceremonial occasions, when sweating became a subsidiary feature or was wholly omitted.

Boats

Native California used two types of boat—the wooden canoe and the tule balsa, a shaped raft of rushes. Their use tends to be exclusive without becoming fully so. Their distribution is determined by cultural more than by physiographic factors.

The northwestern canoe was employed on Humboldt Bay and along the open, rocky coast to the north, but its shape as well as range indicate it to have been devised for river use. It was dug out of half a redwood log, was square ended, round bottomed, of heavy proportions, but nicely finished with recurved gunwales and carved-out seat. A similar if not identical boat was used on the southern Oregon coast beyond the range of the redwood tree. The southern limit is marked by Cape Mendocino and the navigable waters of Eel River. Inland, the Karok and Hupa regularly used canoes of Yurok manufacture, and occasional examples were sold as far upstream as the Shasta.

The southern California canoe was a seagoing vessel, indispensable to the Shoshonean and Chumash islanders of the Santa Barbara group, and considerably employed also by the mainlanders of the shore from Point Concepcion and probably San Luis Obispo as far south as San Diego. It was usually of lashed planks, either because solid timber for dugouts was scant, or because dexterity in woodworking rendered a carpentered construction less laborious. A dugout form seems also to have been known, and perhaps prevailed among the manually clumsier tribes toward San Diego. A double-bladed paddle was used. The southern California canoe was purely maritime. There were no navigable rivers, and on the few sheltered bays and lagoons the balsa was sufficient and generally employed. The size of this canoe was not great, the beam probably narrow, and the construction light; but the sea is normally calm in southern California and one side of the islands almost always sheltered.

The balsa or rush raft had a nearly universal distribution, so far as drainage conditions permitted; the only groups that wholly rejected it in favor of the canoe being the Chumash and the northwestern tribes. It is reported from the Modoc, Achomawi, Northern Paiute, Wintun, Maidu, Pomo, Costanoans, Yokuts, Tübatulabal, Luiseño, Diegueño, and Colorado River tribes. For river crossing, a bundle or group of bundles of tules sufficed. On large lakes and bays well-shaped vessels, with pointed and elevated prow and raised sides, were often navigated with paddles. The balsa does not appear to have been in use north of California, but it was known in Mexico, and probably has a continuous distribution, except for gaps due to negative environment, into South America.

The balsa was most often poled; but in the deep waters of San Francisco Bay the Costanoans propelled it with the same double-bladed paddle that was used with the canoe of the coast and archipelago of southern California, whence the less skilful northerners may be assumed to have derived the implement. The double paddle is extremely rare in America; like the "Mediterranean" type of arrow release, it appears to have been recorded only from the eastern Eskimo. The Pomo of Clear Lake used a single paddle with short broad blade. The canoe paddle of the northwestern tribes is long, narrow, and heavy, having to serve both as pole and as oar; that of the Klamath and Modoc, whose lake waters were currentless, is of more normal shape. Whether or not the southerners employed the one-bladed paddle in addition to the double-ended one, does not seem to be known.

The occurrence of the double-bladed paddle militates against the supposition that the Chumash plank canoe might be of Oceanic origin. It would be strange if the boat—minus the outrigger—could be derived from the central Pacific, its paddle from the Arctic. Both look like local inventions.

Except for Drake's reference to canoes among the Coast Miwok—perhaps to be understood as balsas—there is no evidence that any form of boat was in use on the ocean from the Golden Gate to Cape Mendocino. A few logs were occasionally lashed into a rude raft when seal or mussel rocks were to be visited.

A number of interior groups ferried goods, children, and perhaps even women across swollen streams in large baskets or—in the south—pots. Swimming men propelled and guarded the little vessels. This custom is established for the Yuki, Yokuts, and Mohave, and was no doubt participated in by other tribes.

Fishing

In fresh water and still bays, fish are more successfully taken by rude people with nets or weirs or poison than by line. Fish hooks are therefore employed only occasionally. This is the case in California. There was probably no group that was ignorant of the fish hook, but one hears little of its use. The one exception was on the southern coast, where deep water appears to have restricted the use of nets. The prevalent hook in this region was a single curved piece cut out of haliotis shell. Elsewhere the hook was in use chiefly for fishing in the larger lakes, and in the higher mountains where trout were taken. It consisted most commonly of a wooded shank with a pointed bone lashed backward on it at an angle of 45 degrees or less. Sometimes two such bones projected on opposite sides. The gorget, a straight bone sharpened on both ends and suspended from a string in its middle, is reported from the Modoc, but is likely to have had a wider distribution.

The harpoon was probably known to every group in California whose territory contained sufficient bodies of water. The Colorado River tribes provide the only exception: the stream is too murky for the harpoon. The type of implement is everywhere substantially identical. The shaft, being intended for thrusting and not throwing, is long and slender. The foreshaft is usually double, one prong being slightly longer than the other, presumably because the stroke is most commonly delivered at an angle to the bottom. The toggle heads are small, of bone and wood tightly wrapped with string and pitched. The socket is most frequently in or near the end. The string leaving the head at or near the middle, the socket end serves as a barb. This rather rude device is sufficient because the harpoon is rarely employed for game larger than a salmon. The lines are short and fastened to the spear.

A heavier harpoon which was perhaps hurled was used by the northwestern coast tribes for taking sea lions. Only the heads have been preserved. These are of bone or antler and possess a true barb as well as socket.

The seine for surrounding fish, the stretched gill net, and the dip net were known to all the Californians, although many groups had occasion to use only certain varieties. The form and size of the dip net of course differed according as it was used in large or small streams, in the surf or in standing waters. The two commonest forms of frame were a semicircular hoop bisected by the handle, and two long diverging poles crossed and braced in the angle. A kite-shaped frame was sometimes employed for scooping. Nets without poles had floats of wood or tule stems. The sinkers were grooved or nicked stones, the commonest type of all being a flat beach pebble notched on opposite edges to prevent the string slipping. Perforated stones are known to have been used as net sinkers only in northwestern California and even there they occur by the side of the grooved variety. They are usually distinguishable without difficulty from the perforated stone of southern and central California which served as a digging stick weight, by the fact that their perforation is normally not in the middle. The northwesterners also availed themselves of naturally perforated stones.

Fish poison was fed into small streams and pools by a number of tribes: the Pomo, Yokuts, and Luiseño are specified, which indicates that the practice was widely spread. Buckeyes and soaproot (*Chlorogalum*) as well as other plants were employed.

Bows

The bow was self, long, and narrow in the south, sinew-backed, somewhat shorter, thin, and broad in northern and central California. Of course light unbacked bows were used for small game and by boys everywhere. The material varied locally. In the northwest, the bow was of yew and shorter and flatter than anywhere else; the wood was pared down to little greater thickness than the sinew, the edge was sharp, and the grip much pinched. Good bows of course quickly went out of use before firearms, so that few examples have been preserved anywhere except low-grade modern pieces intended for birds and rabbits. But sinew backing is reported southward to the Yokuts and Panamint, so that the Tehachapi range may be set as the limit. The Yokuts name of the Kitanemuk meant "large bows." This group therefore is likely to have used the southern self bow. On the other hand, a specimen attributed to the Chumash is sinew-backed, thong-wound in the middle, and has a three-ply sinew cord. As the piece is narrower than the northern bows and the wood does not seem to be yew, the attribution is probably correct.

The arrow was normally two-pieced, its head most frequently of obsidian, which works finer and smaller as well as sharper than flint. The butt end of the point was frequently notched for a sinew lashing. The foreshaft was generally set into the main shaft. For small game shot at close range one-piece arrows frequently sufficed: the stone head was also omitted, or replaced by a blunted wooden point. Cane was used as main shaft wherever it was available, but nowhere exclusively. From the Yokuts south to the Yuma the typical fighting arrow was a simple wooden shaft without head, quantity rather than effectiveness of ammunition appearing the desideratum. The same tribes, however, often tipped their cane deer-arrows with stone.

The arrow was bent straight in a hole cut through a slab of wood, and polished with *Equisetum* or in two grooved pieces of sandstone in the north. The southern straightener and polisher is determined by the cane arrow: a transversely grooved rectangle of steatite set by the fire. This Southwestern form extends north at least to the Yokuts; the Maidu possessed it in somewhat aberrant form.

Textiles

Basketry is unquestionably the most developed art in California, so that it is of interest that the principle which chiefly emerges in connection with the art is that its growth has been in the form of what ethnologists are wont to name "complexes." That is to say, materials, processes, forms, and uses which abstractly considered bear no intrinsic relation to one another, or only a slight relation, are in fact bound up in a unit. A series of tribes employ the same forms, substances, and techniques; when a group is reached which abandons one of these factors, it abandons most or all of them, and follows a characteristically different art.

This is particularly clear of the basketry of northernmost California. At first sight this art seems to be distinguished chiefly by the outstanding fact that it knows no coiling processes. Its southern line of demarcation runs between the Sinkyone and Kato, the Wailaki and Yuki, through Wintun and Yana territory at points that have not been determined with certainty, and between the Achomawi (or more strictly the Atsugewi) and the Maidu. Northward it extends far into Oregon west of the Cascades. The Klamath and Modoc do not adhere to it, although their industry is a related one.

Further examination reveals a considerable number of other traits that are universally followed by the tribes in the region in question. Wicker and checker work, which have no connection with coiling, are also not made. Of the numerous varieties of twining, the plain weave is substantially the only one employed, with some use of subsidiary strengthening in narrow belts of three-strand twining. The diagonal twine is known, but practiced only sporadically. Decoration is wholly in overlay twining, each weft strand being faced with a colored one. The materials of this basketry are hazel shoots for warp, conifer roots for weft, and *Xerophyllum*, *Adiantum*, and alder-dyed *Woodwardia* for white, black, and red patterns respectively. All these plants appear to grow some distance south of the range of this basketry. At least in some places to the south they are undoubtedly sufficiently abundant to serve as materials. The limit of distribution of the art can therefore not be ascribed to botanical causes. Similarly, there is no easily seen reason why people should stop wearing basketry caps and pounding acorns in a basketry hopper because their materials or technique have become different. That they do, evidences the strength of this particular complex.

In southern California a definite type of basket ware is adhered to with nearly equal rigidity. The typical technique here is coiling, normally on a foundation of straws of *Epicampes* grass. The sewing material is sumac or *Juncus*. Twined ware is subsidiary, is roughly done, and is made wholly in *Juncus*—a material that, used alone, forbids any considerable degree of finish. Here again the basketry cap and the mortar hopper appear but are limited toward the north by the range of the technique.

From southern California proper this basketry has penetrated to the southerly Yokuts and the adjacent Shoshonean tribes. Chumash ware also belongs to the same type, although it often substitutes *Juncus* for the *Epicampes* grass and sometimes uses willow. Both the Chumash and the Yokuts and Shoshoneans in and north of the Tehachapi mountains have developed one characteristic form not found in southern California proper: the shouldered basket with constricted neck. This is represented in the south by a simpler form, a small globular basket. The extreme development of the "bottle-neck" type is found among the Yokuts, Kawaiisu, and Tüatulabal. The Chumash on the one side, and the willow-using Chemehuevi on the other, round the shoulders of these vessels so as to show a partial transition to the southern California prototype.

The Colorado River tribes slight basketry to a very unusual degree. They make a few rude trays and fish traps. The majority of their baskets they seem always to have acquired in trade from their neighbors. Their neglect of the art recalls its similar low condition among the Pueblos, but is even more pronounced. Pottery making and agriculture seem to be the influences most largely responsible.

Central California from the Yuki and Maidu to the Yokuts is an area in which coiling and twining occur side by side. There are probably more twined baskets made, but they are manufactured for rougher usage and more often undecorated. Show pieces are usually coiled. The characteristic technique is therefore perhaps coiling, but the two processes nearly balance. The materials are not so uniform as in the north or south. The most characteristic plant is perhaps the redbud, *Cercis occidentalis*, which furnishes the red and often the white surface of coiled vessels and is used in twining also. The most common techniques are coiling with triple foundation and plain twining. Diagonal twining is however more or less followed, and lattice twining, single-rod coiling, and wicker work all have at least a local distribution. Twining with overlay is never practiced. Forms are variable, but not to any notable extent. Oval baskets are made in the Pomo region, and occasionally elsewhere, but there is no shape of so pronounced a character as the southern Yokuts bottleneck.

A number of local basketry arts have grown in central California on this generic foundation. The most complicated of these is that of the Pomo and their immediate neighbors, who have developed feather-covering, lattice-twining, checker-work, single-rod coiling, and the mortar hopper, and several other specializations. It may be added that the Pomo appear to be the only central Californian group that habitually make twined baskets with patterns.

Another definite center of development includes the Washo and in some measure the Miwok. Both of these groups practice single-rod coiling and have evolved a distinctive style of ornamentation characterized by a certain lightness of decorative touch. This ware, however, shades off to the south into Yokuts basketry with its southern California affiliations, and to the north into Maidu ware.

The latter in its pure form is readily distinguished from Miwok as well as Pomo basketry, but presents few positive peculiarities.

Costanoan and Salinan baskets perished so completely that no very definite idea of them can be formed. It is unlikely that any very marked local type prevailed in this region, and yet there are almost certain to have been some peculiarities.

The Yuki, wedged in between the Pomo and tribes that followed the northern California twining, make a coiled ware which with all its simplicity cannot be confounded with that of any other group in California; this in spite of the general lack of advancement which pervades their culture.

It thus appears that we may infer that a single style and type underlies the basketry of the whole of central California; that this has undergone numerous local diversifications due only in part to the materials available, and extending on the other hand into its purely decorative aspects; and that the most active and proficient of these local superstructures was that for which the Pomo were responsible, their creation, however, differing only in degree from those which resulted from analogous but less active impulses elsewhere. In central California, therefore, a basic basketry complex is less rigidly developed, or preserved, than in either the north or the south. The flora being substantially uniform through central California, differences in the use of materials are in themselves significant of the incipient or superficial diversifications of the art.

The Modoc constitute a sub-type within the area of twining. They overlay chiefly when they use *Xerophyllum* or quills, it would seem, and the majority of their baskets, which are composed of tule fibers of several shades, are in plain twining. But the shapes and patterns of their ware have clearly been developed under the influences that guide the art of the overlaying tribes; and the cap and hopper occur among them.

It is difficult to decide whether the Modoc art is to be interpreted as a form of the primitive style on which the modern overlaying complex is based, or as a readaptation of the latter to a new and widely useful material. The question can scarcely be answered without full consideration of the basketry of all Oregon.

Cloth is unknown in aboriginal California. Rush mats are twined like baskets or sewn. The nearest approach to a loom is a pair of upright sticks on which a long cord of rabbit fur is wound back and forth to be made into a blanket by the intertwining of a weft of the same material, or of two cords. The Maidu and southern Californians, and therefore probably other tribes also, made similar blankets of feather cords or strips of duck skin. The rabbit skin blanket has of course a wide distribution outside of California; that of bird skins may have been devised locally.

Pottery

The distribution of pottery in California reveals this art as surely due to Southwestern influences. It is practiced by the Yuma, Mohave, and other Colorado River tribes; sporadically by the Chemehuevi; by the Diegueño, Luiseño, Serrano, and Cahuilla; probably not by the Gabrielino; with the Juaneño doubtful. A second area, in which cruder pottery is made, lies to the north, apparently disconnected from the southern California one. In this district live the southern and perhaps central Yokuts, the Tübatulabal, and the Western Mono. This ware seems to be pieced with the fingers; it is irregular, undecorated, and the skill to construct vessels of any size was wanting. The southern Californians tempered with crushed rock, employed a clay that baked dull reddish, laid it on in thin spiral coils, and smoothed it between a wooden paddle and a pebble. They never corrugated, and no slipped ware has been found in the region; but there was some variety of forms—bowls, jars, pots, oval plates, short handled spoons, asymmetrical and multiple-mouthed jars, pipes—executed in a considerable range of sizes. Designs were solely in yellow ochre, and frequently omitted. They consisted chiefly of patterns of angular lines, with or without the corners filled in. Curves, solidly painted areas, and semi-realistic figures were rarely attempted. The ware was light, brittle, and porous.

Musical Instruments

The rattle is of three kinds in the greater part of California: the split clap stick for dancing, the gravel-filled cocoon bunch for shamanistic practices, the bundle of deer hoofs for the adolescent girl. South of Tehachapi these are generally replaced by a single form, whose material varies between turtle shell and gourd according to region. The northwest does not use rattles except in the adolescence ceremony; in which some tribes, such as the Hupa and Sinkyone, employ a modification of the clap stick, the Karok, Tolowa, and others the more general deer hoofs. The latter implement is known as far south as the Luiseño but seems to be associated with hunting or mourning ceremonies at this end of the state. The clap stick penetrated to the Gabrielino.

The notched scraper or musical rasp has been reported only from the Salinans.

California is a drumless region, except in the area of the Kuksu cult. There a foot drum, a segment of a large cylinder of wood, is set at the back of the dance house, and held very sacred. Various substitutes exist: the Yurok beat a board with a paddle, the Maidu strike or rub baskets, the Mohave do the same before a resounding jar. But these devices accompany gambling or shamans' or narrative songs: none of the substitutes replace dance drums.

Whistles of bone or cane are employed far more frequently in dances than the drum—by practically all tribes, in fact, although of course in quite different connections.

The bull-roarer has been reported from several scattered tribes. As might be expected, its use is religious, but its specific service is not well known and may have varied. To the Luiseño it was a summons. It was not used by the northwestern nations.

The only true musical instrument in our sense is the flute, an open, reedless tube, blown across the edge of one end. Almost always it has four holes, often more or less grouped in two pairs, and is innocent of any definite scale. It is played for self-recreation and courtship. The Mohave alone know a flageolet.

The musical or resonant bow, a sort of Jew's harp, the only stringed instrument of California, has been recorded among the Pomo, Maidu, Yokuts, and Diegueño, and no doubt had a wider distribution. It was tapped as a restful amusement, and sometimes in converse with the spirits.

It is remarkable, although abundantly paralleled among other Indians, that the only two instruments capable of producing a melody were not used ceremonially. The cause may be their imperfection. The dance was based on song, which an instrument of rhythm could enrich, but with which a mechanically but crudely produced melody would have clashed.

It is also a curious fact that the comparatively superior civilization of the northwestern tribes was the one that wholly lacked drum, bull-roarer, and musical bow and made minimal employ of rattles.

Money

Two forms of money prevailed in California, the dentalium shell, imported from the far north; and the clam shell disk bead. Among the strictly northwestern tribes dentalia were alone standard. In a belt stretching across the remainder of the northern end of the state, and limited very nearly, to the south, by the line that marks the end of the range of overlay twined basketry, dentalia and disks were used side by side.

Beyond, to the southern end of the state, dentalia were so sporadic as to be no longer reckoned as money, and the clam money was the medium of valuation. It had two sources of supply. On Bodega Bay, perhaps also at a few other points, the resident Coast Miwok and neighboring Pomo gathered the shell *Saxidomus aratus* or *gracilis*. From Morro Bay near San Luis Obispo to San Diego there occurs another large clam, *Tivela* or *Pachydesma crassatelloides*. Both of these were broken, the pieces roughly shaped, bored, strung, and then rounded and polished on a sandstone slab. The disks were from a third of an inch to an inch in diamenter, and from a quarter to a third of an inch thick, and varied in value according to size, thickness, polish, and age. The Pomo supplied the north; southern and central California used *Pachydesma* beads. The Southern Maidu are said to have had the latter, which fact, on account of their remoteness from the supply, may account for the higher value of the currency among them than with the Yokuts. But the Pomo *Saxidomus* bead is likely also to have reached the Maidu.

From the Yokuts and Salinans south, money was measured on the circumference of the hand. The exact distance traversed by the string varied somewhat according to tribe; the value in our terms appears to have fluctuated locally to a greater degree. The Pomo, Wintun, and Maidu seem not to have known the hand scale. They measured their strings in the rough by stretching them out, and appear to have counted the beads when they wished accuracy.

Associated with the two clam moneys were two kinds of valuables, both in cylindrical form. The northern was of magnesite, obtained in or near southeastern Pomo territory. This was polished and on baking took on a tawny or reddish hue, often variegated. These stone cylinders traveled as far as the Yuki and the Miwok. From the south came similar but longer and slenderer pieces of shell, white to violet in color, made sometimes of the columella of univalves, sometimes out of the hinge of a large rock oyster or rock clam, probably *Hinnites giganteus*. The bivalve cylinders took the finer grain and seem to have been preferred. Among the Chumash, such pieces must have been fairly common, to judge from finds in graves. To the inland Yokuts and Miwok they were excessively valuable. Both the magnesite and the shell cylinders were perforated longitudinally, and often constituted the center piece of a fine string of beads; but, however displayed, they were too precious to be properly classifiable as ornaments. At the same time their individual variability in size and quality, and consequently in value, was too great to allow them to be reckoned as ordinary money. They may be ranked on the whole with the obsidian blades of northwestern California, as an equivalent of precious stones among ourselves.

The small univalve *Olivella biplicata* and probably other species of the same genus were used nearly everywhere in the state. In the north, they were strung whole; in central and southern California, frequently broken up and rolled into thin, slightly concave disks, as by the Southwestern Indians of today. Neither form had much value. The olivella disks are far more common in graves than clam disks, as if a change of custom had taken place from the prehistoric to the historic period. But a more likely explanation is that the olivellas accompanied the corpse precisely because they were less valuable, the clam currency either being saved for inheritance, or, if offered, destroyed by fire in the great mourning anniversary.

Haliotis was much used in necklaces, ear ornaments, and the like, and among tribes remote from the sea commanded a considerable price; but it was nowhere standardized into currency.

Tobacco

Tobacco, of two or more species of *Nicotiana*, was smoked everywhere, but by the Yokuts, Tübatulabal, Kitanemuk, and Costanoans it was also mixed with shell lime and eaten.

The plant was grown by the northwestern groups such as the Yurok and Hupa, and apparently by the Wintun and Maidu. This limited agriculture, restricted to the people of a rather small area remote from tribes with farming customs, is curious. The Hupa and Yurok are afraid of wild tobacco as liable to have sprung from a grave; but it is as likely that the cultivation produced this unreasonable fear by rendering the use of the natural product unnecessary, as that the superstition was the impetus to the cultivation.

Tobacco was offered religiously by the Yurok, the Hupa, the Yahi, the Yokuts, and presumably by most or all other tribes; but exact data are lacking.

The pipe is found everywhere, and with insignificant exceptions is tubular. In the northwest, it averages about six inches long, and is of hard wood scraped somewhat concave in profile, the bowl lined with inset soapstone. In the region about the Pomo, the pipe is longer, the bowl end abruptly thickened to two or three inches, the stem slender. This bulb-ended pipe and the bulb-ended pestle have nearly the same distribution and may have influenced one another. In the Sierra Nevada, the pipe runs to only three or four inches, and tapers somewhat to the mouth end. The Chumash pipe has been preserved in its stone exemplars. These normally resemble the Sierra type, but are often longer, normally thicker, and more frequently contain a brief mouthpiece of bone. Ceremonial specimens are sometimes of obtuse angular shape. The pottery making tribes of the south use clay pipes most commonly. These are short, with shouldered bowl end. In all the region from the Yokuts south, in other words wherever the plant is available, a simple length of cane frequently replaces the worked pipe; and among all tribes shamans have all-stone pieces at times. The Modoc pipe is essentially Eastern: a stone head set on a wooden stem. The head is variable, as if it were a new and not yet established form: a tube, an L, intermediate forms, or a disk.

The Californians were light smokers, rarely passionate. They consumed smaller quantities of tobacco than most Eastern tribes and did not dilute it with bark. Smoking was of little formal social consequence, and indulged in chiefly at bedtime in the sweat-house. The available species of *Nicotiana* were pungent and powerful in physiological effect, and quickly produced dizziness and sleep.

Various

The ax and the stone celt are foreign to aboriginal California. The substitute is the wedge or chisel of antler—among the Chumash of whale's bone—driven by a stone. This maul is shaped only in extreme northern California.

The commonest string materials are the bark or outer fibers of dogbane or Indian hemp, *Apocynum cannabinum*, and milkweed, *Asclepias*. From these, fine cords and heavy ropes are spun by hand. Nettle string is reported from two groups as distant as the Modoc and the Luiseño. Other tribes are likely to have used it also as a subsidiary material. In the northwest, from the Tolowa to the Coast Yuki, and inland at least to the Shasta, Indian hemp and milkweed are superseded by a small species of iris—*I. macrosiphon*—from each leaf of which two thin, tough, silky fibers are scraped out. The manufacture is tedious, but results in an unusually fine, hard, and even string. In the southern desert, yucca fibers yield a coarse stiff cordage, and the reed—*Phragmites*—is also said to be used. Barks of various kinds, mostly from unidentified species, are employed for wrappings and lashings by many tribes, and grapevine is a convenient tying material for large objects when special pliability is not required. Practically all Californian cordage, of whatever weight, was two-ply before Caucasian contact became influential.

The carrying net is essentially southern so far as California is concerned, but connects geographically as well as in type with a net used by the Shoshonean women of the Great Basin. It was in use among all the southern Californians except those of the Colorado River and possibly the Chemehuevi, and extended north among the Yokuts. The shape of the utensil is that of a small hammock of large mesh. One end terminates in a heavy cord, the other in a loop. A varying type occurs in an isolated region to the north among the Pomo and Yuki. Here the ends of the net are carried into a continuous head band. This arrangement does not permit of contraction or expansion to accommodate the load as in the south. The net has also been mentioned for the Costanoans, but its type there remains unknown. It is possible that these people served as transmitters of the idea from the south to the Pomo. A curious device is reported from the Maidu. The pack strap, when not of skin, is

braided or more probably woven. Through its larger central portion the
warp threads run free without weft. This arrangement allows them to
be spread out and to enfold a small or light load somewhat in the fashion of a net.

～～～～～

*Many of the studies presented in this book are frankly descriptive.
American Indianists have always had strong interests in distribution,
diffusion, and historical development and culture change in general.
The following article, however, analyzes the cultures of some Northern
California Indians from a very unusual point of view: it employs the
method of analogy to compare Yurok, Hupa, and other tribes of northwest California with the emerging capitalist societies of Europe, as
analyzed by the German sociologist Max Weber. The intent of the
paper is to relate two markedly different groups of cultures, widely removed in space and level of development, wherein a general ethos was
developed which supported the growth of a strong capitalistic structure.
The article is a highly original and valuable contribution, not only to
California ethnology, but also to the social sciences in general.*

26 *Walter Goldschmidt*

BELIEF AND BEHAVIOR IN
NORTHWEST CALIFORNIA
INDIAN SOCIETY*

The sociological analysis of European history has revolved about the
problem of the emergence of capitalism, the development of the industrial economy, and the shift from Catholicism to Protestantism. The two
best-known of the analysts have been Weber, who viewed the "protes-

* Abridged from "Ethics and the Structure of Society: an Ethnological Contribution to
the Sociology of Knowledge," by W. Goldschmidt, in *American Anthropologist*, 53,
506–524, 1951.

tant ethic" as a necessary precondition to the development of capitalism, and Tawney, who does not commit himself as to priority but asserts the interdependence of the two. The study of the relationship of ideas to the character of social action has come to be known as the sociology of knowledge, and its most classical studies have postulated what anthropologists would call a functional relationship between the system of ideas and the structure of the economy and society.

To this body of theory the present paper brings data from the culture of Northwest California, a culture which reflects in surprising degree certain structural and ethical characteristics of emergent capitalistic Europe. This was the culture of the Yurok, Hupa, Karok and some of their neighbors. The existence of these patterns among a primitive people has in itself important implications for the assumptions as to the inherent differences of primitive and industrial societies. The comparison between the relationship of the "protestant ethic" and the "capitalist structure" of Northwest California society and the similar relationship in European society raises important points concerning the interdependence of the two facets of a culture and indicates in passing the need for further conceptualization of functionalism as an approach to the study of cultures. To these considerations we may turn after a brief demonstration of the reality of a "capitalist" structure of the primitive peoples and its particular manifestations, and after discussing the nature of their "protestantism." It should be mentioned that the present essay is but an outline of a larger study that will eventually present greater detail.

One initial point needs to be raised. Weber distinguishes between "capitalistic spirit" and those more nearly universal patterns such as search for riches and large-scale economic enterprises. Particularly, he refers to the organization of production based upon legally free workers for the purpose of procuring profits, toward which end production is rationalized through the mechanism of competition. We see therefore that in this usage capitalism is crucially a form of social organization rather than merely a pattern of economic exploitation. We shall speak, therefore, of the capitalistic structure of society rather than of capitalist economy.

The structure of Northwest California society may be briefly stated. On the economic side there are the following: The universal application of the concept of property, privately and individually held; the use of money as a universal means of exchange; the existence of wealth and its accumulation for purposes of prestige. On the social side these character-istics are paramount: The organization of the tribe into villages and households; the general but not universal patrilineal descent; absence of clans or any other inalienable group affiliations; absence of any vested authoritarian position, and the maintenance of power through control of wealth with social stratification not clearly marked into classes, but of overweening importance. More broadly, Northwest California society was an open class sytem in which prestige and power rested fundamen-tally with the possession of goods.

All property, whether natural resources, money, or items of wealth, are privately (and for the most part individually) owned. By resource property is meant fishing, hunting and gathering grounds. Like no other hunting-gathering people of which I have knowledge (and very few primitive peoples generally), these resources are held as private property by individuals for their own use and control, and not in trust or as titular head for some larger group. This ownership was individual. The sharp definition of title includes such considerations as:

1. The separation of title to separate types of products such as right to stranded whales along a specified segment of seacoast; or the right to the flippers off all sea-lions that are killed by hunters along a section of coastline.

2. The ownership of property rights within the territory of an alien tribe, such as a Hupa family's ownership of a rock on the Yurok coast area from which they obtained clams, and the possession by Yurok of a seed-gathering area in Chilula territory.

3. The division of title to a fishing place between two or more persons by measured time-spans; so that one uses it one day, another the next, etc.

Ownership was complete, with free right of alienation. Land holdings were readily transferred, either in legal disputes or for a consideration. The degree of freedom in this right is indicated by the fact that an owner might transfer his share to a person who was stranger or enemy to his co-owner so that a piece of property might be co-owned by persons with unfriendly relationships.

Where private property is recognized among primitive peoples, its importance is frequently vitiated by the mandatory generosity with re-spect to goods. Not so among the Northwest Californians. Generosity with food is expected as a general thing, but not to the impairment of one's own interests. Poachers, for instance, were shot. This was not a matter of territoriality, but of the transgression of individual rights. Or again, Waterman reports with respect to oak groves that "when acorns were plentiful no one worried much about his 'rights' or 'other people's rights' for that matter. In seasons of scarcity, when the acorn crop fell short (which often happened), or when it failed in certain sections, ownership of places became a very important matter. Permission to pick up acorns in a given spot might in that case be bartered for Indian money" (6:222). Such rental and restriction of the usufruct can hardly be compared to western economic exploitation, but it does show the relationship of ownership to the relative well-being of the individual. Waterman indicates that there is a direct relationship between resource ownership and wealth status.

The close identification of the individual with his property is another feature of the ownership pattern that must receive attention. This is manifested in attitudes toward the more personal forms of property (careful storage, tabus on handling, and the like), but it also appears in respect to real property. This is shown by laws of liability, where harm which befalls one on the property of another is treated as the direct responsibility (indeed the will) of that person.

So developed a concept of property requires the use of money, and in Northwest California money buys everything—wealth, resources, food, honor, and wives. As a form of behavior it is more uniformly applied than it is with us, though not so frequently. The dentalium shell served this purpose, the denominational value varying with its length. This was so much a matter of concern that every man of substance had standardized measurements tattooed on his forearm. This money was carefully preserved in elkhorn purses, each dentalium of value individually wrapped and decorated. Such decoration did not enhance the value of the object, but was merely care, lavished for its own sake, upon a treasured thing.

The third category of property is wealth—goods which served as the recognized goal of the individual, the possession of which marked his social position. Wealth consisted chiefly of paraphernalia used in one or another of the religious ceremonials of the people. These include the skins of albino or other off-color deer, large flint or obsidian blades (both used in the White Deerskin dance), woodpecker crest headbands and a host of lesser items of attire and personal decoration. These are not things which have utilitarian value in any direct sense. But they were used in the transfer of resource property, in legal disputes, and in the purchase of brides, as well as being displayed in the important ceremonial activities. Above all, the amount and value defined the social status of the owner, and his position of power in the community. We will return to this later.

The structure of the Yurok-Hupa social system had an amorphous quality. Though there were functioning social groups to which each person belonged, and though status distinctions were of greatest importance, still the most significant characteristic of the structure was the general absence of pre-ordained group membership and ascribed social position. All social affiliation contained a measure of individual consent, and all social position a measure of personal achievement. Groups to which the individual was attached included the family or household unit, the sweathouse group, the village, and the tribe. The household unit was crucial. It was a moderately extended patrilineal family consisting of man, wife, children, married-in in-laws and their children. Such families shared a dwelling house, about which their activities centered. The sharp delineation of the constitution of a family was prevented by the custom of "half-marriage," a second-rate marital practice in which the man joined the family of his bride, and their children became members of the house of the bride's father. These marriages took place in one out of five cases, so that nearly half the households must have been involved in such a marriage each generation. This custom, more than any other, prevented the family from taking on a crystallized structure because it prevented the juridical definition of family constitution, so frequent among primitive peoples.

Furthermore, a person might break with his family without social disapproval. Thus Spott and Kroeber report one case of a man who left his father's household and set himself up independently across the river, because his father had been niggardly in refusing to assist in the purchase of a bride—and this with public approval and no recrimination. This does not mean that the family was unimportant or that family ties were loosely regarded (the contrary is clearly the case), but only that there was a measure of personal consent and lack of pre-ordained identification even in this basic institution.

The sweathouse group formed a clique of men from three or so neighboring houses who shared the use of a subterranean sudatory. This structure served as sleeping, working, and lounging quarters for the men, as well as a sudatory for the semi-ritualized sweating activity. The personnel at any one time was fixed, and there were clearly marked status positions within the group. Boys about the age of puberty joined the group, presumably that to which the head of their household belonged. Membership of this group was not, therefore, a fixed matter. It was subject to the same vagaries that affected membership in the household. In addition, the data obtained on sweathouse membership suggests that a person was free to join any nearby group, so long as it was mutually agreeable.

These sweathouse cliques appear to have formed the unit (or the nucleus) for two separate, though related functions: (1) a body of men who acted in mutual support in case of dispute or fight, and (2) a group to support an individual presenting a unit of the White Deerskin dance. These political and religious functions are frequently performed by clans in the simpler societies. But significantly the groups were not structured like clans; not merely because they did not have unilinearity of descent, but because an individual's membership was neither foreordained nor eternal, but always contained an element of personal choice.

We may dismiss the village and tribe with a word. Though persons were identified by their village of residence and their tribe of origin, neither of these groups had any direct claim upon the action of the individual; there was no village nor national government, no village or tribal action in wars. Significantly, the affiliation could effectively be broken by moving to a distance or to one of the other tribes within the orbit of the culture.

Social status distinctions were an essential element in the structuring of Hupa and Yurok society. Certain statuses ascribed position to a small minority. Bastards had no social standing by virtue of their illegitimacy. Slaves were held, but their position was not quite so hopeless. Aside from these, there were the rich and the poor, class differentials which represent a continuum of status, not unlike that of the middle class in Western society. Since class status depended upon wealth, which was heritable, class affiliations followed closely according to the parents. Indeed, there was a clear distinction between the man of rich family background and the parvenu. Thus class position was not entirely open.

But in Yurok and Hupa theory it was open. Myths contain repeatedly the element of movement from poverty to riches. The youth is told that he can achieve by proper effort. At least one case is recorded of an individual independently attaining wealth, and his behavior was approved and his position accepted. The situation appears to have been as with us: in theory everyone might achieve status; in actuality models for such movement existed, but in fact only a small proportion of persons significantly altered their social position. There is some evidence that the Yurok class differentiation was more sharply defined and mobility less realizable than among the Hupa or the Tolowa. But it seems to me this is a crystallization which will naturally take place in an open class system because of the tendency of persons of status toward such a definition. Indeed, Weber makes the same point for German society.

The third facet of Northwest California society was the systems of power and authority. Here again the situation was unstructured, for there were no persons vested with authority by virtue of station or public office. Government was strictly *laissez faire*, with order prevailing through the consistent effort of each person to serve his own self interest. Authority rested on a continual threat and show of force by the quick recognition of offense and the insistent demand for retribution. In Northwest California law all offense was against the person—it could hardly be otherwise in the absence of any formalized social unit. A great range of offenses were recognized: murder and adultery, theft and poaching, curses, minor insults.

For each offense there was a more or less clearly indicated fine or indemnity to be paid by the offender to the plaintiff, after proper adjudication through a neutral go-between. Not only were liability, intent and value of damage done recognized in determination of indemnity, but the status of the offended party was also considered, particularly in matters of murder. In view of these variables, it is not surprising that each case was the subject of prolonged litigation and negotiation, in which other considerations than the purely legalistic were brought to play.

For, in final analysis, the only ultimate sanction for legal settlement was the threat of physical force. The community was concerned with justice and its pressures were brought to bear for settlement according to established precedents. But it had no machinery to enforce a peaceful settlement, and an offended person might resort to, and always implicitly threatened to bring, physical retribution. In this use of force the individual counted on the support of his associates—his household group, his sweathouse clique, and a widening circle of supporters. It follows from the nature of the group affiliations that this was no absolute call, but an expectation of support which was subject to the willingness and consent of the supporters. This consent must have been a function in part of the righteousness of the cause and the appropriateness of the conduct of the principal. It was also a function of the social position and system of obligation that he had established.

It follows further that authority rested in large measure with the strong, and that this strength was fiscal strength. It was not merely the differential fines that worked to the advantage of the wealthy, or the higher bride price for their daughters, nor even that the wealthy were in a better economic position to push the limits of propriety and the demands for retribution. These were real but secondary by-products. It was that the owners of resources and of wealth could surround themselves with a greater body of persons willing to stand by them at times of crisis. Directly, the owner of resources could support a larger family. Indirectly, a wealthy man was central in a system of mutual obligations, and lesser persons found it useful to stand with him. Among these obligations might have been economic assistance and support (with his resources) in legal disputes. The pattern of allegiances was established in the presentation of the White Deerskin Dance. In these ceremonials, leadership was taken by several individuals of substance, each of whom presented a set of dances utilizing his own paraphernalia. They were aided by their household and sweathouse group fellows, and by others who felt sufficient obligation or allegiance. These ceremonials were public displays, not only of wealth, but also of power and the ties of mutual obligation. They were institutionalized and canalized expressions of individuated aggressive behavior which served to demonstrate fiscal strength, public power, social allegiances and social status.

The capitalist structure of the society may be summarized as follows: a system in which the individual was placed chiefly by personal acquisition of wealth which in theory was freely attainable by all, with both status and power resting upon the ownership of property.

The ethical pattern in Northwest California may be examined under its three fundamental features: The moral demand to work and by extension to the pursuit of gain; the moral demand of self denial, and the individuation of moral responsibility.

There is a strong compulsion to work heavily emphasized in child rearing, supported by the religious beliefs and demands, and expressed as a basic element in behavior. Northwest Californians were a busy and creative people. In societies living close to the minimum level of subsistence, the emphasis upon industriousness is not surprising. But poverty was not found here. The important thing about the evaluation of industriousness is not that there was such a value; but the moral involvement of the value. Weber was at some pains to show that Franklin's hedonistic arguments for industry were spurious, that Franklin demonstrably held work as a moral end. The same thing is true for the Northwest Californians.

The gathering of sweathouse wood demonstrates this fact. All men, particularly the youths, were exhorted to gather wood for use in sweating. This was not exploitation of child labor, but an important religious act, freighted with significance. Special wood was brought from the mountain ridges; it was used for an important purification ritual. The gathering itself was a religious act, for it was a means of acquiring "luck." It had to be done with the proper psychological attitude of which restrained demeanor and constant thinking about the acquisition of riches were the chief elements. The job became a moral end rather than a means to an end, with both religious and economic involvements.

The second commandment of the Northwest Californians was worldly asceticism. The Northwest Californian was exhorted to abstain from any kind of over-indulgence—eating, sexual gratification, play or sloth. The evidence here is definitive. For instance, sexuality was unclean. The sex act might not be committed in the dwelling house but was performed on the beaches. Youths were exhorted to be continent, and a woman particularly to preserve her virginity until married. Even after marriage, a man was expected to restrain himself. One of Wallace's informants says: "It's not good to be with a woman all the time. It's bad luck in getting money or hunting deer. A man weans himself from doing that as much as he can. . . . Most men have strong minds and good control . . ." and again, "If a man has too many kids, he is thought to be hoggish, like a dog" (5:48, 50).

Again big eaters were viewed as vulgar, and a person of good manners always ate slowly and in moderation, leaving food in his baskets to indicate self control as well as economic well-being. These patterns are clearly articulated by every student of these cultures and need no further elucidation.

But these behavior patterns were not purely secular. Sexual indulgence was not only bad, but sinful. And sin had a peculiarly economic definition. Sexual intercourse was bad because seminal fluid drives out dentalia and other wealth, to which it is abhorrent. Put another way, objects which at one and the same time demonstrated secular power and were associated with sacred ritual were the focal point in the taboo against intercourse. The rejection of sexuality was a religious aversion. It was religious yet it is important to appreciate how closely it was tied to economic well-being. There was constant economic evaluation of moral acts—with the custom of bride purchase, the wages of sin became subject to strict cost accounting.

The sweathouse ritual offered a daily test of other forms of self-indulgence for the men. The subterranean sweathouse had two doors. One was a hatchway in the roof for easy entrance and ordinary use. After sweating, however, the men had to leave through a narrow oval opening at the floor level and climb out a cobble-lined flue. Only a lithe, naked, sweaty body could work its way through this opening. It is obvious that any indulgence in food or sloth would make egress impossible. Here was a test that was daily and absolute, and carried with it the full force of religious sanction. Furthermore the sweathouse activities and sweating itself was attached to the wealth acquisition pattern, for the overt purpose of the sweating ritual was to insure luck for the individual in his economic pursuits.

Asceticism like work therefore was moral behavior which came to be an end itself; an end closely connected with economic and social success on one hand and with deep religious meaning and sanction on the other. Though it had these moral aspects, the "practical" implications of asceticism were recognized. The Hupa youth was told what our own fathers have told us, that if you want to be rich you must leave the women alone.

The third feature of the protestant ethic of Northwest California society is the individuation of moral responsibility; that is, the placing of responsibility for the individual's worth and his acts upon the individual himself. He was neither the creature of some unseen power nor the product of circumstance, but the master of his own fate. To this there were exceptions, such as bastards whose circumstances of birth determined their character, and shamans, whose possession of power was viewed as lying beyond their individual will. But the normal citizen was held personally responsible for his acts, and so conceived of himself.

We may see this conception in legal philosophy, with its recognition of liability and intent. Indeed, liability laws placed responsibility upon an individual in a more far-reaching manner than our own, perhaps because of a certain underlying magical identification between the individual and his property. With respect to Yurok law, Kroeber has written that "damage must be fully compensated for even though inflicted without a shadow of intent; but if the infringement is wilful, or malice is evident, added compensation is due for intent." More impressive, though less direct, are the psychological implications of the recognition that wounding a man is less serious than drawing a bead without shooting. The explanation can only lie in the concept of intent or the philosophical notion of will, where it is assumed that in wounding a man the intent to wound is evident, but in drawing a bead the intent to kill is implicit.

Consider again the nature of the wood-gathering act, in which the youth sought power not by subjecting himself to the will of some unseen spirit, but by directing his thoughts along consciously chosen channels.

Closely associated with this individuated self are the concepts of sin and guilt, which were to be found among the Northwest Californians. Present tribal members regularly use the word "sin" to describe morally disapproved behavior. The White Deerskin Dance is specifically designed to rid the world of the contaminating influence of the cumulative sins of individuals of their community. Descriptions of child rearing practices indicate the direct, overt introduction of these notions in the constant moralizing and placing of responsibility upon the child for his own conduct. The evidence for the internalization of this pattern of responsibility, and its expression in the form of guilt, is somewhat nebulous, but not entirely wanting. Aside from the conceptualization of sin and the expression of deep moral concern over wrongdoing, it appears in one rather unique situation. In the treatment of certain sick children, the shaman decides that there is no intrusive disease object, but that the immoral act of some ancestor is responsible, as in the following:

After she [the doctor] was in a trance state she said, "I see something so big [motioning with her hand] hanging over the boy, and from time to time blood drips on it. By it stands the shadow of his father, who must confess something or lose his boy . . ." . . . Thereupon the boy's mother confessed to whatever she had committed; but nothing she said was to the point. Then finally the father confessed what he had done when he put the blood in the sea lion bladder [i.e., added his own blood to that which would be eaten]. "That is it," said the K'otep doctor. "The boy will recover now." (4:189)

Kroeber says of these stories that "the sin committed is always extremely shameful in native eyes, though to us it may approach the venial. In fact, the nature of the wrongdoing illustrates vividly the Yurok puritanical preoccupation with sin. The guilt is religious: something impure and defiling is involved. But it is also a violation of custom, law, and recognized morals" (4:158). This is not the place to examine in detail the implications of this remarkable practice, with its analogy both to the Catholic confessional and present-day psychoanalytical practice. But it does offer evidence of the personalization of the moral act and the internalization of guilt.

Finally, this pattern of individuation is expressed in the personality characteristics of the people. The Northwest Californian is extremely aggressive in his interpersonal relations; he is hostile to his fellow men and expects hostility toward himself; he never relaxes his barriers of suspicion. The myths demonstrate these components which may be observed in the real world—aggressiveness, bickering and drive toward personal success. They also demonstrate certain reaction patterns—compulsive demand to work, withdrawal in the geographic sense and obedience and submission to the absolute powers of the creator gods.

Other personality traits were also involved. There was a constant theme of loneliness running through the mythology, and loneliness is an expected concomitant of individuation and hostility. More remote, perhaps, is the notion of romantic love, so familiar to us but so rare among primitive peoples. Here again individuation is implicit, for romantic love involves both the individuated self and the individuated other.

In summary, the Northwest Californian ethics placed the focus of moral responsibility upon the individual, a moral responsibility which internalized the command to industriousness, self-denial and personal aggrandizement; a moral demand which produced a pattern of individual guilt and the concept of sin.

The analogy between the California and European examples of the relation between the structural and ethical aspects of society, whatever it contributes to the understanding of each system, raises questions beyond the limits of either. The light that it sheds upon the particular development of our own cultural history, to which I will return, seems secondary to certain theoretical questions which lie implicit in the analogy even though they cannot be fully met with the data at hand.

Specifically, as indicated in the introductory paragraph, it raises questions concerning the meaning and nature of functionalism. I take it that by now the broad postulate of Malinowskian functionalism, that all aspects of a single culture are interrelated, is accepted by anthropologists. Certainly the description presented above supports this idea, so far as it goes. But in this form, the theory is hardly more than a pious negation of anthropological diffusionism; it does nothing to contribute to a positive understanding of society as a dynamic phenomenon. It says only that which is must be. Merton has perhaps been the first to point up the poverty, as well as the diversity, of the functionalist conceptions.

In order to invest meaning into the term, we propose a distinction between *permissive* and *requisite* functional relationships, where the former means no more than that two cultural elements may lie side by side within a culture, whereas the latter means that one cultural element requires the other either as a necessary condition or as an inevitable consequence. Specifically, in the present instance, we would assert a *requisite* functional relationship between "protestantism" and "capitalist structure," as they have already been defined in our analysis of Northwest California society.

The concept of *requisite function* takes us away from a consideration of the particular culture, and becomes a contribution to the theory of society. For its implications are that the relationship transcends the individual culture and is required by the very nature of that phenomenon that we call society. That is, it asserts that if one element appears in any society, it must be accompanied by the second. It goes beyond the position developed by Aberle *et al.*, regarding functional prerequisites necessary to all societies. For it asserts that the quality displayed in one department of a culture will require certain particular qualities in other departments. Actually such a theoretical position underlay the very hypothesis of Weber, and significantly enough he was at pains to show that similar ideological circumstances did not prevail in those other great societies in which capitalism did not develop.

But we are in a position to say more than that there is a requisite relationship between a particular ideology and a peculiar structure; for each of these is made up of a congeries of interrelated cultural characteristics, and while the general features of each aspect of the two societies are alike, the details differ. Thus we can suggest just which of these factors are a party to this requisite social relationship and which may be viewed as incidental to it. In order to point up these details we have tabulated the several crucial elements, placing in italics, the elements which the two cultures share. We are, of course aware that a final formulation of such a requisite pattern needs additional cases of coexistence, a task that yet lies before us.

The tabulation raises to crucial importance: the use of private property and of money as a medium of exchange; the relation between the ownership of wealth on one hand and power and status on the other, as well as the individuated social structure and relatively free social mobility; it reduces the importance of industrial production, rationality in economic and social intercourse, the crucial economic phenomena of the exploitation of labor and the utilization of interest. On the ethical side, it only points up the relative unimportance of the particularistic aspects of a religion, and focuses attention upon its moral imperatives. It is important here to keep in mind that the statements in the preceding paragraph, and hence the content of the tabulation, do not in themselves deny the requisite character of the nonemphasized items as they apply internally to each of the two cultures involved. It may well be that the concept of a stern god-factor was an essential ingredient to the development of the particular kind of capitalism that the West came to know; that rational production and exploitation of labor were equally necessary to European protestantism. What the analysis does assert is

TABLE I

NORTHWEST CALIFORNIA AND EUROPEAN SIMILARITIES

Northwest California	Europe
Socio-economic Structure	
1. The hunting-gathering production	Industrial production
2. Traditional production techniques	Rational production techniques
3. *Private ownership of resources*	*Private ownership of resources*
4. *Money as a medium of exchange*	*Money as a medium of exchange*
5. Capital not profitable to owner	Interest as a source of power and wealth
6. No significant labor exploitation	Labor exploitation basic to economic organization
7. *Wealth status as a determinant of power*	*Wealth status as a determinant of power*
8. *Wealth as an indication of status*	*Wealth as an indication of status*
9. *Putative open class system*	*Putative open class system*
10. *Individuated family structure*	*Individuated family structure*
11. *Absence of fixed group orientation*	*Absence of fixed group orientation*
12. Small homogeneous communities	Increasingly urbanized communities
Ethico-religious System	
1. *Individuated moral responsibility*	*Individuated moral responsibility*
2. *Work as a moral act*	*Work as a moral act*
3. *Asceticism in appetites, food and sex*	*Asceticism in appetites, food and sex*
4. *The concepts of sin and guilt*	*The concepts of sin and guilt*
5. *Morality tales and personal preaching*	*Morality tales and personal preaching*
6. Supernatural beings and spirits	God as a stern Father
7. *Absence of priestly intercessor between man and supernatural*	*Absence of priestly intercessor between man and supernatural*
8. No concept of predestination manifest	Concept of predestination

that they are not generically functional requisites; it deprives them of a use to which they are not infrequently put, namely the imputation of broader imperatives in social life.

The concept of requisite function and the procedure for its determination is of course not limited to these two departments of culture. A similar analysis can be made for the relation between the personality characteristic of a population and its culture, particularly the child-rearing aspects. Here, as in the Weber-Tawney material, functional relationships have been postulated on the basis of one or another single cultural example, and with considerably less rigor of method or clarity of conceptualization.

It will be well to pause to examine this aspect of Hupa-Yurok culture, in part because it adds to our analysis and understanding of the culture itself, in part because it offers further exemplification of the method, and finally because there has emerged from the works of Erikson a wholly different conception of their culture from that which derives from the present analysis. We have already noted certain personality characteristics such as a compulsive concern over asceticism and industriousness, patterns of personal guilt, as well as tendencies toward hostility, competitiveness and loneliness. This group of traits has clear analogs with our own culture. Erikson describes them as anal:

> No student of psychoanalytic literature could avoid the impression that many of the Yurok "traits" correspond to the "anal character" as described by Freud and Abraham. Compulsiveness, suspiciousness, miserliness, etc., are said to characterize "anal-neurotic" individuals, that is, individuals with an infantile history of preoccupation with excretion, with a narcissistic holding on of the "treasures" of the cloaca . . . (1:296)

Psychoanalytic theory, based upon a single culture would derive such a pattern from the child-rearing practices. But Erikson discovered that the child-rearing practices focus no attention on anality; that there are no problems in overt behavior of child rearing which suggest a fixation on the anal phase, and no myth or fable reflects problems in this zone. Erikson is therefore constrained to suggest a "body focus on the *alimentary* zone, in the sense of 'the tubular food-carrying passage extending from the mouth to the anus,' with a positive educational emphasis on the mouth" (1:297).

Erikson is asserting a requisite function relationship (indeed a causal one) between child training and personality traits, but in the absence of methodology he compromises disconformity by finding the nearest loop-hole.

The Yurok-Hupa analogy to the personality formation of Western society, combined with rather radical differences in childhood training, puts a great strain on the theoretical orientation which derives the former from the latter and reduces social structure to a mere end-product. The Yurok-Hupa data and the comparisons with Western society can be brought into a common system of understanding only when we reverse the formulation. That is, the structural character of the society is one which rewards certain personality configurations so that they dominate the social scene and set the patterns. It also creates a con-figuration of demands and tensions which are transmitted through child rearing to successive generations. These patterns may express them-selves in various ways within the family system.

Let us be more explicit. The individuated pattern of social action, the internalized demands for personal success with its road theoretically open to all, the absence of fixity of social position and security in group solidarity, and the importance of property for social advancement and hence for satisfaction of the ego—all these combine to support such traits of character as aggressiveness, hostility, competitiveness, loneliness and penuriousness. Indeed, it is hard to see how a Hupa or Yurok could operate effectively in his society without these traits. That is to say, there appears to be a requisite functional relationship between these two aspects of culture.

But the cultural aspects of the early phases of maturation are not ex-onerated from all involvement. What is held in common would appear to be another requisite functional relationship, and this is an intense parental concern over the behavior of children. This is certainly charac-teristic of the modern culture in which such "anality" is manifested. It is also true of Hupa-Yurok culture, as has already been indicated, where the tensions of adult life are quickly, effectively and consciously trans-mitted to the children. We may certainly believe that such transmission would be unavoidable. At any rate it has been written into the situation for a direct and overt reason, namely, the avoidance of litigation through improper conduct of children.

Again, the concept of requisite functional relationship and the analytic device for comparison alters the specific formulation and focuses upon the necessary rather than the incidental. Significantly, the Yurok and

Hupa child training practices indicate tensions first and foremost with eating habits, secondly with sexual matters, and not significantly with toilet training.

The analysis of the ethical system and the social structure of Northwest California societies, and their analogy to the parallel forms in 16th century Europe has served several purposes. First, it presents a means of understanding the Hupa-Yurok culture itself, a culture which has long been known and frequently alluded to in the literature of anthropological theory, but which has remained enigmatic and inadequately comprehended. Secondly, it has suggested a mode of analysis that can sharpen the concept of functionalism and may lead to a better understanding of the character of the interrelatedness of cultural forms. While the specific contributions remain necessarily tentative in the absence of additional cases, the analogy is itself suggestive that there is a specific interdependence of a particular ethic to a particular social structure which is societal and hence transcends the individual culture. Such assumptions have been implicit in the past when based on only a single case, but their character is seen to alter when comparative material is introduced. This is not only true for these two facets of culture, but applies as well to such other departments as child rearing and personality formation.

Perhaps it is not too much to expect that the California analog contributes also to our understanding of the development of capitalism and its ideological supports in Western society. The case supports the theory of a necessary interrelationship, insofar as this might still be considered a matter of doubt. But it also suggests an alteration of the formula, for the things which remain constant between the two cultures are not precisely what the historians and the sociologists have felt should be emphasized. Always recognizing that the individual culture has its own involvements, its own necessary conditions and inevitable consequences; still, the priority of such factors as rationality in production, of labor exploitation, of interest on capital, would appear to be an overemphasis. From the sociological point of view, the undermining of the basis for the established elite, the movement of population to urban centers and the consequent breaking down of both spatial and status confinements take on a greater importance. It is the social structure, rather than the specific economic implementation of that structure, which seems to have crucial involvement with the ethical system.

$\mathcal{B}$alanophagy" is the eating of acorns, although many people believe that the term must somehow refer to whales. Throughout California, most of the Great Basin and in the Plateau, in the Southwest, in the Eastern Woodlands, in fact, very nearly wherever the oak tree grows—man uses its fruit as food. Making acorns palatable, however, usually requires special tactics. Although acorns from some species are low in tannic acid and may be eaten without treatment, most require that the acid content be reduced in some way. Following processing, the residue of the nut forms a mush which has few characteristics normally associated by Americans with food: it tends (1) to have the consistency of a gelatinous, crunchy peanut butter, (2) to be gritty with sand, (3) to have a semifluorescent surface color reminiscent of gentian violet, and (4) to have a flavor which is a cross between alumized sour cream and Grapenuts. All that really can be said in its favor is that it is an extremely substantial food, of which with a little exposure, one can become extremely fond. Many present-day California Indians, no less than their forebearers, depend on the acorn at least as a garnish to some meals, if no longer as a staple food.

27 Edward W. Gifford

THE USE OF ACORNS IN CALIFORNIA*

Balanophagy, or acorn eating, was probably the most characteristic feature of the domestic economy of the Californian Indians. In fact, the habit extended from Lower California northward through the Pacific states practically wherever oaks grew. The northern limit of abundant oaks was the Umpqua divide in Oregon. Beyond that they were relatively rare and played a correspondingly small part in the native dietary. A few grew in the Willamette valley and in the Puget Sound region.

Wherever hard seeds or grains are eaten, some sort of pulverizing or

* Excerpt from "California Balanophagy," by E. W. Gifford, in *Essays in Anthropology Presented to A. L. Kroeber.* Berkeley: Univ. California Press, 87–98, 1936.

403

grinding device is employed, in order to render the food assimilable. Acorns do not belong in this class of foods. The nuts can be masticated as readily as walnuts or almonds. The universal use of grinding or pulverizing implements on the one hand and the limited distribution of acorn pulverizing on the other hand, point to the likelihood that the former is exceedingly ancient and the latter far less so, and that the acorn industry has here and there taken over the grinding process, not because of the hardness of the food, but for the sake of reducing it to meal, or to aid in leaching it. In California this is further apparent when it is noted that the same species of acorns which were pulverized were sometimes treated by immersion or burial and eaten without pulverizing.

The crux of the Californian acorn industry is the removal of the objectionable tannic acid from the nuts. The discovery of the relatively rapid process of leaching pulverized acorns made available a vast new food supply of high nutritive value. It is likely that once this discovery was made it spread rapidly and resulted in a greatly increased consumption of acorns. It is probable that the cruder method of rendering acorns edible by immersing them in water or mud, without pulverizing, was the antecedent of leaching the pulverized nuts in a sand basin or basket. The immersion or burial method, sometimes accompanied by boiling or roasting of the nuts, was employed to some extent among the Yurok, Hupa, Shasta, Pomo, and Yuki, the last-named burying the acorns in a sandy place with grass, charcoal, and ashes, and then soaking them in water from time to time until they became sweet. Gunther mentions burial or immersion for the Klallam, Nisqually, and Snohomish, and Spier and Sapir describe burial in mud by the Wishram. It should be emphasized that the immersion method dispenses entirely with the mortar and pestle.

Certain species of acorns apparently have less tannic acid than others. Among the Shasta, *Quercus chrysolepis* acorns were sometimes roasted in ashes and eaten without any preliminary burying or boiling. However, burial whole in mud for several weeks was the customary treatment for these acorns.

The striking thing about the acorn eating of the American Pacific coast is the well-nigh universal knowledge of leaching, attributable no doubt to diffusion rather than separate inventions. Leaching of pulverized meal had the advantage of rendering edible at once the acorns which otherwise had to undergo months of immersion in mud and water. The time necessary for the spread of the leaching process throughout the oak districts of California was probably brief. Judged by the rapidity of the spread of maize and tobacco cultivation among primitive peoples in the Old World in post-Columbian times, it seems likely that two or three centuries would be ample for the spread of so important a discovery as the leaching of acorn meal over so small an area as California. However, as to when it spread—whether 1000 years ago or 10,000 years ago—there is as yet no clue.

The uniformity of the Californian acorn-meal leaching process, either in a sand basin or in a basket, contrasts with the multiplicity of pulverizing devices and seems to indicate that leaching carried with it no special pulverizing device, but rather superimposed itself on the local varieties of pulverizing devices which had already developed. Possibly some methods of pulverizing developed after leaching was introduced, but no method is wholly limited to acorns.

Cabrillo's expedition was the first to record the use of acorns in California, but the account, which refers to the Santa Barbara region in 1542, makes no mention of leaching.

Removal of tannic acid by immersion or burial of the nuts is obviously a simple process which might be arrived at through testing the qualities of accidentally immersed acorns. Pulverizing and leaching are more complicated and involved processes, and appear as inventions to improve and hasten the tannic acid removal. The overlapping distribution of the two methods seems to indicate their genetic relationship. Reason dictates that immersion was the earlier process.

However, if leaching is a process which formed part of the original stock of culture of the ancestors of the American Indians, and not an independent Californian invention, we may look upon manioc leaching in South America and acorn and buckeye leaching in California as based upon this early knowledge. But, that leaching is such an ancient invention is by no means assured. The absence of leaching for acorns in the Southeastern area of the United States makes the case dubious. However, there the interest in extracting oils and the development of agriculture may have obliterated an earlier leaching complex. With the development of agricultural products a people would hardly resort to leaching acorns, except in time of famine.

If there was no widespread fundamental concept of leaching, then California would appear to be a region in which the leaching process was independently invented. The only clue, and that uncertain, as to the part of California in which the invention might have been made, is offered by the number of plants treated by leaching. Nevertheless, this criterion is dubious, as a people learning to leach acorns may have been enterprising enough to test the method for other likely foods. However, the opposite case is offered by the Yavapai of Arizona, who leach iron-wood seeds by boiling, but have not applied the method to acorns.

In regard to the acorn industry on the Pacific coast, California seems central, Washington marginal. At least, this view is dictated by the methods of tannin removal. For Oregon it is to be noted that the Takelma leached.

Leaching in a sandy shallow depression or basin seems characteristic of the northwestern Californian culture area and most of the central Californian culture area. The Luiseño and Cahuilla were the only southerners reported to employ this method, but they also employed the southern method of leaching in a basket. The Costanoan and Sierra Miwok of central California also employed both methods. Peoples reported using the sand basin only were the Yokuts, Western Mono, Eastern Mono, Patwin, Southern Maidu, Northern Maidu, Pomo, Chimariko, Hupa, and Yurok. Beals reports leaching on bare hard ground for the Southern Maidu, which may be a degeneration from the sand basin reported by Powers. Reported to employ only the basket leacher were the Salinan, Gabrielino, and Southern Diegueño. The Shasta employed a device which seems to have been sort of a compromise between the sand-basin leacher and the basket leacher. The Kamia used a sand basin covered with a layer of foliage. Some Eastern Mono lined the leaching basin with bark.

Coniferous twigs used to break the fall of the water in leaching acorn meal are recorded for the Miwok, Nisenan, Northern Maidu, Pomo, and Yuki, but probably are used by other tribes, too.

None of the Californian peoples extracted the oil of acorns, as was done in the Southeastern area, where it was used in preparing food and to anoint the body. Chesnut states that oil was extracted by boiling the nuts in water containing the ash of maple wood.

As might be expected among pottery-using peoples, acorn meal was boiled in pots among some Eastern Mono, the Southern Diegueño, the Luiseño, and the Kamia, and in steatite vessels among the Gabrielino. Probably other pottery-using peoples did likewise, but there is no record. Stone boiling of the meal in baskets was the customary central and northwestern practice.

The storage of acorns or corresponding food supplies is provided for in three ways in California. All the southern tribes construct a large receptacle of twigs irregularly interlaced like a bird's nest. This is sometimes made with a bottom, sometimes set on a bed of twigs and covered in the same way. The more arid the climate, the less does construction matter. Mountain tribes make the receptacle with bottom and lid and small mouth. In the open desert the chief function of the granary is to hold the food together and it becomes little else than a short section of hollow cylinder. Nowhere is there any recognizable technique. The diameter is from two to six feet. The setting is always outdoors, sometimes on a platform, often on bare rocks, and occasionally on the ground. The Chumash did not use this type of receptacle.

In central California a cache or granary is used which can also not be described as a true basket. It differs from the southern form in usually being smaller in diameter but higher, in being constructed of finer and softer materials, and in depending more or less directly in its structure on a series of posts which at the same time elevate it from the ground. This is the granary of the tribes in the Sierra Nevada, used by the Wintun, Maidu, Miwok, and Yokuts, and in somewhat modified form—a mat of sticks covered with thatch—by the Western or mountain Mono. It has penetrated also to those of the Pomo of Lake County who are in direct communication with the Wintun.

In the remainder of California, both north and south, large baskets —their type of course determined by the prevailing style of basketry— are set indoors or perhaps occasionally in caves or rock recesses.

Wherever tan oak acorns (*Pasania* [formerly *Quercus*] *densiflora*) were obtainable they seem to have been preferred. This is essentially a northern coast species. Among the other species, the preference varied: *Quercus kelloggii* (*californica*) with the Southern Maidu or Nisenan, Miwok, Shasta, Luiseño; *Quercus dumosa* with the Cahuilla; *Quercus gambeli* with the Southern Maidu (although Beals mentions black oak, presumably *Quercus kelloggii*); *Quercus kelloggii, Quercus chrysolepis,* and *Quercus wislizenii* with the Northern Maidu; and *Quercus agrifolia* with the Pomo. The distribution of the various species of oaks was largely the determining factor as to the species most highly regarded by each tribe and as to the number of species used by each tribe. After *Pasania densiflora, Quercus kelloggii* seems to have been the favorite.

The leaching out of the tannic acid after the nut meats had been reduced to meal seems to have been limited to the Pacific coast. In central Arizona only sweet acorns were eaten by the Yavapai, and the bitter ones neglected. The acorns of *Quercus oblongifolia* were obtained by the Pima from the Papago by trade. After the hulls had been removed they were parched and ground into meal. Consequently, in Arizona a vast supply of bitter acorns was neglected as food. In southern California, the Diegueño, close linguistic relatives of the Yavapai, were thoroughly familiar with leaching. It would seem that the separation of these two groups took place before leaching of acorns was invented, or at least before it had become known to them. It is entirely possible, of course, that the Diegueño, moving into California, came in touch with people already familiar with leaching. Between the Yavapai and Diegueño lies a 200–300-mile stretch of oakless desert country.

Thus, a more or less concentric distribution appears for the methods of acorn utilization in the western United States—a highly specialized leaching process bordered by an area in which only sweet acorns, unleached, were utilized. To the southward, in the highlands of Mexico, lies the peripheral area of complete neglect of acorns. This concentric distribution in western America seems to indicate complete separation from the acorn-boiling area of the Eastern Woodlands.

The second extensive American area of acorn leaching lies in the Eastern Woodlands. It extends, Professor Speck writes me, "from Ontario east to western Maine (perhaps farther east if we had data) and in southern New England to the Narragansett." In addition, the Delaware now residing in Oklahoma eat acorns of two species (bur oak and pin oak) which are roasted. The boiling of acorns was the method of removing tannic acid in the Eastern Woodlands. It preceded pulverizing, whereas the Californian leaching succeeded pulverizing.

The eating of sweet acorns, that is, those containing little tannin, is probably an expectable phenomenon. Such are offered for sale in the markets of Tucson, Arizona, where they are much relished by the Papago and other aborigines. Farther south, however, the Mexicans neglect acorns as food, which seems strange considering their vogue in Spain. Dr. Ralph L. Beals, who has studied various western Mexican tribes, notably Mayo, Yaqui, and Mixe, could find no evidence of human consumption of acorns, even though the higher mountains of Oaxaca where the Mixe live are clothed with great oak forests. Trelease enumerates 253 Mexican species of the genus *Quercus* as against only 84 in the United States.

It should be noted that the acorn-leaching areas (California and Eastern Woodlands) of the New World are in the northern portion of the American oak area which stretches southward to Colombia. In other words, leaching is in the oak regions nearest Asia. As between Middle

American and Asiatic origins for leaching, if the possibility of independent invention could be eliminated, the choice would fall to an Asiatic source. The fading, concentric distribution of acorn utilization in America—leaching, eating sweet acorns only, eating no acorns—roughly parallels the distribution of sinew-backed and simple bow, paddle-and-anvil pottery and that made without paddle and anvil, tailored clothing and no tailored clothing, moccasins and no moccasins, and various other cultural features of North America which connect with the Old World rather than with Middle America.

*A*ll *human societies attempt to control human sexual behavior; and if heterosexual behavioral patterns are everywhere regarded by the majority as the normal, the desirable, the ideal, human cultures must also deal with at least one other human potential—homosexuality—a behavioral alternative probably practiced in all human societies by men, by women, or by members of both sexes. Some societies permit and, under some circumstances such as initiation ceremonies, even encourage widespread homosexual relations. Other societies (the contemporary United States, for example) hide, deny, and even persecute the hapless victims of sexual urges and interests still not well understood by medical or social scientists. As is apparent in the following article, the Mohave regard homosexuals as humorous and deviant; nonetheless the society provides a status for them. Many American Indian societies permitted homosexuals and transvestites to achieve an open, accepted relationship with other individuals and, at times, to become important social figures. Perhaps a greater understanding of potential human sexual fulfillment may be reached through examination of studies such as the following by Devereux.*

It should be noted that the Mohave Indians could be placed with equal ease within either the California or the Southwest culture area. Like other societies discussed in this book, they represent the margin rather than the core of the area in which we perforce group them.

28 *George Devereux*

HOMOSEXUALITY AMONG THE MOHAVE INDIANS*

The Mohave recognize only two definite types of homosexuals. Male transvestites, taking the role of the woman in sexual intercourse, are known as alyha·. Female homosexuals, assuming the role of the male, are known as hwame·. Their partners are not considered homosexuals, and from the evidence of our case-histories appear to have been invariably persons of bisexual tendencies, who did not go through any formal initiation and were not designated by any special name.

While there exists no mention of any transvestite Mohave culture-hero comparable to the culture-hero of the kindred Kamia, homosexuality and the initiation-ceremonies thereto pertaining are mentioned in the creation-myth—the only other section dealing with things sexual being concerned with procreation and the intimately related puberty ceremonies.

The following account was obtained from the late Ñahwera, an almost senile singer, said to be the last person to know the transvestite initiation songs. It has been further expanded by several other informants. Neither the above-mentioned singer nor the informants in question were homosexuals.

From the very beginning of the world it was meant that there should be homosexuals, just as it was instituted that there should be shamans. They were intended for that purpose. While their mothers are pregnant, they will have the usual dreams forecasting the anatomic sex of their child. Thus the mothers of alyha· dream of arrow-feathers and other male appurtenances, while the mothers of hwame· dream of feminine regalia such as beads, etc." (This is curious in view of the fact that beginning with the sixth (lunar) month of elapsed pregnancy the foeti are said to be conscious and dream of their future destinies, sharing to a certain extent their dreams with their mothers, and vice versa.) "At the same time the dreams of their mothers will also contain

* Abridged from "Institutionalized Homosexuality of the Mohave Indians," by G. Devereux, in *Human Biology*, **9**, 498–527, 1937.

certain hints of the future homosexual proclivities of the child about to be born."
(No data as to the nature of these "hints" could be obtained.) "For several
years following birth these homosexual tendencies will remain hidden. They
will come to the fore, however, previous to puberty: that is, the time when
young persons become initiated into the functions of their sex, such as hunting
or cooking, respectively. None but young people will become berdaches as a
rule. Their tendencies will become apparent early enough to cause them to be
tattooed in accordance with the tattooing pattern pertaining to their adopted
sex. Once a young person started off 'right' there is no danger of his or her
becoming homosexual (alyha· or hwame·) even if occasional unions with
homosexuals should occur. They will feel toward their possible transvestite
mate as they would feel toward a true woman, respectively man.

This point is crucial. The transvestite must attempt to duplicate the
behavior-pattern of his adopted sex and make "normal" individuals of
his anatomic sex feel toward him as though he truly belonged to his
adopted sex. Forde describes this situation very accurately. "When he
(i.e., the transvestite) came out of the dream, he put his hand to his
mouth and laughed four times. He laughed with a woman's voice and
his mind was changed from male into female. Other young people noticed this and began to feel toward him as to a woman" (2:157).

Any person who dreamt about becoming a transvestite while in the
maternal womb may turn into one. They then attend to the occupation-
pattern of their adopted sex, except that female transvestites may not be
tribal or war-leaders. Social status, however, seemed to play a certain
role. One female informant, herself a member of a chiefly family, stated
that only persons classified as ipa tahana (person really, i.e., member of
a prominent family) became transvestites, as a rule. Conversely it was
said that only "normal" persons possessing special powers, especially
shamans specializing in the cure of venereal diseases and credited with
special luck in love, may secure transvestite spouses.

OTHER DETERMINANTS OF HOMOSEXUALITY

Beyond the factor of predestination, other factors also influenced the
decision of certain persons to become transvestites.

"The chief may hold gatherings and people became transvestites through
his (spiritual) power." This statement has never been explained. "In recent
times a certain youth at Needles became a homosexual through listening to
the alyha· songs of Ñahwera, who sang his songs at feasts and funerals." (Any

song may be sung on those occasions.) "That youth was a relative of my husband. Eventually he got sores about his rectum and died. Now Ñahwera does not like to sing his songs any more.

"A boy may begin to act strangely just as he is about to reach puberty. At that time other boys try to act like grown-ups and imitate their elders. They handle bows and arrows, ride horses and hunt, and make love to little girls. These boys, however, will shun such tasks. They pick up dolls and toy with metates just as girls do. They refuse to play with the toys of their own sex. Nor will they wear a breech-clout. They ask for skirts instead. They will watch a woman's gambling game which we call the Utah-game—as though they were under a spell. This game will fascinate them. They will try to participate in this game whenever they see it." (This game consists in throwing four dice, one of which is called "male" because it is painted black, and the other "female", because it is painted red. The fall of these dice is accompanied by much obscene comment. When the red die falls on top of the black one comments like "this woman is actively copulating with her mate" are made.)

"Girls will act just the opposite. They like to chum with boys and adopt boys' ways. They throw away their dolls and metates, and refuse to shred bark or perform other feminine tasks. They turn away from the skirt and long for the breech-clout.

"Their parents will eventually notice this strange behavior and comment upon it. 'Well, he may be a boy, but he seems to be more interested in the ways of women.' Corresponding comments are made about boyish girls. Parents and relatives will sometimes try to bully them into normal behavior—especially the girls, but they soon realize that nothing can be done about it. 'If our child wishes to go that way, the only thing we can do is make it adopt the status of a transvestite.' They are not proud of having a transvestite in the family, because transvestites are considered somewhat crazy."

After the above information had been obtained a trip was taken to Needles by the present writer, his interpreter and his chief informant, to obtain the four alyha· songs from Ñahwera. The following is his account. The songs themselves are in a very old-fashioned Mohave, almost unintelligible to the younger generation and consisting of mere catchwords, in accordance with the customary Mohave style of singing.

Ever since the world began at the magic mountain Avi-kwame· it was said that there would be transvestites. In the beginning, if they were to become transvestites, the process started during their intra-uterine life. When they grew up they were given toys according to their sex. They did not like these toys however. At the beginning, the God Matavilye died at Avi-kwame·, not because he had to die, but because he wanted to set mankind an example. There is the house. He is on his death-bed and people are all around him. He tells them that their lives would be different, and some among them would turn into transvestites. Then Matavilye died. All the people went their own way but Matavilye loved mankind so much that, although he was already on his way to heaven, he returned to be cremated in our fashion. Had he not returned to us, we would have been just like the Whites: evil, cruel and grasping. He cared for us so much that he returned to be cremated on earth. If a ghost comes to visit the earth he does it because he likes the earth very much. If from underneath the cremation pit a whirlwind rises, it means a soul went in there, because it thought so much of the earth. Then all things begin in that death-house. When there is a desire in a child's heart to become a transvestite that child will act different. It will let people become aware of that desire. They may insist on giving the child the toys and garments of its true sex, but the child will throw them away and do this every time there is a big gathering. Then people prepare a skirt of shredded bark for the boy or a breech-clout for the girl. If they give them the garments worn by other members of their sex they will turn away from them. They do all they can to dissuade girls who show such inclinations. But if they fail to convince her they will realize that it cannot be helped. She will be chumming with men and be one of them. Then all those who have tried to change her conduct will gather and agree that they had done all that could be done and that the only thing for them to do was to give her the status of a transvestite. These female transvestites (hwame·) are like lewd women who also throw away their house-keeping implements, and run wild. These songs are called alyha· kwayum or alyha· kupama and are for boys. The singer refers to himself as Pameas and describes their actions in these songs.

PHYSIOLOGICAL PATTERN ASSUMED BY HOMOSEXUALS

One of the most peculiar aspects of institutionalized homosexuality is the imitation of the physiological pattern of the assumed sex by homosexuals. They resented any normal nomenclature applied to their genitalia. Alyha· insisted that their penis (moδar) be called a clitoris (havalik), their testes (hama·), labia majora (havakwit), and their anus (hivey), vagina (hiθpan). The hwame· equally resented any reference to the fact that they had vulvae, but it was not stated that they insisted on a corresponding male terminology. It is interesting to note that according to anatomic and embryologic observations the penis and clitoris, the rectum and the vagina, the scrotum and the labia are histologically of the same origin, the rectum and the vagina being formed from the hind gut of the embryo.

Since homosexuals resented such references, they were often teased in that fashion. "Just as a man would not like to be told he had a cunnus or a woman that she had a penis, so an alyha· resented references to his penis, and a hwame· remarks upon her vagina." (A certain Mohave man, upon being asked by his wife to bring her some water, exclaimed: "Perhaps I have a cunnus and should don your skirt too. Give me your skirt and you can have my breech-clout and go hunting.") "You can tease a hwame·, because she is just a woman, but if you tease an alyha·, who has the strength of a man, he will run after you and beat you up. He will assault you many days later, if he could not catch you at once." "A certain man passing by the house of an alyha· said to him in jest, 'How is your penis today?' 'Not penis, cunnus', replied the alyha· angrily. 'Well then, how big is your cunnus?' the man replied, using the word 'erection' instead of 'big.' The alyha· picked up a club and for one or two weeks tried to assault the man whenever he saw him."

Intercourse with an alyha· is surrounded by an etiquette all of its own, to which the partner had better conform "lest one should get into all sorts of trouble."

"This is what Kuwal, who had several alyha· wives, told me," the shaman said. "Kuwal had rectal and oral intercourse with his alyha· wives, but if you copulate too often rectally with an alyha· he will get hemorrhoids, just as our women do when we have too much anal intercourse with them. You may play with the penis of your *wife* when it is flaccid. I often did it, saying, 'Your cunnus is so nice and big and your pubic hair is nice and soft to touch.' Then my alyha· wife would loll about, giggling happily like this, 'hhh.' *She* was very much pleased with herself and me. *She* liked to be told about her cunnus. When alyha· get an erection, it embarrasses them, because the penis sticks out between the loose fibers of the bark-skirt. They used to have erections when we had intercourse. Then I would put my arm about them and play with the erect penis, even though they hated it. I was careful not to laugh aloud, but I chuckled inwardly. At the pitch of intercourse the alyha· ejaculate.

"Kuwal used to tell about these things in public. When we asked him why he did not tell his alyha· wife that *she* had an erection, he used to say, 'I would not dare do it. *She* would kill me. I never dared touch the penis in erection, except during intercourse. You'd court death if you did it otherwise, because they would get violent if you play with their erect penis too much.' "

It is noteworthy that in English all Mohave refer to an alyha· as *she* and to a hwame· as *he*. This becomes quite confusing to the fieldworker, at times, but also proves the highly institutionalized character of this cultural complex.

When an alyha· found a husband, he would begin to imitate menstruation. He took a stick and scratched himself between the legs until blood was drawn. This he referred to as "catamenial flow" and submitted to the whole set of puberty observances, then as well as during subsequent "menstruations." According to the Mohave pattern, when a man marries an unmenstruated girl he has to share a great deal of her puberty taboos when she menstruates for the first time. Since the alyha· claimed this to be his first menstruation, the husband had to submit *nolens volens* to the whole set of observances.

Even more curious are the pretensions of alyha· concerning their hypothetical pregnancies. When they decided to become "pregnant" they ceased faking menstruations. They observed the customary pregnancy taboos as rigidly or even more so than normal women, conforming to many obsolescent customs even, and compelling their husbands to observe their share of taboos, as befits expectant fathers. They publicly boasted of their pregnancy, even though many Mohave women deny being pregnant, even when it has become obvious to all and sundry that they were pregnant. This gave rise to never ending jests, but the alyha· paid no attention to them. In only one way did they fail to conform to the usual pregnancy pattern. Having no other means at their disposal, they continued oral and rectal intercourse with their husbands, even though the former is alleged to harm the foetus' glottis and the latter his bowels. In the absence of their husbands they stuffed rags and bark under their skirts, in increasing quantities, to make their abdomen protrude. In due time they made a decoction of mesquite beans which is said to cause severe constipation. They drank this decoction by sucking it through their teeth, which acted as a sieve and prevented the swallowing of bean-fragments.

Eventually they had severe abdominal pains for a day or two, which they dubbed labour-pains. When the faeces could not longer be withheld the alyha· went into the bushes and defecated sitting over a hole in the traditional posture of parturating women. They had no assistants, and leaned therefore against a tree, as did women who were in travail before any feminine help could be obtained. The faeces were said to be thick, dry and friable and caused a bleeding of the rectum. They then pretended that stillbirth had taken place and buried the faeces and a little log. After that they returned to the house and claimed to have given birth to a stillborn child. They had to pretend it was a stillbirth, because stillborn babies are buried whereas those dying are cremated publicly, and "such ceremonies are past joking." Yet people would hear the alyha·

wailing and mourning for the imaginary child. They clipped their hair and compelled their husbands to clip their hair in the fashion befitting the mourners. Since the Mohave never made any preparations for birth, because boys and girls had to have different cradles, no problem arose from the disposal of empty cradles.

"People used to tease me about my wives' imaginary children," Kuwal is reported as saying. "When I walked about with friends and spoke with regret of the real children I had once and of my beautiful Cocopa and Yuma wives who were real women, they used to say, 'We know all about your beautiful wives. You married those alyha· and believed them when they scratched themselves and pretended to be menstruating, or when they were pregnant with a pillow.' Or else they would kick a pile of animal dung and say, 'Those are your children.' And yet I had real children once and they died. Were they not dead they would now take care of me in my old age."

SOCIAL ASPECTS

Socially speaking Mohave civilization acted wisely perhaps in acknowledging the inevitable. This airing of the abnormal tendencies of certain individuals achieved several aims. It deprived certain modes of atypical behaviour of the glamour of secrecy and sin and of the aureola of persecution. It enabled certain persons swaying on the outskirts of homosexuality to obtain the desired experience and find their way back to the average tribal pattern without the humiliation of a moral Canossa. It created what is known as an "abscess of fixation" and localized the disorder in a small area of the body social. Last of all the very publicity given to their status did not permit homosexuals to insinuate themselves into the confidence of normal persons under false colors and profit by some temporary unhappiness of the latter to sway them. They had to compete with normal blatant sexuality not in the dark groves of Corydon and Sappho but in the open daylight, on the acknowledged playground of normal sexuality, i.e., at gatherings and feasts. This arrangement, while safeguarding homosexuals from the dangers of persecution, also made their unsuccessful courtships doubly painful because of the very publicity given to it. In creating metaphorically speaking, "reserved quarters," for permanent homosexuals and for the passing whim of bisexually inclined active male homosexuals and passive female ones, they gave the latter an opportunity to satisfy their passing longings, and left the door wide open for a return to normalcy.

SECTION VII
The Southwest

The Southwest, whose heartland is comprised of the present states of Arizona and New Mexico, is in many ways the most complicated culture area of native North America. When Coronado passed through the region in 1540, the Southwest contained the following populations: the people of the Pueblos (eighty or more villages, with at least four languages plus dozens of dialects); the Piman-speaking populations (principally the Pima-Papago of Arizona and the Opata of Northern Mexico); the Yuman-speaking groups (Walapai, Havasupai, Maricopa, Yavapai, and the groups on the Lower Colorado River—the Yuma, Mohave, Cocopa, and others); and the Athabascan-speakers (the Apache and Navaho). Nor do these populations complete the inventory. If, following the suggestions of Kirchoff in the first article in this section, we extend the limits of the Southwest to a maximum (to include parts of California, Nevada, Utah, Colorado, Texas, and all of Northwest Mexico), the list of tribes and languages becomes very long indeed.

With respect to culture types, the culture area was again exceedingly complex. In the late prehistoric period, Indians of the lower Gila River region were constructing large communities and small temple mounds; at the same time the Seri Indians on the coast of the Gulf of Lower California were collecting shellfish and cactus fruit in order to survive. As Kirchoff points out, the Southwest contained two dominant cultural orientations based chiefly on subsistence patterns: nomadism on the one hand and farming on the other.

Two realities underlie the history of cultural development in the Southwest: 1) the generally arid nature of the terrain, and 2) the position of the Southwest across the mouth of the funnel which is Northern Mexico. The aridity and general scarcity of water have forced population clustering and emphasis upon plant rather than animal food. Furthermore, the location of the Southwest *vis à vis* Mexico has insured a continuous flow of cultural materials, and perhaps people, from north to south and conversely. It is certain that the ancestors of the Indians in the southern hemisphere passed through Northern Mexico. It is equally certain that features found in the American Southwest diffused to that area from central Mexico, or perhaps from even further south. Early forms of corn, beans, and squash (C-B-S agriculture, as it is sometimes called), the subsistence mainstays of the Southwest, began to arrive as long ago as 6,000 years or more, the estimated time of arrival of primitive corn in the region. In the late prehistoric period a few hundred years prior to the arrival of the Spaniards, Indians on the Gila River (near what is now Phoenix) were building large communities with multistoried buildings, and with such features as ceremonial ball courts and pyramidal temple mounds. At the same time that influences were being felt from the south, the Southwest was experiencing the ancient process of population infiltration from the north: small groups of Athabascan-speakers (the ancestors of the present Apache and Navaho) were drifting along the eastern face of the Rocky Mountains into northern New Mexico and Arizona.

From the viewpoint of ethnography, archaeology, and anthropological linguistics, the Southwest is one of the best known regions of the world. To be sure, major problems still remain; yet all of the native populations have been studied, at least some work has been done on most of the languages, and the archaeologist is able now to consider historical and cultural questions of some detail.

29 Paul Kirchhoff

GATHERERS AND FARMERS IN THE GREATER SOUTHWEST*

Our ideas of the Southwest were originally built around the cultures of the historic and prehistoric peoples of New Mexico and Arizona, but from an early date there has been a tendency to add other groups to this nucleus. In his *Native Culture of the Southwest* Kroeber writes:

Haeberlin long ago did not hesitate to treat the southern Californians as out-right Southwestern . . . Wissler and I, in continental classifications, both extend the Southwest culture south nearly to the Tropic, so that half of it lies in Mexico. No one appears to have challenged this classification, perhaps because data from northern Mexico are so scant. (5:376)

A few years later, in 1932, Beals published "The Comparative Ethnology of Northern Mexico before 1750" in which he established a more precise southern boundary for the Southwestern area. It starts on the West Coast just to the south of the Sinaloa River, and ends on the Gulf Coast on the Soto la Marina, swinging far to the south on the North Mexican Plateau, so as to include some but not all of the nomadic nonagricultural tribes of that area. Beals seems to have regarded this part of the southern boundary as tentative, "in the absence of more defi-nite information on the nomads."

In 1939 Kroeber published his *Cultural and Natural Areas of Native North America,* which is the first, and to date only, attempt to divide the whole of North and Central America, first into a relatively large number of small culture areas and then into a few larger units. One of the larger units is the Southwest, or as Kroeber frequently calls it, the "cultural Southwest." On the American side he includes New Mexico,

* Abridged from "Gatherers and Farmers in the Greater Southwest: a Problem in Clas-sification," by P. Kirchhoff, in *American Anthropologist,* **56,** 529–560, 1954.

Arizona, and southern California, but excludes the Great Basin and central California. On the Mexican side he follows Beals' southern boundary only on the West Coast, stating that for the rest "the question of the Mexican-Southwestern frontier must be left an essentially open one for the present." Actually, east of the Sierra Madre Occidental he includes only the Tarahumara, and even them only with great doubt, counting all the remainder of northern Mexico, that is, all the gatherers and part-farmers of the North Mexican Plateau and the Gulf Coast north of Tampico, in his "Mexico and Central America."

Kroeber's grouping of the North Mexican food gatherers with Mexico-Central America or Mesoamerica may go back to Beals' earlier position when he drew the southern boundary of the Southwest across that region, adding that "this division throws a large portion of the nomadic non-agricultural peoples with the Mexican area, creating an analogous situation to that existing in the Southwest where we have virtually two types of culture coexisting in the same area" (2: 146). But at the North Mexican Conference at which I presented new data on the food gatherers and part-farmers of the northern plateau, Beals abandoned his earlier hesitation regarding the southern portion of this area and included all of it in his Greater Southwest. He argued also, in line with Drucker's earlier proposal, for a southward extension of the agricultural part of the Greater Southwest so as to include the peoples of the Sierra Madre down to and including the Cora and Huichol. (I include these peoples in Mesoamerica.)

As for the northern boundary of the Southwest, I listed in 1942 not only the whole of northern Mexico, including Baja California, but also the Great Basin as belonging to the Greater Southwest or Arid America, as I then proposed to call it, and on my 1943 map I likewise included southern coastal Texas but excluded central California which I then still considered to constitute a separate culture area. Beals, on the other hand, considered it a possibility "that large parts of Central California should be included on climatic and perhaps cultural grounds" (3:94). I have in the meantime arrived at the position that all of California, except its northwestern portion, should be included in the Greater Southwest, on both climatic and cultural grounds.

At the present time, therefore, I should define the Greater Southwest areally to include Central, Southern, and Baja California, the Great Basin, Arizona, New Mexico, southern coastal Texas, and northern Mexico south to the Sinaloa and Panuco Rivers.

NATURE AND CULTURE IN THE GREATER SOUTH-WEST: ONE CULTURE AREA OR TWO?

This large arid or semiarid area offers man on a prefarming and pre-herding level basically similar food resources throughout. These resources may be characterized as: more vegetable than animal food, and vegetable food of a specific type. The few subregions where these proportions are reversed are too small and isolated from each other to affect the total picture. One may anticipate, therefore, that on a cultural level where man essentially takes what nature offers, this broadly uniform situation should result in the formation of but one basic type of culture, in part growing out of, and in part developing around, a specific type of production.

To agricultural man the Greater Southwest offers limited opportunities for farming, in some regions without, and in others only with, irrigation. The areas open for agricultural exploitation on a premachine level are found either in the semiarid sections, or in relatively small, oasis-like portions within the arid parts. Since agriculture does not seem to have sprung up independently in any part of the Greater Southwest (all plants cultivated in pre-European days were of southern origin, except possibly the tepary bean), the utilization of the farming opportunities which the area offered depended upon the arrival, in its various sections, either of farmers or of farming techniques and products handed on from group to group. The absence of farming in areas susceptible of it, like California, is thus due not to natural limitations but to cultural limitations of a historical character—the feebleness of agricultural stimuli.

The Greater Southwest, then, offered two very different sets of conditions and opportunities to two types of culture—one found over the whole area, to gatherers, and one found over limited portions of it, to farmers. At one time in the past, gatherers seem to have lived over the whole area, and even though hunting or fishing may have been more important in particular limited localities than the gathering of vegetable food, the latter must have been the basis of the prevailing type of culture; for that period we may assume the existence of but one culture area in the Greater Southwest. But from the moment farming made its appearance in part of the area, this ceased to be the case, and the question whether we are dealing with one or two or possibly more culture areas arises at this point.

Here are what Beals calls "a few probable characteristics of this hypothetical basic culture":

Perhaps the most significant is the presence of complex techniques for dealing with a large variety of vegetable food sources to form the mainstay of
the diet. The core of the complex is the leaching process and the seed beater
and seed collecting tray, plus the use of one dominant tree-borne fruit
capable of prolonged storage; the piñon, the mesquite and, if California be
included, the acorn. All the non-farming peoples of the region are primarily
gatherers rather than hunters, sharply differentiating them from other North
American peoples. Other elements are techniques for effectively utilizing the
small rodents comprising the bulk of the fauna, social organization necessarily
consisting of small bands, but with a patrilineal bias, ceremonial emphasis
upon puberty rituals, a strong development of witchcraft and magic in place
of true shamanism, etc. (3:195)

This, I would say, is a minimal characterization not only of a
hypothetical culture of the past but of an actual one of the present, one
that exists (or rather existed until the coming of the Whites) over a
large part of western North America. Here are some other traits that
seem to form part of this culture: men go naked, women wear two
aprons, one in front and the other in back; hair worn long; men's skin
or fur cap; "woven" rabbit blanket; coned or domed hut; earth oven;
vision without quest; peacefulness. This list undoubtedly will grow considerably once systematic search begins.

I include in this area both those peoples that subsist exclusively by
gathering, and those that have added some measure of farming but
whose total culture still rests on gathering rather than farming. I also
include those peoples within the Greater Southwest who hunt or fish
more than those tribes which in their subsistence activities are more typical of the Southwestern gathering culture, since in most other respects
they conform to it.

The following subareas of the Southwestern gathering culture may be
distinguished (the order in this enumeration is arbitrary, starting in the
southwest and ending in the southeast):

1. Sonora-Sinaloa Coast (Seri and Guasave)
2. Baja California
3. Southern California
4. Central California
5. Great Basin

6. Northwest Arizona (Yavapai, Walapai, Havasupai)
7. Apache
8. Northern Mexico

Some of the local variations seem to be the result of adaptations to varying ecological conditions. In some restricted localities fishing was more important than gathering of vegetable food, and at some time in the past, when the wooded regions of higher altitude were still in the hands of the gatherers, the latter may have been much more hunters than any of the tribes encountered by the Spaniards. Other local variations may reflect the earlier culture of certain tribes before they either immigrated into the region (Athabascans) or adapted themselves to its increasing aridity. Still other local variations are due to different outside influences.

We may assume that at one time in the past the Southwestern gathering culture was found throughout the Greater Southwest. The arrival from the south of a culture, or possibly several cultures, based on farming reduced the area of the gathering culture considerably, and several of the tribes that shared it may have become geographically disconnected from the main body. Later developments—the withdrawal of some sections of the farming culture from their advanced positions, and possibly the deculturation of others, together with the incorporation into the gathering culture of the Southwest of new arrivals from the north, like the Athabascans—again increased the territory occupied by the gathering culture and re-established geographical continuity among most of its sections.

THE FARMING CULTURE OF THE GREATER SOUTHWEST

Once we eliminate from the traditional Southwest or Greater Southwest culture area the gatherers and part-farmers, we are left with five of Kroeber's "Southwestern" culture areas, viz., Pueblo, Navaho, Cáhita, Pima-Opata, Tarahumara, and Lower Colorado. All these tribes are true farmers in the sense that their culture as a whole, or at least decisive parts of it, has either grown out of or developed around farming as the principal basis of subsistence.

We find, however, marked differences in cultural level and in the degree to which these tribes participate in the most significant aspects of the Southwestern farming culture, between the two "hubs"—the Pueblos and the Pima-Opata. Even within the latter subarea differences are pronounced between the most highly developed and characteristic Lower Pima and Opata, and the considerably simpler Upper Pima, who have quite a number of traits and complexes found in the Southwestern gathering culture. Still less typical is Papago culture which appears to be an impoverished version of Upper Pima culture. But even though the economic importance of farming among the Papago may be lower than among some part-farmers, they have very aptly been called "desert Indians with an agricultural heritage," and on the basis of an evaluation of their agriculture-centered culture as a whole they have to be included in the Southwestern farming culture.

Among the River Yumans agriculture is proportionately more important than among the Papago and it seems to be old (there are even a few agricultural practices unknown to their neighbors), but the role of agriculture in shaping their culture as a whole is less clear than among the Papago. This is undoubtedly due in part to the fact that whereas Pagago culture is an impoverished variant of Pima culture—the inclusion of which in the Southwestern farming culture seems obvious— River Yuman culture in many ways stands quite by itself. Its sociopolitical and specially military organization (which recalls that of certain parts of Mesoamerica) puts these tribes on a level far above that of any of the typical members of the Southwestern gathering culture, and all in all they appear as part of the Southwestern farming culture, though possibly its most divergent part.

My inclusion of the Navaho in the Southwestern farming culture rests not only on the quantitative importance of farming in their economy—Hill ranks them in this respect with the Pueblos, and higher than any other Southwestern tribe—but on the great elaboration of agricultural ritual, which must mean an old and deep-rooted farming complex.

The greater or lesser number of traits and complexes typical of the Southwestern gathering culture which we encounter among the less developed and less typical members of the Southwestern farming culture may be either survivals from a prefarming state, or indications of deculturation and a general weakening of the vigor of the farming culture. Their presence, usually coupled with a lower level of general cultural complexity, has created a number of border cases where assignment either to the Southwestern gathering or farming culture is difficult, but these cases are definitely exceptional, and on the whole the basic contrast between the two regional cultures of the Greater Southwest stands out in bold relief.

There is considerable diversity within the Southwestern farming culture quite aside from differences of level, and when seen only in terms of that culture it may appear so important as to make us wonder whether we are really dealing with one, rather than with two or several, regional cultures. But when contrasted with the Southwestern gathering culture on the one hand, and Mesoamerican culture on the other, the Southwestern farming culture appears as a unit, though a richly variegated one. This situation, however, may be relatively recent. It is quite possible, and in fact likely, that migrations and influences from the south reached the Southwest at different times and over different routes, and that according to the region from which they came they brought different cultural assortments which stimulated different cultural growths, and that these only subsequently fused into one regional culture, different both from that of the earlier inhabitants of the region and from the mother-culture or cultures to the south.

I propose to divide the Pueblos into two subareas: Hopi-Zuni-Keres-Jemez, with exogamous matrilineal clans, multiple kiva organization, emergence from underground, multiple worlds, four or six directions beginning in the north, four and seven as ritual numbers; and the Tanoan-speaking Pueblos, except Jemez, with nonexogamous patrilineal clans, two kivas or two groups of kivas and a general dualism in political and ceremonial organization, emergence from underwater, five directions beginning in the east, and three and its multiples, especially twelve, as ritual numbers. A fuller investigation would undoubtedly multiply the number of specific differences by many times. In spite of the obvious and well-known features which they have in common, these two groups (which do not quite correspond to the customary subdivision into "Western" and "Easter" Pueblos) appear as different from each other as any two of the four agricultural subareas in Kroeber's "Sonora-Gila-Yuma" division.

Together with the Navaho, the Hopi-Zuni-Keres-Jemez and the Tanoan Pueblos form a regional subculture, even though each of the two Pueblo groups, and interestingly enough especially the eastern (Tanoan) one, has a significant number of traits in common with the Pima and Papago (the Opata are too little known to show such resemblances). The traits common to the Tanoan Pueblos and the Pima-Papago (nonexogamous patrilineal clans, a red-white dualism, permanent race tracks, religious leaders who are shamans rather than priests, and specific beliefs, such as, e.g., that enemy scalps may be noisy) seem to be quite old, and some of them are found among the Shoshoneans of Southern California, all of these speaking languages of the Tano-Aztecan group.

Of the four remaining subareas the first three (Cáhita, Pima-Opata, and Tarahumara), all Uto-Aztecan in speech, form another regional subculture. The Hokan-speaking Yumans of the Lower Colorado and Gila stand apart culturally as well as linguistically.

There would then be seven subareas in the farming culture of the Greater Southwest, grouped in three regional subcultures:

1. Tanoan-speaking Pueblos
2. Hopi-Zuni-Keres-Jemez
3. Navaho
4. Cáhita
5. Pima-Opata
6. Tarahumara
7. River Yumans

CONCLUSION

I hope to have demonstrated that, in spite of having been in contact with each other over a long span of time, the two regional cultures of the Greater Southwest have retained their separate identities till the present day. Once separated conceptually, the study of their historical relationships with each other and with other regional cultures, as well as their inclusion in world-wide "types" of culture, become meaningful and useful. The so much older gathering culture appears as one of the most strongly characterized regional variants of the world's food-gathering cultures, and the younger farming culture as a pioneer off-shoot of the great civilizations to the south.

It would be useful to separate these cultures in name as well as in con-cept. Since the descriptive names which I have used in this paper are clumsy, I propose for that of the gatherers the name "Arid America" and "Arid American Culture," and for that of the farmers "Oasis America" and "American Oasis Culture." This implies the abandon-ment of the terms "Southwest" and "Greater Southwest" with refer-ence to a regional type or types of culture, and their use in the future only in the geographical sense.

After much initial hesitation I have come to like the contrast between the two terms proposed, because one, Arid America, stresses the essential dependence of man on nature at a food-gathering level, and the other, Oasis America, his more active intervention on a farming level, through the creation of agricultural and cultural oases in an arid region.

~~~~~~

The Hopi, though not the most typical of the Pueblo people, are one of the best known. The following paper outlines behavior in a society that has a strong emphasis upon matrilineal kinship. Such systems are particularly characteristic of simple agricultural societies in which women tend to do most of the day-to-day agricultural work. The term "matrilineal" should not be confused with the term "matriarchal." Even though one's name, one's right to property or to an office, the regulation of one's possible marriage partners, and even one's residence, are based on one's relationship to women, men nevertheless have great power in Hopi society. A man may have relatively little influence over his own children, but he has very great influence over his sister's children, and ultimately over his sister's daughters' children. The following selection is taken from one of the best and most comprehensive studies ever made of social organization in a relatively simple society.

30 Fred Eggan

THE KINSHIP BEHAVIOR OF
THE HOPI INDIANS*

Despite the voluminous literature available, the social organization of the Pueblos, except in broad outline, is but imperfectly understood. For many groups we have no detailed information at all; for others the ac-

* Abridged from *Social Organization of the Western Pueblos*, by F. Eggan. Chicago: Univ. Chicago Press, 1–42, 1950.

counts are conflicting or confused. The current classifications of Pueblo social organization reflect this situation and are therefore neither comprehensive nor accurate, with the result that historical inferences are frequently misleading and that wider generalizations rest on a faulty base. There are various reasons for this situation—the complexity of Pueblo social structures, the difficulties in the way of ethnographical investigations, particularly in the eastern Pueblos, and the interest of many investigators in other problems and aspects of Pueblo life. The following study is an attempt to remedy this situation, so far as the data allow, for one group of villages—the western Pueblos.

The Pueblos form a cultural unit for comparison with other groups, but closer examination makes it possible to establish various divisions based upon differences in location, language, or institutions. The basic cultural division which is recognized is that between the eastern Pueblos of the Upper Rio Grande drainage and the western Pueblos of the mesa and canyon country to the west. From the standpoint of social organization the situation is more complex. It is not possible at present to deal adequately with the eastern Pueblos—a preliminary survey suggests two or possibly three types of social structure for this group. The far western Pueblos, on the other hand, appear to conform to a single basic type of social structure. To this type the more western Keresan-speaking villages of Acoma and Laguna also belong, so that, for our purposes, the western Pueblos consist of the Hopi villages, Hano, Zuni, Acoma, and Laguna. The line of cleavage is not a sharp one; rather there is a gradual shift in most social institutions as one travels from west to east. Jemez, which is intermediate in certain respects, I have arbitrarily classed with the eastern groups.

These western Pueblos, with the exception of Hano and Laguna, were found by Coronado and his followers in essentially the same locations which they occupy today. Hano was settled by Tewa-speaking peoples who migrated from the Rio Grande region around 1700; Laguna was founded at about the same time by Keresan-speaking migrants from the same region. In historic times these villages have been more isolated from Spanish and American contacts than their eastern neighbors, a factor which needs to be considered in evaluating differences in social organization as well as in religion.

Four linguistic stocks are represented in the Pueblos. In the east are villages speaking various dialects of Tanoan—Tiwa, Tewa, and Towa, the Tewa-speaking Hano being settled among the Hopi. The bulk of the Keresan-speaking villages are likewise in the Rio Grande region, though we have classed Acoma and Laguna with the west. Zuni has its own language, while the Hopi belong with the extensive Uto-Aztekan stock. These linguistic differences suggest different historical origins for certain of the Pueblo peoples and furnish a control for comparisons within the group.

The geographical environment is remarkably uniform throughout the Pueblo area, particularly in the western portions. Here is a high plateau with a distinctive topography—mesas, canyons, and dry washes. The climate is solar and semiarid, with daily and seasonal extremes of temperature and a scanty precipitation distributed primarily in the form of local thunder-showers during the summer months. In the east the higher altitude provides a somewhat greater rainfall and cooler temperature; more important, the Rio Grande and its tributaries furnish a relatively constant water supply in contrast to the greater dependence upon rainfall and seepage in the western villages. The vegetation is characteristic of semiarid regions; the fauna is less specialized than the flora and not very numerous. In the recent past antelopes, deer, mountain sheep, mountain lions, wolves, coyotes, wildcats, bears, badgers, rabbits, and numerous smaller mammals and birds were to be found in the region. Despite their present primary dependence on agriculture, the Pueblo peoples formerly made considerable use of the available flora and fauna, and, as symbols, they pervade the social and ceremonial life.

The external adjustment of the Pueblos to this environment, with minor differences, follows one pattern. The people live in compact communities with stone or adobe houses grouped around plazas, often rising in terraced tiers. These dwellings not only affect the outward appearance of the villages but often reflect their internal organization as well. Each pueblo depends primarily on agriculture for subsistence, corn, beans, and squash being the primary crops, supplemented by plants and animals introduced by the Spaniards. Material culture, including the arts of weaving, pottery, and basketry, is everywhere unmistakably Pueblo. Internal organization, on the other hand, follows several patterns, as we have noted above.

Within the geographical and ecological area which houses the Pueblos are other peoples who are sharply separated in many respects, despite the opportunities for contact and the similarities in environment. For the Pueblo area itself, it may be said that in material culture on the one hand, and in the ideas, beliefs, and sentiments on the other, there is a remarkable unity. Each village has achieved a social integration which has been strong enough to keep the society from disintegration, if not from change.

The Hopi villages, most western and isolated of the Pueblo groups, are located on a series of finger-like projections from Black Mesa in northeastern Arizona. This region is part of the arid and dissected Colorado Plateau which here averages some 6,000 feet in height; drainage is southwestward into the Little Colorado. Rainfall is scarce and variable, averaging only some ten inches per year and falling largely during the summer months. Hack has discussed in detail the geological and geographical factors involved in the Hopi water supply; these have enabled a small population to reside in this area since the later Basketmaker period, dating back to approximately the sixth century A.D.

At the time of Coronado there were some seven Hopi villages on four mesas, but after the Pueblo Rebellion of 1680 important changes took place in the region. Awatovi was abandoned or destroyed around 1700, and other villages located on lower spurs moved to the mesa tops. At this time also a group of Tewa-speaking peoples from the Rio Grande settled Hano, and other refugees from the same region took up temporary abode. Population growth and internal dissension led to further village-building, with the result that today there are some eleven villages, distributed as follows: On First Mesa are Walpi, and its "suburb" Sichomovi, and the Tewa-speaking Hano; on Second Mesa are Mishongnovi, Shongopavi, and the latter's semicolony, Shipaulovi; and on Third Mesa, down to 1906, was Oraibi. Oraibi had occupied the same location long before the arrival of the Spaniards and was by far the largest village; in 1906 internal dissension led to the founding of Hotevilla and Bakavi, and further defections to New Oraibi at the foot of the mesa and to the former summer colony at Moencopi left Oraibi a mere shell of its former self.

The present population of the Hopi villages is around thirty-five hundred, an average of about three hundred to a village. The seventeenth- and eighteenth-century estimates were much larger and probably somewhat exaggerated, but famines and disease have operated to reduce the number severely on occasions. For a long time the population remained more or less stationary at a little over two thousand; in the last decade there has been a gradual increase, brought about by a number of factors. This increase threatens to intensify the situation with reference to their neighbors, the Navaho.

From both a cultural and a geographical standpoint the Hopi represent the westernmost outpost of Pueblo life. Their nearest Pueblo neighbors, the Zuni, are some two hundred miles to the southeast, while the Navaho, recent comers to the Hopi region, now completely surround them. Despite their geographical position, their culture is in no sense marginal but is thoroughly Pueblo. To the west there is a sharp cultural break, though the neighboring Navaho have borrowed much and have given much in return. Because the Spaniards did not return in any force after the Pueblo Rebellion, the Hopi lack certain political and religious institutions imposed on other Pueblos, though they have shared in the material benefits which the Spanish brought.

Each major village is politically independent; the Hopi have acted together only on occasions when their welfare has been seriously threatened or when forced by government pressure. What tribal unity there is lies in their common language and culture. With the exception of Hano, there are only slight dialectic differences from mesa to mesa, and the social and cultural patterns encompass the entire tribe.

A preliminary examination reveals that each village is divided into a series of matrilineal, totemically named clans which are linked or grouped in nameless but exogamous phratries. Each clan is composed of one or more matrilineages, which, though nameless, are of great importance. The basic local organization is the extended family based on matrilocal residence and occupying a household of one or more rooms in common. In addition, there are various associations, both societies and kiva groups, which are involved in the performance of the calendric ceremonies. The structure, social functions, and interrelations of these groups can be best seen in the light of an analysis of the kinship system.

For the Hopi the kinship system is the most important element in their social structure. If kinship is considered as based on genealogical relations which are socially recognized and which determine social relations of all kinds between persons so related, the Hopi have emphasized the *social recognition* at the expense of the *genealogical relations* and have used kinship relations and behavior in ceremonial as well as daily life.

The basic relationships are those between the members of the elementary family, but, because of conditions of descent and residence, certain other relationships of a more distant order come to have great importance among the Hopi. The general relationship and pattern of behavior prevailing between each pair or set of relatives will be outlined;

this will be followed by a summary of the duties and obligations of relatives in connection with the life-cycle. Such an account should illuminate
the native values ascribed to the terminology, as well as the relation of
the individual to the household and clan, and the nature of the correlation between kinship terminology and behavior.

The relation of a father to his child is of a different order from the
relation of a woman to her children. A child belongs to the mother's
lineage and clan but is a "child" of the father's clan; although both are
recognized as kin, the two parental groups are rather sharply differentiated in attitudes, behavior, and residence. The father's obligations to his
sons are primarily economic. While he helps select a "ceremonial father" and makes bows and arrows for his sons at Katcina ceremonies, he
is mainly responsible for preparing them to make a living. He teaches
them to farm and herd sheep, often going into partnership with them in
herding activities. When a son marries, his father may give advice and
aid in the preparations; frequently he will present him with a portion of
the flock and a piece of spare land as well.

The position of a father in relationship to his son is something like
that of an older comrade and teacher. There is affection but little in the
way of punishment, and, while a boy respects his father, he does not ordinarily fear him. In certain respects the relationship is also conceived of
as a reciprocal one. A father teaches his son how to make a living and furnishes him with sheep and other property; in return a father will be
supported in his old age by his sons. A father likewise buries his sons,
and he in turn is buried by one of them, the latter receiving a larger
share of the father's personal property for this service.

The Hopi normally make little distinction between the father and the
father's brothers, although behavior toward more distant "fathers" may
be much attenuated. Close ties are frequently found between a father's
brother and his brother's son; other "fathers" may have close relations
as the result of special circumstances. The "ceremonial father" has the
special duty of seeing his "son" through the various initiations, while
the doctor who brings a child back to life from a severe illness is also considered as a "father." A Hopi's primary obligation is to those "fathers"
who have taken an interest in him and aided him on various occasions.
Since all men of the father's clan and phratry are "fathers," it is possible
to have "fathers" much younger than their "sons"; in such cases the
Hopi preserve the same pattern of behavior but reverse the relationship, the "son" helping the "father" while the latter is growing up and
the "son" being aided in turn when he is old.

The relations of a father to his daughter are more limited in scope. He contributes to his daughter's upbringing but has few specific duties, beyond making Katcina dolls and aiding in the activities surrounding her marriage. The relation of a daughter to her father is affected by his behavior toward her mother and the rest of the household. It is generally affectionate but not very close; when crises arise, the father is usually blamed and often treated as an outsider. Since divorce is common, a girl may have one or more stepfathers whose behavior may be variable.

The mother-daughter relationship, in contrast, is an exceedingly close one, based on clan ties, common activities, and life-long residence together. Sex solidarity is strong among the Hopi, exemplified in the kinship groupings, division of labor, and attitudes toward children. A woman with a female child considers her life complete or at least well under way.

The mother is responsible for both the economic and the ritual training of her daughters. She teaches them to grind corn, to cook, to take care of babies, to plaster and repair houses, and to make baskets, plaques, and pottery. She chooses a "ceremonial mother" to look after their initiations into the Katcina cult and the woman's societies, and she may transmit ritual knowledge pertaining to the clan to one or more of them. At puberty, marriage, and the birth of her daughter's children, the mother has important duties.

A daughter's behavior in most cases is reciprocally one of respect and obedience as well as affection. A good daughter aspires to follow her mother's example and rarely acts in opposition to her wishes, even after she is married and has children. Normally she continued to reside with her mother after marriage, though modern conditions are making it easier to set up a separate household.

The position of the mother's sister is practically identical with that of the mother. She normally lives in the same household and aids in the training of her sister's daughter for adult life. Other clan "mothers" may help on occasion, but usually they are primarily concerned with their own children. The "ceremonial mother" has an important role on ritual occasions and often on others as well.

The relation of a mother to her son is almost as close as that with her daughter, particularly in early life. Even after he leaves home at marriage a son frequently returns for aid and advice. A mother encourages her son not to be lazy and to help his father. She has the primary decision as to his "ceremonial father" and repays the latter with food and gifts. While she does not control the marriage arrangements, she plays an important role in the wedding activities. Her home always remains his "real home"; here he keeps much of his personal and ritual property, here he brings guests, and here he returns in case of separation and divorce. A man shows great respect for his mother as head of the household, consulting her on all important questions. Rarely do mother and son fail to get along, though there may be occasional conflicts with more distant "mothers."

The bond between husband and wife varies with time and circumstances but is seldom very close. Their primary loyalties are to their own lineages and clans, and the ties holding them together are tenuous and easily broken to begin with. The marked sexual dichotomy gives them somewhat different spheres of interest and activity, and their relationship is one of co-operation rather than companionship. In Hopi theory the best farm lands are owned by clans and divided among the households; the women own the houses and the crops. A husband has the economic obligation of helping to support not only his wife but the whole household, and, as such, his efforts are often criticized, with resultant separations.

A wife has certain obligations to her husband. She must wash and care for her husband's hair, particularly for ceremonies, and she must prepare food and extend hospitality to his guests on feast days or other occasions. At such times there may be restrictions on sexual relations if the husband is a participant; there are similar restrictions for forty days after the birth of a first child. There is a good deal of individual freedom in the marriage relation. The main tie seems to be their children, and teknonymous usage is frequent. There is also a religious sanction for marriage—the marriage ceremony is essential in order to prepare a woman for entrance to the land of the dead.

Separation is easy, and there is a fairly high rate of divorce in all the villages—a rate which Titiev has computed at around 34 per cent for Old Oraibi. When serious conflicts arise between spouses, the husband is usually treated as an outsider by the household of the wife and may be made unwelcome, or he may become aggrieved at her conduct. In either case he usually returns to his own household until reconciliation or remarriage. The serious social consequences of separation are cushioned by the extended family structure of the household, which makes such a rate of separation possible without disrupting the whole society. The wife and small children can fall back on the larger family for economic support until remarriage, older children being allowed to go with whichever parent they prefer. Modern conditions are rapidly modifying this situation, with serious social consequences, but the older attitudes often persist. One well-educated modern Hopi girl summed up the relationship as follows: "I don't need my husband any more now that I have my baby girl. My family has some extra land, and my brothers will plant it for me." Even children are not a strong enough tie in the face of lineage loyalties.

The sibling bond, in contrast, is a very strong one and one of the most fundamental in Hopi society, being based on common blood and residence and on mutual aid. The strongest and most permanent tie is that between two sisters; next is the relationship between brothers. Brothers frequently co-operate in economic and ritual activities throughout life, despite living in different households after marriage. An older brother should teach and look after a younger brother, although it is knowledge and not age that is important. They may tease each other, but it should not be carried too far; quarrels are thought to blow over quickly, and a brother's behavior is defended to outsiders. Brothers frequently combine their efforts in caring for a herd of sheep, often in collaboration with their father and their brothers-in-law.

Two brothers occasionally marry two sisters or marry into the same clan, although this is not a definite rule. Such marriages may increase the solidarity of the household group and are supposed to eliminate quarreling between the sisters-in-law. Brothers share equally in the personal property of their deceased father, except that the one carrying out the burial duties usually receives an additional amount. Next to the actual brothers, the mother's sister's sons are the closest, often living in the same household. The father's brother's sons, on the other hand, are "brothers" merely because their fathers are in the same clan. For more distant "brothers" the feeling of relationship and obligation is usually much weaker, unless exceptional circumstances are involved.

The relation of sisters to one another—and to their mother—is the foundation of the Hopi household group. This relationship, based on the closest ties of blood, residence, and common occupation, lasts from birth to death and influences their lives each day. Their children are reared together and cared for as their own; if one sister dies, the other looks after her children and brings them up. When there is an age difference, an older sister may act as a "mother" to her younger sister, but ordinarily there is little difference in their behavior. They co-operate in all the tasks of the household, grinding corn together, plastering the house, cooking, and the like. An older sister helps with the preparations for marriage and initiations into the katcina cult and the women's societies. Despite this close bond, sororal polygyny is not practiced, nor is there any tendency toward the sororate or levirate. A mother sometimes turns over the house to a favorite daughter, but usually the eldest sister inherits the control of the household. While quarrels occur, sisters generally manage to get along together. Any quarrels are usually settled by their brothers or their mother's brothers; if that is not possible, one may move out, but she usually continues to use the household equipment. The extensions of the sister relationship are similar to those for brothers.

The brother-sister bond, while close, is modified by the prevailing division of labor and the rules of residence after marriage. There are no restrictions or avoidances in their behavior, but their contacts are fewer in later life. Before marriage a brother works to support his sister and the other members of the household, and even after marriage he considers his sister's household as his own and is free to come and go as he pleases. The sister, in turn, looks to her brother for aid in various crises and often co-operates with him in ceremonial enterprises belonging to the lineage or clan or in the duties attendant upon "ceremonial parenthood."

An older brother has much in common with a younger brother but less with a younger sister. An older sister, on the other hand, engages equally in the task of taking care of her younger brothers and sisters as part of her training for parenthood. When a brother participates in ceremonies and dances and when he marries, a sister aids in the preparation of food and in other ways. Each has a pride in the other's activities. The strong bond between them is the basis for their relationships to each other's children as well. Brothers and sisters share their patrimony, but sisters usually are given fewer of the sheep from their father's flock. With regard to marriage there is no tendency to brother-sister exchange between households.

The relation of a mother's brother to his sister's children is likewise one of the most important in the Hopi kinship structure. As head of his sister's lineage and household, his position is one of authority and control; he is the chief disciplinarian and is both respected and obeyed. "Our old uncles told us" is sufficient explanation and sanction for custom. The mother's brother has the primary responsibility for transmitting the ritual heritage. He usually selects the most capable nephew as his successor and trains him in the duties of whatever ceremonial position he may control. To make him a good Hopi, he may get his nephew up early to run around the mesa and bathe in cold water; if he is lazy, he will pour water on him. In return a nephew is frequently afraid of his uncle, particularly where punishment is administered, but an uncle usually has his nephew's interests at heart.

A mother's brother has no special duties at birth or initiation but plays an important role at the time of his nephews' and nieces' weddings, especially the nieces'. He often is consulted on the choice of a spouse; he takes charge of the weaving of the wedding garments for his nephew's wife and instructs him in his new duties and the proper behavior toward his new relatives. At his niece's marriage he formally welcomes her husband to the household and looks after her interests in any disputes. Normally a niece has less contact with her mother's brother, since she is more directly under her mother's supervision. She may "joke" or tease her mother's brother concerning his "father's sisters" (her mother's father's sisters). "They don't like you," she will tell him, intimating that she is stronger in affection.

The mother's mother's brother is likewise an important relative. While alive he is the ritual head of the household and is considered to know more than the mother's brother. He may act as a teacher, particularly in regard to clan legends and stories, but he seldom punishes his sister's daughter's children, leaving such tasks to his sister's sons. The relations between the brother, mother's brother, and mother's mother's brother are important ones for Hopi ritual life. They belong to the same lineage and household and have the primary responsibility for the proper transmission of clan and ritual knowledge, including ceremonial offices and duties. Within this group the mother's brother has the primary obligation and disciplinary position; the mother's mother's brother has largely finished his tasks. The Hopi have partly taken him out of the mother's brother's classification and classed him as an "older brother," a comrade and helper rather than an authoritarian instructor and disciplinarian. He might have been considered a "grandfather" but that would not fit into the lineage structuring of the kinship system. Parallel to this is the tendency to class the mother's mother's mother as an "older sister," though such cases are, naturally, quite rare.

The grandparent-grandchild relation is more varied, but in general it is one of great affection and attachment. By reason of residence a mother's father is usually closer to his grandson, often sleeping with him, instructing him in Hopi stories and legends, teaching him songs, and giving him gifts. There is some training in agricultural and herding activities but little in the way of punishment or authority involved. The father's father is in a similar relationship, though, being in a different household, he normally has fewer opportunities. He will take his grandson hunting and to his fields, instructing him in Hopi lore. This latter grandfather, along with the father's sister's husband, enters into a joking relationship with the grandson. The father's father may pour water on his grandson if he sleeps late or may roll him in the snow. When the grandson is older, he attempts to "get even" with his grandfather by doing the same thing. While the father's sister's husband enters into such joking and teasing, the special relations between a man and his father's sisters bring about an additional type of joking, outlined below. The mother's father, perhaps because of his position as husband of the head of the household, does not enter into such teasing to any great extent. The relations of grandfather to granddaughters are less extensive and less marked by teasing or joking but involve the same affection and interest.

Grandmothers likewise treat their grandchildren with kindness and affection, teaching them Hopi ways and helping them out of difficulties. If the mother is too hard on her children, the grandmother will interfere on their behalf. The mother's mother occupies a dominant position in the household and as such must be respected, even by the granddaughters. On occasions of ceremony and marriage she aids in the preparation of food and presents. The father's mother is closer to her grandchildren and shows them more affection. As a woman of the father's household and clan she shares, with the father's sisters, an important joking relationship with the grandson, particularly at the time of marriage. Teasing relationships with the granddaughter seem more developed on First Mesa than on Second or Third. The mother's mother and the father's mother divide the duties attendant upon the introduction of a new grandchild into the world.

The grandparent-grandchild relation is widely extended and includes relatives in several conceptual categories. The grandparent term may be used for any very old person—these should be listened to, "since they know the important things." The father's parents occupy a similar position in a different household from that of the mother's parents; in terms of the differential relations of these households to ego we might expect a difference in terminology, but the Hopi have apparently ignored these differences and classed them together, while behaving somewhat differently toward them. The special position of the father's sister's husband will be further discussed below.

The relation between the father's sister and her brother's child is a very important one in Hopi life. With the father's mother, the father's sisters are involved in all the crises and ceremonial occasions in the life of their brother's child, from birth to death. At birth, puberty, marriage, initiations, ceremonial participation, and preparation for burial the father's sisters play an important role. These relations are closer and more concerned with the brother's son than with his daughter. Not only is her home a second home to ego, but the relationship has a sexual tinge, with many references to sexual play between them, which may be symbolical or refer to actual relations.

This relationship serves to illuminate the role of the father's sisters at marriage and the joking relationship with the father's sister's husband. At the time of the boy's marriage, besides aiding in the preparations, the father's sisters find fault with the bride, comparing her unfavorably to themselves. Sometimes all the women of the father's household and clan descend with mock ferocity on the boy's household, bedaubing the mother and her sisters with mud and disrupting the household, at the same time engaging in spirited repartee. Any damage done is later more than repaid, and, while the show is very realistic, "they don't mean it— it's a means of showing that they care more for the boy than the others." Similar expressions of their regard may continue, even after the groom has gone to live at the bride's household.

This expression of jealousy and regard takes a reciprocal form in the joking and teasing between ego, his father's sisters, and their husbands. The latter, as a "grandfather," may have rolled his grandson in the snow and otherwise teased him as a child, for which direct retaliations are in order. The boy may also tease his father's sister about her husband, telling her that her husband is lazy and "no good" and that he will look after her. The father's sister, in turn, may tell her husband that he is free to leave her at any time, since her "grandchild" will take care of her—"you can go home and I'll take my *imyi* for my husband." A man is expected to stand up for all his "father's sisters" at all times.

The father's sister, while carrying out similar duties toward her brother's daughters, does not have the same close and intimate relationship with them. There are fewer ritual occasions, and there is no teasing or joking involved. Girls aid and co-operate with their father's sisters in plastering houses, in carrying water, and in doing other household tasks. Boys hunt rabbits for their "aunts" and in former times went on expeditions to furnish them with salt.

While a man has many "father's sisters," the closest ones are the actual sisters of his father, who usually reside in his natal household. The father's sister's daughters, when unmarried, are not teased; they choose favorite mother's brother's sons as partners in "Butterfly" and other social dances. A girl who receives aid from her unmarried "father's sisters" at the time of her marriage will reciprocate when the latter marry. More distant "father's sisters," whether clan, phratry, or ceremonial, are regarded with affection and joked with whenever occasions arise. The position of the father's sister in the father's lineage and in behavior is essentially that of a "grandmother," and occasionally she is called that. She calls her brother's children "grandchild," and her husband in turn is called "grandfather." She might be considered as a "little grandmother"; the special terminology serves to segregate the women of the father's clan and phratry from the primary grandparents who have a direct genealogical relationship.

The relations with relatives by marriage, other than the father's sister's husband, take a somewhat different and nonreciprocal form. A man marrying into a household begins to share in the task of supporting the household by cultivating its land, hunting game, and gathering wood. To begin with, he is considered as a "male relative-in-law" and is judged by the household on the basis of his performance. If he gets along well in co-operative activities, there is a tendency for the wife's brothers to call him "brother" rather than "male relative-in-law," and, as he has children, he becomes a "father" to the generation below. At first, also, his connection with the household and lineage is solely through his wife, and he uses for them the same terms that his wife does, extending these to the clan. Two men married to sisters in the same household call each others "partners"; they have similar tasks in relation to the household.

The relations with female relatives-in-law are somewhat different, though equally nonreciprocal. Any woman marrying a man of the lineage (and clan) is considered as a "female relative-in-law" and must be called by the term *imï'wi* from the beginning of the marriage ceremony; in return she uses the terms her husband uses for his clanspeople. The "female relatives-in-law" do not form a localized group but are regarded with affection, except by the father's sisters of their husbands. They have important duties at marriage; whenever a woman of their husbands' clan is being married, they are expected to come and aid in the preparations which are necessary.

The primary obligations of relatives-in-law are to the household and lineage with which they are immediately tied, but these obligations are further extended to the clan and phratry group. The obligations of the household and lineage, in return, amount to relatively little, nor is there any extension to the relatives of these in-laws of the relationships outlined above. These relationships become somewhat more "reciprocal," however, if we look at them from the standpoint of the two households (and lineages) united by a marriage. The husband's household loses an economic worker but gains a "female relative-in-law"; correlatively, the wife's household gains an economic support and furnishes a worker for marriage and other occasions. On a village-wide basis households lose brothers and gain "male relatives-in-law."

As one drives north or west from Tucson, Arizona, the arid homeland of the Pima and the Papago is traversed. These ancient agricultural Indians are descendant from a Cochise, or Desert culture, strata. The Piman-speakers are linguistic relatives of the Hopi and the Shoshone on the one hand, and of the Yaqui and the Aztec on the other. It was probably to the ancestors of the Pima that the early influences of Mexican civilization first came; the Spaniards also came into contact with the peaceful Pima along the Gila River when they moved north from Mexico. Harried by the Apache and the Yavapai, exploited by the Spanish and later by the Americans, the Pima were badly disorganized by the beginning of the twentieth century. The following selection lists some of the food plants available to the Pima, which supplemented those they produced through agriculture. Excluding the cultigens, the basic list of plants and their methods of preparation could be extended over a vast area in the American west and, in time, back perhaps 5,000 to 10,000 years.

31 Frank Russell

PIMA INDIAN SUBSISTENCE*

The Pimas subsist upon a mixed diet in which vegetable food predominates. In the past it would seem probable that the proportion of meat

* Abridged from "The Pima Indians," by F. Russell, in *Annual Reports of the Bureau of American Ethnology*, **26**, 66–78, 1908.

was greater than at present, though they have long been tillers of the soil. Certain articles of their diet appear to be markedly flesh producing, and this tendency is at least not diminished by the habits of life resulting from the semitropical climate of the Gila Valley. They are noticeably heavier than individuals belonging to the tribes on the Colorado plateau to the north and northeast, and many old persons exhibit a degree of obesity that is in striking contrast with the "tall and sinewy" Indian conventionalized in popular thought.

About every fifth year in primitive times the Gila River failed in midwinter, the flow diminishing day by day until at length the last drop of water that could not gain shelter beneath the sands was licked up by the ever-thirsty sun. The fish gathered in the few pools that were maintained by the underflow, the ducks and other water birds took flight, but the deer and antelope could the more readily be stalked because of their resorting to known watering places. Without water in the river and canals there could be no crops, and necessity drove the people to seek far afield for the native plants that in some degree produce fruits or seeds even in dry seasons. The fruit of the saguaro and the seed or bean of the mesquite were the most abundant and accessible resources. When even these failed the Pimas were driven to make long journeys into the Apache country—and whenever they got a mile from their own villages they were in the land of the Apache—in search of animal food, roots, berries, and especially the edible agaves.

At other times the very abundance of water proved disastrous; floods destroyed the canals and swept away the crops. As early as 1697 Padre Kino reported that owing to the fields having been overflowed the Pimas could offer him no pinole, but gave mesquite meal instead. The resort to uncultivated products such as their Papago cousins to the southward wholly subsisted upon did not prevent the Pimas from attaining proficiency in agriculture, and it must many times have preserved them from total extinction. With what success they sought for edible plants may be judged from the subjoined list, which is believed to be fairly complete. It contains 22 plants of which the stems, leaves, or flowers were eaten, 4 that furnished roots or bulbs, 24 with seeds or nuts, and 15 that supplied fruits or berries. And this in a region that appears to the casual visitor to be a desert with but a few thorny shrubs and but one tree that he would deem worthy of the name.

PLANTS USED FOR FOOD

Â'nûk ï'avak, Atriplex bracteosa var.; A. coronata Wats.; A. elegans Dietrich. These saltbushes, with a few others as yet unidentified, are sometimes boiled with other food because of their salty flavor. They are cooked in pits with the fruit of the cactus, Opuntia arborescens, the method of roasting them being described below. The young shoots of some of them are crisp and tender. Commonly known as "sagebrush," these saltbushes are among the most abundant plants in that region. There are both herbaceous and woody species, the former being eaten by stock and the latter being useful for fuel.

A'opa hï'âsĭk, Populus deltoides Marsh. The cottonwood occurs in a thin fringe, with here and there a grove along the Gila and Salt rivers. In February and March the women send some of the barefoot boys into the tree tops to throw down the catkins, which are then gathered in baskets and carried home to be eaten raw by stripping them off the stem between the teeth.

Aot, Agave americana Linn. (possibly a few related species also). Mescal was gathered in times of famine, and it would have been much more extensively used had it not been for the danger from "the enemy," the Apaches, that attended even the shortest journey away from the villages. The plant has ever been a favorite, not only among the Pimas but also with the Papagos, the Apaches, and a score of other tribes. The first day's work after reaching the hills where this plant grows was to seek suitable wood and make digging sticks. Then the men gathered the mescal heads by prying them out with the sticks, and trimmed off the leaves with a knife, leaving one or two, so that the heads might be tied in pairs and slung on a rope for carrying. Thin-leaved specimens were rejected, inasmuch as they not only contain little nourishment, but blister the mouth when eaten. While the men were bringing in the mescal, the women gathered wood for fuel. Pits were dug, and after the fire built in them had died down small stones were placed on the coals. The mescal was then placed on the stones and the whole covered with earth. When it had roasted for twenty-four hours, a small opening was made in the pit and its contents examined; if the cooking was not yet complete, the opening was closed and the pit left undisturbed twelve hours longer. If the roasting was not done when the pit was first opened, it was believed that the incontinence of some members of the party was the cause. The heads of the fruit were opened by removing the envelope on one side; the center was cut out and dried in the sun, when it was ready for use or for storing away.

Mescal is now obtained from the Papagos. It is eaten by chewing until the juice is extracted and rejecting the fiber. It is used alone or together with pinole. Sirup is extracted from the prepared mescal by boiling until the juice is removed, which is then thickened by prolonged boiling until it becomes a black sirup, somewhat similar to sorghum. It is inferior to saguaro sirup.

A'păn, Monolepis chenopoides. The roots are washed, boiled in an olla, and cooled in a basket. The water is squeezed out, and they are again put into the olla with a little fat or lard and salt. After cooking for a few moments they are ready to serve with tortillas. This plant is also used in a similar manner by the Mexicans, who are supposed to have learned its value from the natives. The seeds are boiled, partially dried, parched, ground on the metate, and eaten as pinole.

A'taftak, Cucurbita fœtidissima H.B.K. The seeds of this wild gourd are roasted and eaten.

E'ikâfi. The root of this small plant is gathered, boiled, and eaten without peeling.

Hait''kam, Olneya tesota. The nuts of the ironwood tree are parched in an olla, or, what is more usual, the broken half of one, and eaten without further preparation. The tree grows on the mesas on all sides of the villages, where it is very conspicuous for a few days in May, when it is covered with a mass of purple flowers.

Hâ'kowat, Phoradendron californicum. The berries of the mistletoe that grows on the mesquite are gathered and boiled without stripping from the stem. They are taken in the fingers, and the berries stripped off into the mouth as eaten. Various species of mistletoe are very abundant on the trees along the Gila, but this one only is eaten.

Halt, Cucurbita pepo Linn. The common species of pumpkin grown by the Pimas, as well as by the whites and Mexicans, is cut in strips and dried, when it is known by a number of different names, according to the manner of cutting and the particular variety. This species includes the pumpkins proper, the bush scallop squashes, the summer crook-necks, and the white or yellow warty squashes. The club-shaped, pear-shaped, or long-cylindrical smooth squash is Cucurbita moschata Duchesne. It is extensively grown by the Pimas. The seeds of the pumpkin are parched and eaten. When the dried pumpkin is used, it is softened in water and boiled.

Ha'nûm, Opuntia arborescens. The fruit of this cactus is gathered with an instrument that resembles an enlarged wooden clothespin. It is collected in large quantities and carried home in the kiâhâ, or carrying basket. A pit is dug and a fire built in it, on which stones are heated. As the fire dies down the stones are removed and a layer of the saltbush, Suæda arborescens, is placed over the coals; above this is placed a layer of cactus fruit, then hot stones, and so alternately to the top, over which a thick layer of saltbush is laid with earth outside. The pit is left undisturbed over one night, then its contents are spread out, dried, and the fruit stirred with a stick until the thorns are rubbed off, whereupon it is ready to store away for future use. In its final preparation it must be boiled. It is then salted and eaten with pinole. The acid flavor is usually relieved by the addition of various plants cooked as greens.

Ha'rsany, Cereus giganteus Engelm. The fruit of the giant cactus, or, as it is more generally known in the Southwest, the saguaro, is gathered in June, and so important is the harvest that the event marks the beginning of the new year in the Pima calendar. The supply is a large one and only industry is required to make it available throughout the entire year, as both the seeds and the dried fruit may be preserved. Seeds that have passed through the body are sometimes gathered from the dried feces, washed, and treated as those obtained directly from the fruit, though there would seem to be some special value ascribed to them as in the case of the "second harvest" of the Seri.

The fruit is eaten without preparation when it ripens. It is of a crimson color and contains many black seeds about the size of those of the fig, which fruit it resembles in taste. By a process of boiling and fermentation an intoxicating liquor is obtained from the fresh fruit which has been more highly esteemed than the nutritious food and has rendered this new-year a season of debauchery.

The fruit is dried and preserved in balls 15 or more centimeters in diameter. From either the fresh or dried fruit sirup is extracted by boiling it "all day." The residue is ground on the metate into an oily paste which is eaten without further preparation. The seeds may be separated from the pulp at the time of drying the fruit and may be eaten raw or ground on the metate and treated as any meal—put into water to form a pinole or combined with other meal to bake into bread.

Ha'valt, Yucca bacatta. The fruit is boiled, dried, ground on the mealing-stone, and boiled with flour. It is also eaten raw as a cathartic. The stems are reduced to pulp and used as soap. Y. elata is also used as soap.

Ho'ny, Zea Mays. Corn, the most important crop of the Pueblo tribes, has, in recent years at least, been of less value to the Pimas than wheat. The numerous varieties are all prepared in about the same manner. As the husked corn is brought in by the women, it is piled on a thin layer of brush and roasted by burning the latter, after which it is cut from the cob, dried, and stored away for future use. The shelled corn is ground on the metate and baked in large cakes in the ashes. Corn is also boiled with ashes, dried, and the hulls washed off, then thoroughly dried and parched with coals or over the fire. It is then made into a gruel, but is not so highly regarded as the wheat pinole.

I'saᵛĭk. The thorns of this cactus are removed as soon as gathered, and it is eaten without further preparation.

I'tany, Atriplex sp. The heads of this saltbush are pounded up in the mortar and screened to separate the hulls. The seeds are washed, spread to dry, parched in a piece of olla, and ground on the metate. They are then ready to be eaten as pinole, or dry, in the latter case a pinch of the meal being taken alternately with a sip of water.

Ka'ĭfsa, Cicer arietinum Linn. The chick-pea is raised in small quantities and is also purchased from the traders. This is the garabanzo of Mexico. The name chicos is sometimes applied to this pea as it is to anything small, especially to small or, rather, sweet corn that is just old enough for roasting.

Kâf, Chenopodium murale. The seed is gathered early in the summer and prepared by parching and grinding, after which it may be eaten as pinole or combined with other meal.

Kâ'meûvat. After the August rains this seed is gathered, parched over coals in the parching pan, ground on the metate, and eaten as pinole.

Kan'yo, Sorghum vulgare Pers. Sorghum is cultivated when the water supply permits. It has been obtained recently from the whites, who raise it extensively in the Southwest.

Kĭ'ak. The heads of this annual are gathered and the seeds beaten out with the kiâhâ stick used as a flail. The seeds are moistened, parched, which makes it resemble pop corn, ground on the metate, and eaten by taking alternately pinches of meal and sips of water.

Koĭ, Prosopis velutina. Mesquite beans formed nearly if not quite the most important article of diet of the Pimas in primitive times. They are still extensively used, though the supply is somewhat curtailed by the livestock which feed avidly upon them. As already stated, the crop sometimes fails, "especially in hard times," as one of our informants naively remarked. The mesquite harvest takes place somewhat later than that of the saguaro. The beans are gathered and stored in the pod in cylindrical bins on the roofs of the houses or sheds. While yet on the trees, the bean pods are bored by larvæ of the family Bruchid.

The beans are prepared for use by being pounded up in a mortar with a stone pestle, or, if a large quantity is required, with a large wooden one. The pods may be ground with the beans. Another method of preparation is to separate the beans from the pods, parch them by tossing them up in a pan of live coals, and reduce them to meal by grinding, whereupon they may be eaten as pinole. This has a sweetish taste and is reputed to be very nourishing.

The catkins of the mesquite are eaten without preparation by stripping from the stem between the teeth.

The white gum which exudes from the mesquite limbs is used in making candy.

The inner bark is employed as a substitute for rennet.

Ko'kitcuhûtaki, Parkinsonia microphyla (in the foothills); P. torreyana (on the mesas). The paloverde bean was formerly eaten either as gathered or after being pounded in the mortar. It was not eaten as pinole, but sometimes mixed with mesquite meal.

Ko'mûlt. The heads are gathered and washed, sometimes twice, then boiled in an olla with a little water. Wheat flour and a seasoning of salt are added and the whole is stirred until the heads fall to pieces.

Ko'-okupaltûk. According to tradition the seeds were eaten in primitive times, but no one now knows how they were prepared. The plant is now boiled with meat as greens.

Ko'ûtcĭlt, Prosopis pubescens. Screw beans are abundant along the banks of the Gila. They are cooked in pits which are lined with arrow bushes set on end. The beans are placed in layers alternating with cocklebur leaves, the whole covered with earth and left to stand three or four days, after which they are taken out and spread to dry. They are then ready to use or store away in the arrow-bush basket bins on the house tops. They are further prepared for food by pounding up in a mortar, the fine flour then being ready to be eaten as pinole. The coarser portion is taken up in the hands with water, the juice sucked through the fingers, and the remainder rejected.

Kwa'aolt, Licium fremontii var. The red berry is boiled and eaten.

Mâ-âtatûk. This is described as resembling asparagus. The stems may be eaten raw or boiled or roasted in the ashes.

Me'la, Citrullus vulgaris Shrad. Watermelons are among the most important crops of the Pimas and are eaten during at least six months of the year.

Naf, Opuntia engelmanni. The thorns are brushed off the fruit of the prickly pear before it is gathered. It is then peeled and eaten, the seeds being thrown away. The Papagos make a sirup from the fruit (which is said to cause fever in those not accustomed to its use) and dry the fruit as they do that of the saguaro, but the Pimas make no further use of it than to eat it raw.

Nyi'âtam, Malva sp. This plant is boiled and the liquid used in making pinole in times of famine.

O'-opat, Acacia greggii. The beans of the cat's-claw were eaten in primitive times, but no one of the present generation knows how they were prepared.

Ositcu'wutpat, Zizyphus lycioides. The black berry of this thorny bush is gathered in the basket bowls after it has been beaten down with sticks. It is eaten raw and the seeds are thrown away.

Pap'kam. The heads are tied in bunches and dried in the sun. They are then shelled, screened, the seeds parched, ground on the metate, and eaten as pinole. They are "not sweet."

Pavf(ĭ), Phaseolus vulgaris Linn. At least one variety of the common kidney bean, pole bean, bunch bean, etc., was known to the natives before the advent of the Spaniards. Venegas states that "red frixoles, or kidney beans" (Phaseolus sp.), were cultivated by the natives of lower California, and this may have been the variety known in Pimería.

Pel'tûkany, Triticum sativum Lam. Wheat is the principal crop of the Pimas, and four varieties are known to them. It is ground on the metate to make the flour used in cooking the great loaves that weigh from 10 to 20 pounds. Tortillas resembling those of the Mexicans are now more commonly used than the heavy loaves of former days. A light and toothsome doughnut is fried in bubbling hot suet. One of the commonest methods of preparing wheat is to parch it, grind it on the metate, and eat it as a sort of thin gruel called hak(ĭ) tcoĭ; or the wheat may be boiled before parching, in which case the product is known as pârsâ ʈ tcoĭ. Both are known to the whites by the Mexican term "pinole."

Rsat. The bulb of the wild onion is eaten. It is common on the slopes at the foot of the Estrellas.

Rso'-owût. The fine reddish seed is boiled with flour as a mush.

Rsur'su-ulĭk. This is used as greens with similar plants.

Sâi'tûkam iavik. The leaf of this thorny plant is eaten raw or boiled.

Si'etcu, Cucumis melo Linn. The muskmelon is extensively raised by the Pimas.

Si'vitcĭlt, Rumex hymenosepalus. The canaigre is cultivated by the whites in the Gila valley for tannin, yet it is eaten by the Pimas. The stem is roasted in the ashes or, recently, stewed with sugar. We have seen the children greedily devouring the raw roots in March. Dr. Palmer states that the roots are used to tan deerskin and also as soap.

So'-oaot, Sophia pinnata (Walt) Britton. The seeds are parched, ground, and mixed with water to form pinole. The Mexicans of Arizona use the leaves of this plant in preparing a drink. An infusion made from the leaves is also employed as a remedy for sores.

Tâki, Gosypium sp. The cotton plant is no longer raised, but from pre-Spanish days down to the last quarter of a century it was cultivated both for the fiber and the seeds. The latter were pounded up with mesquite beans in the mortar or they were sometimes parched and eaten without grinding.

Tapk'. These seeds resemble those of flax in appearance. They are eaten either raw or boiled and are yet extensively used.

Tapkalt. This is one of the varieties of squash that is cultivated by the Pimas at the present time.

Tâ'ta â'nûk, Atriplex nuttallii. The stems of this saltbush are boiled with wheat. They are cut in short lengths and used sometimes as a stuffing for roast rabbit.

Tcia, Salvia columbaria Benth. The seeds when infused in water form a pleasant mucilaginous beverage, very popular with the Pimas.

Toi'âldi. The fruit of this cactus is brought by the Papagos and traded to the Pimas. It is cooked in the same manner as Opuntia arborescens.

Tciaaolt, Echinocactus wislizeni. The pulp of the visnaga is considered valuable in lieu of water to those suffering from thirst. It is also eaten after being cut in strips and boiled all day. It is sometimes boiled with mesquite beans, a layer each in the cooking olla. It is occasionally boiled with sugar. It is quite a popular confection among the whites, who, in some places, obtain the raw material from the Papagos.

Tci'-itkwatak, Lithospermum sp. The leaves are eaten without preparation.

Tcil'tipĭn (Sp.). This pepper is raised by the Papagos and brought to the Pimas.

Tco'hokia. The leaves are gathered in spring and sometimes baked in tortillas. In summer the seeds are gathered, ground on the metate, mixed with meal or squash, or they may be parched and ground to be eaten dry.

Tco'tcĭk â'nûk, Suæda arborescens; S. suffrutescens. These are added to greens or cactus fruit to give flavor.

To'a, Quercus oblongifolia. The acorns of this oak are traded from the Papagos. After the hulls have been removed they are parched and ground into meal.

Ω rtam, Atriplex lentiformis. The seed of this saltbush is cooked in pits which are lined with Suæda arborescens and the papery inner bark of the cottonwood moistened and mixed together. The roasting requires but one night, then the seeds are taken out, dried, parched, and laid away for future use. When eaten, it is placed in a cup and water added until a thick gruel is produced.

Vakwai'hai-indûm, Solanum elæagnifolium. The berries are put in the milk from which cheese is made to serve as a substitute for rennet.

Vak'wandam, Rumex berlandieri. This plant is used with the cactus fruit, Opuntia arborescens, in the same manner as the saltbush, Suæda arborescens.

Vi'pinoĭ, Opuntia versicolor. The fruit is sometimes eaten raw, but it is usually prepared in the same manner as Opuntia arborescens.

Dr. Edward Palmer, who collected among the Pimas in 1885, obtained some nuts of the "quinine plant," Simmondsia californica Nutt., which he says are eaten either raw or parched. Professor Thornber states that the Mexicans use the oil as a hair tonic. He also describes an "Indian potato," Hoffmanseggia falcaria Cav., which, when roasted, tastes like the cultivated Irish potato. However, this is a member of the pea family and not a potato. A true Solanum is found native to Arizona, but we have not learned that the Pimas know of it.

At least three kinds of chewing gum are in use. That most highly esteemed is called vi-ipam, "milky"; it is obtained from a plant which somewhat resembles a sweet-potato vine. The pointed pods are gathered, their milk poured into a squash stalk and heated in the ashes, whereupon it is ready to chew. A bush, Encelia farinosa, called *tohafs,* exudes a clear gum; and that on the stems of some of the Compositae is sometimes gathered and chewed by children.

*W*arfare was neither desirable nor particularly common for many of the agricultural societies in the Southwest. However, raids, feuds, and battles were of great importance in the lives of men of the Yuman-speaking tribes both of California and of the Southwest. The Maricopa, *long resident on the Gila River near the Pima, carried on traditional warfare with the Mohave, the Yuma, the Yavapai (all of whom also spoke Yuman languages), and with the Apache as well. War among the Yumans did not have territorial expansion as its end, but territorial expansion was without doubt a frequent result of the destruction and decimation of competing populations. When attacking a settlement, all things living were fair enemy; men, women, children, even dogs were killed. The resultant depopulation weakened some societies to the point that viability was lost. The Halchidhoma, for example, were driven from their Colorado River homeland partially by the military activity of the Yuma and the Mohave.*

32 Leslie Spier

MARICOPA WARFARE*

The Maricopa lived on the southern side of the vast plain in central southern Arizona through which flow the Gila and Salt Rivers. West of their country the rivers join, sweep by mountain barriers in a great arc (Gila Bend), and continue westward through a hundred miles of wide basin to join the Colorado River at Yuma. Immediately north of the Salt and the lower Gila the country rises in a succession of broken mountain ridges to the heights of the plateau that constitutes northern Arizona. The eastern end of the Salt-Gila valley is blocked by the same mountains sweeping southeasterly to the Sierra Madre of Mexico. From the Gila the country rises gradually to the south; a slope broken by many small sharply rising mountain ranges whose trend is northwest to southeast.

The habitat of the Maricopa was on the middle Gila, from its junction with the Salt River for thirty miles eastward to Pima Butte. The Maricopa have no tradition of ever having lived anywhere else. East of them on the Gila were the allied Pima, some of whom lived until the opening of the nineteenth century somewhat further east in the Santa

* Abridged from *Yuman Tribes of the Gila River*, by L. Spier. Chicago: Univ. Chicago Press, 1–2, 160–166, 1933.

Cruz valley. West of the Maricopa were an Halchidhoma speaking group, the Kaveltcadom, hitherto unrecorded. They occupied the Gila from Gila Bend downstream halfway to the Colorado. The highlands south of the Gila from the eastern mountains westward to the Colorado were occupied by Papago. The mountains of eastern Arizona were held by various bands of Apache. Those rising north of the Salt and lower Gila contained Yavapai bands, whose territory extended from near Globe westward to the Colorado. In the valley of the lower Colorado were the Yuma at the Gila confluence, the Cocopa nearer the Gulf of California, and upstream, south of the Colorado gorge, the Mohave. Various smaller tribes (Halchidhoma, Kohuana, Halyikwamai, Cheme-huevi, Kamia, and perhaps others) had shifting loci in the historic pe-riod, now between Yuma and Cocopa, again between Yuma and Mohave.

Warfare occupied an unusually large place in the minds of the Maricopa for a people who by temperament were essentially mild-tempered and sedentary. They maintain that it was forced on them by raids of Yuma and Yavapai which had to be met or anticipated. While this seems much like the usual disavowal of aggression that can be heard from any of our western Indians, in this case I believe it to be true. No great premium attached to the man with a war record: the war leader was held in high regard, but the ordinary man who took a scalp or cap-tive was not socially exceptional. Maricopa weighted dream experiences far beyond exploits of war. Nevertheless they talked a good deal of war, took pleasure in planning it, and brought up their sons to look forward to it.

The Halchidhoma situation was much the same, with this difference; that while they were still on the Colorado, they were caught between Yuma and Mohave, who hammered away at them with repeated at-tacks. While they were by no means supine and did counterattack, they had everything to lose by aggression. In the end, they lost their foot-hold on the river and fled into Mexico.

Both tribes shared unremitting warfare with Yuma, Mohave, Yavapai, and Western Apache. At least after their joint settlement on the middle Gila, this meant especially the Yuma and Yavapai, the nearer of the four. The Yuma were joined by Mohave and Yavapai, the Yavapai by Apache, for descent on the Maricopa villages. Reciprocally, their allies were Cocopa, Kohuana, and perhaps Pima against the Yuma; the Pima against the Yavapai. Word having been dispatched to the Cocopa and the Kohuana, these people stole around through the desert to the east to join in the attack on the Yuma.

Every few years there was a raid or pitched battle important enough to rest in their memories. Culling through the Pima annals recorded by Russell, I find mention of a Yuma raid against the Maricopa in 1883; of the Maricopa against Yuma in 1841; then three Yuma descents on the Maricopa between 1842 and 1845, followed at longer intervals by others in 1850 and 1857. My own information agrees only in that there were conflicts with the Yuma every few years. Kutox emphasized two expeditions apiece as worthy of recollection, yet he mentioned others indirectly. He placed a foray of Maricopa against Yuma as possibly in 1838, the return engagement some time after; again against the Yuma in 1848 or 1849, and the last descent of the Yuma on the Maricopa in 1856. (Documentary evidence makes this 1857 with certainty.) Peace followed in 1862 or 1863. The date 1848–49 is checked twice in the narratives given below. Kutox remembered the battle of 1857 as a boy of nine. Kutox' date 1838 may correspond to the Pima 1841, 1848 or 1849 undoubtedly to their 1850, and they agree on 1856 or 1857. Bartlett mentioned an engagement "a year before" 1852: this is probably Kutox' 1848 or 1849 and Pima 1850. Kutox also mentioned a Maricopa party going to Yuma before he was born (1847); this may be that of 1838. A Mohave raid on Halchidhoma at Gila Bend seens to have been about 1835.

The Pima annals are filled with references to Yavapai and Apache attacks on the Pima as constantly occuring and mention reciprocal engagements. There can be no question that the Maricopa community as frequently suffered the same and went into the mountains to hunt down these enemies. These were different affairs from the pitched battles with the Yuma: a few Yavapai-Apache marauders picking off stragglers about the villages, or the wiping out of isolated enemy families discovered in the mountain caves.

Two quite different modes of warfare were adopted. Against the Yuma and Mohave, the Maricopa followed the Colorado River custom of formally arranging pitched battles. These were preceded by challengers who first pranced up and down shouting insults at their opponents, until they clashed in single combat, followed by a general mêlée in which foemen stood against each other until they were clubbed down. Against the Yavapai, tactics were wholly different. While they still went *en masse*, it was rather in the nature of a foray, a quick blow and a speedy return, resting largely on their ability as bowmen.

Winter was thought the best time to go to war, especially on nights that were stormy. The enemy would think it too cold to leave their houses and would feel safe indoors. This was also the time that the Maricopa expected raids. On stormy nights, cold and windy, when enemies were thought to be about, everyone in the community gathered for security to sleep in the meeting house. It was on such nights that sentries (matŏ'au'm, "standing by himself") were posted. They went around the settlement at a distance, but built no deceptive fires as Russell records for the Pima. Stockades were unknown to informants, although they are reputed to have existed in this area.

A shaman was called on at such gatherings to use his clairvoyant power to find if the enemy were approaching. He invoked the attendance of the spirits of the mountains by sucking up four piles of dirt. The mountains were thought to enter one by one and divulge the whereabouts and intentions of the enemy through the shaman's interpreter.

However strongly they may have felt that winter was the proper time for warfare, the intoxication of the sahuaro drink roused them to frenzy for war at the time of the sahuaro celebration (June). "When they drank this they thought of war." The song peculiar to the celebration tells of "red water," i.e., blood, its appearance and "how it is made": that the enemy has come to join in drinking: they had joined in battle, now they would be together drinking. Intoxication and incitement, with their proximity to the mountains while gathering the fruit, led them to set out at once against the Yavapai.

Further, Russell's Pima annals indicate conflicts rather generally distributed through the year with the greater number in spring and summer. Thus, the Yuma came against the Maricopa in October, 1833, the autumn of 1842, and in the summer of 1843 and 1857. My own information is that the Mohave raided Gila Bend in midwinter (1835?). While this tells nothing of the time their own parties set out, it at least indicates when Yuma and Mohave might be expected. Pima and Maricopa were in much the same situation respecting raids of the Yavapai and Apache and their own retaliating attacks. The Pima annals yield the following where the season is identifiable. The Apache-Yavapai came down in spring five times, in summer the same, in the autumn once, in winter twice. Pima attacks on them, either alone or with Maricopa or Papago allies, were in spring once, summer twice, and winter twice. Bartlett saw a Maricopa party set out in July, 1852.

Dress for battle was no more than everyday wear: breechclout and sandals. Older men coiled the long braids that hung on back and breast around the head, confining them with a head-band. They sometimes let them hang full length until the enemy was neared, then bound them about the crown with one braid, or, like younger men, tied the ends of the braids together as they hung down the back. I am not certain that war paint differed from that on gala occasions. This included a mask-like black stripe across the eyes and horizontal lines in white across the long back hair. Similarly, the feather headdress may have been only the everyday one: a bit of eagle down or an eagle feather pendent by a short cord from the back hair. A feather bonnet, a cap with eagle feathers projecting sidewise and vertically, was worn by some to indicate their bravery, but this also was gala dress.

A war party was observed by Bartlett in July, 1852. "Such as had their own cotton blankets, placed them around their bodies in folds, and over this wound their lariats as tight as possible; for the double purpose, I suppose, of bracing their bodies, and of protecting their vital parts from arrows. Those who possessed neither [trade] shirts nor blankets, remained as nature made them, with the addition of a little paint. On their head dresses, they had all bestowed more attention than on their bodies. Some had them plastered with clay, so as to resemble huge turbans. Others had decorated the great club of hair which hung down their backs with bits of scarlet cloth, but more of them with the richly-figured sashes or belts of their own manufacture. Some again wore their hair in braids tastefully wound around their heads, inter-mingled with pieces of scarlet cloth; while a few, less particular as to their appearance, wore it clubbed up in a huge mass." (1:216)

War parties comprised relatively large bodies of men, at least against the Yuma, although fewer may have participated against the Yavapi. Kutox persistently mentioned two hundred as the number in a party: while this need not be taken literally, it does indicate the order of their numbers. This is in striking contrast to the handful of raiders which the mountain tribes of Arizona mustered at any one time, and indicates clearly that warfare was a national affair of the sort carried on by the lower Colorado tribes. The contrast with the mountain tribes is not one of relative populations because the Maricopa were not very numerous in the second quarter of the last century, the period to which our data relate.

The organization of the parties was simple. There was a battle leader, one or two individuals who bore feathered pikes (the "battle standards" of the Yuma), several champions, and shamans who used their clair-voyant abilities to seek out the enemy and who tended the wounded. All these men had their functions by reason of special powers they had dreamed. Not one of them was more than a leader: they were not officers to issue orders. It seems reasonably clear that the tribal chief was not ordinarily war leader.

There was but one battle leader at a time among the Maricopa. He was the only man who had the requisite dreams of war, and when he died, another dreamed in his stead. The dreams dwelt on surmounting dangers and killing the enemy. In his dreams he saw clouds of little flies (called kumanyihwi') fighting in the air, and by their actions he learned how to make successful issue of the battle. He dreamed only that he would be successful. His personal preparation was like that of all shamans: a series of dreams in which the spirits initiated him in the mysteries of his art until they were satisfied that he was fully prepared. There is a cactus more thorny than cholla, called àxu'l. He dreamed he saw these fighting in the form of humans. When they saw he was fitted for his position, these spirits took him into a large cave, the hollow interior of a mountain located in the enemy country. As he entered he saw a club, a shield, and a pike hanging on the wall. Each time he was taken there, they gave him the opportunity to learn the use of one of these until he was proficient with all. Then he was ready to lead in battle. His song first described the morning star (xomàce' kovàtai'à, "big star"), which in some undefined way is connected with war. Just what was his function in battle was not ascertained. The last of such leaders among the Maricopa was named ka'kaio'.

The bearer of the feathered pike was a functionary known alike to Maricopa and Halchidhoma, and was represented among other lower Colorado tribes. He assumed no-flight obligations which placed him in the forefront of battle and in that sense was a war leader. But while Forde describes the pike of the Yuma as a battle standard sometimes planted in the ground and about which the forces rallied, my informants explicitly and repeatedly denied this function among the Gila River tribes. The pike was carried by a man selected as the best warrior; quite infrequently two men had them. He used it as his weapon, supplemented by a club, and carried no shield. He was not the war captain, nor a dreamer. Carrying it entailed what was practically a no-flight obligation: the bearer must go always forward, never retreat. He was credited with fearlessness: even though his companions retreated, he rushed forward into the enemy's midst, to seize them by the hair and club them to death. Black paint covered his body and was drawn in a band across his eyes. His bangs were daubed red. At his death the pike was destroyed with the remainder of his personal belongings. Whether his position was transmitted was not disclosed.

This pike was a mesquite shaft, pointed at one or both ends, encircled at intervals by bands of red and black paint, and bearing pendant feathers. Kutox gave contradictory evidence regarding details: he stated that it was in length the height of its bearer, again that it was four to five feet long; that it was pointed at one end, again at both. A specimen which he had made for me is pointed at one end only and is forty-three inches in length. Another specimen made by Charlie Redbird is pointed at one end alone. The feathers were the largest plumes of buzzard and eagle, each bound individually to the shaft, leaving a space free for a hand grip at the middle. Halchidhoma and Maricopa made such pikes identically and alike called them hukwilĭ'c.

Armament consisted of bows, short wooden clubs, and circular shields. Rarely a man might arm himself with a wooden pike. A warrior carried either bow, or club and shield; never both. Clubmen and bowmen went into battle as separate divisions; the clubmen always grouped to march in front, the bowmen following. Each of these companies was said to have had its leader, presumably a spontaneous leader, since the absence of any special designation for them argues against formality of their status.

Anthropologists frequently work with "preliterate" cultures—cultures that lack the technique of writing. Consequently, the anthropologist in the field must attempt to build his own knowledge of the native language simply to communicate with his subjects. He usually finds himself studying language as intensively as other aspects of culture. In the following essay, language is seen as far more than merely a set of grammatical rules and a list of words. It is, rather, a living image of the world seen through the eyes of its speakers, a tool which does far more than provide a means of interpersonal communication alone. It is a process whereby traditional world view, traditional knowledge, and traditional experience are translated into an operational means of classifying extant phenomena. People see what their language indicates; the language indicates what has been traditionally important. A more beautiful statement of this thesis than that which follows does not exist in anthropological literature.

33 Clyde Kluckhohn and Dorthea Leighton

THE LANGUAGE OF
THE NAVAHO*

This chapter will be devoted to trying to get a little way inside the Navaho mind. Since the Navahos, like all other peoples, necessarily think with words, at least a superficial conception of the main peculiarities of the Navaho language must be gained before endeavoring to see the world as it appears to The People. The forms of each language impose upon its speakers certain positive predispositions and certain negative restrictions as to the meanings they find in their experience.

From characteristic types of expressions even an outsider may safely infer some of the assumptions which The People make about the nature of things. For example, the Navahos do not say, "I am hungry" or "I have hunger." They always put it as "hunger is killing me" and "thirst is killing me." Similarly, they prefer the active, personalized "water is killing me" to the English description of the impersonal process of natural forces, "I am drowning." From such examples an immediate insight is gained into the Navaho manner of conceiving such events. To The People, hunger is not something which comes from within but something to which the individual is subjected by an outside force. Indeed if an articulate Navaho is pressed for an explanation of this linguistic idiom he is likely to say, "The spirit of hunger sits here beside me."

From the psychological point of view, there are as many different worlds upon the earth as there are languages. Each language is an instrument which guides people in observing, in reacting, in expressing themselves in a special way. The pie of experience can be sliced in all sorts of ways, and language is the principal directive force in the background. It is a great pity that most Americans have so strong an emotional block against the formal analysis of linguistic structures. They have been made to suffer so much from having to memorize rules and

* Abridged from "The Tongue of the People," in *The Navaho*, by C. Kluckhohn and D. Leighton. Cambridge, Mass.: Harvard Univ. Press, 182–215, 1946.

approaching language in a mechanical, unimaginative way that they tend to think of "grammar" as the most inhuman of studies. Looked at in another way, nothing is more human than the speech of an individual or of a folk. No clues are so helpful as those of language in leading to ultimate, unconscious psychological attitudes. Moreover, much of the friction between groups and between nations arises because in both the literal and the slangy senses they don't speak the same language.

For the Navaho case, Robert Young and William Morgan have well put the basic problems:

> The pattern of Navaho thought and linguistic expression is totally unlike that of the European languages with which we are most commonly familiar. We learn such foreign languages as Spanish, French, Italian, and German with a minimum of difficulty because there exist so many analogies, both with respect to grammar and to words, with our own native English. Moreover, the pattern according to which we conceive and express our thoughts in English and in these common European languages is basically the same throughout. We translate readily from one to the other, often almost word for word. And lastly, similar or very closely related sound systems prevailing throughout make the words easy to pronounce and to remember.
>
> On the other hand, the Navaho language presents a number of strange sounds which are difficult to imitate, and which make the words very hard to remember at first. Secondly, the pattern of thought varies so greatly from our English pattern that we have no small difficulty in learning to think like, and subsequently to express ourselves like the Navaho. An understanding of the morphology and structure of the language, and an insight into the nature of the thought patterns involved can go far in aiding to solve the puzzle. (9:40)

The tacit premises that are habitually present in the thinking of Navahos elude the outsider until he actually studies somewhat minutely some native utterances recorded in text and compares them with translations given by several different English-speaking Navahos. Better still, if he learns a little Navaho and tries to express himself—even on very simple matters—he is speedily compelled to realize that the categories in which one classifies experience and tries to communicate it to others are not altogether "given" by the events of the external world. Every language is a different system of categorizing and interpreting experience. This system is the more insidious and pervasive because native speakers are so unconscious of it as a system, because to them it is part of the very nature of things, remaining always in the class of background phenomena. That is, the very fact that Navahos do not stop every time they talk about hunger and say to themselves, "When I talk this way I am personalizing hunger as a force outside myself," makes for difficulty of understanding between whites and The People. They take such ways of thought as much for granted as the air they breathe, and unconsciously assume that all human beings in their right minds think the same way.

It is primarily for this reason that administrators, teachers, missionaries, and others who have to do with the Navahos—or any foreign people—would do well to learn something of the salient features of the linguistic structure. It is also for this reason that anyone who wants to understand the Navahos at all must know something about their language and the way in which it molds thought, interests, and attitudes.

There is no doubt that Navaho is a difficult language, but this is not sufficient cause for throwing up one's hands and avoiding the whole subject like the plague. There is a difference between learning a language and using a language. Few whites have the time or the skill to learn to speak Navaho so well that they can dispense with an interpreter. But mastering the tongue or remaining completely ignorant of it are not the only alternatives. The white person who will make the effort necessary to gain a general orientation to the language will not only find the information intensely interesting but will also discover that he can use even this limited knowledge very effectively. If he will then take the further step of talking a bit, in spite of the mistakes he is certain to make, he will be rewarded for this venture considerably beyond his expectations.

The purpose of this chapter can clearly be neither to give a scientific description of the language nor to provide a manual for learning Navaho. The aim is to sketch some structural features to show the reader how the climate of feeling, reacting, and thinking created by the Navaho language is different from that created by English and other European languages.

NAVAHO SOUNDS

White people despair at learning Navaho not only because of its unfamiliar and difficult sounds but also because Navahos are accustomed to respond to small variations which in English are either ignored or used merely for expressive emphasis. For example, a small clutch of the breath ("glottal closure"), which the speaker of European languages scarcely notices, often differentiates Navaho words. *Tsin* means "log," "stick," or "tree," whereas *ts'in* (the ' representing glottal closure) means "bone." Similarly, *bita'* means "between," but *bit'a'* means "its wing."

The Navahos also distinguish quite separate meanings on the basis of pronouncing their vowels in long, intermediate, or short fashion. For example, the words *bito'* (his water) and *bitoo'* (its juice) are absolutely identical save for the fact that the second vowel in the latter is lingered over.

Finally, the Navahos, like the Chinese, pay very careful attention to the tones of vowels (and of the sound "n" which is sometimes used in Navaho with vowel quantity). Four separate tones (low, high, rising, falling) are differentiated. The only difference between *'azee'* (medicine) and *'azéé'* (mouth) is that the final long vowel of the latter has a high pitch, as indicated by the accent mark. The same thing is true for the difference between *'anaa'* (war) and *'anáá'* (eye). The phonetic variations in the following five words are almost imperceptible to the untrained white ear:

bíni', his mind	*binii'*, his face
bínii', his nostrils	*bini,* in it
binii', his waist	

Perhaps in the case of most nouns, as in the examples just given, meanings would ordinarily become clear from context. But when we come to verbs, differences in pronunciation so slight as to pass unnoticed by those habituated to tongues of Indo-European pattern make for a bewildering set of variations, many of which would be equally suitable to an identical context. For example:

naash'á, I go around with the round object.
naash'aah, I am in the act of lowering the round object.
násh'ááh, I am in the act of turning the round object upside down (or over).
naash'áah, I am accustomed to lowering the round object.

Any of these expressions might easily be confused with *násh'a,* which means "I am skinning it."

The importance of these minute variations in Navaho cuts both ways in complicating the problems of communication between whites and Navahos. These variations make it difficult for whites to speak Navaho, and they also make it difficult for Navahos to learn English sounds accurately. The very fact that the Navahos themselves are sensitized from childhood to these (and not to other) types of sound patterns and alternations makes the phonetics of English or Spanish hard for them to master.

So far as pronunciation alone is concerned, there are languages whose systems of sounds present more problems to the speaker of European background than does Navaho. There are a number of sounds in Navaho that are not found in English, but there are parallels to almost all (except glottalization) in German, Welsh, Polish, and other European languages. The real difficulty with Navaho rests in the fact that the small phonetic differences of the sort that have been illustrated above cannot be by-passed. There is no leeway. In the language of the Sioux Indians there are also long vowels; one can, however communicate quite effectively without rendering them very accurately. But there is nothing slouchy about Navaho. Sounds must be reproduced with pedantic neatness. Tones can be ignored in Chinese for the sake of stress. Not so in Navaho. The language of The People is the most delicate known for phonetic dynamics.

A few white persons (children of traders or missionaries) who have learned Navaho as small children, speak "without an accent." A very few other whites have learned as adults to speak fluent and correct Navaho but have failed to acquire certain nuances in the sheer style of speaking. Learners may take comfort against their mistakes and embarrassment from the realization that the only recipe for pronouncing Navaho perfectly is to take the precaution of being born of or among Navahos. The talk of those who have learned Navaho as adults always has a flabby quality to the Navaho ear. They neglect a slight hesitation a fraction of a second before uttering the stem of the word. They move their lips and mouths too vigorously. Native Navaho has a nonchalant, mechanical flavor in ordinary discourse—almost as if a robot were talking.

NAVAHO WORDS

It is often said that the word range of all "primitive" peoples is small and that vocabularies of more than a few thousand words are rare. This is pure mythology. It is impossible to say how many "words" there are in Navaho without the statement's being susceptible of misunderstanding, for everything depends upon the standard adopted as to what constitutes a separate word, a peculiarly acute problem in Navaho. But it may be asserted without qualification that Navaho has a very rich vocabulary. Some suggestion of extent may be given by noting that there are more than a thousand *recorded* names for plants, that the technical terms used in ceremonialism total at least five hundred, that every cultural specialization or occupation has its own special terminology.

The language has shown itself flexible in its capacity for dealing with new objects (the parts of an automobile, for example) and new experiences. But this has been done, for the most part, by making up new words in accord with old patterns rather than by taking over Spanish and English words and pronouncing them in Navaho fashion. "Tomato" is "red plant." An elephant is "one that lassoes with his nose." Many American Indian languages have enlarged their vocabularies by incorporating European words, but Navaho has admitted very few. An automobile is called by one of two terms (*chidí* or *chuggi*) which imitate the sound of a car. "Gasoline" then becomes *chidi bi tó,* "car's water."

Words are very important to The People. They are things of power. Some words attract good; others drive away evil. Certain words are dangerous—they may be uttered only by special persons under specially defined conditions. Hence there are specialized vocabularies known only to those who are trained in a craft or ceremonial skill. Young Navahos who have spent much time away at a boarding school or among whites will often complain of an uncle or grandfather, "He uses hard words. I can't understand him."

Not only are many words differentiated from each other by small sound changes, but there are many actual homonyms, words which have very similar or identical sounds but quite different meanings. The presence of these homonymous words and syllables give rise to the many puns is which the Navahos delight. For instance, *ha'át'íishą́' nílį* means either "what is flowing?" or "what clan are you?" and The People tell stories with many embellishments about this question's being asked of a man who was standing beside a river. Another favorite pun hangs on the fact that the same verb means either "to decide on the matter" or "to put the round object down." This is often employed to satirize the ponderous dealings of important people or, less kindly, to jibe at the hunched back (round object) of a cripple. Still another worn joke arises from the fact that *hodeeshtał* means equally "I will sing" or "I will kick him." And so there are many anecdotes of this pattern:

"So-and-so has gone over yonder."
"What for?"

"He is going to give one a kick" (i.e., the man [a Singer] will perform a chant).

Many puns are more subtle than they appear on the surface. To enter fully into their humor requires sensitiveness to no less than three or four changes of linguistic front.

A QUICK GLANCE AT NAVAHO GRAMMAR

Navaho grammar is primarily a matter of the verb. The other parts of speech can, however, be used by the beginner to make himself fairly well understood.

Nonverbal Parts of Speech

There are few true Navaho nouns, though the list does include some of the commonest and most basic words in the language. Most words which English speakers are apt to term nouns are really nominalized verbs. Some nouns, in fact, can be conjugated after the fashion of neutral verbs. Adjectives are almost entirely the third-person forms of neuter verbs that denote quality, state, or condition. In the formal sense Navaho has no adjectives. Other parts of speech are: pronouns, postpositions, and particles.

Many pronouns are absorbed in verbs, but they are also used independently or prefixed to nouns and postpositions. Navaho pronouns present features of usage and nuances of meaning which is hard indeed for the European to grasp. For example, "it" as the object of a verb has several different forms, depending upon whether "it" is thought of as definite or indefinite or as a place. The speaker must also choose between a number of possible alternatives for a third person subject of a verb. One of these, which has been called "the person of preferred interest," makes a nice discrimination that is typically Navaho. This form of "he" designates the hero of the story as opposed to others, a Navaho as opposed to a member of another tribe, and so on.

Independent possessive pronouns have two forms, distinguished only by the length of the final vowel. One form signifies merely the state of possession; the other indicates that the owner just came into possession of the object. In the case of body parts, the Navahos make use of another subtle distinction. Thus, *shibeʽ* means "my milk" in the sense of milk which actually came from my breasts, whereas *sheʽabeʽ* means "my milk" in the sense of milk owned by me.

Postpositions are roughly the Navaho equivalent of our prepositions, except that they follow rather than precede their objects. There are a great variety of these, and their usage is relatively simple. They are a godsend to the foreigner, for by combining nouns and postpositions one may communicate many meanings without venturing into the intricacies of the Navaho verb. For instance, one may dodge the very difficult verb "go" by saying, "Your father, how about him?" and the child will state where the father has gone.

Navaho nouns have no gender and, with a few exceptions, have the same forms for singular and plural. Save for a few subtleties in the use of pronominal possessives, nouns are quite easy to handle. Thus, a white man can say a good deal in Navaho if he learns a few hundred nouns and ten or twenty postpositions.

The particles (numerals, "adverbs," "conjunctions," etc.) are many and varied and bafflingly idiomatic. A few of the directional enclitics will illustrate the idiomatic quality and also the precision that is so characteristically Navaho. By selecting among them, the Navaho divides space into zones and circles or into lines and directions, or indicates many other refinements of these ideas. For example, *kodi* (near me) and *kojí* (nearer me than you) show zones and circles thus:

> *ńlaáhdi*, at a point away from me and from you
> *ńláahjí*, at a point distant from both you and me

They can indicate lines and directions in this fashion:

> *ńleídi*, way over there where he is
> *nahjí*, away from where we are

Navaho Verbs

Navaho has a peculiarly intricate construction of verbs which derive quite definite meanings from the assembling of elements that are generalized and colorless in themselves. Indeed, it might be called a chemical language. That is, the basic process is that of utilizing the varying effects of small elements in different combinations. Syntax, to the Navaho consciousness, is locked up, confined within the verb.

In a sense, the conjugation of the verb is primarily a matter of making the proper alterations in the prefixes. The verb stem conveys an image which remains constant. However, this nuclear notion is much more minutely specific than is that of the vast majority of English verbs. Verbs of going, for example, are a great nuisance in all Athabascan languages. The first difficulty is that there are usually entirely different stems when one, two, or three or more persons are involved in the action. Thus one stem for the simplest kind of "going" is *-gháάh* in the singular, *-ʿaash* in the dual, and *-kááh* in the plural.

deesháάł, I shall go.
diitʿash, We (two) will go.
diikah, We (more than two) will go.

The complications are bewildering to a white person:

nił deeshʿash, I'll go with you. (The verb has a singular subject but the dual stem is used because two persons are involved in the action.)

nihił deeshkah, I'll go with the two of you. (The subject is still singular but the plural stem must be used because more than two people are involved.)

On the other hand:

deʿnohhááh, One of you come here. (*-noh-* refers to plural "you" but, since only one person is expected to act, the stem is singular.)

deʿnínááh, Come here (you, singular).
deʿnohkááh, Come here (you, plural, in a group).
deʿhohkááh, Come here (you, plural, one after another).

In short, where English is loose, Navaho is fussy about the finest shades of meaning, which it expresses by small permutations of verbal elements.

Navaho is compact as well as precise. The last example above shows how with great economy the Navaho language by the simple substitution of a monosyllable conveys ideas which take many words in English. Take two more examples along the same line:

dadiikah, We will each go separately.
hidiikah, We will go one after another, in succession.

Some of these prefixes are difficult to distinguish in English translation. For instance, *ná-* and *náá-* are ordinarily both rendered by "again," but actually there is a significant shade of difference.

deeskʿaaz hazlíį,   It (the weather) got cold.
deeskʿaaz náhásdlíį, It got cold again.
deeskʿaaz nááhásdlíį, It got cold again.

But really the third form means "it got cold *back*"; that is, a return to a previous state is specified.

Navaho is likewise very finicky in expressing agency. *Tsinaaʿeeł shił niʿééł, tsinaaʿeeł shił ʿaníłééł,* and *tsinaaʿeeł níłʿééł* may all be rendered: "I came by boat." But the first form implies that the boat floats off of its own accord, the second that the movement is caused by an indefinite or unstated subject, the third that the movement of the boat was caused by the speaker.

A great many verbs have alternating stems, depending upon the type of object which is acted upon or is the subject of a positional verb. These class stems embrace such categories as the following: the long-object class (a pencil, a stick, a pipe); the slender-flexible-object class (snakes, thongs, certain pluralities including certain types of food and property); the container-*and*-contents class; the granular-mass class (sugar, salt, etc.); the things-bundled-up class (hay, bundles of clothing, etc.—if they are loose and not compact); the fabric class (paper, spread out leather, blankets, etc.); the viscous-object class (mud, feces, etc.); the bulky-round-object class; the animate-object class; and others. Thus there is no such thing as saying "I give" in Navaho—there are more than twenty different forms, one of which must be chosen to accord with the nature of the object given.

It is really a distortion to say that there is any Navaho verb stem meaning "to give." With greater correctness we might say that "give" in Navaho is the transitive correspondent of "come." You cause something to come to one. "To give A to B" becomes, as it were, in Navaho "to handle such and such an object (the precise stem will depend, of course, upon the class of object) completively to or for such and such a person." To generalize: one cannot decide what stem to use in Navaho on the basis of the nuclear idea in English. The structure is too different. The Navaho language represents an importantly different mode of *thinking* and must be regarded as such.

The inflections of the verb in most European languages perform as one of their principal functions those distinctions between past, present, and future which we call "tense." It is an arguable question whether there are tenses in the European sense in Navaho. The language of The People is interested primarily in the category the grammarians call "aspect."

Aspect defines the geometrical character of an event, stating its definability with regard to line and point rather than its position in an absolute time scale or in time as broken up by the moving present of the speaker. Traces of aspect inflection may be found in modern Greek,

German, and Spanish, but only in Slavic languages such as Russian and Polish does it have any systematic importance among contemporary European tongues. Aspect indicates different types of activity. Thus, the momentaneous aspect in Navaho means that action is thought of as beginning and ending within an instant, while the continuative suggests that action lasts. Inceptive, cessative, durative, imperfective, and semelfactive, are some of the other aspects in Navaho—with a different paradigm of every verb stem for each.

Grammarians also consider modes as one of the principal verbal categories in Navaho. Some modes are similar to, but not identical with, the tenses of English. Others indicate the way an act is performed—repeatedly or customarily, etc. For example, *biih náshdááh* (iterative mode) means "time and again I put it on," whereas *biih yísháah* (usitative mode, means "habitually I put it on." The usitative mode implies the speaker's interest is general, not in a specific event. Often it should be translated "our custom is so and so." It may indeed refer to events that are hypothetical so far as the speaker is concerned. Hence sometimes it must be rendered "if I were to" or "whenever." The iterative, in contrast, refers to actual repetition of acts.

Future, present, and past time may be left unspecified or may be indicated by suffixes, but sometimes they are made clear by the combination of aspect and mode. For instance, *'ááshłííł* (imperfective aspect, progressive mode) may be rendered "I am (progressively) making it." The imperfective aspect most often conveys a sense analogous to that of English indefinite present. But the primary idea which The People express through this aspect is that of uncompleted action. So far as time is concerned, the act may take place in the past, provided that the act is uncompleted. Or it may refer to the future when one is about to do or in the act of doing something. Depending upon context and upon the mode with which it is combined, therefore, the imperfective must be rendered "I am in the act of" or "I was in the act of" or "I am about to be in the act of," and in a great variety of other ways.

Navahos are perfectly satisfied with what seem to whites rather imprecise discriminations in the realm of time sequences. On the other hand, they are the fussiest people in the world about always making explicit in the forms of the language many distinctions which English makes only occasionally and irregularly, more often than not leaving them vague or to be clarified from context. In English one says "I eat," meaning "I eat something." The Navaho point of view is different. "I eat" means "I eat it." If the object thought of is actually indefinite, then *'a-* ("something") must be expressed. Furthermore, Navaho always specifies through the form of the verb the contrast between status and action. All verbs in Navaho are divided by grammarians into two groups: neutral and active. "Neutral" designates those verbs that do not change their character. "Active" refers to verbs that denote activities or that do change their character. There is, in Navaho, all the difference in the world between the type of idea suggested by English "I am friendly" and that suggested by "I habitually do friendly acts." The English phrases are rendered by distinct Navaho forms. Each type of verb may also be either transitive or intransitive. "To be tall" is neutral-intransitive. "To hold it" is neutral-transitive. "I see it" (in the sense of "I have it visible") is the neutral-transitive form, whereas "I look at it" is neutral-active.

Because so much is expressed and implied by the few syllables that make up a single verb form, the Navaho verb is like a tiny Imagist poem. A free translation of such a microcosm of meaning must normally become a somewhat extended paraphrase before even the main significance can be included. One Navaho word more often than not turns into a whole sentence in English. The single word *shínii'á*, for instance, means "the rigid object (such as a gun) leans against me."

Let us look at some further examples showing the extent of definition required to convey the sense of a Navaho verb:

haadinsh'aa,   I hand it over to him by word of mouth.

shii'įįd,   He gave me a piece of his mind.

shan'doo'aal,   Would that you might give me back permission to speak.

'aajíyígháàh,   He is getting to that point there by you.

ni'á,   A set of round objects extends off in a horizontal line, or: I brought it.

'o'ó'áál,   Would that the sun (or moon) might set.

híínáál,   You are shuffling along sidewise.

'eeshdéél,   I have eaten some berries (apples, buns, or any plural separable objects) one at a time.

nándįįh,   Time and again you (sing.) eat it.

ná'íldil,   You are accustomed to eat plural separable objects one at a time.

hanlcóós,   You take a fabric-like object out of an enclosed space.

The above translations are no more than crude approximations that by no means transmit the total sense of the Navaho. In the first example the "him" is not just any "him" but a person being addressed politely or respectfully. The verb form is a somewhat stereotyped formula used in making certain types of gifts, especially of land. However, in some contexts it must be rendered "I promise it to him," and in others, "I forgive him." The optative form illustrated in the third example may also have the sense of a polite prohibitive, meaning, "Please don't give me back the floor." In the ninth example the form makes it plain that "it" is a definite "it" not "something" (indefinite), which would be a different form (*ná'idį́į́h*). The subtle distinctions inherent in the aspect and tense-mode forms used in the Navaho verbs are left completely unexpressed in the English renderings given. In short, it would take literally pages to analyze the full implications of these eleven words.

Most American Indians had little love for a corpse, even that of a close relative. Indeed, many Indians intensely feared the threat believed to come from a deceased kinsman. Because of this fear, hasty burials, quick decampments, name-use taboos, and excessively apparent grief and mourning were often quickly attendant upon a death scene. Apache and Navahos, as well as most of the Yuman-speaking groups, believed that ghosts emanated from the dead which were responsible, in one form or another, for most sickness and death.

34 Morris E. Opler and William E. Bittle

THE DEATH PRACTICES OF
THE KIOWA APACHE*

Because of the excessive fear of the ghost among the Apachean-speaking tribes of the Southwest and Southern Plains, death is a

* Abridged from "The Death Practices and Eschatology of the Kiowa Apache," by M. E. Opler and W. E. Bittle, in *Southwestern Journal of Anthropology*, **17**, 383–394, 1961.

traumatic experience for them, one which focuses attention on all possible allies of dark forces and which evokes elaborate ritual defenses. Understandably, therefore, it is an area of culture rich in interesting concepts and symbolism. As a result it has received a good deal of notice in the literature and has been the subject of a number of studies. This paper is meant to add to that series and to help pave the way for a comparative study that it is hoped will throw light upon the history, differentiation, and interrelations of the Apacheans.

The Kiowa Apache believed that the ghosts of dead relatives came to conduct the dying to the afterworld. A seriously ill person might mutter: "They come after me; I've got to go. I've lived pretty poor on this earth. My mother, my father, come after me" (6:121). That these visits of the ghosts of the departed are associated with death and ill fortune is indicated by the kind of appeal addressed to the corpse as soon as death occurred: "Don't you ever turn your face to us." "Don't look back, keep on going; when I get old and die I will see you." "If you look back evil will come upon us" (6:121).

Among the Kiowa Apache the reaction to a death was immediate and violent. Close relatives wailed, tore their clothes and exposed their bodies without shame; some shaved the head, lacerated the body, and cut off a finger joint. Women made a greater demonstration of grief than men, and the spouse of the dead person was expected to mourn most ostentatiously of all. A widow might dress in a garment made of smoke-blackened material from old tipi flaps, and she remained in this abject condition until relatives of her deceased husband, usually his sisters, released her from some of the mourning obligations and dressed her in good clothes. Similarly a widower went to great lengths to show his grief. Sometimes he requested relatives of his wife to gash his forehead or to cut off all his hair and gave presents to the one who performed the service.

The corpse, and particularly the skull, was considered a source of danger and contamination; the word for skull symbolizes not only the corpse but all the material and polluting aspects of death. It was believed hazardous even to get too close to the dead. Fainting spells, insanity, and facial paralysis could result from such exposure or contact. Consequently the body was prepared and disposed of with all dispatch. A close relative, usually a woman, washed the body with yucca suds, combed the hair, and painted the face, often with red and yellow ochre. Occasionally an outsider or a nonrelative was induced to prepare the body and was paid handsomely for this disagreeable task. The dead person was dressed in his best clothes. If death occurred during the day, the funeral took place before sundown. If the death occurred at night, the body was disposed of the following day. A prompt burial reduced the possibility that the ghost would linger and "talk" to relatives. The doorway of the Kiowa Apache tipi opened to the east; but because "the doorway is for the living," the corpse was removed from the north, west, or south side. Usually only close relatives followed the travois and made up the burial party. If someone who was not a kinsman attended, he was given a gift. Whenever possible, the corpse was placed in a shallow, rocky crevice in hilly country. Burial near streams was avoided for fear that the body would wash out. The personal belongings of an individual, such as his weapons and shield, might be buried with him. One eye-witness account mentions that the body of a Kiowa Apache chief was interred face downward, but this may have been happenstance. The favorite horse of the deceased was killed at the site of the grave by piercing it in the neck or shooting it in the head. As the animal collapsed, the wife of the dead man might grasp its neck, become spattered with its blood, and fall to the ground with it. In the case of a chief or prominent man, a number of animals might be sacrificed. On one occasion two horses and a mule were dispatched at the grave of a Kiowa Apache chief. Rocks and thorny branches were placed on top of the grave to discourage marauding animals. After the burial the site of a grave was strictly avoided.

Upon the return of the funeral party any remaining property of the deceased was destroyed. Most of the possessions which were combustible were burned; even the ordinary tipi was destroyed, though heraldic tipis were preserved and passed on to close male kin. A warrior's designed shield was buried with him or destroyed, but the right to make a similar shield was inherited by the nearest male relative. Surplus clothes of the dead person were not burned but were thrown into a river; ". . . you gave them to the river for some future return" (4). Apparently there was some vague idea that the property disposed of at the time of death would be of use in the after-life. However, any property or ceremonial knowledge a person had given to others before his death could be retained. The personal ceremonial equipment of the deceased was destroyed, but ritual objects of tribal importance, such as medicine bundles, were inherited in the male line or, in the absence of male kin, were placed in the custody of female relatives. If a man owned many horses, those which were not killed at his grave became the honored and pampered property of his brother. Their manes were trimmed and their tails were cropped, and they were ridden only to battle. If they perished in war, it was considered a credit to the deceased. Relatives of the dead wailed and mourned anew when they saw these horses about the camp and made a particular show of grief if any of them failed to return from an encounter.

Members of the burial party changed clothing upon their return. Those who had not cut their bodies washed with water. Those who had gashed their bodies rubbed fat on the cuts and could not wash until the wounds were healed. The mourners rubbed themselves liberally with sage. All close kinsmen of the dead person and those who had been involved in the funeral rites fumigated themselves freely with smoke from fires in which cedar, sage, or the root of a plant called "medicine fat"—powerful prophylactics against ghosts—were burned. In fact, sage, cedar, and "medicine fat" were used whenever the fear of ghosts or thoughts and dreams about the dead aroused anxieties. To ward off hazards associated with death and ghosts, a cross of cedar ash was traced on the forehead, also. Death rendered a locality unclean and dangerous. If a family in which a death occurred had been camping with others, the entire group moved from the place where the person had died. The immediate family of the deceased stayed at some distance from the others for a while. During this period of semi-isolation the mourners would go to elevated spots to wail and there would be visited by friends who sought to comfort them.

Not only was the memory of the dead person suppressed by the destruction of his property and of objects associated with him, but there could not be any direct reference to him. His name could not be mentioned, particularly in the presence of his relatives, and words that were similar to or identical with his name could not be uttered. Persons who had used a certain kinship term for the deceased now addressed those of similar relationship with secondary terms. Because of the strictness and extensions of these usages, names were not conferred upon children until it was fairly certain that they would survive.

The elaborateness of practice and the intensity of anxiety in respect to death varied with the age and status of the deceased. The whole group engaged in mourning for a chief; but because of their innocence and lack of rancor, the bodies and ghosts of children caused little concern, and much the same can be said about very old people who had lived their life out to the full. Nor was the slain enemy feared. Explained an informant: "You don't have to worry about being hurt by the ghost of an enemy. When you kill someone in battle, he is totally eliminated.

There is nothing left, not even his ghost" (4). It was the corpses and ghosts of Kiowa Apache who had died in the prime of life which caused most worry to the living.

The most usual method of disposal of the dead was interment, but in the case of warriors scaffold burial also was practiced. There is the possibility that lodge or tipi burial, at least of a temporary nature, occasionally occurred, too. An informant asserted that the body of a prominent man was sometimes left for a day or two in a tipi before final disposal in the hope that he would be restored to life. Two stories have been collected from the Kiowa Apache which include descriptions of tipi burial.

The close relatives of the deceased, particularly the brothers of a dead man and the sisters of a dead woman, not only mourned energetically but were careful to see that the memory of their dead kinsman was treated with proper respect. If the dead man belonged to one of the male dancing societies, the organization had to obtain consent from his closest male relatives before it could hold its next function. If it failed to do this, the outraged brother, father, or uncle could invade the place of meeting, destroying the drum and other property, and prevent the dance from continuing. The organization would then have to mollify the relatives with gifts and to smoke and mourn for the departed. If some of the members of a war party were slain, the victory dance was postponed out of respect for the dead and regard for the feelings of the bereaved. The blood kin of the deceased kept a close watch on his spouse to make sure that mourning obligations were not taken lightly. If this person had been a good husband or wife and well liked by the family, the burden could be lightened and shortened; but unmistakable evidence of grief was ordinarily expected for an initial period. The close blood kin of the dead person also expected to have a good deal to say about the future marriage arrangements of a surviving widow or widower. There was a strong feeling in favor of sororate-levirate arrangements. If a woman who died had an unmarried sister, it was she who ordinarily took care of any children left motherless by the death. She was also the leading candidate for the hand of the widower, once the mourning period was over. In fact, the mourning period could be shortened if a marriage between the women and her dead sister's husband was agreed on. If the deceased woman had no eligible sister, real or classificatory, the widower still had to wait at least a year before he could make marriage arrangements for himself independently, had to present gifts to his relatives-in-law, and had to gain their consent. If he acted too hastily or without permission, his wife's sisters had the right to beat him and his new wife without interference. On the other hand, if he acted with due respect, even though he ultimately married outside his former wife's family, his ties with its members remained strong. The affinal terms they had used to each other were continued, and his new wife was treated with courtesy and addressed by a kin term. The same principle held if it was a man who died. Then his wife was expected to mourn ostentatiously and in time to wed an unmarried brother of her deceased husband, if his family so desired. In fact, this man was obligated to look after the welfare of his dead brother's wife and children, and the marriage was essentially a sharpening and formalizing of the responsibility. In case there was no marriageable brother-in-law, if a woman honored the memory of her dead husband long enough and obtained permission for an outside alliance, the former ties with her relatives-in-law were retained and even extended to her new husband. On the other hand, any lack of seriousness in mourning or a marriage outside the family without permission was resented and brought swift reprisals. The brothers of the dead man could then beat the woman or cut off the tip of her nose and also destroy the property of the man she had married. In addition, a supernatural punishment menaced a widow or widower who married without permission before the mourning period ended. Such a person and his mate were likely to be persecuted by the affronted ghost of the deceased. Sometimes the relatives of a person who had become the target of the ire of a dead man's kin would try to pacify them by inducing them to smoke with them and forgive the couple.

The burial and mourning practices which have been summarized are best understood in terms of the concepts which enter into Kiowa Apache eschatology. There are three main concepts of this kind to keep in mind: a vital force or animating spirit which continues as a neutral or harmless spirit after death; "evil tendencies" which develop during life and continue on in association with the ghost in after-life; and the ghost which comes into being at death and is a potential source of danger to the living thereafter. The "evil tendencies" do not appear in personified form; rather, they are the background and dynamics of the ghost's activities. It is the ghost which assumes definite shapes and which uses recognized instrumentalities to achieve its dark ends.

The life principle or animating spirit in man is called dà·γą́·'. Dying can be described by saying, "Dà·γą́·' is fading," or "Dà·γą́·' is going." We shall arbitrarily refer to dà·γą́·' as "spirit." At death the spirit leaves the body for an afterworld, usually considered to be sky world or heaven. The spirits of all human beings, regardless of whether they have been good or evil on earth, have the same destination. The spirits of those whose conduct was questionable in life are purified and capable only of good in heaven. Spirits do not interfere in earthly affairs and cannot assume the form of animals or natural forces. They remain in their sky world and enjoy a perpetual existence of abundance and pleasure. Kiowa Apache who participated in the Ghost Dance Religion and who fell down in trance have claimed, on their recovery, to have been in heaven and seen departed relatives there. Obviously the living had no sense of persecution by these spirits.

Less pleasant and much less easy to label by a single term is the notion of bà'é·h. Linguistically the form is probably related to the word for "gray." Semantically the matter is more complex. Bà'é·h causes the individual to do destructive and antisocial acts in anger. It is involved in feats that show power and magical immunity but about which there is something unsavory and weird. It is absent in the newborn child, and an exceptionally good person may be the repository of very little of it at the end of his life. The conduct of a woman who marries too soon after the death of her husband is explained by bà'é·h, and so is the behavior of the shaman who traffics with owls and ghosts to his own advantage. Perhaps the closest we can come to conceptualizing bà'é·h, is to think of it as the evil tendencies, powers, and impulses that accumulate during life. Bà'é·h enters Kiowa Apache eschatology because death does not terminate it. It is as much a component of the ghost as it is of the nature of the living adult; and it is, of course, far more dangerous and uncontrollable in the ghost. These precipitates of human malice, perpetuated beyond the grave, take no separate shape and are not seen or felt as such. But they furnish the motive power for ghosts which seek to return to the encampments of the people and spread terror and sickness.

Whereas the "evil tendencies" in an individual have their origin in life and continue into the after-life, the čį̀·yé or "ghost" (literally, the word conveys the meaning of "to be no good") comes into existence only at death. The proper destination of the ghost is an afterworld, generally conceived of as an underworld. It, too, is a place of "no scarcity" and of comfort. McAllister was told that it is located under a mythological northern lake from which one of the important medicine bundles was obtained. A Kiowa Apache who entered the lake and secured the ceremony and bundle saw the ghosts of his dead friends and relatives there and, while sitting in a tipi, "he heard the ordinary sounds of camp life—the murmuring gossip of women, the scraping of hides, and the barking of dogs" (8:162–163).

As long as ghosts are content to travel to their afterworld and remain there, they do no injury to living men. But they tend to resist the termination of their life: they linger about the corpse, the place of burial, their former haunts and possessions; and, even when they do go to the afterworld, they have the power to return to persecute or harass those with whom they have scores to settle. No ghost comes back except on frightening errands; no ghost is seen or heard by a human being without a sense of terror and despair. The least violent act a ghost can perform is to lead a new shade to the afterworld. Even this is interpreted by the living as a threat; the ghosts are constantly trying to extinguish life, to draw the living to the dead.

Although children who died were not feared, their very helplessness and vulnerability to supernatural attack made them ready targets of ghosts and particularly susceptible to evil influences associated with death. Consequently it was important to keep children from seeing or touching a corpse or from watching funeral processions. Because ghosts sometimes appear as whirlwinds or as sparks (lightning?) that move ahead of whirlwinds, children were taught to look away or cover the eyes at the approach of a whirlwind, and the face of a baby was shielded by an older person so he would not see this phenomenon. Also, because of concern over the ghost's undue interest in children, the footprints of a child who was learning to walk were rubbed out. If an infant had to be left alone, a stick was placed across the cradle at the chest to protect it from ghosts. Older children were trained to ignore whistling noises, for ghosts try to attract attention to themselves by such means.

There are also a number of birds and animals that are associated with death and the ghost. It is Crow who is charged with the origin of death. Angered because he was not given the plumage of the eagle in the early days of the world, he threw a rock into the water, saying, "If this comes up there will be no death, but if it sinks there will be death" (7:22). Though the crow is unloved for this, there is no evidence of direct association between it and the ghost on this account.

Dogs, coyotes, and wolves are also connected with thoughts and portents of misfortune and death. It is said that the coyote howls before a death occurs and that the howling of a dog or wolf is also warning of death or bad luck. For this reason howling dogs are often driven from camp. Certain animals and birds are sufficiently feared to be used as bugaboos. Children who misbehave are told that the wolf, coyote, or owl will get them unless they mend their ways.

If the ghost alters its appearance, it is as an owl that it is most likely to return. Accordingly, the presence of an owl about the encampment arouses liveliest apprehensions, and the hooting of the owl is interpreted as a threatening message. Since the owl is active in the nighttime, it is believed that attacks by ghosts occur mostly after nightfall. One of the names for ghosts is "They move around at night," probably a reference to the malignant ghost in the form of an owl.

There are shamans with ceremonies to control ghosts and owls and to cure ghost sickness, but it is a question whether these religious practitioners are not ultimately as much feared as the malady they claim to heal. Since they can influence ghosts and owls, they are suspected of practicing witchcraft through them on occasion, of sending owls and ghosts to sicken those who have offended them, or even, for a fee, of dispatching ghosts to trouble someone who has done them no harm. Moreover, it is hinted that some of them use their knowledge first to strike down a fellow tribesman with ghost sickness and then to cure him of it in exchange for fine presents. These shamans are considered by many to have more than a fair share of "evil tendencies" and are believed to be prominent among those who return as injurious ghosts after death. In their ritual they claim to employ the owl as a messenger between themselves and the dead, and they make much use of feathers of the eagle and the swift-hawk in their ceremonies.

It is interesting to consider from what direction ghost sickness is thought to come and who is most likely to be affected by it. It is agreed that there is not much need to fear the ghost of a good and kindly person, but one must not overlook the possibility of masked or suppressed antagonism, either. Consequently there are few dead persons who are not suspected at all. An undercurrent of fear permeates the whole thought area. Perhaps the most potent curse in the language is to call a person a ghost. If conflict with an individual prior to his death was open and sharp, there is even more cause for alarm, for "if the dead person has a grudge against somebody, the ghost comes back and causes sickness in that person" (4). The close and constant interaction between kin makes it almost inevitable that a good share of the "grudges" and guilt feelings remain within the family circle. As a Kiowa Apache put it: "It bothers mostly the members of the family. . . . I think that the more closely related you are to the dead person, the more the ghost may bother you. My wife always believes this, and she thinks that her father's ghost may come back"(4).

Women and children are considered more vulnerable than men to ghost sickness and witchcraft.

Ghost or owl sickness has certain rather standard characteristics of development and symptom. After the death of a relative or friend, a person may be gloomy and depressed. He may dream of the dead and of death; and since such dreams are portents of what may happen, he fumigates generously with sage, cedar, and "medicine fat" and prays that the events pictured in the dreams will not come to pass. He seeks to forget the matter, for thinking and dreaming of the deceased are likely to induce the return of the ghost. If his thoughts and dreams are of a kinsman, the cultural prescriptions place him in an ambivalent, anxiety-provoking position. He destroys the property of his relative and refrains from mentioning his name in order to banish his memory and to prevent the musings that lead to visits from ghosts. Nevertheless, he must re-member to play the mourner in regard to dress, social life, and other matters for some time. This alternation of repression and exhibition makes it really impossible to put the dead person out of mind, and his inability to accomplish this feeds his dread of the return of the ghost. The process is circular and self-defeating and may account for the exces-sive amount of anxiety that surrounds the death complex of the Kiowa Apache and other Apachean groups.

If the symptoms are no more severe than depression and bad dreams, the situation is usually handled by means of the common remedies for dealing with ghosts. But an acute case may involve hysteria, insanity, or paralysis, particularly facial paralysis. Then a shamanistic ceremony is required. Ghost or owl sickness, and especially sickness of this kind sent by a witch, usually is marked by a twisted mouth and a "twisting" of the eyes. In fact, ghost sickness is traditionally associated with ailments of the upper part of the body. More recently polio has been attributed to ghost sickness, the affected part being the area touched by the ghost.

Kiowa Apache culture was badly shattered and impoverished by the time the first serious study of it was made by McAllister in 1933–34. There are now only a few members of the Kiowa Apache tribe who can speak the language with any fluency, and there are even fewer who to-day know much about the older cultural traditions. It is almost certain that details of the Kiowa Apache death practices have been lost which can never be recovered. Yet we can be thankful that we have as good an outline as we do, and we can look forward to using it to good advantage in comparative studies.

For example, even the most cursory review of the materials shows some extremely significant agreements between the Kiowa Apache and the Lipan Apache in respect to practices and beliefs at death. Besides the core of traits that all Apacheans share, such as the fear of ghosts, hasty burial, etc., there are others in which the two tribes tend to correspond closely and contrast with most of the others. For instance, the Lipan, like the Kiowa Apache, make a distinction between the life principle or spirit and the ghost; and they ask the corpse not to look back during its journey to the afterworld. They also shoot the favorite mount of the dead person in the throat and trim the manes and tails of the horses that are spared. They, too, move the whole encampment when a death occurs. Likewise, isolation of the family of the deceased for some time is practiced, and the same custom of the comforting of the bereaved by outsiders is found among them. For both of these tribes juniper is a purifying agent useful against ghosts, and widows and widowers who marry too soon have reason to fear persecution at the hands of the ghost of the former mate. There are many Kiowa Apache parallels to Jicarilla Apache practices, too, which need to be scrutinized; but these do not seem to be quite as impressive as the Kiowa Apache-Lipan resemblances. At any rate, those who are prone to see the Kiowa Apache as an offshoot of the Sarsi or as the remnant of a separate migration into the Plains will have to consider evidence of this kind.

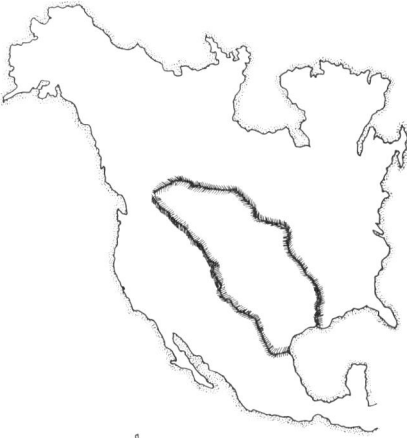

SECTION VIII
The Plains

No Indian group so caught the fancy of the twentieth century as did the Plains Indians. Yet no group of North American Indians was more atypical than the hawk-nosed, feather-wearing, buffalo-hunting Sioux, Cheyenne, or Crow. Glorified through "wild-west" shows, immortalized on the buffalo-head nickel, the Indian of the northern Plains has become the prototype of the aboriginal North American. In reality the despised "digger" of the Great Basin, or the nonromantic Pima of the Southwest, or the haughty Kwakiutl of the Northwest Coast would have served as a more valid stereotype.

The Plains Indian depicted by Hollywood was a product of acculturation, a result of the pervasive changes following the introduction of the horse and the gun. Prior to the seventeenth century, the central portion of North America (a broad band extending from Saskatchewan and Alberta on the north to the Gulf of Mexico on the south) was inhabited by simple horticulturalists, and probably by some nomadic groups as well. Both of these populations were to a degree dependent upon the enormous herds of buffalo that roamed the Plains until their destruction by hunters near the close of the nineteenth century; but it was only after the introduction of the horse and the gun in the eighteenth century that Indians of the Plains took their characteristic pose.

The most typical of the Plains tribes [the Arapaho, Assiniboin, Blackfoot, Cheyenne, Comanche, Crow, Dakota (Sioux), Kiowa, and others] were to be found in a 300- to 400-mile-wide strip fronting the eastern slope of the Rocky Mountains. Here were the grassy steppes where buffalo hunting reached its zenith, as Lowie points out. Further to the east, on what have been called the tallgrass "prairies," precipitation was nearly double that of the western plains (prairie range = 20–40 inches annually). The prairies were inhabited by cultural and linguistic relatives of the farming peoples in the eastern portion of North America who, for perhaps thousands of years, had occupied the wooded banks of the western tributaries of the Mississippi.

The earliest occupants of the Plains were apparently hunters of large game animals associated with the terminal Pleistocene period, chiefly mammoth and bison. This occupation dates back at least 10,000 years, and perhaps much earlier (see Willey, p. 15). The period between 5000 B.C. and approximately 2000 B.C. is the "Dark

Ages" for the Plains; little archaeological evidence has as yet been uncovered for this period.

Influences dated at 4,000 years ago from the eastern portion of the continent are clearly present in the Prairies, and at approximately the same time a "Desert culture" form is found throughout the western Plains. By 1000 b.c. in what is now Kansas, Woodland-type cultures ("Hopewellian") were present and left such remains as pottery, carefully worked ground stone tools and ornaments, native copper objects, burial mounds, and fairly extensive village debris. Sometime after the time of Christ, the Plains "Village" people departed their extensive and well-known sites to rely heavily upon river-bottom horticulture and upon the hunting of buffalo herds. It is likely that Europeans encountered descendants largely of the Plains "Village" people when they penetrated the Plains for the first time, in the sixteenth and seventeenth centuries.

During the eighteenth and nineteenth centuries the story of the Plains Indians is, if filled with temporary splendor, marked by an ever-increasing rate of cultural decline. Hard hit by diseases introduced by the "white man" (especially smallpox), ever more restricted by the incursions of hunters, trappers, and finally settlers, the Plains Indians either stood and fought, or slowly succumbed. In either case the result was essentially the same: loss of land, loss of culture, loss of dignity. Despite the existence of numerous reservations on the Plains both in the United States and Canada, little eighteenth- and nineteenth-century Plains culture has survived. And, tragically, the memories of the surviving descendants of the Plains tribes are memories which go back only to the period of the gun and the horse—memories which extend only to the period when decimation and destruction were already upon them.

35 Robert H. Lowie

THE CULTURE-TYPE OF THE PLAINS INDIANS*

"Plains" is a geographical term that may be construed loosely to include the area between the Mississippi and the Rocky Mountains, along with adjacent parts of Canada. Or it may be limited so as to exclude the "Prairie" belt. However, it is not possible to apply the narrower definition at all strictly. The Plains proper are supposed to be marked off by their short-grass vegetation, a result of aridity; and the Prairie soil is allegedly distinguishable by its dark color. However, neither of these criteria is absolute. The shift in the character of the soil is gradual as one travels eastward, so that any line of demarcation drawn on this basis would be arbitrary. The true Plains are arid, with an average rainfall of less than 20 inches a year against 30 inches or more in other farming regions of our country. Hence the lack of trees and the dominant part of drought-resisting grama and buffalo grass in the vegetation. However, in this respect also no rigid definition will hold. In 1894 the town of Hays, Kansas, had a precipitation of only 11.80 inches, whereas in another year it rose to 35.40 inches. In some years the whole area will suffer from exceptional drought or share unusual humidity, but more frequently there will be no such uniformity in the several sections of the Plains. In consequence of such fluctuation the difference in vegetation from the Prairies may disappear, wet years bringing taller species of grass. Great variation also occurs with reference to temperature; in the same year subareas differ noticeably, so that in Texas the mercury may rise to 100° Fahrenheit for 30 consecutive days, whereas in North Dakota there may be only two such days during the same month; in the following year the figures may be reversed.

* Abridged from "Introduction," in *Indians of the Plains*, by R. H. Lowie. Garden City, N. Y.: Natural History Press, 1–11, 1963.

Even within a restricted section of the territory, appreciable differences are found. In South Dakota the southeastern valleys have an elevation of 1,100 feet against that of 5,000 feet in the Black Hills; and
while the annual precipitation in the former district averages 30 inches,
it drops to only 14 in the northwestern part of the state.

It is thus impossible to give a strict definition of the Plains Area in
geographical terms. Culturally it would be even more arbitrary to set up
absolute boundaries, for it is a matter of historical record or trustworthy
tradition that many tribes of the Plains emigrated into them from the
Prairies and Woodlands of the east. Hence we cannot confine ourselves
to the short-grass regions, but shall include in our survey the natives of
southern Alberta, Saskatchewan, and Manitoba; of Montana, Wyoming, Colorado, the Dakotas, Nebraska, Kansas, Oklahoma, and
northern Texas; and of Minnesota, Iowa, Missouri, and Arkansas. As a
matter of fact, it will not be possible to avoid mention of adjoining districts in any direction, their natives being conveniently referred to as
"marginal."

THE PLAINS TRIBES

Primitive peoples are most conveniently classified according to their
linguistic affiliations. Groups whose speech is so similar that they are
able to communicate with each other, notwithstanding minor differences, are said to be speaking *dialects* of the same language; if the
differences are too great for mutual intelligibility, we speak of distinct
languages. However, in many instances of the latter kind, the languages
show many resemblances that can be explained only on the assumption
that they have diverged from a common parental tongue, perhaps centuries or even millenniums ago. This holds true for English, Dutch, and
Swedish, but even Russian proves to be connected with these languages
when their vocabularies and grammars are closely examined. Such ultimately related languages jointly form a *family* (*stock*). In a large family it may happen that two or more of the languages are closer to each
other than to the rest, in which case the family is for convenience divided into *branches*. Thus, most European languages plus certain
Asiatic ones form the Indo-European family, which comprises the Ger-
manic, Romance, Slavic, and other branches, most of them composed of
several distinct languages, which in turn may split up into various dialects.

This mode of grouping, when applied to the Plains Indians leads to the recognition of six families. If we hyphenate the names of political groups speaking identical or virtually identical languages, we arrive at the following tabulation:

Algonkian family	Blackfoot (Piegan–Blood–Northern Blackfoot)	Plains Cree Plains Ojibwa (Plains Chippewa)
	Cheyenne Arapaho–Gros Ventre	
Athabaskan family	Sarsi	Kiowa Apache
Caddoan family	Pawnee–Arikara	Wichita
Kiowan family	Kiowa	
Siouan family	Mandan Hidatsa Crow	Dakota–Assiniboin Iowa–Oto–Missouri Omaha–Ponca–Osage–Kansa
Uto-Aztecan family	Wind River Shoshone–Comanche	Ute

Though the several Plains tribes spoke so many different languages, they were not without a common medium of communication, *viz.*, a sign language not identical with that of deaf-mutes, but comparable to it. The gestures employed to designate various ideas were generally understood throughout the Plains. To illustrate the system, "cold" was indicated by clenching both hands and crossing the forearms in front of the chest with a trembling motion. "Chief" was represented by raising the forefinger, pointing it vertically upward, then reversing the finger and bringing it down. For "rain" or "snow" the gesture was to hold the hands at the level of the shoulders, the fingers hanging down, the palm down, and then to push downward. Though it might seem that this was an inferior system of communication, its possibilities were far greater than might be supposed. A Cheyenne could thereby recount his war deeds to a group of Crow Indians incapable of understanding one word of his speech. A Shoshone once explained to the author how the folk tale of a giant bird that snatched and ate people could be told wholly by signs; and the Kiowa correspondingly gave General Hugh Lenox Scott an account of their complex Sun Dance ceremonial.

PLAINS CULTURE

These tribes share a sufficiently large number of cultural traits to be classed together as representing a distinctive mode of life. Inasmuch as they inhabit a continuous territory, it is proper to speak of a "Plains" culture area, using the geographical term in its wider sense. In characterizing such an area we must keep in mind neighboring areas, for only by comparison can a type of culture stand out clearly. This means that lacks as well as positive occurrences must be noted. The Plains peoples, then, were typically large-game hunters, dependent for a considerable part of their diet on buffalo and using buffalo hides and deerskin for clothing and receptacles. Unlike the Basin and Plateau tribes to the west, they made little or no use of fish and of such small game as rabbits. Houses of stone or adobe, such as are still inhabited by the Pueblos of New Mexico and Arizona, were wholly absent. During at least part of the year the Plains Indians lived in conical skin-covered tents (tipis); these were larger than the similarly shaped tents of the Mackenzie River region to the north and further differed from them and from the occasionally skin-covered Eastern Woodland tents in having a special arrangement for a smoke vent. Characteristic was the seasonal grouping of tipis in a large circle.

The only aboriginal domestic animal was the dog, eaten by a few of the tribes, more generally used for packing and traction. The Spaniards introduced horses, which vitally altered hunting and transport methods, secondarily also affecting other aspects of life. The Plains Indians, favored by their environment, turned into equestrian nomads, sharply contrasting with Pueblo, Woodland, and Basin peoples. However, this transformation does not antedate the eighteenth century. The Spanish settlements in present New Mexico were the source of supply, and the new feature spread slowly toward the north. Equestrian culture and its derivatives are therefore typical of the whole area only from well into the eighteenth century. Travel before and after the introduction of the horse was by land, the Woodland bark or dugout canoe being conspicuously absent among all but the easternmost tribes of the area.

As regards crafts, Plain Indians were good skin dressers and extensively used hides and dressed skins. In glaring contrast to their western and southwestern neighbors they displayed next to no aptitude for weaving and basketry. Woodwork likewise was not developed. However, the women made a good deal of fine porcupine-quill embroidery, and some skill was displayed in the attachment of feathers for decoration.

Several nonmaterial traits require mention at this point. Like the Eastern Indians, the Plains tribes were very warlike, thus again differing sharply from the natives of the Basin and the Plateau. A periodically functioning police force is another characteristic of the area, and clublike organizations promoting the military spirit as part of their functions were widespread. The number and complexity of ceremonials again distinguishes the Plains from the Basin and Plateau, the climax being attained in the usually annual festival of the Sun Dance. Decorative art in painting, quillwork, and beadwork emphasized straight-lined geometrical designs, the style of painted figures on rawhide containers being highly distinctive. Except near the eastern border of the area, the absence of floral patterns until recent times separated Plains from Woodland art.

The foregoing diagnostic traits suffice to set off the Plains from other areas. However, some supplementary statements are required. In the first place, a few of the outlying tribes, such as the Ute and Shoshone, share the external features rather than the religious and social traits, which tend to be at best attenuated among them. Secondly, the Southern Siouans together with the Pawnee, Mandan, Hidatsa, and Arikara unquestionably represent a distinct subculture. That is, while displaying most or all of the Plains criteria, they show additional traits, notably agriculture and a semisedentary existence with pottery-making and part-time residence in fixed villages of earthlodges.

Finally, any classification on cultural and geographical lines has an element of arbitrariness in borderline cases. Whether to include certain peripheral groups is optional. Thus, the Upper Kutenai, recently living in the extreme north of Idaho and Montana as well as in British Columbia, but once living east of the Rockies, were buffalo hunters and adopted a few traits, such as the Sun Dance, from the Blackfoot or Cree. They have been regarded both as a stock by themselves and as another Algonkian group. Several other Plateau groups—Flathead, Nez Percé, Yakima, Spokane—also periodically invaded the Plains to hunt, but apart from dress and certain decorative art designs, they took over very little from the Plains tribes.

Two additional Uto-Aztecan tribes, the Bannock and the Northern Shoshone of Idaho, likewise exhibited a few Plains features. Finally, the Jicarilla Apache (Athabaskan) of northern New Mexico and southern Colorado similarly shared some Plains Indian traits. In all these instances, however, the similarities are of comparatively recent date and relate to superficial features. Thus, though the Jicarilla hunted buffalo in the Plains, they never felt comfortable there and promptly hurried out of the unfamiliar territory. According to Professor Morris Opler, who has made a comparative study of most Apache groups, "psychologically they are anything but a Plains people." Corresponding remarks hold for the other dubious cases. For example, the Northern Shoshone (Idaho) discovered by Lewis and Clark in 1805 largely depended on a fish diet and sometimes resorted to their ancient grass lodges for dwellings; their social and ceremonial life was always extremely meager, and their myths conformed to the Basin rather than the Plains pattern. Other borderline cases include members of the inadequately known Caddoan stock, encountered by the Spaniards as early as 1541 and 1542, and the Quapaw or Arkansas Indians. However, both are properly put into the Southeastern culture area, though linguistically the Quapaw are one with the Omaha subdivision of the Siouan family.

POLITICAL, LINGUISTIC, CULTURAL UNITS

The term "tribe" may be used in a political sense, corresponding to the "nation" of civilized peoples. This is unobjectionable *provided* we remember the linguistic and political groups need not coincide. As the use of the same language did not prevent the American colonists from founding a new nation, so Omaha and Ponca Indians separated and at times even fought each other. In other words, linguistically they remained one, politically they became two tribes. The Piegan, Blood, and Northern Blackfoot differ only in minutiae of speech, but politically they were independent. The Dakota, popularly known as "Sioux," fall into three dialectic groups, roughly distinguishable by the use of d, n, or l: the Eastern dialect has "Dakota" for the tribal name of the speaker, the Central dialect (of which Assiniboin is a subvariety) substitutes "Nakota," the Western dialect "Lakota." So close are these variants that when missionaries reduced the language to writing in the Santee (Eastern) form the Teton (Western) groups read it without trouble, merely pronouncing the words after their own fashion—precisely as an American reads "clerk" in a British book though the author pronounced it "clark." Politically, however, there were many distinct Dakota groups.

In short, it is necessary to be clear whether the term "tribe" is to be understood politically or linguistically.

If two groups are identical, or nearly so, in speech, it seems a fair assumption that their separation took place a relatively short time ago, that accordingly both have preserved essentially the same mode of life. However, there is no regularity about this; a change of environment may bring with it new adaptations or the loss of adaptations to an earlier habitat. The Teton could not have split off from other Dakota many centuries ago, but by 1700 they were neither gathering wild rice nor paddling canoes after the Santee fashion. Of great importance in this connection are the alien contacts experienced, which may profoundly alter a people's culture. The Sarsi language differs very slightly from that of the Beaver Indians but moving southward, possibly about 1700, they soon attached themselves to the Blackfoot and assimilated the essentials of their culture, so that they are in historic times incomparably closer to the natives of the northern Plains than to their linguistic congeners. Naturally a complete transformation is rarely achieved within a short space of time; the Cree clung to snowshoes even in the Far West, and the Uto-Aztecan buffalo hunters preserved the Basin type of mythology.

Many classic papers have been written on the influence of the horse and gun on the way of life of the Plains Indian. The tracing of the introduction and of subsequent events is a monument to the combined skills of archaeologists, ethnohistorians, and ethnologists. The following exposition is, to be sure, an excellent example of the type of work which the historically inclined anthropologist is capable. But it is more than that. It is one of the best studies made of the long-term cultural effects subsequent to the introduction of foreign elements—the horse and the gun. There is a valuable lesson to be learned from this case. If the short-term effect of the horse and gun was cultural grandeur, the long-term result was cultural disintegration. The mid-twentieth century is a time when American and other cultures are avidly introducing innovations wherever and whenever possible: medicines, cosmetics, religions, Coca-Cola, Volkswagens, and on and on. One can only speculate as to the possible long-term effect of such innovations.

36 John C. Ewers

THE HORSE COMPLEX IN PLAINS INDIAN HISTORY*

THE NATURAL AND CULTURAL SETTING

The vast herds of buffalo that roamed the grassy plains between the Mississippi River and the Rocky Mountains made that area one of the finest natural hunting grounds in the world. From the time of Folsom Man, some 10,000 or more years ago, until the extermination of the buffalo ca. 1880, dependence upon the buffalo was a characteristic of the Indian cultures of this area. In the period immediately preceding the spread of the Spanish horse over the Great Plains the dominant culture of the area was shared by those tribes living along the fertile river valleys, in semisedentary villages, growing crops of corn, beans, and squash. Undoubtedly, these tribes relied heavily upon buffalo meat to supplement their vegetable diet. Presumably they hunted buffalo extensively during those periods of the year when they were not actively engaged in planting, cultivating, or harvesting their crops. The distances traveled in these hunts must have depended upon the relative scarcity or availability of buffalo near their villages. The Mandan in the north, the Pawnee in the Central Plains, and the Wichita in the south were the westernmost of these horticultural tribes. Westward of them, on the High Plains, lived several tribes who were nomads, depending upon the wandering buffalo herds for their livelihood, which they followed on foot carrying their portable lodges and meager possessions with them on dog travois and on their own backs. It seems most probable that these tribes included the Blackfoot in the north, the Shoshoni-Commanche in the Montana-Wyoming area, and the Kiowa, and Apache (Coronado's "Querechos and Teyas") farther south. There may have been other tribes that have since disappeared or were absorbed by known tribes. Compared with the toil and uncertainty of the nomad's life, that of the

* Abridged from "The Horse in Blackfoot Indian Culture; with Comparative Material from Other Western Tribes," by J. C. Ewers, *in Smithsonian Institution, Bureau of American Ethnology, Bulletin* **159**, 331–339, 1955.

gardening tribes must have appeared relatively easy and secure to the Indians of the time.

Their experience with dogs as transport animals prepared the Plains Indians for acceptance of the horse as a stronger and more useful "big dog," which would relieve them of carrying heavy burdens and expedite buffalo hunting. The Indians were fortunate also that their grasslands afforded excellent range for horses on which these herbiverous animals would thrive and increase in numbers with relatively little care. Cultural and natural conditions greatly encouraged the ready acceptance of the horse by the Plains tribes and their rapid conversion from pedestrians to horsemen.

I believe the role of the horse complex in the history of the Plains Indians can best be comprehended in terms of three periods, as follows.

1. Period Of Diffusion And Integration (from the first acquisition of horses by Plain Indians to about 1800). In view of the elemental simplicity of Plains Indian methods of breaking horses and teaching individuals to ride, I see no reason to believe that any prolonged period was required for the conversion of pedestrian Indians to horsemen. I believe that the most important determinant of the rate of diffusion of horses from tribe to tribe was the number of animals available, and that the number of horses traded or captured from Spanish or Pueblo Indian sources increased as the 18th century progressed. This increase, combined with the natural increase in the herds possessed by Indians, made possible wider distribution of horses over broader areas. Although tribes on the periphery of the Spanish Southwest may have begun to acquire them as early as 1640, horses were a novelty to the majority of the northern Plains tribes a century later. The great period of horse diffusion in a northern portion of the Great Plains was from ca. 1740 to 1800. A Blackfoot Indian, born ca. 1725, could have witnessed the acquisition of the first horse by his people and lived to see the relative stabilization of tribal horse holdings among them by ca. 1800.

In the northward spread of horses trade appeared to have been the most important avenue of diffusion. The primary center of diffusion was the Spanish Southwest from which horses were traded or stolen and driven northward to secondary diffusion centers among the Shoshoni in western Wyoming or Montana, and at or near the horticultural villages on the Missouri. From these secondary centers horses were traded to other tribes of the northern Plains, sometimes passing through tertiary centers of diffusion such as the annual trading fair on the James River where horses obtained by the Teton from the Arikara were traded to other Dakota tribes. The number of tribes engaged as primary intermediaries in supplying the secondary centers gives a clue to the expanding nature of this trade. Presumably the Ute were the earliest suppliers of the Shoshoni center, while the Comanche entered this trade after 1705. The Kiowa and Kiowa Apache seem to have been the earliest suppliers of the horticultural tribes on the Upper Missouri. Sometime after 1750 the Comanche appear to have shifted their trade to the horticultural tribes. Prior to 1800 the Cheyenne and Arapaho had entered the trade between the primary center and the horticultural tribes, while the Crow became active in acquiring horses at the Shoshonean center and trading them at considerable profit on the Missouri.

Raiding for horses appears to have been a secondary avenue of diffusion, necessitated by the inability of Indians to purchase needed horses at prices they could afford to pay for them. Certainly horse raiding was common throughout the area from the Spanish frontier to the Saskatchewan Plains in the last quarter of the 18th century.

The 18th century witnessed the widespread adaptation of horses to their three primary uses among the Plains Indians—i. e., as riding animals in hunting and warfare and as burden bearers in moving camp. Whether the Indians preferred to use horses for riding or for transporting equipment in the early years of their experience with these animals, when their horse holdings were limited, is an interesting question. In 1719 La Harpe and Valverde noted that the Lipan and El Cuartelejo Apache transported their lodges by dog traction, while they employed horses in warfare. Although these data are not sufficient to fully justify such a conclusion, they suggest the possibility that those tribes in direct contact with horse-using Spanish peoples may have adopted the horse initially as a riding animal, while some tribes remote from the primary diffusion center preferred to employ their first horses as a replacement for dogs as beasts of burden. Yet Hendry witnessed "Arthithinue" Indians riding horses in the buffalo chase on the Saskatchewan Plains in 1754. We know that the Pawnee of the Central Plains hunted buffalo on horseback before 1700.

Undoubtedly, the hostile pressure from Ojibwa, armed with firearms, was an important factor in the westward movement of Algonquian and Siouan tribes from Minnesota and the eastern Dakotas toward the High Plains. However, once these tribes had become Plainsmen and had acquired horses their greater mobility enabled them to halt the westward movement of their pedestrian enemies at the forest margin. In 1798, an Ojibwa chief explained to David Thompson:

> While they (Sioux) keep to the Plains with their Horses we are no match for them; for we being footmen, they could get to windward of us, and set fire to the grass; when we marched for the Woods, they would be there before us, dismount, and under cover fire on us. Until we have Horses like them, we must keep to the Woods, and leave the plains to them. (8:264)

Before 1800 the Arapaho, Gros Ventres, Crow, and Cheyenne, traditionally horticultural tribes, had become nomadic hunters and all except the Gros Ventres had become actively engaged in supplying horses to the secondary diffusion centers on the Upper Missouri. Although the Arapaho-Gros Ventres may have begun to move westward as a result of pressures from the eastward before horses reached the Missouri River area, it appears most probable that they did not relinquish horticultural practices until they became aware of the advantages of hunting buffalo on horseback. I should prefer to look upon the conversion of all those formerly horticultural tribes to nomadism as part of the great movement leading to the concentration of many hunting tribes in the formerly lightly populated High Plains, where buffalo were most numerous, in the 18th century. This movement of tribes proceeded from both east and west, into the High Plains. The powerful Dakota tribes moved westward, with the Teton in the lead. Farther north the Assiniboin and Cree moved in the same direction. From the west, and probably somewhat earlier owing to their earlier acquisition of horses, the Shoshoni, Flathead, Pend d'Oreille, and Nez Percé entered the High Plains only to be later driven back by the southwestward movement of the aggressive Blackfoot. Yet those tribes continued to make periodic hunting excursions in force to the buffalo plains. Within the High Plains there was a general southward movement of tribes toward the primary diffusion center for horses. The Apache were pushed southward by the powerful Comanche and the Kiowa and Kiowa-Apache followed, being in turn forced to move by the advancing Teton. While this movement continued in the 19th century with the southward drift of the Arapaho and Cheyenne as well as the Blackfoot, it was set in motion long before 1800.

Once strange peoples then came into frequent contact on the High Plains. Their meetings resulted in exchanges of objects and ideas among which were traits of the horse complex itself. As might be expected, this close proximity also caused conflicts over hunting grounds and horses. Ambitious young men, needing horses to gain economic and social status among their own people, stole them from neighboring tribes. Horse raiding not only engendered intertribal wars but tended to perpetuate them.

During the 18th century the culture of the nomadic horse-using buffalo hunters became the dominant culture of the Great Plains. Tabeau in 1803, explained the abandonment of horticulture by the Cheyenne on the Missouri a few years earlier as a direct result of their unfavorable competition with the nomadic Sioux:

> The Sioux always wandering, left little for capture to the enemy, who often knew not where to find them, and the Cheyennes, settled there were every day exposed, in spite of their superior courage, to some particular catastrophe. To lessen this disparity more, they abandoned agriculture and their hearths and became a nomadic people. (7:151-153)

Farther to the southwest a similar drama was being enacted, in which Apache tribes were forced to abandon their fields and flee southward to escape the pressure of the aggressive, better armed Comanche.

Before 1800, the stability which the growth of crops had given to the horticultural tribes, and which in pre-horse times had made their way of life more secure than that of the nomadic hunters, had become a handicap. Their sedentary villages were surrounded by mobile horsemen who attacked and insulted them or made peace to obtain garden produce in exchange for surplus products of the chase, at will. Penned up in their compact villages, the horticultural tribes on the Missouri suffered heavy losses from the white man's plagues, beginning with the smallpox epidemic of 1781.

Even though many of the traits in the Plain Indian horse complex were not specifically mentioned in the literature until after 1800, it appears most probable that the great majority of the traits in this complex were widely diffused over the area before that date. Even the distinctive horse medicine cult, first mentioned in Tabeau's description of the Arikara in 1803, was probably an 18th-century innovation.

Whether or not the horse complex was sufficiently well formulated in the minds of members of some of the tribes engaged in supplying horses to the secondary diffusion centers in the middle of the 18th century to permit its being borrowed almost in toto by some of the northern tribes is questionable. However, it does seem reasonable to suppose that ideas regarding the care, training, and use of horses and attitude toward horses, as well as the animals themselves were exchanged at those primitive market places. Certainly extensive borrowing must have taken place long before the establishment of white men's trading posts on the Upper Missouri or the inauguration of white traders' rendezvous in the Wyoming country. We may even question whether the fur traders' rendezvous itself was not an adaptation of the Indian horse traders' fair in the same general region in protohistoric times.

2. *Period Of Crystallization And Maximum Utilization* (from about 1800 until the extermination of the buffalo). Before 1800 the use of horses had spread among the Indian tribes to the natural limits of the Great Plains in the northeast and across the Rockies beyond the Plains in the northwest. The first eight decades of the 19th century constituted the heyday of Plains Indian Horse Culture. By and large, traits of the horse complex observed at or near the beginning of the century persisted until the extermination of the buffalo. The horn pommel and cantle pack saddle appears to have been the only material culture trait in the complex invented within this period. It spread rapidly over the Plains and into the Plateau. There was a tendency during this period for horse raiding to replace trading as the most common means of acquiring horses. Among those tribes which were not poor in horses there was a tendency toward the abandonment of the buffalo drive and the surround in favor of the chase. It was probably during this period, after memories of the first acquisition of horses had become dim, that the beautiful mythological explanations of the origin of horses became popular.

The relative wealth in horses of the tribes of the area changed little during this period. No tribe is known to have advanced from poverty to wealth in horses, nor was a wealthy tribe reduced to poverty. Individuals were actively increasing their herds through breeding and capture of enemy horses. Their activities were offset by loss of horses stolen by the enemy and through deaths.

The horticultural tribes of the Upper Missouri continued to decline in numbers and relative importance, offering little in the way of furs to the traders and limited opposition to the advancing frontier of white settlement. The powerful, nomadic, buffalo-hunting tribes, the Teton Dakota, Arapaho, Cheyenne, Comanche, and Kiowa were the principal fighters of the Plains Indian wars aimed at preventing white invasion of their beloved hunting grounds.

3. Period Of Disintegration (from the extermination of the buffalo to the present). With the extermination of the buffalo, settlement of the Indians in permanent dwellings upon reservations, and the end of intertribal warfare, the three primary functions of horses in their traditional culture—their use in hunting, moving camp, and warfare—were rendered obsolete. In their adjustment to a new way of life, with the encouragement of the Government, Indians adopted white men's horse usages. Even the Indian pony has become nearly or entirely extinct. Yet there remain among other tribes, as among the Blackfoot, survivals of customs and attitudes which are remainders of their Horse Culture heritage.

OLD THEORIES AND NEW INTERPRETATIONS

Two opposing theories regarding the influence of the horse upon Plains Indian culture have been presented by able and experienced students of Plains Indian life.

Clark Wissler, in his pioneer study entitled, "The Influence of the Horse in the Development of Plains Culture," expressed the belief that the traits which he regarded as most characteristic of Plains Indian culture of the historic period (the tipi, the travois, the foot war party, the coup, the Sun Dance, the camp circle, men's societies, and the circumscribed range with summer and winter camps) were, or probably were known to the Plains Indians before they acquired horses. He concluded that "There is no good evidence at hand to support the view that the horse led to the development of the important traits," That "no important traits, material or otherwise, were either dropped or added," and that "from a qualitative point of view the culture of the Plains would have been much the same without the horse." He believed that "as an intensifier of original Plains traits, the horse presents it strongest claim."

Kroeber, in "Cultural and Natural Areas of Native North America," warned against such an "essentially static conception" of Plains Indian culture history.

Could any good-sized group have lived permanently off the bison on the open plains while they and their dogs were dragging their dwellings, furniture, provisions, and children? How large a tepee could have been continuously moved in this way, how much apparatus could it have contained, how close were its inmates huddled, how large the camp circle? How often could several thousand people have congregated in one spot to hold a four or eight days' Sun Dance? By the standard of the nineteenth century, the sixteenth-century Plains Indian would have been miserably poor and almost chronically hungry, if he had tried to follow the same life. Showy clothing, embroidered footgear, medicine bundle purchases, elaborate rituals, gratuitous and time-consuming warfare, all these he could have indulged in but little—not much more than the tribes of the intermountain or southern Texas regions. (2:76–77)

These views of both Wissler and Kroeber reflect the paucity of specific information on the details of the pre-horse culture of the Plains Indians which existed when they prepared their statements and still exists (and which is a handicap under which any student of the problem must labor), as well as the lack of a careful analysis of the Plains Indian horse complex as a basis for their reasoning. Kroeber appears to have been unduly skeptical of the possibility of groups of communal bison hunters existing on the Great Plains before the introduction of horses. Rugged as their life may have been compared with that of later horse-using nomads, we have both archeological and early historical proof of its existence. From the time of Folsom Man until the appearance of horticultural practices only a few centuries prior to the introduction of the horse into the area, the inhabitants of the Great Plains were hunting peoples. Spanish explorers in the 16th century met sizable villages of pedestrian hunters dwelling in portable skin lodges, moving camp with the aid of dogs, and impounding buffalo on the southern Plains, whose sustenance "comes entirely from the cows, because they neither sow nor reap corn." The archeologist Waldo R. Wedel cautiously observed:

It does seem possible, though, that the "Querecho-Teyas" type of life in 1541 was already rather old, and furthermore that it was very similar to, if not a direct continuation of, cultural habits deduced by the prehistorian from remains at the few geologically old sites which have thus far been intensively worked in western Nebraska and northern Colorado. (9:327)

It does not seem probable that the numerous buffalo drive sites in Montana and southern Alberta were used entirely by horse-using peoples. I am of the opinion that *the* reason European explorers failed to find a pedestrian buffalo-hunting people on the northern High Plains was that horses had already been introduced to that region before white men reached it.

It is my contention that the horse complex was adapted to a pre-existing pedestrian buffalo-hunting economy the bearers of which readily recognized that horses would be of great advantage to their way of life. The culture of the pedestrian hunters may have included most if not all of the traits Wissler had ascribed to it as well as other traits which survived with little modification in the Horse Culture Period. Nevertheless, I cannot believe that Plains Indian life in the Horse Culture Period, which included such elements as the daily care, breeding and training of horses, the teaching of children to ride, the chase, specialized riding and transport gear adapted to the use of horses, new methods of packing and transporting camp equipment, frequent horse raiding and mobile scalp raiding, extensive trade in horses, social status based upon property ownership, important role of the horse in children's play, horse racing, and the horse medicine cult, did not differ qualitatively as well as quantitatively from Plains Indian life in the Pedestrian Culture Period. The use of horses not only enriched the material culture of the tribes who acquired them but it altered their habits of daily life, served to develop new manual and motor skills, changed their concepts of their physical environment and the social relationships of individuals.

Probably the most distinctive new trait of the Horse Culture Period was social rather than material in nature. The adaptation of horses to the Plains Indian economy brought about a change from a relatively classless society to a society composed of three classes, which graded almost imperceptibly into one another, and in which membership was determined largely upon the basis of horse ownership—a privileged but responsible upper class, a relatively independent middle class, and an underprivileged and dependent lower class. The influence of this class system not only was apparent in Indian care and use of horses, but it was active in trade relationships between individuals, in marriage, in legal procedures and religious practices. Failure to recognize the existence of these classes has, in the past, resulted in an idealized portrayal of Plains Indian culture based primarily upon the activities and attributes of the wealthy.

I find closest analogies to this class system not among the pre-horse cultures of the Great Plains, but among horse-using nomadic peoples of other continents. Patai has briefly described the three-class system, based upon relative wealth in horses within the local groups among the nomads of Central Asia. Murdock recognized "social gradations based upon wealth or military prowess" as a distinctive characteristic of the horse-using nomads of the South American pampean area (4:421–22). Does it not seem probable that a tendency toward a class system based upon ownership of property (particularly in horses) was characteristic of horse-using nomadic peoples, and that this characteristic distinguished their cultures qualitatively from that of pedestrian nomads?

It appears to me that the influence of the horse permeated and modified to a greater or lesser degree every major aspect of Plains Indian life. Considering the rapidity of its adaptation, the number and diversity of the horse's associations in Plains Indian culture was truly remarkable. Edward Sapir, in his brilliant work entitled "Time Perspective in Aboriginal American Culture, a Study of Method," has proposed as one test for inferring the relative age of an element in culture that, "The more frequently an element is associated with others, the older, generally speaking, it will be felt to be. . . . One feels that it takes considerable time for an element of culture to become so thoroughly ramified in the cultural whole as to meet us at every step" (5:21). The application of this test to the case of the horse in Plains Indian culture of the third quarter of the 19th century, when horse associations in the culture greatly outnumbered dog associations, would lead to the totally erroneous conclusion that these Indians had known and used horses for a longer period that they had employed dogs. In the case of the horse, the remarkable number and diversity of its associations must have been due to the readiness with which these Indians accepted this new animal and the remarkable adaptability of the culture and the horse to one another.

The Sun Dance is an excellent example of a ceremony which served many social purposes alongside its dominantly supernatural concerns. The occasion of the Sun Dance, for most of the Plains Indians, was a time of convivialty and pleasure. For many spectators, it was sheer entertainment. For others, however, the impetus toward participation was quite different. The loss of a relative in war, the search for supernatural solutions to personal problems, individual feeling that all was not well with the world—any of these motives, plus infinitely more, could lead to the organization and presentation of a Sun Dance ceremony. Most of the tribes in the Plains encouraged participating dancers to engage in forms of self-torture or self-mutilation. The most common form of such prac-

tices was that of placing thongs tied to the central pole through slits in the flesh of the dancer's breast or back; the dancer would then dance until he could tear free. In 1904 the U. S. Department of the Interior banned the Sun Dance; it was again permitted in 1935.

37 *Leslie Spier*

THE KIOWA SUN DANCE*

No Plains ceremony is more popularly known than the sun dance, and with justice, since it ranks all other ceremonies that combine the spectacular with the sacred. Among the Arapaho, for example, it easily takes precedence in native esteem over the performances of the age-societies, with which it is classed, while, on the other hand, it rivals in seriousness the unwrapping of the sacred flat pipe, the tribal palladium, a proceeding which is entirely lacking in the spectacular. In fact it is everywhere considered so important for their welfare that the entire tribe is involved in its undertaking. Among some tribes, as the Cheyenne, Oglala, and Kiowa, the attendance of every able-bodied adult of the tribe is compulsory.

Incidentally, "sun dance" is a misnomer, since the dance is by no means connected solely with the sun. On the contrary, it probably is concerned with it to no greater degree than is Plains religion as a whole. Its popular name is presumably derived from the Dakota *wiwanyag wacipi*, "sungazing dance," which is applied particularly to the torture dance.

The sun dance is found throughout the Plains area, except among the southern and the southeastern marginal tribes. It has been reported for the Piegan, Blood, and North Blackfoot, Sarsi, Kutenai, Gros Ventre, Assiniboin, Plains-Cree, Plains-Ojibway, Arikara, Hidatsa, Crow, Wind River and Fort Hall Shoshoni, Bannock, Uintah and Southern Ute, Oglala, Yanktonai, Wahpeton (including the Canadian group) and Sisseton Dakota, Arapaho, Cheyenne (both northern and southern

---

* Abridged from "Notes on the Kiowa Sun Dance," and "The Sun Dance of the Plains Indians: Its Development and Diffusion," by L. Spier, in *The Sun Dance of the Plains Indians*, C. Wissler (ed.). *Anthropological Papers of the American Museum of Natural History*, **16**, 437–462, 1921.

groups), Sutaio, and Kiowa. Among all of these groups, except the Canadian Dakota, the sun dance is a tribal ceremony. The apparent exceptions are the Crow, where the River and Mountain divisions usually held separate ceremonies, and the Plains-Cree and Plains-Ojibway, where the dance may be given simultaneously by several bands; but these instances only emphasize the fact that it is the political unit which functions at this time as a ceremonial unit.

These several sun dances are not only complex in ideation and procedure, but their composite character is easily recognized, for like other widely distributed ceremonies, they have a varied content. Furthermore, many of their rites are repeated in other complex ceremonials of the same tribe, as in the Blackfoot and Arapaho women's dance, the Eastern Dakota round dance, and one of the Hidatsa Above-women ceremonies. Some Plains tribes, which cannot be credited with the sun dance, have ceremonies closely resembling it in some respects; such as the Mandan *ōkī'pʌ*, the Omaha *hedewatci*, and the Pawnee four-pole ceremony. Finally, many of the rites, such as sweatbathing, smoking the pipe, etc., are quite common among all these Plains tribes and even beyond the limits of the area.

The performance of the ceremony coincides very nearly with the summer buffalo hunt, on which occasion the entire tribe comes together from their separate winter quarters and camps in a great circle. The sun dance week is also the occasion for a host of minor ceremonies, many of which are considered necessary accompaniments of the dance. McClintock's account of the Blackfoot festivities, of example, clearly shows that this is the time *par excellence* for the performance of ceremonies, the opening and transfer of medicine bundles, social dances, etc. The tribe as a whole is involved in the undertaking, both by reason of its seriousness and through the participation of great numbers of people.

The sun dance is usually initiated by some man or woman in fulfilment of a vow made at a time of distress, when supernatural aid is invoked and received. It is, however, not so much a thanks-offering as a new occasion for supplicating supernatural power. On the formation of the camp circle, a tipi is pitched near its center in which the secret preliminary rites take place. Here the pledger and his associates are instructed in its esoteric significance by the priests conducting the ceremony, regalia are prepared, and painting and songs rehearsed. At the same time more public preliminary activities are going forward. Some tribes prepare buffalo tongues for use during the dance, while special hunters are sent out to obtain a buffalo bull hide. Other parties are engaged in gathering timbers and brush for the dance structure, which they erect at the center of the camp circle. The spectacular performance begins when the great mass of people set out to fetch the center pole for the dance lodge: they scout for a tree, count coup on it, and fell it as if it were an enemy. The pledger and priests now leave the secret tipi for the dance lodge. A bundle of brush, the buffalo bull hide, cloth, and other offerings, are tied in the forks of the center pole; the pole is raised, and the structure soon completed.

Before the serious dancing commences, warriors dance in the lodge and an altar is built there. The pledger and his associates, who deny themselves food and drink throughout this period, now begin to dance in supplication for supernatural power, steadily gazing the while at the sun or the offerings on the center pole. This lasts intermittently for several days and nights. Their sacrifice culminates in the so-called torture feature: skewers are thrust through the flesh of breast or back; by these they are tethered to the center pole, dancing and tearing against these bonds until the flesh gives away.

The Kiowa sun dance ($k'o^u du^n$, specifically the name for the lodge) was an annual tribal affair, in which the associated Kiowa Apache freely joined. It was danced in an effort to obtain material benefits from, or through, the medicine doll in the possession of the medicineman, who is at the same time director and principal performer.

> This is a small image, less than 2 feet in length, representing a human figure dressed in a robe of white feathers, with a headdress consisting of a single upright feather and pendants of ermine skin, with numerous strands of blue beads around its neck, and painted upon the face, breast, and back with designs symbolic of the sun and moon. [Martinez says the face is entirely obscured by hanging beads.] The image itself is of dark-green stone, in form rudely resembling a human head and bust, probably shaped by art like the stone fetishes of the Pueblo tribes. It is preserved in a rawhide box in charge of the hereditary keeper, and is never under any circumstances exposed to view except at the annual sun dance, when it is fastened to a short upright stick planted within the medicine lodge, near the western side . . . The ancient *tai'me* image was of buckskin, with a stalk of Indian tobacco for a headdress. This buckskin image was left in the medicine lodge, with all the other adornments and sacrificial offerings, at the close of each ceremony. The present *tai'me* is one of three, two of which came originally from the Crows, through an Arapaho who married into the Kiowa tribe, while the third came by capture from the Blackfeet. (3:240)

The bundle containing the image is usually hung outside of its keep-er's tipi. It is not customary to expose the image except at the sun dance, but tobacco is placed with it from time to time. Its function outside of the dance is identical with its use there: those who need its aid make vows to it, which they fulfil by sacrificing horses, etc., and making sweat-lodges. The image is the property of one man, or more properly of his family, since it may be inherited by his blood relatives.

There are ten or twelve minor images (*ta'lyúkà*) which strongly re-semble the *tai'me* in function, as they are essentially war medicines. Most of them were in the keeping of men other than the sacred doll owner, but two were kept by him for a time. They have little or no part in the sun dance.

The sun dance was normally an annual ceremony, but sometimes a year passed without one. The dance was theoretically dependent on someone going to the keeper and saying, "I dreamed of it (*i. e.*, the sun dance)," or on the keeper himself dreaming of it. On two occasions a second dance was held in the dance lodge after the keeper had removed the sacred doll at the close of the first dance, because a second man had also dreamed of it. After the dream is announced the keeper hangs the image on his back and rides out to all the camps, announcing, as he cir-cles them, that he will conduct the ceremony the following spring (May or June). This announcement was sometimes made immediately after the close of the preceding dance, but usually it came just before they intended to hold the dance. The keeper fasts while he is making the announcement, even if it takes three days, as may happen when the camps were scattered. When they know the dance is to be held, others vow to dance for a specified number of days, and all gather near the dance ground. No one may absent himself: they are all afraid of his medicine. When the tribe is assembled, the keeper circles the camp, again bearing the sacred doll on his back.

Two young men are selected by the keeper from one of the military societies to scout for a tree to serve as center pole for the dance lodge. While searching, they must refrain from drinking. About this time all those intending to dance are building sweatlodges to purify themselves: the keeper must enter each of these to direct the proceedings; this en-tails considerable work for him. Should he be sick at this time, the doll is carried into the sweatlodge by the captive in his stead. It is incumbent on the *tai'me* shield owners to accompany this captive and help him per-form the necessary ceremonies. When the tree for the center pole has been selected, the whole camp moves after the keeper and his family to the dance ground. A dozen or more old men follow immediately after him. The main body is guarded front, rear, and both flanks by the military societies, as is customary when a camp moves. The procession halts four times on its journey while the keeper smokes and prays. Next, the soldier societies charge on the dance ground, or rather on a pole erected there before the camp circle is established.

The next morning the man who has that privilege sets out with his wife to get the hide of a young buffalo bull. When such a person dies, the keeper appoints one of his kin to take his place. The couple must fast while on this hunt. If the buffalo is killed with a single arrow, it is a favorable omen, if many are needed, the opposite is indicated. The buffalo must be killed so that he falls on his belly with his head toward the east. A broad strip of back skin, with the tail and head skin attached is carried to the keeper's tipi, where feathers are tied to its head.

The next morning they set out to fetch the center pole. Scott describes a parade around the camp circle by the military societies which then proceed to charge the tree selected for the center pole, which is defended in sham combat by one of the men's societies (*akiaik'to*, war with the trees). After the chiefs have recited their coups, and prayers have been said by the sacred doll keeper and his wife, who have brought the doll there, the tree is chopped down by a captive Mexican woman. A captive is always selected for this difficult task, so that any harm due to an error on her part may not fall on a tribesman. This function is always performed by a Mexican woman: when she dies, the keeper appoints her successor. As the tree falls, they shout and shoot in the air. The pole is carried to the dance ground by a society designated by the keeper, where a hole to receive it has been dug by a men's military society. The pole is set upright by a single medicineman who owns this privilege.

The center pole is not painted.

After the center pole is in place, everyone, but especially the military societies, assists in building the enclosing structure. The lodge is like those of the Arapaho and Cheyenne: it is circular, the rafters rest on the center pole, and the covering of boughs extends a third of the way to the center of the roof. An entrance is left on the east side. A flat stone is placed here so that every dancer passing through must set his foot on it. Wet sand is spread over the ground in the dance lodge and heaped around the base of the center pole. Two little round holes, walled in with mud, are dug near the rear of the lodge to hold incense smudges.

A screen of cottonwood and cedar branches is constructed just north of these.

This business continued through the day, except for an hour or two in the middle of the afternoon, when the old women—the grandmothers of the tribe—had a dance. The music consisted of singing and drumming, done by several old women, who were squatted on the ground in a circle. The dancers —old, gray-headed women, from sixty to eighty years of age—performed in a circle around them for some time, finally striking off upon a waddling run, one behind another; they formed a circle, came back and, doubling so as to bring two together, threw their arms around each other's necks, and trudged around for some time longer; then sat down, while a youngish man circulated the pipe, from which each in turn took two or three whiffs, and this ceremony ended.

When the dance lodge was completed, the soldiers of the tribe then had a frolic in and about it, running and jumping, striking and kicking, throwing one another down, stripping and tearing the clothes off each other. . . . Before this frolic was over, a party of ten or twelve warriors appeared, moving a kind of shield to and fro before their bodies, making, in some manner (as I was not near enough to see how it was done), a grating sound, not unlike the filing of a mill-saw.

In the afternoon, a party of a dozen or more warriors and braves proceeded to the medicine house, followed by a large proportion of the people of the encampment. They were highly painted, and wore shirts only, with headdresses of feathers which extended down the backs to the ground, and were kept in their proper places by means of an ornamented strap clasping the waist. Some of them had long horns attached to their head-dresses. They were armed with lances and revolvers, and carrying a couple of long poles mounted from end to end with feathers, the one white and the other black. They also bore shields highly ornamented with paint, feathers, and hair.

They took their station upon the side opposite the entrance, the musicians standing behind them.

Many old women occupied a position to the right and near the entrance, who set up a tremulous shrieking; the drums began to beat, and the dance began, the party above described only participating in it.

They at first slowly advanced towards the central post, followed by the musicians several of whom carried a side of raw hide (dried), which was beaten upon with sticks, making about as much music as to beat upon the sole of an old shoe, while the drums, the voices of the women, and the rattling of pebbles in instruments of raw hide filled out the choir.

After slowly advancing nearly to the central post, they retired backward, again advanced, a little farther than before; this was repeated several times, each time advancing a little farther, until they crowded upon the spectators, drew their revolvers, and discharged them into the air.

Soon after, the women rushed forward with a shrieking yell, threw their blankets violently upon the ground, at the feet of the retiring dancers, snatched them up with the same tremulous shriek that had been before produced, and retired; which closed this part of the entertainment. The ornamented shields used on this occasion were afterwards hung up with the medicine. (1:168–172)

These may be the shields which are associated with the *tai'me*. Later, after the sacred doll has been brought into the lodge, they are either hung with it on the cedar screen as Battey observed, or on stakes set up outside the dance lodge to the west, i. e., behind the image, where Martinez saw them. No offerings are made to them there. It is incumbent on a *tai'me* shield owner to dance with the associates (*g.uołg.uàt'*) in every sun dance so long as he continues to own the shield. He is not considered one of the associates however. Shield owners always help the image keeper when he asks their aid. They must also assist his captive substitute when officiating in a sweatlodge. A shield owner cannot sell his shield, but he may give it to his son in anticipation of his death, receiving presents in return. Otherwise, on the death of its owner the shield is placed on his grave. Should a son or nephew dream of it, he has the right to make a duplicate with the help of the doll owner in order to keep it in the family. However, if any other man dreams of it and wants to make the duplicate, he must pay the owner. The shield is usually hung outside of its owner's tipi. The shield owners must not eat buffalo hearts, or touch a bearskin, or have anything to do with a bear. Like the associates, they must not smoke with their moccasins on, or kill, or eat any kind of rabbit, or kill or touch a skunk. These shields are used only in war as their owner's personal medicine: no offerings are ever made to them.

Late in the day, a number of men who have vowed to take part in the subsequent dance, together with one woman who has the privilege, are garbed in buffalo robes to represent the living animals. They gather to the east of the lodge where they simulate the actions of a herd of buffalo. A man, called a scout, starts from the entrance of the lodge with a firebrand and circles about the herd until he meets a second man, mounted and carrying a shield and a straight pipe, who thereupon drives the buffalo toward the dance lodge, which they circle several times before negotiating the entrance. Once inside they lie down; the man with the pipe dismounts and enters. Picking up the hairs on the back of first one animal and another, he says, "This is the fattest animal.

: is our protector in war." Then he recites a coup. This designated (or
kes?) a brave man of that buffalo. Both the man with the firebrand
d he with the pipe ought to be medicinemen. The present incumbent
the first office also has the privilege of erecting the center pole. When
ese men die, the sacred doll keeper selects successors from their fami-
s.

That evening after sunset the dance proper begins, to last four nights
d days, ending in the evening. The doll keeper proceeds to his own
i, where with the assistance of seven other medicinemen (*tai'me*
ield keepers and some others not otherwise connected with the cere-
ony), he unwraps the *tai'me*. Carrying it on his back, he walks to the
nce lodge and completely circles it four times, feigning to enter each
ne he passes the entrance. After entering, he goes around by the south
e to the northwest quadrant, where he plants the image hanging on a
ff. Formerly two or more of the minor images, *ta'lyŭkà*, were placed
ith the *tai'me*. After the image is in place the dancers enter to per-
rm for the night.

The keeper dances throughout the whole four-day period. He is
inted yellow, with a design representing the sun, and sometimes an-
her for the moon, drawn on his chest and back. "His face was painted,
e that of the Taimay itself, with red and black zigzag lines downward
om the eyes." He wears a yellow buckskin kilt, a jackrabbit skin cap
th down attached, and sage wristlets. He is barefoot. He carries a
nch of cedar in his hand, and an eagle bone whistle from which an
gle feather is pendent.

Beside the *tai'me* keeper there are three classes of persons who
nce; the associates (*g.uołg.uát'*), the *tai'me* shield keepers, and the
mmon dancers. The four associates must dance throughout the whole
ur-day period. They appear in four successive dances (normally four
ars), after which they choose successors from among those young
en, eighteen to thirty years old, who have made the best records in
ir. These young men, with the assistance of their relatives, pay horses
d buffalo robes for the privilege, receiving the regalia in return. One
io is chosen cannot refuse; if he does, he may expect a calamity. The
ociate may belong to any of the military societies. His office does not
pose obligations of foolhardiness in war (such as the no-flight idea),
t he is obliged to act the part of an intrepid warrior, because he enjoys
urity in battle. The associate must not look in a mirror lest he become
id, nor can he touch a skunk or jackrabbit, nor remain near a fire
ere someone is cooking. Dogs must not be permitted to jump over an

associate. He must remove his moccasins before he smokes, but others may keep theirs on when smoking in his presence. The associate dances in order to live long and to be a great warrior. His body is painted white or yellow: a round spot representing the sun is painted on the middle of his chest, and a crescent moon (the concavity upward) on both sides of the sun, and the same decoration is repeated on his back. The skin is cut away as a sacrifice and to make these designs permanent after his first dance. A scalp from a *tai'me* shield hangs on his breast with two eagle feathers; another on his back. His face is "ornamented with a green stripe across the forehead, and around down the sides of the cheeks, to the corners of the mouth, and meeting on the chin." He wears a yellow buckskin kilt, with his breechclout hung outside, like the Arapaho and Cheyenne sun dancers. Bunches of sage are stuck into his belt, others tied around his wrists and ankles, and carried in each hand. On his head is either a cap of jackrabbit skin in which is stuck an eagle feather or a sage wreath with down attached. He carries a bone whistle. Like the sacred doll keeper and all other dancers, he is barefoot.

The *tai'me* shield owners, who dance with the associates are sometimes painted yellow or green with pictures of the sun and moon on their bodies, but otherwise they wear the regalia of the common dancers.

The rank and file of the dancers are men, never women. Anyone may vow to dance a certain number of days, with the object of becoming a better warrior and living long.

They believe that it warded off sickness, caused happiness, prosperity, many children, success in war, and plenty of buffalo for all the people. It was frequently vowed by persons in danger from sickness or the enemy. (6:347)

Sometimes a medicineman danced to intercede for a sick man. A sick man who had vowed to attend the dance in order to be cured would be carried into the dance lodge, but he would not dance. These dancers make offerings to the *tai'me*. They do not pay the doll keeper in order to enter the dance, and they have no right in any subsequent performance by reason of having once participated. Like all other dancers they must fast and go without water during the period that they dance; they can, however, smoke provided the proper rites are observed.

These dancers are painted white; they wear white buckskin kilts, with the breechclout outside, carry bone whistles, and are barefoot. They have no headdress, wrist or ankle ornaments. They paint themselves.

There is only one style of paint used by either the principal or the common dancers throughout the sun dance.

The dancers form a line on the east side of the lodge facing the
image. Their step is that characteristic of the sun dance of other tribes:
they stand in place, alternately bending their knees and rising on their
toes. They dance intermittently throughout four days and nights; the
common dancers leave as the periods for which they have vowed to
dance have elapsed or when they can no longer stand the combined
strain of fasting, thirsting, and dancing. The "four days and nights"
which are specified are in reality only three nights and days; evidently
the first day of preliminary dancing is included to fill out the quota to
the magic "four."

At the end of the ceremony, the image keeper chews up some medicine root and prepares a drink, of which the dancers are permitted to
imbibe a little.

After the image has been removed, old clothing is hung on the center
pole as a sacrifice. Once Martinez saw a horse tied to the center pole as a
sacrifice to the sun. It remained there until it starved to death. Horses
were also painted and placed, together with blankets and similar valuables, on high hills as sacrifices. Others beside the associates sacrificed
their flesh to the sun at this time, or in fact, whenever they wanted to, as
Martinez has done. The Kiowa never suspended their dancers, as in the
self-torture dance of other tribes, neither in the sun dance, nor when an
individual sought a vision while fasting alone in the mountains.

The night the dance closes everyone joins in a hilarious time in the
dance lodge. Next morning the camp circle breaks up, and the warriors
soon go off to war. They do not molest the dance lodge, though other
tribes passing that way may do so: the Kiowa do not care.

*P*ersonal bravery, zeal in war, and early death in battle were the
ideals of the male youth of the Plains Indians. To survive to become
a decrepit relic was to suggest that one had not been a model youth. Yet
to these Indians war was not an action which should lead to vast blood-
letting, great territorial gains, or even any great risk of death. The "massacre," such as that of General Custer and his men at the Little Big Horn,

*was a foreign concept which came into prominence only with the advent
of the U.S. Army on the Plains. Among themselves, the Indians were
interested in the accumulation of prestige, horses, and guns, and in the
counting of "coup." The roots of Plains Indian warfare are clearly to be
seen in the East where, among the Winnebago, the Creek, the Caddo,
and other tribes, the taking of scalps (or entire heads) and the diligent
pursuit of personal prestige motivated men to go "on the warpath."*

38 *George B. Grinnell*

COUP AND SCALP AMONG THE PLAINS INDIANS*

In early days, after subsistence, the first requirement of life, had been
attended to, war was the most important pursuit of certain plains tribes.
Among the war customs, two of those best known and most written
about are scalping and counting coup. These are very generally misunderstood and are ill defined in the books. It seems the more important to correct existing errors because these customs are no longer
practiced and are now known only to old men.

In a periodical, which described a collection of Indian clothing and
implements, the following words occur:

> In former times, the most notable achievement of an Indian was the taking
> of a scalp, but with the introduction of rifles the killing of a man became so
> easy and there were usually so many scalps taken after a battle that this trophy
> began to lose its importance. The Indians considered it a much braver act to
> touch the body of a fallen foe with a coup stick under fire of the enemy.

In the Handbook of Indian Tribes it is said:

> Coups are usually "counted"—as it was termed—that is, credit of victory
> was taken for three brave deeds, viz., killing an enemy, scalping an enemy or be-
> ing the first to strike an enemy either alive or dead. Each one of these entitled

* Abridged from "Coup and Scalp Among the Plains Indians," by G. B. Grinnell, in
American Anthropologist, **12**, 296–310, 1910.

a man to rank as a warrior and to recount the exploit in public; but to be first to touch the enemy was regarded as the greatest deed of all, as it implied close approach during battle.

The first of these quotations is—except the last sentence—fantastically untrue, while the second is also misleading, since the killing or scalping of an enemy seems to be given equal rank with touching the enemy. Among the plains tribes with which I am well acquainted—and the same is true of all the others of which I know anything at all— coming in actual personal contact with the enemy by touching him with something held in the hand or with a part of the person was the bravest act that could be performed.

To kill an enemy was good in so far as it reduced the numbers of the hostile party. To scalp an enemy was not an important feat and in no sense especially creditable. Enemies were not infrequently left un- scalped. If scalped, the skin of the head was taken merely as a trophy, something to show, something to dance over—a good thing but of no great importance; but to touch the enemy with something held in the hand, with the bare hand, or with any part of the body, was a proof of bravery—a feat which entitled the man or boy who did it to the greatest credit.

When an enemy was killed, each of those nearest to him tried to be the first to reach him and touch him, usually by striking the body with something held in the hand, a gun, bow, whip, or stick. Those who fol- lowed raced up and struck the body—as many as might wish to do so. Anyone who wished to might scalp the dead. Neither the killing nor the scalping was regarded as an especially creditable act. The chief applause was won by the man who first could touch the fallen enemy. In Indian estimation the bravest act that could be performed was to count coup on—to touch or strike—a living unhurt man and to leave him alive, and this was frequently done. Cases are often told of where, when the lines of two opposing tribes faced each other in battle, some brave man rode out in front of his people, charged upon the enemy, ran through their line, struck one of them, and then, turning and riding back, returned to his own party. If however, the man was knocked off his horse, or his horse was killed, all of his party made a headlong charge to rescue and bring him off.

When hunting, it was not unusual for boys or young men, if they killed an animal, especially if it was an animal regarded as dangerous, to rush up and count coup on it. I have been told of cases where young men, who, chasing a black bear on the prairie, had killed it with their arrows, raced up to it on foot to see who should count the first coup.

It was regarded as an evidence of bravery for a man to go into battle carrying no weapon that would do any harm at a distance. It was more creditable to carry a lance than a bow and arrows; more creditable to carry a hatchet or war club than a lance; and the bravest thing of all was to go into a fight with nothing more than a whip, or a long twig—sometimes called a coup stick. I have never heard a stone-headed war club called coup stick.

It was not an infrequent practice among the Cheyenne—as indeed among other plains tribes—for a man, if he had been long sick and was without hope of recovery, or if some great misfortune had happened to him and he no longer wished to live, to declare his purpose to give his body to the enemy. In practice this meant committing suicide by attacking enemies without any suitable means of offense or defence, doing some very brave thing, and being killed while doing it. This, of course, was a most honorable way of dying, far more so than to kill one's self by shooting, by the knife, or by the rope, though there was no disgrace in self-destruction. Suicide by hanging, however, was usually confined to girls who had been crossed in love.

There is still living in Montana a man who, when seventeen or eighteen years of age, after a long illness to which there seemed no end, declared to his father that he wished to give his body to the enemy. The father assented, fitted out the son with his strongest "medicine," and sent the boy off with a party to the south, armed only with a little hatchet. After the party had reached the country of the enemy, two of these, who were Omaha, were discovered returning from the hunt. Both had guns. The Cheyenne charged on them, and the boy, Sun's-road, having been provided with his father's best war horse, led. He overtook one of the enemy who turned and tried to shoot at him, but the gun snapped. Sun's-road knocked the man off his horse with his little hatchet and riding on overtook the other man, who turned and shot at him; but Sun's-road dropped down on his horse, avoided the bullet, and knocked the Omaha off his horse. Both enemies were killed by the Cheyenne who were following Sun's-road. The young man had now fulfilled his vow. He received from the members of the war party, and from the tribe when he returned to the village, the greatest praise. He recovered his health, and now at the age of seventy-four or seventy-five years still tells the story of his early adventures.

The Cheyenne counted coup on an enemy three times; that is to say, three men might touch the body and receive credit, according to the order in which this was done. Subsequent coups received no credit. The Arapaho touched four times. In battle the members of a tribe touched the enemy without reference to what had been done by those of another allied tribe in the same fight. Thus in a fight where Cheyenne and Arapaho were engaged the same man might be touched seven times. In a fight on the Rio Grande del Norte, where Cheyenne, Arapaho, Comanche, Kiowa, and Apache defeated the Ute, the counting of the coups by the different tribes resulted in tremendous confusion.

When a Cheyenne touched an enemy the man who touched him cried "ah haih'" and said "I am the first." The second to touch the body cried "I am the second," and so the third.

It is evident that in the confusion of a large fight, such as often took place, many mistakes might occur and certain men might believe themselves entitled to honors which others thought were theirs. After the fight was over, then, the victorious party got together in a circle and built a fire of buffalo chips. On the ground near the fire were placed a pipe and a gun. The different men interested approached this fire, and, first touching the pipe called out their deeds, saying, "I am the first," "second," or "third," as the case might be. Some man might dispute another and say, "No, I struck him first," and so the point would be argued and the difference settled at the time.

Often these disputes were hot. I recall one among the Pawnee about which there was great feeling. A Sioux had been killed and Baptiste Bahele, a half-breed Skidi and sub-chief, and a young man of no special importance, were racing for the fallen enemy to secure the honor of touching him first. Baptiste had the faster horse and reached the body first, but, just as he was leaning over to touch it, the animal shied and turned off, so that what he held in his hand did not actually touch the body, while the boy who was following him rode straight over the fallen man and struck him. Baptiste argued plausibly enough that he had reached the body first and was entitled to be credited with the coup, but acknowledged that he did not actually touch the body, though he would have done so had his horse not shied. There was no difference of opinion among the Indians, who unanimously gave the honor to the boy.

Once two young Cheyenne were racing to touch a fallen enemy. Their horses were running side by side, though one was slightly ahead of the other. The man in advance was armed with a sabre, the other, almost even with him, was leaning forward to touch the enemy with his lance. A sabre being shorter than a lance, the leading man was likely to get only the second coup, but he reached down, grasped his comrade's lance, and gave it a little push, and it touched the enemy as they passed over him. Although the owner of the lance still held it, yet because his hand was behind his fellow's on its shaft, he received credit only for the second coup. If a man struck an enemy with a lance, anyone who touched or struck the lance while it was still fixed in or touching the enemy's person, received credit for the next coup.

A man who believed he had accomplished something made a strong fight for his rights and was certain to be supported in his contention by all his friends, and above all by all his relatives. When disputes took place, there were formal ways of getting at the truth. Among the Cheyenne a strong affirmation, or oath, was to rub the hand over the pipe as the statement was made, or to point to the medicine arrows and say, "Arrows, you hear me; I did (or did not do) this thing." The Blackfeet usually passed the hand over the pipe stem, thus asseverating that the story was as straight as the hole through the stem.

With the Cheyenne, if there was a dispute as to who had touched an enemy, counting the first coup, a still more formal oath might be exacted. A buffalo skull, painted with a black streak running from between the horns to the nose, red about the eye sockets, on the right-hand cheek a black, round spot, the sun, and on the left a red half-moon, had its eye sockets and its nose stuffed full of green grass. This represented the medicine lodge. Against this were rested a gun and four arrows, representing the medicine arrows. The men to be sworn were to place their hands on these and make their statements. Small sticks, about a foot long, to the number of the enemies that had been killed in the fight which they were to discuss were prepared and placed on the ground alongside the arrows and the gun.

In a mixed fight where many people were engaged there were always disputes, and this oath was often—even usually—exacted. A large crowd of people, both men and women, assembled to witness the ceremony. The chiefs directed the crier to call up the men who claimed honors, in the order in which they declared that they had struck an enemy; the man who claimed the first coup first, he who claimed the second coup second, and so on. The man making the oath walked up to the sacred objects and stood over them, and stretching up his hands to heaven said, *Mā ĭ yŭn ăsts′ nī āh′tŭ,* "Spiritual powers, listen to me." Then, bending down, he placed his hands on the objects, and said, *Nā nĭt'shŭ,* "I touched him." After he had made his oath he added, "If I tell a lie, I hope that I may be shot far off."

He narrated in detail how he charged on the enemy and how he struck him. Then were called the men who counted the second and third coup on this same enemy and each told his story at length. Next the man who touched the second enemy was called, and he was followed by those who had counted the second and third coup on the same individual. In the same way all claimants told their stories.

If, under such circumstances, a man made a false statement, it was considered certain that before long he or some one of his family would die. The Cheyenne feared this oath, and, if a man was doubtful as to whether he had done what he claimed, he was very likely not to appear when his name was called. On the other hand, each of two men might honestly enough declare—owing to error—that he first touched an enemy. Or, a man might swear falsely. In the year 1862, a man disputing with another declared that he had first touched the enemy. The next year, while the Cheyenne were making the medicine lodge on the Republican River, this man died, and everyone believed, and said, that he had lied about the coup of the year before.

When two men were striving to touch an enemy and others were watching them, and the thing was close, the spectators might say to one of the two, "We did not see plainly what you did, but of what he did we are certain." In this way they might bar out from the first honor the man concerning whose achievement they were doubtful. As already said, the relatives of each claimant were active partisans of their kinsmen.

If enemies were running away and being pursued, and one fell behind or was separated from his party, and was touched three times, if he escaped serious injury and later got among his own people once more, the coup might again be counted on him up to the usual three times.

As an example of the odd things that have happened in connection with the practice of touching the enemy, according to Cheyenne rules, the curious case of Yellow-shirt may be mentioned. In the great battle that took place on Wolf Creek in 1838, between the allied Kiowa, Comanche, and Apache on one hand, and the Cheyenne and Arapaho on the other, coup was counted on Yellow-shirt, a Kiowa, nine times. When the charge was made on the Kiowa camp, Yellow-shirt was fighting on foot and was touched three times, but not seriously injured. Later, he reached his village, mounted a horse, came out to fight and was touched three times on horseback. Almost immediately afterward his horse was killed and his leg broken, and he sat on the ground, still fighting by shooting arrows, and was again touched three times and killed. So in all nine coups were counted on this man, all of which were allowed. In another case coup was counted nine times on a Pawnee, who was not killed and finally got away.

If, through some oversight, the third coup had not been formally counted on an enemy, the act of taking off his moccasins as plunder has been decided to be the third coup, because the man who removed them touched the dead man's person. Coup, of course, might be counted on man, woman, or child. Anyone who was captured would first be touched.

There were other achievements which were regarded as sufficiently noteworthy to be related as a portion of a triumph, but which were in no sense comparable with the honor of touching an enemy. Such brave deeds, among the Blackfeet, were the taking of a captive, of a shield, a gun, arrows, a bow, or a medicine pipe, any of which acts might be coupled with touching an enemy.

Among the same people it was highly creditable to ride over an enemy on foot, and in the old time dances of the different bands of the All-comrades, horses were frequently painted with the prints of a red hand on either side of the neck and certain paintings on the breast intended to represent the contact of the horse's body with the enemy.

Among the Cheyenne the capture of a horse or horses was such a brave deed, and, if the man who had touched an enemy took from him a shield or a gun, the capture of this implement was always mentioned. The drum would be sounded for touching the enemy, sounded again for the capture of the shield, again for the capture of the gun, and—if the man had scalped the dead—for the taking of the scalp.

I believe that the high esteem in which the act of touching the enemy is held is a survival of the old feeling that prevailed before the Indians had missiles and when—if they fought—they were obliged to do so hand to hand, with clubs and sharpened sticks. Under such conditions only those who actually came to grips, so to speak, with the enemy— who met him hand to hand—could inflict any injury and gain any glory. After arrows came into use it may still have been thought a finer thing to meet the enemy hand to hand than to kill him with an arrow at a distance.

The general opinion that the act of scalping reflects credit on the warrior has no foundation. The belief perhaps arose from the fact that, when an enemy was killed or wounded, brave Indians rushed toward him. White observers have very likely inferred that those who were rushing upon an enemy were eager to take his scalp. As a matter of fact they cared little or nothing for the scalp but very much for the credit of touching the fallen man. Most people are untrustworthy observers and draw inferences from their preconceived notions, rather than from what actually takes place.

As already said, among the plains tribes a scalp was a mere trophy and was not highly valued. It was regarded as an emblem of victory and was a good thing to carry back to the village to rejoice and dance over. But any part of an enemy's body might serve for this, and it was not at all uncommon among the Blackfeet to take off a leg or an arm, or even a foot or hand, to carry back and rejoice over for weeks and months. Very commonly, a party returning from war would give one or more scalps to a group of old men and old women, who would paint their faces black and carry the scalp all about through the village dancing at intervals, singing the praises of the successful warriors, making speeches in their honor, and generally rejoicing. Scalps were sometimes sacrificed among all these tribes, perhaps burned, as by the Pawnee, or among Cheyenne and Blackfeet tied to a pole and left out on the prairie to be rained on and finally to disappear in the weather. Scalps were used to trim and fringe war clothing—shirts and leggings—and to tie to the horse's bridle in going to war. Usually the scalps taken were small, a little larger than a silver dollar, but like any other piece of fresh skin they stretched greatly.

When, on the warpath, a scalp had been taken by a young Cheyenne who had never before scalped an enemy, it was necessary that he be taught how to treat the scalp, how to prepare it for transportation to the village. Instruction in this ceremonial was given by some older man familiar with such things, who in times past had himself been taught by a man older than he how the scalp should be handled. Before any work was done, the pipe was filled and lighted and held toward the sky and to the ground, and then the stem was held toward the scalp and a prayer was made asking for further good fortune. The instructor lighted the pipe and made the prayer.

Previous to this a large buffalo chip had been procured, and it was placed on the ground before the instructor and between him and the fire. The instructor took in his mouth a piece of bitterroot and some leaves of the white sage, and masticated them a little. The learner stood before the instructor and held his hands out before him, palms up and edges together, and the instructor spat ceremonially on the palm of each hand. The young man made the usual motions, rubbing his hands together and then passing the right hand over the right leg, from ankle to thigh, and the left hand over the right arm from wrist to shoulder, using the left hand on the left leg and the right hand on the left arm. He then passed his hands over his face, and then backward over his hair and the sides of his head. These, of course, are the usual ceremonial motions.

The scalp was now placed on the buffalo chip, flesh side up. The instructor sat close by the young man and directed each one of the various operations which follow. The learner took from the fire a bit of charcoal and rubbed it over both sides of a knife, from hilt to point; he held the knife over the scalp and said, "May we again conquer these enemies; and, if we do so, I will cut this again in the same way." With the point of the knife he now made a cross-cut over the scalp from north to south, and another from east to west, always beginning at the edge of the skin away from himself, or toward the fire, and drawing the knife toward him. The point of the knife passed through the flesh still remaining on the skin and down to the skin, dividing this flesh or fascia into four sections. The learner now took the scalp in his hands and beginning at the outer side of the circle shaved off the flesh from the quadrant toward the east and placed it on the buffalo chip. Next he shaved off from the skin the quadrant toward the south, and this flesh so taken off was put in its place on the buffalo chip. The quadrant toward the west was then taken off and placed on the chip, and the last quadrant toward the north was removed and put on the chip. Thus, the four sections of flesh trimmed from the scalp lay on the buffalo chip in their proper relations.

Now some young man was called up and was told to carry the buffalo chip away, and leave it on the prairie. Before he started, the learner told him that he must ask the *Măĭyŭn'* (the Mysterious Ones, the Spirits) to take pity on him, that he might be aided to count a coup.

The young man now bent a willow twig, already provided, into a hoop, lashing the two ends together with a sinew. Then with sinew and awl the margin of the scalp was sewed to the hoop to stretch it. If the hoop was too large and the scalp did not reach it, the scalp was made larger by cutting short holes about the margin and parallel to it. The sewing was done from east to south, to west, to north, and to east. A slender willow pole six feet long, trimmed and peeled, and sharpened at the butt, with a notch cut in the other end, had already been prepared. By a string tied to the hoop the scalp was fastened to this pole, the sharpened butt of which was then thrust into the ground. If convenient, all this was done on the day the scalp was taken, at all events as soon as possible. When travelling, the willow pole to which the scalp was attached was carried on the left arm. The scalp was taken back to camp on this pole and remained attached to it during all the dancing that took place.

Among the Cheyenne the scalp dances of modern times have not been at all the same as those of earlier days. The last of those, I am told, took place in 1852.

Anyone familiar with Indians and Indian ways will understand that the various dances that they practice are not merely haphazard jumpings up and down and posturings, to the music of chance singing. The ceremonial of the various dances is perfectly well defined, and the songs are well known and as invariable as if they had been printed. There was a regular way and ceremonial about the old time scalp dance. While in a sense a triumph dance, it was also very largely social in character. The account which I give of it comes to me from George Bent, son of the famous Colonel William Bent, whose mother was a Cheyenne woman, and who has lived with the Cheyenne practically all his life. He is a man of good intelligence and some education, and entirely trustworthy.

These old time scalp dances were directed by a little group of men called "halfmen-halfwomen," who usually dressed as old men. All belonged to the same family or group to which Oak (Ōūm'sh) belonged. It was called Ŏttŏ ha nĭ', "Bare legs." It is possible that this may be the same band or clan which I have elsewhere spoken of under the name Ŏhk tō ŭn'a. Of these halfmen-halfwomen there were at that time five. They were men, but had taken up the ways of women. Their voices sounded between the voice of a man and that of a woman. They were very popular and especial favorites of young people, those who were married as well as those young men and young women who were not married, for they were noted matchmakers. They were fine love talkers. If a man wanted to get a girl to run away with him and could get one of these people to help him, he seldom failed. When a young man wanted to send gifts for a young woman, one of these halfmen-halfwomen was sent to the girl's relatives to do the talking in making the marriage.

The five men above referred to were named Wolf-walking-alone, Buffalo-wallow, Hiding-shield-under-his-robe, Big-mule, and Bridge. All these men died a long time ago, but in more recent times there were two such men, one living among the Northern Cheyenne and the other among the Southern. These men had both men's names and women's names. The one among the Northern Cheyenne was named Pipe and his woman's name was Pipe-woman. He died in 1868. The one who lived with the Southern Cheyenne was named Good-road and Good-road-woman. He died in 1879. These were the two last of these people in the Cheyenne tribe.

When war parties were preparing to start out, one of these persons was often asked to accompany it, and, in fact, in old times large war parties rarely started without one or two of them being along. They were good company and fine talkers. When they went with war parties they were well treated. They watched all that was being done and in the fighting cared for the wounded. They were doctors, or "medicine men," and were skilful in taking care of the sick and wounded.

After a battle the best scalps were given to them, and when they came in sight of the village on their return they carried these scalps on the ends of poles. When they came to the village the men who carried the pipes—the leaders of the war party—and the halfmen-halfwomen carrying the scalps went ahead of the party and ran along outside the village and waved the scalps tied to the poles. This took place usually in the early morning, so that the village should be taken by surprise. The old men, the women, and the children, rushed out to meet the war party. If the members of a war party had their faces blackened when they came in, this showed that the party had not lost any of its members. If one of the party had been killed, the scalps were thrown away and there were no scalp dances on the return. If a person had counted a coup and had been killed, the scalp dance went on just as if no one had been killed. It was a great honor for a person to count coup first, and then afterward to be killed in the same fight. His relations did not mourn for him, but, instead, joined in the scalp dance which took place that night.

The great scalp dance took place in the evening in the center of the village. The halfmen-halfwomen went to each lodge and told the owner to send some wood to the center of the village for the big dance that was to take place that night. As the people brought the wood, the halfmen-halfwomen built it up as a pile, in the shape of a lodge. It was a cone, wide at the bottom and small at the top, made by standing the sticks of wood on end. All about and under it was put dried grass ready for the fire at any time. This pile of wood was called "Skunk" (hkā'ō). The "skunk" was lighted when a majority of the good singers with their drums reached the place. The singers were chiefly middle-aged men, all married. Then the singers and drummers began their songs, and everybody came to the dance, all of them painted with red paint and black paint. All the older persons had their faces and bodies painted black. The men wore no shirts, and the old women had their bodies blackened from the waist up. In the center of the village the drummers stood in a row, facing the opening in the circle. The young men stood in a row facing the north; the young women stood in a row facing the young men, and so looking south. The old women and the old men took their places down at the lower end of the young people, and faced west. The halfmen-halfwomen took their places in the middle of this square and were the managers of the dance. No one was allowed in the middle of the square except these persons.

The dance now commenced. The women began to dance in line toward the center, and the young men all walked around behind the drummers to the girls' side of the square, placed themselves behind their sweethearts, and each put one arm through an arm of one of the girls and danced with her in that way. This was called "the sweethearts' dance."

After dancing for a time they returned to their places and stood in rows as before. The halfmen-halfwomen danced in front of the drummers, holding the poles to which scalps were tied and waving the scalps while dancing. At the other end old women danced, also carrying scalps tied on poles. The old men whose sons had counted coup also danced at the lower end. These old men and old women often acted as clowns, trying to make the people laugh. Some of them were dressed like the enemies that had been killed.

The next dance was called "the matchmaking dance," and the songs sung were different from those sung in the one before. If in this dance there were two of these halfmen-halfwomen, one went over to the line of young men and one to the line of young women and asked the different dancers whom they would like for partners. Then the two halfmen-halfwomen came together in the center and told one another whom to select. All this time the singers and drummers were making their music. The halfmen-halfwomen then walked to the young men and took them by the robes and led them across to where their sweethearts were standing, and made the men stand by the girls. In this dance no one might begin to dance until every woman had her partner. Two men might not stand together. Men always stood between women.

After all the women had their partners, all those in this row danced toward the center and then danced back not turning at all. Several times they danced back and forward; then the halfmen-halfwomen said to the young men, "Go back to your places."

If the night was dark the big fire was kept up by the boys, but if the moon was full less firelight was needed.

After a time the halfmen-halfwomen called out the third dance, telling what dance it was. The young men and young women danced toward each other in two long rows, and then danced back again. After a time the halfmen-halfwomen called out "Select your partners," and each man crossed over to get his sweetheart as a partner, and the young women when told to select their partners also crossed over and met their sweethearts. After all had partners—for the men and the women were equal in number—they formed a ring around the big fire and danced about it. In this circling dance the drummers and singers also fell in, and the whole ring danced to the left about the fire. The old women and the old men got in the center of the ring, holding the scalps which they waved in the air. The halfmen-halfwomen danced around outside the ring, and danced to the right hand. With the scalps tied to poles they kept the young girls and the boys away from the dancers, for the boys and girls were afraid of the scalps. In this way they kept the children from crowding close to the dancers.

After dancing for some time in this way, the halfmen-halfwomen told the drummers and singers to put the women inside in this round dance. While the young men were going around the ring, now and then one of them would step inside and put an arm around his sweetheart's neck. After this had gone on for some time, all fell back as before into their old places—the drummers and singers to their places, and the young men and women to theirs.

Soon the fourth dance was called by the halfmen-halfwomen, and the singers started up a different song for this. This dance was called "the slippery dance." In this only women danced, two of them together; in other words, they danced in pairs. These women danced up to their sweethearts and took hold of their robes and then danced back to the center, leading the young men out. The young men did not dance, for the slippery dance was practiced by women only. The young men walked after those who were holding them and were held by their sweethearts until the men's sisters had presented to the sweethearts a ring or a bracelet. This process was called "setting them free." Sometimes a young fellow went up and presented a ring or a bracelet to have his friend set free.

After this dance the halfmen-halfwomen told the dancers to rest for a time and asked that some one should bring water for the dancers. The assembly partly broke up. Women would go away to tie up their legs, for, as they wore buckskin dresses, and the next dance was to be a stooping dance, the dresses might get in their way, be stepped on, and trip them up. This was the last dance, called "the galloping buffalo-bull dance."

When all had returned the halfmen-halfwomen told the people to sit down, and all took their places. The drummers and singers also sat down. When the singing and drumming began three or four women arose and danced toward the men, and when they had come close to them stooped down and turned their backs toward the men and danced before them. Then just as many men as there were women stood up and danced, joining the women; the men stooped also, just like the women. More women danced out and men joined them, and at length all the men and women came together and the whole party of them danced in a long row, all stooping down, dancing like a bull galloping. The halfmen-halfwomen would then say, "Go round in a circle," and all the dancers stood erect and began the circle dance of round dances, while the drummers and singers joined them in the circle. In this round dance everyone sang as they went around. By this time it was nearly morning, and the dance at last broke up, the people returning to their homes.

SECTION IX
*The Eastern
Agriculturists*

The major zone of agriculture in aboriginal North America was to be found south of the Great Lakes and the Ottawa River and generally east of the Mississippi River. This region witnessed the highest development of civilized arts and skills north of Mexico prior to the arrival of Europeans in the New World. Sadly, it was also this cultural province which suffered the first heavy onslaught of European colonists and settlers; consequently, the Indians of the agricultural East are those who were first, and thoroughly, de-culturated. Disease, war, land deprivation, and insidious innovations (such as the gun and alcohol) took an early heavy toll of the aboriginal populations of the eastern seaboard and, by the time serious students of aboriginal life had begun their work in the early twentieth century, little was left of the traditional life-ways of the Indians in the eastern portion of the United States. The Natchez, the Tunica, the Choctaw, and the Creek are best known through accounts left by explorers, or through documents from the colonial period. The Powhatan, the Cherokee, the Iroquois and a few other tribes survived somewhat longer as cultural entities, but by the end of the nineteenth century little was left of the formerly well-organized and independent native societies.

As elsewhere on the continent, the East was anciently occupied by foragers armed with spears or darts with "fluted" points. Following the decline in numbers of the large postpleistocene animals, the easterners began to adjust to the forest clime in which they found themselves. Regionally variable due to differences in ecological detail, some populations adapted to coastal or riverine environments while others developed adaptations useful in the more forested regions. The Archaic cultures, those which clearly predate the introduction of agriculture in the East, were most probably gatherers and hunters who, as time went on, were the recipients of diffused knowledge (pottery and horticulture mainly) from Mexico. As in the Southwest, cultural growth and development was stimulated by Mexican introductions which implemented already existent nonagricultural adaptations. The archaeological record of the Mississippi Valley, the Gulf Coast shelf, the Ohio River drainage, and other portions of the East as well, all document the gradual shift from a dependence upon forest products to an increasing reliance upon agricultural produce. Nevertheless, the cultures of the East were strongly dependent throughout their history upon game, nuts, berries, fish, wild rice, and other wild products.

The precise pattern of cultural growth in the East is still not clear. Neither is the exact date of the introduction of agricultural plants certain, nor how and when contacts with Meso-American centers were initiated; nor, for that matter, is there full agreement regarding the pre-European distribution of tribes and language groups.

Following European contact, and perhaps prior to it, many of the tribes of the East had amalgamated into confederacies for the purpose of economic or military cooperation. The renowned Iroquois, the Powhatan, and the Creek (among other lesser known Indian groups), established political and military power over wide areas through alliances and conquest. But, as in the Plains, their hegemony was to be of short duration. The powerful Indian societies inevitably became entangled with the expanding colonial frontier, or were caught between the rivalries of competing European powers (usually the French and the English), or became pawns in the hands of international economic forces when they became dependent upon trade, especially for furs—and the adaptive bases upon which Indian cultures had traditionally depended were inexorably worn away. Like the Indians of the Plains, the Indians of the East either fought and lost, cooperated and lost, or fled and lost. No true accommodation was possible.

In the opening article of the section, Albert Spaulding offers a widely accepted outline for the development of culture in the East, from the Archaic to the Middle Mississippi culture which he suggests was still flourishing in the sixteenth century.

39 Albert C. Spaulding

PREHISTORIC CULTURES OF THE EAST*

THE ARCHAIC CULTURE

The Archaic Culture type is a rather shaky classificatory union of a large number of small components scattered over practically the entire area under consideration. Indeed, the reported presence of Archaic sites in any particular region seems to be pretty much a function of the intensity of archeological field work. The major unifying feature of the Archaic components on the positive side is the small size of the sites (this statement will be qualified later) and the presence of large flint projectile points, although this is not meant to imply that small sites and large projectile points are absent from other culture types. It is much easier to describe the Archaic sites in terms of what is absent from them; they do not show pottery, smoking pipes, mounds and other earth construction, or evidence of substantial buildings, and these absences are good evidence for their generally early time position. It has been inferred from the negative evidence that the Archaic peoples gained their subsistance through hunting, fishing, and gathering rather than agriculture. Dart throwers were certainly used to hurl projectiles (actual specimens have been found), and the prevailingly large flint projectile points suggest that the bow and arrow were entirely unknown.

It is clear from the information at hand that significant cultural subgroupings existed at the Archaic level. There were western variants, for example the non-pottery sites discovered by the Smithsonian River Basin Surveys in recent years. Farther to the east, complexes which

* Abridged from "Prehistoric Cultural Development in the Eastern United States," by A. C. Spaulding, in *New Interpretations of Aboriginal American Culture History*, B. Meggers and C. Evans (eds.). Anthropological Society of Washington, 12–27, 1955.

come to mind are the distinctive and well-known shell heap sites of the Savannah, Tennessee, and Green Rivers; a variety of coastal sites from Maine to Florida (often marked by extensive shell heaps); an aberrant non-pottery culture in the lower Mississippi Valley best known from the sites of Jaketown in Mississippi and Poverty Point in Louisiana; and two cultural entities in New York and New England, the Lamoka Culture and another sometimes called the Laurentian Culture. The differences observed between these groupings are in large part to be explained on geographical grounds to judge by the quite well-defined regions into which the component sites cluster. It is probably fair to say that much of the observed variation can be attributed to regional developments from a common and widespread Paleo-Indian base. But certain of the differences are of such nature as to suggest that time differences within the period of Archaic Culture domination and derivation from distinctive cultural backgrounds are also to be considered.

A brief comparison of four of the Archaic sub-units mentioned above will illustrate the problem. The first of these is the Indian Knoll Culture of the Green River in Kentucky, a representative of the southeastern river-shell-heap type of culture. The Indian Knoll people lived on the river banks in favored spots where mussels were abundant. They were deer hunters, fishermen, and gatherers of the local flora and river mussels. Although an Indian Knoll community was at any one time undoubtedly a small village (probably no more than a hundred or so persons), continual occupation for a very long period resulted in impressive refuse deposits composed primarily of tons of mussel shells, abundant deer and other animal bones, and other debris. The refuse mounds are almost literally riddled with burial pits, and the grave goods found in them demonstrate that some leisure was available for the production of beautifully finished polished stone dart thrower weights, bone and antler dart throwers, nicely decorated bone pins, stone and shell beads, and other luxury goods. The presence of conch shells from Florida waters and copper from the Lake Superior region clearly shows that the extensive trade routes of later periods had their inception here. Heavy woodworking was accomplished with fully gooved stone axes, and a variety of chipped flint scrapers and knives served for lighter tasks. Large flint projectile points are, of course, commonly found, and numerous stone pestles suggest preparation of vegetable food. The relatively early time position of the Indian Knoll Culture type is plain because, like other Archaic complexes, it lacks a number of traits universally present in the area in protohistoric and early historic times. This inferential dating is amply confirmed by eight radiocarbon dates ranging from about 5000 B.C. to about 2000 B.C.

At approximately the same time, on the basis of radiocarbon dating, a second Archaic Culture type existed in western New York. It is best known from a site at Lamoka Lake and is usually called the Lamoka Culture. Although the subsistence pattern of the Lamoka people must have been much like that reported from Indian Knoll and many similarities in artifact types can be detected, there are also significant differences. Work in marine shells is virtually absent at Lamoka, and the grooved axe of Indian Knoll does not occur at all, its place as a heavy woodworking tool being taken by crude flaked stone choppers and several kinds of polished stone adzes. There are enough differences in the bone and antler tools to characterize them as overlapping but distinctive assemblages. It can hardly be argued that such differences in detail were a direct response to sharply distinct environmental circumstances— Kentucky is not so different from New York as all that and there is no particular reason to think that the two regions were less like each other a few thousand years ago. Moreover, the actual distance between the cultures was not great, and there is no formidable geographical barrier intervening. Under these circumstances, the explanation which seems most likely is that Lamoka and Indian Knoll were peripheral representatives of culture types which did develop in relative isolation under distinctly different ecological circumstances. The main ties of Indian Knoll are clearly to the southeast, where numerous sites of similar character are found. On the other hand, the Lamoka culture had certain northern overtones. Thus the beveled adze is found in greatest quantity along the north shores of Lake Erie and Lake Ontario, and a preference for the adze as a woodworking stool is a strong and ancient boreal tradition from Scandinavia to Labrador. The Lamoka beaver tooth knives point in the same direction. However, Lamoka can scarcely be thought of as a transplanted boreal culture owing to the absence of certain commonplace northern artifact types, especially barbed bone points. It would seem to be basically a variant of the eastern United States Archaic Culture type which was influenced to a certain extent by the alien culture of the spruce-fir forests to the north.

A third subtype which falls within the very broad definition of Archaic is the poorly defined Laurentian Culture, a term which I will use to include a number of manifestations scattered from Wisconsin to New England. Although we are handicapped by a bad sampling situation, some evidence of local specialization, and probably time difference, it is possible to describe the Laurentian Culture as producing a variety of chipped stone forms, barbed bone points, winged bannerstones, ground slate and copper projectile points, and ground stone and copper adzes and gouges. Stratigraphic evidence indicates that the Laurentian succeeds the Lamoka Culture in New York, and it apparently presisted for a time after the introduction of pottery. From our standpoint, the important feature of the Laurentian is that it cannot be derived satisfactorily from the preceding cultures. It represents a new complex of elements associated with a new physical type in the northeastern part of our area. The gouges, ground slate points, and other elements point to a northern origin, and an actual movement of people from the Canadian forest seems to be the most likely explanation. The ultimate origin of the Laurentian complex need not concern us here, but it is surely in some sense a representative of the north European-Siberian-North American cultural tradition of the boreal forest zone, and its appearance in the northeastern fringe of our area is a reflection of the proximity of that fringe to the northern forests. Indeed, certain parts of the area of Laurentian occupancy such as the Upper Peninsula of Michigan can be considered essentially of boreal forest type from the standpoint of ecology.

A final special subtype of the Archaic to be discussed is the Poverty Point complex of Louisiana and Mississippi. It is included with the Archaic Cultures because of its lack of pottery vessels, but in many respects it is a strange bedfellow. The culture is not known in every detail, but outstanding features of Poverty Point sites include great quantities of more or less crudely modeled clay objects of unknown function. Fragments of stone vessels are also a characteristic feature. It is thought that the vessels were imported from the southern Appalachian region, the nearest available source of the soapstone and closely related minerals used for their manufacture. A still more surprising feature is the recent discovery of large numbers of small, ribbon-like blades of flint at several sites; their association with the other Poverty Point materials is not certain but seems highly probable. The most striking feature of all, however, is the presence of earthworks. At the Poverty Point site itself these include a tremendous octagonal figure composed of six concentric banks of earth, the whole being some three-quarters of a mile in diameter, and a mound 70 feet high situated on the west side of the octagon. The amorphous clay objects, flint work, and earth construction are quite unlike anything reported from other Archaic Cultures, and some sort of special explanation is in order. Geographical isolation may be involved in part, but the lower Mississippi Valley is not exactly remote from the Tennessee-Alabama-Georgia area with its more orthodox cultures, and the soapstone is good evidence of actual contact between the two areas. A second explanation is isolation in time from the better known Archaic Cultures, and one radiocarbon date of 400 B.C. supports this line of reasoning. The radiocarbon date produces difficulties almost as formidable as those it is supposed to solve because by this time there were well-established agricultural and pottery making groups in the Illinois-Ohio area. But, if the date is reasonably close, we can derive the earthworks and perhaps the ribbon flakes from the Hopewell Culture as Ford has suggested. The Hopewell Culture (to be discussed below) was a pottery making, agricultural complex, and I am at a loss to explain why the Poverty Point people failed to make pottery of Hopewell type if such a connection existed. A third explanation is that the Poverty Point Culture as described here did not exist at all—that we have assembled a group of incongruous elements on the basis of accidental geographical association. On this view, the clay objects and stone sherds would already have been archeological specimens when the earth embankments and the mound were built. In short, we will leave Poverty Point as an enigma.

Our résumé of the Archaic has discussed four differing culture types. The Indian Knoll type was presented as a characteristic example of a native culture developed in the southeast from a Paleo-Indian base over a period of several thousand years, and it was indicated that related although not identical cultures of similar origin could be found in most parts of the eastern United States. The Lamoka Culture was thought to be fundamentally of the same origin but visibly influenced by an alien tradition at home in the subarctic zone. The Laurentian Culture was said to be derived from the subarctic zone, and the mode of introduction seems to have been outright invasion into the boreal fringe of our area. The Poverty Point Culture was presented as an anomaly which cannot be explained with any degree of satisfaction from the evidence at hand.

THE ADENA CULTURE

We now leave the simple hunters and gatherers for the second of our major culture types, the entity commonly known as the Adena Culture. The Adena Culture is a well-defined type with a restricted geographical range in the southern part of Ohio, southeastern Indiana, northern Kentucky, northwestern West Virginia, and southwestern Pennsylvania.

Within this area, and especially in Ohio, there are numerous sites marked by more or less conical burial mounds and sometimes circular or other types of earth bank enclosures. Most of the information about the culture is derived from excavation of the burial mounds and the scanty village site refuse found in the vicinity of the mounds. The mounds and their associated material reveal a culture which is of quite a different order from that of the Archaic people, although the absence of adequate data on village refuse is a serious deficiency in our knowledge of Adena.

On the basis of the sheer size of the mounds (one of them is about 70 feet high) and the complexity of the mortuary practices associated with them, we can safely infer a complex social organization and an efficient economic base. It would appear that on occasion the body of an important dignitary would be placed in a log tomb in a house floor together with artifacts and other bodies, perhaps those of retainers slain for the purpose, and that the tomb would then be covered temporarily. After a suitable interval, the bones would be painted and a small earth mound erected over the tomb. The next step consisted of burning the house containing the tomb and its primary mound, and finally the main mound was constructed over the remains of the burned house, the primary mound, and the tomb. In some cases, additional tombs were placed in the final mound at various stages in its construction. Simple cremation in the village areas seems to have been the prevailing custom for ordinary folk.

Other Adena traits clearly indicate a substantial way of life. Houses were circular with sturdy outward slanting supporting posts; they ranged from about 20 to nearly 70 feet in diameter. There are in addition some circles of post molds about 100 feet in diameter. If the latter were completely roofed, one house would have been capable of sheltering a sizable village. Even the smaller circles indicate houses of very respectable dimensions and capacities. Pottery vessels of simple forms, some having four-footed bases; tubular stone pipes; stone, copper, shell, and mica ornaments; stone celts; textiles; and other artifacts have been found. A human effigy tubular pipe from an Ohio mound shows a man clad in a decorated breech cloth with a bustle-like appendage and wearing circular ear plugs. I think that most archeologists infer that the Adena people cultivated corn, tobacco, gourds, and presumably other plants, although direct evidence is scanty or lacking. Finally, the Adena people were physically quite distinct from the Indian Knoll people of the same general area, and they accentuated this distinctiveness by the practice of head deformation.

If it is true that the Adena culture represents the first appearance of this general cultural complex in the area, and the weight of evidence seems to indicate that it is true, then the question of Adena-Archaic rela tionships is critical. We should first point out that corn as a cultivated crop is on botanical grounds almost certainly of Middle or South American origin and hence must be an imported trait. It seems equally clear that a reasonably efficient corn agriculture must underlie such an elabo rate cultural development, and we are forced to postulate some sort of direct or indirect connection with Middle or South America. That this connection did not take place through the southwestern United States is suggested by the fact that the corn of the closely related and nearly con temporaneous Hopewell Culture is a Guatemalan type not normally found in the early agricultural horizons of the Southwest. It would ap pear then that northeastern Mexico is the most likely source. An alternative route through the Antillean islands is said to be most un likely by specialists in that area. But it is not absolutely certain that Adena is the first corn-growing culture of the area on the evidence of radiocarbon dating. One radiocarbon date for a Kentucky Adena site is about 700 B.C., a second for the same site is 220 B.C., but another Ken tucky mound yielded a date of A.D. 780 and an Ohio mound dated at A.D. 440. This time range begins a little earlier but for the most part overlaps that of the Hopewell Culture, making it impossible to decide on this evidence alone whether or not the Adena people were the first agriculturalists of eastern United States. Even if we accept the chrono logical priority of Adena, a view which was standard before radiocarbon dating, we are still in an area of sharp disagreement about the manner in which it originated.

One point of view is that the Adena complex in essentially complete form was brought by a rapid migration from northeastern Mexico to the Ohio Valley, thus accounting for the simultaneous appearance of a new physical type and a radically different cultural orientation. Unfortu nately, no one has as yet discovered an unmistakable ancestor in the proper part of Mexico. It is not impossible that an appropriate predeces sor will be discovered in the future, however, and such traits as ear spools, large round houses, celts rather than grooved axes, perhaps burial mounds, burial in house floor, and so on, do have a faintly Mid dle or even South American flavor. Opponents of this view suggest a bare minimum of Mexican influence—a diffusion of corn and a few other plants without actual migration of people—followed by a local development of burial practices and other elaborate features. Apparent continuities with the local Archaic, for example in chipped stone tools and use of shell and copper, are emphasized, and the new physical type is explained by evolution in place or by a population increment from the north as exemplified by the Laurentian situation. I think that there is not sufficient evidence at hand to attempt any final adjudication of these opposing theories, although I regard the migration theory as less cumbersome. The problem is an extremely important one because it deals with a fundamental cultural reorientation involving the establishment of a set of basic practices which persisted until the obliteration of Indian culture in the eastern United States.

THE HOPEWELL CULTURE

The Hopewell Culture represents a third distinctive culture type, but its distinctiveness with relation to Adena is a matter of detail rather than of basic subsistence and ceremonial patterns. The geographical distribution and character of Hopewell sites suggest two primary areas of concentration, southern Ohio and the valleys of the Illinois and Mississippi Rivers in Illinois. Other centers with clear Hopewell affinities are found in Louisiana, the Florida coast, the Kansas City area, and in various other localities scattered from New York to Oklahoma. In its most highly developed form, which occurs in southern Ohio, the Hopewell culture produced some exceedingly impressive remains. Very large burial mounds, hilltop enclosures, and literally miles of earthworks arranged in geometrical enclosures and parallel walls are found at Ohio sites and offer the clearest possible evidence of effective group labor. Scarcely less impressive are quantities of fine art products deposited in the burial mounds. Raw materials for these products were imported from such remote sources as the Appalachian region of Virginia and North Carolina, the Rocky Mountains, the Lake Superior region, and the Florida coast. The art products and mounds are expressions of an elaborate mortuary cult, and the peculiar geometric shapes of the earthbank enclosures strongly suggest ceremonial functions. Information on ordinary Hopewell village sites is quite scanty, but it can be said that they were comparatively humble with little evidence of impressive permanent buildings or the fine art goods associated with the burial mounds. Subsistence was obtained by gardening (actual examples of corn have been found) and by hunting and gathering wild products. The bow and arrow seem to have been unknown, the dart thrower being the device used to hurl projectiles as was the case with Archaic and Adena Cultures. In general, there is little evidence of notable differences between Adena and Hopewell in basic subsistence techniques. The greater brilliance and geographical extent of the Hopewell Culture accordingly cannot be attributed to any markedly superior economic techniques; it appears rather to be the result of more effective social organization along the general lines introduced by the Adena people.

But Hopewell Culture cannot be considered simply an intensification or elaboration of the Adena pattern. We can logically postulate an Adena source for the basic agriculture and many of the ceremonial practices, especially the earthbank enclosures and burial mounds. It is perhaps justifiable to speculate about possible Adena prototypes for such Middle American-like Hopewell traits as copper earspools, negative painted cloth, and panpipes. There are, however, other Hopewell traits which point to a direct connection with the Archaic people rather than to the Adena Culture. Examples of such traits are the presence in Hopewell of the grooved stone axe, stone plummets, and cut animal jaws. In this connection, it is important to note that the Hopewell physical type is predominantly that of the Archaic people, although some genetic influence from the Adena people is evident. A third group of Hopewell elements does not look like either the Middle Western Archaic or like Adena, but seems rather to have a northern stamp; here one can include ribbon-like flint flakes used as knives, conoidal bottomed pottery finished with a cord-wrapped paddle and decorated by impressions of a cord-wrapped stick or a toothed tool, bilaterally symmetrical decoration reminiscent of northern art in birchbark, and skin moccasins (shown on clay figurines). A final group of culture elements was surely invented by the Hopewell people themselves. An excellent example is the characteristic platform smoking pipe.

When we add to these factors the radiocarbon dates for Hopewell (beginning slightly later but having roughly the same range as those of Adena), the following interpretation is suggested:

1. Following the introduction of the Adena Culture, it dominated its restricted area and strongly influenced an Archaic population to the west, particularly in Illinois. This population had already received influence from the north, just as did the Archaic people of New York.

2. Archaic, Adena, and northern influences fused into a vigorous

Hopewell Culture which expanded to the east and took over the Adena area in Ohio but not in northern Kentucky, where the Adena people were able to maintain their cultural and physical identity for a considerable period.

3. Concurrently, Hopewell ideas and to some extent Hopewell people expanded widely over the eastern United States. It seems likely that in many areas the Hopewell rather than the Adena people were responsible for the introduction of burial mounds and agriculture, and that many simple mound-building, pottery-making groups now considered to be pre-Hopewell were actually contemporaneous with Hopewell.

4. There followed a period of decline marked by abandonment of the great Ohio and Illinois ceremonial centers and development of a number of local traditions which carry on certain of the Hopewell ideas in an impoverished form.

The reader is warned that this reconstruction is based upon something less than universally accepted evidence; indeed, it is no more than a point of view from which to reappraise existing evidence and to seek new data. It is impossible to predict whether or not future work will confirm or deny the general scheme, but it does seem to account best for the material at hand.

There does not appear to be any simple explanation for the fading out of Hopewell Culture. Certainly, there is no clear evidence of military conquest by incoming peoples or the advent of any sweeping economic changes. Whatever the reason, or reasons, for the decline may have been, it does seem to be true that in most (or perhaps all) of the areas of highly developed Hopewell Culture an interlude of comparatively simple cultures separates the Hopewell peak from the next great culture type, the Middle Mississippi.

THE MIDDLE MISSISSIPPI CULTURE

In the strictest sense, the Middle Mississippi Culture type is represented by a limited number of great sites situated roughly in an east-west belt from north central Georgia through northern Alabama and Mississippi to western Tennessee and Kentucky, southern Illinois, and southeastern Missouri. In addition to these great centers, Middle Mississippi influences radiated far and wide to modify outlying groups which had strong cultural roots in the preceding period. Outstanding elements in the new cultural configuration are (1) tremendous ceremonial centers having a plaza arrangement of pyramidal temple mounds and sometimes a ditched and palisaded fortification; (2) large village sites (not always directly associated with mound groups) with accompanying cemeteries; (3) a new pottery complex in which the clay was mixed with crushed burned shell, many new vessel forms were made, and handles, modeled decoration, and painting were emphasized; (4) a number of new art concepts executed in clay, carved stone, sheet copper, engraved shell, and other media; and (5) various other new types of artifacts, of which an example is a small triangular arrow point of flint.

Dating of Middle Mississippi Culture on the more recent end of the scale offers no difficulty; the culture was flourishing when the De Soto party made its way across the southeast in the mid-sixteenth century. The problem of how far back in time it extends is not so easy. Existing radiocarbon dates for Middle Mississippi sites are capricious and internally inconsistent, but it seems safe to estimate that the earlier sites were in existence by about A.D. 1000. There is evidence of cultural development within the Middle Mississippi tradition in the form of changing pottery styles and the addition of new motifs in ceremonial art, but cultures that are plainly transitional between Hopewell and Middle Mississippi are not known.

This absence of developmental stages suggests the importation of ideas to the eastern United States, and the pyramidal mounds and the art forms again point to Mexico as the source. Portrayals of winged snakes, dancing men with bird attributes and speech scrolls issuing from their mouths, human skulls and long bones, and other items have a definite Middle American appearance, although no object of actual Mexican origin has been reported. But the new culture is not plainly associated with a new physical type, there is no evidence of linguistic connection with Mexico, and many Middle Mississippi traits have their origin in the Hopewell or earlier periods in the United States. It looks very much as if a group of Mexican religious ideas and perhaps forms of social organization was added to, and assimilated by, the native post-Hopewell Culture. The small arrow points probably signify the replacement of the older dart thrower by the bow and arrow as the major weapon for warfare and hunting, but it is not known whether or not new crops or important new varieties of old crops appeared. In any case, the very large size of the ceremonial centers and villages testifies to a productive economic system, an effective social organization and a preoccupation with religious activities.

The mechanism by which such a cultural change could be effected can only be guessed at. Some sort of contact with Mexico, again probably northeastern Mexico on geographical grounds, is indicated, and the contact must have been of such nature as to permit the dissemination of ideas without extensive movement of material objects or people. Perhaps the rich ceremonialism and generally impressive level of Mexican cultures proved irresistible to visitors from Missouri or Arkansas, who returned to their homeland as missionaries with a vivid impression of Mexican religious ideas and paraphernalia. Certainly, the Pueblo area of New Mexico and Arizona cannot be the source of the Mexican influence since Middle Mississippi was in some respects much closer to Mexican practices than were the Pueblo peoples.

The complex chiefdoms and proto-states of the Southeast are known only through early historical documents. Even at that time, the middle and late seventeenth century, considerable population destruction is believed to have occurred due to epidemic European diseases. At the time of the passage of De Soto (1540–1542), the Creek and Cherokee were still using the ceremonial mounds of the region and perhaps were still building them. Little descriptive material is found regarding these early encounters between the Indians and the Spanish; the most useful early documents are those left to us by the French in the late seventeenth and early eighteenth centuries. The Natchez, described in the sources quoted in the following article, have inspired quantities of commentary on the plausibility, even the possibility, of the type of social structure outlined for them. Recent interpretations of the entire Gulf Coast region suggest that the elaborate sociocultural position achieved by the Natchez was shared by most of the other populations along the lower Mississippi, and by those located on the coastal margins also.

John Swanton is widely recognized as one of the outstanding authorities on the North American Indian and was for many years associated with the Bureau of American Ethnology.

40 *John R. Swanton*

EARLY ACCOUNTS OF THE NATCHEZ*

The Natchez villages were scattered along St. Catherine's Creek, east of the present city of Natchez, at short intervals. According to Tonti, it was 3 leagues from the French camp on the Mississippi to the Natchez village whither La Salle had been invited. This would probably be the Great Village, which, according to later writers, was not more than a league from the river, but La Salle's camp, instead of being at the nearest point on the river, was probably below, near the mouth of St. Catherine's creek. Iberville was told that the Natchez or "Theloël" occupied nine villages, whose names were given him, and, so far as the number is concerned, this statement is confirmed by Pénicaut, while De Montigny says "ten or twelve."

The cabins constituting these villages were so far apart that the latter might rather be described as neighborhoods, and in consequence they often covered a considerable tract of country. De la Vente states that "the Natchez, the Tonicas, the Chattas, the Chicachas, etc., are in villages of 6, 10, and as many as 20 leagues" (1:47), while on the other hand St. Cosme says that the Natchez and the Arkansas cabins were often a quarter of a league apart.

Pénicaut describes the general location of the Natchez villages in the following romantic and decidedly exaggerated manner:

The village [meaning either the Natchez villages collectively or the Great Village] of the Natchez is the most beautiful one can find in Louisiana. It is situated one league from the shore of the Mississipy. It is embellished with very beautiful walks, which nature has formed there without artifice. There are prairies around it, ornamented with flowers, cut up with little hillocks, on which are groves of all kinds of fragrant trees. Many little rivulets of very clear water come from under a mountain, which appears at 2 leagues from

* Abridged from "Indian Tribes of the Lower Mississippi Valley and Adjacent Coast of the Gulf of Mexico," by J. R. Swanton in *Smithsonian Institution, Bureau of American Ethnology, Bulletin* **43**, 45–46, 100–107, 1911.

these prairies, and, after having watered very many places, they unite into two great rivulets, which pass around the village, at the end of which they join, to form a little river [St. Catherine's], which runs over a fine gravel and passes through three villages, which are half a league apart, and finally, 2 leagues from there, it falls into the Mississipy. Its water is very agreeable to drink, because it is cold as ice in summer, and in winter it is tepid. (5:444)

SOCIAL ORGANIZATION

Aside from their temple nothing attracted more attention from visitors to the Natchez than their peculiar strongly centralized form of government. Following are the statements regarding it recorded by various writers.

From the Luxembourg Memoir:

The chief of the entire nation is the great Sun and his relations little Suns, who are more or less respected according to their degee of proximity to the great chief. The veneration which these savages have for the great chief and for his family goes so far that whether he speaks good or evil, they thank him by genuflections and reverences marked by howls. All these Suns have many savages who have become their slaves voluntarily, and who hunt and work for them. They were formerly obliged to kill themselves when their masters died. Some of their women also followed this custom; but the French have undeceived them regarding such a barbarous usage. All these relatives of the Sun regard the other savages as dirt. (2:143–144)

From Pénicaut:

This great chief commands all the chiefs of the eight other villages. He sends orders to them by two of his servants (*laquais*), for he has as many as 30 of them who are called *loüés*, in their language *tichon*. He also has many servants who are called *Oulchil tichon* (Great Sun servants) who serve him for many ends. The chiefs of the other villages send him what has been obtained from the dances of their villages. His house is very large; it can hold as many as 4,000 [!] persons. This grand chief is as absolute as a king. His people do not come near him through respect. When they speak to him, they are 4 paces distant. His bed is at the right on entering the cabin; there are [under it] four wooden posts, 2 feet in height, 10 feet apart one way and 8 the other. There are crossbars going from one post to another, on which the planks are placed which form a kind of table, which is very smooth, of the same length and breadth as that of the bed, which is reddened all over. On this kind of table there is a mat made of fine canes and a great bolster of goose feathers, and for covering there are the skins of deer for summer and the skins of bison or bear for winter. Only his wife has the right to sleep there with him. Only she, too, can eat at his table. When he gives the leavings to his brothers or any of his relatives, he pushes the dishes to them with his feet. On rising, all the relatives or some old men of consideration approach his bed, and raising their arms on high, make frightful cries. They salute him thus without his deigning to notice them.

It must be noticed that a grand chief noble can marry only a plebeian, but that the children which come from this union, whether boys or girls, are nobles; that, if he happens to die before his wife, his wife must be strangled to accompany him into the other world. In the same manner a girl noble, that is to say, a daughter of a wife of a chief noble, when she wishes to marry, is only able to marry a plebeian, and if she dies after she is married before her husband, the latter has to be put to death also to accompany her in the other world. The children who come from these marriages are reputed nobles or Suns.

Their nobility is very different from that of our Europeans, for in France the more ancient it is the more it is esteemed. Their extraction, on the contrary, is no more esteemed noble at the seventh generation; moreover, they draw their nobility from the woman and not from the man. I have asked them the reason for this, and they have replied to me that nobility can come only from the woman, because the woman to whom children belong is more certain than the man. (5:449–451)

From Charlevoix:

What distinguishes them more particularly is the form of their government, entirely despotic; a great dependence, which extends even to a kind of slavery, in the subjects; more pride and grandeur in the chiefs, and their pacific spirit, which, however, they have not entirely preserved for some years past.

The Hurons believe, as well as they, that their hereditary chiefs are descended from the Sun; but there is not one that would be his servant, nor follow him into the other world for the honor of serving him there, as often happens among the Natchez.

The great chief of the Natchez bears the name of the Sun; and it is always, as among the Hurons, the son of the woman who is nearest related to him that succeeds him. They give this woman the title of woman chief; and though in general she does not meddle with the government, they pay her great honors. She has also, as well as the great chief, the power of life and death. As soon as anyone has had the misfortune to displease either of them, they order their guards, whom they call *allouez*, to kill him. "Go and rid me of that dog," say they; and they are immediately obeyed. Their subjects, and even the chiefs of the villages, never approach them but they salute them three times, setting up a cry, which is a kind of howling. They do the same when they retire, and they retire walking backward. When they meet them they must stop and range themselves on both sides of the way, and make the same cries till they are gone past. Their subjects are also obliged to carry them the best of their harvest, and of their hunting and fishing. Lastly, no person, not even their nearest relations, and those who are of noble families, when they have the honor to eat with them, have a right to put their hands to the same dish, or to drink out of the same vessel.

The daughters of the noble families can marry none but obscure persons; but they have a right to turn away their husbands when they please, and to take others, provided there is no relationship between them.

If their husbands are unfaithful to them they can order them to be knocked on the head, but they are not subject to the same laws themselves. They may have besides as many gallants as they think fit, and the husband is not to take it amiss. This is a privilege belonging to the blood of the great chief. The husband of any one of these must stand in the presence of his wife in a respectful posture; he does not eat with her; he salutes her in the same tone as her domestics. The only privilege which such a burdensome alliance procures him is to be exempt from labor and to have authority over those who serve his wife.

The Natchez have two war chiefs, two masters of the ceremonies for the temple, two officers to regulate what is done in treaties of peace or war; one that has the inspection of works, and four others who are employed to order everything in the public feasts. It is the great chief who appoints persons to these offices, and those who hold them are respected and obeyed as he would be himself. (4:162–163, 165)

From Le Petit:

The sun is the principal object of veneration to these people; as they can not conceive of anything which can be above this heavenly body, nothing else appears to them more worthy of their homage. It is for the same reason that the great chief of this nation, who knows nothing on the earth more dignified than himself, takes the title of brother of the sun, and the credulity of the people maintains him in the despotic authority which he claims. To enable them better to converse together, they raise a mound of artificial soil, on which they build his cabin, which is of the same construction as the temple. The door fronts the east, and every morning the great chief honors by his presence the rising of his elder brother, and salutes him with many howlings as soon as he appears above the horizon. Then he gives orders that they shall light his calumet; he makes him an offering of the first three puffs which he draws; afterward raising his hand above his head, and turning from the east to the west, he shows him the direction which he must take in his course.

There are in this cabin a number of beds on the left hand at entering; but on the right is only the bed of the great chief, ornamented with different painted figures. This bed consists of nothing but a mattress of canes and reeds, very hard, with a square log of wood which serves for a pillow. In the middle of the cabin is seen a small stone, and no one should approach the bed until he has made a circuit of this stone. Those who enter salute by a howl, and advance even to the bottom of the cabin without looking at the right side where the chief is. Then they give a new salute by raising their arms above the head and howling three times. If it be anyone whom the chief holds in consideration he answers by a slight sigh and makes a sign to him to be seated. He thanks him for his politeness by a new howl. At every question which the chief puts to him he howls once before he answers, and when he takes his leave he prolongs a single howl until he is out of his presence.

When the great chief dies they demolish his cabin and then raise a new mound, on which they build the cabin of him who is to replace him in this dignity, for he never lodges in that of his predecessor. The old men prescribe the laws for the rest of the people, and one of their principles is to have a sovereign respect for the great chief as being the brother of the sun and the master of the temple.

These people blindly obey the least wish of their great chief. They look upon him as absolute master, not only of their property but also of their lives, and not one of them would dare to refuse him his head, if he should demand it; for whatever labors he commands them to execute, they are forbidden to exact any wages. The French, who are often in need of hunters or of rowers for their long voyages, never apply to anyone but the great chief. He furnishes all the men they wish, and receives payment, without giving any part to those unfortunate individuals, who are not permitted even to complain. One of the principal articles of their religion, and particularly for the servants of the great chief, is that of honoring his funeral rites by dying with him, that they may go to serve him in the other world. In their blindness they willingly submit to this law, in the foolish belief that in the train of their chief they will go to enjoy the greatest happiness.

The government is hereditary; it is not, however, the son of the reigning chief who succeeds his father, but the son of the sister, or the first princess of the blood. This policy is founded on the knowledge they have of the licentiousness of their women. They are not sure, they say, that the children of the chief's wife may be of the blood royal, whereas the son of the sister of the great chief must be, at least on the side of the mother.

The great chief nominates to the most important offices of state; such are the two war chiefs, the two masters of ceremony for the worship of the temple, the two officers who preside over the other ceremonies which are observed when foreigners come to treat of peace, another who has the inspection of the public works, four others charged with the arrangement of the festivals

with which they publicly entertain the nation and such strangers as come to
visit them. All these ministers, who execute the will of the great chief, are
treated with the same respect and obedience as if he personally gave the orders. (6, vol. 68:126–137)

From Dumont:

In each of the savage nations, as in all the nations of the earth, two kinds
of men may be beheld, of which the one seems born to command and to enjoy all the honors, the other to obey and to grovel in obscurity. It is these
which we name the great and the people. The first are, among the savages,
the chiefs, the Suns, and the Honored men. All those who are not embraced
in this class and decorated with one of these titles compose the people and
are called Stinkards (*Puants*).

The submissiveness of the savages to their chief, who commands them with
the most despotic power, is extreme. They obey him in everything he may
command them. When he speaks to them they howl nine times by way of
applause and to show him their satisfaction, and if he demands the life of any
one of them he comes himself to present his head. But at the death of this
chief his children, boys or girls, never inherit his power and never succeed to
the command. His descendants reenter the rank of Stinkards, and it is for the
boys to perform actions of valor which may raise them to the dignity of Honored men. It appertains only to the female Sun, whom they call also the white
woman, to perpetuate the stem from which spring their chiefs. She has more
power so long as she lives than the chief himself, who may be her son or her
brother, and never her husband, whom she is able to choose if she wishes from
among the Stinkards and who is rather her slave than her master. The males
who spring from this woman are the chiefs of the nation, and the girls become, like herself, female Suns or white women.

In order to understand this propagation of the nobility and the government
in these savage nations let us go back as far as the law which establishes the
succession among them, and let us suppose that at the time of this establishment there remained only one *Oüachill-Tamaïll*; that is to say, one female
Sun or white woman. Let us suppose, besides, that this woman has two children, a boy and a girl. Then, according to the law which wills that the nobility be perpetuated through the women and degenerate through the men,
this boy sprung from the white woman will be established as the true *Oüachill-
Liquip*; that is to say, great chief or great Sun, but at his death his children
are only nobles. The children of these become simply Honored, and the children of these last fall back into the rank of Stinkards. On the other hand, of
the sons of his sister, who was herself white woman or female Sun, the eldest
will be great chief or great Sun, the second little Sun, chief of war, and the
others only Suns, their children degenerating successively, as I have noted.
As to her daughters, they are not only white women or female Suns but it

is also through them that the Suns and the nobility will be perpetuated in the nation.

When these savages are asked the reason for the establishment of this law they reply that, as in accordance with their usage at the death of the great chief or great Sun, his wives must also die with him, as well as his male and female servants, without which he would be without wives and without followers in the other world, it happens from that that the female Suns never desire to be married to the great chief, who for this reason is always obliged to marry Stinkard women. "But if it should happen," say they, "that this Stinkard woman should by chance yield herself to a Stinkard man and the child that arose from this intercourse came to command us, it would follow that we would be governed by a Stinkard, which would not be in order." "On the other hand," they added, "whether the female Sun has children by her husband or by any other person whatever, it matters little to us. They are always Suns on the side of their mother, a fact which is most certain, since the womb can not lie."

With regard to the Honored men, it is seen by what I have just said that birth gives this rank to all the grandchildren of the great chief. But besides birth there are other means by which a Stinkard may raise himself to this degree of nobility in the nation. One of the most usual is to render himself famous by some action of valor and bravery. The scalp of an enemy, for example, which a warrior may have carried away, or even the tail of a mare or of a horse will suffice to enable him to obtain this title, and to give him, as well as his wife, the right to disfigure the body by carrying on their skins strange figures, which, as I have said, form their principal adornment.

Here is still another means by which a Stinkard, provided he is married, may attain to the rank of the Honored. If this Stinkard, at the death of the great chief of the nation, has a child at the breast, or at any rate of very tender years, he repairs with his wife and his child to the cabin where this chief is laid out. As soon as they have arrived there the father and mother wring the neck of their infant, which they throw at the feet of the body, as a victim which they immolate to the manes of their chief. After this barbarous sacrifice they roll between their hands some twists of Spanish beard, which they put under their feet, as if they would signify by that that they are not worthy to walk on the earth, and in this condition they both remain standing before the corpse of the great chief without changing their positions or taking nourishment all day. During that time the cabin is visited by all kinds of persons who come, some from curiosity, others to see one time more the one who had governed them and to desire him a good passage. Finally, when the sun has set, the man and the woman come out of the cabin and receive the compliments of all the warriors and Honored men, to the number of whom they have been added by this strange and cruel ceremony. (2:175–187)

From Du Pratz:

The Natchez Nation is composed of nobility and people. The people are called in their language *Miche-Miche-Quipy*, which signifies *Puant* (Stinkard), a name, however, which offends them, and which no one dares to pronounce before them, for it would put them in very bad humor. The Stinkards have a language entirely different from that of the nobility, to whom they are submissive to the last degree. That of the nobility is soft, solemn, and very rich. The substantive nouns are declined, as in Latin, without articles. The nobility is divided into Suns, Nobles, and Honored men. The Suns are so named because they are descended from a man and woman who made them believe that they came out of the sun, as I have said more at length in speaking of their religion.

The man and woman who gave laws to the Natchez had children, and ordained that their race should always be distinguished from the mass of the nation, and that none of their descendants should be put to death for any cause whatsoever, but should complete his days calmly as nature permitted him. The need of preserving their blood pure and safe made them establish another usage of which examples are seen only in a nation of Scythians, of which Herodotus speaks. As their children, being brothers and sisters, were unable to intermarry without committing a crime, and as it was necessary in order to have descendants that they marry Stinkard men and Stinkard women, they wished in order to guard against the disastrous results of the infidelity of the women that the nobility should be transmitted only through women. Their male and female children were equally called Suns and respected as such, but with this difference, that the males enjoyed this privilege only during their lives and personally. Their children bore only the name of Nobles, and the male children of Nobles were only Honored men. These Honored men, however, might by their warlike exploits be able to reascend to the rank of Nobles, but their children again became Honored men, and the children of these Honored men, as well as those of the others, were lost in the people and placed in the rank of Stinkards. Thus the son of a female Sun (or Sun woman) is a Sun, like his mother, but his son is only a Noble, his grandson an Honored man, and his great-grandson a Stinkard. Hence it happens, on account of their long lives—for these people often see the fourth generation—that it is a very common thing for a Sun to see his posterity lost among the common people.

The women are free from this unpleasantness. The nobility is maintained from mother to daughter, and they are Suns in perpetuity without suffering any alteration in dignity. However, they are never able to attain the sovereignty any more than the children of the male Suns, but the eldest son of the female Sun nearest related to the mother of the reigning Sun is the one who mounts the throne when it becomes vacant. The reigning Sun bears the title of great Sun.

As the posterity of the two first Suns has become much multiplied, one perceives readily that many of these Suns are no longer related and might ally themselves together, which would preserve their blood for the most part without any mixture, but another law established at the same time opposes an invincible obstacle, namely, that which does not permit any Sun to die a violent death. It is this, that it was ordered that when a male or female Sun should come to die his wife or her husband should be put to death on the day of the funeral, in order to go and keep him company in the country of spirits. That could not be carried out if the wife and husband were both Suns, and this blind and barbarous custom is so punctually observed that the Suns are under the pleasing necessity of making mesalliances. (3, vol. 2:393–397)

Concerning the despotic authority of the great Sun, Du Pratz says:

In fact these people are reared in such perfect submission to their sovereign that the authority which he exerts over them is a veritable despotism, which can be compared only to that of the first Ottoman emperors. He is, like them, absolute master of the goods and life of his subjects, he disposes of them according to his pleasure, his will is his reason, and, an advantage which the Ottomans have never had, there is neither any attempt on his person nor seditious movements to fear. When he orders a man who has merited it to be put to death, the unhappy condemned individual neither begs nor makes intercession for his life, nor seeks to escape. The order of the sovereign is executed on the spot and no one murmurs. The relatives of the great chief share more or less of his authority in proportion to the nearness in blood, and the Tattooed-serpent has been seen to have three men put to death who had arrested and bound a Frenchman whom he loved much, in order to kill him, although we were then at war with the Natchez. (3, vol. 2:352–353)

The great chief or great Sun wore, as a mark of his preeminent position and authority, a feather crown.

This crown is composed of a cap and a diadem, surmounted by large feathers. The cap is made of a netting, which holds the diadem, which is a texture 2 inches broad and presses together behind tightly as is desired. The cap is of black threads, but the diadem is red and embellished with little beads or small white seeds, as hard as beads. The feathers which surmount the diadem are white. Those in front may be 8 inches long, and those behind 4 inches. These feathers are arranged in a curved line. At the end of these feathers is a tuft of hair (*houpe de poil*) and above a little hairy tassel (*aigrette de crin*), all being only an inch and a half long and dyed a very beautiful red.

This crown or feather hat is an object very pleasing to the sight. (3, vol. 2:201)

Nevertheless, the Sun also had a council to advise him, and sometimes his authority was considerably curtailed by it, as well as by the
more prominent and energetic village chiefs, a fact which comes out
clearly in the course of the last Natchez war. De la Vente seems to have
the Natchez in mind when he speaks of a council composed of the principal warriors in which the more ancient always occupied the highest
places. "They are listened to like oracles," he writes, "and the young
people make it a point of honor to follow their opinions to the point of
veneration" (1:42). It appears that the great Sun and the great war
chief could also be controlled by them—a very important fact.

The essence of the Natchez system, so far as it is revealed to us by
French writers, may be shown diagrammatically as follows:

Nobility:
　　Suns: Children of Sun mothers and Stinkard fathers.
　　Nobles: Children of Noble mothers and Stinkard fathers, or of Sun
　　fathers and Stinkard mothers.
　　Honored People: Children of Honored women and Stinkard fa-
　　thers, or of Noble fathers and Stinkard mothers.
Stinkards:
　　Children of Stinkard mothers and Honored men, or of Stinkard fa-
　　thers and Stinkard mothers.

The Suns were a purely hereditary body, and, as might be inferred
from this diagram, were the smallest of all classes. La Harpe states that
in 1700 there were 17 Suns, but it is not clear whether he includes only
those in the Grand Village or the entire number, and whether the Suns
of both sexes are referred to. Le Petit (1730) gives 11 Suns. The intermarriage of Stinkards is nowhere directly mentioned, but it must be
assumed, for otherwise Stinkards would in time become as few as Suns,
whereas it is evident that they constituted the largest part of the population.

O*ne of the best known of all American Indian tribes is the Cherokee, who quickly adopted European social and technological forms
and came to be included as one of the "five civilized tribes." Involvement with Europeans, participation in Indian wars, and conflict with settlers led to their removal to reservations in Oklahoma in 1838–39.*

*Employing ethnohistorical sources in the following paper, Fred
Gearing attempts a re-creation of the differing factors influencing social
participation of the eighteenth–century Cherokee.*

41 Fred Gearing

THE CHEROKEE IN THE
EIGHTEENTH CENTURY*

The notion of structural pose, which is offered here, draws attention to
the well-established fact that the social structure of a human community
is not a single set of roles and organized groups, but is rather a series of
several sets of roles and groups which appear and disappear according to
the tasks at hand. The notion of structural pose elevates that known fact
to a position of central importance in structural analysis. In every
human community, a series of social structures come and go recurrently.
A Cherokee village in 1750, faced with a community task such as holding a village council, divided that work and coordinated it by arranging
all villagers into one social structure. Whenever the white flag was
raised over a village council house to call the council, a young male villager assumed with little or no reflection a defined set of relations with
every other villager. At the moment before, perhaps, his most en-
grossing relations had been with other men of his own age; now his
mind's eye shifted to the old men of the village. Before, perhaps, his
fellow clansmen had been dispersed and variously occupied with diverse
interests; now they all came to sit together and were engrossed with
him in a common task and were a corporate group among other like
groups. Faced with another task, such as negotiating with an alien

* Abridged from "The Structural Poses of the 18th Century Cherokee Villages," by F.
Gearing, in *American Anthropologist*, **60**, 1148–1157, 1958.

power, the community rearranged all villagers into still a different structure of roles and organized groups.

The notion of structural pose firmly fixes the mind of the student to that long-evident fact: human communities typically rearrange themselves to accomplish their various tasks. Orthodox studies of social structure do not. On most pages of the usual American structural studies, structural elements—clans, households, mother's brothers—are treated as if those groups and roles were ever-present. The usual operation is to elicit from observed events the shared understanding of the actors as to who is acting. The student sees one man speaking and other men listening. A participant, on questioning, reveals that the man speaks and is listened to because he is a man among men, because he is old among others younger, and because he is a fellow clansman. The student therefore knows that this society "has" these elements in its social structure. Having discovered the sundry elements of structure, the student usually proceeds to discover fit and ill fit—systematic interconnection—among the elements, treated as if ever-present. In obvious fact, all the elements are not operative all the time; one combination of elements operates, then another combination. When structural studies choose to give intensive attention to one or a few societies, the fact often intrudes that all elements are not operative at all times, but on the whole it remains in the background; when the studies move by drawing actuarial tables of correlation, the fact virtually disappears. British structural analyses of segmentary societies have, at the point where segmentariness itself is under discussion, given this temporal dimension of structure its deserved attention.

The thesis here is that the orthodox conceptualizations of social structures are a cumbersome reification of structural fact and that those conceptualizations hinder the articulation of structural studies with studies of personality and of ethos. I do not imagine that I here disclose a social fact which is new. Rather, I suggest here a less cumbersome and more profitable way of analyzing a known fact. In a word, a human community does not have a single social structure; it has several. Put otherwise, the social structure of a society is the sum of the several structural poses it assumes around the year.

I will illustrate the notion of structural pose by describing the four recurrent structural poses assumed by the male population of any 18th century Cherokee village as that village moved through its annual round of village tasks.

The aboriginal Cherokee kinship system was of the Crow type.

Whenever any two Cherokee came together, the presence or absence of a kinship relation was a major fact determining their behavior and, among kin, behavior was patterned by the particular nature of that kinship connection. Gilbert has described the total set of relations among kin.

Differentiation according to age and sex also affected behavior whenever any two Cherokee came together. Two sex statuses were employed. Men hunted and warred; women tilled gardens, cooked, and raised infants. The sexual division of labor was rather complete, but certain phases of agricultural labor fell to the men, and female warriors apparently existed under rare circumstances. Both sexes participated in ceremonies, but men acquitted the major responsibilities. Male age statuses were boy, young man, and beloved man. Female age statuses were probably parallel. A boy joined his first war party in his teens, but between 25 and 30 years of age, probably after he had established a family, he would receive a war rank and thus pass into the status of young man. Between 50 and 60 years of age a young man would cease to join war parties and thus become a beloved man. The age status of beloved man carried much prestige and influence; young men were expected to speak their minds to beloved men, but decorously, and to defer to their judgments when disagreement arose.

The Cherokee kinship system and the sex and age statuses meshed and at no visible points were in conflict. Indeed, their separation is an intellectual act which would probably not occur to a reflective Cherokee. Fortes has termed this set of shared understandings which patterned the behavior of every villager toward any other villager the "woof" of society.

Beyond this, the Cherokee joined in organized groups, the "warp" of Cherokee village structure. These groups were 30 or 40 households which were ideally matrilocal but were often neolocal, the local segments of seven matrilineal clans, a body of elders which included all men over about 55 years of age, and a war organization.

In each such group, kinship relations and age and sex categories patterned behavior. But each kind of organized group brought together a different combination of relatives and nonrelatives and a different proportion of persons of the age and sex categories. While ideas about proper behavior between father and son were constant, father and son were not always together; hence that relationship was not always operative. Father and son were usually together whenever the household was together; they were necessarily apart whenever the clans were gathered; and they may or may not have been together, depending on their ages, when the body of elders or the war organization was acting.

The notion of structural pose points up the systematic, rhythmic way in which Cherokees joined in first one set of organized groups and then another. There were four structural poses. In each pose, different groups operated, singly or in combination. During every minute of the Cherokee year, villagers guided themselves by the set of relations of one or another of those four poses, or at least understood that they should. For the hunt and for other tasks, the Cherokee village was one structural pose, an aggregate of independent households. Beginning soon after the Cherokee New Year in October, young men in small parties, usually fewer than ten, left the village for the winter hunt. The principal prey was deer. Hunters stalked their prey; there was no premium on large parties, and success depended less on coordination of the group than on individual skill. Parties could be gone a full six months, but shorter trips were probably more common. They returned to the village in time for a festival in early April which marked the end of winter and the beginning of summer. After the crops were in the ground and before the harvest, the young men again went out, this time for a shorter summer hunt. The division of labor—who would hunt and who would not—was an internal household matter. The relations among members of hunting parties was a household matter or at most a matter of voluntary association among men from a few households. The disposal of the catch and its preparation was a household matter.

A variety of other tasks fell to the aggregate of independent households. The household bore the major responsibilities connected with birth and the socialization of the child. It prepared food and provided shelter. In the event of illness, the household called in a priest-specialist and nursed the sick.

Occasionally, and at no predictable time, the rhythm of such household activities was disturbed by a murder. For purposes of punishing a killer, the village assumed a second structural pose. For this task and others, the seven local clan-segments became the significant groups and the village became an aggregate of independent clan-segments. A murder was a signal; fathers left their wives and children, conceptually or physically, to join with their mother's brothers, their brothers, their sisters' sons, to accomplish the task at hand. Each clan-segment was for this task a corporate individual; all local clansmen were guilty if a fellow clansman had killed, and all male clansmen were responsible for revenge if a fellow clansman had been killed. The killer (or one of his clan) was usually killed if he had murdered intentionally; otherwise some other settlement was possible.

To the clan-segments fell also the regulation of marriage. That regulation included the selection of a clansman's mate outside the clan and preferably in his father's father's clan. Marriage was further regulated through the beating of widows or widowers who violated mourning regulations by clanswomen of the deceased, and through punishment of men who deserted or neglected their wives and children by clanswomen of the neglected women and children.

For the purpose of reaching certain decisions, the village became a third structure. Now it was not an aggregate of smaller independent groups, but a single organized whole. At the time of the New Year Festival in late October, the village met in its most important general council of the year. (Other village councils were called as needed; they probably tended to occur in conjunction with the annual cycle of religious festivals.) A white pole was raised with an eagle feather and a white flag at the top, and the whole population came into the council house; village council houses which could seat 500 were not uncommon. The variety of decisions a village made was probably not great. For example, public buildings might need repair or might have to be built. Or, since farming lands were limited in the mountainous sections and since slash and burn techniques sometimes exhausted the soil faster than the floods replenished it, villages were sometimes forced to move.

Villagers organized themselves into a single whole by again gathering the seven clan-segments and by adding another, cross-cutting, organized group—the body of elders. The body of elders contained all male villagers over about 55 years of age—the beloved men. The principal officials were four priests and one secular officer: the village priest-chief, his right-hand man, the keeper of the council house, the messenger, and the secular village speaker. These men lived near the council house and probably acted, during general councils, as if without clan affiliation. But a second order of officials were simultaneously clansmen and members of the body of elders. These were the priest-chief's seven-man inner council of clansmen; one man was drawn from each clan-segment and each was the voice of his segment during the councils. The remaining beloved men also acted during councils both as clansmen and as elders. The rest of the village, those not in the body of elders, sat with their fellow clansmen, women apart from men. All male villagers could speak to points under consideration. Decisions were reached along two structural axes: each clan-segment came to an opinion and those opinions were reconciled in the body of elders, though not in the simple two-phase manner implied. Decisions had the semblance of unanimity in the sense that they were delayed until overt opposition ceased.

The Cherokee village assumed this same structural pose in two other major activities. First, in religious festivals the village expressed its basic ideas about the nature of the relations between man and god, between man and nature, and between man and man; the beloved men, organized as the body of elders, served the clan-segments as the channel of that expression by leading the ritual acts. Second, to organize agricultural work, the village probably assumed the same structural pose.

To carry on offensive war, the Cherokee village assumed a fourth structural pose. When a general council decided for war, the red standard of the village was raised and a new combination of organized groups went into operation. The village became an order of command. The age status of beloved men remained organized as the body of elders, excepting four who removed themselves from the elders to assume major war roles. The age status of young men plus those persons from the age status of boys who had passed adolescence left their fellow clansmen; these joined warriors of their respective war ranks, became the village war organization, and left the village. Women, children, and young men not able-bodied acted as members of their several clan-segments through clan representatives in both the body of elders and the war organization.

The major village war commanders were four beloved men with priestly esoteric knowledge necessary for war—the war priest, the war chief, the speaker for war, and the surgeon. The village war chief, and probably the other three top war officials, were elected by warriors. Those major war officials appointed four junior officers, probably ad hoc, from among the young men: a man with priestly knowledge to be flag bearer; a stand-in for the war priest to accompany the war party; two special war leaders, one a priest and one without priestly knowledge. There was also a seven-man council for war—probably a prominent warrior from each clan-segment—and a set of four scouts. The command functions were divided among those officers. Beneath the officials, the war organization was hierarchically stratified by four ranks which were earned through war deeds.

The day after a decision for war, the priestly war officials conjured; warriors fasted; a dance lasted through the night. Deeds were recounted to excite emulation. At dawn the young men went to the river and plunged seven times; again the priests conjured. The war speaker made a speech and the war party, carrying its standard and war ark, marched out of the village in a formal procession ordered by the offices and ranks of the war organization.

Three other village activities utilized this fourth structure. First, rather than decide for war with a particular tribe or colony, the village general council might decide to send a party to negotiate. Negotiations were handled by the war organization, and relationships among members of the negotiating party were the same relations that obtained among those persons during offensive war. The party carried instructions from the general council and, unlike war parties, usually maintained close communication with the body of elders during negotiations. Second, periodically during the summer, when warfare was rare, the young men joined for ball games with other villages. They assumed a set of relations with each other and with the village at large which duplicated the structure of the village for war. Third, in the event of attack on a village by an enemy, the village was organized under the war organization hierarchy.

To any Cherokee villager, each recurrent task was a signal to assume a certain set of relations with every other villager. For the variety of village tasks here reviewed, the male villagers organized themselves into four distinguishable structures. In other words, Cherokee village social structure was the rhythmic appearance and disappearance of those four structural poses.

For purely descriptive purposes, this notion of structural pose has no apparent advantage over the more usual conceptualizations found in structural studies. For certain theoretical purposes, it has significant advantages. I will briefly suggest two.

First, analysis in terms of structural pose provides an easier bridge to the individual, and hence an easier articulation with bodies of theory which deal with the individual and how he comes to be what he is. Structural pose holds the student's attention to the fact that individuals must move, recurrently and constantly, into and out of required relations with others. With analysis in terms of structural pose, a man's typical year, or typical lifetime, is immediately and concretely visible; his recurrent roles are laid out in the approximate sequence and frequence in which he must take them up and lay them down. A Cherokee young man, as he moved back and forth from the structural pose for war activities to the pose for village councils, shifted his loyalties and his relative status. Most importantly, he shifted from coercion-tinged war relationships, in which he feared the wrath of the prominent war leaders and perhaps was feared by warriors in ranks beneath him, to non-coercive deferential relations with gentle clan elders and village priest officials. The notion of structural pose reminds us and permits us to inquire in what way, and perhaps at what cost, the Cherokees could require any individual successfully to combine in himself the behavior required of warrior and young clansman.

The answers to that question cannot come from structural studies per se, but require help from disciplines which deal with the psychologies of individuals—role theory and depth psychology. Role theory tends to assume great flexibility in men; it anticipates and explains well the frequently large degree of success in the conscious and purposeful adjustment of a man's behavior as he moves from one role to another; the major maladjustments are expected when contradictory roles are demanded of him simultaneously. In contrast, Freudian psychology tends to insist more on the limitations of human adaptability in virtue of inborn qualities and early childhood experience; it anticipates more frequent failure, and accounts for such failures. In order to see successful flexibility or unsuccessful inflexibility, both psychologies need an image of a man's movement through the variety of social niches his society lays out for him.

Both psychologies help illuminate Cherokee social behavior. The required ritual purification of warriors on their return to the village comes to be seen as a device which insisted that the young men lay down their coercion-tinged relations with fellow warriors and assume the proper noncoercive relations with their families, clans, and with villagers at large. Most young Cherokees, with the assistance of this ritual event, were successful in this recurrent adjustment. The more prominent warriors typically were not. These few remained improperly overbearing in their relations with fellow villagers, and suffered the displeasure of their fellows; they were given war honors, but otherwise avoided. Further, after prominent warriors entered the body of elders, they usually enjoyed little influence or honor. Role theory and depth psychology seem respectively best equipped to explain the usual successes and the less usual but recurrent failures. Both need structural data. Those data, in the form of structural-pose analysis, are immediately applicable to the problem; the same data, in the form of more orthodox structural analyses, are not.

Second, structural pose provides a more adequate backdrop for understanding ethos than do orthodox structural studies. It is common knowledge that human groups deem an act good in one relationship and bad or irrelevant in another. So much is easily seen in the usual structural studies. But a community also deems an act morally appropriate in one situation and inappropriate in another. Structural pose permits an easier movement of the mind from structure to situation, and therefore from structure to the situational aspect of value. Situations evoke appropriate social groupings and, in and among those groupings, moral codes. Cherokee villagers valued personal freedom—or more accurately, they disvalued coerciveness. Yet Cherokee warriors were typically coercive. That social fact is not much illuminated by speaking of theory versus practice, or of a dual value system. It is, in the Cherokee instance, a complex matter of pervasive moral ideal, of certain allowed exceptions to that ideal, of certain characteristic violations of it, and of certain cultural devices for isolating those exceptions and violations into one corner of village life. In the event of war, the war organization formed; and the proper, allowed exceptions and the characteristic, expected, but improper violations both materialized in the relations within the war organization. The crisis situations in which war parties typically found themselves required command relations. Among the devices which bottled up that bothersome aspect of the Cherokee moral life was the custom of causing the war organization to disband when its immediate job was done. Cherokee value, situation, and structure were in reality of a piece.

Communities always divide their labor among social segments. The tasks require different operations of the different segments and the different operations can require different forms of leadership behavior within the different segments. Sometimes, the pattern of leadership within a segment unavoidably diverges from ideas about proper conduct because of the nature of the tasks that segment must perform. A society might conceivably exist where ethos floats evenly down over all tasks and all social segments, but assumptions of that condition have caused misinterpretations which are still accepted as truth. For example, Benedict put the Pueblo and the Plains groups at opposite poles of a continuum through this error. In effect, she compared the moral notions operative during a Pueblo general council with the partly immoral relations among a Plains war party. Yet some Pueblos had war parties which behaved not unlike Plains war parties, some Plains groups had general councils which behaved not unlike Pueblo general councils, and in both groups, the general council and related ritual were thought of as the clearest expression of the good life. Differences in emphasis surely existed, and those differences probably made for two quite different

kinds of men. But the comparisons would more accurately begin with
the basic pattern shared by both Plains and Pueblo societies. Structural
pose allows us to leave value, situation, and structure interconnected,
and therefore helps us to understand their interconnections.

Redfield argues that all of us should deem it worthwhile that some of
us work toward conceptualizations that permit us to view the complex
life of a human community as a single, systematic whole. Analyses such
as social structure, personality and culture, and ethos grasp some aspect
of that complex whole, but each grasps a different though overlapping
aspect. I take it that a modification of one kind of analysis which allows
an easier articulation with another kind is a good modification—in the
sense that it allows us to hope that what was seen as two systems can
now be seen as one. I believe that the notion of structural pose might be
such a modification. It offers the possibility that things known from
studies of social structure can be joined with things known from studies
of personality and culture and from studies of ethos, and that all of
them can be seen simultaneously and in their systematic interconnections.

*The Iroquois have been of interest to scholars since the pioneer
work among them by Lewis Henry Morgan in the nineteenth century.
During the United States' colonial period, the militaristic, expansionistic
member tribes (the Oneida, the Onondaga, the Cayuga, the Mohawk,
the Seneca, and later the Tuscarora) became middle-men between the
European on the northeastern seaboard and the inland tribes, such as
the Huron, the Erie, the Neutral, and various Algonkian-speaking peoples. Supported first by the Dutch, then by the English, the Iroquois
with an egalitarian, if strong, centralized political machinery came to occupy a dominant position vis à vis their neighbors. Trading in guns and
furs and gradually developing territorially aggressive warfare, the Iroquois destroyed or conquered most of their Indian competitors by 1700.
In the War of Independence (1776) the majority of the Iroquois sided
with the English against the colonists and, as a result of this unhappy
choice, most of the Indians were driven to Canada or otherwise dispossessed of their territory in the former colonies.
Alexander Goldenweiser, a prominent student of Franz Boas', pub-*

lished widely in the 1920's and 1930's and made many important con-
tributions to the development of anthropological theory.

42 Alexander A. Goldenweiser

IROQUOIS SOCIAL ORGANIZATION*

SOCIAL ORGANIZATION

The Phratry

Each of the five tribes of the confederacy is divided into clans which are grouped in two "phatries." These dual divisions do not, among the Iroquois, have any names, nor is there any evidence of a former existence of such names. The clans of one division or "side" call each other "brothers," while the clans of the other "side" are their "cousins," and vice versa. No origin myths referring to these divisions were obtained except the account contained in the Deganawida myth. Although my genealogies do not extend far enough back to bear witness to the former exogamy of the "sides," the frequency of intra-phratric marriages seems to be less in the older sections of the genealogies. Moreover, all of the older informants are agreed as to the ancient exogamy of the "sides" and remember incidents falling into the period of transition when the ancient rule began to give way, presently to be superseded by another exogamous regulation, that of the clan. There can, therefore, be no reasonable doubt that in ancient times the two main divisions of an Iroquois tribe were exogamous. The functions of the sides are manifold and all-important. At games, such as the peach-stone game, or lacrosse, the "sides" are lined up against each other. The "brothers" and "cousins" are similarly divided at contests such as the snow-snake game or target practice with bow and arrow. At all feasts the action as well as the spatial arrangement of the participants reveal the presence of the two

* Abridged from "On Iroquois Work, 1912," by A. A. Goldenweiser, in *Summary Report of the Canada Geological Survey* (Seasonal Paper), **26**, 464–475, 1913.

"sides." The same is true of ceremonies of adoption, ceremonies at which "friends" are made; night wakes, memorial ceremonies, and burial. In the latter instance, the functionaries at the burial ceremonial are always selected from the "side" opposite to the one of the deceased. At all great periodic festivals, such as the Strawberry Festival, the Green Corn Festival, etc., which are held in the ceremonial longhouses, the members of the two "sides" are always spatially divided and face each other. A speaker represents each side and, in the course of the performance, always addresses the opposite side. At the preliminary meetings of officials which always precede the festivals, two men are usually appointed to go from house to house and solicit contributions to the feast; these men always represent the "brothers" and "cousins" respectively. The Death Feast Society and the tribal Medicine Societies, the so-called "Little Water" or "Real Life" societies, follow in their performance, the phratric division. The same seems to be true of the performances of the other medicinal societies, the False-faces, Otters, Buffaloes, etc. At the election of chiefs the "sides" are functionally represented, a point to be presently referred to more specifically. At name-giving ceremonies, the name is bestowed by the "side" opposite to the one to which the recipient of the name belongs. In the dream-guessing ritual the guesser must belong to the "side" opposite to that of the dreamer.

At councils, on the other hand, that is, at all meetings of an administrative or judicial character, a tripartite arrangement takes the place of the dual division.

The Clan

We now pass to the consideration of the social units embraced in the phratry, the clans. The number of clans in an Iroquois tribe is not always the same; the Seneca, Cayuga, and Onondaga have now (at Grand River) and seem to have had for some time past more than eight clans each, while the precise number of clans is different for each tribe. To the Mohawk and Oneida we shall return presently. Not every clan is represented by a chief in the Confederacy. One informant states that the arrangement of clans into phratries differed before and after the formation of the Confederacy. While the historical reference is doubtless wrong, the statement is not without significance. The clans of the Seneca before Confederacy (B. C.) and after Confederacy (A. C.) can be represented as follows:

B. C.

Turtle	Hawk
Bear	Deer
Wolf	Snipe
Ball	Duck
	Eel

A. C.

Turtle	Hawk
Bear	Little Snipe
Wolf	Great Snipe
(Ball)	(Duck)
	(Eel)

Of the latter list, the Duck, Eel, and Ball clans were never repre-sented by chiefs in the Confederacy. No individuals belonging to the Eel or Duck clans can at present be found among the Grand River Seneca. As stated before, the arrangement of the clans at councils did not follow phratry lines. The Seneca chiefs, for instance, when in coun-cil, were grouped as follows:

GROUP I ("in control")

1 Turtle Chief
1 Little Snipe Chief

GROUP II	GROUP III
1 Turtle Chief	1 Hawk Chief
1 Bear Chief	1 Little Snipe Chief
1 Wolf Chief	1 Great Snipe Chief

For purposes of discussion there was a further subdivision. The Tur-tle chief (II) conferred with the Hawk chief (III), the Bear (II) with the Little Snipe chief (III), the Wolf (II) with the Great Snipe chief (III); the Turtle and Little Snipe chiefs (I) had the deciding voice. This grouping of clans and phratries had its analogue in the grouping of tribes of the Confederacy. On ceremonial occasions the grouping was as follows:

Mohawk	Oneida
Onondaga	Cayuga
Seneca	

When in council, the tribes assumed the tripartite arrangements:

ONONDAGA ('in control')

Mohawk	Oneida
Seneca	Cayuga

The Mohawk and Oneida seem to have had only three clans each. These were the Turtle, Wolf, and Bear clans. However, among the Oneida of Oneida Reserve (near St. Thomas, Ont.) these three clans are each subdivided into three groups differentiated by the size or species of the eponymous animal. These minor groups, moreover, have their distinct sets of individual names and of the nine Oneida chiefs each is associated with one of the minor divisions. These facts were fully verified by genealogies. Their significance may become clearer in my further investigations.

Whether the clan systems of the Iroquois tribes are derived from a common historical source it is impossible to say. It cannot be doubted, however, that for a long period of time the clans, Wolf, Bear, etc., of one tribe were in no way associated with the corresponding clans of the other tribes. During the formation of the Confederacy and since, the intimacy of relations between clans of identical name but belonging to different tribes became very great. It always remained an equalization, however, not a fusion. And to this day each clan of each tribe must be regarded as the social unit. The practice of exogamy, it is true, has been extended to all clans of identical name; the clans of each tribe, on the other hand, have preserved their distinct sets of individual names. Owing to the disappearance of many individual names, cases where this last rule was disregarded have of late been known to occur. Whenever this happens, however, the act is freely criticized and disputes arise.

From the beginning of my investigations I was on the look-out for any beliefs or practices which might have pointed to the former existence of some special relations between the clansmen and the eponymous animal of their clan. All inquiries in that direction, however, led to negative results. There was no prohibition on the killing or eating of the eponymous animal; no idea of descent from it was entertained; the eponymous animal was not a guardian or protector, nor was it a brother or friend of the clansman. Carved representations of clan animals certainly used to be placed over the entrance-doors of longhouses presumably associated with the particular clan; the practice of wearing carved miniature figurines of clan animals or of painting or tattooing them on the breast may have existed; vague references are also made to a former belief in the power of clansmen to hunt their eponymous animal successfully. Individual names among the five tribes of the Confederacy never refer to the clan animal or bird. The only indisputable fact about these eponymous animals is that they were eponymous. The animal names of clans, however, are by no means the terms by which they are commonly designated. For this purpose collective terms referring to some quality or habit of the eponymous creature are used, such as "the people of dark complexion" (Bear), "the people with small hoofs" (Deer), etc. Only on those occasions when the clan membership of an individual must be specifically indicated, for instance at condolence ceremonies, are the animal names used. In a description of the social organization of the Seneca, recorded in Seneca text, in which the arrangement of clans, etc., is systematically discussed, the clans are not once referred to by their animal names. The distinctive traits of an Iroquois clan may be summarized as follows: (1) the clans are exogamous (as this trait became extended so as to embrace the clans of identical name in all tribes, the clan in each tribe can no longer be regarded as an exogamous unit); (2) each clan has its own set of individual names; (3) the majority, although not all, clans claim a chief in the confederate body and participate in his election; (4) in ancient times a clan certainly owned a burial ground and possibly communal lands; (5) in ancient times clans may have been associated with longhouses, although probably not in the sense of one clan occupying or predominating in, only one longhouse; (6) in ancient times clans may have been associated with villages; (7) a clan has the right to adopt an outsider into the clan; (8) although the clans as such do not figure at ceremonies, they elect their own ceremonial officials.

No separate clan origin myths were found. When questioned on that topic, the Iroquois invariably refer to the Deganawida myth. I have recorded this myth in Onondaga text.

It must be noted as possibly significant that in the myths so far recorded no mention is made of clans and chiefs; instead, villages and headmen are always spoken of.

The Family

Under this heading two distinct units in Iroquois sociology must be considered. On the one hand a family was constituted by one's relatives on the father's and the mother's side. This group was united by the ties of the classificatory system of relationship; one's father's brothers, for instance, were one's fathers just as one's mother's sisters were one's mothers, etc. The group also figured in a number of family ceremonies, and was important in connexion with marriages; it was also appealed to by the individual in numerous matters of personal behaviour, such as assuming a second name, or joining a society, or starting an important undertaking. Of far greater significance, however, was the group we may designate as maternal family. It embraced the male and female descendants of a woman, the descendants of her female descendants, and so on. The entire group was thus united by the ties of blood on the female side. The woman who at any time stood at the head of such a group wielded most powerful influence over its members. Moreover, the group as such had certain religious and ceremonial prerogatives. These functions of the maternal family have now become obsolete, and my material to date throws but little light on the old condition. In my subsequent studies I shall make a systematic attempt to penetrate more deeply into the nature and significance of this social grouping. The genealogies indicate that whereas the chiefs are identified with clans, the actual succession follows the maternal family. The same is true of the ceremonial officials, of whom each clan has three male and three female. To a limited extent this also applies to individual names, which show a certain tendency to be passed down in the maternal family, commonly by skipping one generation.

The Raising of Chiefs and the Functions of Women

The judicial and executive powers of the Iroquois Confederacy were vested in a body of fifty chiefs. Of these nine came from the Mohawk, nine from the Oneida, fourteen from the Onondaga, ten from the Cayuga, and eight from the Seneca. These chiefs must be strictly distinguished from the warrior chiefs who were elected whenever occasion required, whose office was not hereditary, and whose powers expired with the termination of the raid or other military undertaking which had brought them into being. In the case of the fifty civil chiefs the elective and hereditary principles were curiously combined. Every chief was associated with a clan—although not every clan was represented by a chief; but the hereditary right to elect a chief belonged to a smaller unit, the maternal family, or a body of persons united by the ties of consanguinity. Small genealogies collected with this special point in view, show clearly the extent of the elective principle within these small social bodies. There seems to have been no age limit to the office of a chief; but an aged chief feeling his powers waning, would of his own accord resign, leaving his place free to be filled by a younger man. When a man was made chief, he laid aside his individual name and assumed a chief's name, which was his while he continued to be chief and then passed on to his successor, and so on *ad infinitum*. Every chief's name had a definite place in the set of chiefs' names, and at condolence ceremonies, when the names were recited, the fixed order was strictly adhered to. The differences of rank probably once associated with these names cannot now be clearly discerned, except in the case of a few names.

When a chief died, the women of his tribe and clan held a meeting at which a candidate for the vacant place was decided upon. A woman delegate carried the news to the chiefs of the clans which belonged to the "side" of the deceased chief's clan. They had the power to veto the selection, in which case another women's meeting was called and another candidate was selected. Usually, however, the first choice of the women was confirmed by the chiefs of their own "side" and then by the chiefs of the opposite "side." Thereupon the candidacy was carried to the Confederate Council to be ratified, first by the Confederate phratry of the deceased, then by the opposite phratry (see section on "Clan"). This was followed by a public condolence ceremony in the course of which the chief was formally "raised," instructed in the rights and duties of his office, and adorned with the horns of the deer, the symbol of his high station. The condolence ceremony is fully described in the Deganawida myth.

The participation of the women in the procedure did not end there. The woman delegate, the same who had carried the announcement of the candidate to the chiefs, had to keep close watch over the ways and actions of the young chief. If he displayed an inclination to deviate from the accepted code of behaviour, the woman delegate appeared before him and tried to persuade him to desist from his evil practices. If after a time she discovered that her appeal had no effect, she repeated the visit. If that also proved of no avail, she was joined by a warrior chief of her clan, and together they made a last attempt to induce the chief to reform. If their efforts proved unsuccessful, the woman delegate called a meeting of the women of her clan and publicly denounced the chief. The impeachment then passed through the various bodies referred to before, up to the final ratification by the Confederate Council. Thereupon the chief was formally deposed, and his place was declared vacant.

The prominent part played by women in the election and deposition of chiefs marks her high social status among the Iroquois. Of the six ceremonial officials who were hereditary in each clan, three were men and three women. The preparation and conduct of almost all ceremonies were in the hands of these officials. Some of the most important ceremonial societies, such as the Dark Dance and the Death Feast societies, were not only run by the women but the latter also constituted the larger part of the membership in these societies. Although women had no formally recognized voice at councils, nor ever appeared, so far as known, as appointed speakers at ceremonies, speeches were often made by women in council as well as on ceremonial occasions. Some women, a few within the memory of men now living, were reputed as skilful orators and must have wielded strong personal influence. Woman was pre-eminently the owner of property. Whereas the husband, in ancient times, could regard as his own only his weapons, tools, and wearing apparel, his wife owned the objects of the household, the house itself, and the land. The children who, of course, followed the mother's clan, belonged to her. The individual names, in each clan, were also regarded as belonging to the women. In the arrangement of marriages woman was the determining factor. Not, indeed, the bride, but her mother, together with the mother of the bridegroom. The two women had full power to arrange the match, and the wisdom of their decision was seldom questioned. The oldest woman of the clan, or the woman most respected for her wisdom and experience, was a most powerful factor in the affairs of the clan, and none, not even the chief, could with impunity disregard her advice. Nor did her influence end there, for she also exercised authority over the children of her clansmen, who (the children) belonged to many clans and widely scattered districts. Thus the entire social structure of the Iroquois was permeated by a maze of channels through which keen-witted women guided the affairs of the people.

CEREMONIES

In every clan we find three male and three female officials whose duty it is to plan and superintend the ceremonial performances. Of these the most conspicuous are the periodic harvesting festivals. When early in spring the strawberries begin to ripen, the Strawberry Festival is held, an outline description of which I secured. In the course of the performance the motions gone through by the berry-pickers are imitated by the dancers. Similar festivities occur when the beans and raspberries are ripe. The Raspberry Festival I recorded in outline; while the Bean Festival was taken down in Onondaga text (in part translated). The ripening of corn becomes the occasion for an important four-day ceremony, the Green Corn Festival. Of this a fairly detailed, although not complete, description is in my hands. The most important periodic ceremonial of the year is the Mid-winter Festival which lasts five days and is followed by a period of another two or three days during which games are played. Of this ritual I have an outline description, and part of it is recorded in Onondaga text. The sequence of events in the above series of festivals may be summarized as follows. About the time when a festival is usually held, the officials meet and deliberate as to the main features of the forthcoming feast. Then two men are sent out who go from house to house and collect contributions in victuals and, in modern times, money. A second meeting of officials is called at which the contributions are examined. If the amount is sufficient, a date for the feast is fixed upon. If the contributions are scanty, the two men are sent out for another round; then the date is fixed at a third meeting. The festival opens with the selection of two speakers who are appointed by the officials. Then follows an appeal to the Great Spirit and a thanksgiving address to the powers of Nature, in particular to the three sisters, Corn, Bean, and Squash. This address is repeated in practically the same form at all of the above festivals. Next in order are songs and dances for men, for women, or for both, accompanied by rattles or tomtoms handled by men especially appointed for that purpose at each feast. During the period of the dances, which in the Green Corn and Mid-winter Festivals occupy from two to three days, the religious societies also hold their performances. On the second day of the Green Corn and on the second or third days of the Mid-winter Festivals, babies are brought in by their mothers, and names are officially bestowed upon them. Dream-guessing is a special feature of the mid-winter rituals. Persons who had dreams announce that fact to the chiefs, and the dreams are guessed by persons of the opposite "side" in the course of the feast. The one who guesses the dream must make for the dreamer a miniature object, a canoe, rattle, lacrosse stick, etc., around which the dream centres. The object is kept by the dreamer and is supposed to bring luck and ward off disease. In the morning of the fifth day of the Mid-winter Festival the Sacrifice of the White Dog takes place. I have witnessed and recorded the rite. The significance of the entire performance is, however, by no means clear to me. It is to be hoped that further intensive study of the ceremonies, a study which may extend over two or three years, will throw light on this somewhat puzzling ritual.

As regards other ritualistic performances, brief descriptions were secured of: (1) wakes; (2) memorial feasts; (3) death feasts, in the family and the tribe; (4) adoption ceremonies, of an individual or a group of individuals, in the family, clan, and Confederacy; (5) ceremonies at which "friends" were made. A full description of the condolence rituals is contained in the Deganawida myth. Some of the so-called "societies" also hold ceremonial meetings, in particular the Death Feast Society and the Medicine Societies, into the Onondaga branch of which I was initiated, having previously been adopted into the Seneca tribe and the Wolf clan.

SOCIETIES

The societies of the Iroquois, whatever their history may have been, are at the present time medicinal in their functions. The society in each tribe which is most influential and sacred is the so-called Medicine Society referred to in the section on "Ceremonies". Ritualistically it falls into two divisions, of which the "Little Water" or "Real Life" division is by far the more secret in its performances and powerful in its social bearings. The only way of joining this division of the society is by having a dream of a certain fixed type. The other division may be joined by any one who has met with an accident, had some bone broken, and was cured by the members of the society. The other societies are known as the False-face (or Corn Husk), the Otter, Bear, Buffalo, and Eagle societies. The Dark Dance and the Death Feast societies comprise a much more elaborate ritual than the other societies, excepting the "Real Life," and stand in a group by themselves. All of these societies are in full swing at the Grand River Reserve as well as among the Seneca of New York State (as revealed by Mr. A. C. Parker's data). There can, therefore, be no doubt that prolonged research will result in a much fuller body of information than has so far been obtained.

Membership in a society is secured in one of a limited number of ways. A man (or woman) may fall sick and dream of an otter or buffalo; he (or she) then calls in the corresponding society, who perform their rites, whereupon the patient finds himself cured. He (or she) then joins the society and thenceforth invites its members to a feast at certain indefinite intervals, usually about once a year. There may be sickness, but no dream. Then the parents of the patient, or an old relative or a "prophet," are consulted. These "prophets" are men or women well versed in the traditional magical lore. They tell dreams, practice divinations, and in an inconspicuous way continue to wield a rather powerful influence among the modern Iroquois. Following the advice of the parent, relative, or prophet, the patient appeals to a society for a cure, and if their efforts prove successful, which is usually the case (for the time being, at any rate), he or she joins the society. Unless this is accompanied by the periodic festivities referred to above, the society takes revenge and the patient may again become afflicted. Some societies are appealed to as specialists in certain diseases. The False-faces, for example, are particularly efficacious in cases of swelling of the face, tooth-ache, inflammation of the eyes, nose-bleeding, sore chin, and ear-ache. One woman dreamed that she was crossing a river over an ice-bridge. The bridge gave way and she found herself afloat on a chunk of ice which continued to revolve, intermittently plunging her into the water and then bringing her to the surface again. She awoke and, after consultation with a prophet, became a member of the Otter society, which is intimately associated with water. Another woman joined the same society after dreaming that an otter carried her across a stream in a miniature canoe which the otter held in its mouth. One man, a skilled false-face carver, when he was a young boy, used to amuse himself by carving small false-faces. His parents objected to the practice and put a stop to it. About two months later the boy fell sick. Then his parents advised him to join the False-faces. He was cured by them and became a member of the society. Some three years ago an Oneida man of powerful frame and great strength, suddenly became ill. He could not locate the source of his trouble but felt his strength waning from day to day. His weight was rapidly decreasing. While he was thus afflicted, it so happened that he was travelling alone through the woods. Suddenly he heard a strange whistle which he readily identified as the voice of the False-face. Being of a skeptical disposition, he did not pay much heed to the incident, and reached home. Meanwhile his illness grew worse, and twice the False-face appeared to him in a dream, and spoke to him. Then he resolved to call in the False-faces. They performed their rites, and presently he felt relieved. Of course, he joined the society. (This personal experience is recorded in Oneida text.)

In addition to their activities as visiting physicians, some of the societies practice ceremonial rites or exercise medicinal functions of a more generalized kind. The Medicine Societies hold elaborate ceremonial meetings (see section on "Ceremonies"). The False-faces, twice a year, in spring and in autumn, separate into two bands. The members of each band, wearing false-faces, rattles in hand, and garbed in appropriate costume, go from house to house and amidst singing and rattling of the turtle shells, drive away the disease spirits. Then the two bands reunite, and a ceremonial meeting is held at the tribal Long House.

The numerous semihorticultural tribes of the Upper Great Lakes region are often overshadowed by their more glamorous neighbors. Existing between the strongly horticultural Iroquoian groups to the east and the buffalo hunters to the west, the Sauk, the Fox, the Miami, the Winnebago, the Ottawa, the Potawatomi, and the Chippewa tribes among others, shared marginally in the cultural patterns of both the Plains and the East, but basically exhibited similarities to the Algonkian-speaking hunters and foragers to the north.

George Quimby, long curator of North American archaeology and ethnology at the Field Museum of Natural History, has written extensively on the archaeological and historical aspects of aboriginal culture development.

43 George I. Quimby

THE INDIAN TRIBES OF THE UPPER GREAT LAKES REGION*

The Indian tribes of the Upper Great Lakes region during the Early Historic period were the Huron, Ottawa, Chippewa or Ojibwa, Potawa-

---

* Excerpt from *Indian Life in the Upper Great Lakes: 11,000 B.C. to A.D. 1800*, by G. I. Quimby. Chicago: Univ. Chicago Press, 108–112, 1960.

tomi, Winnebago, Menomini, Sauk, Fox, and Miami. These at least are the tribes that would have been counted by the first census taker, had there been one in the region at the time.

There were no census takers, but from the reports and diaries of European explorers, missionaries, and fur traders estimates of population have been obtained, and these provide the basis for the first census of the Upper Great Lakes region.

There were 45,000 to 60,000 Indians in the Huron-Tionontati tribes; 3,000 to 3,500 Ottawa Indians; some 25,000 to 35,000 Indians among the various bands of the Chippewa tribe; 4,000 Potawatomi Indians; 3,800 persons in the Winnebago tribe; 3,000 Menomini Indians; 3,500 Sauk Indians; 3,000 Fox Indians; and 4,500 persons in the Miami tribe.

These estimates suggest that there was a population of at least 100,000 Indians occupying the Upper Great Lakes region at the beginning of the Early Historic period.

In the Upper Great Lakes region there are about 144,000 square miles of land and inland lakes.

A population of about 100,000 persons occupying and using about 144,000 square miles of land and inland lakes and rivers suggests a population density of less than one person per square mile. This certainly was not a dense population judged by modern standards, but it may have been considered so in terms of the standards of the Indian occupants. After all, about 10 per cent of the prehistoric owners of North America north of Mexico seem to have lived in the Upper Great Lakes region.

The greatest population density in the Upper Great Lakes region seems to have been in Ontario, in the region between Lake Simcoe and Georgian Bay and the adjacent land westward and southwestward to Lake Huron. In A.D. 1600 this area was the homeland of the Huron and Tionontati people. Within this area of perhaps 4,500 square miles, there probably lived at least 45,000 Indians, a population density of ten persons per square mile.

The most sparse population density seems to have been in the Lake Superior basin of upper Michigan and Ontario. In this area there were perhaps some 20,000 Chippewa using an area of about 49,000 square miles, a population density of less than one person per two square miles.

These differences in density of population within the Upper Great Lakes region reflect the subsistence level and the limitations of environment. The highest density of population was found among Indians who obtained their subsistence by farming and did relatively little hunting. Under these conditions the least amount of land would support the most people.

The lowest density of population was found in the northern parts of the region where farming was impossible. Here the Indians obtained their subsistence by hunting and the size of the population was geared directly to the size of the animal population in a predator-prey relationship.

In other parts of the Upper Great Lakes region there were tribes of Indians who gained their subsistence by a combination of farming and hunting in almost equal parts. Their population densities varied in relation to the size of the areas they utilized for hunting. If measured only in terms of their villages and farm lands they would have had a relatively high density of population. Their relatively low population densities were as much a measure of the territory they were able to control as a measure of subsistence level.

Each of the Indian tribes in the Upper Great Lakes region had its own language and each of these languages belonged to one of three major language families or stocks, Iroquoian, Algonkian, or Siouan.

The language of the Hurons belonged to the Iroquoian family of languages. The Winnebago language belonged to the Chiwere division of the Siouan linguistic stock. All of the other tribes in the Upper Great Lakes region possessed languages belonging to the Algonkian family.

Chippewa and Ottawa were dialects of essentially the same Algonkian language. Potawatomi, although a separate language, was closer to Chippewa-Ottawa than to any other Algonkian language. Menomini, although separate, seems to have been most closely related to the Sauk and Fox (with Kickapoo) group of Algonkian dialects. The Miami, along with the Illinois, who lived south of the Upper Great Lakes region, formed another linguistic division of the Algonkian family.

Upon the basis of linguistic relationships there was the following grouping of tribes within the Upper Great Lakes region: The Huron stood alone; the Ottawa, Chippewa, and Potawatomi formed a group of related tribes; the Winnebago stood alone; the Menomini, Sauk, and Fox (and Kickapoo on the western edge of the region) formed a group of related tribes; and the Miami (with the Illinois to the south of them) were a separate group.

In terms of social organization, particularly the systems of classifying relatives and regulating marriage and inheritance, there were significant groupings of tribal cultures within the Upper Great Lakes region. These groupings are as follows:

The Huron, Chippewa, Ottawa, and Potawatomi formed one group in terms of their common system of classifying relatives and regulating marriage. However, the Huron reckoned descent in the female line—they were matrilineal, whereas the Chippewa, Ottawa, and Potawatomi were patrilineal. Thus the Chippewa, Ottawa, and Potawatomi form one group and the Huron, though similar, constitute a separate grouping.

The other tribes of the Upper Great Lakes, the Winnebago, Menomini, Sauk and Fox, Miami, and their neighboring tribes to the south and west of the region have in common a different system of classifying relations and regulating marriage, and thus comprise a third grouping.

Another way to classify these various tribes of Indians is by their modes of subsistence. The Hurons were intensive farmers and engaged in a limited amount of hunting, primarily to obtain raw materials for clothing and tools. The Chippewa, on the other hand, were essentially hunters. The rest of the Upper Great Lakes tribes had a subsistence based about equally upon farming and hunting. The Menomini, however, combined their farming with the gathering of wild rice, probably to a greater degree than any other tribe in the region.

Those tribes oriented toward the southern and southwestern parts of the region, the Sauk, Fox, and Miami, undertook communal hunts in the prairies. The northern tribes, such as the Ottawa and Potawatomi who hunted in the forests, separated into small family groups when hunting. The Winnebago and Menomini seem to have been intermediate.

All of the tribes in the Upper Great Lakes, except the nomadic Chippewa, were essentially sedentary. And even the Chippewa tended to congregate in larger groups in summer, especially at favorable fishing places.

The arrival of European explorers, fur traders, and missionaries in the Upper Great Lakes region was responsible for a number of changes in the native tribal cultures. In the period from 1600 to 1760 this culture change was not as rapid as it was later. The first changes were in relation to material things such as weapons, tools, and utensils.

Iron knives were substituted for stone knives, iron hoes replaced wooden and bone or shell hoes, iron axes were substituted for stone axes, and iron and brass points replaced the chipped-stone points on arrows.

French type bastions and gates were added to the aboriginal type of wooden stockades, and brass kettles were introduced to compete with pottery vessels of native manufacture.

Porcelain beads in abundance were preferred to the old beads of marine shell, and brass rings and bracelets were worn by the women. Lengths of French sword blades were hafted to wooden spears instead of shorter blades of chipped flint. Guns were introduced and used along with bows and arrows.

French clothing came to have value in terms of prestige and was worn for show on top of the native clothing made of animal skins. Even some food plants, such as peas and watermelons, were introduced by the French, who also were responsible for the addition of house cats, pigs, geese, ducks, and chickens. Pigs came to be used at feasts in place of especially fattened bears and dogs.

In non-material aspects of culture the changes were not particularly great. Religion was the cultural field of greatest interest to the missionaries, and change in religious ideas was very slow. Some inroads were made, however, because as early as 1679 some remnants of the Huron gave a dance at Christmas to celebrate the birth of Christ and his arrival at their village.

The changes in tribal culture were earlier in the eastern part of the Upper Great Lakes region than they were in the western and northern portions; for it was there that the Indians first encountered the Europeans. Moreover, in much of this period the quantity of goods introduced was not sufficient to cause the Indian to abandon his old handicrafts. The old and the new persisted until near the end of the period, at which time some of the old handicrafts became extinct through lack of use. By 1760 pottery-making had ceased and brass kettles were used almost exclusively. Guns had finally replaced the bow and arrow, and wars and the fur trade had brought about a number of changes in the various tribal cultures.

*B*ecause of our own concern with national identities and with social and political boundaries, it is all too easy for even anthropologists to forget that a specific human social group exists in a matrix of similar social groups. *War, trade, marriage exchange, and reciprocal ceremonialism are forms of universal intersocietal interaction. In most societies the individual members acquire at birth continuing relationships with other individuals involving exchange of items of worth. Such exchanges serve to circulate wealth, to maintain economic equality, to foster continuing interpersonal and intergroup ties and, in many other ways, to weave together the various individuals and social segments which compose the larger society.*

In the following paper, perhaps the best of its type written about an American Indian society, Mary Herman examines in detail the forms and contexts involved in Huron exchange relationships.

44 Mary W. Herman

THE SOCIAL ASPECTS OF HURON PROPERTY*

Ownership patterns found among the cultures of the world have interested anthropologists almost as long as there has been a science of that name. However, most students have confined their attention to certain traditional questions, particularly the size and composition of the group in physical possession of land, capital goods, and items of personal use. This is not an adequate conception of the problem since not only the form of ownership patterns, but their interrelationships with other aspects of the culture, have been found to vary markedly between different societies. A full understanding of the institution of property therefore requires an investigation of the social setting in which it functions, or what Hallowell has called the "social aspect of property."

The ownership rights of individuals or groups can be encompassed within the socially recognized power to acquire, use, dispose of, or destroy property. In no known instance is an owner given completely free rein in the exercise of these rights. There are usually numerous customs, not all directly related to legal ownership, which limit and direct the owner's behavior and determine his attitudes with respect to property.

* Abridged from "The Social Aspects of Huron Property," by M. W. Herman, in *American Anthropologist*, **58**, 1044–58, 1956.

In other words, ownership in the social sense can best be understood as a more or less interrelated collection of culturally prescribed rights, duties, and beliefs concerning property.

A systematic review of the material on the seventeenth-century Huron acquisition, use, and disposal of food and certain of the goods circulating in the fur trade (particularly wampum, furs, and small items of French manufacture) reveals an integration of these activities with aspects of culture not generally discussed in connection with property relationships in the anthropological literature. The resulting analysis is presented below to illustrate by a concrete example the manner in which such interrelationships may operate, and to suggest their broader applications in the study of property rights.

Following an introductory discussion of Huron trade, the material is organized by the types of occasion on which substantial transfers of ownership took place—informal gift-giving, formal presentations, curing and burial ceremonies, theft, and gambling. In addition, two factors motivating the disposition of property, the sense of communal responsibility and the importance of generous gift-giving in determining social status and power, are discussed separately.

HURON TRADE IN THE SEVENTEENTH CENTURY

The main sources on which a description of seventeenth-century Huron culture must depend are the accounts of Samuel de Champlain, based on a nine months visit to Huronia in 1615; Gabriel Sagard, a Recollect father who spent the year 1623–24 among the Huron; and the yearly reports of the Jesuit priests on the Huron, which extend from 1635 until the dispersal of this tribe by the Iroquois in 1649. By the time of the earliest of these sources, the Huron had already established an organized trading arrangement in which they carried maize, nets, tobacco, wampum, and small items of French manufacture to bands of Algonkian-speaking hunters living north of the St. Lawrence River, in exchange for furs which the Huron sold to the French. Some of the maize and tobacco involved in this trade was obtained from the Neutral and Petun who did not engage directly in the Algonkian trade. The Huron also traded with a neighboring Algonkian tribe, the Nipissing, with whom they exchanged maize for fish, game, and magical charms. From all reports the Huron were good businessmen and made every effort to get the best possible returns in their trading activities.

By means of trade, which constituted a large part of the men's sphere of work, and the agricultural labor of the women, some households acquired large stocks of trade items and surplus maize. It was not made clear by the seventeenth century observers whether any of these goods were owned exclusively by individuals and whether any belonged to conjugal families or compound households. In some instances they attribute the disposition of movable property to specific individuals, as in gambling losses, while in others it is attributed to the household.

COMMUNAL RESPONSIBILITY

The feeling of communal responsibility among the Huron rested on the belief (1) that all members of the community had a right to the basic necessities of life, and (2) that the whole community benefited by certain types of expenditure, which resulted from obligations of the group and which therefore the group should pay. The latter category included reparations payments arising out of a murder committed by a member of the village, payments involved in prisoner exchanges or peace treaties, tolls for crossing another chief's territory, and goods needed for curing dances and formal feasts. A stock of goods—wampum necklaces, glass beads, axes, knives, and other small wealth objects—was maintained for the discharge of obligations of this type. This fund was to some extent replenished by payments made to the village as a whole on occasions similar to those on which the community paid out gifts or tolls, but contributions were sometimes needed, at which time "every man taxes himself freely with what he can pay, and without any compulsion gives of his means according to his convenience and good will" (7:266–67).

Such contributions might also be required when the Huron were away from home. For example, when Sagard was accompanying some Huron to Quebec to trade, they were stopped by a group of Algonkin and Montagnais and obliged to make special presents to be allowed to pass. Another instance occurred in 1642 when the Huron attended a Nipissing feast of the dead. An individual Huron delegate secured a prize in the games by unfair means, and the other tribal members taxed themselves in order to make a suitable retribution payment to the Nipissing. There were also numerous occasions in connection with special emergencies and curing ceremonies where particular objects were required, when direct appeals for donations were made and, as will be noted below, responded to by the Huron to the best of their ability.

When a member of a Huron village was without food or shelter, a council would be called to make arrangements to provide them. The custom of communal co-operation in building houses is described by Sagard, and instances in which this occurred are recorded in the *Jesuit Relations*. In 1637 a fire burned down the house of a Huron family, and the other households of the village bound themselves to furnish three sacks of corn and whatever else they felt they could contribute. This was decided in a council of the old men and, according to a French observer, the participants acted very generously. The same year the people of Ossosané, a Huron village, held a council at which they agreed to build a chapel for the Jesuit priests. This incident presumably indicates an extension to the Jesuits of membership in the community, or a recognition of their services. Sagard explains a similar service performed for his party as follows:

> But as regards us, who were strangers to them and newcomers, it was a great thing that they should show themselves so full of human kindness as to put up a building for us with good feeling so general and universal, since as a rule to strangers they give nothing for nothing, except to deserving persons or those who have obliged them greatly, although they themselves always make demands, especially upon the French. (7:79)

INFORMAL ENTERTAINING AND GIFT GIVING

All the French visitors to the Huron noted their extensive hospitality, both to one another and to those outsiders who were accepted as friends. Many of the Huron were absent from the villages during the spring and summer, the men to engage in trading and war, the women in agricultural pursuits. But during the winter, feasts and informal gatherings frequently took place. Of the people of the Bear district, who were particularly noted for their sociability, Brebeuf said: "When they are not busy with their fields, hunting fishing, or trading, they are less in their own Houses than in those of their friends. . . . If they have something better than usual, they make a feast for their friends, and hardly ever eat it alone" (6, vol. 10:213).

In similar fashion, Indians visiting from other villages or tribes, or accepted Europeans, found that they could lodge almost indefinitely with those Huron who could afford to have long-term visitors. Although it was customary to give presents to one's host on such occasions, particularly if the visitor were a European, the exchange was not supposed to be one of value given for value received, but rather a formalized expression of friendship. There was some disagreement among European observers on this point, but the bulk of the evidence tends to support the above contention.

For example, Brebeuf, who had stayed with a wealthy Huron in the village of Toanché for six weeks in 1635, said:

> You can lodge where you please; for this Nation above all others is exceedingly hospitable towards all sorts of persons, even toward Strangers; and you may remain as long as you please, being always well treated according to the fashion of the country. (6, vol. 8:93–97)

From Frenchmen, however, they expected some compensation on leaving. On the same subject Sagard says:

> Whenever we had to go from one village to another for some necessity or business we used to go freely to their dwellings to lodge and get our food, and they received us in them and treated us very kindly although they were under no obligation to us. For they hold it proper to help wayfarers and to receive among them with politeness anyone who is not an enemy, and much more so those of their own nation. (7:88)

Bressani, in a summary report on the Huron after their dispersal, concluded that they "received every comer to their houses as they would members of the family". Champlain received similar friendly treatment, being given a warm welcome and feast in his honor at each of the villages he visited.

Visitors to the Huron were also expected to give presents to friends who came from far and near to see them on their arrival. When Brebeuf returned to the Huron in 1635, he spent the first evening and the next day in "exchanges of affection, visits, salutations, and encouraging words from the whole village." On the following days, persons with whom he had been acquainted in other villages came to see him "and all took away with them, in exchange for their visit, some trifling presents." Of this custom the Jesuit says, "This is a small thing in detail, but on the whole it exerts a great influence and is of great importance in these regions" (6, vol. 8:97). Sagard also mentions the custom of exchanges of presents between friends when they visited one another, and says that on such occasions they accepted whatever was offered. For this reason, he says, they despise the behavior of the French merchants, "who will bargain for an hour to cheapen [the price of] a beaver's skin."

At a later date Father Chaumonot complains that, "these savages practice among themselves certain rules of hospitality, with us they apply them not. We are, therefore, obliged to carry with us a few little knives, awls, rings, needles, earrings, and such like things, to pay our hosts" (6, vol. 8:19). In view of the extensive evidence to the contrary, this point of view seems best explained as a misinterpretation of Huron culture. It is possible, however, that the treatment which Father Chaumonot experienced may have reflected a deterioration in the relations between Jesuit and Huron, the priests having been suspected of causing by sorcery the frequent epidemics from which the Huron began to suffer shortly after receiving the Jesuits to their villages.

Another aspect of the custom of giving gifts to friends which, however, is almost as formal in character as the diplomatic gifts to be discussed below, was that of sympathy gifts. Presents usually accompanied other expressions of sympathy on such occasions as the death of relative, fires, or droughts. The best examples of such behavior on the village level are cases in which the Jesuits made condolence presentations to the Huron, but their accompanying remarks indicate that in doing this they were conforming to Huron mores. One such occasion occurred in 1637 when the Jesuits, having obtained some deer, gave a feast to the Huron to testify their sympathy for their suffering because of the current epidemic, and "in order to proceed after the manner of the country, we made them a present of 400 Porcelain beads, a couple of hatchets, and a Moose skin." These priests later visited the family of one of their converts to console the members on a number of deaths which had occurred among their relatives, and as "according to the custom of the country, a person who is in affliction hardly considers himself comforted if you give him nothing but words, the Father made them a present of 400 porcelain beads and 2 little hatchets" (6, vol. 13:151; vol. 14:27).

DIPLOMATIC FEASTS AND EXCHANGES OF PRESENTS

In many instances the smooth functioning of social relations both within the tribe and with other societies was facilitated by formally patterned feasts and gift exchanges. As a Jesuit observer stated it: "[Feasts] . . . are the oil of their ointments . . . the general instrument or condition without which nothing is done" (6, vol. 17:209). Regarding the role of presents on public occasions, Brebeuf said that "inasmuch as all affairs of importance are managed here by presents, and as the Porcelain that takes the place of gold and silver in this Country is allpowerful, I presented in this Assembly a collar of twelve hundred beads of

Porcelain, telling them that it was given to smooth the difficulties of the road to Paradise" (6, vol. 10:29). In addition to the attitude of friendliness associated with the giving of a present, the custom had special significance because the presentation was viewed as a voucher of the sincerity of the speaker and proof for posterity of what had been said. Because of this special meaning attached to formal gifts, Huron spies sent presents along with their reports to vouch for their truth, and each phase of diplomatic negotiations with other tribes was backed up in tangible form. Some idea of the range of occasions on which formal feasting and exchange of presents were customary is indicated below.

First, among the Huron themselves, it was the custom for a private person to invite his friends and the leading men of the village to a feast if he wished to make any kind of public announcement regarding his affairs or if he merely wished to win renown. At the yearly general assemblies or councils at which representatives of the four political districts and numerous villages of Huronia gathered to renew their friendship and plan for their common interests, great feasts and dances took place and presents were exchanged between the various groups involved.

Numerous incidents illustrating the use of gifts in intertribal diplomacy were recorded by seventeenth-century Huron observers. Messages from one tribe to another were usually accompanied by a gift, a custom illustrated by the presentation of fifty beaver skins and four strings of wampum to Champlain in 1611 to confirm Huron friendship with the French and to invite the latter to their country. Another instance was recorded when the Algonkin of Allumette Island sent twenty-three collars of porcelain beads to the Huron to urge them to join in battle against the Iroquois in 1636. Gifts were also the medium by which permission was obtained to cross the territory of other tribes on trading expeditions, and by which a Huron chief could be induced to allow outsiders to trade with the tribes which were his special prerogative.

In councils between nations, feasts and exchanges of presents were as essential as the speeches themselves. Every year when the Huron went to the French settlements to trade their furs, "The day of their arrival they erect their huts; the second, they hold their councils and make their presents; the third and fourth, they trade. . . . When it is over they take one day more for their last council, for the feast which is generally made for them, and the dance; and early the next morning they disappear like a flock of birds" (6, vol. 5:265).

The exchange of presents was also a regular feature of councils held to negotiate peace settlements. Excerpts from an account of an assembly of various Algonkian tribes, the Huron, French, and Iroquois in July, 1644, illustrate the form of these councils, the type of speeches, and the role played by presents.

The council took place in the courtyard of the fort at Three Rivers, over which large sails had been spread for shade. The French governor and his attendants were on one side, with the Iroquois seated at the governor's feet, since they had requested that they be on his side as a mark of affection. The Algonkin and Montagnais representatives were opposite them; to one side were the Huron, to the other, the French. Two poles were erected in the center, and a rope stretched between them "on which to hang and tie the words that they; the Iroquois; were to bring us—that is to say, the presents they wished to make us, which consisted of seventeen collars of porcelain beads. . . ." (6, vol. 27:251–255)

The Iroquois speaker arose with the first collar in his hand and began his speech in a loud voice:

"Onontio, lend me ear. I am the mouth for the whole of my country. . . . We have a multitude of war songs in our country; we have cast them all on the ground; we have no longer anything but songs of rejoicing." Thereupon he began to sing; his countrymen responded; he walked about that great space as if on the stage of a theatre; he made a thousand gestures; he looked up to Heaven; he gazed at the Sun; he rubbed his arms as if he wished to draw from them the strength that moved them in war." (6, vol. 27:255–267)

Then, after thanking the governor for saving the life of an Iroquois prisoner the previous autumn, he fastened the first collar to the rope.

In a similar manner he took up each of the remaining sixteen presents, explaining their meaning in eloquent words and theatrical gestures—one returned a French prisoner, and another assured his listeners that the Iroquois no longer mourned their people who had been killed in previous encounters and would not try to avenge their deaths. Other presents were offered to clear the river of hostile canoes, to smooth the rapids and waterfalls, and to bind together all the peoples represented at the council. To illustrate the meaning of this last present, the orator "took hold of a Frenchman, placed his arm within his, and with his other arm he clasped that of an Alguonquin. Having thus joined himself to them, 'Here,' he said, 'is the knot that binds us insepably; nothing can part us' " (6, vol. 27:255–267).

This meeting was concluded with a dance in which the French and all the tribes participated. The day following this speech the governor gave a feast, and on the next day replied to the presents of the Iroquois by fourteen gifts, each with its meaning. Councils at which the Huron and Algonkian tribes added their endorsements to the peace negotiations were held after they had time to consult with their people at home.

REPARATIONS PAYMENTS

Whether one Huron murdered another, or a person from another tribe, the only socially recognized method for healing the breach without resort to further bloodshed was by gift giving. As noted in the discussion of communal responsibility, the unit involved in such a property transfer was the village rather than the principals themselves or their immediate families, except presumably in cases where both parties were members of the same community. In general, a much larger quantity of goods had to change hands when the offense involved persons of different tribes. According to Brebeuf, at least sixty presents, each worth as much as a beaver robe, were required as reparations for murder. The first nine gifts should be strings of wampum (having about 1000 beads apiece). A later writer, Ragueneau, says the thirty presents sufficed if both parties were Huron men, forty if the victim were a woman, and still more were necessary if the injured party belonged to another tribe. He describes in some detail an occasion on which more than 100 presents were given by the Huron to the French to wipe out the offense felt at the murder of a Frenchman.

The goods required for reparations payments were collected at a council held in the offender's village, and everyone present appeared to French observers to strive to give all they could afford. When the parties involved were of different tribes, the payment was made at a public gathering with much formality and rhetorical speeches of the type characteristic of important occasions. For instance, in the council witnessed by Ragueneau in 1647, presents were given "in order that the door might be opened," "to wipe away thy tears . . . ," as a drink "to restore the voice which thou hast lost, so that it may speak kindly." Then followed nine presents to erect a sepulcher for the deceased Frenchman; then eight chiefs each brought an offering to represent the principal bones of the body. Ragueneau made a return gift of 3,000 porcelain beads "to make their land level so that it might receive them more gently when they should be overthrown by the violence of the reproaches that . . . [he] was to address to them for having committed so foul a murder."

The next day the Huron erected a kind of stage in a public place, from which were hung the fifty presents that constituted the principal part of the reparations payment and bore that name. These were inspected by the French, and any declared not satisfactory had to be replaced by others. Gifts were then given to represent the clothing worn by a person of the rank of the deceased. Others followed "to draw out from the wound the hatchet," more for each blow struck, "to close the earth, which had gaped in horror at the crime," and "to trample it down." Then all the men danced to manifest their joy that the earth was closed. Still another present was given to throw a stone upon the hole so that it could not be reopened, after which the Jesuits responded with a few final gifts to assure the villagers that the incident would be forgotten now that reparations had been made (6, vol. 33:239–249).

GIFTS REQUIRED FOR CURING CEREMONIES

Certain types of curing ceremonies and burials were also important occasions for gift giving. Large amounts of goods were given away for these purposes, and there were strong social pressures on Huron villagers to contribute to the fullest extent of their means on these occasions.

In Huron theory, there were three main forms of illness, differentiated on the basis of their cause. Wounds and some minor bodily ills were believed to have natural causes and were treated with medicines and sweat baths; certain diseases were the result of sorcery and could be cured only by the counter-operations of another sorcerer; and the third category of ills comprised those caused by unfulfilled desires of the soul. The curse for sickness of the last type have the most relevance for the present inquiry because friends and neighbors were called upon to give freely of their possessions to determine and satisfy hidden desires of the soul.

Ragueneau explains Huron beliefs concerning unfulfilled desires of the soul by stating that, in addition to the desires one has voluntarily,

. . . which arise from a previous knowledge of some goodness that we imagine to exist in the thing desired, the Hurons believe that our souls have other desires, which are, as it were, inborn and concealed. These, they say, come from the depths of the soul not through any knowledge, but by means of a certain blind transporting of the soul to certain objects . . . our soul makes these natural desires known by means of dreams, which are its language. Accordingly, when these desires are accomplished, it is satisfied; but, on the contrary, if it be not granted what it desires, it becomes angry, and not only does not give its body the good and the happiness that it wished to procure for it, but often it also revolts against the body, causing various diseases, and even death. (6, vol. 33:189)

It appears that the soul's desires were sometimes revealed directly to the individual through the good offices of his guardian spirit, who appeared in a dream. Many persons, however, became ill with no intimation of the cause and had to rely on the supernatural contacts of a shaman to determine their hidden desires.

The desires revealed in either way commonly called for feasts, dances, or gambling matches, as well as particular presents such as canoes, porcelain collars, skin robes, and even household utensils. The desired ceremonies were often already known and in the possession of medicine societies, whose members would perform them for those who needed them. Sometimes, however, a new ceremony was called for in a dream, in which case each detail of its execution was revealed. One of the curing societies which required many presents for its performances was that of the *Ononhara*, or mad men. Their activities involved the assumption of a frenzied manner, in which condition the members proceeded from house to house propounding riddles wherein was concealed the gift which they desired. They accepted everything offered whether it was the right answer or not, but the sick person could not improve until the correct answer had been found.

When the stricken individual was a person of importance in the village, provision of the necessary presents became a community project. The chiefs would call a council to make arrangements for the ceremonies and to request donations. These might be of considerable quantity and value, as for example, in the case of a rich old man for whom ceremonies were conducted which lasted two weeks, and another in which twenty specific presents were required in addition to those given to the "Madness Society." Furthermore, the Jesuits inform us that as on other occasions where public spirit could be shown by generous donations, there was great rivalry to make lavish presentations.

At the conclusion of a successful cure, the relatives of the sick person provided a munificent feast to which large crowds were invited. The number and extent of these feasts and ceremonies caused the Jesuits to express the view that, "Such is the occupation of our Savages through the Winter; and most of the products of their hunting, their fishing, and their trading, and their wealth, are expended in these public recreations . . ." (6, vol. 33:209).

BURIAL GIFTS

The Huron buried their dead twice, once soon after death and again at regularly recurring ceremonials at which all who had died since the last joint burial were reinterred in a common grave. On both occasions lavish presents were expected, received, honored, and displayed.

According to contemporary reports, the Huron frequently informed a man of his approaching death and prepared him for its occurrence. Such a person was dressed in his finest clothes and attended his own farewell feast. When he died, word was sent to the other villages and the relative on whom the special responsibility fell, came to make arrangements for the burial. Friends and relatives gave presents, some of which were put in the grave and some returned to the close associates of the dead man "for their trouble" in helping with the funeral. A chief announced what each present was and who had given it, and they were sometimes displayed hanging from poles along the sides of the house. After the death of a man of importance, his name was taken by someone still living, or "resuscitated." This was again the occasion for an elaborate feast, and, in the case of chiefs, gifts were given to the new leader by each of the four Huron districts.

The feasts of the dead, at which the souls of all who had died were honored and then reburied, were held every ten or twelve years. It was customary for each of the four districts, which were both political divisions and familistic units, to hold its own ceremony and commit its dead to a common grave. The bones of those who had died earlier and the bodies of the more recently dead were cleaned and wrapped in new furs and porcelain collars and then carried to the grave, where the packages of bones were hung on a surrounding scaffold.

At one such ceremony witnessed by Brebeuf, the grave was lined with forty-eight beaver robes before the bodies and packages of bones were lowered. Then damaged kettles, porcelain collars, and netfuls of corn were placed in the grave and covered over with mats, bark, sand, poles, and wooden stakes. The entire morning was spent distributing presents. "Twenty were given to the master of the feast, to thank the Nations which had taken part therein. The dead distributed a number of them, by the hands of the Captains, to their living friends; some served only for show and were taken away by those who had exhibited them," and a number were thrown to the crowd (6, vol. 10:301).

It was a point of honor to bring many presents, and the description of the ceremonies clearly indicates that it was evident to all present just what and how much each person or household contributed. Persons would strip themselves of their possessions to make a good showing, so that it appeared to one observer almost as if "all their exertions, their labors and their trading, concern almost entirely the amassing of something with which to honor the Dead. Robes, axes and porcelain, the whole riches of this Country are used for burial. They may go without warm enough clothing to save robes for this purpose" (6, vol. 10:265).

WEALTH AND SOCIAL STATUS

Among the Huron, wealth appears to have been highly regarded as evidence of industry and supernatural favor, and because it facilitated expression of the desirable qualities of generosity and hospitality. Some of the evidence on which this generalization is based has already appeared in the discussion of the various occasions at which public contributions were required. The present section will further explore the mechanisms by which community pressures and rewards operated to induce generosity on the part of individual Huron, in particular on those of more than average wealth.

Public opinion could operate effectively as a mechanism for redistributing property in part because of the public nature of the occasions on which contributions were pledged. As noted earlier, contributions to the public fund or for special communal needs were made openly in council and therefore became common knowledge. There were still further opportunities for publicity in the displaying of presents at the curing and burial ceremonies. Furthermore, the rewards for generosity on the part of important men in the community were not limited to satisfying public opinion or gaining a good reputation, but consisted of more tangible returns as well.

It was noted by a Jesuit observer that only the dreams of a person of some wealth whose dreams had been found true in the past were accepted with full credulity, and that only in these cases was the carrying out of the instructions derived from the dream made a community project. Elsewhere we read that when someone of importance falls sick, the chief goes to inquire on behalf of the old men what he had dreamed or what he desired for his health. The community then made every effort to provide it. In 1638 Father Le Mercier mentioned that he and his associates had to wait two weeks to talk to the Indians because daily feasts were being held for a rich old man in response to a dream that this would cure him.

The wealthy individual who had given generously to help cure someone might be rewarded by honors such as the following:

Afterwards the relatives of the sick person give very splendid feasts, to which large crowds are invited; the choicest morsels fall to the lot of the most notable persons, and of those who have made the best show during these days of public magnificence. (6, vol. 33:209)

The burial ceremonies, and particularly the feast of the dead, were other public occasions at which the rich outshone their less fortunate brethren in munificence, and received much honor for it. Brebeuf mentions in 1636 that some persons were almost stripped of their possessions because several of their friends had died for whose soul they had made presents. And in describing a feast of the dead he says, "The middle classes and the poor . . . suffer much, in order not to appear less liberal than the others in this celebration. Every one makes it a point of honor" (6, vol. 10:303–305). Not only were the wealthy in a position to make larger presentations, but, being important persons in the community, they were honored by larger and more numerous offerings at death than were those of ordinary stature. Everyone received presents from friends and relatives, but if the deceased had been a man of importance, chiefs of other villages also came in person and gave presents. When death necessitated the selection of a new chief, one of the factors considered in appraising the eligible candidates appears to have been the ability to acquire and distribute wealth properly.

One incident reported by the Jesuits suggests that on occasion the threat of physical violence might force a redistribution of property if a person of unusual good fortune did not offer to share his abundance with his neighbors. Brebeuf was staying with one of the wealthiest Huron in the village of Toanché where fires had twice wiped out the houses and possessions of most of the other villagers, but had miraculously spared those of his host. As a result,

. . . jealousy having been enkindled against him, and some wishing to destroy his cabin that the fire had spared, at once he caused a large cauldron to be hung, prepared a good feast, invited the whole village, and, having assembled them, delivered this harrangue: "My Brethren, I am very deeply grieved at the misfortune that has happened; but what can we do about it? It is over. For myself, I know not what I have done for Heaven, to be spared before all others. Now, in order to testify my desire to share in the common misfortune, I have two bins of corn" (they held at least one hundred and twenty bushels); "I give one of them freely to the whole village." This action calmed their jealousy and put an end to their wicked designs. . . ." (6, vol. 8:95)

The existence of differences in wealth in Huron villages, and the motives and rewards for liberal disposition of goods in socially accepted ways, are summed up in Lalemont's explanation of the Hurons' response to exhortations for contributions to reparations payments: "It seems as if they vied with one another according to the amount of their wealth, and as the desire of glory and of appearing solicitous for the public welfare urges them to do on like occasions" (6, vol. 28:51).

GAMBLING

Further insight into the Huron concept of property may be obtained by a consideration of their attitude toward gambling losses. We have already encountered gambling as a ceremony designed to cure illness, but it also had a purely recreational aspect. There were three games on which stakes were commonly laid; la crosse, several variations of the peach-stone game, and straws. Gambling was extremely popular among the Huron of both sexes; they devoted much of their leisure time to this pursuit and, as a consequence, sometimes lost goods of considerable value. The circumstances under which a gambling match might take place ranged from informal games between friends to large assemblies where two or more villages joined to gamble and feast.

Several writers report that objects of great value, such as porcelain collars or beaver robes, were lost at gambling encounters; and that after the choicer items were gone, the players staked their clothing or whatever else they possessed. In one instance, a Huron staked and lost his wife to a Frenchman, who, however, returned her the following day. Instances are also given in which one village played another for their household utensils. At one intervillage rivalry, thirty porcelain collars were lost.

Sagard says that the Huron players "lose as cheerfully and patiently when chance does not favor them as if they had lost nothing," and other observers make similar comments. This appears to have been the ideal pattern, and it is consistent with the high value placed on a stoical attitude toward hardship in other circumstances. It is also consistent with the Huron emphasis on the use of property as opposed to individual accumulation. However, it must also be noted that in spite of the ideal attitude of disinterestedness toward loss of wealth, feeling at times ran high at gambling matches, and quarrels and injuries arose out of them. One case of suicide is recorded in which the motive was alleged to have been remorse at having lost some valuable goods at gambling. A chief's son committed suicide after having lost a beaver robe and porcelain collar.

THEFT

Theft was common among the Huron, who stole not only from strangers but from each other as well. Sanctions could be invoked against a thief, but the prevalence of stealing suggests that it was not considered a seriously antisocial act. Some writers go so far as to assert that skill in theft was highly regarded accomplishment. The redress permitted by custom consisted of the injured person's right to take back not only his own property but that of his depredator as well, if he could discover him. Retaliation was an individual act, however, and commanded none of the communal action available in the case of murder. As a result, the cleverness and relative importance of the parties involved were significant factors in determining what action was taken in any given instance.

The importance of property in Huron society must then be reconciled with widespread expropriation and an absence of strong social sanctions protecting the owner. As in the case of gambling, the apparent conflict can be resolved to a considerable extent by assuming that Huron approbation of property accumulation was based on the subsequent use of that wealth in socially approved ways. Theft merely involved a transfer of ownership, and when carried out at the expense of strangers, it even increased the disposable wealth of the community. The Huron also greatly appreciated skill and cleverness, and apparently viewed cases of theft as contests of skill between owner and depredator in which the superior man won both the property and social approval.

CONCLUSIONS

An analysis of the seventeenth-century material on Huron attitudes and behavior with respect to certain types of movable property leads to several conclusions: (1) they had a strong feeling of communal responsibility; (2) there was widespread institutionalization of gift giving; (3) high value was placed on generosity; (4) social status accrued to the liberal and wealthy man; and (5) a disinterested attitude toward ownership per se was encouraged. The broader pattern of encouragement of a disinterested attitude toward the mere acquisition or loss of property is derived both from the positive value of generosity and the negative attitude toward extravagant emotions or sanctions on occasions of property loss.

Since a substantial quantity of goods and services were involved in voluntary transfers for which no immediate or precisely equal return was expected, it may be concluded that to a Huron, ownership of many items of movable wealth (including food) had meaning only in the light of the communal pressures which forced him to alleviate the misfortune of his fellow men, to contribute to community payments, to share his good fortune with his friends by giving feasts and presents, to make honorable contributions for curing and burial ceremonies, and, in general, to regard the holding of property per se as of little importance. As noted briefly in the discussion of Huron trading practices, these attitudes were largely confined to intratribal contacts (except for certain formal presentations) and were not applied in trading situations or dealings with complete strangers.

*C*ritics *of ethnographic reports frequently comment on the overemphasis upon the role of males in the studies of native societies. The criticism is well taken. Most ethnographers have been males and, even in the not infrequent case of the female ethnographer, the fieldworker finds himself (or herself) forced to deal with the more overt, the more visible, the seemingly more cogent life of the men. Among the Hopi, the Iroquois, and among many Indians of the Plains, women held high status and sometimes political and ceremonial offices. Several American Indian societies were markedly egalitarian in the prestige and power allocated alike to males and to females.*

In the following brief paper, an excerpt from a much longer study, Louise Spindler comments on the role of women among the Menomini of the Upper Great Lakes area.

45 *Louise S. Spindler*
WOMEN IN MENOMINI CULTURE*

The Menomini Indians are a Central Algonkian tribe, belonging to the "Woodland" culture area and the Algonkian language stock. There existed in aboriginal times an underlying uniformity in culture throughout the entire northern area to the extent that an Algonkian "core" culture can be isolated, as represented most closely by the Naskapi and Montagnais, which represent the basic elements of all Algonkian cultures within the area. A brief skeleton of this core culture consists of: subsistence by hunting, fishing, and gathering; the family hunting group with patrilineal extended family and an atomistic political structure; girls' seclusion at puberty with menstrual taboos connected with hunting luck; an extreme fear of famine; divination; respect observances toward game animals (especially the bear); emphasis upon the boy's first game kill; shamanistic practices and guardian spirit complex; the importance of dreams and "power"; the shaking tent rite for curing or finding lost objects through the medium of the turtle; the use of the sweathouse for magico-religious purposes and curing; the trickster cycle and reference to skeleton beings in the folklore; the spring feast of thanksgiving; mild mother-in-law, son-in-law avoidances; the naming feast for the child; marriages arranged by the parents.

The Menomini and the Southern Ojibwa may both be viewed as subgroups within this great common area of culture and language which extends throughout the forested lands of eastern and central United States and Canada. There were differences in the cultures of these two groups due to a greater degree of specialization than was found in the more northerly groups and also to the addition of complexes from the south and through contacts with the Iroquois. Nevertheless, beneath the deceptive overlay of elaborations and specializations of cultural traits

* Excerpt from "Menomini Women and Culture Change," by L. S. Spindler, in *Memoirs of the American Anthropological Association*, **91**, 14–20, 1962.

and complexes, the identifiable Algonkian "core" culture is basic to Menomini culture.

Some of the cultural items of the northern Algonkian hunters (Montagnais, Naskapi) which became elaborated among the Menomini were: the power of the chief and a council of elders who held formal trials for crimes; cross-cousin marriage and the probability of the practice of levirate and sororate; formalized joking relationships; respect avoidances between parent-in-law and children-in-law; elaborate rites for the dead. New cultural items which were added from Siouan and southern sources were the clan organization with exogamous phratries and moieties with a probably neo-Omaha kinship system; the war complex with war chiefs; horticulture; the role of the number four in religion and magic; and the feast of the dead.

Elements in Menomini culture traceable to Iroquoian sources: the eating of dog flesh at ceremonial feasts; the La Crosse game; thunderbeings; the concept of the milky way as a path to the land of the souls; catlinite pipes; and the long-house.

In contrast to the relatively undifferentiated shamanism of the simple Algonkian cultures of the far north, there were many classes and societies of people possessing unusual powers. Aside from the *mete·o* (leaders) of the *Metɛ·wen* Lodge, there were two doctors' cults—*Wa·beno* and *Cese·ko*, two religious cults (thunder and buffalo), and a well-organized witches society of eight members. The shaking tent rite was performed by one of the specialized doctors' cults. There was a notable lack of the windigo starvation psychosis among the Menomini, or any extreme fear of famine.

SOME PSYCHOLOGICAL IMPLICATIONS

On the basis of the cultural homogeneity for the entire Northeast area of North America, Hallowell posits a similarity in psychological patterns for the area, which existed in pre-contact times and is represented at present by less acculturated Algonkian groups such as the Berens River Ojibwa. This interpretation may be generalized to include the Menomini in that they shared in large measure their values and beliefs with the other groups of the area. Further, it was revealed in the study of Menomini males that the least acculturated Menomini and the least acculturated Ojibwa share a similar personality structure.

Hallowell explains that the earliest explorers and missionaries reported a general intelligence of the Indians of the area equal to that of

Europeans. These men described a pattern of emotional restraint or in-hibition which applied to all the woodland peoples. It was from these early reports that the stereotype of "the Indian" as a *stoical* type of human being grew. In reference to Algonkian women in Canada in 1710, Father Jouvency writes:

> Whatever misfortune may befall them they never allow themselves to lose their calm composure of mind, in which they think that happiness especially consists. . . . Even the pangs of childbirth, although most bitter, are so con-cealed or conquered by the women that they do not even groan . . . (6:277)

There were consistent reports from the explorers and missionaries concerning the keen sense of humor possessed by members of the entire area. The Indians would laugh readily in the face of trials. Anger was never expressed in interpersonal relationships, which were characterized by gentleness, humanity, and friendliness. An extreme independence and individualism were noticed by all observers. Little discipline was exercised upon children, since these Indians felt that the only way to avoid anxiety was to restrain one's self and comply with the demands of others. For this reason, there was also an extreme reluctance on their part to refuse a favor outright. Hallowell feels that the strong beliefs in sorcery noted by the Jesuits and others were an expression of indirect aggression, necessary since direct aggressions were not culturally ap-proved. And further, the inhibitory pattern of emotional restraint has characteristics of a defense mechanism against anxieties. Since the same general picture of psychological manifestations are prevalent in the en-tire northeastern area where the groups possess similar cultures, Hallo-well feels that they are culturally determined.

WOMEN'S ROLES IN ABORIGINAL MENOMINI CULTURE

It would seem logical to infer from the data that the aboriginal Menomini culture, like that of the Ojibwa, was male-oriented. The more important activities of the culture were centered around the male. The boys were given names of the most powerful beings, while the girls were given protective names. The boys' first game kill was recognized by a formal ceremony, while excellence of performance shown in any task by the girl was never celebrated. Special celebrations were held for the young males victorious in war, while their sisters stood by and ac-cepted the scalps. The women were, in the main, spectators of many of the most important events in Menomini life.

In spite of this emphasis on male activities, Menomini women were included in rites and given cult membership to a greater extent than the Ojibwa women, which might be due to stronger Iroquoian influences. There were often very powerful elderly Menomini women who ranked in importance with the men in making decisions.

Gaining Power. Both boys and girls fasted at puberty for a guardian spirit. The powers were for the most part related to qualities that would make a man a good hunter and provider. Visions came to the girl in the form of the sun or the wind and insured qualities such as long life and happiness, unless an evil power came as an unsolicited visitation, causing the girl to become a witch.

The more common pattern of informal dreaming for inspiration for beadwork patterns or power to prophesy or cure prevailed among women.

Menstruation. While women sought powers of their own, they were defined in certain situations as killers of men's power. During menstruation and following childbirth, women were considered unclean and extremely dangerous to men and children. When the girl's first menstruation period began, she was isolated for 10 days in a special lodge. After that the period was shortened to two or three days. She used her own utensils and refrained from touching herself or looking up, which might offend the gods above. If a man were to eat food prepared by her at this time, he was in danger of losing his guardian spirit, which lived inside him, it was believed, in the form of a tiny turtle or fish. If he found out about the woman's condition in time, he could take an emetic and vomit the food before it killed the little animal. The menstruating woman was careful not to feed, touch, or even breathe upon a small child for fear of causing its death.

Child Training. Discipline and care of the young children was left largely to the woman. The infant was kept in a cradle board until the age of two or until she (or he) could walk. The penis of the male child was pinched after birth to keep it from growing to an abnormal size and so that he would be able to control his sexual passions as an adult. A child was nursed for as long as it would reach for the breast and weaning was not sudden. The naming ceremony for the infant was an important familial event. And later, the feast for the boy's first game kill was of equal importance.

Children and aged people, both supposedly very close to the supernatural, were the favored persons in Menomini culture. All adults were especially kind to infants. Otherwise, the belief was that the infant's soul, fresh from the land of the spirits, would get homesick. The mother constantly watched a small child for any evidences of unusual behavior, such as stopping in the middle of play to stand quietly or crying excessively, since this might signify that one of the gods (especially Thunderers) had been reincarnated in the body of the child. Or sometimes a deceased relative's spirit was reincarnated. A special seer or shaman who understood baby talk was called in if this happened. Frequently it was found that the source of the infant's trouble was simply that his proper name had not been recognized, and this was immediately remedied by giving a naming ceremony.

There was no physical punishment of children until after eight years of age. Then they were sometimes whipped—on the legs only—with a strap or would have water thrown in their faces. For the most part, coercion took the form of threats from some evil being such as the owl, who personified witchcraft and evil powers. Training for physical endurance was rather severe, however. Boys, and sometimes girls, were sent to break the ice of the river and bathe in the cold water.

As the children grew older, the mother relied more and more upon other members of the group for the transmission of cultural values. Older children were assembled around some respected elder who would tell them how to live, using stories to illustrate his points. In a more informal fashion, fathers and grandparents would transmit important Menomini values by relating folk tales in the evening around the fire for hours at a time.

The persistent theme which ran through all the prescriptions for children's behavior was constraint and deep self control. Behavior during the puberty fast symbolized these characteristics as did the main themes of the tales and exhortations of the elders.

Witchcraft. Menomini women practiced witchcraft to the same degree as men. During the early days of the reservation period, some of the most famous witches were women. Evil powers came through dream visions, often in the form of the horned hairy serpent. The witch was then obliged to feed her (or his) bag by killing victims; otherwise, it was believed, one of her own family would die.

The witch's services could be bought for a fee. If the sorcerer possessed an owl bundle, she would kill the victim by performing rituals and commanding the owl skin to come to life and fly to the home of the victim to kill him with a magic arrow (a small cowrie shell). If the sorcerer owned a bear bundle, she killed the victim by pointing the bear paw at him. It was believed that the witches sometimes flew long distances to accomplish the task with the aid of feather quills contained in the bear paw bundle. When witches walked, they were said to follow invisible trails in the woods, often along riverbeds. The location of these trails is common knowledge to many Menomini today. Sometimes victims were killed or maimed by manipulation of carved wooden dolls or the use of hair, clothing, and nail parings, in the same pattern as that of the users of sympathetic and contagious magic in Europe.

After the victim was buried, the witch came to the grave in the form of an animal—usually a dog or turkey—to consume the vital organs. Sometimes relatives watching the grave were able, after taking a protective medicine to keep them awake, to shoot·the animal, which always then crawled home to die. If a person suspected of witchcraft died at this time, she (or he) was identified as the witch.

There is evidence that the magic bundles were inherited when fasting for power disappeared. Also, in later years there occurred a fusion of functions for the witch. The same person who performed the acts of witchcraft could protect one from all evil powers, give love medicines and herbs for curing disease, and foretell the future.

Religious Ceremonies. Not much is known concerning women's participation in the pre-contact ceremonial organizations. They did actively participate in the War Dance and continued to do so until the present. The *metɛwen,* or Medicine Lodge, probably of early post-contact origin included women on an equal membership basis with men. They were given medicine bags (inherited or made of otter or mink for the occasion and filled with medicines) and fully installed into the lodge. The main intent of the lodge was to prolong life, insure good health, and offer protection against witches.

The Dream Dance (*ni·mihɛ twan*) was introduced to the Menomini sometime between 1865 and 1885 by the Potawatami and Chippewa. The women members had auxiliary groups—one for each drum. Each woman had a partner, and on special occasions decorated sticks were stuck up around the drum during the meeting and the women took their special places behind the drum-beaters. Otherwise, they arranged for the feasts, secured clothing for the adoption ceremonies, danced hesitatingly, and sang in muted tones behind the men.

It is interesting to note that it is believed that a woman messiah introduced the Dream Dance to the Menomini. The members believe that the "great gentle spirit," *Kesɛ·maneto·w,* became angered because the Metɛwen was becoming corrupted and thus gave the Menomini a purer ritual and dance. He sent a woman messiah from the West, who had fled from warring Indians (Sioux). After hiding in the water under lily pads, she emerged to give the message to Indians that they should live in peace, not drink, speak the truth, and not strike back if struck.

When the Peyote Cult was first introduced to the reservation by the Winnebago or Potowatimi in 1914, women were excluded. It was soon agreed that women should be admitted to membership. Thereafter, they took their places reclining behind the men at the meetings. They partook of the peyote to a lesser degree than men and a few of them had full-blown visions. A woman was appointed to serve the meal in the morning according to the prescribed rituals. The women members used peyote extensively as a medicine in an informal fashion, for such things as childbirth, earache, or for inspiration for beadwork patterns in much the same manner as the dream was used.

Review of Longer Term Dynamics. There was theoretically a division of labor between the sexes. Traditionally, Menomini women were supposed to stay home and make lodge furnishings, tan, cook, make fish nets, pick berries, collect herbs, bear and care for children, and harvest wild rice and maple sugar with the men. However, the men's activities were culturally defined as being the important jobs and severe economic pressures supported those definitions. Thus a woman who fished well, raced well, hunted well, or danced like a man was highly respected. The deviant woman has always had alternatives for the traditionally defined women's roles except for those specifically defined male roles (usually religious in nature). She could find support and security by staying at home, performing women's tasks, and listening by the hour to the tales of her grandmother, or she could perform a wide range of male activities which might appeal to her.

In recent years women have filled a wide variety of men's roles. For example, they now fill the roles of judge, advisory council members, political roles, and roles of consultants in the mill office.

POST-CONTACT DEVELOPMENTS

The Menomini were found by the French missionary-explorer, Jean Nicollet, in 1639, not far from their present reservation site on the Menomini River. The warring Iroquois had split the central group of Algonkians, to which the Menomini belong, from the Eastern Algonkians by driving a wedge between them. As a result of this separation, significant divergent trends later developed among the Menomini, who were virtually stranded on a cultural island. By 1664, the Menomini had been practically decimated by wars with neighboring tribes, but from this point on the population underwent a striking increase.

With the coming of the French fur trader around 1667, the sedentary village pattern of the Menomini disintegrated and the tribe divided into roving bands with family hunting grounds, organized for the purpose of trapping furs. A cycle was then introduced which placed the Indians in the roles of debtors. They were encouraged to charge large amounts of supplies at the French trading posts in the summer with their promise to repay in furs during the winter. Since this arrangement destroyed the old pattern of village life, the primary extended family groups became split into roving bands of smaller families. Under the domination of the French government, however, the Menomini were fairly satisfied. The French army men, fur traders, and government representatives entered into tribal life and intermarried extensively, as witnessed by the preponderance of French names on the reservation today. As close allies of the French, the Menomini prospered and became one of the dominant tribes in the area (1736).

When the English came in 1761, they were not readily accepted. Strong lines of cleavage existed with little intermarriage. The paternalistic attitude of the English, coupled with extensive gift giving, finally won the support of the Menomini.

In 1815, control of the Menomini went to the Americans. Then in 1852, the tribe, consisting of 2,002 men, women, and children, entered their present reservation area—an area with plentiful sturgeon and wild rice beds, numerous small lakes, streams and creeks, and plentiful game. The game and fish, however, were not sufficient for an indefinite period for the large numbers in the limited area, and some Menomini began to turn to farming.

The United States government agents and the bureaucratic reservation government, strongly supporting the Catholic church, presented real problems in adjustment for the Menomini. This type of organization represented an extreme polarity in terms of the atomistic Menomini social organization. As a group, the Menomini reacted to the situation by refusing to cooperate until they were allowed to have their own tribal council and to run their successful lumber mill as they might decide. These concessions were made by the government and exist today as an integral part of the Menomini government.

SECTION X

The Indian in the Modern World

Since the period of exploration began, the successful colonialist everywhere in the world has faced a problem of what to do with the native populations surviving the initial periods of culture contact. Inevitably the native populations are poorly equipped to participate in the dominant society because of racial, linguistic, or cultural barriers. For native peoples wanting to maintain some degree of cultural separateness, such as those of the Yaqui of Sonora, Mexico, or the Hopi of Arizona, the problem is further complicated. Such separateness inevitably carries certain drawbacks. Absorption in infancy of an indigenous cultural heritage may handicap the individual's adult participation in the dominant culture. For example, a youth who speaks English only poorly is denied access to many positions in the society at large. On the other hand, membership in a small, tradition-oriented society may provide to the individual a secure web of social relationships which the urban world of the mid-twentieth century rarely approximates.

Schools, hospitals, roads, and stores are to be found wherever populations are dense and incomes high. In competition for the tax dollar, the Indian necessarily loses since he is frequently exempt from most taxes. The Indian, then, often is among the last citizens to receive the material benefits of modern American Society, as are other minority group members who lack political power and economic substance.

William H. Kelly is a well-known authority on contemporary Indians, especially those of the American Southwest. In the first article of this section he discusses the general socioeconomic position of Indians in the United States of our time.

46 *William H. Kelly*

SOCIOECONOMIC CONDITIONS OF CONTEMPORARY AMERICAN INDIANS*

Compared with the population of the United States, Indians are relatively few in number. In a total population of 183 million people, there are about 550,000 Indians.

Unlike the situation in other countries, it is comparatively easy to define, and therefore to enumerate, Indians in the United States. These are the people who are members of an Indian tribe and thus entitled to special benefits, such as free medical care and property tax exemptions. They are usually, but not always, of at least one-quarter Indian blood but are not defined by the language they speak nor by economic or cultural factors.

The greatest single concentration of Indians is in the Southwestern states of Arizona and New Mexico where there are about 140,000 Indians as compared with 2,136,000 non-Indians: about 6.5 per cent of the total. The largest tribe in the United States, the Navajo, with a population of about 90,000, is in this area.

Other states with important Indian populations are: Alaska, 43,091; California, 39,014; Montana, 21,181; North Carolina, 38,129; Oklahoma, 64,689; South Dakota, 25,794; and Washington, 21,076. As can be seen, the Indian population of the United States is concentrated in the West, including Alaska, where about 458,000 of the 550,000 reside.

The tendency for Indians to leave their reservations to live and work in non-Indian communities is shown in recent figures compiled by the Bureau of Indian Affairs. The 1960 Indian population by states, and by reservation residence within states, is given below:

* Abridged from "United States," by W. H. Kelly, in *Indianist Yearbook*, Inter-American Indian Institute, Mexico, **22**, 115–124, 1962.

TABLE I

LOCATION OF INDIANS, 1960

State	Total Population	Live On Reservations	Reservation Area in Acres
Alaska	43,081	3,685	2,993,270
Arizona	83,387	67,657	23,821,457
California	39,014	7,280	593,374
Colorado	4,288	1,101	865,955
Florida	2,504	616	78,933
Idaho	5,231	3,910	676,372
Iowa	1,708	485	3,476
Kansas	4,109	589	35,577
Louisiana	3,587	111	422
Michigan	9,701	869	22,527
Minnesota	15,496	9,420	827,045
Mississippi	3,119	2,910	16,620
Montana	21,181	17,473	6,130,736
Nebraska	5,545	2,139	71,178
Nevada	6,321	3,433	1,336,309
New Mexico	56,255	47,568	3,147,981
North Carolina	38,129	5,216	56,115
North Dakota	11,736	7,806	1,544,390
Oklahoma	64,689	53,076	2,393,727
Oregon	8,026	2,860	1,671,184
South Carolina	1,098	353	4,249
South Dakota	25,794	24,040	4,860,483
Utah	6,961	4,397	1,127,465
Washington	21,076	9,033	2,688,759
Wisconsin	14,297	5,801	431,199
Wyoming	4,020	3,772	2,057,702
Other States	50,555	. . .	None
Total:	550,908	285,600	57,456,505

During the Nineteenth Century it was probably true that the Indians of the United States were decreasing in numbers. This is decidedly not the case today. The annual rate of increase is now estimated at 28 per 1,000.

INDIAN ECONOMICS

The majority—perhaps three-fourths—of the Indians in the United States make their entire living through wage work on and off their reservations. Even so, Indians attach a great social and symbolic significance to their land and, almost universally, choose to remain on their land as selfemployed farmers or livestock growers until economic necessity forces them to abandon agriculture or supplement income from this source through seasonal or temporary wage work.

This change toward wage work reflects a growing Indian population on a fixed land base, an abandonment of subsistence agriculture, and a desire for a higher standard of living which can only be secured, in agriculture, through an increase in size of land holdings.

In spite of this shift, however, the Bureau of Indian Affairs estimates that reservations are "overpopulated." In this calculation they estimate that farming and livestock raising could support, at a reasonable standard of living, only one-half to two-thirds of the Indian families now attempting to make their living by this means. Measures to correct this situation, and thus maintain the reservations as a home area for those who desire to live there, include the following: educational and training programs to increase the efficiency of Indian farmers, provision of additional capital and credit for resources development, and the development of industrial and business enterprises on or near reservations.

INDIAN FAMILY INCOME

Indian families must support themselves, the same as non-Indians. For the United States as a whole, the 1950 Census reported a median family income of $983 for reservation Indians. This figure does not include the value of income "in kind," such as food produced and consumed in the home and free living quarters. Neither does it include the value of special economic advantages enjoyed by most Indians: freedom from property taxes and some income taxes, free medical care, free subsistence for children in boarding schools, and many free services found on some reservations such as water for agriculture and domestic use.

The 1950 Census figure itself is probably low since enumerators, especially in the Indian case, could not be expected to secure knowledge of income from all sources. In any event, it is known that Indian income has risen, even more proportionately than non-Indian family incomes, during the past ten years. Recent estimates of income on a number of reservations suggest that those groups with extremely low incomes in 1950 have improved their economic condition to a considerable degree. The Navajo, for example, have greatly increased their income from wage work and other sources with the result that the average family income of $526 in 1950 has been increased to $3,225 in 1960.

More recent figures for the Colorado River Tribes and for the Papago, to take two additional examples, show the same trend. In 1950 Colorado River average family income was reported to be $2,444. In 1958 it was estimated at $4,624. In 1950 Papago average family income was reported to be $1,111. In 1961 it was estimated at $2,200.

Navajo family income is worth reporting in detail since it reveals an increased dependence upon wage work and the comparative unimportance of agriculture.

TABLE 2

SOURCES OF NAVAJO INCOME, 1960

Sources	Amount
A. *Earned cash income:*	
Payroll, Bureau of Indian Affairs	$ 7,590,000
Payroll, U. S. Public Health Service	1,607,842
Payroll, Navajo Tribe	3,707,500
Payroll, Other reservation sources	5,175,705
Wages, Navajo Tribe	4,786,000
Wages, Off-reservation agriculture	1,368,000
Wages, Off-reservation non-agriculture	3,294,200
Unemployment compensation	1,255,800
Reservation agriculture (sold and consumed)	3,950,000
Arts and crafts sales	500,000
Individual mineral leases	803,178
Miscellaneous	1,500,000
B. *Unearned cash income:*	
Social Security	$ 3,000,000
General welfare assistance	363,552
Tribal scholarships	254,823
Old Age and Survivors Insurance	2,500,000
C. *Unearned non-cash income:*	
Tribal welfare, various	$ 926,086
School children's clothing	750,000
Boarding school meals	3,428,270
Tribal stock feed program	510,000
Surplus commodities, welfare	353,249
Value free health services	4,000,000
Total:	$51,624,205
Total cash income:	$41,656,600

Navajo average family income is based upon an estimate of 80,000 reservation Indians and 16,000 reservation families. When only cash income is considered, average annual family income is estimated at $2,600.

It is important to note that more than half of family income on the Navajo Reservation in 1940 was from farming and livestock and that this had dropped to about 8 per cent in 1960.

OCCUPATION GROUPS

Figures on income are in keeping with information on Indian occupational groups. These figures show the heavy percentage of Indians in the United States in low income jobs and in types of work which permit periodic and seasonal employment. Information is from the 1950 Census which does not list multiple sources of income, but gives a single occupation determined by the source from which the principal income was received during the census week. Statistics for both Indians and non-Indians are based upon civilian males fourteen years of age and older.

TABLE 3

PERCENTAGES BY OCCUPATION OF EMPLOYED UNITED STATES
INDIAN MALES AND OF ALL UNITED STATES MALES

Major Occupational Group	Per Cent of Indian Males	Per Cent of All Males
Professional, technical, and kindred workers	2.54	7.35
Farmers and farm managers	24.24	10.52
Managers, officials, and proprietors, except farm	1.96	10.66
Clerical, sales, and kindred workers	3.15	13.04
Craftsmen, foremen, and kindred workers	11.00	18.85
Operatives and kindred workers	13.09	20.32
Private household workers	.25	.18
Service workers, except private	3.63	5.94
Farm laborers, unpaid family workers	8.26	1.53
Farm laborers, except unpaid and farm foremen	14.10	3.40
Laborers, except farm and mine	17.78	8.21
	100.00	100.00

CHARACTERISTICS OF THE LABOR FORCE

On the whole, wage work represents an acceptable mode of economic adjustment for all Indians. Indian interests and attitudes, however, stand in their way when there is an opportunity to step up to permanent skilled or semiskilled employment. One reason for this is that Indian values do not lead the individual to consider work, in itself, as a virtue or as a source of personal prestige. Wage work, in their eyes, is a means to an end and, in most cases, the end desired represents a relatively low standard of living. Wealth, as a symbol of success and prestige, which is so common in non-Indian society as a motive for economic effort, is not important to most Indians outside the north Pacific coast. In the extreme case, among the Indians of southern Arizona and southern California, wealth was, until quite recently, entirely meaningless.

Not all Indians, however, who would elect to improve their economic position are able to do so. Most reservations are isolated from industrial and trading centers. In Arizona, 66 per cent of the Indian population lives in counties containing 3.4 per cent of the non-Indian population. Under such conditions, relatively few Indian boys and girls have had the opportunity to secure training in the kinds of jobs which so frequently prepare other young men and women for skilled and semi-skilled types of employment. Added to this is the general lack of education, formal and informal, in the skills and social patterns associated with permanent off-reservation employment.

Perhaps the greatest present deficiency in Indian training for permanent employment is the small number of students who receive an adequate formal education. During 1955–56 only 13 per cent of Indian children in Indian Service Schools were in high school as compared with more than 23 per cent for the United States as a whole. Present trends, however, indicate that there will be a considerable improvement in this situation in the next few years.

TRIBAL INCOME

Even though tribal land on most reservations has been allotted to individual members, tribes have retained some land that is held in common and, on some reservations, the entire reservation is held by the tribe. In many instances such land is assigned rent free to Indian families, but where valuable resources exist, particularly timber or minerals, they are developed by a tribal corporation or, more commonly, leased to non-Indians. In addition, many tribes operate reservation stores, farms, ranches, packing plants, hotels, and other tribal enterprises and derive revenue, in the form of taxes or fees, from industrial and business enterprises when operated by non-Indians on tribal land. Not all tribal enterprises show a profit, and none are conducted within the pattern of American business because of the restrictions imposed by the federal trust responsibility. Another serious hindrance to the development of tribal enterprises as an avenue for training in the American economic system has been tribal council control. This has resulted, in many instances, in operations that are dictated by Indian values and tribal politics. Where attempts have been made to operate enterprises along business lines, the council has most frequently employed non-Indian managers who, under instructions to show a profit, cannot spend the time and money necessary to train Indian successors.

In some instances, tribal income is passed along to members in the form of per capita payments, but in most cases it is used by the tribe for the support of tribal government, welfare programs, and for range improvement and other forms of resources development.

There are no published statistics on tribal income. Data from the Southwest, however, indicate that it is quite uneven. The Hopi, Papago, and Salt River Pima tribes have incomes of less than $10 per year per capita. The Gila River Pima, Navajo (1955) and Taos Pueblo have incomes of less than $50 per year per capita. Other incomes are: San Carlos Apache, $103 (1955), and Mescalero Apache, $280.

GOVERNMENT ATTITUDE TOWARD THE INDIAN

Unlike most Indian groups in Latin America, reservation Indians in the United States have retained their right to local self-government, live in relative isolation on lands held in trust for them by the federal government, and are not subject to state laws nor state property taxes. As indicated in Table 1, however, it must be kept in mind that many Indians have chosen to leave their reservations in which case they are treated the same as other citizens of the state. The following information, therefore, refers only to reservation Indians.

The policy of the federal government with respect to Indians has remained relatively unchanged during the past 35 years. Briefly stated, this can be described as the protection and preservation of Indian land holdings and the preparation of Indians through educational and other programs for participation in American life. The result of this policy has been federal management and control of Indian economics, resources development, education, health care, general welfare assistance, and many similar services.

The system has been under constant attack by those who believe that the isolation and protection of Indians have retarded their advancement and their integration into American life. It has been defended by those who believe that without federal protection, Indians would lose their land holdings, and without federal operations and subsidies, Indians could not receive the quality of services and assistance needed to overcome economic, social, and educational disadvantages. The idea that federal protection and services for Indians should be dissolved as quickly as possible was generally accepted by both the Congress and the Bureau of Indian Affairs as recently as ten years ago. The present administration, however, has declared its willingness to continue the attempt to find a satisfactory adjustment for Indians under the existing system of federal aid and protection, and to terminate federal programs only when requested to do so by the Indians concerned.

In the spring of 1961, Stewart Udall, the newly appointed Secretary of the Interior under President John F. Kennedy, appointed a special committee to make a study of Indian Affairs and to make recommendations with respect to future policies and programs. The findings of this committee, of which the present Commissioner of Indian Affairs, Dr. Philleo Nash, was a member, were approved by Secretary Udall and adopted as the policy of his administration.

On the whole the service functions of the Bureau remain unchanged and involve the operation and expansion of a school system designed to provide at least twelve years of education for all Indians. Welfare, relocation, health, law and order, and similar programs will continue as formerly.

The important change is in the areas of resources development, industrial and business development, and vocational training programs for adults. The spotlight has thus been shifted from routine programs of education, property management, law and order, welfare, and the like, to programs aimed at an improvement of Indian economic conditions.

Development of Resources. The committee report emphasizes resource surveys and master plans for purposes of future development, along with a continuation of existing resources development projects. To accomplish such planning, the Bureau of Indian Affairs has joined with another federal department, the Area Redevelopment Agency, and has secured funds under the Area Redevelopment Act for a series of studies on Indian reservations.

Credit.   A recommendation was made for the expansion of the existing revolving loan fund for Indians which would enable more individuals to secure funds for higher education, housing, agriculture, and small business enterprises.

Vocational Training and Relocation.   The great demand among Indians for vocational training, and for assistance in securing jobs in areas surrounding their reservations, was recognized by the committee in its recommendation that these programs be expanded. As a consequence, during 1961 more Indians than ever before were benefited by these programs. More than 3,000 were assisted to relocate and more than 4,000 were receiving vocational training. In addition, another 2,000 Indians were given special help to permit them to secure on-the-job training.

Industrial Development.   Emphasis upon industrial development is reflected in the annual report of the Commissioner of Indian Affairs for 1961. He said:

> The purpose of the Bureau's Industrial Development Program is to assist the Indian people in cooperating with their neighboring communities in the development of plans and programs which will attract industry to the areas surrounding the reservations and thus provide employment opportunities and improve economic and social conditions.
>
> During fiscal year 1961, continued emphasis was placed on (1) working with tribal leaders to explain the basic concepts of industrial development and the need for cooperation with communities near the reservations; (2) assisting tribal and community groups in organizing industrial development foundations and similar entities in order that they will be in a better position to negotiate with industrialists interested in reservation area locations; (3) gathering necessary basic information on resources available and assisting in the preparation of fact sheets and brochures; and (4) providing information and assistance to industries which have indicated interest in expansion of their present production facilities in reservation areas.
>
> The growing interest of Indian tribes in industrial development is shown by the fact that several tribal groups have taken action to earmark their own tribal funds for industrial development purposes. (7)

A total of $1,556,000 was set aside for this purpose in 1961. In addition, other tribes are in the process of developing programs and earmarking funds for use in attracting industries to the reservation areas.

The sources of funds being programmed are from judgment awards and damages due to flooding of resources by dam construction, and from leases and royalties, and other income.

The philosophy of federal administration of Indian affairs is set forth in the conclusion to the committee report:

. . . In spite of the many difficulties which the Bureau [of Indian Affairs] has encountered in discharging its often-conflicting directives, the assistance which it and other agencies have provided to the Indians has made it possible for this group of Americans to progress toward fuller and more effective participation in the social, cultural, political and esthetic life of the United States. A greater percentage of Indians today vote, seek elective office, attend school, enjoy good health, have attained prominence in the arts, and are socially accepted by their non-Indian neighbors than at any other time in the nation's history. On the other hand, the number of Indians for whom these changes have not taken place is still large, is increasing rapidly, and presents a continuing challenge.

Much of the progress which the Indians have made has occurred during the past forty years. They have been considered citizens only since 1924 and, in Arizona and New Mexico, their right to vote was not confirmed in the courts until 1948. Statutory authority for the organization of tribal governments was provided by Congress just a little over 25 years ago, and Indian youth have been drafted for military service only since World War II.

The events of these past forty years have done much to make Indians aware of the fact that they cannot alone decide the kind of future world they will inhabit. Furthermore, their experiences have shown them new ways of making their lives more secure and comfortable. Now, the desire of many for better incomes, more formal education, better health, and more voice in their own affairs rivals their desire to retain older ways.

The Task Force [committee] believes that in the foreseeable future, the proper role of the Federal Government is to help Indians find their way along a new trail; one which leads to equal citizenship, maximum self sufficiency, and full participation in American life. In discharging this role, it must seek to make available to Indians a greater range of alternatives which are compatible with the American system, and where necessary, to assist Indians with choosing from among these alternatives. As a part of this responsibility, it must mobilize and direct the vast reservoir of good will toward Indians which is found throughout the country. Finally, since many of the problems relating to Indian development are local problems, it must use its influence to persuade local governments, as well as those who live near Indian reservation, to recognize their stake in the Indian future and to work with the Indians and with the Federal Government in preparing the new trail.(7)

INDIAN ORGANIZATIONS

There is only one important Indian organization in the United States with direction exclusively in the hands of Indians. This is the National Congress of American Indians. It has come to have a strong voice as a spokesman for the Indian point of view, and has consistently endorsed the continuation of the existing federal program.

Indian organizations, composed of both Indians and whites, include the Indian Rights Association, 1505 Race Street, Philadelphia 2, Pennsylvania; and the Association on American Indian Affairs, 475 Riverside Drive, New York 27, New York. Both these organizations concern themselves with the promotion of improvements in the federal program for Indians, and in the protection of Indian rights, both tribal and individual.

The Bureau of Indian Affairs, a branch of the federal government, fills the role of the National Indian Institutes found in Latin American countries. The Indian Health Division of the National Public Health Service is responsible for all Indian health programs.

*C*ontroversy has surrounded White-Indian relations from the time of earliest contact. Those with the power to make Indian policy had to deal with those who shaped it—the elected political officials versus the legislators and the appointed administrators. Finally, local officials, both civil and military, were required to implement decisions that were made. From the time of the pronouncements from the Spanish throne, through the Northwest Ordinance, until the Indian Reorganization Act, well-intentioned administrative officials have meant only good for the Indian. Yet, regarding, for example, the plagues and pox of early contact, the shove westward in early colonial times, and the direct military pacification and genocide of the late nineteenth century, the Indian has been forcibly modified culturally and assimilated socially. In the following article, D'Arcy McNickle, himself a member of the Flathead tribe of Montana and long a professional worker with the Bureau of Indian Affairs, presents a scholarly treatment of the history of contact until the infamous Dawes Act (General Allotment Act) of 1887.

47 *D'Arcy McNickle*

INDIAN AND EUROPEAN: INDIAN-WHITE RELATIONS FROM DISCOVERY TO 1887*

It is a source of continuing surprise that the American Indians have not adjusted their lives to the national life, that their special problems persist, and that their ethnic identity does not dissolve. This surprise is not limited to the uninformed person who rarely has occasion to concern himself about such matters, but is particularly experienced by individuals who have an occupational interest in the fate of the American Indian: administrative officials, educators, legislators, missionary workers, and the like.

A review of the historical relations between the first inhabitants of the Western Hemisphere and the later coming Europeans may have an uncommon importance in our day, if in reconstructing this past we can identify and describe not the events alone but the attitudes and passions and judgments which lay behind the events. The value would consist in helping us to see ourselves as other people have seen us, and from our own performance—especially its failures—learn to improve our methods in the field of human relations. The present review must be brief, but it can be suggestive.

THE PERIOD OF DISCOVERY

It was a fateful concurrence that the New World should be discovered at a time when Europe was awakening from its long medieval sleep and moving in many directions simultaneously to assert the mastery of Western man. In a single lifetime (1450–1520) spanning Columbus' momentous voyages, the printing press came into use in Eu-

* Abridged from "Indian and European: Indian-White Relations from Discovery to 1887," by D. McNickle, in *Annals of the American Academy of Political and Social Sciences*, **311**, 1–11, 1957.

rope, making it possible, in time to come, to spread knowledge to the masses; seafaring men overcame their fear of unknown land and water and pushed exploration westward into the Atlantic and southward along the coast of Africa; humanist scholars were translating the lost literature of classical Rome and Greece; and the Protestant Reformation was in full motion. In such events, and in others that preceded and followed, were the makings of the modern world.

What was beginning to emerge and would be more clearly defined in the years during which discovery and settlement progressed in the Americas, was a European society—varying in detail from country to country, but intrinsically similar—based on a belief in the perfectability of man. Exploration, invention, and discovery, working to reinforce each other, and to refute and confound an older society of static values, opened European minds to the idea of progress along an upward curve of goodness and happiness. It was a new idea in the world, a sharp departure from an earlier notion that man had been perfect in the past, in the Garden of Eden, and had fallen from grace; or from the still earlier belief that man moved through a series of descending phases from a golden age to barbarity, and back again.

In time the new belief would be vulgarized by equating progress with increased material conveniences and comforts, but in its beginnings it grew from a concern for the moral improvement of mankind, a seeking after heaven on earth, or (in the Calvinist interpretation) a seeking to be among the elected few who would find heaven hereafter. And it was more than an emotional outreaching, for it had behind it the solid thinking of men like Francis Bacon, Descartes, Newton, and Locke: men who demonstrated the uses of reason in examining and explaining the physical world. "It was reason that would lead man to understand nature and by understanding nature to mold his conduct in accordance with nature" (4:121).

MEN WITH A MISSION

Thus, the men who came out of Europe into what they pleased to call the New World were men with a mission. The mission might be secondary to their immediate needs of security, but it was never wholly absent and at times it was of dominating interest in the actions of individual settlers. The nature of the mission was variously phrased, but essentially it amounted to an unremitting effort to make Europeans out of the New World inhabitants, in social practices and in value concepts.

One of the first orders of the Spanish monarchs, Isabella and Ferdinand, to Ovando, first governor of The Indies (1501), was to require the Indians to be brought together in towns.

Each Indian was to be given a house of his own for his family and a farm for cultivation and cattle raising. . . . The Indians were to be persuaded to go about dressed, like "reasonable" men. . . . The Indians were to be persuaded to abandon their ancient evil ways, "and they are not to bathe as frequently as hitherto, as we are informed that it does them much harm." (12:28–29)

The mission theme is clearly stated by the Englishman, Robert Gray, in his *A Good Speed to Virginia* (1609):

. . . It is not the nature of men, but the education of men, which makes them barbarous and uncivill, and therefore chaunge the education of men, and you shall see that their nature will be greatly rectified and corrected; seeing therefore men by nature so easily yielde to discipline and government upon any reasonable shewe of bettering their fortunes, it is everie man's dutie to travell both by sea and land, and to venture either with his person or with his purse, to bring the barbarous and savage people to a civill and Christian kinde of government, under which they may learne how to live holily, justly, and soberly in this world, and to apprehend the meanes to save their soules in the world to come. . . . (8:10)

IMPACT ON THE INDIANS

Wherever Europeans settled in the Indian world changes occurred, in living habits, in the use of tools and weapons, and in some nonmaterial practices. In the northern regions hunting tribes were induced to change from a subsistence to a commercial type of hunting, even though, with the greater killing power of the weapons they obtained from European traders, they threatened their own basis of livelihood. When beaver disappeared from northern New York and the Iroquois nations faced a total loss of a rich trade and the political power to which they were accustomed before the arrival of the Europeans, they turned to violence as a means of compelling the tribes farther west to bring their furs into Iroquois country rather than to Canada.

The great role of the Iroquois was that of middlemen between the "far Indians" and the English, a role which enabled them not only to obtain material benefits, but to retain that position of superiority over the Indians of the eastern half of the United States which they . . . could no longer hope to hold by mere force alone, since their fighting men had so diminished in numbers and their enemies had obtained weapons as good as their own. (14:xlii)

Thus the long effort of the Iroquois people to build a League of Peace was destroyed in competition for the material goods which were part of the cultural baggage of the incoming white man.

EUROPEANS' MISUNDERSTANDING OF INDIAN WAYS

The efforts by Europeans to modify Indian practices with respect to land use and tenure profoundly influenced the relationship between the two races. Attitudes toward Indian rights of occupancy often reflected either total lack of knowledge or erroneous understanding of Indian custom. A common assumption was that the Indians were too primitive to have developed a property system. Thus, the Reverend Richard Hakluyt described them as "more brutish than the beasts they hunt, more wild and unmanly than that unmanned wild countrey, which they range rather than inhabite" (8:7).

Even more common was the notion that the Indians were hunters to the exclusion of all other occupations, a notion that gave comfort to those settlers who regarded agriculture as a higher use of land and so justified themselves when they encroached upon Indian lands. Some of the first settlements were located in areas of such low fertility that as a practical matter they might have been reserved for hunting only; yet wherever soil, moisture, and growing season permitted, the Indian inhabitants planted fields of corn, beans, squash, and tobacco. The passengers who went ashore from the *Mayflower* to settle on the Massachusetts coast found the Indians fertilizing the ground with the fish (alewives) that ran so plentifully in the early spring: "You may see in one township a hundred acres together set with these fish, every acre taking a thousand of them; and an acre thus dressed will produce and yield so much corn as three acres without fish" (15:231). The place they chose for settlement was "a high ground, where there is a great deal of land cleared, and hath been planted with corn three or four years ago . . . and on the further side of the river also much corn ground [has been] cleared" (15:167–168).

Agriculture, like hunting, was for subsistence, hence operations were planned to meet the needs of consumption and to provide reserves against a lean year; but they were not on a scale to provide surpluses for commercial exchange or foreign export.

When European settlers encountered the Indians and dealt with them as if they were members of European political communities, they did so, in part, under the moral persuasion of their times. This moral concept was variously phrased, and in Spain it took the form of advice which Francisco de Vitoria prepared for the Emperor Charles V: That the Indians, though "unbelievers," were the true owners of their land; were entitled to their own customs and government; and might not be enslaved or despoiled of their property unless they should be so inconsiderate as to war against the Spanish.

THE BIBLE AS GUIDE

In the English-speaking countries, no individual spoke out so clearly and so specifically on the rights of the Indians, yet sentiments like those expressed by Vitoria were current by the beginning of the seventeenth century. An English phrasing of the moral principle might be taken from the first letter of instructions from the Massachusetts Bay Company to Captain John Endecott (1629), in charge of the colonizing group sent out by the company.

Above all, we pray you to be careful that there be none in our precincts permitted to do any injury, in the least kind, to the heathen people; and if any offend in that way, let them receive due correction . . . if any of the savages pretend right of inheritance to all or any part of the lands granted in our patent, we pray you endeavor to purchase their title, that we may avoid the least scruple of intrusion. (16:159)

On occasion, the Bible itself was cited as authority for policy in dealing with the Indians, as in the case of a Virginia statute (1633) quoting Genesis, Chapter I, verse 28 ("And God blessed them, and God said unto them, Be fruitful, and multiply, and replenish the earth, and subdue it"), also Psalm CXV, verse 16 ("The heaven, even the heavens, are the Lord's: but the earth hath he given to the children of men"). This Virginia statute then provided that "what lands any of the Indians in this jurisdiction have possessed and improved, by subduing the same, they have just right unto"; while grants made to Englishmen, according to the act, were also based on the authority of Genesis, and on "invitation of the Indians." The last phrase would suggest that the Bible alone was not deemed a sufficient warrant for Englishmen to assume possession of Indian lands, unless there was Indian consent.

Practices varied in the English colonies, but generally the first settlers negotiated with the Indians and, though there may not have been a meeting of minds, a friendly exchange took place. The Europeans thought they were "purchasing" a title, the Indians as certainly thought they were performing their duty toward a stranger by sharing hospitality with him.

There were other considerations involved in these transactions. European law-ways required a man to have a piece of paper to show ownership; it was as important that this piece of paper change hands as it was that the real property pass from one to another. Even in the case of venturing companies to which grants of territory had been made by ruling heads of government (as in the case of Lord Baltimore and William Penn), the Europeans took the precaution of paying the Indians for the land, thus acquiring documentary title which other Europeans would recognize.

The consideration which probably overshadowed all of these, in determining the behavior of the first Europeans toward the Indians, was the very practical one of winning and keeping the good will of the tribes. It was a consideration which dominated much of the policy of individual colonies, and it continued to have critical importance in the policy of the United States until at least through the War of 1812.

BEGINNINGS OF A POLICY

The evolution of a policy which would meet at once the various needs and demands of the Indians as well as the requirements of the several colonies, was never completed by the British government, although the elements of such a policy had been under discussion for more than twenty years prior to the American Revolution. From the early days of settlement until the middle of the eighteenth century, each colony was allowed to deal directly with the Indians within its borders. Most of the colonies indeed had adopted measures designed to regulate trade and land purchases. But practices between the colonies varied so greatly and the administration of their own rules was often so inadequate that Indians complained of their treatment and either threatened or actually resorted to armed resistance. In addition to these proper grievances, the French in Canada and in the West lost no opportunity to aggravate the fears of the Indians by insisting that the English would not be satisfied until they had completely removed the Indians. The French had not been colonizers, but had been satisfied to trade and to build fortified posts to thwart competition. Hence, they could assure the Indians that they were not competing with them for the land.

MEETINGS AND DECISIONS

One of the first efforts of the British to effect a consolidated policy for the American colonies was the calling of the Albany Congress in June, 1754. The conference was attended by the governors of New York, Virginia, Maryland, Pennsylvania, New Jersey, New Hampshire and Massachusetts, under instructions of the British Board of Trade. Specifically, the colonies were directed to complete an agreement for a joint management of Indian affairs. Instead of working out such a plan, the representatives of the several colonies drafted a plan of union providing for a representative council or legislature, and an executive to be appointed by the Crown. The plan was rejected by the several colonial assemblies and rejected even more firmly by the home government, which then proceeded to appoint two officials, one for the northern tribes and one for the southern, and placed in their hands authority to exercise political control in Indian matters, leaving the control of trade in the separate colonies. The defeat of General Braddock (July 1755), recently appointed Commander in Chief of colonial troops, spurred the British to further efforts to bring order and responsibility in Indian affairs. Even more disturbing to the British ministers was Pontiac's success in achieving an alliance of the tribes in the Great Lakes-Ohio River Valley and the capture of the line of forts leading into the Northwest.

The growing crisis resulted in the issuance of the Royal Proclamation of October 7, 1763. The proclamation dealt with a number of questions, but of chief interest are its declarations on the relations of Europeans and Indians in the New World. These may be summarized as: (1) The Indians have a right to be protected in the peaceful possession of their lands, (2) Definite boundaries should be established and recognized, beyond which no settlement should occur except by mutual consent of the Indians and the King's representatives, and (3) Persons settled upon Indian lands the title to which had not been ceded by the Indians were ordered to be removed.

Even before the issuance of the proclamation negotiations with the Indians south of the Ohio River had established a boundary line between Indian holdings and the colonial settlements; negotiations were now entered into with the northern tribes, and by October, 1768, a line had been agreed upon running from the eastern end of Lake Ontario all the way to the Gulf of Mexico in northwest Florida. This boundary, by agreement with all the tribes affected (some twenty-five or thirty in number) and representatives of the several colonies, was offered as a barrier against any further settlement westward except as the tribes might consent.

FAILURE OF PLAN

What the British did not succeed in achieving was the means of enforcing these agreements. Having failed to establish centralized control over Indian affairs and having no funds to pay the costs of such a centralized agency, the government had to fall back upon the several colonies to provide police power. By December, 1773, it was reported that not less than sixty thousand people had settled between Pittsburgh and the mouth of the Ohio River, and the Iroquois complained bitterly that "the provinces have done nothing and the trade has been thrown into utter confusion by the traders being left to their own will and pleasure and pursuit of gain, following our people to their hunting grounds with goods and liquor" (3:20–52).

TRANSFER OF RESPONSIBILITIES

United States policy in its beginnings had the same problems to meet as those which the British had faced and failed to solve. Generally, these were problems of understanding, or the lack of it; they stemmed from the inflexible habit of expecting Indians to act like Europeans.

The moral law, or natural law, which Europeans cited as the basis of Indian rights in the land, was itself the creation of European minds. The formal procedure of negotiated purchase had a legal meaning for Europeans which had no counterpart in Indian society. Land was not merchantable, in the European sense, among any of the North American tribes. Individual right of occupancy and use was recognized and protected, and under given conditions trespass could be punished; boundary lines were respected, as between tribes, and between clans or other groupings within a tribe. Such concepts were the cultural results of experiences which differed from the experiences of European men, concepts that were designed to serve a different kind of social purpose. They explain why it was that, in effort after effort, the early Indians tried to drive the settlers off land which previously they had "sold"; why tribes sometimes turned upon certain of their own headmen and destroyed them for giving away what belonged to the whole group; and they explain what lay behind the appeal of the Ohio River tribes, writing to the government at Washington in the winter of 1786:

> Brothers: We are still of the opinion . . . that all treaties carried on with the United States, on our parts, should be with the general voice of the whole Confederacy (of tribes). . . . Any cession of our lands should be made in the most public manner, and by the united voice of the Confederacy. . . . Brothers: Let us pursue reasonable steps; let us meet halfways . . . we beg that you will prevent your surveyors and other people from coming upon our side of the Ohio River. (1:8–9)

THE INDIAN POSITION

If the Indians were to maintain their cultural integrity, and that was what they were demanding (the British had promised to protect this right on the eve of the Revolutionary War, and as a result of that promise Joseph Brant led his Mohawk people to the side of the British), it was essential that a boundary line be maintained. The Atlantic coast had been such a boundary, at the beginning of the seventeenth century, between Europe and the Indian world. That barrier had been breached in a series of transactions which held certain meanings and served certain purposes for the European settlers; the same transactions carried quite different meanings for the Indian people and, for them, served no useful purposes. The result, after seven generations, was that the Indians found themselves in a position where they had to insist on fending off the incoming white man. Their continued existence, they thought, depended on it.

THE NEW MASTER

At the outset, the United States government tried with some firmness to adhere to the policy promulgated by the British government: a policy of recognizing Indian boundaries and providing legal machinery for the peaceful liquidation of those boundaries. Henry Knox, first Secretary of War under the Constitution and the first federal official in charge of Indian affairs, stated the position on June 15, 1789:

> By having recourse to the several Indian treaties, made by the authority of Congress, since the conclusion of the war with Great Britain, it would appear

that Congress were of the opinion, that the treaty of peace of 1783 absolutely invested them with the fee of all the Indian lands within the limits of the United States; that they had the right to assign, or retain such portions as they should judge proper.

But it is manifest, from the representations of the confederated Indians at the Huron Village, in December 1786, that they entertained a different opinion, and that they were the only rightful proprietors of the soil; and it appears by the Resolve of the second of July 1788, that Congress so far conformed to the idea, as to appropriate a sum of money solely to the purpose of extinguishing the Indian claims to lands they had ceded to the United States, and for obtaining regular conveyances of same. . . .

The principle of the Indian rights to the lands they possess being thus conceded, the dignity and interest of the nation will be advanced by making it the basis of the future administration of justice towards the Indian tribes. (1:12–14)

A CHANGING WORLD

In the colonial period, it had been taken for granted that Indians would accept European ways and incorporate them into their own lives. They needed only the opportunity; and missionaries, educators, and statesmen labored mightily to make this opportunity clear and visible to the Indian people. Many strong souls, rapt in their vision of the beatitude of European institutions, accepted martyrdom at the hands of what seemed callous and unworthy savages (actually, men who valued life in their own way, who pursued quite different objectives) to bring Europe into the New World. As the colonial period closed, the mood changed. Possibly there were still as many men who believed Indians could be educated—that is, civilized—but their numbers were swallowed up in the waves of population that rolled westward after independence had been won. Moving westward, meant progress, growth, greatness.

A recent writer summarizes the changing situation:

The American solution [to the problem of the savage] was worked out as an element in an idea of progress, American progress. Cultures are good . . . as they allow for full realization of man's essential and absolute moral nature; and man realizes this nature as he progresses historically from a lesser to a greater good, from the simple to the complex, from savagism to civilization. . . . The Indian was the remnant of a savage past away from which civilized men had struggled to grow. To study him was to study the past. To civilize him was to triumph over the past. To kill him was to kill the past. (8:48–49)

Evidence for the manner in which these ideas came into American thinking will be found, for example, in the oration of John Quincy Adams before the Sons of the Pilgrims, December 12, 1802:

There are moralists who have questioned the right of the Europeans to intrude upon the possessions of the aborigines in any case and under any limitations whatsoever. But have they maturely considered the whole subject? The Indian right of possession itself stands, with regard to the greatest part of the country, upon a questionable foundation. Their cultivated fields, their constructed habitations, a space of ample sufficiency for their subsistence, and whatever they had annexed to themselves by personal labor, was undoubtedly by the law of nature theirs. But what is the right of a huntsman to the forest of a thousand miles over which he has accidently ranged in quest of prey? Shall the liberal bounties of Providence to the race of man be monopolized by one of ten thousand for whom they were created? . . . Shall the lordly savage not only disdain the virtues and enjoyments of civilization himself, but shall he control the civilization of a world? . . . No, generous philanthropist! (10:536)

METHODS AND DEVICES

In the forty-odd years between the enactment of the Northwest Ordinance of 1787 and Andrew Jackson's Second Annual Message, delivered December 6th, 1830, the United States moved away from the potential which was inherent in colonial attitudes, of allowing the Indian people a chance to maintain their integrity as a people. Boundaries could be in the minds of a people; they might not hold the Appalachian watershed, but they could still hold to a system of values they understood. They did not ask to remain static, but to grow into new conditions, as they became ready, while retaining their dignity in their own eyes. From the latter date onward, it became a question of how soon, and by what devices, the extinguishment of the Indian past would be effected.

In its Indian provisions, the Northwest Ordinance read:

Article III. . . . The utmost good faith shall always be observed towards the Indians; their land and property shall never be taken from them without their consent; and in their property, rights, and liberty, they never shall be invaded or disturbed, unless in just and lawful wars authorized by Congress; but laws founded in justice and humanity shall from time to time be made, for preventing wrongs being done to them and for preserving peace and friendship with them.

Here, once again, was the promise of fair dealing which Europeans since Francisco de Vitoria had urged as policy, which the British actually adopted but could not enforce; and now the United States had accepted it, and in its turn would discover that it had not the means of carrying it into force. The reasons it could not carry it into force are the real subject matter of President Jackson's Second Annual Message, though he appears to talk about other considerations. He said:

Humanity has often wept over the fate of the aborigines of this country, and Philanthropy has been long busily employed in devising means to avert it, but its progress has never for a moment been arrested, and one by one have many powerful tribes disappeared from the earth. . . . But true Philanthropy could not wish to see this continent restored to the condition in which it was found by our forefathers. What good man would prefer a country covered with forests and ranged by a few thousand savages to our extensive Republic, studded with cities, towns, and prosperous farms, embellished with all the improvements which art can devise or industry execute, occupied by more than twelve million happy people, and filled with all the blessings of liberty, civilization, and religion? (9:520–521)

Some months previously (May 28, 1830), President Jackson had signed the Indian Removal Act, which placed in the hands of the President authority to remove all Indians west of the Mississippi River. The proposal had been under discussion and indeed had been hotly debated for several years. Passage of the measure was precipitated finally by actions taken by the state of Georgia.

The state had insisted since its establishment that the United States purchase the lands occupied by Indian tribes (Creeks and Cherokees) within her borders. Some purchases had been made, but the time came when these Indians refused to sell any more of their land, on the grounds that they needed it for their own existence. Georgia retaliated against the Cherokees by enacting legislation which extended her laws over the Cherokee nation. The Cherokees challenged the right of Georgia to assume such jurisdiction, and in two famous cases (*Cherokee Nation* vs. *Georgia* and *Worcester* vs. *Georgia*) tested the ability and the willingness of the United States to protect an Indian tribe in its efforts at self-determination. The Cherokees lost, not because their cause was wrong, but because of a defect in the American system of government. The Supreme Court, with Chief Justice Marshall writing the opinion, held that the State of Georgia had no authority to extend its law over the Cherokees and therefore its action was a nullity. Georgia chose not to recognize the opinion, and the President of the United States refused to be disturbed by Georgia's position.

The Removal Act of 1830 was a discretionary act, authorizing the president (not directing him) to negotiate treaties with the eastern Indians, the treaties to provide the following: lands would be offered west of the Mississippi; payment would be made for lands and improvements relinquished in the east; title to the new lands would be guaranteed in perpetuity, or so long as the tribe should exist; the right of self-government would be respected. The removal was to be based on agreement, but when the Cherokees and the Seminoles attempted to exercise the choice of remaining, they were answered with the United States Army; forced removal followed.

After 1830, Indian tribes continued to be moved, some of them three or four times, like inanimate pieces on the checkerboard of the nation's destiny. A writer has observed:

> For a time the scheme of moving the Indians to lands west of the Mississippi seemed to offer a practical solution to their problem. Jedidiah Morse believed that the Indians possessed the capacity for making progress in the arts of civilized life if only they were given government aid and an education. . . . However, in most of the arguments for the removal of the Indian tribes . . . the emphasis was placed on the advantages to the white man which would result from the displacement of the noble savage, and the idea of progress was invoked . . . to give a rationalization of inevitable justice to the forced migration. (5:41)

The decision by Congress in 1871, in the form of a rider to an appropriation act, that "Hereafter no Indian nation or tribe within the territory of the United States shall be acknowledged or recognized as an independent tribe or power with whom the United States may contract by trading," followed logically on the events that have been reviewed here. It was the recognition of a reality, that Indian friendship and support were no longer needed by the nation.

THE UNKINDEST ACT

It is fitting to close this brief review with mention of the General Allotment Act, also called the Dawes Act, of February 8, 1887. Here, again, was permissive legislation authorizing the President of the United States, in his discretion, to divide an Indian reservation into individual holdings, assign a parcel of land to each man, woman and child, and declare all remaining land surplus to the needs of the Indians. The "surplus" lands were then opened for homesteading and paid for at $2.50 per acre, as and when the lands were taken up by homesteaders. By this and other devices contained in the Act, the Indians were relieved of some ninety million acres, or almost two-thirds of their land base, between the years 1887 and 1930. Without cost to itself, the federal government thus transferred large acreages from Indian to white ownership, even requiring the tribes to pay the costs of surveying and allotting. In every case where allotment was carried out, the Indian tribe objected; and in most cases the lands were covered by treaties in which the United States obligated itself to protect the tribe in its right of possession.

In the speeches in support of the bill while it was pending in Congress, are echoes of that sense of urgent mission which Europeans carried with them into the new world; which moved Queen Isabella and King Ferdinand to insist that the Indians be persuaded to dress up and to bathe less frequently, and led Robert Gray in 1609 to believe that the right education was all that was needed to make a European out of an Indian.

Now, in the 1880's, arguing for the legislation which would become the General Allotment Act, Senator Pendleton of Ohio declared:

> They must either change their mode of life or they must die. We may regret it, we may wish it were otherwise, our sentiments of humanity may be shocked by the alternative, but we cannot shut our eyes to the fact that that is the alternative, and that these Indians must either change their modes of life or they will be exterminated. . . . In order that they may change their modes of life, we must change our policy. . . . We must stimulate within them to the very largest degree, the idea of home, of family, and of property. These are the very anchorages of civilization; the commencement of the dawning of these ideas in the mind is the commencement of the civilization of any race, and these Indians are no exception. (2)

In the heat of such a discussion, it would not have occurred to any of the debaters to inquire of the Indians what ideas they had of home, of family, and of property. It would have been assumed, in any case, that the ideas, whatever they were, were without merit since they were Indian.

*S*ocial *groups have come into contact with one another since earliest human times; no process is more characteristic of man than miscegenation, both cultural and biological. Since the mid-1930's anthropologists have become extremely interested in the sequence of events which occur when two cultures meet. The process of change which ensues in both cultures has been labeled "acculturation." Important to the study of any single "acculturation situation" are the natures of the respective cultures, the type, duration, and results of contact, and the response of the cultures over a longer span of time. North America has provided a natural laboratory for acculturational studies due to the varied reactions of Indian societies to White intervention. In the next paper, Professor Evon Vogt, a well-known student of Navaho culture, examines the effects of contact on the North American Indian, region by region.*

48 Evon Z. Vogt

THE ACCULTURATION
OF AMERICAN INDIANS*

By the mid-twentieth century it has become apparent to social scientists studying the American Indian that the Indian population of the United States is markedly increasing and that the rate of basic acculturation to white American ways of life is incredibly slower than our earlier assumptions led us to believe. During the latter part of the nineteenth century and the early part of this century, the American Indians were prevailingly thought of in American public opinion as a "vanishing race." Vestiges of this opinion are, indeed, still with us as illustrated by the fact that an impressive "Memorial to the American Indian" is shortly to be built on the outskirts of Gallup, New Mexico—at the edge of the Navaho Indian country where the Navaho population has increased from 15,000 (at most) in 1868 to almost 80,000 in 1956 and where Navaho culture persists with great vigor!

We were led to these comfortable assumptions about the vanishing

* Abridged from "The Acculturation of American Indians," by E. Z. Vogt, in *Annals of the American Academy of Political and Social Sciences*, **311**, 137–146, 1957.

American Indian by the fact that there *were* important population declines earlier in our history—many Indian tribes, in fact, became extinct —and by the observation that the Indians *had* undergone impressive changes in certain aspects of their cultures. It was anticipated that the population decline would continue and that the acculturative changes would proceed apace with all tribes and in all aspects of their culture as white American institutions impinged upon them. Earlier generations of young anthropology students were urged to go into the field and collect ethnographic data on Indian culture before it completely disappeared.

It has also been felt strongly that just as European immigrant groups are becoming Americanized within a few generations in the great American "melting pot" so, too, will the American Indians become assimilated. However, students did not stop to raise seriously enough the question of the vast difference between the American Indian and the Europeans. European immigrants all came from the same general stream of Western culture and they, by and large, were motivated toward assimilation when they migrated to the United States. Not only were the Indians linguistically and culturally completely different from the peoples of Europe, but they also had little choice in the matter. European culture came to them in their native habitat and proceeded by force to overrun the continent.

The acculturative changes which formed the basis for our earlier observations involved several different kinds of processes. These processes have been in operation in varying degrees since 1540 when Coronado arrived at Xuni and established the first contact between Europeans and American Indians within what are now the continental borders of the United States. In the first place there has been an important "drifting out" process from almost all American Indian populations over the centuries in which individuals and families have left their native settlements to take up residence in American communities. In some cases, this rate of migration has been great enough to involve almost all of the Indian population; but in many other cases, it has had the effect of "draining off" the most acculturated segment of the population each generation and of leaving a conservative reservoir of more traditional culture carriers intact to carry on their Indian way of life. We now also perceive clearly that we must differentiate between acculturative changes taking place in these individuals and families that are drifting away from the traditional ways of life and the Indian sociocultural system which may be undergoing quite a different type of change and at a much slower rate. This difference between *individual* change and *system* change in acculturation situations is fundamental, and it means that we should not jump to the conclusion that full acculturation will soon take place simply because we observe a certain segment of the population leaving Indian country to take up residence in the white world.

A second widespread and continuing process has been the replacement of Indian material culture with goods, techniques, and technological equipment of the white American way of life. There is no American Indian tribe today who is living close to the aboriginal level in its patterns of food, clothing, and shelter. But it is now clear that just because Zuni Indians, for example, build more modern type houses with running water and electric lights, invest in radios and refrigerators, and drive new automobiles, it does not mean that they necessarily abandon their kinship obligations or give up dancing in Katchina dances. Indeed, it has been startling to many of us to observe how completely the inventories of material culture in Indian households are composed of items derived from white American culture, and, yet, how relatively slow the rate of change is in social organization and religion in the same community.

All American Indian populations have also been undergoing a process of increasing involvement with our white American sociocultural system: in economic relationships to our market economy; in crucial adjustments to our state and national political systems, which now hold the ultimate control of force; and to our educational system, which now provides schools for almost all Indian children; in important connections with Christian missionary movements that now touch every Indian population. The earlier isolation of Indian populations from the main streams of modern life has decreased markedly in the past few decades, and today only one tribe—the Havasupai living deep in a branch of the Grand Canyon in northern Arizona—cannot be reached by automobile. As a result, the languages, social structures, and religions have all shown some change as the modern world closes in upon the Indian cultures.

But what is interesting to the close observer is that, despite all these pressures for change, there are still basically Indian systems of social structure and culture persisting with variable vigor within conservative nuclei of American Indian populations. It would be rash indeed to predict now that these cultural features will completely disappear in the course of acculturation in one, two, or even several generations.

This proposition raises the fundamental question as to why we have had to alter our earlier expectations concerning the rate of American Indian acculturation and why full acculturation to white American ways of life is not occurring in the contemporary scene. In this article I shall outline a conceptual framework for the analysis of American Indian acculturation, provide a brief synoptic review of the acculturation situation in different areas of the United States, and then discuss the limiting factors to full acculturation by comparing the situation of the United States with that in Mexico. The final section will consider the development of "Pan-Indianism" as an emerging stage in American Indian acculturation.

CONCEPTUAL FRAMEWORK FOR THE ANALYSIS OF ACCULTURATION

Although students of American Indian acculturation are not yet ready to provide a definitive synthesis of the processes, we have developed a framework for understanding the general outlines in terms of two sets of variables: (a) *the nature of the two cultures which come into contact,* involving such questions as the types of sociocultural integration, settlement pattern, attitudes toward strangers, and so forth, and the intercultural compatibility of these patterns; and (b) *the contact conditions,* involving such questions as whether the contact is "forced" or "permissive," of long or short duration, intensive or sporadic, and so forth. The interaction between these two sets of variables leads to the types of intercultural relationships we observe and to a complex and varied set of processes of change that are just beginning to be understood adequately. These processes are of two major orders which may be differentiated by the terms "microscopic" and "macroscopic." The microscopic comprise specific recurring sequences of events in acculturation, such as the diffusion of concrete objects between the two cultures—the replacement of stone by steel axes being a classic example of this type of process. The macroscopic comprise the more pervasive patterns of change which persist over long-time spans and involve alterations in the sociocultural systems. In the first case the results have more to do with simple additions, subtractions, or replacements in cultural and linguistic *content;* in the second instance the results have more to do with *structural* and *pattern* changes, of which we are able to identify a number of different types— "additive," "fusional," "isolative," "nativistic," "assimilative," and so forth.

SYNOPTIC REVIEW OF THE
ACCULTURATION SITUATION

My purpose here is merely to outline certain of the major trends in acculturation in terms of the two sets of variables we utilize to account for the processes.

East of the Mississippi. By and large, the Indian populations were forcibly removed from the areas east of the Mississippi River as the American population expanded and the frontier moved West. It is significant that the conditions of contact were such that it did not make much difference as to whether the aboriginal cultures were loosely integrated, scattered small bands of Northeastern Algonquian peoples or more complexly organized agricultural peoples such as the Southeastern Cherokee, Creek, Choctaw, and Chickasaw. By about 1845 the removal was substantially completed, and today only scattered small pockets of Indian population remain, principally in isolated regions—the Eastern Cherokee in the Great Smoky Mountains of North Carolina; the Seminoles, a subdivision of the Creek, who found refuge in the everglades in Florida; six small clusters of Iroquois in New York State and the Oneida who moved to Wisconsin in 1832; several groups of Algonquian peoples in the northern woods of Michigan, Wisconsin, and Minnesota; and a few other remnants such as the Abnaki in Maine.

But, even in this region, where the pressures for acculturation have been maximal, certain basic Indian cultural patterns persist with surprising vigor.

The Plains. In the prairie and plains between the Mississippi and the Rocky Mountains, removal took place later and was not carried to the same extremes. Oklahoma on the Southern Plains was utilized as a region in which to resettle many of the displaced Eastern tribes and a large number of the Prairie and Plains tribes. In the Dakotas and eastern Montana a number of large Indian populations, especially the Dakota, or Sioux, remain on reservations. Other small remnants include the Mesquakie, or Fox, in Iowa, and the Omaha and Ponca in Nebraska.

The removal or reduction of the Plains tribes involved a great deal of violence in the latter half of the nineteenth century. The development of strong warfare patterns and the use of the horse and gun made these tribes into formidable opponents for the United States Army. The Indian wars which took place on the Plains have so impressed themselves on the national consciousness as to make the Plains Indian into the pre-vailing stereotype of the American Indian. It is also significant that some of the most important nativistic reactions to occur in the United States came in the wake of these developments on the Plains—the Ghost Dance, followed by the less nativistic, more transitional Peyote Cult.

Again, although pressures for acculturation throughout this area have been great and the acculturation which has occurred has involved much personal frustration and demoralization for individual Indians, certain basic Indian ways of life persist in almost all cases, even in such appar-ently highly acculturated groups as the Mesquakies near Tama, Iowa.

Intermontane Region. It is certainly no geographic accident that all the large remaining Indian populations of the United States are located west of the 20-inch rainfall line. Here the land is much less desirable for farming without irrigation, and the total population density continues to present a marked contrast to that of the more humid eastern half of the nation. An additional important historical dimension was added to this picture by the fact that the main frontier of white settlement leaped across the arid intermontane region in the mid-nineteenth century when gold was discovered on the Pacific coast. These facts had special signifi-cance for the Southwest which I shall discuss below, but they were also important in lessening the pressures for early and forced acculturation in the territory to the north.

Through much of the intermontane region, especially in the Great Basin of Utah and Nevada, the aboriginal cultures were at such a low level of technological development and sociocultural integration as to create a contact situation in which these Shoshonean peoples had little to lose and much to gain by attaching themselves by small kinship units to the scattered ranches and mining camps. In this situation acculturation has proceeded quite rapidly and with relatively little strain.

Pacific Coast. In the Pacific coast region strong acculturative forces were set in motion by the middle of the nineteenth century after gold was discovered in California and desirable lands were made available for settlement in Oregon and Washington. White-American population increased rapidly, and the Indian cultures were not organized to with-stand much pressure. The result was the complete extinction of many groups and the reduction of others to small remnant populations living, in most cases, on reservations made up of a number of different Indian cultures. The Warm Springs reservation in Oregon with a combination of Wascos, Sahaptins, and Paiutes is a good example. In these cases Indian cultural patterns have not completely disappeared, but the process of acculturation has moved much further than it has in the Southwest, for example, and within a much shorter time period.

The Southwest. There is not much doubt that we find the largest and most conservative nuclei of American Indian populations in the Southwest. Here the time span of European contact has extended over four centuries, but the earlier Spanish control did not effectively reach the scattered encampments of the Apachean tribes, nor penetrate effectively to such tribes as the River and Upland Yumans. The major efforts were directed toward the Eastern Pueblos; the Hopi villages were never brought under effective control and the Zuni villages only periodically. The Pueblos were characterized by a relatively high degree of sociocultural integration in aboriginal times. The major effect of the Spanish effort seems to have been to add a few material culture items—such as wheat, domestic livestock, and a veneer of Catholicism —but it also increased the effectiveness of their boundary-maintaining mechanisms which operated against further acculturation in social organization and religion.

Since gold was discovered in California right after the United States acquired this territory, the American frontier also tended to leap across the Southwest, leaving the Indian lands and cultures intact for an additional generation. Effective Anglo-American control did not come until late in the nineteenth century, following the roundup of the Apachean tribes and the coming of the railroad. Only in the past fifty years have contact conditions been such as to lead to new trends in acculturation. As of 1956, the acculturation situation is changing fast; but at the same time, Indian populations are increasing throughout the Southwest, and conservative nuclei of most tribes will certainly maintain Indian patterns for many generations to come.

LIMITING FACTORS TO FULL ACCULTURATION

A number of hypotheses have been advanced to account for the persistence of Indian culture in the face of increasing pressure from white American society toward full acculturation and the complete assimilation of Indian populations. To mention only a few of the common hypotheses, there is, in the first place, the argument, often advanced by the lay public, that isolation of the Indian populations on remote reservations administered by the Indian Bureau has insulated them from proper exposure to educational facilities, mass communications, and so forth and has prevented them from obtaining the means for assimilation. This hypothesis has undoubted merit, but it certainly fails to account for the many cases of Indian groups which have been subjected to a great deal of contact, yet who continue to maintain many of their old patterns. Witness, for example, the Tuscarora living on the outskirts of Niagara Falls, New York, or the Isleta Pueblo located within fifteen miles of Albuquerque, New Mexico.

A more interesting hypothesis, also emphasizing contact conditions, has been advanced by Dozier and others to the effect that "forced" acculturation, if not so extreme as to lead to early absoption of the subordinate group, will result in a high degree of resistance to change in indigenous cultural patterns. This formulation appears to work well for cases like the Southwestern Pueblo where the aboriginal sociocultural systems were highly enough organized to develop patterns of resistance when "forced" acculturation occurred. It applies less well to tribes with a low level of aboriginal sociocultural integration, and, of course, does not apply at all to cases where the acculturation process was relatively "permissive" and the groups still maintain their old patterns.

A third type of hypothesis, involving a theory about the nature of culture, has been the thesis that while the material aspects of a culture can change readily, family and kinship institutions are more persistent; that the aspects of a way of life which have been labeled as core culture, implicit values, cultural orientations, and personality type, are still more persistent. This type of hypothesis appears to apply to certain tribes and to some ranges of our data. But the formulation in its present form will not account for all the variability we observe in rates of change in different aspects of American Indian culture. It also does not answer the basic question as to why *any* Indian patterns should be preserved at all considering the kind and degree of pressure for change many Indian tribes have experienced.

Still a fourth hypothesis stresses the importance of an organized communal structure. Eric Wolf has characterized this structure as a "corporate" community that maintains a bounded social system with clear-cut limits, in relation to both outsiders and insiders, and has structural identity over time. His thesis is that in Latin America the persistence of Indian-culture content seems to have depended primarily on maintenance of this structure and that where the structure collapsed, traditional cultural forms quickly gave way. This formulation has not been systematically explored with United States-Indian data; but it strikes me as an attractive hypothesis, especially in accounting for the high degree of persistence we observe among still very conservative tribes living in compact communities, like the Southwestern Pueblos. It is also crucial in explaining many of the differences between the acculturation of the American Negroes and the slower acculturation of the American Indians. But what concerns us more in this attempt to understand the limiting factors to full acculturation is why some important Indian patterns continue to persist among groups whose corporate structure has been shattered.

In all of these hypotheses, and others which cannot be discussed for lack of space, it is my impression that we have tended to de-emphasize recently, in our analyses of United-States-Indian data, what is perhaps the most important factor of all: our persisting Anglo-American "racial" attitudes, derived historically from Puritan Colonialism, which strongly devaluate other physical types bearing different cultural traditions. These inflexible attitudes are of course directly related to the superordinate-subordinate structural character of Indian-white relationships in the United States. They are also related to the lack of a large mixed Indian-white population which would provide cultural models and reference groups along the continuum of acculturation for the conservative nuclei still living in the native-oriented Indian communities.

We pay lip service to the idea of Indians being the "First Americans," we now manifest considerable interest in their customs, and we decorate our homes with Indian rugs and pottery and dress our women in fashionable "squaw dresses" derived from Indian styles; but the barriers to full acceptance measured by such an index as the rate of intermarriage are still formidable in most areas of the United States. There are, of course, exceptions in some localities, as among the Menominee of Wisconsin, among the Wascos on the Warm Springs reservation in Oregon, or in parts of Oklahoma where intermarriage is more frequent. There has also undoubtedly been some admixture in all areas over the centuries. But taking the nation as a whole and considering especially the localities of high Indian population, such as the Southwest, the rate of miscegenation with whites continues to be astonishingly low.

The contrast with Mexico is sharp and illuminating. In Mexico interbreeding between Spanish and Indian began almost immediately after the Spanish conquest. Even though miscegenation was prohibited during the late Colonial period, the total process has moved far enough to produce a profoundly "mestizo" nation. There are still relatively unacculturated and unassimilated Indians remaining in various parts of the nation; but when Indian groups enter a transitional stage and begin to move in the direction of integration, there are cultural models and reference groups for them all along the continuum of acculturation, from the most native-oriented Indian communities to the sophisticated urban life in Mexico City. The sociocultural system is also open for the ambitious and talented Indian individual like Benito Juarez who began his career in an isolated Zapotec Indian village and went on to become one of Mexico's greatest presidents. But, even more important, the system is relatively open for transitional Indian groups as they proceed generation by generation along the continuum to fuller integration and acculturation. There is now a conscious and conspicuous positive valuation of the Indian heritage on the part of Mexico's political and intellectual leaders.

In the United States, on the other hand, the path to full acculturation is confusing and frustrating, and an ultimate ceiling is still firmly clamped down by our persisting Anglo-American "racial" attitudes. Instead of proceeding generation by generation along a continuum to full acculturation, it is as if an American-Indian group must at some point leap across a spark gap to achieve a fully integrated position in white American society.

I do not mean to imply that biological interbreeding per se affects the process, but that biological miscegenation leads to profoundly different self-conceptions and evaluations; to the kinds of reference groups that seem to provide a kind of natural "ladder of acculturation" in many areas of Mexico that is so conspicuously lacking in the United States; and to a much more permeable barrier at the extreme end of the acculturation continuum.

PAN-INDIANISM

Since a kind of ultimate lid or ceiling has been placed upon full acculturation and assimilation in the United States, it is now pertinent to raise the question as to what is happening to Indian groups who become reasonably well educated by our standards and move a great distance from their aboriginal ways of life without becoming fully integrated in the larger United States society. One way of looking at the problem is that we shall continue with a type of cultural pluralism for some generations to come. But in a vast number of cases, the process has moved too far for Indian groups to continue to find much meaning in their own particular aboriginal cultures, and what appears to be emerging is an interesting type of "Pan-Indianism."

This Pan-Indianism is assuming a form in which increasing numbers of American Indians are participating in customs and institutions that are describable only as Indian. These customs and institutions are being synthesized from elements derived from diverse Indian cultures and to some extent from white American culture. There exists also in many regions, and especially in Oklahoma, a loosely knit, informally organized grouping of Indians who have joined forces to participate in these Pan-Indian activities.

Historically, the beginnings of this type of Pan-Indianism are found in many of the nativistic movements which followed in the wake of conquest, the spread of the Ghost Dances being a classic type of example. The later emergence of the Peyote Cult, which involved not only the exchange of customs and ideas among Indian tribes and the incorporation of Christian concepts, but also intertribal participation in the same ceremonies, carried the process much further and continues to be one of the focal points in Pan-Indianism.

Conspicuous more recent developments are the various powwows and intertribal ceremonial gatherings. Some are organized by the Indians themselves, especially in Oklahoma and the Middle West; others, like the annual Gallup Inter-Tribal Indian Ceremonial, are managed by white businessmen to promote local business interests. But in both types, there is enthusiastic intertribal participation on the part of the Indians and a strong encouragement of Pan-Indianism.

Although the cultural elements found in this emerging Pan-Indian movement are derived from diverse Indian sources, it is highly significant that a high proportion of these elements are drawn from Plains culture: the war bonnet, the Plains-type war dance, and so forth. These elements have become symbols of Indianism to the Indians themselves to a degree that bears little relationship to the aboriginal facts. And it is probable that their importance as symbols derives in part from the fact that these elements are central features of the prevailing white-American stereotype of the American Indian. They are the features of Indian culture which white tourists expect to find when they attend intertribal ceremonials, and Indians are rewarded by the whites for behaving in conformity to the stereotype. This phenomenon is evident at the Gallup Inter-Tribal Ceremonial where a close-to-aboriginal Navaho or Apache dance receives only a scattering of applause, but a Plains-type war dance enjoys a thundering ovation from the white audience, regardless of whether the dance is performed by the Kiowas or by the Zunis! The result is that more and more tribes are adopting Plains styles of dancing, and Pan-Indianism proceeds apace.

Other features of Pan-Indianism include intertribal visiting and inter-marriage, which are also of crucial importance, and the national Indian organizations such as the National Congress of American Indians which, to date, are less important than the powwows.

The significance of this Pan-Indianism in general terms is that it pro-vides a social and cultural framework within which acculturating Indian groups can maintain their sense of identity and integrity as Indians as long as the dominant larger society assigns them to subordinate status. In the future, it is probable that this Pan-Indianism will develop greater political significance than it has at present, and that organiza-tions like the National Congress of American Indians will speak more effectively for a more highly organized American-Indian minority which will begin to take the franchise more seriously and be more care-fully listened to in the halls of the United States Congress in Washing-ton.

Hallucinogenic drugs are becoming socially more important because of the increasing interest of respectable citizens in such agents as marijuana and lysergic acid diethylamide (LSD). But American Indi-ans have long known of, and used, a number of comparable agents. From such seemingly innocuous drugs as tobacco (which, as smoked by the Indians, was capable of inducing severe physiological reactions), to the "mescal bean" (Sophora secundiflora) and "black drink" of the Southeastern agriculturalists, and finally to "peyote" (Lophophora wil-liamsii) and "toloache" or Jimson Weed (Datura sp.), the American Indian was familiar with agents that could please, or intoxicate, or kill. One of these—peyote—has become important in the ceremonials of the Native American Church, a syncretic Indian religion. Indians have fought court battles to secure the constitutionally guaranteed right to freedom of religious worship, against local and state authorities, who have frequently classified peyote as a harmful narcotic, and accordingly outlawed its use. James Slotkin, who was a practicing member of the Native American Church as well as a trained anthropologist, has recorded the sentiments associated with the use of peyote.

49 James S. Slotkin

THE PEYOTE WAY*

Peyote (*Lophophora williamsii*) is a spineless cactus which grows in the northern half of Mexico and for a short distance north of the Texas border. It has attracted attention because it is used as a sacrament in religious rites conducted by Indians in the United States and Canada belonging to the Native American Church. The Peyote Religion or Peyote Way, as it is called by members, is the most widespread contemporary religion among the Indians, and is continually spreading to additional tribes.

From the viewpoint of almost all Peyotists, the religion is an Indian version of Christianity. White Christian theology, ethics, and eschatology have been adopted with modifications which make them more compatible with traditional Indian culture. The religion probably originated among the Kiowa and Comanche in Oklahoma about 1885.

The Peyote rite is an all-night ceremony, lasting approximately from sunset to sunrise, characteristically held in a Plains type tipi. Essentially the rite has four major elements: prayer, singing, eating the sacramental Peyote, and contemplation. The ritual is well defined, being divided into four periods: from sunset to midnight, from midnight to three o'clock, from three o'clock to dawn, and from dawn to morning. Four fixed songs sung by the rite leader, analogous to the fixed songs in the Catholic mass, mark most of these divisions.

The rite within the tipi begins with the Starting Song; the midnight period is marked by the Midnight Water Song; there is no special song at three o'clock; at dawn there is the Morning Water Song, and the rite ends with the Quitting Song. At midnight sacred water is drunk again and a communion meal eaten.

* Abridged from "The Peyote Way," by J. S. Slotkin, in *Tomorrow,* **4,** 64–70, 1956.

Usually five people officiate at the rite. Four are men: the leader, often referred to as the Roadman because he leads the group along the Peyote Road (that is, the Peyotist way of life) to salvation; the drum chief who accompanies the leader when he sings; the cedar chief who is in charge of cedar incense; and the fire chief who maintains a ritual fire and acts as sergeant-at-arms. A close female relative of the leader, usually his wife, brings in, and prays over, the morning water.

In clockwise rotation, starting with the leader, each male participant sings a set of four solo songs; he is accompanied on a water drum by the man to his right. The singing continues from the time of the Starting Song to that of the Morning Water Song; the number of rounds of singing therefore depends upon the amount of men present. On most occasions there are four rounds, so that each man sings a total of sixteen songs.

During the rite Peyote is taken in one of the following forms: the fresh whole plant except for roots (green Peyote), the dried top of the plant (Peyote button), or an infusion of the Peyote button in water (Peyote tea). Some people have no difficulty taking Peyote. But many find it bitter, inducing indigestion or nausea. A common complaint is, "It's hard to take Peyote."

The amount taken depends upon the individual, and the solemnity of the ritual occasion. There is great tribal variability in amount used, and accurate figures are virtually impossible to obtain. But in general one might say that under ordinary circumstances the bulk of the people take less than a dozen Peyotes. On the most serious occasions, such as rites held for someone mortally sick, those present take as much Peyote as they can; the capacity of most people seems to range from about four to forty Peyote buttons.

Peyotists have been organized into the Native American Church since 1918. These church groups run the gamut of comprehensiveness from the single local group on the one extreme, to the intertribal and international federation known as the Native American Church of North America, on the other extreme.

In a series of other publications I have discussed the early history of Peyotism, presented an historical and generalized account of the religion and given a detailed description of the Peyote Religion in a single tribe —all from the viewpoint of a relatively detached anthropologist. The present essay is different. Here I concentrate on the contemporary uses of, and attitudes toward, sacramental Peyote, and write as a member and officer of the Native American Church of North America. Of course the presentation is mine, but I think substantially it represents the consensus of our membership.

Long ago God took pity on the Indian. (Opinions vary as to when this happened: when plants were created at the origin of the world, when Jesus lived, or after the white man had successfully invaded this continent.) So God created Peyote and put some of his power into it for the use of Indians. Therefore the Peyotist takes the sacramental Peyote to absorb God's power contained in it, in the same way that the white Christian takes the sacramental bread and wine.

Power is the English term used by Indians for the supernatural force called *mana* by anthropologists; it is equivalent to the New Testament *pneuma*, translated as Holy Spirit or Holy Ghost. Power is needed to live. As a Crow Indian once remarked to me as we were strolling near a highway, man is like an auto; if the car loses its power it cannot go. Physically, power makes a person healthy, and safe when confronted by danger. Spiritually, power gives a person knowledge of how to behave successfully in everyday life, and what to make of one's life as a whole. The Peyotist obtains power from the sacramental Peyote.

Physically, Peyote is used as a divine healer and amulet.

For sick people Peyote is used in various ways. In a mild illness Peyote is taken as a home remedy. Thus when a man has a cold, he drinks hot Peyote tea and goes to bed. In more serious illnesses Peyote is taken during the Peyote rite. Such an illness is due not only to lack of sufficient power, but also to a foreign object within the body. Therefore a seriously sick person who takes Peyote usually vomits, thus expelling the foreign object which is the precipitating cause of the illness; then more Peyote is taken in order to obtain the amount of power needed for health.

In cases of severe illness, the rite itself is held for the purpose of healing the patient; it is often referred to as a doctoring meeting. In addition to having the sick person take Peyote, as in less desperate cases, everyone else present prays to God to give the patient extra power so he or she will recover.

Members may keep a Peyote button at home, or on their person, to protect them from danger. The latter is particularly true of men in the armed forces. The power within the Peyote wards off harm from anything in the area of its influence. In cases of great danger, as when a young man is about to leave for military service, a prayer meeting is held at which everyone present beseeches God to give the man extra power to avoid harm.

Spiritually, Peyote is used to obtain knowledge. This is known as learning from Peyote. Used properly, Peyote is an inexhaustible teacher. A stock statement is, "You can use Peyote all your life, but you'll never get to the end of what there is to be known from Peyote. Peyote is always teaching you something new." Many Peyotists say that the educated white man obtains his knowledge from books—particularly the Bible; while the uneducated Indian has to obtain his knowledge from Peyote. But the Indian's means of achieving knowledge is superior to that of the white man. The latter learns from books merely what other people have to say; the former learns from Peyote by direct experience.

A Comanche once said, "The white man talks *about* Jesus; we talk *to* Jesus." Thus the individual has a vividly direct experience of what he learns, qualitatively different from inference or hearsay. Therefore the Peyotist, epistemologically speaking, is an individualist and empiricist; he believes only what he himself has experienced.

A Peyotist maxim is, "The only way to find out about Peyote is to take it and learn from Peyote yourself." It may be interesting to know what others have to say; but all that really matters is what one has directly experienced—what he has learned himself from Peyote. This conception of salvation by knowledge, to be achieved by revelation (in this case, through Peyote) rather than through verbal or written learning, is a doctrine similar to that of early Middle Eastern Gnosticism.

The mere act of eating Peyote does not itself bring knowledge. The proper ritual behavior has to be observed before one is granted knowledge through Peyote. Physically, one must be clean, having bathed and put on clean clothes. Spiritually, one must put away all evil thought. Psychologically, one must be conscious of his personal inadequacy, humble, sincere in wanting to obtain the benefits of Peyote, and concentrate on it.

Peyote teaches in a variety of ways.

One common way in which Peyote teaches is by heightening the sensibility of the Peyotist, either in reference to himself or to others.

Heightened sensibility to oneself manifests itself as increased powers of introspection. One aspect of introspection is very important in Peyotism. During the rite a good deal of time is spent in self-evaluation. Finally the individual engages in silent or vocal prayer to God, confessing his sins, repenting, and promising to follow the Peyote Road (that is, the Peyotist ethic) more carefully in the future. If he has spiritual evil within him, Peyote makes him vomit, thus purging him of sin.

Heightened sensibility to others manifests itself as what might be called mental telepathy. One either feels that he knows what others are thinking, or feels that he either influences, or is influenced by, the thoughts of others. In this connection a frequent phenomenon is speaking in tongues, which results from the fact that people from different tribes participate in a rite together, each using his own language; Peyote teaches one the meaning of otherwise unknown languages.

For example, during the rite each male participant in succession sings solo four songs at a time. Recently a Winnebago sitting next to me sang a song with what I heard as a Fox text (Fox is an Algonquian language closely related to Menomini, the language I use in the rite), sung so clearly and distinctly I understood every word.

When he was through, I leaned over and asked, "How come you sang that song in Fox rather than Winnebago (a Siouan language unintelligible to me)?"

"I did sing it in Winnebago," he replied. The afternoon following the rite he sat down next to me and asked me to listen while he repeated the song; this time it was completely unintelligible to me because the effects of Peyote had worn off.

A second common way in which Peyote teaches is by means of revelation, called a vision. The vision is obtained because one has eaten enough Peyote under the proper ritual conditions to obtain the power needed to commune with the spirit world. The vision provides a direct experience (visual, auditory, or a combination of both) of God or some intermediary spirit, such as Jesus, Peyote Spirit (the personification of Peyote), or Waterbird.

The nature of the vision depends upon the personality and problems of the individual. The following are typical: He may be comforted by seeing or hearing some previously unexperienced item of Peyotist belief, or departed loved ones now in a happy existence. He may be guided on the one hand by being shown the way to solve some problem in daily life; on the other hand, he may be reproved for evil thoughts or deeds, and warned to repent.

A third way in which Peyote teaches is by means of a mystical experience. This is relatively uncommon. It is limited to Peyotists of a certain personality type among the more knowledgeable members of the church; roughly speaking, they have what white people would call a mystical temperament. These Peyotists, in turn, rarely have visions, and tend to look upon them as distractions. The mystical experience may be said to consist in the harmony of all immediate experience with whatever the individual conceives to be the highest good.

Peyote has the remarkable property of helping one to have a mystical experience for an indefinite period of time, as opposed to most forms of mystical discipline underwhich the mystical experience commonly lasts for a matter of minutes. Actually, I have no idea of how long I could maintain such an experience with Peyote, for after about an hour or so it is invariably interrupted by some ritual detail I am required to perform.

What happens to the Peyotist phenomenologically that makes possible the extraordinary results I have described? It seems to depend on both the physiological and psychological effects of Peyote.

Physiologically, Peyote seems to have curative properties. Many times, after a variety of illnesses brought about by fieldwork conditions, I have left a Peyote meeting permanently well again.

Another physiological effect of Peyote is that it reduces fatigue to an astonishing extent. For instance, I am not robust, but after taking Peyote I can participate in the rite with virtually no fatigue—a rite which requires me to sit on the ground, cross-legged, with no back rest, and without moving, for 10 to 14 hours at a stretch; all this in the absence of food and water.

Psychologically, Peyote increases one's sensitivity to relevant stimuli. This applies to both external and internal stimuli. Externally, for example, the ritual fire has more intense colors when I am under the influence of Peyote. Internally, I find it easier to introspect upon otherwise vague immediate experiences.

At the same time, Peyote decreases one's sensitivity to irrelevant external and internal stimuli. Very little concentration is needed for me to ignore distracting noises inside or outside the tipi. Similarly, extraneous internal sensations or ideas are easily ignored.

Thus, on one occasion I wrote in my field diary, "I could notice no internal sensations. If I paid very close attention, I could observe a vague and faint feeling that suggested that without Peyote my back would be sore from sitting up in one position all night; the same was true of my crossed legs. Also, my mouth might be dry, but I couldn't be sure."

The combination of such effects as absence of fatigue, heightened sensitivity to relevant stimuli, and lowered sensitivity to irrelevant stimuli, should make it easier to understand how the individual is disposed to learn from Peyote under especially created ritual conditions.

To any reader who becomes intrigued by Peyote, two warnings should be given. First, I have discussed the effects of Peyote on those who used it as a sacrament under ritual conditions. The described responses of white people to Peyote under experimental conditions are quite different; in fact, they tend to be psychologically traumatic. Second, Peyote is a sacrament in the Native American Church, which refuses to permit the presence of curiosity seekers at its rites, and vigorously opposes the sale or use of Peyote for non-sacramental purposes.

Whether in Arizona, Alaska, Georgia, or Newfoundland, the American Indian is a citizen of a twentieth-century nation which makes available to him goods and services commensurate with his geographical and social position. As we have noted before, the Indian is often too poorly situated in either social or geographic respects to receive education, public health and hospital care, welfare or family assistance, or any of the multiple services which the modern state is able to provide. Furthermore, if and when the situational problems are overcome, cultural barriers remain. In the following synthesis, a renowned expert on cross-cultural educational problems, Robert J. Havighurst, comments on the educational history of the American Indian.

50 *Robert J. Havighurst*

EDUCATION AMONG
AMERICAN INDIANS:
INDIVIDUAL AND
CULTURAL ASPECTS*

Education is as old as human society, and every human society has its own particular ways of making its children into full-fledged adult participants in its culture. The American Indian tribes having different cultures used different forms of education, but all were alike in giving education *informally* through parents, other relatives, the old people of the tribe, religious societies, hunting and war, and work parties.

TRADITIONAL INDIAN EDUCATION

As long as they preserve their cultures, the Indian tribes educated their children successfully in this informal way. A few tribes, all living in the American Southwest, have preserved their cultures well-nigh intact into the twentieth century and have continued to educate their children in the traditional ways. Among these, the Pueblo groups have succeeded remarkably well in maintaining the tribal cultures in the face of competition from the surrounding culture of white Americans. One of the Pueblo tribes is the Hopi whose members live in villages of close-packed stone houses on the mesas of north central Arizona. A Hopi chief, now a man of about seventy, has given us in his autobiography an account of the education he received as a boy. He says:

Learning to work was like play. We children tagged around with our elders and copied what they did. We followed our fathers to the fields and helped plant and weed. The old men took us for walks and taught us the

* Abridged from "Education Among American Indians: Individual and Cultural Aspects," by R. J. Havighurst, in *Annals of the American Academy of Political and Social Sciences,* **311,** 105–115, 1957.

uses of plants and how to collect them. We joined the women in gathering rabbitweed for baskets, and went with them to dig clay for pots. We would taste this clay as the women did to test it. We watched the fields to drive out the birds and rodents, helped pick peaches to dry in the sun, and gather melons to lug up the mesa. We rode the burros to harvest corn, gather fuel, or herd sheep. In house-building we helped a little by bringing dirt to cover the roofs. In this way we grew up doing things. All the old people said that it was a disgrace to be idle and that a lazy boy should be whipped. (11:51–52)

This man, when he was six or seven years old, went through the first initiation, in which all Hopi children learn the simplest of the religious mysteries. Before that he had received some of his early moral education through the visits of katcinas, villagers disguised as supernatural beings. Of this he says:

I saw some giantlike Katcinas stalking into the village with long black bills and big sawlike teeth. One carried a rope to lasso disobedient children. He stopped at a certain house and called for a boy. "You have been naughty" he scolded. "You fight with other children. You kill chickens. You pay no attention to the old people. We have come to get you and eat you." The boy cried and promised to behave better. The giant became angrier and threatened to tie him up and take him away. But the boy's parents begged for his life and offered fresh meat in his place. The giant reached out his hand as if to grab the boy but took the meat instead. Placing it in his basket, he warned the boy that he would get just one more chance to change his conduct. I was frightened and got out of sight. I heard that sometimes these giants captured boys and really ate them. (11:45)

The education of a Hopi boy had much that was similar to that of a Zuni or Zia boy, since these were all Pueblo tribes, but there were great differences between the education of Hopi children and that of the Navahos, who dwelt in isolated family units and lived a semi-nomad life; and there were other differences characteristic of the plains-dwelling and buffalo-hunting Sioux; or the desert-dwelling Papago; or the salmon-fishing Yurok; or the maize-growing Pequots of New England. It is to be remembered that there were 500 different Indian languages in North America and more than that number of tribes, each with its own particular culture which it taught to its children.

Toward the close of the nineteenth century, those Indian tribes which were left settled down to a peaceful coexistence among themselves and with the white man; and the latter felt some responsibility for educating their children. For some years from the end of the Indian wars until the 1920's, the American government Indian policy was to educate the Indian children into the white culture, and for this purpose there were established government schools, many of them boarding schools, to which Indian children of various tribes were sent.

The period of boarding schools had its heyday from about 1890 to 1920. In this period soldiers were sometimes sent out to round up Indian children and bring them into boarding schools. Several of the Indian schools became quite well-known for one feature or another. For example, the Carlisle School in Pennsylvania was made famous by the fact that Jim Thorpe, the great all-round athlete of the period between 1910 and 1920, got his athletic start there.

The boarding schools were changed a great deal after the Meriam Report made to the government in 1928 on *The Problems of Indian Administration*. Among other things this report called attention to the value of bringing up children in their home environment and asked that the boarding schools be "humanized" and used only for older children.

In this earlier time, Sun Chief, the Hopi whom we have quoted on his Indian education, attended boarding schools first on the edge of the Hopi country and later in California. He adjusted himself fairly well to the California school, until he was taken with a severe illness during which he was unconscious for a time and had a vision of his "Hopi Spirit Guide." During a long convalescence, he concluded that he should return to the ways of his fathers. He says:

As I lay on my blanket I thought about my school days and all that I had learned. I could talk like a gentleman, read, write, and cipher. I could name all the states of the Union, with their capitals, repeat the names of all the books of the Bible, quote a hundred verses of scripture, sing more than two dozen Christian hymns and patriotic songs, debate, shout football yells, swing my partners in square dances, bake bread, sew well enough to make a pair of trousers, and tell "dirty stories" by the hour. It was important that I had learned how to get along with white men and earn money by helping them. But my death experience had taught me that I had a Hopi Spirit Guide whom I must follow if I wished to live. I wanted to become a real Hopi again, to sing the good old Katcina songs, and to feel free to make love without the fear of sin or a rawhide. (11:34)

Sun Chief's irony should not be taken as an adequate summary or evaluation of the education given in Indian boarding schools during the period 1890 to 1920, but nevertheless it is the reflection of the experience of an intelligent man who became a leader of his own tribe in his adult years.

THE INDIAN AS A MAN OF TWO CULTURES

Education is always a process of teaching a culture, and the education provided by the whites for the Indians has always been aimed at teaching the white culture, or at least some elements of it, to people who have been reared in another culture. In the period of "Americanization" of the Indians, the whites' education was more explicitly aimed at making "white men" out of Indians than it has been since 1930. Since then, it has been designed as a supplement to the tribal education rather than a rival or a replacement for the tribal education. Nevertheless, white education has represented a new and different culture to the Indian, even when planned as supplementary to tribal education by teaching only certain white agricultural and home-making skills and the 3 R's and by leaving matters of religion, family life, and vocational choice to the traditional tribal processes. Therefore, the Indian who is subjected to white education becomes a man of two cultures. Sometimes the Indian culture predominates and sometimes the white culture wins. Generally, the individual makes his own combination of the two by adopting such white "ways" as are useful and pleasant to him including farming and homemaking skills, artisan skills, and often a form of Christianity.

The existence in the Indian's experience of parallel but different cultures is illustrated by a study made in the early 1940's of Navaho Indian children having different degrees of contact with white culture in two different communities. The Shiprock community is located on a well-traveled highway and has substantial economic relations with neighboring white communities. This was probably the most acculturated of Navaho communities in the early 1940's. In contrast, the Navaho Mountain community was probably the least acculturated. Situated far away from any highway, in an area almost never visited by white men, many of the Navaho children had never seen a white person except the school teacher; and many of the children never attended school. A few of the older children attended a boarding school in Tuba City, which was on a secondary highway, but still relatively apart from the world of white Americans.

The Shiprock children were closer to the average of white American children on a number of tests of attitudes and abilities than were the

Navaho Mountain children, but still the Shiprock children showed many significant differences from the white children, indicating the persistence of the Indian culture in their lives.

Attitude Towards Games

Among other things the Indian children were asked about the games they played, who had made the rules, and who could change the rules. These questions had been asked of Swiss children and of American white children at various ages. The following tribes were studied in this way, Pueblo (Hopi, Zuni, Zia), Sioux, Papago, and Navaho. The games mentioned by the children were all "white"—that is, part of the surrounding white culture—such as basketball, baseball, marbles, and "jacks." Concerning these "white" games the Indian children showed the same kind of change of attitude with age as is shown by white children. That is, the younger children said that rules were made by powerful people or people in authority, and that these rules could not be changed; while the older children said that rules are made by experts or by committees of players. However, the change to a more mature set of attitudes was generally slower in coming to the Indian children.

At Navaho Mountain, the isolated Navaho community, some of the children had never seen "white" games and gave answers concerning traditional Navaho games. This suggested to one of the researchers that she might ask systematically about Navaho games as well as about "white" games, and she was able to get information concerning attitudes toward the rules of games from thirty-eight boys and girls in the Navaho Mountain area, of whom twenty-four had had experience with both kinds of games.

Concerning the "white" games, they generally said that the rules were made by the coach, or the teacher, or some person in authority, and that these rules would be changed by agreement among the people playing the game. This kind of answer is given by white children. But when asked about rules of traditional Navaho games, the Navaho Mountain youth said unanimously that the rules were first made by the "holy people," or by the "ancient ones," or by the "animals"—who in the ancient days possessed human characteristics—and that no human could change the rules.

For example, an 18-year-old Navaho boy had gone away to an Indian boarding school and had obtained a relatively large degree of contact with white culture. He spoke about football and said that "coaches or head people" get together and make or change the rules. But concerning Navaho games he said that the rules could not be changed "because the holy people taught us them. It's not right to change them."

Thus we see that these young people learn one kind of attitude toward rules of games that they see in the "white" culture, and probably toward rules of life in general; and they learn a different kind of attitude toward such rules that are part of the Navaho culture. Truly they are growing up to be people of two cultures, subject to two contrasting kinds of education; and they must make their own combination or synthesis of the two cultures and the two kinds of education.

The "white" education is part of the white American culture. The Indian child comes to this conditioned by the culture his family and community have taught him. Some Indian groups are now quite thoroughly acculturated to the white way of life—notably in Oklahoma. Their children learn little of the traditional Indian culture and take on the culture of the white school quite easily. Other Indian children, like those of Navaho Mountain, get very little experience of white society and learn very little from the white school. Most Indians are between these two extremes. In general, we should expect the Indian child to do well in American schools by "white" standards only if he and his family are a part of the white culture.

EQUIPMENT OF INDIAN CHILDREN FOR EDUCATION

Thus the culture of the Indian child equips him well or poorly for education in American schools, depending on how well his culture matches that of the American society which surrounds him. Where his Indian community has been largely absorbed into the white community and the adjustment has been successful, as is true of the Oklahoma Indians, the Indian child may be expected to do as well as white children in the schools, unless he has some biological "racial" difference which gives him an advantage or a disadvantage over white children. There is no evidence that such a biological difference exists.

When his culture is quite different from that of the surrounding white community, as in the case of the Pueblo and Navaho Indians, or when his tribal culture has disintegrated and his group has not yet adjusted well to membership in the surrounding white culture, as was true in the 1940's of the Sioux, the Indian child may be expected to do rather poorly in schools that are run according to white standards.

In addition to this general statement about the equipment of Indian children for success in schools, there are two general questions whose answers throw some light on Indian experience with white schooling.

The first question is whether Indian children are well motivated for work in school. A form of motivation which is important in American education is the individual's desire to compete with and do better than his fellows. This is a notable aspect of the white American culture, especially of the middle class. Consequently, school children are rewarded by parents and teachers for doing better than other children. Some Indian tribes are traditionally individualistic and competitive, but most of those that survive today are co-operative in their basic attitudes. They work and share together in large families and in neighborhood groups, and they value sharing and co-operation more than individual differences and competition. The Indians of the Southwest, and especially the Pueblo tribes, are notably co-operative. Consequently, if a teacher in a government school, who has been accustomed to assume that children are competitive, tries to appeal to this kind of motivation by using spelling contests or by encouraging children to call attention to the mistakes of other children, the teacher may be perplexed to find that such teaching methods do not work very well. The Indian children may not parade their knowledge before others nor try to appear better than their peers.

In a situation like this, the teacher would do well to discover other forms of motivation for school work, including the use of group procedures and the provision of activities which the Indian children enjoy in themselves. Drawing and painting and other crafts seem to have such an intrinsic appeal to Indian children.

Motivation for education is also poor, by white standards, when a tribe has lost its traditional culture and has not yet successfully fitted into the white culture. Such a situation is described by MacGregor in his study of two Sioux communities where the people were just beginning to be successful as cattle raisers, but many were eking out a poor existence as laborers in nearby white communities or were making a bare living as farmers. The children of these communities were mixed in their attitudes toward schooling. Many of them started out well, and then in adolescence seemed to lose their drive for education.

Intelligence of Indian Children

Studies of the intelligence of Indian children may be divided into two groups—those reported before and after 1935. The first group of studies tended to show that Indians were less intelligent than white children. The second group tended to show that there was no difference in average intelligence between Indian and white children, except for such differences as were explainable on the basis of cultural differences.

The following is a brief summary of the studies of the intelligence of Indian groups in particular, including the tests used and the results obtained. The earliest reported study dates back to 1914 when Rowe administered Stanford-Binet examinations to 268 Indians and found 94 per cent of them to be below the norm for whites on the basis of chronological age. Hunter and Sommermeier in 1921 gave the Otis Classification Test to 715 mixed- and full-blood Indians and found a correlation of .41 between degree of white blood and the intelligence quotient. Garth administered the National Intelligence Test to Indians of various tribes and localities as well as to Mexicans and other ethnic groups. His findings substantiate largely those of Hunter and Sommermeier. Garth found Mexicans to do better than full-blood Indians, but not as well as mixed-blood Indians. Garth and his associates also found public-school Indian students to be slightly superior to the United States government school Indians and that there was a rise in IQ with school grade. The last finding led Garth to weigh heavily the factor of education in test performance. Haught administered the Pintner-Cunningham Mental Test to little children, the National Intelligence Test to children of intermediate age, and the Terman Group Test of Mental Ability to those in the upper-age levels. He concluded that "Indians make lower scores than whites because they are lower in native ability (6:137–142)." The results heretofore described were obtained mainly with the use of paper-and-pencil tests of general intelligence in which the verbal component is quite prominent.

These studies of Indians using verbal intelligence tests give results rather similar to the well-known studies by Sherman, Gordon, and others on white children living in isolated mountain hollows in Virginia, on canalboats in England, and in isolated rural areas where there is very little schooling. These children tend to fall below the average of white children and to suffer a decrease in IQ as they grow older. Such findings suggest that the observed differences of intelligence may not be due to racial differences.

To determine the effect of language on test results, Jameson and Sandiford administered both nonlanguage and language tests of intelligence to 717 mixed-blood Indians and obtained a difference of 5 points in IQ in favor of the nonlanguage test. The more significant attempts to appraise the intelligence of Indians within the past ten to fifteen years have been made with the use of performance or relatively "culture-free" tests.

Klineberg administered the Pintner-Paterson series of six tests to Indian and white children on the Yakima Indian reservation and found (1) that Indian children took longer with form boards but made fewer errors, (2) that comparison of Indian and white groups in terms of total number of points obtained on the Pintner-Paterson Point Scale showed no differences between the two because the Indians made up in accuracy for their inferior speed, and (3) that correspondence of score with degree of white blood was lacking. Whereas preceding investigations pointed to the superiority of the whites over the Indians on tests of intelligence, Klineberg's study is among the first to offer contradictory evidence and to suggest that test performance may be affected by cultural factors.

A later study by Garth and Smith, employing a nonlanguage and a language test with the same subjects, found (1) that Indian children consistently show a performance on the Pintner-Paterson test more nearly equal to white performance than they do on the verbal test, (2) that the IQ's on the performance test were 10 to 14 points higher than those on the verbal test.

Recent Intelligence Test Studies

In more recent testings on Indian children, the general contention has been that the verbal component in tests of general intelligence handicaps the Indian child. Tests that are relatively culture free, of a performance variety, are considerably more appropriate than tests requiring facility with the English language.

An extensive testing program with Indian children was carried through by a University of Chicago group as part of the *Study of Indian Education*. The Grace Arthur Point Performance Scale in a shortened form was used with 670 Indian children aged 6 through 15 in communities of the Navaho, Hopi, Zuni, Zia, Papago, and Sioux Indian tribes. The Arthur test consisted of a battery of nonverbal performance tests—The Porteus Maze, Mare and Foal, Seguin Form Board, Kohs Block Design, and Knox Cube tests. Nonverbal tests were used because it was thought that tests requiring oral or written work in English would penalize the Indian children, since most of them spoke an Indian language at home and very few of them were fluent in English.

Practically all the children tested were full-blood Indians except the Sioux, where the sample of children conformed to the pattern of blood-mixture on the reservation. In most communities, either practically all children within the age range or a representative sample of them were tested.

On this test battery, most of the Indian groups gave almost exactly the same quality of performance that white children do. There were two Indian groups who fell substantially below the norms for white children—one Papago and one Navaho group—and these children also fell substantially below other groups from the same tribes. However, the Hopi groups performed definitely above the level of white children. The results of this study indicate that Indian children do about as well as white children on a performance test of intelligence, and that differences exist between tribes and among communities within a tribe—differences of the degree that are also found among white children in various types of communities.

The results of this test on the Sioux children are of special interest because they can be compared with the results of a Kuhlmann-Anderson (verbal) intelligence test which was administered to some of the same children shortly after they had taken the Arthur test. A total of thirty boys and girls took both tests. The average IQ of this group on the Kuhlmann-Anderson test was 82.5, with a standard deviation of 13.5. The average Arthur test IQ of this group was 102.8, with a standard deviation of 19.1. The product-moment correlation coefficient between the two sets of scores was .53 ±.09. A group with an average IQ of 83 is generally supposed to be a very dull group, very few of whom are even average in intelligence when compared with a normal group. This conclusion might have been drawn concerning Sioux children from the verbal test. Yet, in the performance test of intelligence, the same group averaged 103, slightly above the average for white children.

In a study made on these same Indian children of five tribes, another nonverbal test of intelligence showed a considerable superiority of Indian children over white children. The test was the Goodenough Draw-A-Man Test. This requires the child to use a pencil to draw a figure of a man. The drawing is scored for accuracy in proportion and detail, and not for other esthetic qualities. Between the ages of 6 and 11 the scores on this test have been found to be closely related to other measures of intelligence. The Draw-A-Man test has been used with various Indian groups since 1926, with a general finding of a minor degree of inferiority of Indian children compared with white children. However, a 1942 study by Rohrer compared Osage (Oklahoma) Indian children with white children in the same public school classrooms. The Osage Indians are well off economically and speak English in their homes. The mean IQ of the Indian children was 103.8; of the white children, 102.9.

When the test was given to the same groups who were tested with the Arthur Performance Test, the results showed the Indian children to be superior to white children. Average IQ's ranged from 117 (one of the Hopi groups) to 102 (one of the Sioux groups). This was not taken to mean that Indian children are actually superior in native intelligence to white children. The results are best explained as due to cultural differences between the Indian and white children and between the Indian groups. The Indian children, especially the boys, are stimulated culturally to take an active interest in the world of nature and are given much opportunity to form and express concepts of natural objects, including the human body, on the basis of their observations. Furthermore, drawing is done more commonly by adults in several of the Indian tribes than it is by white adults. The Hopi boys exceeded the girls very greatly on this test. This may be explained as due to the greater amount of stimulation received by boys than by girls in this culture to take an active interest in the world of nature: in man, animals, clouds, and other natural phenomena.

The conclusion which is drawn by most social scientists from the data on Indian cultures and Indian intelligence is that the American Indians of today have about the same innate equipment for learning as have the white children of America. But in those Indian tribes which have preserved their traditional cultures to some extent, there is a limited motivation of children for a high level of performance in schools and colleges.

CURRENT TRENDS IN INDIAN EDUCATIONAL ACHIEVEMENT

In 1928 the Meriam Report proposed major changes in Indian education, principally the following:

1. Keep education on the reservation as far as possible and keep it closely related to family and tribal life. Avoid sending children away from home as much as possible.

2. Make the day schools on the reservations into community centers which teach adults as well as children.

3. Humanize the boarding schools; limit them to older children.

4. Make Indian education fit the facts of postschool life for most

Indians—stress vocational training in agriculture and handicrafts, health, homemaking, and so forth. Pay attention to occupational placement of graduates.

5. Provide high school and college opportunities for those who do well in school, through more secondary schools and through scholarship aid for able Indian students who wish to attend college.

These proposals have been generally followed in the years since 1928. However, Indian life has been changing, and the educational program of the Indian Service has been affected by the growing acculturation of the Indians and by their growing tendency to leave the reservations and to live in centers of modern culture. For instance, the Navahos, who up to 1940 were generally not interested in schooling for their children and tended to keep to themselves, have recently been asking for more educational opportunities. They have sent many of their adolescent children to off-reservation boarding schools which have offered a special five-year program for adolescent youth who have had little or no prior schooling. By 1955, approximately 1,200 young men and women had graduated from this program and 50 per cent of these graduates were employed off the Navaho reservation, while only 7 per cent were employed on the reservation—the remainder being housewives, students, or unemployed.

Another example of movement away from the reservation is provided by the Sioux of the Pine Ridge reservation in South Dakota. In 1938–39 a study of graduates of the Pine Ridge schools showed that 98 per cent of them stayed on the reservation to make a living. In 1951 a study was made of 1,542 Pine Ridge boys and girls who had been enrolled in reservation schools between 1937 and 1947. Of this group, 54 per cent were still on the reservation. Most of the remainder were living in white communities near the reservation.

Studies of Educational Achievement

There have been several studies of the educational achievement of Indian children since 1945 made with standardized tests which permit comparison among the various groups of Indian and white children.

There were striking differences among Indian groups on the tests of school achievement in the areas of reading, vocabulary, spelling, arithmetic, health and safety, and natural resources. The groups with the greatest degree of contact with modern culture did best. Most of the Indian groups were below public school white children who lived in the neighborhood of these Indians. On two tests the differences between white and Indian children were small. These had been prepared by Indian Service personnel to test knowledge of health and safety procedures and knowledge of the use of local natural resources of tools. For these two tests, the Indian children had about the same kind of practical background and school experience as the white children of neighboring communities. In the entire battery of tests, Indian children who live *off* an Indian reservation generally did better than Indian children who live *on* a reservation. Further, Indian pupils who live in towns achieved somewhat better than those who live in the open country.

When comparisons of Indian and white pupils are made at various grade levels, it is found that the Indian children compare more favorably with white children in elementary grades than in high school. This is probably due to the fact that the material taught in elementary grades is closer to the life experience of the Indian children—more practical— than is the more abstract teaching of the high school. Thus the home and community life of the Indian child tend to aid him in learning the simple mental skills taught in elementary school, but they contribute little toward helping him with high-school subjects.

Educational Facilities

During recent years there has been an increase of provisions for secondary education by the Indian Service. For instance, in 1936 there were 13 high schools operated by the Indian Service, compared with 33 in 1951. The most rapid gains in school enrollment among Indian children have been in secondary schools. Very few high-school graduates go on to college, though even here there has been a relative gain. In 1936 about one out of fifty Indian high-school graduates found his way to college, while, in 1950, one in six of the 597 graduates of Indian Service high schools entered college. Still, this is a small number, and the total of Indians entering college, from all kinds of secondary schools, is in the neighborhood of 200. It appears that Indian youths are doing what white working-class youths also tend to do; increasingly they set their sights on high-school graduation, but relatively few of them go to college.

CONCLUSIONS

It is clear that, generally speaking, American Indian groups have not taken part in American education at the secondary and higher levels as have the European immigrant groups such as the Germans, Irish, Scandinavians, and Italians. Most Indian groups have clung to enough of their traditional cultures to prevent them from adopting fully the white American culture, including its attitudes toward education and its use of education as a means of social mobility and occupational achievement.

Those Indian groups who move into the stream of dominant American culture will gradually make more use of schooling and will perform better as scholars. This may take a long time. It seems that the Indian groups who do move into the American culture do so at the lower economic levels and require a generation or two to learn the ways of upward mobility, including the use of education for this purpose.

Individual Indians have done very well in the American educational system by committing themselves to learning the dominant American culture and living in it. The number of such people is relatively small and gives evidence of the great holding power of many of the traditional Indian cultures upon their members, even in the face of pressure and temptation to seek the advantages of the American culture.

⁓⁓⁓

A highly controversial article by Robert Manners is presented as the final selection in the book, accompanied by a spirited exchange with John Collier, Sr., U.S. Commissioner of Indian Affairs from 1933 until 1945. The author and his critic each represent important points of view: one regards assimilation of the Indians into the dominant culture as desirable and inevitable; the other espouses cultural self-determination as a possibility, and moreover, as the only tenable humanistic position. The reader may decide for himself the merits of the respective cases, as both Manners and Collier urge. These articles represent a common form of conflict resolution in the academic-scientific world; the subject which they discuss—the alternatives available to the present state of worldwide cultural pluralism—has far more than continental implications.

51   *Robert A. Manners*

PLURALISM AND THE
AMERICAN INDIAN*

After almost two years of litigation, the right of the New York State
Power Authority to condemn part of the Tuscarora Indian Reservation
for the Niagara Power Project was upheld by the U. S. Supreme Court
in March 1960.

That the legal issues involved in the case are complex is indicated not
only by the 6 to 3 decision of the Supreme Court but by judicial dis-
agreements that cropped up all along the line to the final determination.
Questions of whether the land constituted a genuine reservation or not,
or whether an act of Congress should be required before condemnation
could proceed, or whether agreements entered into by the government
with other tribes at other times and other places were appropriate
precedents for this particular case have been involved in the Supreme
Court's determination. It would be absurd and presumptuous of me to
try to assess the legal propriety of the decision.

But there are aspects and implications of the Tuscarora case which go
beyond the decision and this particular group of Indians. These do need
airing now. I am referring to the significance of the dispute for the way
in which it revealed the ambiguous status of the Tuscaroras in American
culture and, by implication, the ambiguities of status and behavior of
all reservation Indians—and many others as well—in the United States
today.

In point of fact, I don't think it really matters whether the Tuscarora
reservation was a "legal" reservation or not. What does matter to the
Tuscaroras and to all other American Indians, it seems to me, is how
their present relationship to the land and to the institutions of the society of which they are technically a part affects their status as citizens of
the United States. It is in this context that I view the position taken by

---

* Abridged from "Pluralism and the American Indian," by R. A. Manners, in *America Indigena*, **22**, 25–38, 1962.

the Tuscaroras and their attorneys as harmful to them in the long run. Their insistence upon maintaining at all times the forms of an antique relationship which treated them as part of an Indian "nation" and which concomitantly assigned them to an inferior and degraded status can only have the effect of prolonging that status and that degradation.

It is my belief that American Indian self-interest might be better served by abandoning certain legal-technical inmunities and privileges which Indians now enjoy as a result of treaties and agreements arranged long ago and under very different conditions than by attempting to hold on to them in the face of the social burden that these often involve. This is a view that suggests that the second-class citizenship endured by many American Indians today is at least in part derived from certain inconsistencies in their own thinking about themselves and where they stand in relation to the larger society which surrounds them. It is a view which holds that some of the very Indian groups which would like to improve their condition within the dominant white world along white-world lines have jeopardized their chances of so doing by clinging at inappropriate moments to the quasi-wardship status which at other moments is admittedly the main source of their security and protection.

I would not wish to minimize the very real threats which would be posed to the surviving groups of reservation Indians in the United States should they suddenly, and in accordance with the wishes of some Federal administrators and legislators, be deprived of specific Federal protections and left to the mercies of certain state functionaries and private individuals. But I should prefer to emphasize an approach to the Indians' problem of inferior citizenship which leans less on opportunistic selectivity of the phantom "best" in both worlds and more on a recognition of the realities of their present involvement in the world of today.

It is significant that the U. S. Court of Appeals panel which, on July 24, 1958, ordered a halt to the seizure of Tuscarora lands noted in their opinion that if the Indians were to claim and enjoy equal protection under the laws "it may well be that they should bear some of the burdens, including that of having their lands condemned for public purposes." In short, the decision to decline condemnation seems to have been booby-trapped with more long-range potential consequences for harm than they could have realized. For it publicized—to the benefit of those who would make use of these issues for an attack on any significant and costly program of aid for the Indians—one of the truly vulnerable facets of Federal protection.

I am not implying that a solution of the difficulties created by many of the treaties and agreements entered into with the various Indian groups is to be found in unilateral abrogation by the government whenever its obligations under such agreements become burdensome to a government agency. Nor am I suggesting that certain of the special benefits which now accrue to some Indian communities in the United States are nearly adequate to compensate for the many indignities and disadvantages which fall to them. However, it appears to me that the link between these benefits and the perpetuation of the Indians' unfavorable situation in the American social, economic, and political scene may be stronger than we realize.

This does not mean that I would, for example, advocate immediate termination of Federal watchdog functions over activities of the Indians with regard to the sale or other disposition of their lands. The termination of Federal controls or supervisory functions must be performed with great care, and only when and where such action is warranted by circumstances which guarantee no betrayal of the Indians' real interests. But it is precisely because I believe that the best interests of the Indians will be served by a greater degree of protected involvement in the enveloping white culture that I question the wisdom of appeals from such proposals as it had been involved in the Tuscarora land condemnation case. For it is the sad truth that anything that serves to perpetuate the Indians' distinctiveness from the rest of the American community may serve also to perpetuate their second-class status in that community.

If the laws which protect the mass of white Americans from sharpers of one kind or another are more or less adequate for them, then it remains for us to create the proper conditions among Indians throughout the United States in order to guarantee the same adequacy of protection for them. The chief reason that they are in general more likely to be victimized than most of the rest of us is that they are, as a group, less sophisticated, less well-equipped by education and experience to recognize the perils and pitfalls the law holds as well as its protections.

INDIANS AND THE WHITE FRIENDS OF INDIANS

The various organizations set up to protect Indian rights, most of the attorneys who fight their cases for them, and the mass of white Americans who give the matter any thought at all are clearly "on the side of the Indians." That is, they have some knowledge of the vast injustices visited upon the Indians by whites during the past three or four hundred years. They not only believe that compensation should be made to the living descendants of those who have been wronged, but that these same descendants should have the opportunity of deciding for themselves how they should like to live. Few would want to challenge the rectitude of a struggle for Indian rights which embraced these goals. But there is, unfortunately, a vast gulf between the academic decision to allow people to choose their own way of life, or to filter out those elements of their culture which—in their opinion—are worth saving, and the practical means of implementing these choices.

Many American whites have little or no choice about their way of life, even less choice about the elements of their culture which they would like to preserve as part of their individual heritage. However, we are uniformly committed to the value that the *individual* should have a fair opportunity at least to choose the occupation, the career, and the locale within which he will pursue his "way of life."

It is my belief that some of the best-meant struggles to insure freedom of choice to the Indian may turn out in the long run to have had the opposite effect. In the first place, these struggles are generally geared to what the *group* shall be guaranteed, or what the *group* shall be aided in doing. Secondly, the emphasis is implicitly conservative, i.e., it ordinarily assumes that the assistance given shall be as little disruptive of the group's culture as possible. But it should by now be clear that the American Indian has, by and large, a far better chance of achieving personal (hence collective) freedom in a democratic society under a program which aims for his full participation in life in the American community than he does while operating under the distinguished-status handicaps now functioning part-time. This kind of distinction may confer certain shortrun advantages and quasi-advantages, but in the long run it makes the Indian a more visible target for discrimination and chronically inferior citizenship.

I am suggesting that some of the excellent energies which are presently dissipated in pursuit of preservation of a way of life which is, for the most part, gone or doomed, be focussed more realistically on procuring genuine guarantees of full citizenship to the American Indians. This involves a renewal of and/or a concentration upon the old-fashioned struggle for an end to all kinds of economic, legal, and social discrimination. These are endeavors to which the many active friends of the Indians have long dedicated themselves. But they have also, in their understandable respect for Indian tradition and Indian culture, fought the anachronistic battle—*often, contrary to the deepest wishes of many of the Indians themselves*—against the loss of these traditions and this culture. It is this kind of *unconscious* rearguard action against themselves and the people to whose interests they are genuinely dedicated that has, it seems to me, delayed the inevitable resolution of the difficulties, prolonged the agonies of the Indians, and sapped the energies of the combatants whose common and intrinsic goal is the dignity of each American Indian in our society.

The aim should be not to protect the American Indians against the risks to which most white members of our society are subject, *but to elevate them to a status and a competence in which they are equipped to face those risks with the same chances of "success" as the whites.* The Tuscarora land condemnation procedures, it seems to me, offered an opportunity for public attack on the very real inequalities to which even eastern American Indians are subject. It was muffed. It was muffed not because the friends of the American Indian had abandoned their efforts to protect the Indian against discrimination, but because they had misprotected them in a manner reminiscent of the paternalistic overprotection which, in its excesses, they rightly and repeatedly condemn. Having secured the best financial settlement possible, they would have been in a strategic position to point out that the seizure was just another in a long series of historical developments and changes which not only revealed the Indians' involvement with white decisions over which they had no control but emphasized as well the futility of any attempts to carry on in the "old way." The Tuscarora cannot and do not any longer depend upon the land directly to take care of all of their needs—or even a sizeable part of them. If even this inadequate resource is to be whittled down to satisfy the "larger society," then concrete steps must be taken to equip the disprivileged Indians for survival in the seriously altered and constantly altering conditions of their life.

It has never been necessary to prove that the Indian is basically handicapped in his struggle for survival in a society where he must compete with better-equipped whites. The trouble has been that he is caught up in a situation in which he is unrealistically expected to survive in an enclave *inside* that society. Thus, in their efforts to shield him from the unfair competition with whites—as well as to preserve certain admirable features of the pre-contact culture—the friends of the American Indian have urged him to cling to whatever remains of his ancient lands and his ancient ways. They have observed with horror some of the consequences of involvement and the unequal competition. And so they have counselled a kind of selective disengagement, forgetting, so it seems, that disengagement of this kind is not a voluntary thing. Like all the rest of us, the Indians *are* engaged. They should be encouraged to confront the meaning of this engagement and not led to believe that all choices any longer lie with them.

WHAT KIND OF HELP FOR THE INDIANS?

The handicap of most American Indians today consists in the fact that they are inadequately equipped by cultural circumstances and by a lack of proper financial assistance to assume fairly their place in America's competitive scheme. Since the overwhelming majority of them cannot survive in the "old way," they must be given the means to survive in the "new way."

It is interesting, in this connection, to note that the voluntary relocation program sponsored by the Indian Bureau placed 31,259 Indians in Western and Midwestern cities between the time it was launched in 1952 and February, 1960. The Indian Commissioner, Glenn Emmons, reports that "about 70 per cent of [these Indians] have become self-supporting in their new homes." In view of the special burdens of readjustment under which these volunteers have operated, it is rather remarkable that as few as 30 per cent found they could not stick it out. This adjustment, and the recent serious discussions of some Indian leaders about the possibility of persuading the Government to extend Point IV aid to such tribes as request it suggests a genuine willingness on the part of many Indians to allow their lives to be transformed if the transformation offers them a "living."

It is true that others might still prefer an impossible return to the past. But the chief reason for this is that they see no other way out. For even many of those who have most sincerely sought to help them have often cast their eyes backwards in a devotion to remedies which are clearly anachronistic. Ruth Underhill remarks: "Those who tried to keep the old life intact have, perhaps, only deferred the pains of acculturating without preventing them" (13:341).

The struggle for American Indians should no longer be concentrated on an impractical enclave or ghetto survival. The present situation demands that this fight for their rights be dedicated to assuring them full opportunity to come voluntarily into what is now "white American life" on a fair competitive basis. If the tools are provided and the opportunities are genuine, they will, I am sure, enter into this way of life which is ours (whatever we may think of it) more fully and in far greater numbers than any of their friends would have dreamed. It is, I believe, the Indians' recognition of their handicaps more often than it is reverence for a past which none can remember that often impels them to favor solutions in the framework of the old, and all too often misleads some of their wellwishers into the conviction that the Indians would really turn the clock back even if we made it possible for them to participate equally in American culture with the rest of us.

If we are agreed that virtually all of the material culture and most of the social forms which characterized the pre-contact eastern Indians are already gone, then it would seem to me there should be few impediments to further agreement among their friends on the broad features of a program which would accomplish their *proper* integration into the larger society. For it is presently an improper and a biased integration from which they suffer. They are eccentrically incorporated into the political body, increasingly involved in our economic activities, but virtually outside the social realm of the whites. If the present form of their integration into American society is not to remain a device by which they are permanently saddled with inferior status, it must be revised. It must take the full form of cultural assimilation, i.e., incorporation on a basis of equality with others in *all* spheres of our culture.

It would be difficult to press for a program of this kind while at the same time certain Indian groups continued to insist upon remaining immune from their obligations as citizens. For example, a program for full and equal social and economic opportunities could expect little support from legislators or the white citizenry at large while Indians insisted upon such civil immunities as were revealed in the Tuscarora case.

In 1958, 1100 families (white) in Worcester, Massachusetts, learned that they would have to be removed to make room for a ten-mile segment of the new Federal highway system. Translated into individuals, and in terms of the entire $50,000,000,000 highway program, it looks as if around 3,400,000 people will receive eviction notices within the next ten years or so—just as a consequence of this particular road building scheme. And this is only a part of the road-building, watershed, dam, and electrification projects which will involve the movements of at least hundreds of thousands more in the same period.

It is true that few of the people whose lives will be altered by these forced movements can point to a treaty with the U.S. government guaranteeing them the inviolability of their homes and homesteads. But the vast majority had probably assumed that their title deeds, backed up by the Constitution, the Bill of Rights and the Fourteenth Amendment, were all that they needed to insure their occupancy for as long as they wished to remain.

The right of eminent domain is an ancient one. Its exercise frequently works serious hardships on the dispossessed. But while all cases in which it is applied call for justice and consideration of the hardship potentialities, none demands that the state should abandon its obligations to further the apparent interests of the community at large. It is obvious from the circumstances of their present way of life and from the nature of the settlement offered, that the Tuscarora Indians were not confronted with extraordinary difficulties by the proposed plan of removal. It would have been far better, I believe, had they been urged to accept the settlement, further cementing their claims to full citizenship, emphasizing the obstacles along the road to that status which confront them, and pointing as well to the probable means of its achievement. In short, Indian public relations would have been better served by such a stand than by the one taken. Such a decision would have called attention to the fact that the Tuscaroras do not want to be second-class, protected citizens in the worst sense, and it would simultaneously have illuminated the need for more basic solutions of their ambiguous status in white America.

It may seem paradoxical to advocate, on the one hand, a rapid assumption of the full obligations of citizenship and, on the other, a continuation of certain Federal guarantees which confer privileged status upon the Indians. But it is not, for the two are complementary aspects of the same general position. The position is that the assertion of full citizenship rights, privileges and obligations involves equal opportunities and that where discriminations are practiced equal opportunities are curtailed. In order that Indians may acquire first-class citizenship they must indicate their willingness to abandon privilege while they simultaneously insist upon their right to be protected against predation.

THE RELATION BETWEEN INDIANISM AND INDIAN RIGHTS

Since I advocate protection of the Indians' rights as individuals I am opposed to forced and artificial preservation of their Indianism. No North American Indians today have preserved unchanged the patterns of their aboriginal or early contact culture. The degree to which they have become acculturated varies from those who are completely assimilated—generally by biological amalgamation—to those, like the

Hopi of Arizona, who still maintain in some of their villages the main features of their aboriginal social structure and religion, plus a somewhat modified economy, etc. But even the Hopi are undergoing rapid change. They are changing not so much under *direct* pressure from outside, but rather under the influence of the more indirect and perhaps more persuasive pressures of the wonder-world around them. Despite the many resistances to change built into Hopi social structure, the desire for the material things which only money can bring is effecting important alterations in the lives of many Hopi individuals. It is certain that this "infection" will spread.

While most of us would be reluctant to applaud wholeheartedly our white—or Western—culture, it apparently has some lures for those "outside" it as well as for those of us who are caught up more fully in it. In any case, it is not our function to decide for the Indians whether they should partake of our television and H-bomb culture. Part of it they may be able to decide for themselves; most of it will be decided for them anyway. What *we* may decide, however, is that they should be provided with every opportunity to become citizens who can make their own choices and their own mistakes without any special handicaps.

The truth seems to be that we cannot preserve the old ways without at the same time perpetuating features which are inconsonant with even minimal democratic ideals. We may deplore the loss of the old Indian cultures, the disappearance of whole congeries of admirable traits and practices that accompanies increasing participation in the white world. But the economic base that made the old life possible, that permitted an independent existence for them as Indians is gone almost everywhere. At the same time the Indians have come to want many of the things that the white world reveals. Much of what they reject in this world they reject because they cannot afford. And much of the rest they do not even try to get, for they have been taught through experience that what is held out is often in fact not meant for them and is withdrawn as they reach to embrace it.

It is not only a matter of television and Volkswagens. Most Indians talk longingly about the land and the old days and the lost security and/or excitement. But anyone who has spent some time among them knows that virtually all of the younger—and a good many of the older Indians as well—realize the dreamlike quality of the world they talk about. They know that they are overstating the case for the glories of the past. But what is even more important is that most of them would not have it if it were handed to them on a platter if they were simultaneously offered the alternative of equal participation in the world of the whites. In short, I am saying that ever-increasing numbers of Indians would renounce completely what is left to them of their own world and elect to be full participants in the white world surrounding them *if only they could be assured competitive equality, if they could be protected from the humiliation and the degradation to which they are frequently subjected when they try to participate.*

For better or worse, most American Indians are in many ways involved in white American culture. None are completely enclaved "outside" of it. It is not the job of the rest of us to decide that the old way of life was better than the one we hold out. We and they do not have the power to decide *whether* they shall be involved. We may still, I believe, decide *how* they shall be involved. If we think it is sad, or horrible, or amusing that we should be a part of a world that seems to be on the edge of extinction, it is still neither within our capacity, nor is it morally defensible that we should try to impose restrictions or to foster actions which, in effect, seek to wed the Indians to a badly watered-down old way of life between two worlds.

ASSIMILATION OR INTEGRATION
WITHOUT DISCRIMINATION

Since the Indians will come increasingly and with increasing rapidity into the mainstream of white American culture, it seems that the best thing that can be done for them is to insure that they shall not come in uniformly as a lower class and disprivileged group. Protective treatment against discriminatory exploitation during this period of assimilation is essential. And the obverse is implied. Thus, insulation of the Indians from the operation of apparently *non*-discriminatory practices like the Tuscarora land alienation attempt could serve to delay the very ends towards which many of them are striving.

It will not help the Indians to think of themselves—or to urge others to think it of them—and their relationship to the land in terms that were appropriate 300 or more years ago. It seems a clear disservice to the shredded dignity of the American Indians to encourage him in the preservation and production of revised and synthetic forms whose original functions disappeared generations ago.

There is overwhelming evidence that many of the enclaved reservation cultures are segregated and ghettoized cultures in the very worst sense of the words. They are at present in the sorry position of sharing some of the poorer features of both worlds. It is impossible for them to recreate the old world *in toto* even if they should want to do so. And they are shut out from the new world by civic, economic, and social disabilities easily preserved and enhanced by their isolation. They have not always chosen the isolation or the concomitant struggle to maintain themselves by inadequate adaptations of old patterns. In effect, then, not only the isolation but the quixotic battle against the encroachment of the white world have been the only effective answers of most American Indians to the pattern of discriminations under which they labor. Certainly they, like any other minority group in our society, have the academic right to decide whether they should like to be dropped in the melting-pot or left outside. If they have chosen and been helped to choose to remain mostly outside it is not necessarily because they cherish the beads, the blankets, and the long hair of the past. It may be because they have not been given a fair boost to where they can get their hands on the rim of the pot.

THE PROBLEM OF CULTURAL PLURALISM AND DEMOCRACY

Cultural pluralism seems an admirable thing, and from any enlightened point of view a way of life much closer to the inner meaning and ideal of American democracy than the melting-pot concept. But the unhappy reality is that pluralism here and elsewhere frequently involves exploitation and inferior status. The right of the Indians to try to maintain certain features of the old culture cannot be gainsaid. But so far the exercise of this right and the more potent pressures that have compelled it have meant virtual ghettoization. The Indians have for the most part succeeded only superficially in maintaining the "core of inner meanings" and the respected practices of the past.

Most American Indians, like all American Negroes, are chronic victims of discrimination. In the present struggles over school and lunch counter integration in the South it is pointed out that segregation is a major manifestation of and at the same time a contributory cause to the overall patterns of discrimination. Attempts at cultural isolation and preservation work similar hardships on the American Indian. While it is true that the American Negro long ago lost virtually every vestige of his African culture, this is not true of the Indians. But wherever the attempt to retain features of this unextinguished culture involve outmoded isolation and economic deprivation we should, it seems to me,

reconsider the worth to the Indians themselves of such efforts at retention.

*I would insist that as long as any group of American Indians really
reckons that the advantages of partial physical and/or cultural isolation
outweigh the disadvantages that group should be allowed to make the
decision of isolation for itself.* But if this admittedly partial isolation is a
refuge into which they draw *unwillingly* because they have no other
weapons with which to fight against discrimination, then it seems to me
we should devote our efforts to helping them secure the full political, social, and economic support they will need in order to achieve equality of
opportunity—even if the securing means they shall lose what's left of
the old culture and be swallowed up by the new.

I do not believe that the various disadvantaged American Indian
groups should be forced against their wishes to abandon their physical
or cultural reserves. I am simply hopeful that we and they may evaluate the alternatives open to them, and that together we may be in position to implement a broad program of assimilation for those who wish
it—one which will bestow upon them the status of first-class citizen by
removing the impediments of generations of second-class status under
which they have been obliged to exist. In any such program acceptance
of responsibilities must go hand-in-hand with categorical rejection of
discrimination. And since an end to discrimination (or a very significant
reduction in same) implies massive expenditures on Indian education as
well as a tightening of legislation in various fields, then the funds for
implementation must be found at once.

CONCLUSION: ANOTHER LOOK AT INDIAN RIGHTS

The problem of the American Indian is an old one and one of our
own creating. However, the responsibility for its persistence down to the
present does not lie alone with those who fought to keep the Indians in
an inferior status but also, ironically, with some of their best friends. It
will require, rechannelized, the selfless devotion and energies which
these friends of the American Indian have demonstrated over the years
to solve the problem now.

It would seem to me that all they need do is to agree that their struggles in defense of the Indian's right to his own way of life and his own
traditions involved an intention of "doing something for the Indians."
If they will accept the truth of this proposition—and it should not be
difficult—it may not be much harder for them to decide that "doing

something" could mean more than defending the right of the Indian to try to live as he "wished." Perhaps they will also be willing to concede that often in our kind of world tradition may *have* to be abandoned if people are to be saved. We may then hope that the proved energies of the many friends of the American Indians will be concentrated in a new struggle to provide the Indian with the tools he will need for voluntary assimilation. And we may hope further that while they continue to urge respect for the Indian's way of life and restitution for the wrongs he has suffered, his friends will allow that deprivation and discrimination in an avowed democracy may be more distasteful than the loss of a culture trait; and, finally, that these deprivations and discriminations may themselves be related to the Indian's preservation—enforced and voluntary—of his differences.

In order to meet the intensifying problem of a contracting land base —with reference to a growing population—most groups of American Indians will, as I said earlier, require massive financial assistance. This must come primarily from the Federal government. It will mean imposed administration to a degree which goes beyond anything now experienced by the Indians. But solution of their difficulties cannot be achieved without assistance and impositions of this kind. The Indians, like most other people in the world today, cannot survive isolated and unaided in an environment which has ceased to provide them with the means of survival in the old way. For good or evil, they have become a part of the larger world, and it is in this setting, and with a recognition of all that this implies that problems of most Indians are to be evaluated and a solution for them sought. The very least we can do for the depressed, discriminated-against, citizen-wards of our white government would be to include them wholly, whole-heartedly, realistically, and immediately in our administrative plans for the whole of the United States.

I do not think that many American Indians would be likely to resist such changes as would enable them better to cope with the job of staying alive. The problem of Indian survival has been viewed by some (and this is a basic tenet of the new Indian policy inaugurated by the Indian Reorganization Act of 1934, subsequently guided by Professor John Collier) as the problem of maintaining an Indian "way of life," whatever that may be. I have been suggesting that in order that most American Indian groups may grow or live at all, it may be necessary that they abandon their Indian "way of life," whatever that may be. If sheer survival demands the loss of their "identity" as a group it is too bad, but others have had to pay this price before. It may well be the price most American Indians will have to pay for their continued existence as individuals.

～～～⁓⁓

52 John Collier vs. Robert A. Manners

DIVERGENT VIEWS ON "PLURALISM AND THE AMERICAN INDIAN"*

The thirteen-page essay by Dr. Robert A. Manners in the January, 1962, issue of *America Indígena* necessitates a commentary. The essay does not represent the thinking of anthropologists and social scientists in the United States. It represents, instead, the thinking and the powerfully determined will of influential non-scientific groups and masses in the United States and, doubtless, in some other countries. The language used by these groups and masses is not the old-fashioned language of unashamed exploitation. It is a different language, derived from what is called Madison Avenue in the United States. Madison Avenue is the advertising and "public relations" industry, and its language is that of sweetness and light. Individuals and groups who are different from the pulverized, un-structured masses are to be pitied, and not as in an earlier time to be scorned or hated. They are to be charitably saved from themselves through being made partners in the material and cultural dominance of the White, Western, economically affluent, socially atomistic, and spiritually featureless society which in this H-bomb epoch is being herded toward its own and the world's doom. Not guns or the lash or, in the main, not jails, are to be used in the grinding of human differences into the faceless dead-level of White-decreed West-

* Abridged from "John Collier Comments on the Essay of Robert A. Manners, Pluralism and the American Indian," *America Indígena*, **22**, 205–208, 1962.

ern economic man; instead, that which Madison Avenue calls the "engineering of consent" is to be used.

Of this kind, it appears to me, is Dr. Manners' essay. The Indians are to be saved from themselves, but not through the old-fashioned coercion and expropriation. They are to be saved from themselves by themselves, through accepting as final and as life-sufficing and as their own destiny the Western White Man's jungle and slough of despond in this middle Twentieth Century. Voluntarily abandoning their grouphoods, their un-dying pasts, their cultures, their Indianhood, they are to take what they can get within the jungle and slough of despond. What they can get, as "go-getting" isolates, will not be much, but at least they will be self-saved from their ethnic shame.

Dr. Manners will think that these are hard words. But I think that his essay invites and deserves them. Stripped of its somewhat glittering, wordy camouflage, the essay appears as nothing except the old, familiar, ethno-centric assertion by the White man that he—the White man, in this dying age when his own White-Man values are being killed by his own steam-roller is human destiny.

Dr. Manners' essay reiterates and reiterates opinion. I can find in it only three statements of his own of fact, and each of these is in error. I specify:

1. The Tuscarora Indian reservation. Many years ago, the Corps of Army Engineers very carelessly adopted an engineering project which entailed the destruction of the homeland of the Tuscaroras. The Army Engineers "sold" their engineering plan to the City of Pittsburgh, and Pittsburgh clamored for the execution of their engineering plan. Then entered into the situation Dr. Arthur Morgan, eminent as an engineer, who had served under President Roosevelt as the chairman of the Tennessee Valley Authority. Dr. Morgan resurveyed the various potentials for flood control and power development, and found that a project different from that of the Army Engineers would insure more electric power and more flood control and would leave the Tuscaroras' homeland undisturbed. The Tuscaroras and their numerous friends struggled to have the two opposing projects scientifically evaluated side by side. The Army Engineers, prestige-proud, resisted such an evaluation; and their lobbying power in Congress proved irresistible. Hence, the Tuscaroras' homeland is to be destroyed. Dr. Manners leaves un-mentioned Dr. Morgan's alternative plan, and views the resistances of the Indians and their many friends as outmoded sentimentality.

2. Dr. Manners states: "The recent serious discussions of some In-

dian leaders about the possibility of persuading the Government to extend Point IV aid to such tribes as request it, suggests a genuine willingness on the part of many Indians to allow their lives to be transformed if the transformation offers them a 'living.' " The "some Indian leaders" mentioned by Dr. Manners were the National Congress of American Indians acting unanimously. That Indian Congress stands for all that Dr. Manners objects to. And the "Point IV" aid would have been funds for irrigation, reforestation, economic loans, etc., increased health services, broadened education, within those Indian landholdings which Dr. Manners denominates "enclaves" or "ghettos." (The present Indian Administration, which Dr. Manners disparages without using so many words, is doing now the very things that the National Congress of American Indians has been asking for).

3. Dr. Manners concludes: "The problem of Indian survival has been viewed by some (and this is a basic tenet of the new Indian policy inaugurated by the Indian Reorganizaion Act of 1934, subsequently guided by Professor John Collier) as the problem of maintaining an Indian 'way of life,' whatever that may be." Dr. Manners' ignorance appears to be extreme. The Indian Reorganization Act brought to an end the forced individual "allotment" of Indian lands, whose results had been ruinous; it provided for an increase of the land-base of the tribes; it provided a revolving loan fund for Indian economic enterprises; it provided for higher education of Indian youth; it left to each Indian tribe the free choice between making the Act its own law or rejecting the Act. Parallel enactments put an end to the hounding of Indian religions by the Indian Bureau, revoked the Indian Bureau's power to exclude scientific workers from the Indian lands, and authorized the tribes to contract for services with States and local governments and with scientific bodies. However, none of the above is cited by Dr. Manners. His animus is directed against the philosophy and spirit which made the Indian Reorganization Act and the Indian New Deal. That philosophy and spirit was that men must make their own choices and go forward from where they are; and that the Indian grouphoods and cultures should be permitted and helped to function dynamically as they had done for ten thousand years, but had been forbidden to do, by the Government, for the preceding century. The response of the tribes and their members was creative and immense, as it continues to be in the present.

Why do I give importance to Dr. Manners' essay? Partly because, while it will have no effect upon present Indian policy in the United

States, and momentarily appears as a voice of a dead past, that dead past will press hard to come alive again. It did come alive in the years 1950 to 1957 in the United States, and wrought a complete ruin on one Indian tribe and on its long-conserved forest wealth. That tribe was the Klamaths of Oregon. It sought the complete ruin of the Menominee tribe in Wisconsin; a ruin which the tribe averted through help from the State of Wisconsin. And the dead past in Indian affairs may yet come alive again. And the Manners article has importance as an attack against the fundamental policy of the Inter-American Indian Institute; I quote the words of that policy at the end of this communication.

But the Manners article has a wider significance if not importance. It seeks to rationalize the intentions of forces in the United States more powerful and more determined than all the social scientists. These forces intend, as implied at the beginning of this communication, that through polite "engineerings of consent," or if need be through brute force, there shall come about a dead manipulable flatness of human life in the United States and in the rest of the world; that the individual isolate, "freed" from grouphood, culture and home, an atomized "go-getter," shall become—each individual—one among three billion interchangeable grains of sand in an unstructured sand-heap of the world.

Yes—here I repeat in part—the tooth-and-claw philosophy of the later nineteenth century is upon us once more, although temporarily the tooth and claw are hidden in gloves and masks. Plain speech and rough words for the time being are used no more, as Thomas Henry Huxley used them in the 1880's and the Indian Bureau of old times used them. Our Madison Avenue has taught us to use words of soft selfrighteousness; now it is in behalf of the soul of man that we shall erode, denigrate, and crumble into the sand-heap, the grouphoods, cultures and homes of men.

Dr. Manners' essay, if they chance to read it, will be practically meaningless to the United States Indians and their numerous friends and the Indian Affairs administration; meaningless, yet bodeful, because it is a voice of a past which confidently expects to return, and to be permanent, and to rule: to rule not only in Indian affairs but in the United States as a whole and in much of the world. I do not suggest that Dr. Manners consciously asserts or implies the doom of the United States and of the world. I mean, the spiritual doom; his essay treats of the Indians and Indian policy of the United States. But the concept which appears to rule his thinking is, so to speak, a *tropism* within, a wider compulsion in the United States and much of the Western world. That compulsion is toward the culture-surrendering un-structured sand-heap of our part of the world.

I quote now the basic declaration of the Inter-American Indian Institute, as initially adopted in plenary session by the Nations at Patzcuaro in 1940, and as faithfully adhered to by the lamented Dr. Manuel Gamio and by his thoroughly adequate successor, doctor Miguel Leon-Portilla:

"The nations of the Americas shall adopt and intensify the policy of offering the amplest opportunity for the display of the capacity of their Indian groups, to the end that the Indian cultures shall not die but shall endure to enrich the culture of each nation and of the world and contribute to the energies of the nations."

ROBERT A. MANNERS ANSWERS *

Professor Collier's long devotion to the welfare of the American Indians, and the impressive record of his efforts on their behalf are without parallel among social scientists in the United States. More than anyone else he has earned the right to be known as the kind of devoted friend of the American Indian to whom I respectfully referred in my essay, "Pluralism and the American Indian." Perhaps, however, it is the very quality and intensity of his devotion to a *particular kind* of philosophy and program that make it difficult for Prof. Collier not only to accept but even to *see* a somewhat different point of view than his own. Thus, it should not come as a complete surprise that his attachment to his own analysis and plans have blinded him to my essay's main analytic features and led him to indict me as one of those who wish to "erode, denigrate, and crumble into the sand-heap, the grouphoods, cultures and homes of men." He has confused analysis with advocacy, confounded recommendations for meeting problems posed by culture change with a calculated sell-out.

Not only has Professor Collier missed the entire point of my essay, but in his zeal to expose me as an apostle of the new "exploitation," and the "engineering of consent" he has charged me with error in each of the "only three statements . . . of fact" contained in the essay.

The first "error" concerns my failure to mention Dr. Arthur E. Morgan's "alternative plan" for one proposed by the Army Engineers for the "City of Pittsburgh!" Dr. Collier observes that the original army

* Abridged from "Robert A. Manners Answers John Collier's Comments on His Article," *America Indigena*, **23**, 71–75, 1963.

plan "entailed the destruction of the homeland of the Tuscaroras." (!)

In his anxiety of impugn my competence and good intentions, Professor Collier has carelessly confused the facts in the case. Dr. Morgan was retained by the *Seneca Indians* (another tribe of the Iroquois Nation) in connection with another entirely different dam and flood control project, the Kinzua dam scheme in Northern Pennsylvania. He proposed the alternative Conewango-Cattaraugus site (north of Kinzua, Pennsylvania, and Jamestown, New York) as cheaper and more desirable than the army engineer-backed Kinzua dam proposal. *Dr. Morgan and this particular project had nothing at all to do with the Tuscarora Indians and the Niagara Power Project of my essay.* Professor Collier has confused the Seneca with the Tuscarora, Kinzua with Niagara and the Army Engineers with Robert Moses. And even if he had not done so, there would still be no excuse for referring to the alleged omission as an "error."

The second "error" concerns my reference to the recommendation of some "Indian leaders" who favored extending "Point IV and to such tribes as requested it." Professor Collier points out that these Indian leaders "were the National Congress of American Indians acting unanimously." He says that they stand "for all that Dr. Manners objects to." That is not so as any careful reading of my essay will show—but it does not, in any case, constitute an error of fact to refer to them as "some Indian leaders." And it is clear that these same Collier's-favored leaders were advocating a kind of massive economic assistance which could have no other outcome than to move the Indians so aided a few steps closer to "assimilation."

The third and final "error" Professor Collier attributes to me is that I said that maintaining an Indian "way of life" was "a basic tenet of the Indian Reorganization Act of 1934." And he adds that my "ignorance appears to be extreme" because I do not enumerate the specific provisions for economic betterment and insured tribal autonomy proposed by the act. I knew of these provisions and I have always approved of those features of the act which advanced the education and improved the economic welfare of the Indians.

Is Professor Collier trying to say that inclusion of these particulars would have revealed the "error" of my assertion about a "basic tenet" of the new Indian policy? I hope not. For it is apparent from his own description—in the same paragraph—of "the philosophy and spirit which made the Indian Reorganization Act and the Indian New Deal" that "maintaining an 'Indian way of life'" was indeed central to the new Indian policy "guided by Profesor John Collier." Where, then, is the third "error?"

The rest of Professor Collier's comments are less specific, hence the accusations are even more fanciful and remote from the substance of my essay. He accuses me of being against "the philosophy and spirit" [that] "men must make their own choices" when I specifically stated the contrary: *"I would insist that as long as any group of American Indians really reckons that the advantages of partial physical and/or cultural isolation outweigh the disadvantages that group should be allowed to make the decision of isolation for itself.* But if this admittedly partial isolation is a refuge into which they draw *unwillingly* because they have no other weapons with which to fight against discrimination then . . . we should devote our efforts to helping them secure the full political, social, and economic support they will need in order to achieve equality of opportunity . . .

"I do not believe that the various disadvantaged American Indian groups should be forced against their wishes to abandon their cultural or physical reserves. I am simply hopeful that we and they may evaluate the alternatives open to them, and that together we may be in a position to implement a broad program of assimilation for those who wish it . . ."

There is no point in pursuing further and point-by-point the completely tangential criticisms of Professor Collier. And I see no need either to defend myself against the personal vilification which is so significantly a part of this stylishly written but inappropriate critique. For those who read but do not run the essay itself is ample defense against Professor Collier's charges.

I am not opposed to free choice (although I suspect its exercise has serious limitations), or the undoubted virtues of cultural variety. I am not—and my essay makes this quite clear too—in favor of relaxing Federal protection of Indian groups while this protection remains necessary to defend them against the many forms of privation to which they have been subjected. Nor am I terribly enamored of the civilization to which I have "invited" American Indian participation. I have merely said that it is not our function to decide for the Indians whether they should partake of our television and H-bomb culture. Part of it they may be able to decide for themselves; most of it will be decided for them anyway.

The point of the essay, and a point which Professor Collier's remarks completely overlook, is that the Indians *are* involved, they are involved unfairly, and it would be the better part of decency if we did everything in our power to help them—*where they want it*—to be involved with greater advantage and fewer disadvantages than they now enjoy.

In case it should seem that I have taken a position contrary to the wishes and perceptions of all American Indians, I should like to recommend a careful reading of the Progress Reports issued prior to the American Indian Chicago Conference in 1961. These contain comments from Indians around the nation. And while it is apparent, as Ruth Hill Useem notes, that most Indian assumptions are negative, unenthusiastic and fearful—the outlook of a beaten people—it is significant that many of the respondents clearly expressed the desire for a more equitable share in the nation's material riches, and a number call for a more democratic integration of Indians in the American community.

Thus, the Governor and the Council of the "Penobscot Nation" say: "We feel that we are prevented from moving ahead in the modern world. We feel that it is time for a change . . . [our people] want to take their place in a modern world."

From Oraibi, Arizona: The Indian Service should be "devoting its main energies to the social and economic advancement of the Indians, *so that they may be absorbed into the prevailing civilization* or be fitted to live in the presence of that civilization . . . To what degree the Indians will be absorbed or be permitted to be absorbed into the prevailing civilization will work itself out as time goes on" (emphasis added).

From Fort Wayne, Indiana comes a poignant "recommendation" that the conference should work to have "Congress set aside all treaties and all laws on the books and place the Indian on the tax rolls and give him full responsibility under the law as a citizen . . . work to scrap ALL treaties and laws made just for Indians and fight to get us citizenship or deport us *en masse* to Mexico or Canada as non-citizens not fit to live within the borders of the United States."

From Lodge Grass, Montana: Among the many problems of the Indians are "lack of adequate education to meet on equal terms all non-Indians in their contests to hammer out a livelihood in the business world of today and under the highly complex and competitive economic order of our country."

And, finally, I can think of no better way to close this rejoinder to Professor Collier than by reproducing, *in toto,* from the fourth report of the AICC, three paragraphs devoted to the "Indian Problem" by a "full-blooded Indian" from Albuquerque who is, I would guess, neither

Madison Avenue, a new exploiter, an "engineer of consent," or an American Indian quisling—even though his comments parallel those of my own to which Professor Collier has taken such bitter exception.

"Albuquerque, New Mexico, April 5, 1961. The aim of the forthcoming 'Indian Powow' as stated in the *Albuquerque Journal* (March 28, 1961) is so absurd and preposterous that it would hardly be expected to originate or receive impetus from a University such as the University of Chicago. To assume that the Indian and his culture are unchanged and unchangeable is to make a baseless assumption. Furthermore, any attempt to revivify and sanction an antiquated, superannuated way of life is to impede his progress toward individual responsibility and self-improvement, the lack of which will inevitably keep him 'at the bottom of our heap in health, education and economic well being.' He will improve himself in these areas only when he ceases to live in the past.

"The Indian needs not 'an Indian Bill of Rights to fit the oldest frontiersman of the new frontier' or any special charters, but more individual responsibility and encouragement to face the new frontiers like any American citizen. Anything short of this will put the new frontiersman in an old frontier of no progress when all about him progress continues to march on.

"Therefore, as a full-blooded Indian who believes in progress, and who knows well the detriments of antiquity, let me urge you to formulate plans that will help the Indian keep up with a modern way of life rather than to put him in a situation that will require his catching up later."

FINAL REPLY OF JOHN COLLIER *

I am grateful for your courtesy in inviting a reply from me to Dr. Manners' commentary upon my remarks which were occasioned by his original essay. In the main, I would simply refer the reader back to Dr. Manners' original essay, and to my commentary on that essay in the July *America Indigena*. I would, however, like to state my appreciation of Dr. Manners' friendly reference to myself; and to point out that my commentary did not contain, as he states in his rejoinder, any "personal villification" of himself. My commentary set forth an impersonal point of view which differed from Dr. Manners' point of view; and I suggested that Dr. Manners' point of view was similar to the point of view of many non-anthropological individuals in our Western world of

* Abridged from "Final Reply of John Collier," *America Indigena*, **23**, 76–77, 1963.

today. Such a statement as mine was not "personal villification" but sociological classification.

It was not personal villification but a serious impersonal statement when I wrote that "the concept which appears to rule his (Dr. Manners') thinking is, so to speak, a *tropism* within a wider compulsion within the United States and much of the Western world. That compulsion is toward the culture-surrendering, un-structured, sand-heap of our part of the world."

Dr. Manners quotes, at the close of his rejoinder, words of an unidentified "full-blood" Indian. He states that this Indian's "comments parallel those of my (Dr. Manners') own." I suggest that with these words Dr. Manners "villifies" himself; for I do not believe that Dr. Manners' own thinking is as crude as the extremely un-Indian thinking of the "full-blood" Indian, which, he states, parallels his own thinking.

Seriously, I here remark: Dr. Manners writes in his rejoinder that "my (Collier's) devotion to a *particular kind* of philosophy and programs makes it difficult for me (Collier) not only to accept but even to see a somewhat different point of view from my (Collier's) own." In truth, I see that different point of view only too well. I have seen it across the greater part of my life; and have struggled against it not only in relation to American Indians but in relation to ethnic minorities and dependencies all over the world, and in relation to ourselves in the United States. The forceful drive, and the polite persuasion through "engineerings of consent," toward the crushing or the surrender of human differences, operates within the very *zeitgeist* of contemporary Western man. It is a conscious drive and persuasion and also, and more profoundly, an unconscious drive. In Dr. Manners it may be unconscious, or partly so. Whichever be the case, it is not "personal villification" of Dr. Manners to suggest, as above, that "the concept which appears to rule his thinking is, so to speak, a *tropism* within a wider compulsion in the United States and much of the Western world."

I accept one of Dr. Manners' corrections. The Seneca Indians are of course not the Tuscaroras. Each of these two groups has resisted what it believed was the un-necessary destruction of its homeland.

Dr. Manners is accurate in stating that there are some Indians who vocally appear to advocate the surrender of Indianhood. A case in point may be viewed today, at Santa Fe in New Mexico. Yet superficially viewed it is a mis-leading case. At Santa Fe, the new Indian Administration (U.S.A.) is taking steps to create an Institute of American Indian Art. This Institute will re-establish and expand in behalf of all Indian youths, an earlier Indian Arts work at Santa Fe, a work whose results across thirty years, in the intensification of Indian art production while persuading Indian art to be faithful to the ancient Indian genius, became famous all over the world.

Today, before the Institute of American Indian Art has even commenced to operate, a stubborn attack against it is being carried on in the press. And nominally, at least this attack is being led by *an Indian* who is one of my own closest Indian friends—a friend across forty years and into the present. This Indian friend, I surmise, has become confused through white pressures of local and personal nature. Superficially, momentarily, this Indian friend of mine might be made to appear to be supporting Dr. Manners' thesis. Yet fundamentally and permanently, this friend of mine is Indian to the core; he has worked across more than a generation to keep whole and strong the Pueblos' life-way, while helping to lead that life-way, in all of its age-old profundity, onward into the world.

In conclusion, I suggest that the issue raised in Dr. Manners' original essay is a wider, profounder issue than perhaps he himself, as yet, knows.

REFERENCES QUOTED

SECTION I: *INTRODUCTION*

1. ALLEE, J. A., and K. P. SCHMIDT (1951). *Ecological Animal Geography*. 2nd ed. New York: Wiley.
2. ALLEN, L. (1931). Siouan and Iroquoian, *International Journal of American Linguistics*, **6**, 185–193.
3. BLOOMFIELD, L. (1946). Algonquian, in *Linguistic Structures of Native America*, Harry Hoijer *et al.* New York: VFPA, 85–129.
4. BLUMENBACH, J. F. (1865). De Generis Humani Veritate Nativa, in *The Anthropological Treatises of Blumenbach and Hunter*. (Trans. T. Bendyshe.) London: Anthropological Society. 145–276.
5. BOAS, F. (1912a). Migrations of Asiatic Races and Cultures to North America, *Scientific Monthly*, **28**, 110–117.
6. —— (1912b). The History of the American Race, *Annals of the New York Academy of Sciences*, **21**, 117–183.
7. BRINTON, D. G. (1887). A Review of the Data for the Study of the Prehistoric Chronology of America, *Proceedings of the American Association for the Advancement of Science*, **36**, 283–301.
8. DENIKER, J. (1889). "Essai d'une Classification des Races Humaines, Basee Uniquement sur les Characteres Physiques, *Bulletin de Societe d'Anthropologie de Paris*, 3 Ser, **2**, 320–336.
9. DIXON, R. B. (1923). *The Racial History of Man*. New York: Scribner.
10. D'ORBIGNY, A. (1839). *L'Homme Americain (de l'Amerique Meridionale) Considere sous ses Rapports Physiologiques et Maraux*, Vol. 1. Paris: Levrault.
11. FLINT, T. (1826). *Recollections of the Last Ten Years Passed in Occasional Residence and Journeyings from the Valley of the Mississippi from Pittsburg and the Missouri to the Gulf of Mexico, and from Florida to the Spanish Frontier*. Boston: Cummings, Hilleard.

12. HOOTEN, E. A. (1937). Aboriginal Racial Types in America, in *Apes, Men, and Morons*. New York: Putnam, pp. 155–186.

13. ———— (1946). *Up from the Ape*. 2nd ed. New York: Macmillan.

14. HRDLICKA, A. (1912). The Derivation and Probable Place of Origin of the North American Indian, *Proceedings of the 18th International Congress of Americanists*, London, pp. 57–62.

15. ———— (1925). The Origin and Antiquity of the American Indian, *Smithsonian Institution Annual Report for 1923*, Washington, pp. 481–494.

16. HUMBOLDT, BARON A. VON (1822). *Political Essay on the Kingdom of New Spain*. 3rd ed., Vol. 1. London: Longman, Hurst, Rees, Orne, & Baron.

17. KEITH, SIR A. (1949). *A New Theory of Human Evolution*. London: Watts.

18. MOLINA, J. I. (1808). *The Geographical, Natural and Civic History of Chile*. (Trans. "An American Gentleman.") Vol. 1. Middletown, Conn.: Riley.

19. MORTON, S. G. (1844). *An Inquiry into the Distinctive Characteristics of the Aboriginal Race of America*. 2nd ed. Philadelphia: Penington.

20. PATTERSON, H. S. (1871). Memoir of the Life and Scientific Labors of Samuel George Morton, in *Types of Mankind*, Nott, J. S. and Glidden, G. (eds.). Philadelphia: Lippincott, pp. 17–57.

21. PUTNAM, F. W. (1901). A Problem in American Anthropology, *Smithsonian Institution Annual Report for 1899*, Washington, pp. 473–486.

22. SCHREIDER, E. (1951). Anatomical Factors of Body Heat Regulation, *Nature*, **167**, 823–824.

23. TAYLOR, G. (1927). *Environment and Race*. London: Oxford Univ. Press.

24. ULLOA, A. DE (1944). *Noticeas Americanas. Entretenimiento Físico-Histórico sobre la América Meridional y la Septentrional Oriental.*

25. VIRCHOW, R. (1890). La Craniologie Americaine, in *Report of the 7th International Congress of Americanists*, 1888, pp. 250–262.

26. WILSON, D. (1876). *Prehistoric Man; Researches into the Origin of Civilization in the Old and New World*. 3rd ed., Vol. 2. London: Macmillan.

27. WISSLER, C. (1917). *The American Indian*. New York: McMurtrie.

SECTION II: *THE ESKIMO*

1. KROEBER, A. L. (1948). *Anthropology*. New York: Harcourt, Brace and Company.

2. LAUGHLIN, W. S. (1951). A New View of the History of the Aleutians, *Arctic*, Vol. 4, No. 84.

3. LOWIE, R. H. (1952). The Heterogeneity of Marginal Cultures, *Selected Papers of the 29th International Congress of Americanists*. Chicago: Univ. Chicago Press, pp. 1–7.
4. SAPIR, E. (1916). Time Perspective in Aboriginal American Cultures: a Study in Method, *Memoirs of the Canada Department of Mines, Geological Survey*, No. 90, Anthropological Series No. 13.

SECTION III: *THE NORTHERN HUNTERS*

1. BIDNEY, D. (1953). *Theoretical Anthropology*. New York: Columbia Univ. Press.
2. DORSON, R. M. (1952). *Bloodstoppers and Bearwalkers: Folk Traditions of the Upper Peninsula*. Cambridge, Mass.: Harvard Univ. Press.
3. GREENBERG, J. H. (1954). Concerning Inferences from Linguistic to Non-Linguistic Data, in *Language in Culture*, Hoijer, H. (ed.). Chicago: Univ. Chicago Press.
4. HALLOWELL, A. I. (1934). Some Empirical Aspects of Northern Saulteaux Religion, *American Anthropologist*, **36**, 389–404.
5. ——— (1955). *Culture and Experience*. Philadelphia: Univ. Pennsylvania Press.
6. LOVEJOY, A. O., and BOAS, G. (1935). *Primitivism and Related Ideas in Antiquity*. Baltimore: Johns Hopkins Press.
7. RADIN, P. (1914). Religion of the North American Indians, *Journal of American Folklore*, **27**, 335–373.
8. REDFIELD, R. F. (1952). The Primitive World View, *Proceedings of the American Philosophical Society*, **96**, 30–36.
9. THOMPSON, S. (1946). *The Folktale*. New York: Dryden Press.

SECTION V: *THE NORTHWEST COAST*

1. BENEDICT, R. (1934). *Patterns of Culture*. Boston: Houghton Mifflin.
2. BOAS, F. (1897). The Social Organization and Secret Societies of the Kwakiutl Indians, *Report of the U.S. National Museum for 1895*, pp. 311–738.
3. ——— (1936). Die Individualität Primitiver Kulturen, in *Reine und angewandet Soziologie* (Volume in honor of Tönnies). Leipzig.

SECTION VI: *CALIFORNIA*

1. ERICKSON, O. (1943). Observations on the Yurok: Childhood and World Image, *University of California Publications in American Archaeology and Ethnology*, Vol. 35, No. 10.
2. FORDE, C. (1931). Ethnography of the Yuma Indians, *University of California Publications in American Archaeology and Ethnology*, Vol. 28.

3. KROEBER, A. L. (1926). Law of the Yurok Indians, *Atti del XXII Congresso Internazionale degli Americanisti,* Vol. 2.

4. SPOTT, R., and KROEBER, A. L. (1942). Yurok Narratives, *University of California Publications in American Archaeology and Ethnology,* Vol. 35, No. 9.

5. WALLACE, J. (1946). *Hupa Education: A Study in Primitive Socialization and Personality Development.* Unpublished Ph.D. thesis, University of California, Berkeley.

6. WATERMAN, T. T. (1920). Yurok Geography, *University of California Publications in American Archaeology and Ethnology,* Vol. 18, No. 5.

SECTION VII: *THE SOUTHWEST*

1. BARTLETT, R. (1856). *Personal Narrative of the Explorations and Incidents in Texas, New Mexico, California, Sonora, Chihuahua, etc.,* 2 vols. New York.

2. BEALS, R. (1932). The Comparative Ethnology of Northern Mexico before 1750, *Ibero-Americana,* **2,** 93–225.

3. ———— (1943). Northern Mexico and the Southwest (El Norte de México y el Sur de Estados Unidos), *Tercera Reunión de Mesa Redonda sobre Problemas Anthropológicas de México y Central America.*

4. BITTLE, W. E. (1959). Unpublished Kiowa Apache Field Notes.

5. KROEBER, A. L. (1928). Native Culture of the Southwest, *University of California Publications in American Archaeology and Ethnology,* Vol. 23.

6. MCALLISTER, J. (1935). *Kiowa Apache Social Organization.* Unpublished Ph.D. thesis, University of Chicago.

7. ———— (1949). Kiowa Apache Tales, in Boatright, M. C., (ed.), *The Sky is My Tipi,* pp. 1–141. Dallas.

8. ———— (1955). Kiowa Apache Social Organization, in *Social Anthropology of North American Tribes,* 2nd ed. Eggan, F. (ed.) pp. 99–169. Chicago: Univ. Chicago Press.

9. YOUNG, R. W., and MORGAN, W. (1943). The Navaho Languages, *Publication of United States Indian Service, Educational Division.*

SECTION VIII: *THE PLAINS*

1. BATTEY, T. C. (1876). *The Life and Adventures of a Quaker among the Indians.* Boston.

2. KROEBER, A. L. (1939). Culture and Natural Areas of Native North America, *University of California Publications in American Archaeology and Ethnology,* Vol. 38.

3. MOONEY, J. (1900). Calendar History of the Kiowa Indians, *17th Annual Report, Bureau of American Ethnology*, Part I.

4. MURDOCK, G. P. (1951). South American Culture Areas, *Southwestern Journal of Anthropology*, **7**, 415–436.

5. SAPIR, E. (1916). Time Perspective in Aboriginal American Culture, *Memoirs of the Canada Department of Mines, Geological Survey*, No. 90, Anthropological Series 13.

6. SCOTT, H. L. (1911). Notes on the Kado or Sun Dance of the Kiowa, *American Anthropologist* (N. S.), **13**, 345–379.

7. TABEAU, P. (1939). *Tabeau's Narrative of Liosel's Expedition to the Upper Missouri*. Abel, A. H. (ed.). Norman: Univ. of Okla. Press.

8. THOMPSON, D. (1916). David Thompson's Narrative of His Explorations in Western America, 1784–1812, Tyrell, J. B. (ed.). *Champlain Social Publication No. 12*.

9. WEDEL, W. (1940). Culture Sequence in the Central Great Plains, *Smithsonian Miscellaneous Collection*, **100**, 291–352.

SECTION IX: *EASTERN AGRICULTURISTS*

1. DE KERLEREC (1704). *Rapport du Chevalier de Kerlerec in Compte Rendu du Congres International des Americanistes, 15eme Session*, Vol. 1.

2. DUMONT DE MONTIGNY (ed. *Le Mascrier*) (1753). *Memoires Historiques sur la Louisiane*. 2 vols. Paris.

3. DU PRATZ, LE PAGE (1758), *Histoire de la Louisiana*, Vols. 1, 2, 3.

4. FRENCH (1851). *Historical Collections of Louisiana.*

5. MARGRY, P. (ed.) (1877–1886). *Decouvertes et Establissements des Francais dans l'quest et dans le Sud de l'Amerique*. Septentrionale (1614–1754), Paris.

6. THWAITES, R. G. (ed.) (1896–1901). *The Jesuit Relations and Allied Documents*. 73 vols. Cleveland: Burrows.

7. WRONG, G. M. (ed.) (1939). The Long Journey to the Country of the Hurons, *Publications of the Champlain Society*, Vol. 25.

SECTION X: *THE INDIAN IN THE MODERN WORLD*

1. ANONYMOUS (1831). *American State Papers*. Class II, Bureau of Indian Affairs, Vol. 1, Gales and Seaton, Washington, D.C.

2. ANONYMOUS (1881). Congressional Record, Vol. 11. 46th Congress, 3rd Session.

3. ANONYMOUS (1908). The Genesis of the Proclamation of 1763. *Historical Collections*, Michigan Pioneer and Historical Society, Vol. 36.

4. BRINTON, C. (1953). *The Shaping of the Modern Mind*. New York: New York Library.

5. EKIRCH, A. A. (1944). *The Idea of Progress in America, 1815–1860.* New York: Columbia Univ. Press.

6. HAUGHT, B. F. (1934). Mental Growth of the Southwestern Indians, *Journal of Applied Psychology,* **18**, 137–42.

7. KELLER, W. W. *et. al.* (1961). Report to the Secretary of the Interior by the Task Force on Indian Affairs, Bureau of Indian Affairs, Washington, D.C. (mimeographed).

8. PEARCE, R. H. (1953). *The Savages of America.* Baltimore: Johns Hopkins Press.

9. RICHARDSON, J. D. (ed.). *A Compilation of the Messages and Papers of Presidents, 1789–1897,* Vol. 2. U.S. Gov. Printing Office.

10. ROYCE, C. C. (1899). *Indian Land Cessions in the United States.* 18th Annual Report of the Bureau of American Ethnology, Part 2.

11. SIMMONS, L. (ed.) (1942). *Sun Chief.* New Haven, Conn.: Yale Univ. Press.

12. SIMPSON, L. B. (1929). *The Encomienda in New Spain, Forced Native Labor in the Spanish Colonies, 1492–1550.* Berkeley: Univ. California Press.

13. UNDERHILL, R. (1953). *Red Man's America.* Chicago: Univ. Chicago Press.

14. WRAXALL, P. (1915). *Wraxall Abridgement of the New York Indian Records, 1768–1851.* Harvard Historical Studies, No. 21.

15. YOUNG, A. (ed.) (1841). "*Letters of Edward Winslow*" *Chronicles of the Pilgrim Fathers of the Colony of Plymouth from 1602–1625.* Boston: Little, Brown.

16. ——— (1846). *Chronicles of the First Planters of the Colony of Massachusetts Bay, 1623–1636.* Boston: Little, Brown.

ADDITIONAL READINGS LIST

SECTION I: *INTRODUCTION*

ALEXANDER, B. (1964). *North American Mythology.* New York: Cooper Square Publishers.

COLLIER, D. (1959). *Indian Art of the Americas.* Chicago: Chicago Natural History Museum.

COLLIER, J. (1947). *Indians of the Americas.* New York: Mentor Books.

DEUEL, T. (1958). American Indian Ways of Life, Springfield, Ill.: Illinois State Museum. Story of Illinois Series, No. 9.

DRIVER, H. E. (1961). *Indians of North America.* Chicago: Univ. Chicago Press.

———— (1964). *The Americas on the Eve of Discovery.* Englewood Cliffs, N.J.: Prentice-Hall.

EDMONSON, M. S. (1958). Status Terminology and the Social Structure of North American Indians, MAES.* New York: J. J. Augustin.

EGGAN, F. (ed.) (1955). *Social Anthropology of North American Tribes.* 2nd ed. Chicago: Univ. Chicago Press.

HAGAN, W. T. (1961). *American Indians.* Chicago: Univ. Chicago Press.

HODGE, F. W. (ed.) (1907–1910). Handbook of American Indians North of Mexico, BBAE, Vol. 30, 2 vols.

HOIJER, H. (1946). Linguistic Structures of Native America, VFPA, Vol. 6.

HYMES, D. (ed.) (1964). *Language in Culture and Society: A Reader in Linguistics and Anthropology.* New York: Harper & Row.

JENNINGS, J. E., and NORBECK, E. (eds.) (1964). *Prehistoric Man in the New World.* Chicago: Univ. Chicago Press.

KROEBER, A. L. (1939). Cultural and Natural Areas of Native North America, UCP, Vol. 38.

* Abbreviations are explained on p. 715.

699

LaFarge, O. (1956). *A Pictorial History of the American Indian*. New York: Crown.

Martin, P. S., Quimby, G. I., and Collier, D. (1947). *Indians before Columbus*. Chicago: Univ. Chicago Press.

Murdock, G. P. (1960). *Ethnographic Bibliography of North America*. Behavior Science Bibliographies, *Human Relations Area Files*, 3rd ed. New Haven, Conn.

Powell, J. W. (1891). Indian Linguistic Families of America North of Mexico, ARBAE, Vol. 7, 7–142.

Sapir, E. (1916). Time Perspective in Aboriginal American Culture, MCDM, No. 90.

Schoolcraft, H. R. (1853–1857). *Information Respecting the History, Condition and Prospects of the Indian Tribes of the United States*. Philadelphia: Lippincott.

Spencer, R. F., Jennings, J. D. *et al.* (1965). *The Native Americans*. New York: Harper & Row.

Stirling, M. W., *et al.* (1955) *Indians of the Americas*. Washington, D.C.: National Geographic Society.

Swanton, J. R. (1946). The Indian Tribes of North America, BBAE, Vol. 145.

Tschopik, H. (1952). *Indians of North America*. New York: American Museum of Natural History.

Underhill, R. M. (1953). *Red Man's America*. Chicago: Univ. Chicago Press.

———— (1965). *Red Man's Religion*. Chicago: Univ. Chicago Press.

Wauchope, R. (1962). *Lost Tribes and Sunken Continents*. Chicago: Univ. Chicago Press.

Willey, G. R., and Phillips, P. (1958). *Method and Theory in American Archaeology*. Chicago: Univ. Chicago Press.

Wissler, C. (1940). *Indians of the United States*. New York: Doubleday.
———— (1950). *The American Indian*, 3rd ed. New York: Peter Smith.

Wormington, H. M. (1957). Ancient Man in North America, Denver Museum of Natural History, Popular Series No. 4, 4th ed.

SECTION II: *THE ESKIMO*

Birket-Smith, K. (1924). Ethnography of the Egesminde District, MG, Vol. 66. Copenhagen.

———— (1929). The Caribou Eskimos, RFTE, Report 5. Copenhagen.

———— (1953). The Chugach Eskimo, National-musets Skrifter. Ethnografisk-Raekke, Vol. 6, Copenhagen: National Museum.

———— (1958). The Eskimos, 2nd ed. New York: Humanities Press.

Boas, F. (1888). The Central Eskimo, ARBAE, Vol. 6, 390–669.

———— (1901–1907). The Eskimo of Baffin Land and Hudson Bay, BAMNH, Vol. 15.

CARPENTER, E., VAELEY, F., and FLAHERTY, R. (1959). *Eskimo.* Exploration Series No. 9. Toronto: Univ. Toronto Press.

COLLINS, H. B. (1954). Arctic Area, Program of the History of American Indigenous Period, Vol. 1, No. 2. Comision de Historia, Instituto Panamericano de Geografia Historia, Mexico, D.F.

DAMAS, D. (1963). Igluligmiut Kinship and Local Groupings: A Structural Approach, BNMC, No. 196, Anthropological Series No. 64.

HARPER, F. (1964). Caribou Eskimos of the Upper Kazan River, Keewatin, University of Kansas Museum of Natural History, Miscellaneous Publications No. 36.

HAWKES, M. W. (1916). The Labrador Eskimo, MCDM, Vol. 91.

HUGHES, C. C. (1960). *An Eskimo Village in the Modern World.* Ithaca: Cornell Univ. Press.

JENNÈSS, D. (1922). The Life of the Copper Eskimo, RCAE, Vol. 12.

———— (1928). *The People of the Twilight.* Chicago: Univ. Chicago Press.

KROEBER, A. L. (1899). The Eskimo of Smith Sound, BAMNH, Vol. 12, 265–327.

LANTIS, M. (1946). The Social Culture of the Nunivak Eskimo, TAPS, Vol. 35, 151–323.

———— (1960). Eskimo Childhood and Interpersonal Relationships; Nunivak Biographies and Geneologies, MAES, Seattle: Univ. Washington Press.

MATHIASSEN, T. (1928). Material Culture of the Iglulik Eskimos, RFTE, Vol. 6.

MURDOCH, J. (1892). Ethnological Results of the Point Barrow Expedition, ARBAE, Vol. 9, 3–441.

NELSON, E. W. (1899). The Eskimo about Bering Strait, ARBAE, Vol. 18, 3–518.

OSWALT, W. (1963). *Napaskiak: An Alaskan Eskimo Community.* Tucson: Univ. Arizona Press.

RAINEY, F. (1947). The Whale Hunters of Tigara, APAM, Vol. 41, 231–283.

RASMUSSEN, K. (1908). *The People of the Polar North.* London: Paul, Trench, Trubner.

———— (1929). Intellectual Culture of the Iglulik Eskimos, RFTE, Vol. 7, No. 1.

———— (1930). Observations on the Intellectual Culture of the Caribou Eskimos, RFTE, Vol. 7, No. 2.

———— (1931). The Netsilik Eskimos, RFTE, Vol. 8, Nos. 1, 2.

———— (1932). Intellectual Culture of the Copper Eskimo, RCAE, Vol. 16.

SPENCER, R. F. (1959). The North Alaskan Eskimo: A Study in Ecology and Society, BBAE, No. 171.

STEENSBY, H. P. (1910). Contributions to the Ethnology and Anthropo-geography of the Polar Eskimos, MG, Vol. 34, 253–405.
THALBITZER, W. (1911). Eskimo, BBAE, Vol. 40, 967–1069.
VANSTONE, J. W. (1962). *Point Hope: An Eskimo Village in Transition.* American Ethnological Society (unnumbered series). Seattle: University of Washington Press.
WEYER, E. M. (1932). *The Eskimo.* New Haven: Yale Univ. Press.

SECTION III: *THE NORTHERN HUNTERS*

BALIKCI, A. (1965). Vunta Kutchin Social Change: A Study of People of Old Crow, Yukon Territory, NCRC, Department of Northern Affairs and Natural Resources. Ottawa.
BARNOUW, V. (1950). Acculturation and Personality Among the Wisconsin Chippewa, MAAA, No. 72.
BIRKET-SMITH, K. (1930). Contribution to Chippewyan Ethnology, RFTE, Vol. 5.
———, and DELAGUNA, F. (1938). *The Eyak Indians of the Copper River Delta.* Copenhagen: Levin and Munskgaard.
BUCKLEY, H., KEW, J. E. M., and HAWLEY, J. B. (1963). The Indians and Metis of Northern Saskatchewan: A Report on Economic and Social Development, Center for Community Studies, Saskatoon.
CALLENDER, C. (1962). Social Organization of the Central Algonkian Indians, PAMPM, No. 7.
COHEN, R. (1962). An Anthropological Survey of Communities in the Mackenzie-Slave Lake Region of Canada, NCRC, No. 62. Department of Northern Affairs and Natural Resources. Ottawa.
DENSMORE, F. (1926). Chippewa Customs, BBAE, No. 86.
DUNNING, R. W. (1959). *Social and Economic Change Among the Northern Ojibwa.* Toronto: Univ. Toronto Press.
GODDARD, P. E. (1916). The Beaver Indians, APAM, Vol. 10, 201–293.
HELM, J. (1961). The Lynx Point People: The Dynamics of a Northern Athapaskan Band, BNMC, No. 176, Anthropological Series No. 53.
———, and LURIE, N. O. (1961). The Subsistence Economy of the Dogrib Indians of Lac La Nartre in the Mackenzie District of the Northwest Territories, NCRC, Department of Northern Affairs and Natural Resources. Ottawa.
HONIGMANN, J. J. (1949). Culture and Ethos of Kaska Society, YUPA, Vol. 40.
——— (1954). The Kaska Indians: An Ethnographic Reconstruction, YUPA, Vol. 51.
——— (1956). The Attawapiskat Swampy Cree, UAAP, Vol. 5, 23–82.
——— (1961). Foodways in a Muskeg Community: An Anthropological

Report on the Attawapiskat Indians, NCRC, Department of Northern Affairs and National Resources, Ottawa.

HOWLEY, J. P. (1915). *The Beothucks or Red Indians.* Cambridge: Harvard Univ. Press.

JENNESS, D. (1935). The Ojibwa Indians of Parry Island, BCDM, Vol. 78.

———— (1937). The Sekani Indians of British Columbia, BCDM, Vol. 84.

———— (1938). The Sarcee Indians of Alberta, BCDM, Vol. 90.

KINIETZ, W. V. (1947). Chippewa Village: The Story of Katikitegon, BCIS, No. 25.

LANDES, R. (1937). Ojibwa Sociology, CUCA, Vol. 29. New York: Columbia Univ. Press.

———— (1938). The Ojibwa Woman, CUCA, Vol. 31. New York: Columbia Univ. Press.

LEACOCK, E. (1954). The Montagnais "Hunting Territory" and the Fur Trade, MAAA, Vol. 78.

McGEE, J. T. (1961). Cultural Stability and Change Among the Montagnais Indians of the Lake Melville Region of Labrador, CUAS, No. 19. Washington, D.C.: Catholic Univ. of America Press.

McKENNAN, R. A. (1959). The Upper Tanana Indians, YUPA, Vol. 55.

MELCHING, W. H. (1958–59). The Malecite Indians with Notes on the Micmacs, Anthro., Vols. 7, 8.

OSGOOD, C. (1936). Contributions to the Ethnography of the Kutchin, YUPA, Vol. 14.

———— (1937). The Ethnography of the Tanaina, YUPA, Vol. 16.

———— (1958). Ingalik Social Culture, YUPA, Vol. 53.

———— (1959). Ingalik Mental Culture, YUPA, Vol. 56.

RADIN, P. (1916). The Winnebago Tribe, ARBAE, Vol. 37, 33–550.

———— (1950). Winnebago Culture as Described by Themselves, MIJL, Vol. 3.

SLOBODIN, R. (1962). Band Organization of the Peel River Kutchin, BNMC, Vol. 179, Series No. 55.

SPECK, F. G. (1935). *Naskapi.* Norman: Univ. Oklahoma Press.

———— (1940). *Penobscot Man; the Life of a Forest Tribe in Maine.* Philadelphia: Univ. of Pennsylvania Press.

WALLIS, W. D., and WALLIS, R. S. (1955). *The Micmac Indians of Eastern Canada.* Minneapolis: Univ. Minnesota Press.

———— (1957). The Malecite Indians of New Brunswick, BNMC, Vol. 148.

SECTION IV: *THE BASIN-PLATEAU*

BARRETT, S. A. (1910). The Material Culture of the Klamath Lake and Modoc Indians of Northeastern California and Southern Oregon, UCP, Vol. 5, 239–60.

BARRETT, S. A. (1917). The Washo Indians, BPMCM, Vol. 2, 1–52.

CLINE, W., *et al.* (1938). The Sinkaietk or Southern Okanagon of Washington, GSA, Vol. 5.

CRESSMAN, L. S. (1962). *The Sandal and the Cave: The Indians of Oregon.* Portland, Ore.: Beaver Books.

GATSCHET, A. S. (1890). The Klamath Indians of Southwestern Oregon, CNAE, 2 vols.

JENNINGS, J. D. (1957). Danger Cave, MSAA, Vol. 14.

KELLY, I. T. (1932). Ethnography of the Surprise Valley Paiute, UCP, Vol. 31, 67–210.

LOWIE, R. H. (1908). The Northern Shoshone, APAM, Vol. 2, 169–306.

———— (1924). Notes on Shoshonean Ethnography, APAM, Vol. 20, 185–314.

———— (1939). Ethnographic Notes on the Washo, UCP, Vol. 36, 301–332.

MURPHY, R. F., and MURPHY, Y. (1960). Shoshone-Bannock Subsistence and Society, AR, Vol. 16, No. 7.

RAY, V. F. (1932). The Sanpoil and Nespelem, UWPA, Vol. 5.

———— (1938). Lower Chinook Ethnographic Notes, UWPA, Vol. 7, 29–165.

SHIMKIN, D. B. (1947). Wind River Shoshone Ethnography, AR, Vol. 5, 245–288.

SPIER, L. (1930). Klamath Ethnography, UCP, Vol. 30.

———— and SPIER, E. (1930). Wishram Ethnography, UWPA, Vol. 3, 151–300.

SPINDEN, H. J. (1908). The Nez Percé Indians, MAAA, Vol. 2, 165–274.

STERN, B. J. (1934). The Lummi Indians of Northwest Washington, CUCA, Vol. 17.

STEWARD, J. H. (1933). Ethnography of the Owens Valley Paiute, UCP, Vol. 33, 233–350.

———— (1938). Basin Plateau, Socio-Political Groups, BBAE, No. 120.

———— (1941). Nevada Shoshone, AR, Vol. 4, 209–259.

STEWART, O. C. (1939). Northern Paiute Bands, UCP, Vol. 2, No. 3, 127–149.

———— (1941). Northern Paiute, AR, Vol. 4, 361–446.

TEIT, J. A. (1900). The Thompson Indians, MAMNH, Vol. 2, 163–392.

————(1906). The Lillooet Indians, MAMNH, Vol. 4, 193–300.

———— (1909). The Shuswap, MAMNH, Vol. 4, 447–758.

———— (1928). The Middle Columbia Salish, UWPA, Vol. 2, 98–108.

———— (1930). The Salishan Tribes of the Western Plateau, ARBAE, Vol. 45, 295–396.

Turney-High, H. H. (1937). The Flathead Indians of Montana, MAAA, Vol. 48.

———— (1941). Ethnography of the Kutenai, MAAA, Vol. 56.

Whiting, B. B. (1950). Paiute Sorcery, VFPA, Vol. 15.

SECTION V: *THE NORTHWEST COAST*

Barnett, H. G. (1955). *The Coast Salish of British Columbia.* Eugene: Univ. Oregon Press.

———— (1957). *Indian Shakers.* Carbondale: Univ. So. Illinois Press.

Boas, F. (1895). Social Organization and the Secret Societies of the Kwakiutl Indians, RUSNM, 1895, 311–738.

———— (1909). The Kwakiutl of Vancouver Island, MAMNH, Vol. 8, 307–515.

———— (1916). Tsimshian Mythology, ARBAE, Vol. 31, 29–979.

———— (1921). Ethnology of the Kwakiutl, ARBAE, Vol. 35, 43–1481.

Codere, H. (1950). Fighting with Property, MAES, No. 18.

Colson, E. (1953). *The Makah Indians.* Minneapolis: Univ. Minnesota Press.

de Laguna, F. (1960). The Story of a Tlingit Community, BBAE, Vol. 172.

Drucker, P. (1951). The Northern and Central Nootkan Tribes, BBAE, Vol. 144.

———— (1955). *Indians of the Northwest Coast.* New York: McGraw-Hill.

———— (1958). The Native Brotherhoods: Modern Intertribal Organizations on the Northwest Coast, BBAE, Vol. 168.

———— (1965). *Cultures of the North Pacific Coast.* San Francisco: Chandler.

Ford, C. S. (1941). *Smoke from Their Fires.* New Haven: Yale Univ. Press.

Garfield, V. E. (1939). Tsimshian Clan and Society, UWPA, Vol. 7, 167–349.

———— *et al.* (1951). The Tsimshian: Their Arts and Music. PAES, No. 18.

Gunther, E. (1927). Klallom Ethnography, UWPA, Vol. 1, No. 5, 171–314.

Haeberlin, H. K. and Gunther, E. (1930). The Indians of Puget Sound, UWPA, Vol. 4.

Hawthorn, H. B., Belshaw, C. S., and Jamieson, S. M. (1958). *The Indians of British Columbia.* Berkeley: Univ. California Press.

Inverarity, R. B. (1950). *Art of the Northwest Coast Indians.* Berkeley: Univ. California Press.

Krause, A. (1956). The Tlingit Indians, MAES, Vol. 26, Seattle.

McIllwraith, T. F. (1948). *The Bella Coola Indians.* 2 vols. Toronto: Univ. Toronto Press.

Olson, R. L. (1936). The Quinault Indians, UWPA, Vol. 6, No. 1,

RAY, V. F. (1938). Lower Chinook Ethnographic Notes, UWPA, Vol. 7, 29–165.

SMITH, M. W. (1940). The Puyallup-Nisqually, CUCA, Vol. 32.

SWANTON, J. R. (1909). Contributions to the Ethnology of the Haida, MAMNH, Vol. 8.

SECTION VI: *CALIFORNIA*

BARRETT, S. A., and GIFFORD, E. W. (1933). Miwok Material Culture, BPMCM, Vol. 2, 117–376.

BAUMHOFF, M. A. (1958). California Athabascan Groups, AR, Vol. 16, 157–237.

BEALS, R. L. (1933). Ethnology of Nisenan, UCP, Vol. 31, 335–410.

DIXON, R. B. (1905). The Northern Maidu, BAMNH, Vol. 17, 119–346.

———— (1907). The Shasta, BAMNH, Vol. 17.

———— (1911). Maidu, BBAE, Vol. 40, 679–734.

DIXON, R. B. and KROEBER, A. L. (1919). Linguistic Families of California, UCP, Vol. 16, 47–118.

DEVEREUX, G. (1961). Mohave Ethnopsychiatry, BBAE, Vol. 175.

DRIVER, H. E. (1936). Wappo Ethnography, UCP, Vol. 36, 179–220.

DRUCKER, P. (1936). The Tolowa and Their Southwest Oregon Kin, UCP, Vol. 36, 221–300.

DuBois, C. (1935). Wintu Ethnography, UCP, Vol. 36.

FOSTER, G. M. (1944). A Summary of Yuka Culture, AR, Vol. 5, 155–244.

GARTH, T. R. (1953). Atsugewi Ethnography, AR, Vol. 14, 123–212.

GAYTON, A. H. (1948). Northern Foothills Yokuts and Western Mono, AR, Vol. 10, 143–302.

———— (1948). Tulare Lake, Southern Valley, and Central Foothills Yokuts, AR, Vol. 10.

GIFFORD, E. W. (1926). Clear Lake Pomo Society, UCP, Vol. 18, 287–390.

———— (1931). The Kamia of Imperial Valley, BBAE, Vol. 97.

———— (1932). The Northfork Mono, UCP, Vol. 31, 15–65.

———— (1939). The Coast Yuki, A, Vol. 34, 292–375.

GODDARD, P. E. (1903). Life and Culture of the Hupa, UCP, Vol. 1.

GOLDSCHMIDT, W. (1951). Nomlaki Ethnography, UCP, Vol. 42, 303–443.

HEIZER, R. F., and WHIPPLE, M. A. (1951). *The California Indians: A Source Book*. Berkeley: Univ. California Press.

————, DAVIS, J. T., KROEBER, A. L., and ELSASSER, A. B. (1963). *Aboriginal California: Three Studies in Cultural History*. Berkeley: Univ. California Press.

JOHNSTON, B. (1962). California's Gabrielino Indians, PHAPF, Vol. 8.

KROEBER, A. L. (1908). Ethnography of the Cahuilla Indians, UCP, Vol. 8, 29–68.

———— (1925). Handbook of the Indians of California, ARBAE, Vol. 78.

———— (1932). The Patwin and Their Neighbors, UCP, Vol. 29, 253–364.

MASON, J. A. (1912). The Ethnology of the Salinan Indians, UCP, Vol. 10, 97–240.

MEIGS, P. (1939). The Kiliwa Indians of Lower California, IA, Vol. 15.

MERRIAM, C. H. (1955). *Studies of California Indians.* Berkeley: Univ. California Press.

NOMLAND, G. A. (1938). Bear River Ethnography, AR, Vol. 2, 91–123.

RAY, V. F. (1963). *Primitive Pragmatists: The Modoc Indians of Northern California.* Seattle: Univ. Washington Press.

SPARKMAN, P. S. (1908). The Culture of the Luiseno Indians, UCP, Vol. 8, 187–234.

VOEGELIN, E. W. (1938). Tubatulabal Ethnography, AR, Vol. 2.

SECTION VII: *THE SOUTHWEST*

ABERLE, D. F. (1965). The Peyote Religion Among the Navaho, VFPA, Vol. 42.

ABERLE, S. D. (1948). The Pueblo Indians of New Mexico, MAAA, Vol. 33.

ADAMS, W. Y. (1963). Shonto: A Study of the Role of the Trader in a Modern Navaho Community, BBAE, Vol. 188.

AMSDEN, C. A. (1949). *Navaho Weaving.* Albuquerque: Univ. New Mexico Press.

BEAGLEHOLE, E. (1935). Hopi of the Second Mesa, MAAA, Vol. 44.

———— (1937). Notes on the Hopi Economic Life, YUPA, Vol. 15.

BEALS, R. L. (1945). The Contemporary Culture of the Cahita Indians, ARBAE, Vol. 142.

BELLAH, R. N. (1952). *Apache Kinship Systems.* Cambridge: Harvard Univ. Press.

BENNETT, W. C., and ZINGG, R. M. (1935). *The Tarahumara: An Inland Tribe of Northern Mexico.* Chicago: Univ. Chicago Press.

BUNZEL, R. L. (1929). The Pueblo Potter, CUCA, Vol. 8.

———— (1930). An Introduction to Zuni Ceremonialism, ARBAE, Vol. 47, 467–544.

———— (1930). Zuni Katcinas, ARBAE, Vol. 47, 837–1086.

CASTETTER, E. F., and OPLER, M. E. (1942). *Pima and Papago Indian Agriculture.* Albuquerque: Univ. New Mexico Press.

CASTETTER, E. F., and BELL, W. H. (1951). *Yuman Indian Agriculture.* Albuquerque: Univ. New Mexico Press.

DiPeso, C. C. (1956). The Upper Pima of San Cayetano del Tumacacori, PAF, No. 7.

Dozier, E. P. (1954). The Hopi-Tewa of Arizona, UCP, Vol. 44, 259–376.

Eggan, F. (1950). *Social Organization of the Western Pueblos*. Chicago: Univ. Chicago Press.

Ellis, F. H. (1964). A Reconstruction of the Basic Jemez Pattern of Social Organization with Comparison to Other Tanoan Social Structures, UNMPA, No. 11.

Ezell, P. H. (1961). The Hispanic Acculturation of the Gila River Pimas, MAAA, Vol. 90.

Forbes, J. D. (1960). *Apache, Navaho, and Spaniard*. Norman: Univ. Oklahoma Press.

Forde, C. D. (1931). Ethnography of the Yuma Indians, UCP, Vol. 28, 83–278.

Gifford, E. W. (1932). The Southeastern Yavapai, UCP, Vol. 29, 177–252.

———— (1933). The Cocopa, UCP, Vol. 31, 257–334.

———— (1936). Northeastern and Western Yavapai, UCP, Vol. 34, 247–354.

Goldfrank, E. S. (1927). The Social and Ceremonial Organization of Cochiti, MAAA, Vol. 33.

Goodwin, G. (1942). *The Social Organization of the Western Apache.* Chicago: Univ. Chicago Press.

Haury, E. W. (1950). *The Stratigraphy and Archaeology of Ventana Cave.* Albuquerque: Univ. New Mexico Press.

Johnson, J. B. (1950). The Opata, UNMPA, Vol. 6.

Joseph, A., Spicer, R., and Chesky, J. (1949). *The Desert People*. Chicago: Univ. Chicago Press.

Kluckhohn, C., and Leighton, C. (1946). *The Navaho*. Cambridge: Harvard Univ. Press.

Kroeber, A. L. (1931). The Seri, SWMP, Vol. 6, 1–60.

———— (1935). Walapai Ethnography, MAAA, Vol. 42.

Lange, C. H. (1959). *Cochiti*. Austin: Univ. Texas Press.

Leighton, A. H., and Leighton, D. C. (1944). *The Navaho Door*. Cambridge: Harvard Univ. Press.

Leighton, D. C., and Kluckhohn, C. (1947). *Children of the People*. Cambridge: Harvard Univ. Press.

McCombe, L. E., Vogt, E. Z., and Kluckhohn, C. (1951). *Navaho Means People*. Cambridge: Harvard Univ. Press.

McGee, W. J. (1898). The Seri Indians, ARBAE, Vol. 17, 9–298.

Opler, M. E. (1941). *An Apache Life-Way: The Economic, Social, and Religious Institutions of the Chiricahua Indians*. Chicago: Univ. Chicago Press.

———— (1946). Childhood and Youth in Jicarilla Apache Society, PHAPF, Vol. 5.

PARSONS, E. C. (1925). *The Pueblo of Jemez.* New Haven: Yale Univ. Press.

———— (1929). The Social Organization of the Tewa of New Mexico, MAAA, Vol. 36.

———— (1930). Isleta, ARBAE, Vol. 47, 193–466.

———— (1936). Taos Pueblo, GSA, vol. 2.

———— (1939). *Pueblo Indian Religion.* 2 vols. Chicago: Univ. Chicago Press.

REICHARD, G. A. (1928). Social Life of the Navaho Indians, CUCA, Vol. 7.

———— (1950). *Navaho Religion: A Study of Symbolism.* 2 vols. Bollingen Series. New York: Pantheon.

ROBERTS, J. M. (1956). Zuni Daily Life, NLAUN, Vol. 3.

RUSSELL, F. (1908). The Pima Indians, ARBAE, Vol. 26, 3–390.

SASAKI, T. T. (1960). *Fruitland, New Mexico: A Navaho Community in Transition.* Ithaca: Cornell University Press.

SMITHSON, C. L. (1959). The Havasupai Woman, APUU, Vol. 38.

SONNICHSEN, C. L. (1958). *The Mescalero Apaches.* Norman: Univ. Oklahoma Press.

SPICER, E. H. (1940). *Pascua: A Yaqui Village in Arizona.* Chicago: Univ. Chicago Press.

———— (1954). Potam: A Yaqui Village in Sonora, MAAA, Vol. 77.

———— (1962). *Cycles of Conquest: The Impact of Spain, Mexico, and the United States on the Indians of the Southwest.* Tucson: Univ. Arizona Press.

SPIER, L. (1928). Havasupi Ethnography, APAM, Vol. 29, 83–392.

———— (1933). *Yuman Tribes of the Gila River.* Chicago: Univ. Chicago Press.

STEVENSON, M. C. (1904). The Zuni Indians, ARBAE, Vol. 23.

THOMPSON, L. (1950). *Culture in Crisis: A Study of the Hopi Indians.* New York: Harper & Row.

————, and JOSEPH, A. (1945). *The Hopi Way.* Chicago: Univ. Chicago Press.

TITIEV, M. (1944). Old Oraibi, PMP, Vol. 22, 1–277.

UNDERHILL, R. M. (1939). Social Organization of the Papago Indians, CUCA, Vol. 30.

———— (1946). *Papago Indian Religion.* New York: Columbia Univ. Press.

———— (1956). *The Navahos.* Norman: Univ. Oklahoma Press.

VOGT, E. Z. (1951). Navaho Veterans, PMP, Vol. 41.

WHITE, L. A. (1930). The Acoma Indians, ARBAE, Vol. 47, 17–192.

———— (1932). The Pueblo of San Felipe, MAAA, Vol. 33.

———— (1935). The Pueblo of Santo Domingo, MAAA, Vol. 43.

WHITE, L. A. (1942). The Pueblo of Santa Ana, MAAA, Vol. 40.
——— (1962). The Pueblo of Sia, New Mexico, BBAE, Vol. 184.
WILSON, H. C. (1964). Jicarilla Apache Political and Economic Structures, UCP, Vol. 48, No. 4.

SECTION VIII: *THE PLAINS*

ANDRIST, R. K. (1964). *The Long Death: The Last Days of the Plains Indians.* New York: Macmillan.
BOWERS, A. W. (1950). *Mandan Social and Ceremonial Organization.* Chicago: Univ. Chicago Press.
DENIG, E. T. and EWERS, J. C. (eds.). (1961). *Five Indian Tribes of the Upper Missouri: Sioux, Arickaras, Assiniboines, Crees, and Crows.* Ewers, J. C. (ed.). Norman: Univ. Oklahoma Press.
EWERS, J. C. (1939). *Plains Indian Painting.* Palo Alto: Stanford Univ. Press.
——— (1955). The Horse in Blackfoot Indian Culture, BBAE, Vol. 159.
——— (1958). *The Blackfeet.* Norman: Univ. Oklahoma Press.
FLANNERY, R. (1953). The Gros Ventres of Montana, Part 1: Social Life, CUAS, Vol. 15.
FLETCHER, A. D., and LaFLESCHE, F. (1906). The Omaha Tribe, ARBAE, No. 27.
GRINNELL, G. B. (1923). *The Cheyenne Indians.* New Haven, Conn.: Yale Univ. Press.
——— (1956). *The Fighting Cheyennes.* Norman: Univ. Oklahoma Press.
HOEBEL, E. A. (1940). The Political Organization and Law-Ways of the Comanche Indians, MAAA, Vol. 54.
——— (1952). *The Comanches: Lords of the Southern Plains.* Norman: Univ. Oklahoma Press.
——— (1960). *The Cheyennes: Indians of the Great Plains.* New York: Holt, Rinehart & Winston.
HOWARD, J. H. (1965). The Plains Ojibwa or Bungi: Hunters and Warriors of the Northern Prairies with Special Reference to the Turtle Mountain Band, Anthropological Papers, South Dakota Museum, Vermillion, South Dakota.
HYDE, G. E. (1951). *Pawnee Indians.* Denver, Colo.: Univ. Denver Press.
KROEBER, A. L. (1902–1907). The Arapaho, BAMNH, Vol. 18, 1–229, 279–454.
——— (1907). Ethnology of the Gros Ventre, APAM, Vol. 1, 145–281.
LLEWELLYN, K. N., and HOEBEL, E. A. (1941). *The Cheyenne Way.* Norman: Univ. Oklahoma Press.
LOWIE, R. H. (1910). The Assiniboine, APAM, Vol. 4, 1–270.
——— (1922). Plains Indian Age Societies, APAM, Vol. 11, 877–992.
——— (1935). *The Crow Indians.* New York: Holt, Rinehart & Winston.

——— (1954). *Indians of the Plains.* New York: McGraw-Hill.

MacGregor, G. (1946). *Warriors Without Weapons: A Study of the Society and Personality Development of the Pine Ridge Sioux.* Chicago: Univ. Chicago Press.

Mandelbaum, D. G. (1940). The Plains Cree, APAM, Vol. 37, 155–316.

Marriot, A. (1945). *The Ten Grandmothers: A Contribution to the Ethnology of the Kiowa Indians.* Norman: Univ. Oklahoma Press.

Matthews, W. (1877). Ethnography and philology of the Hidatsa Indians, U. S. Geological and Geographical Survey, Miscellaneous Publications. Vol. 7. Washington, D.C.

Mishkin, B. (1940). Rank and Warfare Among the Plains Indians, MAES, Vol. 3.

Secoy, F. R. (1953). Changing Military Patterns of the Great Plains, MAES, Vol. 21.

Spier, L. (1921). The Sun Dance of the Plains Indians: Its Development and Diffusion, APAM, Vol. 16, Part 7.

Wallace, E., and Hoebel, E. A. (1952). *The Comanches.* Norman: Univ. Oklahoma Press.

Wallis, W. D. (1947). The Canadian Dakota, APAM, Vol. 148.

Wedel, W. R. (1961). *Prehistoric Man on the Great Plains.* Norman: Univ. Oklahoma Press.

Weltfish, G. (1965). *The Lost Universe (Pawnee).* New York: Basic Books.

Whitman, W. (1937). The Oto, CUCA, Vol. 28, 1–32.

Will, G. F., and Spinden, H. J. (1906). The Mandans: A Study of Their Culture, Archaeology and Language, PMP, Vol. 3.

Wissler, C. (1910). Material Culture of the Blackfoot Indians, APAM, Vol. 5, 1–175.

——— (1911). The Social Life of the Blackfoot Indians, APAM, Vol. 7, 1–64.

——— (1912). Societies and Ceremonial Associations in the Oglala Division of the Teton-Dakota, APAM, Vol. 11.

——— (1927). *North American Indians of the Plains.* New York, American Museum of Natural History Handbook Series.

SECTION IX: *THE EASTERN AGRICULTURALISTS*

Caldwell, J. R. (1958). Trend and Tradition in the Prehistory of Eastern United States, MAAA, Vol. 88.

Corkran, D. H. (1962). *The Cherokee Frontier: Conflict and Survival, 1740–62.* Norman: Univ. Oklahoma Press.

DeForest, J. W. (1964). *History of Indians of Connecticut from the Earliest Known Period to 1850.* Hamden, Conn.: Archon Books.

FENLON, W. N., and GULICK, J. (eds.) (1961). Symposium on the Cherokee and Iroquois Culture, BBAE, Vol. 180.

FOREMAN, G. (1934). *The Five Civilized Tribes*. Norman: Univ. Oklahoma
Press.

GEARING, F. (1962). Priests and Warriors: Social Structure of Cherokee
Politics in the 18th Century, MAAA, No. 93.

GIBSON, A. M. (1963). *The Kickapoos: Lords of the Middle Border*. Norman: Univ. Oklahoma Press.

GILBERT, W. H., JR. (1943). The Eastern Cherokee, BBAE, Vol. 133,
No. 23, 169–414.

GRIFFIN, J. (ed.) (1952). *Archaeology of the Eastern United States*. Chicago: Univ. Chicago Press.

GULICK, J. (1960). *Cherokee at the Crossroads*. Chapel Hill: University of
North Carolina, Institute for Research in Social Science.

HAGAN, W. T. (1958). *The Sac and Fox Indians*. Norman: Univ. Oklahoma Press.

HUNT, G. T. (1960). *The Wars of the Iroquois: A Study of Intertribal
Trade Relations*. Madison: Univ. Wisconsin Press.

JONES, W. (1939). Ethnography of the Fox Indians, BBAE, Vol. 125.

KEESING, F. M. (1939). The Menomini Indians of Wisconsin, MAPS, Vol.
10.

LEWIS, T. M. N., and KNEBERG, M. (1958). *Tribes That Slumber: Indian
Tribes in the Tennessee Region*. Knoxville: Univ. Tennessee Press.

MACCAULEY, C. (1884). The Seminole Indians of Florida, ARBAE,
Vol. 5, 469–531.

MASON, R. J. (1962). The Paleo-Indian Tradition in Eastern North America, *Current Anthropology*, **3**, 227–278.

MORGAN, L. H. (1954). *League of the Ho-De-No-Sau-Nee or Iroquois*.
(Reprint from 1901.) New Haven, Conn.: Yale Univ. Press.

PARSONS, E. C. (1941). Notes on the Caddo, MAAA, Vol. 57.

PEITHMANN, I. M. (1964). *Red Men of Fire: A History of the Cherokee
Indians*. Springfield, Ill.: Thomas.

QUIMBY, G. I. (1960). *Indian Life in the Upper Great Lakes (11,000 B.C.
to A.D. 1800)*. Chicago: Univ. Chicago Press.

RITZENTHALER, R. E. (1950). The Oneida Indians of Wisconsin, BPM-
CM, Vol. 19, 1–52.

——— (1953). The Potawotami Indians of Wisconsin, BPMCM, Vol.
19, 99–174.

———, and PETERSON, F. A. (1956). The Mexican Kickapoo Indians,
PAMPM, Vol. 2.

SILVERBERG, J. (1957). The Kickapoo Indians, WA, Vol. 38.

SKINNER, A. (1921). Material Culture of the Menomini, INM, No. 20.

——— (1923–25). Observations on the Ethnology of the Sauk Indians,
BPMCM, No. 5.

———(1926). Ethnology of the Ioway Indians, BPMCM, Vol. 5, 181–354.

——— (1924–27). The Mascoutens or Prairie Potawotami Indians, BPM-CM, Vol. 6.

SPECK, F. G. (1907). The Creek Indians of Taskigi Town, AA, Vol. 2, 99–164.

——— (1909). Ethnology of the Yuchi Indians, UPMAP, Vol. 1, 1–154.

——— (1925). The Rappahannock Indians of Virginia, INM, Vol. 5, 25–83.

——— (1928). Chapters on the Ethnology of the Powhatan Tribes, INM, Vol. 1, 277–445.

——— (1945). The Iroquois, BCIS, Vol. 23, 1–94.

——— (1949). *Midwinter Rites of the Cayuga Longhouse.* Philadelphia: Univ. Pennsylvania Press.

SPINDLER, G. (1955). Sociocultural and Psychological Processes in Menomini Acculturation, ACPCS, Vol. 5.

SPOEHR, A. (1942). Kinship System of the Seminole, FMAS, Vol. 33, 31–113.

SWANTON, J. R. (1928). Social Organization and Social Usages of the Indians of the Creek Confederacy, ARBAE, Vol. 42.

——— (1931). Source Material for the Social and Ceremonial Life of the Choctaw Indians, BBAE, Vol. 103.

——— (1946). The Indians of the Southeastern United States, BBAE, Vol. 137.

TOOKER, E. (1964). An Ethnography of the Huron Indians, 1615–1649, BBAE, Vol. 190.

SECTION X: *THE INDIAN IN THE MODERN WORLD*

BAERREIS, D. A. (1956). *The Indian in Modern America.* Madison: State Historical Society of Wisconsin.

BERKHOFER, R. F., JR. (1965). *Salvation and the Savage: An Analysis of Protestant Missions and American Indian Response, 1787–1862.* Lexington: Univ. Kentucky Press.

DuBois, C. (1938). The 1870 Ghost Dance, AR, Vol. 3.

FENTON, W. N. *et al.* (1957). *American Indian and White Relations to 1830.* Chapel Hill: Univ. North Carolina Press.

FEY, N. E., and McNICKLE, D. (1959). *Indians and Other Americans.* New York: Harper & Row.

HALLOWELL, A. I. (1957). The Impact of the American Indian on American Culture, AA, Vol. 59, 201–217.

LaFARGE, O. (ed.) (1942). *The Changing Indian.* Norman: Univ. Oklahoma Press.

LINTON, R. (ed.) (1940). *Acculturation in Seven American Indian Tribes.* New York: Appleton-Century-Crofts.

LORAN, C. T., and McILWAINE, T. F. (1943). *The North American Indian Today*. Toronto: Univ. Toronto Press.

LURIE, N. (1961). The Voice of the American Indian: Report on the American Indian. Chicago Conference. *Current Anthropology*, **2**, No. 5, 478–500.

MADIGAN, L. (1956). *The American Indian Relocation Program*, New York: *Association of American Indian Affairs*.

McNICKLE, D. (1949). *They Came Here First*. Philadelphia: Lippincott.

———— (1962). *The Indian Tribes of the United States: Ethnic and Cultural Survival*. Institute of Race Relations. London: Oxford Univ. Press.

MOONEY, J. (1896). The Ghost Dance Religion, ARBAE, Vol. 14.

SELLIN, T. (ed.) (1957). American Indians and American Life, APSS, Vol. 311.

SPICER, E. H. (1961). *Perspectives in American Indian Culture Change*. Chicago: Univ. Chicago Press.

TAX, S. (ed.) (1952). *Heritage of Conquest*. Chicago: Univ. Chicago Press.

WASHBURN, W. E. (ed.) (1964). *The Indians and the White Man*. Garden City, N.Y.: Doubleday.

ABBREVIATIONS USED IN
ADDITIONAL READINGS LIST

A	Anthropos. Modling/Wien.
AA	American Anthropologist. Washington, D.C.
Anthro	Anthropologica. Ottawa.
APAM	Anthropological Papers of the American Museum of Natural History. New York City.
APSS	Annals of the American Academy of Political and Social Sciences. Philadelphia.
APUU	Anthropological Papers of the University of Utah. Salt Lake City.
AR	Anthropological Records, University of California. Berkeley.
ARBAE	Annual Reports of the Bureau of American Ethnology. Washington, D.C.
BAMNH	Bulletin of the American Museum of Natural History. New York City.
BBAE	Bulletin of the Bureau of American Ethnology. Washington, D.C.
BCDM	Bulletins (and Annual Reports) of the Canada Department of Mines, National Museum of Canada. Ottawa.
BCIS	Bulletin of the Cranbrook Institute of Science. Detroit.
BNMC	Bulletin of the National Museum of Canada. Ottawa.
BPMCM	Bulletins of the Public Museum of the City of Milwaukee. Milwaukee.
CNAE	Contributions to North American Ethnology. Department of the Interior, U.S. Geographical and Geological Survey of the Rocky Mountain Region. Washington, D.C.

CUAS	Catholic University of American Anthropological Series. Washington, D.C.
CUCA	Columbia University Contributions to Anthropology. New York City.
FMAS	Field, (Chicago) Museum (of Natural History), Anthropological Series. Chicago.
GSA	General Series in Anthropology. Menasha, Wis.
IA	Ibero-Americana. Berkeley, Calif.
INM	Indian Notes and Monographs, Museum of the American Indian, Heye Foundation. New York City.
MAAA	Memoirs of the American Anthropological Association. Menasha, Wis.
MAES	Monographs of the American Ethnological Society.
MAMNH	Memoirs of the American Museum of Natural History. New York City.
MAPS	Memoirs of the American Philosophical Society. Philadelphia.
MCDM	Memoirs of the Canada Department of Mines, Geological Survey. Ottawa.
MG	Meddelelser om Gronland. Copenhagen.
MIJL	Memoirs of the International Journal of American Linguistics, or Indiana University Publications in Anthropology and Linguistics. Bloomington, Ind.
MSAA	Memoirs of the Society for American Archaeology. Salt Lake City.
NCRC	Northern Coordination and Research Center. Ottawa.
NLAUN	Notebook of the Laboratory of Anthropology of the University of Nebraska. Lincoln.
PAES	Publications of the American Ethnological Society. New York City.
PAF	Publications of the Amerind Foundation. Dragoon, Arizona.
PAMPM	Publications in Anthropology of the Public Museum of the City of Milwaukee. Milwaukee.
PHAPF	Publications of the Frederick Webb Hodge Anniversary Publication Fund, Southwest Museum. Los Angeles.
PMP	Peabody Museum Papers (Archaeological and Ethnological Papers of the Peabody Museum), Harvard University. Cambridge, Mass.
RCAE	Report of the Canadian Arctic Expedition. Ottawa.
RFTE	Report of the Fifth Thule Expedition. Copenhagen.
RUSNM	Reports of the United States National Museum. Washington, D.C.
TAPS	Transactions of the American Philosophical Society. Philadelphia.
UAAP	Anthropological Papers of the University of Alaska. Fairbanks.

UCP	University of California Publications in American Archaeology and Ethnology. Berkeley and Los Angeles.
UNMPA	University of New Mexico Publications in Anthropology. Albuquerque.
UPMAP	University of Pennsylvania Museum Anthropological Publications. Philadelphia.
UWPA	University of Washington Publications in Anthropology. Seattle.
VFPA	Viking Fund Publications in Anthropology. New York City.
YUPA	Yale University Publications in Anthropology. New Haven, Conn.
WA	Wisconsin Archaeologist. Milwaukee, Wis.

EDUCATIONAL FILMS ON
THE AMERICAN INDIAN

There are 251 educational films on the American Indian in the list which follows. All major university film catalogues, catalogues from governmental and foreign sources, the Library of Congress guides, and other such inventories, have been examined. Despite efforts to make the film guide as complete as possible, it is probable that some important films have escaped our notice.

Film titles are meant to be complete and accurate. In regard to projection time, color, appropriate audience age level, and producer, information is often lacking in the sources and sometimes varies from one catalogue to another. Rental prices also differ considerably. Where we have been able to find a film in a contemporary catalogue (1965–66), we have so indicated. Where no such citation is to be found, it is possible that the film has been withdrawn from circulation, has undergone a name change, or is very scarce. All films have sound unless noted as silent, and are 16mm. The appropriate age level indicated (p = primary, j = junior high school, s = senior high school, c = college, a = adult) is taken from the sources and is often unreliable. The major difference among most of the film classifications is in the level of narration. Much excellent footage is to be found in films narrated for children or adolescents.

The titles have been organized into regional categories consistent with the organization of this book. It should be noted that all of the films obviously deal with twentieth-century American Indians, and, at best, those films which purport to depict aboriginal life are simulations of earlier conditions. At worst, some of the films are visually misleading and have narrations which are inaccurate or distorted. The cautious student of the American Indian would be well advised to use the films only to supplement careful examination of the extensive anthropological literature which deals with the Indians.

718

SECTION I: *INTRODUCTION*

Title of Film	Time	Color	Level	Producer	Catalogue
AMERICAN INDIANS BEFORE EUROPEAN SETTLEMENT. Relation of culture to environment in five regions of U.S.: Woodlands, Plains, South, Southwest, and Northwest Coast.	11	bw	j–s	COR *	MP
ARCHAEOLOGISTS AT WORK. Archaeology in Southwest; techniques of dendrochronology and Carbon[14].	14	yes	s–c	FAC	UIN
BEFORE THE WHITE MEN CAME. Portrays precontact Indian tribes; types of shelter, hunting, and winter migration.	18	bw	j–s	ILA	MP
CARBON FOURTEEN. Explains "half-life" of Carbon[14] in tracing growth and decay in living things; its use in dating techniques.	1 reel	—	h–a	EBF	—
CLUE TO ANCIENT INDIAN LIFE. A field trip with an archaeologist.	11	yes	e–c	DEP	LFR
DANGEROUS RIVER. Documentary by Smithsonian Institution; archaeological exploration of Big Horn River in Wyoming and Montana.	17	yes	j–c	BFS	UCB
DIGGING INTO HISTORY: PART I —EXPLORATION. Archaeological exploration by University of Illinois uncovers house site forty feet in diameter; finds skeleton of old man, child, and dog.	14	yes	j–a	UIL	UIL
DIGGING INTO HISTORY: PART II —AN EARLY ILLINI. Modeling of clay over features of Hopewell Indian cranium; attempts to determine features of the living man.	14	yes	j–a	UIL	UIL
GLEN CANYON ARCHAEOLOGY I, II, III. Salvage archaeology in Glen Canyon of Colorado River.	42 each	bw	a	UTA	MP

* Abbreviations are explained on p. 742.

Title of Film	Time	Color	Level	Producer	Catalogue
GLIMPSE OF THE PAST. Archaeologist demonstrates by exhibits and diagrams how prehistoric American Indians lived.	10	c/bw	a	UIN	MP
INDIAN DANCES. Indian music; four rhythm patterns used to express relationships with nature.	11	yes	j	EBF	MP
INDIAN HOUSE. Architecture of Southwestern U.S., including cliff dwellings, Spanish influences, and American contributions from East.	8	bw	—	G	—
INDIAN INFLUENCES IN THE UNITED STATES. Influence of Indian on American life through names, language, and art forms.	11	c/bw	j	COR	UIL
INDIAN MUSICAL INSTRUMENTS. Importance of music in Indian life; construction and playing of drums, flutes, rattles, and whistles; songs and dances from various tribes.	13	yes	c	UOK	PSU
INDIANS OF EARLY AMERICA. Daily life of Indians throughout U.S. and Canada; divided into four major culture areas.	22	bw	j–s	EBF	MP
LEARNING ABOUT THE PAST. Work and activities of archaeologists at an Indian mound site; dioramas of various American Indian cultures.	10	yes	j	UIN	UIN
MAKING INDIAN MOCCASINS. Making Indian moccasins.	17	bw	—	BYU	MP
MAKING PRIMITIVE STONE TOOLS. Techniques used in manufacture of stone arrowheads, axes, knives, and skin scrapers.	11	yes	p–a	NFB	NYU
MAN AND CULTURE (Nos. 1–29). Films taken from educational television anthropology course taught by Jesse D. Jennings (check catalogues for specific contents).	29 each	bw	c–a	UTA	MP

Title of Film	Time	Color	Level	Producer	Catalogue
OBSIDIAN POINT MAKING. Pressure flaking by Tolowa Indian of Northern California.	13	yes	p–a	UCB	UCB
PEOPLE ARE TAUGHT TO BE DIFFERENT: CULTURAL PATTERNS OF INFANT REGULATIONS. Cultural differences in early training of infants: southern urban Negroes, the Manus of Admiralty Islands, and Hopi Indians of Northern Arizona.	30	bw	s–a	NET	UIN
PEOPLE ARE TAUGHT TO BE DIFFERENT: THE IMPACT OF PERSONALITIES. Development of personality types in three cultures: American, Alorese of Melanesia, and Hopi Indians.	30	bw	s–a	NET	UIN
POINT OF PINES. Excavation of prehistoric sites at summer field camp in Arizona.	22	yes	j–a	—	NYU
POTTERY MAKING. Making pottery by four methods, including Indian "coil and scrape."	11	bw	p–a	EBF	UAR
SALVAGING AMERICAN PREHISTORY: PART I. Salvage archaeology in the United States.	28	yes	c–a	UT	UT
SALVAGING TEXAS PREHISTORY: PART VI. Methods of archaeology; checking of hypotheses.	28	yes	c–a	UT	UT
SEARCH FOR THE PAST. Search for information on West Coast tribes.	7	bw	—	USC	USC
SHELL MOUNDS IN THE TENNESSEE VALLEY. Home building, from American Indians to modern homes.	21	bw silent	—	TVA	FF
THEFT OF FIRE, THE. Animated cartoon based on Indian folklore tells how people captured fire from Thunder and made it their own.	7	yes	p	THF	NYU
WOODLANDS, THE: PART II. Locating, excavating, and publishing an archaeological site.	28	yes	c–a	UT	UT

SECTION II: *THE ESKIMO*

Title of Film	Time	Color	Level	Producer	Catalogue
ALASKA: NATIVE ALASKA. Visit with Eskimos and Indians and discussion of their problems as modern world confronts them.	29	bw	s—a	KCTA	UIN
ALASKAN ESKIMO. Eskimo father-son teaching relationship on hunting trip; overall view of life during winter, including winter and spring ceremonials.	27	yes	j—s	BYU	MP
ANGOTEE. Eskimo boy's life from birth to adult hunter.	32	c/bw	a	CCG	MP
ANNANACKS. Eskimos in the Hudson Bay region; the founding of an Eskimo cooperative; and the reaction of three Eskimos to city life of Montreal.	60	yes	j—c	CFI	LCC
ARCTIC EXPLORATION. Centers on difficulties of supplying settlements in the arctic; views Eskimos mining coal.	6	bw	j—a	WPN	UTA
ARCTIC OUTPOST. Yearly round of town in Northwest Territories in Canada where Eskimos come to trade.	21	yes	j	IFB	SYR
ARCTIC SEAL HUNTER. Eskimo hunters processing walrus, polar bear, and hair seals.	12	yes	a	BFS	MP
DOWN NORTH. Mining, fishing, and Eskimo activities around Mackenzie River Delta, Great Slave, and Bear Lakes.	30	yes	j—a	NFB	MP
EARLY JOURNEY OF VILHJALMUR STEFANSSON, THE. Stefansson discusses his expedition (1906–1907) up the Mackenzie River; describes his life among the Eskimos.	28	bw	j—c	NFB	LCC

Title of Film	Time	Color	Level	Producer	Catalogue
ESKIMO. No description available.	2 reels	bw	—	FFC	—
ESKIMO ARTS AND CRAFTS. Craftsmanship in bone and ivory; fashioning of clothing and hunting instruments; community rituals and recreation.	22	yes	a	CCG	UCB
ESKIMO CHILDREN. A family living on Nunivak Island off coast of Alaska.	10	bw	p–j	EBF	MP
ESKIMO FAMILY. Eskimo's use of manufactured goods and employment at semiskilled and construction work.	17	c/bw	a	EBF	MP
ESKIMO HUNTERS (NORTHWESTERN ALASKA). Illustrates division of labor; father and son demonstrate hunting of caribou while mother makes skin clothing.	20	bw	s	UW	MP
ESKIMOS (WINTER IN WESTERN ALASKA). Illustrates method of obtaining food and clothing; portrays household activities.	10	yes	—	EBF	UCO
ESKIMO RIVER VILLAGE. Eskimo village of 130 people in Central Alaska.	12	c/bw	j	NF	PSU
ESKIMOS IN LIFE AND LEGEND. Spring and summer hunting whose success is related to sympathetic magic produced by first sculpting image of animal to be hunted.	22	c/bw	p–a	EBF	NFB
ESKIMO SEA HUNTERS. Life of Eskimo family.	20	bw	j	UW	SYR
ESKIMO SUMMER. Illustrates importance of group activities for Eskimo bands in struggle for survival.	16	yes	—	IFB	UCB
ESKIMO TRAILS. Father Hubbard's adventures; missionary priest.	1 reel	bw	—	CF	UIN
FISHING ARCTIC STYLE. Methods of fishing with seines, gill nets, and	12	bw	j–a	BFS	MP

Title of Film	Time	Color	Level	Producer	Catalogue
barbless hooks, in summer and winter; also pictures Indian fish-wheel on Yukon River.					
FISHING AT THE STONE WEIR: PART I. Depicts life of Eskimos during summer when use is made of a stone weir.	29	yes silent	a	ESI	—
FISHING AT THE STONE WEIR: PART II. Continuation of Part I.	29	yes silent	a	ESI	—
GREENLAND'S NEW LIFE. Assim-ilation of Eskimo by Danish com-munity; gradual development into settlement-oriented commercial fishermen.	10	yes	j–c	ABP	UIN
HOW TO BUILD AN IGLOO. Con-struction of igloo in hour and a half.	11	bw	j	MHB	UIL
HUNTERS OF THE NORTH POLE. Eskimo life in Greenland.	10	bw	j–a	SFI	MP
IKPUCK THE IGLOO DWELLER. Coronation Gulf Eskimos; tech-nology involved in obtaining food, clothing, and shelter.	11	c/bw	j–a	BH	UAR
KENOJUAK. Eskimo artists at the Cape Dorset art center in Alaska.	19	yes	e–a	CFI	—
KUMAK THE SLEEPY HUNTER. Table-top puppets and a "once-upon-a-time" narrative of sleepy hunter who receives special power and becomes best hunter in village.	13	yes	p	FI	NYU
LAND OF THE LONG DAY—WIN-TER AND SPRING: PART I. Hun-ter tells of his life, his family and campsite, and the seal hunt.	19	yes	j–a	IFB	NFB
LAND OF THE LONG DAY—SUM-MER AND AUTUMN: PART II. Adult males, women, and children in an encampment; making of clothes and preparation of seal skins; whale hunt.	19	yes	j–a	IFB	NFB

Title of Film	Time	Color	Level	Producer	Catalogue
LAND OF THE ESKIMO. Fishing activities in Manitoba.	5	bw	j–c	WPN	MP
LEGEND OF THE RAVEN. Eskimo carvings and associated legends.	14	yes	s	CCG	FF
LIFE IN COLD LANDS (ESKIMO VILLAGE). Hunting, fur trapping, putting up summer tent, and trading.	10	bw	j	COR	MP
LITTLE DIOMEDE. Maritime Eskimos in Bering Strait; climate, geography, plant and animal life.	19	yes	j	NF	UIL
LIVING STONE, THE. Spring and summer hunting whose success is related to sympathetic magic produced by first sculpting image of the animal to be hunted.	31	c/bw	p–a	EBF	NFB
NANOOK OF THE NORTH. Nanook and his family as they wander about the arctic in search for food.	54	bw	c	A	MP
NEXT DOOR TO SIBERIA. Maritime Eskimos of Little Diomede Island; walrus hunt.	11	yes	j–a	BFI	MP
NOMADS OF THE NORTH. Herders protecting their reindeer herds in Alaska.	11	yes	j–a	BFS	MP
PANGNIRTUNG. Fifteen Canadians in arctic settlement who provide for health and welfare of Eskimos living nearby.	30	yes	—	CCG	FF
PEOPLE OF THE ARCTIC. Geography, resources, and people of Alaska, Labrador, Greenland, and Northern Siberia.	18	bw	j	KB	UCB
PEOPLE OF THE ROCK. Eskimo turned prospector and miner, part of Canada's plan for Eskimo integration.	14	yes	—	NFB	—
SEAL HUNT. A sportsman's expedition into west coast of Hudson's Bay; Eskimos celebrating successful hunt.	22	yes	s–a	CFC	UIL

Title of Film	Time	Color	Level	Producer	Catalogue
TIGERIA: AGELESS CITY OF THE ARCTIC. A 3,000 year old site in Alaska; reconstruction of sod and whale bone houses of former inhabitants.	12	yes	j–a	BFS	MP
WALRUS HUNTING WITH THE ESKIMO. Ingenuity of Eskimos; hunting walrus and white whale.	10	bw	c–a	BH	UAR
WEDDING OF PALO. East Greenland Eskimos; dialogue in Eskimo.	70	bw	c–a	BFS	—

SECTION III: *THE NORTHERN HUNTERS*

	Time	Color	Level	Producer	Catalogue
ATTIUK. A group of Montagnais Indians as they travel from the St. Lawrence River in search of caribou.	28	bw	j–e	CFI	LCC
CARIBOU HUNTERS. Cree and Chippewa Indians of Northern Manitoba in search of Caribou, their main source of food.	18	c/bw	h–c	NFB	NFB
CEREMONIAL PIPES. Origin and ceremonial use of the peace pipe; various types illustrated and described.	16	yes	j–a	—	PSU
CHIPPEWA INDIANS. Changing ways of Chippewa Indians of Red Lake, Minnesota, reservation.	10	yes	c–a	UTA	MP
FUR COUNTRY. Life of Indian trapper in North Woods.	23	yes	c–a	IFF	SYR
GLOOSCAP COUNTRY. Ancient legend of Micmac Indians of Nova Scotia.	14	yes	—	CCG	FF
HOW INDIANS BUILD CANOES. Demonstration by Algonkin Indians of building of birch bark canoes. (cf. PORTAGE; TRAPPERS AND TRADERS).	10	yes	—	IFB	SYR
INDIAN CANOEMEN. Canoeing, fishing, and family encampment of Indians of Northern Quebec.	11	yes	—	NFB	—

Title of Film	Time	Color	Level	Producer	Catalogue
INDIAN HUNTERS. Canadian Indians scouting for new hunting and fishing ground.	10	bw	j–a	SFI	MP
KA KE KI KU. The problems of education of the children of a group north of the St. Lawrence River.	27	bw	j–c	CFI	LCC
LAKE MEN, THE. French-Canadian culture as observed in the life of a Metis Indian, his family, and the Metis communities on Lac la Biche, Alberta.	27	bw	j–c	NFB	LCC
LONGER TRAIL. Young Indian from reservation near Calgary, Alberta, faces problems of modern world.	29	bw	—	NFB	—
MAHNOMEN-HARVEST OF THE NORTH. Chippewa legend of wild rice; past and present methods of harvesting are pictured.	17	yes	s	FRC	SYR
MODERN CHIPPEWA INDIANS. General pattern of life and work on Chippewa reservation in Minnesota.	11	bw	j–a	SMI	UIL
NO LONGER VANISHING. Progress being made by Canadian Indians towards conducting their own affairs.	28	c/bw	—	NFB	FF
PEOPLE ARE TAUGHT TO BE DIFFERENT: DOCTORS ALL. Diagnosis and treatment of illness in three cultures: modern American, Ojibway of Canada, and Djuka Negroes of Dutch Guiana.	30	bw	s–a	NET	UIN
PORTAGE. Activities of Indian trapper in Hudson Bay region; demonstration of birch bark canoe construction (cf. HOW INDIANS BUILD CANOES; TRAPPERS AND TRADERS).	20	yes	j–j	IFB	SYR

Title of Film	Time	Color	Level	Producer	Catalogue
SILENT ENEMY. Northern Woodland Indians' quest for game.	6 reels	bw	s–a	NA	—
TRAPPERS AND TRADERS. Indian tends his traplines and travels to Montreal to sell his skins (cf. PORTAGE; HOW INDIANS MAKE CANOES).	10	yes	j–s	IFB	SYR
VILLAGE IN THE DUST. Excavation fifteen miles from Toronto; skeleton, pottery, and other objects recovered.	20	yes	j–c	NFB	LCC
WOODLAND INDIANS OF EARLY AMERICA. Family life of Chippewa Indians prior to European influence; hunting and gathering of seeds.	10	c/bw	p–i	COR	MP

SECTION IV: *THE BASIN-PLATEAU**

GRASS IS GOLD. Indian Service advises Shoshone on land conservation.	20	yes	—	USB	—
PINE NUTS (A FOOD OF PAIUTE AND WASHO INDIANS). Demonstrates processing of pine nuts, from harvest to final preparation.	13	yes	—	UCB	UCB
PLATEAU AND PACIFIC. Sites on Snake River in southeastern Washington; 8,000-year-old history of area.	28	yes	c–a	UT	UT
TOMESHA LAND. Death Valley, its geology, flora and fauna, and resident Paiute Indians.	27	bw	j–a	SRF	UOR

SECTION V: *THE NORTHWEST COAST*

BLUNDEN HARBOR. Kwakiutl living at Blunden Harbor, British Columbia.	20	bw	—	BFS	MP

* See also films listed for other sections. Many films on California and the Northwest Coast are relevant to the Great Basin (e.g., *The Loon's Necklace*). The Northern Hunter area may also be used to illustrate aspects of life in the Plateau region.

Title of Film	Time	Color	Level	Producer	Catalogue
DANCES OF THE KWAKIUTL. Pantomimic dances with music recorded on location.	10	bw	j–a	BFS	MP
DIGGING UP THE PAST. Detailed processing of a site by University of Washington students.	23	yes	s–a	NF	LFR
FORT RUPERT. Kwakiutl at Fort Rupert; Hamatsa Cannibal Society ritual.	15	yes	j–a	DFP	MP
HAIDA CARVER. A slate-figurine carver of Queen Charlotte Island.	12	yes	—	NFB	—
LAST SALMON RUN OF THE CELILO INDIANS, THE. Celilo Indians and the ceremonial rites at their last salmon feast.	18	bw	j–c	OHS	LCC
LEGEND OF FATHER OCEAN. A Quinault symbolically illustrates legend of origin of Pacific Northwest.	10	yes	j	MM	UIL
LOON'S NECKLACE. Pantomimic use of Indian masks to illustrate legend of origin of loon's white neckband.	5	yes	p–a	EBF	MP
MISSIONARIES CARRY THE WORD. Religious beliefs of Indians before advent of Christianity.	15	bw	—	OSS	—
PEOPLE OF THE POTLATCH. Painting and woodcarving of Indians of Northern British Columbia.	21	yes	—	NFB	UIN
PEOPLE OF THE SKEENA. Tsimshian of the Skeena River Valley and their way of life.	15	yes	j–a	NFB	FF
QULLAYUTE STORY. From native culture to modern world: Shaker religion, smelt fishing, dances, and sports; salmon fishing and clam bakes.	25	yes	j–a	OFD	PSU
SILENT ONES, THE. Techniques used to preserve totem poles removed from abandoned Haida village.	27	yes	c	NFB	LCC

Title of Film	Time	Color	Level	Producer	Catalogue
SKEENA RIVER TRAPLINE. Trapline of Getikshan Indian of Northern British Columbia.	16	c/bw	—	NFB	—
TIMBER AND TOTEM POLES. Construction and restoration of totem poles in Southwest Alaska.	10	yes	j–a	USD	UAR
TOTEM POLE. Development of totem poles and house posts.	27	yes	c	IFB	UCB
TOTEM POLE, THE. The history, function, and art of totem pole carvings.	27	yes	s–a	UC	LFR
TOTEMS. Carved and painted poles of Indians of British Columbia.	11	yes	c	IFB	UCB
WOODEN BOX MADE BY STEAMING AND BENDING. Detailed construction of aboriginal-type wooden box.	33	yes	c	UCB	UCB

SECTION VI: *CALIFORNIA*

ACORNS: STAPLE FOOD OF CALIFORNIA INDIANS. Preparation and use of acorns as food.	28	yes	c–a	UCB	MP
BASKETRY OF THE POMO (TECHNIQUES). Pomo women collect materials and demonstrate basket-weaving techniques.	33	yes	c–a	UCB	UCB
BASKETRY OF THE POMO (FORMS AND ORNAMENTATION). Forms and ornamentation of Pomo basketry; mythology and taboos associated with basketry.	20	yes	c–a	UCB	UCB
BEAUTIFUL TREE-CHISHKALE, THE. Influence of the acorn on the way of life of the central California Indians.	20	yes	j–a	UCB	UCB
BREAD FROM ACORNS. Processing of acorns into breadlike food.	15	bw silent	—	BFS	—
BUCKEYES: A FOOD OF THE CALIFORNIA INDIANS. Nisenan Indians harvest buckeyes and process them by leaching and stone-boiling.	13	bw	c–a	UCB	UCB

Title of Film	Time	Color	Level	Producer	Catalogue
DANCES OF THE KASHIA POMO; THE BOLEMARU RELIGION (WOMEN'S DANCES). Five dances; indications of influences of Christianity and World War II upon century-old cult.	30	yes	c–a	UCB	UCB
DANCES OF THE POMO INDIANS: MEN'S DANCES. Male Pomo at Kashia in ceremonial dress perform four dances with songs and music.	—	yes	c–a	UCB	UCB
DANCES OF THE POMO INDIANS: WOMEN'S DANCES. Women perform five ceremonial dances in costume with songs and ritual.	—	yes	c	UCB	UCB
GAME OF STAVES. Pomo boys explain individualized ornamentation of staves and counters.	10	yes	c–a	UCB	UCB
HUPA INDIAN—WHITE DEERSKIN DANCE. Old cultural patterns retained by Hupa of Northwestern California.	12	yes	j–a	ABP	UCB
INDIANS OF CALIFORNIA: PART I (VILLAGE LIFE). Customs and traditions of disappearing culture.	15	yes	p–i	ABP	MP
INDIANS OF CALIFORNIA: PART II (FOOD). Making of arrowheads, stalking of deer, and women gathering acorns.	14	yes	p–i	ABP	MP
INDIAN FAMILY OF THE CALIFORNIA DESERT. A Cahilla woman recalls her childhood; adaptation to desert and mountains; weapon-making, basket-weaving, and hunting.	15	yes	—	EH	USC
KASHIA MEN'S DANCES: (SOUTHWESTERN POMO INDIANS). Dances by Southwestern Pomo.	40	yes	c–a	UCB	UCB
MISSION DAYS. Story of mission development in California; Indian life within mission community.	15	bw	p	KQED	—

Title of Film	Time	Color	Level	Producer	Catalogue
MISSION LIFE: ALTA CALIFORNIA. Tasks of Indians in California Missions.	20	yes	j	ABP	UCB
POMO SHAMAN. Second and final night of acorn ceremony held by Kashia group of Southwestern Pomo.	20	bw	c–a	UCB	UCB
SINEW-BACKED BOW AND ITS ARROWS. Construction of sinew-backed bow and arrows by a Yurok.	24	yes	c–a	UCB	UCB

SECTION VII: *THE SOUTHWEST*

	Time	Color	Level	Producer	Catalogue
ALTARS OF SAND. Role of sand painting in religion and curing ceremonies.	9	yes	c	UAR	UAR
APACHE INDIAN. Puberty ceremony and The Gon dance depicted.	10	yes	j–a	COR	MP
APACHE INDIAN CAMP LIFE. Basket maker weaves and waterproofs a basket; others grind corn, cook beans, and tend crops.	15	yes silent	j–a	TN	UAR
BE-TA-TA-KIN. Tour of eleventh century cliff-dwelling in Canyon de Chelly in Northwestern Arizona.	11	c/bw	p–c	NYU	NYU
BOY OF THE NAVAJOS. Living habits and activities of Navaho family with emphasis on teen-age son.	11	c/bw	—	COR	MP
CEREMONIAL DANCES OF THE SOUTHWEST TRIBES. Thirteen different ceremonial dances of Southwestern Indians.	10	bw	a	AFP	—
CIBECUE WATERSHED. Stock management on Fort Apache reservation.	22	yes	j–a	USI	—

Title of Film	Time	Color	Level	Producer	Catalogue
DESERT, THE: PART IV. The use, by archaeologists, of the different scientific fields of knowledge to arrive at their conclusions.	28	yes	c–a	UT	UT
DESERT PEOPLE. Papago Indians who have lived in desert for centuries.	25	yes	j–a	USB	UAR
EXPEDITION ARIZONA: MISSIONS OF OLD ARIZONA. Mission San Xavier del Bac and contributions of Father Kino.	27	bw	j–a	FNB	UAR
EXPEDITION ARIZONA: SHARDS OF THE AGES. Three major cultures of Southwest: Hohokam of low desert, Mogollon of mountains, and Anasazi of plateau regions of Arizona.	27	bw	j–a	FNB	UAR
FAMILY LIFE OF THE NAVAHO INDIANS. Development of a Navaho child into an adult.	31	bw silent	j–a	NYU	NYU
FATHER OF THE SOUTHWEST. Father Kino and his role in colonizing the Southwest.	13	yes	—	ADP	UAR
HOPI INDIAN. Customs and ceremonies involved in daily life.	10	c/bw	p–j	COR	MP
HOPI INDIAN ARTS AND CRAFTS. Arts and customs of Hopi Indians: weaving, basket-making and ceramics.	10	bw	p–j	COR	MP
HOPI INDIANS. Indians as farmers, herders, craftsmen, and traders.	21	yes	j–c	SDF	UIN
HOPI KACHINAS. How common kachina doll provides understanding of Hopi culture.	10	bw	c	JB	UAR
HOW THE INDIANS MADE THE DESERT BLOOM. Hohokam irrigation works and their later use by European settlers.	6	bw	j–a	WPN	MP

Title of Film	Time	Color	Level	Producer	Catalogue
INDIAN ARTS AND CRAFTS. Navajo and Pueblo silver, rugs, baskets, and pottery.	20	yes	j–a	USI	—
INDIAN BOY OF THE SOUTHWEST. Life of a Hopi boy; history of pueblos.	14	yes	j	FAC	UIL
INDIAN COUNTRY. The culture of tribes living in the Southwest.	28	yes	j–c	JG	LCC
INDIAN LIFE IN THE SOUTHWEST. Dances of Southwest: the Horse Tail, Pony, Hoop, Buffalo, and Eagle.	11	bw	j–s	AFP	UIL
IN SEARCH OF A CITY. Archaeologists work on Indian burials in Mesa Verde National Park in Colorado.	9	c/bw	j–a	NET	UIN
IN THE LAND OF THE NAVAHO. Home life of the Navaho; rug-weaving, bread-baking, and a wedding ceremony.	90	yes silent	—	EPH	—
LITTLE INDIAN WEAVER. Little Navaho girls learn art of weaving.	16	bw silent	p	P	UIN
MIRACLE ON THE MESA. Arizona mesa country and agriculture, arts, crafts, and dances of Hopi.	20	bw	j–a	ASP	MP
MONUMENT VALLEY. Herding of goats and sheep, preparation of wool, and weaving of blankets.	17	yes	j–a	HDP	MP
NAVAHO—A PEOPLE BETWEEN TWO WORLDS. Frustrations that arise from culture conflict and how this affects Navaho.	18	yes	j–a	UTA	MP
NAVAHO CANYON COUNTRY. Influence of Navaho homeland on history, economy, and culture.	13	yes	j–a	ADP	MP
NAVAHO CHILDREN. Navaho children experience problem of seasonal migration.	11	bw	j	EBF	MP
NAVAHO COUNTRY. Nomadic life in Northwestern Arizona; weaving and jewelry-making.	10	yes	c	UMI	MP

Title of Film	Time	Color	Level	Producer	Catalogue
NAVAHO INDIAN. Daily life; silver-smithing; weaving; ceremonials and general customs.	11	yes	s–c	COR	UIN
NAVAJO INDIAN CAMP LIFE. Different types of hogans, wrapping a baby in a cradle board, planting melon seeds, grinding corn, and making bread.	15	yes silent	j–a	TN	UAR
NAVAHO INDIAN LIFE. General life of Indians in Arizona.	10	yes silent	j–c	BFS	UCB
NAVAHO INDIAN RUG WEAVING. Details of rug-making: shearing, carding, spinning, erecting the loom, and weaving.	15	yes silent	j–a	TN	UAR
NAVAHO INDIANS. Young Navaho couple building home, tilling soil, tending sheep, and carding wool.	11	bw	j	EBF	UIN
NAVAHO INDIANS OF THE PAINTED DESERT. General scene of: homes, clothing, crafts, and industries.	9	bw	j	AAP	MP
NAVAHO LIFE. Everyday life in Canyon de Chelly.	9	yes	j–a	NET	UIN
NAVAHOS LOOK AHEAD. Life on reservation at Paradox Basin, Utah; rodeo, tribal fair, and housing projects.	13	bw	p–j	HO	—
NAVAHO SILVERSMITH. Daily life of Navaho in harsh environment.	11	yes	c	JB	UAR
PEACEFUL ONES. Life in Hopi Indian village.	12	yes	s–a	ADP	UAR
PUEBLO ARTS. Discovery of pottery and art expression that grew from it.	11	yes	j–a	IFB	MP
PUEBLO BOY. Indian rodeo at Gallup, New Mexico; dances and music.	24	yes	p–a	FMC	UIL
PUEBLO HERITAGE. History of people from ancient Mesa Verde to present-day pueblos of Taos, Acoma, and Zuni.	20	yes	p–a	ASP	MP

Title of Film	Time	Color	Level	Producer	Catalogue
RAINBOW OF STONE. Navaho boy and friend attempt to find pasture by following legend.	23	yes	j–c	TFC	MP
RED ROCK COUNTRY. Tour of archaeological and topographical points of interest in Northern Arizona.	25	yes	j–a	GLP	UAR
RIVER PEOPLE. Reconstruction of Pima history from folklore and legend.	25	yes	j–a	USI	UAR
SEARCH FOR AMERICA: PART I, THE NAVAHO. Questions are put to Navaho family to discover values held by them.	29	bw	s–a	UIN	UIN
SEARCH FOR AMERICA: PART II, THE NAVAHO. Tribal Council discusses problems of tribal organization and of continuing force of tradition that shape their solutions.	29	bw	s–a	UIN	UIN
SMOKI SNAKE DANCE. Presents three dances performed by professional dance group called the Smoki.	13	yes	p–c	ADP	UIL
SOUTHEAST HERITAGE. A man attempts to recreate style and texture of old Indian paintings.	6	yes	j	USC	USC
SOUTHWESTERN INDIAN DANCES. Dances of many tribes at Gallup, New Mexico; includes Eagle and Hoop dances.	10	bw	j–a	CD	MP
SPIRIT OF THE WHITE MOUNTAINS. White Mountain Apaches and how they have developed resources of their reservation.	12	yes	c–a	ADP	UIN
SUPAI INDIANS. Life of Indians in Grand Canyon.	10	yes	p–j	COR	MP
TO! CIL! (WATER! GRASS!). History of Navaho and life on reservation.	28	bw	j–a	USD	MP

Title of Film	Time	Color	Level	Producer	Catalogue
TRIBE OF THE TURQUOISE WATER. Life in Cataract Canyon in Arizona where Havasupai live, raise cattle, and farm.	12	yes	j–a	ADP	UAR
VALLEY OF THE STANDING ROCKS. Navaho life in remote area of Arizona and Utah.	24	yes	c	BP	—
VILLAGES IN THE SKY. Hopi villages in Northern Arizona; transportation, manufacture of pottery, baking of bread, and tribal ceremonies.	12	yes	j–a	ADP	UAR
WARRIORS AT PEACE. Apache wickiup, basketry, livestock, and ancient Pollen Blessing Way.	12	yes	j–a	ADP	UAR
WAY OF THE NAVAHO. Problems arising from impact of modern world.	22	—	c	MHB	PSU
WEAVERS OF THE WEST. Navaho life with emphasis on weaving.	13	yes	c–a	ADP	UIL
WHERE THE PADRES WALKED. Activities for a tourist in Tucson, a fiesta in Mexico, Indian reservation at Sacaton, and missions.	25	yes	j–a	GLP	UAR
WHITE MOUNTAIN APACHE. Progress in development of reservation resources.	15	yes	j–a	USI	—

SECTION VIII: *THE PLAINS*

	Time	Color	Level	Producer	Catalogue
AGE OF THE BUFFALO. Recollections of Plains Indian and relation of buffalo to his culture.	14	yes	—	NFB	—
BUFFALO LORE. Importance of bison to Indian; includes shots of rare white bison and battle between two bulls.	8	bw	j–a	SFI	UIL
CALUMET, PIPE OF PEACE. Legends of the Plains Indians that ascribed miraculous powers to the Calumet pipe.	23	yes	i–c	UCB	UCB

Title of Film	Time	Color	Level	Producer	Catalogue
CHILDREN OF THE PLAINS INDIANS. Division of labor in Plains Indian Tribe as it would have been about 1750.	15	—	j	MHB	UIL
CIRCLE OF THE SUN. Sun Dance of contemporary Blood Indians in Alberta, Canada.	30	yes	c–a	CFI	UCB
FALLEN EAGLE. Heritage of Sioux Indians and their present-day existence in South Dakota.	21	c/bw	—	ASP	MP
GREAT PLAINS TRILOGY: DATING THE PAST. Dating techniques, including Carbon[14].	29	bw	c	NU	PSU
GREAT PLAINS TRILOGY: THE FORAGERS. Life of ancient Indians from 2000 B.C. to 500 A.D. as revealed by archaeology.	29	bw	c	NU	PSU
GREAT PLAINS TRILOGY: PLAINSMEN OF THE PAST. Prehistory of Plains until arrival of Europeans.	29	bw	c	NU	PSU
INDIAN BIBLE. Supernatural beliefs of the Indians.	10	bw	—	HFE	—
INDIAN FAMILY OF LONG AGO. How Sioux Indians hunted and used buffalo.	14	c/bw	j	EBF	MP
INDIANS OF THE PLAINS: LIFE IN THE PAST. Past importance of bison to Plains Indians.	1 reel	yes	—	AF	PSU
INDIANS OF THE PLAINS: PRESENT-DAY LIFE. Blackfoot Indians adjusting to modern world.	1 reel	yes	—	AF	PSU
INDIANS OF THE PLAINS: THE SUN DANCE CEREMONY. Process of erecting tipi and sweat lodge; performance of Sun Dance.	1 reel	yes	—	AF	PSU
INDIAN TIPI. Origin of tipi and how it is constructed.	8	bw	j–a	BSA	MP
INJUN TALK. Plains Indians' sign language.	30	yes	j–a	SOC	MP

Title of Film	Time	Color	Level	Producer	Catalogue
MEET THE SIOUX INDIAN. Life of Sioux Indians and their adjustment to environment.	11	yes	j–s	AFA	MP
NAPE EVAPI, "TALKING HANDS." Sign language of Plains Indians.	22	yes	c–a	UOK	UIN
OLD CHIEF'S DANCE. Attempt to do dance of Chief One Bull, nephew of Sitting Bull.	7	yes	c–a	UOK	UIN
PLAINS, THE: PART III. Excavation by the Smithsonian Institution of a fortified earth-lodge village on the Missouri River.	28	yes	c–a	UT	UT
SHADOW OF THE BUFFALO. Story of the bison and its near extinction.	9	c/bw	c–a	NET	UIN
SPIRIT IN THE EARTH. The Indian's story of "Old Faithful" in Yellowstone National Park.	21	yes	j–a	ASP	MP
TALKING HANDS. Sign language used by North American Indians.	20	yes	j–a	UOK	PSU
TIPI-HOW, WITH THE LAUBINS. Erecting large tipi on windy prairie; its convenience for nomadic life.	12	bw	s	TF	UIN
VANISHING PRAIRIE: PIONEER TRAILS, INDIAN LORE AND BIRD LIFE OF THE PRAIRIE, THE. Probable origin of Indian art forms and dances; types of bird life on prairie.	14	yes	j–a	D	MP
VISION QUEST. Ceremonial smoking, sweating, and tipi life of a young warrior.	30	bw	j–c	—	PSU

SECTION IX: *THE EASTERN AGRICULTURALISTS*

Title of Film	Time	Color	Level	Producer	Catalogue
AMERICA'S FIRST GREAT LADY. Life of Pocahontas.	27	bw	s–a	RAC	MP
BOY OF THE SEMINOLES. Activities of teen-aged Seminole Indian boy and his family in Florida.	11	c/bw	j	COR	MP

Title of Film	Time	Color	Level	Producer	Catalogue
CHUCALISSA INDIANS' CRAFT. Photographed in restored Indian Village at Chucalissa State Park near Memphis, Tennessee; ancient handicrafts of Choctaw Indians.	40	yes	j–c	TDC	FF
FALSE FACES, THE. Study by Marius Barbeau in 1961 at Quebec City, when Iroquois and Huron met for first time since 1649.	54	yes	e–a	—	LCC
FRENCH AND INDIAN WAR: SEVEN YEARS WAR IN AMERICA. Contrasts French and English ways of dealing with Indians.	16	yes	j–s	EBF	UIL
INDIAN CORN. Importance of corn to both Indians and settlers.	15	bw	p	KQED	—
INDIAN VALHALLA. Explains reasons for conflicts with Indians and their ultimate defeat.	29	bw	—	UIN	—
LAND OF THE CHEROKEE. Cherokee Indians of Quall reservation in Great Smokey Mountains.	13	bw	c	AFR	—
LONGHOUSE PEOPLE. Ceremonies of remnant Iroquois in Ontario, Canada.	24	yes	c	EBF	UIL
SEMINOLE INDIANS. Seminole Indian Village in Florida Everglades, as seen by an artist.	11	yes	j–a	IFB	MP
SEMINOLE OF THE EVERGLADES. Seminole Indians and great swamp area in which they live.	21	yes	j–a	PLC	MP
TOM SAVAGE-BOY OF EARLY VIRGINIA. White boy given to Indians as indentured servant by Jamestown settlers.	21	yes	j	EBF	MP

SECTION X: *THE INDIAN IN THE MODERN WORLD*

Title of Film	Time	Color	Level	Producer	Catalogue
ALL INDIAN POW-WOW AND RODEO. General view of rodeo at Flagstaff in which 7,000 Indians participated.	10	—	j–s	BAP	—

Title of Film	Time	Color	Level	Producer	Catalogue
AMERICAN INDIANS OF TODAY. Life on and off reservation; Apache, Sioux, Seneca, and other tribes.	16	yes	j–a	EBF	MP
BECAUSE THEY ARE DIFFERENT. Discusses problems associated with integration of Canada's Indians.	28	bw	a	NFB	—
EXILES, THE. A night in the life of relocated Indians in Los Angeles.	72	bw	a	CFI	—
GREAT SPIRIT ON THE PLAINS. Emphasis is upon Christianized Indians in Oklahoma.	27	yes	s	BMC	—
INDIAN CEREMONIALS. Scenes at intertribal ceremonials at Gallup, New Mexico.	18	yes	—	SFF	FF
INDIAN COWBOY. How former nomadic Indians were encouraged to take up agriculture and stock-raising.	20	yes	j–c	USB	—
INDIAN POW-WOW. Intertribal gathering; beauty contest, rodeo and roping; various tribes in their traditional dress.	12	yes	j–a	ADP	MP
INDIAN SUMMER OF DARWIN KAW-AWN-KEE. Depicts a few days in the life of a teen-aged boy who lives in Oklahoma.	27	bw	j–c	WKY	LCC
PROJECTIONS IN INDIAN ART. Southwest Indian art including basketry, pottery, weaving, jewelry, and watercolors.	8	yes	s–a	UAR	UAR
RICH MAN! POOR MAN! Contemporary life of Indians, and examination of common misconceptions.	25	bw	j–a	USB	USB

ABBREVIATIONS USED IN FILM LIST

A	Athena Films
AAP	Allen and Allen Productions
ABP	Arthur Barr Productions
ADP	Avalon Daggett Productions
AF	Academy Films
AFA	Association of Film Artists
AFP	Ambrosch Film Productions
AFR	American Film Review
ASP	Alan Shilan Production
BAP	Barbre Productions
BFI	Brandon Films Incorporated
BFS	Bailey Films Service
BH	Bell and Howell
BMC	Board of the Mission and Church Extension of the Methodist Church
BP	Bengal Pictures
BSA	Boy Scouts of America
BYU	Brigham Young University
CCG	Canadian Consulate General
CD	Carl Dudley
CF	20th Century Fox
CFC	Crawley Films, Canada; Calvert Distillers, Ltd., Canada; Canadian Travel Films Library.
CFI	Contemporary Films Incorporated
COR	Coronet Films

D	Disney
DFP	Delta Films Productions
EBF	Encyclopedia Britannica Films
EH	Education Horizons
EPH	E. P. Hunt
ESI	Educational Service Incorporated
FAC	Film Association of California
FF	Free Films Catalog
FFC	Fox Film Corporation
FI	Film Images
FMC	Ford Motor Company
FNB	First National Bank of Arizona
FRC	Film Research Company
G	Gateway
GLP	Green-Loomis Productions
HDP	Hoefler-Disney Productions
HFE	Hollywood Film Enterprises
HO	Humble Oil and Refining Company
IFB	International Film Bureau
IFF	International Film Foundation
ILA	International Library of Audio-Visual Aids
JB	Jack Breed
JG	Joseph Gayek
KB	Knowledge Builders
KCTA	KCTA-Television
KQED	KQED Kinescope
LCC	Library of Congress Catalogue
LFR	Lander Film Reviews
MHB	McGraw-Hill Book Company
MM	Martin Moyer
MP	Mountain-Plains Catalog
NA	Nu Art
NET	National Educational Television
NF	Northern Films
NFB	National Film Board of Canada
NU	University of Nebraska
NYU	New York University
OFD	Olympic Film Distributor
OHS	Oregon Historical Society
OSS	Oregon State System of Higher Education
P	Pathe
PLC	P. Lorillard Company
PSU	Pennsylvania State University
RAC	Radio Artists Corporation

SDF	Social Documentary Films
SFF	Santa Fe Films Bureau
SFI	Sterling Films Incorporated
SMI	Simme-Meservey Incorporated
SOC	Standard Oil of California
SRF	Sears Roebuck Foundation
SYR	Syracuse University
TDC	Tennessee Department of Conservation
TF	Teton Films
TFC	Teaching Film Custodians
THF	Thorne Films
TN	Tad Nichols
TVA	Tennessee Valley Authority Films Service
UAR	University of Arizona
UCB	University of California, Berkeley
UCO	University of Colorado
UIL	University of Illinois
UIN	University of Indiana
UMI	University of Minnesota
UOK	University of Oklahoma
UOR	University of Oregon
USB	U.S. Bureau of Indian Affairs
USC	University of Southern California
USD	U.S. Department of Agriculture
USI	U.S. Indian Service
UT	University of Texas
UTA	University of Utah
UW	United World
WKY	WKY-Television
WPN	Warner Path News

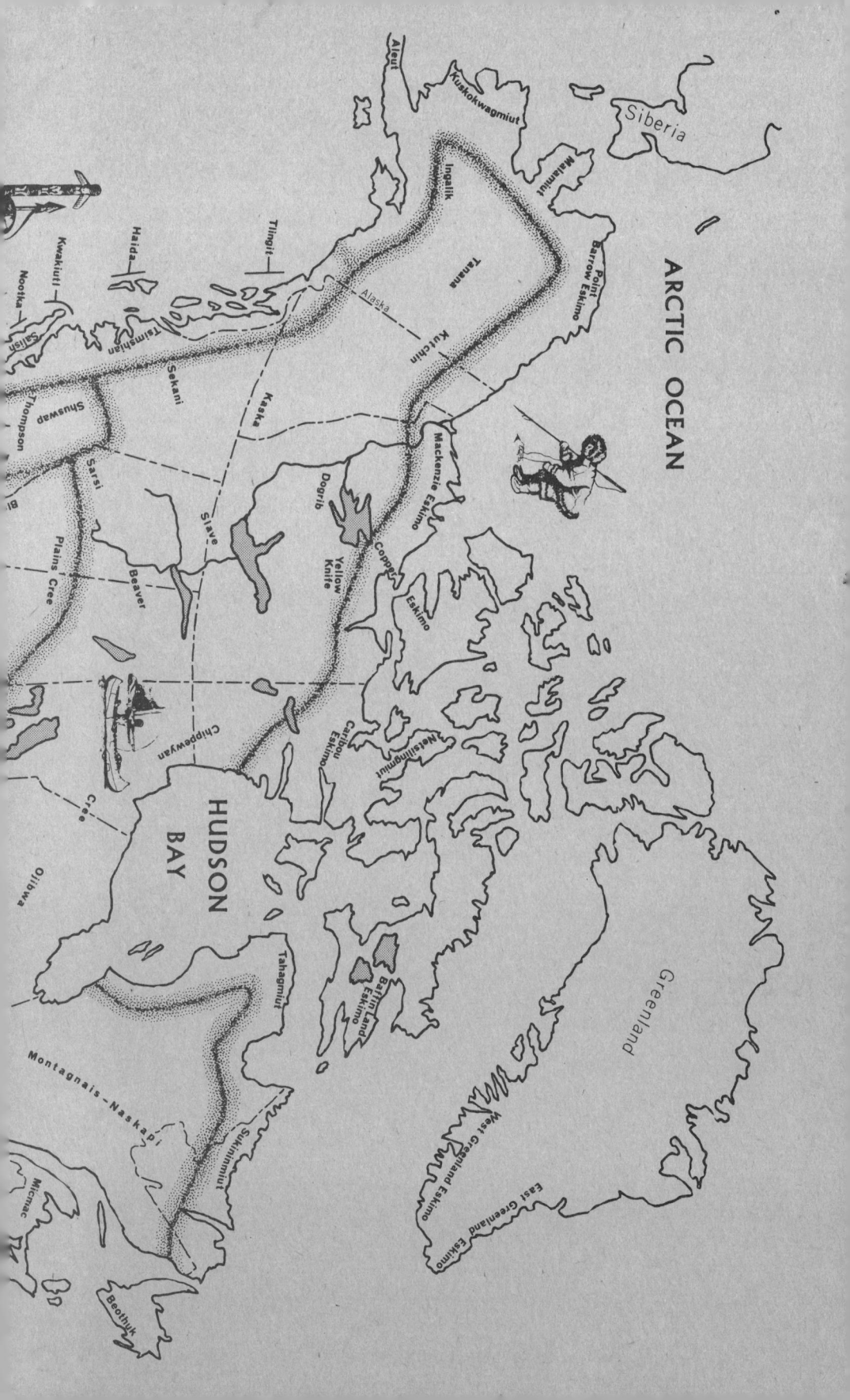